Andrew Newcombe

 FRES    .R

ID685875

Andrew Newcombe

T +33 1 44 56 54 04 Ligne Directe
F +33 1 44 56 44 00/01/02/03
T +33 6 85 01 01 16 Mobile
E andrew.newcombe@freshfields.com

The Jurisprudence of GATT and the WTO

Insights on treaty law and economic relations

This book contains a selection of essays and articles by John H. Jackson previously published over four decades and now collected together into one volume. Each article has been selected for its continued timeliness and relevance to contemporary issues in international trade. Particular attention has been given to making available articles which have previously been less accessible. For the most part articles are republished in their original form but, where appropriate, the author has clearly marked some omissions and added updating material. An indispensable addition to every international trade library.

JOHN H. JACKSON is University Professor at Georgetown University Law Center, Washington DC.

The Jurisprudence of GATT and the WTO

Insights on treaty law and economic relations

John H. Jackson

PUBLISHED BY THE PRESS SYNDICATE OF THE UNIVERSITY OF CAMBRIDGE
The Pitt Building, Trumpington Street, Cambridge, United Kingdom

CAMBRIDGE UNIVERSITY PRESS
The Edinburgh Building, Cambridge CB2 2RU, UK
40 West 20th Street, New York, NY 10011–4211, USA
10 Stamford Road, Oakleigh, VIC 3166, Australia
Ruiz de Alarcón 13, 28014 Madrid, Spain
Dock House, The Waterfront, Cape Town 8001, South Africa

http://www.cambridge.org

First published 2000
Reprinted 2000

Printed in the United Kingdom at the University Press, Cambridge

Typeset in Times 10/12pt [VN]

A catalogue record for this book is available from the British Library

Library of Congress Cataloguing in Publication data
Jackson, John Howard, 1932–
The jurisprudence of GATT and the WTO/John H. Jackson.
    p.   cm.
Includes index.
ISBN 0 521 62056 2 (hardback)
1. Genmeral Agreement on Tariffs and Trade (Organization)   2. World Trade
Organization.   3. Tariff–Law and legislation.   4. Foreign trade regulation.
I. Title.
K4602.21999a
341.7′54–dc21   99–24202   CIP

ISBN 0 521 62056 2 hardback

Contents

Preface

In some ways it is a pleasure to be able to publish a selected portion of one's scholarly production. Partly this book responds to requests from various persons to make some of these articles more accessible through a collection such as this. Over several decades, some of these works were published in journals or volumes which are not as readily available in some libraries of the world as might be desired. Also, this book brings together a number of works on related topics to provide more convenient access and therefore a better opportunity to detect general trends running through them as well as to compare a single author's approaches to various subject matters.

However, the task of producing this volume proved much more difficult than anticipated. Primarily this was due to the difficulty of selection from an extensive list, which even when pared severely resulted in too much material for a reasonable volume. Thus, this volume can in no way be considered as a complete representation of my work. The initial selection criteria focused on works which were as relevant to scholars and policy-makers today as they were when first published. But even that list proved far too long, so other criteria had to be used to influence the final selection. An author's pride in the works he produced became an obstacle to overcome, and works which seemed sometimes too focused on relatively narrow issues (even though still relevant) were subject to exclusion, as were works which were relatively accessible to the likely audience having appeared in journals which would be most likely to be found in relevant libraries around the world. No attempt was made to make this volume a "complete" account of the subject matter in the sense of an embracing logical outline. Readers will need to address this author's books for such approach, and the selection for presentation here avoided material published in books which are separately available.

But as is often the case with scholarship developed over a period of time, some innovative and relatively unique ideas get expressed in shorter published works that do not necessarily fit into the scheme of a larger book manuscript. These thoughts thus also motivated some of the selection decisions made for this volume. A brief select bibliography of my work is included at the end of this volume to lead interested readers to other material of mine, while also including in such bibliography all the works excerpted in this volume.

For the most part the works included in whole or in part speak for themselves. I have not tried to change or update these texts, which are reproduced as near to those as originally published as feasible (except for omissions which are noted with ellipses). The references in the footnotes have been updated to ensure consistency throughout the volume.

The book is logically divided into six parts. Each work presented or excerpted is a chapter for this book, no matter how short, and these chapters are grouped under the six parts according to subject matter that ties them together. I have written a short introduction for each part, to explain how the articles interrelate, and in some cases to provide some current background information to help the reader understand the particular chapters grouped under a part.

Part I is an introduction and overview designed to set the stage or context for the subject of international economic law. This text is drawn from a relatively recent article of mine, as described at the outset of Part I.

Part II contains subject matter about the General Agreement on Tariffs and Trade (GATT, predecessor to the WTO) and the peculiar origin of GATT which shaped its history so deeply.

Part III presents several articles on particular trade policy fundamentals. This part could obviously be much longer, but a reader interested in other trade policy issues will need to address various chapters in several of my books.

Part IV then collects several articles about the dispute settlement system, both under GATT and now under the WTO Agreement and texts. These procedures are in many ways the central legal feature of these institutions. No attempt is made here to give the details of the procedure or to cover all features both under GATT and under the WTO. Rather, the articles here probe certain fundamental jurisprudential issues relating to those procedures.

Part V turns to a broader context, and particularly deals with the relationship of international economic law (including the GATT and the WTO) to the laws and constitutions of nation-states. Again, the approach is to probe certain fundamental policy and jurisprudence issues, while not trying to explain the details of the national laws.

Finally, Part VI draws some conclusions and perspectives, partly in the context of the completion of the Uruguay Round of trade negotiations and the creation of the World Trade Organization, perhaps the supreme accomplishment of the Uruguay Round.

Acknowledgments

The author wishes to acknowledge the extraordinary and efficient efforts of Mr. William Naugle, the Faculty Manuscript Assistant for the Georgetown University Law Center. The diligence and efforts of Mr. Naugle, and the entire faculty support staff, were clearly an essential prerequisite for the completion of this manuscript. The author also wishes to acknowledge and thank the following publishers for granting permission to use the articles or portions of articles comprising this collection of work: Blackwell Publishers, the Institute for International Economics, the *Journal of World Trade*, Kluwer Law International, *Law & Policy in International Business* of the Georgetown University Law Center, the American Society of International Law, the British Institute of International and Comparative Law, the Michigan Law Review Association, and the *Washington & Lee Law Review* of the Washington & Lee University School of Law.

Chapter 1 is based on John H. Jackson, "Global Economics and International Economic Law" (1998) 1 *Journal of International Economic Law* 1–23.

Chapter 2 is based on John H. Jackson, "The Puzzle of GATT: Legal Aspects of a Surprising Institution" (1967) 1 *Journal of World Trade Law* 2, 131–161. I wish to acknowledge the assistance of the University of California School of Law, Berkeley (where I was Professor of Law until the summer of 1966), in providing resources and leave time for conducting research on the law of GATT. I also wish to acknowledge the cooperation of various members of the GATT Secretariat in Geneva, Switzerland, as well as members of various delegations there.

Chapter 3 is based on John H. Jackson, "The Birth of the GATT–MTN System: A Constitutional Appraisal" (1980) 12 *Law and Policy in International Business* 21–58. During 1978–1979, I was legal consultant to the US Senate Finance Committee on matters relating to the implementation of the Multilateral Trade Negotiations Agreements. Substantial portions of this article were drawn from a report I made to the Senate Finance Committee.

Chapter 4 is based on John H. Jackson, "GATT Machinery and the Tokyo Round Agreements" in William R. Cline (ed.), *Trade Policy in the 1980s* (Institute for International Economics, Washington, DC, 1983), chapter 5.

Chapter 5 is based on John H. Jackson, "Equality and Discrimination in International Economic Law: The General Agreement on Tariffs and Trade" in *The British Yearbook of World Affairs* 1983 (London Institute of World Affairs, 1983), 224–239.

Chapter 6 is based on John H. Jackson, "Consistency of Export-Restraint Arrangements with the GATT" (1988) 11 *World Economy* 4, 485–500. The author wishes to acknowledge the able assistance of Thijs Alexander and Ross Denton, both postgraduate students in law, from the Netherlands and the United Kingdom, at the University of Michigan during 1987–1988.

Chapter 7 is based on John H. Jackson, "Perspectives on Countervailing Duties" (1990) 21 *Law and Policy in International Business* 739–756.

Chapter 8 is based on John H. Jackson, "Regional Trade Blocs and the GATT" (1993) 16 *World Economy* 2, 121–130. The original article was partially adapted from a paper delivered at a conference in Buenos Aires, Argentina, July 1992. Comments from an anonymous referee are gratefully acknowledged.

Chapter 9 is based on John H. Jackson, "The Jurisprudence of International Trade: The DISC Case in GATT" (1978) 72 *American Journal of International Law* 747–781.

Chapter 10 is based on John H. Jackson, "The Legal Meaning of a GATT Dispute Settlement Report: Some Reflections" in Niels Blokker and Sam Muller (eds.), *Towards More Effective Supervision by International Organization: Essays in Honour of Henry G. Schermers* (Martinus Nijhoff Publishers, Dordrecht, Boston and London, 1994).

Chapter 11 is based on Steven P. Croley and John H. Jackson, "WTO Dispute Procedures, Standard of Review, and Deference to National Governments" (1996) 90 *American Journal of International Law* 2, 193–213. This article was originally adapted from a chapter prepared for a symposium book edited by Professor Ulrich Petersmann, as part of a project by the International Trade Committee of the International Law Association.

Chapter 12 is based on John H. Jackson, "The WTO Dispute Settlement Understanding – Misunderstandings on the Nature of Legal Obligation" (1997) 91 *American Journal of International Law* 1, 60–64.

Chapter 13 is based on John H. Jackson, "Dispute Settlement and the WTO: Emerging Problems" (1998) 1 *Journal of International Economic Law* 3, 329–351. This article was a revision and extension of a manuscript first presented at the WTO conference in Geneva on April 30, 1998, commemorating the fiftieth anniversary year of the GATT.

Chapter 14 is based on John H. Jackson, "The General Agreement on Tariffs and Trade in United States Domestic Law" (1967) 66 *Michigan Law Review* 249–316. I am indebted to Walter Hollis, Legal Advisor's Office, United States State Department, who generously read the manuscript of this article and made a number of useful suggestions. I am also indebted to members of the GATT Secretariat in Geneva for assisting my general research into GATT for this article.

Chapter 15 is based on John H. Jackson, "United States–EEC Trade Relations: Constitutional Problems of Economic Interdependence" (1979) 16 *Common Market Law Review* 453–478. During 1975–1976 I was a Rockefeller Research Fellow, residing in Brussels, Belgium, for the purpose of observing the legal affairs of the European Economic Community related to external relations, and I wish to express my appreciation to the Rockefeller Foundation for that assistance.

Chapter 16 is based on John H. Jackson, "Perspectives on the Jurisprudence of International Trade: Costs and Benefits of Legal Procedures in the United States" (1984) 82 *Michigan Law Review* 1570–1587. A preliminary and summary version of this article was presented by invitation at a panel chaired by Professor Robert Baldwin of the University of Wisconsin, at the annual meeting of the American Economic Association in San Francisco, December 27, 1983.

Chapter 17 is based on John H. Jackson, "United States" in Francis G. Jacobs and Shelley Roberts (United Kingdom National Committee of Comparative Law) (eds.), *The Effect of Treaties in Domestic Law* (Sweet & Maxwell, London, 1987), chapter 8. I wish to acknowledge the able assistance of Mr. P. Van den Bossche, a graduate student in the law from Belgium, in the preparation of this paper and the documentary support of its text.

Chapter 18 is based on John H. Jackson, "Status of Treaties in Domestic Legal Systems: A Policy Analysis" (1992) 86 *American Journal of International Law* 2, 310–340. I was General Counsel for the Office of the US Trade Representative in the mid-1970s. Some of the arguments and reflections in this article are derived from this and similar experience. I would like to express gratitude for the counsel and advice on various drafts of this article from Professors William Davey, Francis Jacobs, Richard Lauwaars, Meinhard Hilf, Marc Maresceau, Mitsuo Matsushita, Henry Schermers, Eric Stein, and Pieter van Dijk. In addition, I would like to express my gratitude for information received from Carlos Bernal of Mexico; Thomas Cottier of the Government of Switzerland; Professor Yuji Iwasawa of Osaka City University, Japan; Professor Autar K. Koul of the University of Delhi, India; and Matthew Schaefer (regarding Australia). I would also like to recognize the able research assistance of Yves Renouf and Daniel Nelson, students at the University of Michigan Law School.

Chapter 19 is based on John H. Jackson, "The Great 1994 Sovereignty Debate: United States Acceptance and Implementation of the Uruguay Round Results" (1997) 36 *Columbia Journal of Transnational Law* 157–188.

Chapter 20 is based on John H. Jackson, "The World Trade Organization: Watershed Innovation or Cautious Small Step Forward?" (1995) *The World Economy* 11.

Chapter 21 is based on John H. Jackson, "World Trade Rules and Environmental Policies: Congruence or Conflict?" (1992) 49 *Washington and Lee Law Review* 4, 1227–1278.

Chapter 22 is based on John H. Jackson, "Global Economics and International Economic Law" (1998) 1 *Journal of International Economic Law* 1–23.

Abbreviations

DSB	Dispute Settlement Body
DSU	Understanding on the Settlement of Disputes
FCN	friendship, commerce and navigation treaty
FTA	free trade agreement
GATS	General Agreement on Trade in Services
GATT	General Agreement on Tariffs and Trade
ICITO	Interim Commission for the International Trade Organization
IEL	international economic law
ITC	International Trade Commission
ITO	International Trade Organization
MFN	most favored nation
MTA	multilateral trade agreements
MTN	multilateral trade negotiations
MTO	multilateral trade organization
NAFTA	North American Free Trade Agreement
NTB	nontariff barrier
PPA	Protocol of Provisional Application
SII	Structural Impediments Initiative
TPRM	Trade Policy Review Mechanism
TRIPS	trade-related intellectual property
VER	voluntary export arrangements
VRA	voluntary restraint agreements (or arrangements)
WTO	World Trade Organization

Part I

A view of the landscape

An essay of mine written for the first issue of a new *Journal of International Economic Law* sets out the context of this subject matter and develops some of the policy objectives which influence this subject. The first part of this essay neatly summarizes my views which would introduce this volume. The last part of this essay, by contrast, neatly summarizes some of my current views about the ongoing direction of the world trading system and the WTO. This last part thus provides a nice ending to this volume, and readers will find that at the end of Part VI, so that this single essay becomes the "bookends" to this endeavor.

1   Global economics and international economic law

1.   The global economic landscape and implications of interdependence: of stock markets, bananas, and pumpkins

It surprises few people today to see comments about the profound and growing extent of international economic interdependence and linkages. The causes of these developments are numerous: incredible advances in efficiency of communication, extraordinary reductions in transport costs, growing prevalence of instant tele- and cyber-transactions, treaty and other norms causing reduction of governmental barriers to trade, an economic climate more favorable to principles of market economics, cross-border influences of competition which have driven increases in production and service efficiencies, and, last but not least, the blessing of relative peace in the world.

Manifestations of this "globalization" abound: stock market trends that flow quickly around the world; impacts of national government monetary and fiscal decisions; effects of fraud within certain banking or other financial enterprises; worries about health and safety of products moving across borders such as foodstuffs, pharmaceuticals, machinery, appliances; effects of governmental mismanagement and sometimes corruption; worries about the power of nongovernment and private enterprises and their capacity in some cases to operate on the global economy while largely ignoring particular national governmental regulatory protections; and flows of "cultural" influences involving various media often moving swiftly with new communication techniques to transmit music or drama across borders (with substantial economic implications and other effects, even to cause a new taste in Paris for Halloween pumpkins!). A road-map of the various links and cause-effects of a multitude of economic actions becomes an impenetrable maze of pathways, commonly without clear guidebooks to assist their understanding.

Almost every conceivable type of government economic regulation now

---

* This chapter is based on John H. Jackson, "Global Economics and International Economic Law" (1998) 1 *Journal of International Economic Law* 1–23.

must take account of the international and competitive implications of its activity, and often national government officials feel frustrated at their relative inability to control economic forces that vitally affect their constituents and prevent fulfillment of official goals and promises on behalf of their constituents. Sometimes governments are tempted to utilize their power to influence economic forces to benefit better their own constituents at the expense of other societies (a beggar-thy-neighbor approach). In some of these cases competition among governments to capture such benefits can result in damaging the welfare of all participants – a phenomenon suggesting a "prisoner's dilemma" analysis. One astute experienced political leader has said: "All politics is local."[1] But another astute economic writer has noted: "All economics is international."[2] When juxtaposed, these pithy comments reflect some of the policy dilemmas with which political leaders must grapple.

In recent years, particularly, as the Cold War and its threat of major disaster seems to have receded, there has been much discussion and speech-making about the shifting emphasis from "geo-politics" to "geo-economics" (or some would say to the game of "geo-monopoly"). News media attention has begun to refocus on economic matters, with front page attention given to international trade, legislative initiatives relating to trade, problems of food safety, World Trade Organization (WTO) cases about bananas, the activity of financial institutions such as the World Bank or the International Monetary Fund (IMF), and many other economic subjects relating to investment, competition policy, etc. Scholarly efforts and governmental policy studies have also been giving increased attention to the problems mentioned above. Nevertheless, the careful observer is struck by how much we do not know, and how often scholarship and studies seem only to repeat the obvious or emphasize advocacy of preconceived positions or struggle without adequate empirical data on which to make judgments.[3] Very high government officials have been known to disparage solidly accepted economic wisdom or make statements about legal norms that are misleading or plain wrong. It seems clear to this observer that there is great need and opportunity for reflective scholarly attention to many different systemic and "constitutional" issues about our globalized economy.

The degree to which treaties and international law now appear to "intrude" on national and subfederal government decision-making seems

---

[1] See Tip O'Neill and Gary Hymel, *All Politics is Local* (1994).
[2] Peter F. Drucker, "Trade Lessons from the World Economy" (1994) *Foreign Affairs* 99.
[3] See, for example, the papers delivered at a conference at Harvard University Center for Business and Government, October 1995 on "World Trade and Services," which discuss the lack of accurate empirical information concerning trade in services.

to support the statements made above. Governments sometimes feel hemmed in, and sometimes object that they cannot take action sought even by their democratic constituencies. The North American Free Trade Agreement (NAFTA) in some respects went very far in its measures seeking national government changes arguably necessary to fulfill the NAFTA international obligations. This was true for the NAFTA investor protection rules, and also in relation to environment and labor standards.[4] World Trade Organization provisions, perhaps particularly those in the intellectual property agreement[5] which require governments to fulfill certain standards regarding their court systems, and also some of the detailed agreements relating to services (especially financial services or telecommunications),[6] appear to insert their rules quite deeply into national legal systems. Of course, one answer to at least some of the criticisms of international rules which operate to constrain governments, is that the global market forces already constrain governments, and sometimes in ways which are not as healthy as the negotiated treaty text.

The remaining parts of this article will explore some particular facets of the problems outlined above. Part 2 will note the importance which significant thinkers and theorists attach to human institutions and the role of legal rules associated with such institutions.

Part 3 will look at the meaning of the phrase "international economic law," noting some of the dimensions of such a subject title, and some of the difficulties for policy, theoretical, and scholarly work focusing on this subject. Part 4[7] will then look at some traditional market economic concepts regarding the role of government action (presumably to enhance the effective working of markets) and suggest how these concepts are affected by globalization and the legal rules of international institutions.

Part 5 will briefly reflect on some attributes and activities of existing international economic institutions, with a focus on the newest and arguably the most important of these, namely the WTO (although most of the discussion could easily apply to other international economic organizations). Finally, Part 6 will examine some of the thinking about future directions of the world trading system and its constitution, and reflect on the implications of those for scholarship on subjects embraced within the broad topic of "international economic law."

---

[4] North American Free Trade Agreement, entered into force January 1, 1994. See especially chapters 11 and 18, as well as the NAFTA Side Agreements on Labor and Environment.

[5] Final Act Embodying the Results of the Uruguay Round of Multilateral Trade Negotiations, opened for signature April 15, 1994, Marrakesh, Morocco, 33 ILM 1140–1272 (1994) (hereinafter WTO). See WTO Annex 1C, "Agreement on Trade-Related Aspects of Intellectual Property Rights."

[6] WTO, Annex 1C (TRIPS) and 1B (Services).

[7] Parts 4, 5, and 6 of this article are at the end of this volume in chapter 22.

Throughout these parts, however, there is at least one common focus for the discussions found in this article. This is the notion that we are dealing with a form of "constitutional law," involving in this area the broad concept of "constitution" going considerably beyond a written document, and embracing a variety of interconnected governmental institutions as well as evolving practice of many such institutions. The focus is truly the "world trading system," and its legal framework – that which we can here call the "constitution."

2.   Markets and governments and the role of law

Whether economic policies which are based on market principles[8] are the best approach for maximizing human satisfaction is, of course, controversial. Various alternatives have been much debated, and many of those largely rejected, but substantial arguments are made in favor of some sort of mixture of policies, perhaps to temper the perceived negative effects of "too pure market approaches." Whatever mixture may appeal to certain societies, however, it seems reasonably clear that markets can be very beneficial,[9] and, even when not beneficial, market forces demand respect and can cause great difficulties when not respected.[10]

Yet even when stressing the benefits of market economics, important thinkers note the importance of human institutions which guide and shape markets. Two Nobel Prize-winning economists stress this proposition. Ronald Coase has stated:[11]

It is evident that, for their operation, markets . . . require the establishment of legal rules governing the rights and duties of those carrying out transactions . . . To realize all the gains from trade . . . there has to be a legal system and political order . . . Economic policy consists of choosing those legal rules, procedures and administrative structures which will maximize the value of production.

More recently, Douglas North said:[12]

---

[8] See Richard Lipsey, Paul Courant, Douglas Purvis, and Peter Steiner, *Microeconomics* (10th edn., 1993); Avinash K. Dixit and Barry J. Nalebuff, *Thinking Strategically* (1991); Max Corden, *Trade Policy and Economic Welfare* (1974); Peter B. Kenen, *The International Economy* (1994); and Paul Krugman, *International Economics: Theory and Policy* (1994).

[9] For an overview of the economic principles which support policies of liberal international trade rules, see Alan O. Sykes, "Comparative Advantage and the Normative Economics of International Trade Policy" (1998) 1 *Journal of International Economic Law* 49–82.

[10] See, e.g., James Flanigan, "Turmoil is Free Market Watershed," *Los Angeles Times* (home edition), October 29, 1997.

[11] Ronald Coase, *The Firm, the Market and the Law*, chapter 5. See also C. A. E. Goodhart, "Economics and the Law: Too Much One-Way Traffic?" (1997) 60 *Modern Law Review* 1.

[12] Douglas C. North, *Institutions, Institutional Change and Economic Performance* (1990).

That institutions affect the performance of economics is hardly controversial . . . Institutions reduce uncertainty by providing a structure to everyday life . . . Institutions affect the performance of the economy by their effect on the costs of exchange and production.

Human institutions embrace many structures and take many forms, but it is very clear that law and legal norms play the most important part of the institutions which are essential to make markets work. The notion that "rule of law" (ambiguous as that phrase is) or a rule-based or rule-oriented system of human institutions is essential to a beneficial operation of markets, is a constantly recurring theme in many writings.

With respect to international economics, the world is fortunate to have the advantage of institutions such as the Bretton Woods system (including the General Agreement on Tariffs and Trade, GATT) established through the vision of statesmen, scholars and diplomats at the end of World War II. At least some of the credit for relative peace and economic growth of the past half-century goes to those institutions and their rules.[13] And now, of course, we have a major new organization established on January 1, 1995 in our landscape of economic institutions, namely, the WTO, with an extraordinarily elaborate set of rules.

A critical question almost always asked by anyone confronted with an international law rule is "Why do they matter?" Put another way, there exists much cynicism about the importance or effectiveness of international law rules. Frequently the public can read news of violations of such rules by major and minor nations. In some cases such violations, even when admitted to be such (often there is bitter and inconclusive argument on this question), are rationalized or declared "just" by national leaders. Thus the cynicism about international rules cannot be surprising.

A more careful examination of the role and effectiveness of international rules is necessary, however. First, it should be observed that not all domestic rules are always obeyed either. Yet there are many international rules which are remarkably well observed. Why this is so has been the subject of much speculation[14] which will not be repeated here. Notions of reciprocity and a desire to depend on other nations' observance of rules lead many nations to observe rules even when they do not want to.

At least in the context of economic behavior, however, and particularly when that behavior is set in circumstances of decentralized decision-making, as in a market economy, rules can have important operational

---

[13] John H. Jackson, *World Trade and the Law of GATT* (1969), chapter 2. At least some credit for over fifty years of relative peace (avoiding a World War III) can be attributed to the reasonably successful activities of the International Monetary Fund and the World Bank.

[14] See Louis Henkin, *How Nations Behave* (2nd edn., 1979); Roger Fisher, *Improving Compliance with International Law* (1981), 12–16; and Abram Chayes, *The New Sovereignty: Compliance with International Regulatory Agreements* (1995).

functions. They may provide the only predictability or stability to a potential investment or trade-development situation. Without such predictability or stability, trade or investment flows might be even more risky and therefore more inhibited than otherwise. If such "liberal trade" goals contribute to world welfare, then it follows that rules which assist such goals should also contribute to world welfare. To put it another way, the policies which tend to reduce some risks, lower the "risk premium" required by entrepreneurs to enter into international transactions. This should result in a general increase in the efficiency of various economic activities, contributing to greater welfare for everyone.

Assuming then that institutions are important, and that law plays a significant role in those institutions, what legal principles can we identify that play such a role? Obviously this can be a vast subject, certainly ripe for scholarly and policy attention of various kinds for years to come. But perhaps one particular principle can here be mentioned, namely the value of a "rule-oriented" approach to the design of international institutions relating to economic activity.[15]

The "rule-oriented approach" focuses the disputing parties' attention on the rule, and on predicting what an impartial tribunal is likely to conclude about the application of a rule. This in turn, will lead parties to pay closer attention to the rules of the treaty system, and this can lead to greater certainty and predictability which is essential in international affairs, particularly economic affairs driven by market-oriented principles of decentralized decision-making, with participation by millions of entrepreneurs. As noted above, such entrepreneurs need a certain amount of predictability and guidance so that they can make the appropriate efficient investment and market-development decisions.[16]

The phrase "rule orientation" is used here to contrast with phrases such as "rule of law," and "rule-based system." Rule orientation implies a less rigid adherence to "rule" and connotes some fluidity in rule approaches which seems to accord with reality (especially since it accommodates some bargaining or negotiation). Phrases that emphasize too strongly the strict application of rules sometimes scare policy-makers, although in reality they may amount to the same thing. Any legal system must accommodate the inherent ambiguities of rules and the constant changes in the practical needs of human society. The key point is that the procedures of rule application, which often center on a dispute settlement procedure, should be designed so as to promote as much as possible the stability and predicta-

---

[15] See, e.g., John H. Jackson, *The World Trading System* (1997), 109; and John H. Jackson, *The World Trade Organization: Constitution and Jurisprudence* (Cassell Academic, 1998), chapter 4.

[16] See, e.g., North, *Institutions*.

bility of the rule system. For this purpose the procedure must be creditable, "legitimate," and reasonably efficient (not easy criteria).

For example, suppose countries A and B have a trade dispute regarding B's treatment of imports from A to B of widgets. One technique would involve a negotiation between A and B by which the most powerful of the two would have the advantage. Foreign aid, military maneuvers, or import restrictions on other key goods by way of retaliation would figure in the negotiation. A small country would hesitate to challenge a large one on whom its trade depends. Implicit or explicit threats (e.g., to impose quantitative restrictions on some other product) would be a major part of the negotiating technique employed. Domestic political influences would probably play a greater part in the approach of the respective negotiators in this system, particularly on the negotiator for the more powerful party.

On the other hand, a second technique suggested – reference to agreed rules – would see the negotiators arguing about the application of the rule (e.g., was B obligated under a treaty to allow free entry of A's goods in question?). During the process of negotiating a settlement it would be necessary for the parties to understand that an unsettled dispute would ultimately be resolved by impartial third-party judgments based on the rules so that the negotiators would be negotiating with reference to their respective predictions as to the outcome of those judgments and not with reference to potential retaliation or actions by the exercising of the power of one or more of the parties to the dispute.

In both techniques negotiation and settlement of disputes is the dominant mechanism for resolving differences; but the key is the perception of the participants as to what are the "bargaining chips." Insofar as agreed rules for governing the economic relations between the parties exist, a system which predicates negotiation on the implementation of those rules would seem, for a number of reasons, to be preferred. The mere existence of the rules, however, is not enough. When the issue is the application or interpretation of those rules (rather than the formulation of new rules), it is necessary for the parties to believe that if their negotiations reach an impasse the settlement mechanisms which take over for the parties will be designed to apply or interpret the rules fairly. If no such system exists, then the parties are left basically to rely upon their respective "power positions," tempered (it is hoped) by the good will and good faith of the more powerful party (cognizant of its long-range interests).

As the world becomes more economically interdependent, more and more private citizens find their jobs, their businesses, and their quality of life affected, if not controlled, by forces from outside their own country's boundaries. Thus they are more affected by the economic policy pursued by their own country on their behalf. In addition, the relationships become increasingly complex – to the point of being incomprehensible to even the brilliant human mind. As a result, citizens assert themselves, at least within a democracy, and require their representatives and government officials to respond to their needs and their perceived complaints. The result of this is increasing citizen participation, and more parliamentary or Congressional participation in the processes of international economic policy, thus restricting the degree of power and discretion which the executive possesses.

This makes international negotiations and bargaining increasingly difficult. However, if citizens are going to make their demands heard and influential, a "power-oriented" negotiating process (often requiring secrecy, and executive discretion so as to be able to formulate and implement the necessary compromises) becomes more difficult, if not impossible. Consequently, the only appropriate way to turn seems to be towards a rule-oriented system, whereby the various citizens, parliaments, executives, and international organizations will all have their inputs, arriving tortuously at a rule which, however, when established will enable business and other decentralized decision-makers to rely upon the stability and predictability of governmental activity in relation to the rule.[17]

The degree of desired flexibility for rules is a subject discussed by important writers, sometimes with a suggestion that certain rules be raised to "constitutional status" and embedded in national legal systems.[18]

With these "policy-building blocks" in mind, we can now turn to several other dimensions of the subject of international economic law.

3.   Understanding international economic law

It is appropriate to ask what we mean by "international economic law." This phrase can cover a very broad inventory of subjects: embracing the law of economic transactions; government regulation of economic matters; and related legal relations including litigation and international institutions for economic relations. Indeed, it is plausible to suggest that 90

---

[17] Adapted from John H. Jackson, "Governmental Disputes in International Trade Relations: A Proposal in the Context of GATT" (1979) 13 *Journal of World Trade Law* 3–4 and John H. Jackson, "The Crumbling Institutions of the Liberal Trade System" (1978) 12 *Journal of World Trade Law* 98–101; John H. Jackson, *The World Trading System* (2nd edn., 1997).

[18] See, e.g., Ernst-Ulrich Petersmann, *Constitutional Functions and Constitutional Problems of International Economic Law* (1991). Professor Petersmann has also written profoundly on this theme in some of his other numerous writings. See also Thomas Cottier and Krista Nadakavukaner Schefer, "The Relationship Between World Trade Organization Law, National and Regional Law" (1998) 1 *Journal of International Economic Law*; and Ernst-Ulrich Petersmann, "How to Promote the International Rule of Law? Contributions by the World Trade Organization Appellate Review System" (1998) 1 *Journal of International Economic Law*.

percent of international law work is in reality international economic law in some form or another. Much of this, of course, does not have the glamour or visibility of nation-state relations (use of force, human rights, intervention etc.), but does indeed involve many questions of international law and particularly treaty law. Increasingly, today's international economic law (IEL) issues are found on the front pages of the daily newspapers.[19]

To some extent IEL can be divided into two broad approaches which cut across most of the subjects embraced by IEL. These approaches can roughly be termed "transactional" or "regulatory." Both have their place, but activities of research and policy formulation can be substantially different, and should be understood.

Transactional IEL refers to transactions carried out in the context of international trade or other economic activities, and focuses on the way mostly private entrepreneurs or other parties carry out their activity. Much of the literature, for example, is descriptive. It can be valuable as instruction for potential players, to show "how to do it," and warn against pitfalls. It can also go further and make suggestions for change.

Regulatory IEL, however, emphasizes the role of government institutions (national, local or international). Although it can be argued that the international trade transaction is the most government regulated of all private economic transactions (usually requiring at least a report for each transaction, e.g. a customs declaration), nevertheless, most traditional attention to IEL has been focused, perhaps for practical and pragmatic reasons, on transactions. Yet arguably in today's world the real challenges for understanding IEL and its impact on governments and private citizens' lives, suggest a focus on IEL as "regulatory law," similar to domestic subjects such as tax, labor, antitrust, and other regulatory topics.

But apart from its breadth, what are some of the characteristics of IEL which, for example, might affect the approach to it of scholars or policymakers? The following are some tentative ventures to explore these characteristics, but they are obviously by no means complete.

1. International economic law cannot be separated or compartmentalized from general or "public" international law. The activities and cases relating to IEL contain much practice which is relevant to general principles of international law, especially concerning treaty law and practice. Conversely, general international law has considerable relevance to economic relations and transactions. It is interesting, for

---

[19] A more elaborate version of some of these thoughts is expressed in John H. Jackson, "International Economic Law: Reflections on the 'Boilerroom' of International Relations" (1995) 10 *American University Journal of International Law Policy* 595–606.

example, to compare the number of cases handled by the GATT dispute settlement system (approximately 250)[20] to those handled by the World Court (approaching 100). Numbers do not tell the whole tale, but there certainly are some GATT cases that have had as profound conse-quences on national governments and world affairs as have Interna-tional Court of Justice (ICJ) cases. The GATT cases are rich with practice relating to the general question of international dispute resol-ution, and some of this practice has broader implications than simply for the GATT (and now WTO) system itself.

2. The relationship of international economic law to national or "munici-pal" law is particularly important. It is an important part of understand-ing international law generally, but this "link," and the interconnections between IEL and municipal law are particularly significant to the operation and effectiveness of IEL rules. For example, an important question is the relationship of treaty norms to municipal law, expressed by such phrases as "self-executing" or "direct application."[21]

3. As the title phrase "international economic law" suggests, there is necessarily a strong component of multidisciplinary research and think-ing required for those who work on IEL projects. Of course, "econ-omics" is important and useful, especially for understanding the policy motivations of many of the international and national rules on the subject. Obviously, it is just as important to understand some of the criticisms of economic analysis, and to treat with skepticism some of the economic "models." Likewise, there are alternative value structures which should balance some economic notions of "efficiency." Thus, various lifestyle choices and certain long-range value objectives can at least appear, and perhaps be contradictory to some economic objec-tives, as some of those economic objectives are phrased by certain writers. In addition to economics, of course, other subjects are highly relevant. Political science (and its intersection with economics found generally in the "public choice" literature) is very important, as are many other disciplines, such as cultural history and anthropology, geography etc.

4. Work on IEL matters often seems to necessitate more empirical study than some other international law subjects. Empirical research, how-

---

[20] See Robert Hudec, *Enforcing International Trade Law: The Evolution of the Modern GATT Legal System* (1993), 417–585 (indexing 207 GATT complaints from July 1948 to Novem-ber 1989).

[21] See John H. Jackson, "Status of Treaties in Domestic Legal Systems: A Policy Analysis" (1993) 86 *American Journal of International Law* 310 (examining policy issues concerning the relationship between international treaties and domestic law); see also Cottier and Schefer, "The Relationship Between World Trade Organization Law, National and Re-gional Law."

ever, does not necessarily mean statistical research, in the sense used in many policy explorations. For some key issues of international law there are too few "cases" on which to base statistical conclusions (such as correlations), so we are constrained to use a more "anecdotal" or case-study approach. This type of empiricism, however, is nevertheless very important, and a good check on theory or on sweeping generalizations of any kind. Since this often requires a study of particular cases, or at least of certain groups of cases, with considerable quantitative elements, it is frequently necessary to master a considerable amount of detail to understand some of the interplay of forces affecting international economic relations and the law concerning those relations.

5. Another characteristic of IEL, or at least of the problems of research and producing scholarship about IEL, is that, like many subjects of international relations, there is often a substantial problem with obtaining information. Diplomatic habits and sometimes legitimate needs of governments for confidentiality can impose special burdens on scholars, although in recent years a variety of special information sources, such as focused newsletters and internet sites, have ameliorated some of these burdens.

6. As the subjects of international economics became more central to government policy decisions and studies, these subjects also became more prominent in the news media and more deeply interconnected with political groups and agenda. Of course, historically there have been periods of intense public debate about international economic policies such as tariffs, or "antidumping" and unfair trade arguments.[22] But with a post-Cold War shift to "geo-economics" and with developing fears among certain citizen groups about the influence of globalization on their personal and family well-being[23] the "politicization" of international economic policy issues, and therefore of legal issues related to them, has led to various studies by different groups on IEL issues (such as those involved in the debate about the "fast-track" procedure with respect to the USA's treaty-making rules involving the US Congress).[24] These competing studies, sometimes with vastly different conclusions, obviously pose risks to the careful scholar.

What does all this imply for research? Clearly it influences the selection of priorities for research and successfully carrying out IEL research. Empiricism, multidisciplinary approaches, and the breadth of legal understand-

---

[22] For example, discussion about the Smoot–Hawley Tariff Act of 1930, and debate in 1948–1951 about an International Trade Organization (ITO).

[23] Debates during the May 1997 French elections and the 1994 debate in the US on WTO acceptance come to mind.

[24] See, e.g., the numerous news articles in the US during October and November 1997.

ing to relate not only general international law principles with IEL, but also both with national constitutional and other law, create quite a burden.

In some cases (maybe most) it would seem preferable to shape research so as to be useful for the "active users," the legal professionals (government or private) who must regularly cope with international law concepts and legal rules. This is a "policy research" preference rather than a "theory" preference, although obviously there are many situations in which theory has important relevance to policy. But such theory needs to be "good theory," and normally good theory must be tested, usually by empirical observation.

. . .

Part II

The GATT and its troubled origins

The details of the unusual "birth" of the GATT, in 1947 and 1948, along with the unfortunate story of the failure of the vision at that time to create an ITO – an International Trade Organization – have been extensively set forth in several books of mine, particularly my 1969 book, *World Trade and the Law of GATT*. Chapter 2 is an early (1967) article of mine and gives a brief introduction to that history (most of this article is omitted from the chapter). Chapters 3 and 4 deal with the results of the Tokyo Round of negotiations, which was the seventh major negotiating round under GATT held from 1973 to 1979. This round addressed questions about the direction of the trading system, particularly how to shift the focus from the reduction of tariffs to the perplexing problems of nontariff barriers which were becoming increasingly important. The GATT "birth defects" were beginning to be more troublesome, both in the dispute settlement procedures (taken up in Part IV), and in connection with the legal structure of GATT and the difficulty of amending its rules. The Tokyo Round approach was to negotiate a series of "side agreements," each of which was optional, and each of which addressed a particular set of trade barriers. The eighth and final trade round under the GATT, the Uruguay Round (1986 to 1994) reacted to the problems engaged in the Tokyo Round by, *inter alia*, massively revising the trade rules with the development of a totally new agreement to replace the GATT (keeping the GATT text as an annex) and requiring almost all of this new text to be accepted by all adherents. This was the so-called "single package" approach. In addition, the Uruguay Round (briefly discussed in Part VI below) created a new organization, the World Trade Organization (WTO), to attempt to remedy most of the GATT birth defects. It also overhauled the dispute settlement rules, moving them a giant step towards "rule orientation" (as we see in Part IV below).

Some of the text below deals with national implementation of the negotiations such as the Tokyo Round. For more detail on this, however, the reader is referred to J. Jackson, J. Louis, and M. Matsushita, *Implementing the Tokyo Round: National Constitutions and International Economic Rules* (University of Michigan Press, 1984) (dealing with the US, Europe, and Japan), and more recently John H. Jackson and Alan O. Sykes (eds.), *Implementing the Uruguay Round* (1997), with eleven specific country authors.

2   The puzzle of GATT: legal aspects of a surprising institution*

Nineteen years ago last October delegates of twenty-two nations signed a temporary agreement involving tariffs and international trade.[1] Today, two decades later, this "temporary agreement" is one of the principal regulating institutions for the international trade of over seventy nations.[2]

If one were asked in the early years of the General Agreement on Tariffs and Trade (GATT) whether or not it would survive long, the answer no doubt would have been very pessimistic. With scarcely any institutional framework, with no provision for a secretariat,[3] and with

---

* This chapter is based on John H. Jackson, "The Puzzle of GATT: Legal Aspects of a Surprising Institution" (1967) 1 *Journal of World Trade Law* 2, 131–161. I wish to acknowledge the assistance of the University of California School of Law, Berkeley (where I was Professor of Law until the summer of 1966), in providing resources and leave time for conducting research on the law of GATT. I also wish to acknowledge the cooperation of various members of the GATT Secretariat in Geneva, Switzerland, as well as members of various delegations there.

[1] General Agreement on Tariffs and Trade, October 30, 1947, 55 UNTS 194.
[2] The latest status of the GATT membership is set forth in GATT Press Release 973 of November 1, 1966. There are seventy contracting parties to the GATT, plus four countries which have acceded provisionally, two countries which participate in GATT under special arrangements, and eight countries which apply GATT *de facto* pending final decision as to future commercial policy. GATT documentation is extensive. Letter and number document designations in this article are GATT documents unless otherwise specified. Citations to GATT documentation in this article will utilize the following abbreviations and symbols: "PR" for press release; and "L/" followed by a number, indicates the "L" series of documents. The *Basic Instruments and Selected Documents* are a series of volumes, usually one per year, containing selected documents from GATT. Recently, GATT has completely revised its policy of derestricting documents, so as of December 8, 1966 a large number of GATT documents have become available to the public for the first time. See INF/121, L/2647, and INF/122.
[3] The General Agreement itself contains no mention of a secretariat. The original idea was that the secretariat of the International Trade Organization (ITO) would service GATT, and at the beginning of GATT the "Interim Commission for the International Trade Organization" (ICITO) performed the services of the secretariat. To this day, the legal structure, when it is not blurred, consists of this relationship. Rule 15 of the Rules of Procedure for the Contracting Parties of GATT provides: "[T]he usual duties of a Secretariat shall, by agreement with the Interim Commission for the International Trade Organization, be performed by the Executive Secretary of the Interim Commission on a reimburs-

legal ties to an organization that failed to materialize,[4] the GATT would hardly have qualified as "most likely to succeed" among the international organizations set up in the years immediately following World War II. Indeed, in theory at least, GATT was not an "international organization" at all – merely an "agreement."[5] Despite the lack of an institutional framework, despite lack of financial support except of the most meager sort,[6] and despite the powerful forces for trade protectionism which killed the International Trade Organization (ITO)[7] and tried to kill GATT,[8] GATT survived. The fact that GATT did survive, and that it has become a major force in international relations today, is not only surprising but instructive.

It is instructive because it tends to indicate that legal structures or institutions have less to do with the development of affairs than dimly understood political or economic forces, aided by the efforts of dedicated men. One could argue that, despite the apparent obstacles, GATT survived and developed because history "required" it to do so. These explanations, more appropriate for the historian, the political scientist, or the economist than for the lawyer, suggest that constitutional form may not be as significant in international institutions as it seems.

These reflections suggest the danger of a "legal approach" to the GATT. This is reinforced when one observes GATT work at close hand. Lawyers' considerations seem to play a small part. The secretariat which serves GATT presently has no position for a lawyer. Delegates and secretariat members often express an attitude such as "Let's not be concerned with legal technicalities." The GATT has consciously abandoned an attempt to

---

able basis." Further discussion of the many interesting legal problems of the Secretariat of GATT had to be omitted from this article due to space limitations.

[4] The International Trade Organization (ITO) Charter was drafted at the Havana Conference 1947–1948, but when the US President finally decided in 1950 not to submit the ITO Charter to Congress for ratification, the ITO died. See Diebold, "The End of the ITO . . ." (Princeton Essays in International Finance No. 16, 1952); and Gardner, *Sterling–Dollar Diplomacy* (Clarendon Press, Oxford, 1956), 378.

[5] The General Agreement refers to "contracting parties" and to "CONTRACTING PARTIES." The latter, according to Article XXV(1) means the contracting parties "acting jointly." At one of the preparatory sessions for GATT is was decided to use the term "contracting parties," instead of "committee" or some other term, in order to remove any connotation of formal organization. GATT, *Analytical Index to the General Agreements* (2nd revision, 1966), 133. See UN Doc. EPCT/TAC/PV/12, 3.

[6] The total GATT budget today is about US$3 million (L/2694), as compared to about US$18 million for the International Monetary Fund, US$19 million for the International Labor Organization, and US$21 million for the Food and Agriculture Organization.

[7] See Diebold, "The End of the ITO"; and Gardner, *Sterling–Dollar Diplomacy.*

[8] There is a history of hostility in the US Congress against GATT. One example of this is still in 19 USC 1351 where Congress states: "[T]he enactment of the Trade Agreements Extension Act of 1955 shall not be construed to determine or indicate the approval or disapproval by the Congress of the executive agreement known as the General Agreement on Tariffs and Trade."

solve some legal problems which seemed perplexing and irreconcilable, proceeding on to other business.[9]

Yet legal problems there are. The GATT is being invoked before national courts.[10] Certain provisions of GATT have proved very confining and yet have been respected.[11] Some delegates to GATT have expressed a plea to "know where we stand, to know our rights," and others have been pushing for greater sanctions in the event of breach.[12]

The purpose and commission of this article is to survey the legal aspects of the GATT. It is not an easy assignment because any selection of problems is certain to leave out interesting and important topics, and because most of the problems selected for treatment here can each form the focus of a lengthier work. Nevertheless, this discussion may serve as a starting point for those who wish to study GATT law.[13]

This article will discuss legal aspects of GATT under five major headings as follows:

I. The fundamental treaty law of GATT.
II. Tariff negotiations and tariff bindings.
III. Protecting the value of tariff concessions.
IV. Exceptions and escape clauses: continuous negotiation in GATT.
V. Dispute resolution in GATT.

---

[9] See, for example, GATT, "Report of the Working Party on the Association of Overseas Territories with the European Economic Community including Commodity Trade Studies" (GATT Doc. L/805/Rev. 1, 1958), 5. See also GATT, Report by the Intersessional Committee, "The Treaty Establishing European Economic Community," para. 3, reprinted at *Basic Instruments and Selected Documents*, 7th Supplement, 69, 70.

[10] See, for example, US *amicus curiae* brief in the case of *Tupman Thurlow Company Inc.*, v. *W. F. Moss, Commissioner*, 252 F. Supp. 641 (1966), 5 ILM 483; *Baldwin-Lima-Hamilton Corp.* v. *Superior Court*, 208 Cal. App. 2d 803, 25 Cal. Reptr. 798 (1962) (hearing denied December 19, 1962). See also Comment, "GATT, the California Buy American Act, and the Continuing Struggle Between Free Trade and Protectionism" (1964) 52 *California Law Review* 335; Comment, "National Power to Control State Discrimination Against Foreign Goods and Persons: A Study in Federalism" (1960) 12 *Stanford Law Review* 355; Comment, "California's Buy-American Policy: Conflict with GATT and the Constitution" (1964) 17 *Stanford Law Review* 119.

[11] See the discussion of Article XXX of GATT concerning amendments in Part I.C below.

[12] For proposals to amend Article XXIII of GATT to establish rules increasing sanctions for breach of GATT, see GATT Doc. COM.TD/F/1–4.

[13] See, in addition, Seyid Muhammad, *The Legal Framework of World Trade* (Praeger, New York, 1958); and Note, "United States Participation in the General Agreement on Tariffs and Trade" (1961) 61 *Columbia Law Review* 505. For a more general treatment from an economist's viewpoint, see G. Curzon, *Multilateral Commercial Diplomacy: The General Agreement on Tariffs and Trade and Its Impact on National Commercial Policies and Techniques* (Michael Joseph, London, 1965).

I.   The fundamental treaty law of GATT

The basic treaty, the "General Agreement" itself, was completed in October 1947. It has technically never come into force,[14] being applied by a "Protocol of Provisional Application" described below.[15] The GATT has been amended a number of times,[16] and affected by other protocols, including some not technically "in force" themselves,[17] so that even the basic treaty is a complex set of instruments, applying with different rigor to different countries. For the lawyer to ascertain, at any given time, the precise legal commitments between any two nations is no easy task.[18] This part will outline the steps necessary to make such a determination, in four subtopics:

1. a brief survey of the preparatory work for GATT with an analysis of its relevance to GATT and its relation to the ITO which was drafted at the same time;

[14] Article XXVI of GATT governs how governments may accept the Agreement itself, and provides a formula for ascertaining when a sufficient number of governments has accepted the agreement so that it enters into force. From the GATT documentation it appears that only one country, Haiti, has accepted the General Agreement itself. See L/2375/Add. 1, 20 (March 5, 1965 document, reprinting a document of September 25, 1958).

[15] See subpart B below.

[16] Lists of protocols and treaties affecting the GATT may be found in UN Doc. ST/LEG/3, Status of Multilateral Conventions, for instruments drawn prior to February 1, 1955 and deposited with the Secretary-General; and GATT Doc. PROT/2 (as revised through August 1966) for instruments drawn subsequent to February 1955. Some of these instruments actually amend the text of GATT, while others simply affect the rigor or force, or the parties involved, of various clauses in GATT. There are thirty-six treaty instruments including the General Agreement itself listed in UN Doc. ST/LEG/3. GATT Doc. PROT/2 lists sixty-seven instruments up to July 1966. For protocols subsequent to July 1966, see L/2714 (December 2, 1966). It should be noted that, in addition to the instruments listed in the two official lists as relating to GATT, there are certain other instruments with treaty force or treaty-like characteristics which also relate to GATT. Some are in force and some not. Among these are, of course, the Havana Charter itself (see UN Doc. ICITO/1/4; and UN Doc. E/CONF.2/78), two GATT "Certifications of Rectifications and Modifications"; Long-term arrangement regarding international trade and cotton textiles (GATT 1963). There are also others, including a number of bilateral agreements between parties to GATT which relate to their GATT obligations.

[17] GATT Doc. PROT/2 indicates which of the instruments listed therein are in force, and to which countries they apply.

[18] For instance, obligations relating to subsidies found in Article XVI(4) of GATT are affected by a series of Declarations and "procès-verbaux." Since some newly independent countries became members of GATT under sponsorship procedures outlined in this article below at subpart D of this part, and since such independent countries are deemed to have the same position in GATT as the sponsoring country at the time of sponsorship, such new GATT parties might be considered to have the same position with respect to Article XVI(4) as the sponsoring country at the time of the sponsorship. Yet an examination of GATT Doc. PROT/2, 42 regarding the Declaration Giving Effect to the Provisions of Article XVI(4) indicates that no new independent, less developed country which entered GATT under sponsorship is deemed to be applying this clause of the GATT. It is not clear why this is the case, although added information from specific governments concerned might enable one to rationalize this position.

2. the Protocol of Provisional Application and its relation to GATT, to introduce the problem of what is the legal force of GATT;
3. the amending process of GATT; and
4. a short introduction to the complex "membership" law of GATT, suggesting an approach to the question of which nations are legally bound by portions of the General Agreement.

A. Preparatory work

The collapse of international trade in the 1930s and its effects on peace and war led some world leaders to conclude that new international economic institutions were essential.[19] The goals envisaged for such institutions were as much political as economic – the prevention of war and the establishment of a just system of economic relations were as important as the economic benefits that might derive from international trade and economic stability.[20] During World War II preparations were made for developing such institutions.[21] The Bretton Woods Conference and the resulting agreements were the early result of these preparations.[22] But even at that conference it was recognized that an international organization to regulate trade was a necessary complement to the IMF and the IBRD.[23]

The US State Department had prepared a draft charter of an International Trade Organization.[24] At the first session of the United Nations, the Economic and Social Council resolved[25] that a conference to draft a charter for an ITO should be called, and that a preparatory committee for this conference be established.

In all, four international conferences were held to draft an ITO charter, three of which were "preparatory."[26] The first was a meeting of the

---

[19] See Gardner, *Sterling–Dollar Diplomacy*; US State Department, "Sumner Welles Speech 1941" (Commercial Policy Series No. 71), and US State Department, "Harry Hawkins Speech 1944" (Commercial Policy Series No. 74).

[20] In addition to the speeches and materials referenced in the previous footnote, see the general policy speeches made by delegates at the opening of the Second Session of the Preparatory Committee at the Geneva Conference in 1947, UN Doc. EPCT/PV2/1–4.

[21] See Gardner, *Sterling–Dollar Diplomacy*.

[22] See Bretton Woods Proceedings, the Articles of Agreement of the International Monetary Fund, and of the International Bank for Reconstruction and Development.

[23] Bretton Woods Proceedings, vol. 1, 941. The conference resolved "complete attainment of . . . purposes and objectives [of the IMF] . . . cannot be achieved through the instrumentality of the fund alone," and recommended that the governments seek agreement "to reduce obstacles to international trade and in other ways promote mutually advantageous international commercial relations."

[24] US State Department Doc. 2411, December 1945.

[25] UN Economic and Social Council Resolution 1/13, February 18, 1946, UN Doc. E/22.

[26] The documents of all conferences are officially United Nations documents. The first three bear the document numbers E/PC/T (herein shortened to EPCT) plus other letters and numbers designating sub-bodies of the Preparatory Committee. The fourth, the Havana

"Preparatory Committee" in London from October 15 to November 26, 1946.[27] The second was a meeting of the "Drafting Committee" of the Preparatory Committee, held at Lake Success, New York, from January 20 to February 25, 1947[28] to edit and draft a charter in light of the London meeting, with alternatives for provisions on which the London meeting could not agree. The third was the Geneva Conference, officially the Second Session of the Preparatory Committee, which was held from April 10, 1947 to October 30, 1947.[29] This conference had a dual function. On the one hand the Committee continued its drafting of an ITO charter, preparing for the Havana Conference. On the other hand, twenty-two nations undertook negotiations with a view to reducing tariffs and embodied the results of these negotiations in the General Agreement on Tariffs and Trade.[30]

Fourthly, the Havana Conference itself was held from November 21, 1947 to March 24, 1948 for the purpose of finally drafting an ITO charter.[31]

Clearly from the point of view of GATT problems, the Geneva Conference was the most important. The GATT was finally drafted there (a previous draft had been prepared at Lake Success[32]) and transmitted to governments.[33] But in an important sense all preparatory work for the ITO charter is relevant to GATT. Much of the GATT was taken verbatim from the draft of the ITO charter as it stood at the end of the Geneva Conference deliberations on ITO.[34] The General Agreement was expressly tied to the prospective ITO.[35] For example, certain clauses resulting from the Havana

Conference, bears the document numbers E/CONF.2/-. See GATT, *Analytical Index to the General Agreements* (2nd revision, 1966), ii and iii.

[27] Report of the First Session of the Preparatory Committee of the United Nations Conference on Trade and Employment, London, October 1946.

[28] Report of the Drafting Committee of the Preparatory Committee of the United Nations Conference on Trade and Employment, Lake Success, New York, EPCT/34, March 5, 1947.

[29] Report of the Second Session of the Preparatory Committee of the United Nations Conference on Trade and Employment, Geneva, August 1974, EPCT/186; Final Act adopted at the conclusion of the Second Session etc., 55 UNTS 188 (October 30, 1947).

[30] The documents of the Geneva Conference most relating to GATT were in a series EPCT/TAC/- (the Trade Agreement Committee).

[31] Final Act and related documents, United Nations Conference on Trade and Employment, April 1948. UN Doc. ICITO/1/4 and E/CONF.2/78. See also ICITO, September 1948, Reports of Committees and Principal Subcommittees [of United Nations Conference on Trade and Employment held at Havana, Cuba], UN Doc. ICITO/1/8.

[32] Report of the Drafting Committee of the Preparatory Committee, EPCT/34, 65 (note 28 above). See also "Resolution regarding the negotiation of a multilateral trade agreement embodying tariff concession," in Report of the First Session of the Preparatory Committee, EPCT/33, 47.

[33] Final Act adopted at the conclusion of the Second Session etc. (note 29 above).

[34] See EPCT/189, August 30, 1947, the draft of the General Agreement on Tariffs and Trade taken from the Preparatory Committee's text of corresponding Articles in the draft Havana Charter as embodied in EPCT/180.

[35] Article XXIX of GATT is entitled "The Relation of the Agreement to the Havana Charter."

Conference were to be substituted in the General Agreement, absent objection, if the ITO came into effect, and later amendments to GATT reflected Havana Conference work on the ITO.[36] Finally, when the ITO failed to come into being, the GATT had to fill the gap in international relations.[37] However, persons dealing with the GATT were often those who had drafted the ITO and their attitudes towards GATT were undoubtedly colored by their experiences in the ITO negotiations.[38]

The function of the preparatory work for ITO in the interpretation of the GATT is thus complex. Although a broad brush generalization would state that all ITO preparatory work is relevant to GATT, a stricter view would conclude that the ITO preparations must be specifically traced as a source of language in the GATT, to be relevant.

Even when the ITO preparatory work relates to a clause of the ITO charter which was selected for inclusion in GATT, there is arguably a difference in the effect of that preparatory work on interpretation of GATT. The GATT was drafted as a "trade agreement," including only those clauses which the draftsmen felt were normally found in trade agreements,[39] and which were considered essential to protect the value of tariff concessions.[40] Consequently the preparatory work pointed to interpretations of GATT which would fulfill these two criteria. GATT was not considered an "organization,"[41] it was merely a contract with specific limited purposes. It is fair to state that the subsequent development of GATT has pushed it far beyond this initial image.[42] The extension of

[36] Article XXIX(2) of GATT as it was originally worded stated: "[O]n the day on which the Charter of the International Trade Organization enters into force, Article I and Part II of this Agreement shall be suspended and superseded by the corresponding provisions of the Charter; Provided that . . . any contracting party may lodge . . . an objection . . ." See GATT, *Analytical Index to the General Agreements* (2nd revision, 1966), 125.
[37] The official death of the ITO is considered to be the press release of the President of the United States announcing that he would not submit the ITO Charter to the Congress. Gardner, *Sterling–Dollar Diplomacy*, 378.
[38] For instance, L. D. Wilgress of Canada was a signatory of the Final Act of the Geneva Conference in 1947 and the Havana Conference in 1948, and was Chairman of the Contracting Parties of GATT from their first through to the fifth and their ninth through to the eleventh sessions (spanning the first nine years of GATT existence).
[39] UN Doc. EPCT/TAC/PV/11, 34–35 (September 5, 1947, discussion at Geneva conference).
[40] UN Doc. EPCT/TAC/PV/1, 24 (August 5, 1947, Geneva conference discussion).
[41] See note 5 above, and discussion in the preparatory work at Geneva, 1947, UN Doc. EPCT/TAC/PV/12 (September 16, 1947).
[42] This is evidenced by the continual development of the committee structure in GATT including the early Balance of Payments Committee and the Intersessional Committee, culminating in the development of the "Council" (see *Basic Instruments and Selected Documents*, 9th Supplement, 7, 1961). Another action reflecting the attitude of the Contracting Parties towards the GATT is a decision of March 23, 1965 changing the title of the "Executive Secretary" to "Director-General," thus conforming the title of the chief executive to that of a number of other international organizations. *Basic Instruments and Selected Documents*, 13th Supplement, 19.

GATT's role can be justified not only on the basis of its practice and custom (if one is prepared to accept this as a basis) but also on the basis of continued participation, policy statements, and the utilization of GATT institutions by many of the governments concerned.[43] Coupled with a right to withdraw on relatively short notice,[44] this continued participation suggests an ongoing basic consensus that one can use to rationalize the flexible and pragmatic approach that has characterized GATT during its existence. In any event it is clear that in practice GATT will continue to be treated as a major international organization.

B.   The legal force of GATT and the Protocol of Provisional Application

In August 1947 at Geneva, the parties to the GATT negotiations were faced with a dilemma. There was the desire to put the tariff concessions into effect as soon as possible in order to prevent market disruption and speculation as well as political opposition that could ensue if details of the concessions leaked or became public information before the Agreement became effective. Against this was the legal necessity for some nations to obtain legislative changes in laws inconsistent with parts of the GATT.[45] The solution chosen was "provisional application," by a protocol which stated that eight named governments undertake:

provided that this Protocol shall have been signed on behalf of all the foregoing Governments not later than 15 November 1947, to apply provisionally on and after 1 January 1948:
(a) Part I and III of the General Agreement on Tariffs and Trade, and
(b) Part II of that Agreement to the fullest extent not inconsistent with existing legislation.[46]

The Protocol allowed other Geneva participants to sign, and stated that any nation could withdraw on sixty days' notice (compared to the six months' notice required in the General Agreement).[47]

This Protocol became effective when the eight named countries signed before November 15, 1947,[48] and it is still effective. The General Agreement

---

[43] For instance, the Council of GATT has no authorization in the General Agreement itself, but is set up by decision of the Contracting Parties. Yet a considerable number of the contracting parties participate in the work of the Council. Any contracting party who desires can become a member of the Council if it is willing to assume the responsibilities.

[44] See subpart B below.

[45] See the preparatory discussion, Geneva, 1947, UN Doc. EPCT/TAC/PV/1–5.

[46] 55 UNTS 308.   [47] Ibid.; cf. GATT Article XXXI.

[48] The signatures, including some with reservations, are set out at 55 UNTS 312–316. The eight named countries, essential for the Protocol to come into force, were Australia, Belgium, Canada, France, Luxembourg, Netherlands, the United Kingdom, and the United States.

is applied through this Protocol or similar protocols signed by governments which later became contracting parties to GATT.[49]

What is the effect of this on GATT? There are two major effects; first, the withdrawal period is shorter, as stated above; and, secondly, a large portion of GATT obligations are effective only to "the extent not inconsistent with existing legislation." The first effect needs no additional explanation, except to note that it reinforces the "continuing consensus" interpretation of GATT mentioned above. The second effect needs some elaboration. It might also be argued that the word "provisional" affects the interpretation of the whole GATT agreement because the Protocol applies the entire GATT "provisionally." No instance where the term "provisional" has resulted in any noticeable difference in the approach or application of GATT has been found except as just stated above. "Provisional" seems to be defined by the remainder of the Protocol, and apparently that means only the "fullest extent not inconsistent with existing legislation" (for Part II).

The concept "not inconsistent with existing legislation" needs elaboration. There are three problems that merit discussion. First, "existing" at what point of time? Secondly, whose legislation, that of local subdivisions as well as that of the nation? Thirdly, what does "inconsistent" mean, especially in the context of legislation that is not mandatory but permissive, i.e. which authorizes (but does not require) executive action or regulation which would be inconsistent with GATT Part II?

First, what point of time is relevant? At the third session of the GATT Contracting Parties, an issue was raised whether "existing legislation" in the Protocol meant that which existed at the date a nation signed the Protocol, or the date in the last paragraph of the Protocol (October 30, 1947). After consideration the then chairman of the Contracting Parties ruled that it refers to the latter.[50] The procedure is perhaps more intriguing than the substantive result of this ruling, i.e. the apparent acceptance by states of a ruling of a chairman of a group of government representatives as a definitive interpretation of treaty language.

Secondly, whose legislation is relevant? In a federal state, does "existing legislation" also include legislation of the federal subdivisions? Although this issue has arisen in litigation,[51] it is not easy to answer. The preparatory

---

These eight signatures were completed before November 15, 1947. Subsequently fourteen other governments signed the Protocol, but four (China, Syria, Lebanon, and Liberia) later withdrew. Curzon, *Multilateral Commercial Diplomacy.*

[49] The protocols of accession are listed in GATT, *Analytical Index to the General Agreements* (2nd revision, 1966), 155–157.

[50] *Basic Instruments and Selected Documents,* vol. II, 35, Ruling on August 11, 1949.

[51] *Baldwin-Lima-Hamilton Corp.* v. *Superior Court,* 208 Cal. App. 2d 803, 25 Cal. Reptr. 798 (1962) (hearing denied December 19, 1962).

work for GATT does not completely settle it.[52] In the subsequent practice of GATT only one reference to this issue can be found. (India in reporting on "existing legislation" expressly excepted specified subdivision legislation from its report because it had not had the time to study it).[53] Article XXIV, paragraph 12 relates to this problem also and leads one to an analysis that depends heavily on the constitutional law of the nation concerned, both as to the supremacy or non-supremacy of the federal treaties and as to the effect of GATT and the Protocol of Provisional Application as municipal law (without additional implementing legislation).[54]

The third problem concerning the Protocol that must be discussed is the question of what is the "fullest extent not inconsistent with existing legislation." This issue is best posed by a hypothetical.

Legislation of nation A (signatory in 1947 of the Protocol) existing on October 30, 1947 *"authorizes* the President to limit imports by quota whenever they injure a domestic producer, for such time as the President shall determine." Such quotas would be inconsistent with Article XI of the GATT.

1. Prior to October 30, 1947 the President of A had limited imports of perfume to one million units per year, effective indefinitely.
2. In 1948 the President proclaims a quota on wheat of one million units per year.

In either case is A violating its international obligations? If the key word in A's legislation were "requires" instead of "authorizes," one would probably conclude that neither case 1 nor case 2 were a violation of the Protocol. But what about "authorizing" legislation? This issue has generated some controversy in GATT resulting in practice which suggests a conclusion that both cases are a violation of GATT.

When the issue was initially raised in GATT, a working party report adopted by the GATT concluded that measures are within the "existing legislation" exception of the Protocol:

provided that the legislation on which it is based is by its terms or expressed intent of a mandatory character – that is, it imposes on the executive authority requirements which cannot be modified by executive action.[55]

This ruling was reaffirmed in 1955, at a time when the GATT members considered and accepted a proposal that would allow members to accept

---

[52] Mention of the problem is found at UN Doc. EPTC/TAC/PV/11, 44; and UN Doc. EPCT/TAC/PV19, 33.
[53] L/2375/Add. 1, 11.
[54] Article XXIV(12) of GATT reads: "Each contracting party shall take such reasonable measures as may be available to it to ensure observance of the provisions of this Agreement by the regional and local governments and authorities within its territories."
[55] *Basic Instruments and Selected Documents,* vol. II, 62.

the GATT "definitively" (i.e., directly, without application through the appropriate Protocol), while expressing a reservation as to that legislation "existing" within the Protocol's meaning.[56]

Several cases have arisen testing this concept of "not inconsistent with existing legislation." In each case the GATT official position was in accord with the discussion above.[57] However, in at least one case a waiver was issued by GATT to the nation concerned, in a sense "legitimizing" its action which that nation claimed was allowed in any case under the Protocol.[58]

C.   Amending the GATT

Article XXX provides the basic framework for amending GATT, requiring unanimous consent to change Part I (i.e., Articles I and II and the Schedules incorporated by reference), Article XXIX and Article XXX itself. Other amendments become effective "in respect of those contracting parties which accept them" upon acceptance of two-thirds of the members.

Article XXX has proven one of the most troublesome and restricting in GATT. The unanimity requirement has engendered an almost hopelessly confusing situation regarding the schedules (the author has been told that some nations do not even know the true status of their *own* tariff concessions in GATT). In addition, the provision that amendments which are authorized by two-thirds vote apply only to those governments who accept them, has the potential for needless procedural confusion. Three problems in particular will be discussed: the unanimity requirement and schedule adjustments; the relation of waivers under Article XXV to amendments; and procedural difficulties caused by Article XXX.

The schedules of tariff concessions are by Article II "hereby made an integral part of Part I of this Agreement." A schedule is a detailed list of products for a specific GATT party, which states for each product that party's maximum allowable tariff. Thus a schedule for the United Kingdom might list "Widgets – 10 percent," meaning that the UK has promised or "bound" itself to impose a tariff on widgets that will never exceed 10 percent *ad valorem*. The schedules fill many volumes and altogether contain some 65,000 items. Because errors are found, and because the GATT contains procedures for modifying or renegotiating items on the schedules

---

[56] *Basic Instruments and Selected Documents*, 3rd Supplement, 249.

[57] *Basic Instruments and Selected Documents*, 1st Supplement, 61, *Basic Instruments and Selected Documents*, 6th Supplement, 60–61, *Basic Instruments and Selected Documents*, 7th Supplement, 104–107.

[58] Waiver to West Germany for its marketing laws which apply quantitative restrictions to certain agricultural products, decision of May 30, 1959, *Basic Instruments and Selected Documents*, 8th Supplement, 31. This waiver has apparently expired.

(see Part II below), the schedules are constantly being changed. Since its inception there have been twenty-six protocols of "rectification, modification, or supplementary concessions" amending the schedules, of which six are technically not in force.[59] Protocols completed for signature as long ago as 1955 are still not in force.[60] However, oddly enough, and again illustrative of the pragmatic approach of the GATT, these schedule changes are treated by GATT parties as if they were in force.[61]

In 1955 an attempt was made, at the major review session of GATT, to amend Article XXX to provide:

any amendment to the schedules . . . which records rectifications of a purely formal character or modifications resulting from action taken under paragraph 6 of Article II, Article XVIII, Article XXIV, Article XXVII or Article XXVIII, shall become effective on the thirtieth day following certification to this effect by the C*ONTRACTING P*ARTIES: *Provided* that prior to such certification, all contracting parties have been notified of the proposed amendment and no objection has been raised, within thirty days of such notification by any contracting party on the ground that the proposed amendments are not within the terms of this paragraph.[62]

Because one nation still has not accepted this amendment, it remains technically not in effect.[63] Yet subsequent changes to the schedules have been embodied in a series of "certifications" which state:

on the date of the entry into force of paragraph 3 of Article XXX this decision shall constitute a certification by the C*ONTRACTING P*ARTIES on that date . . .[64]

These certifications are also treated by GATT parties as if they were in effect![65]

The relation of Article XXV to Article XXX has posed an intriguing legal problem. Article XXV paragraph 5 provides that by two-thirds votes including half of the members, GATT contracting parties may "In exceptional circumstances not elsewhere provided for in this Agreement . . . waive an obligation imposed upon a contracting party by the Agreement."

[59] GATT Doc. PROT/2, revised to August 1966.   [60] *Ibid.*
[61] This was stated to be the case in discussions which the author had with various government and secretariat personnel, and is illustrated by the fact that no complaints of breach of GATT obligations have been brought when nations institute the tariff changes resulting from the changes to the GATT schedule.
[62] GATT, Final Act adopted at the Ninth Session of the Contracting Parties and Protocol Amending Part I and Articles XXIX and XXX of the General Agreement, etc. March 10, 1955, Geneva, 28.
[63] GATT Doc. PROT/2, 5. L/2575 (March 10, 1966).
[64] GATT, Certification Relating to Rectifications and Modifications of Schedules to the General Agreement on Tariffs and Trade, January 15, 1963, Geneva; GATT, Second Certification Relating to Rectifications and Modifications of Schedules to the General Agreement on Tariffs and Trade, April 29, 1964, Geneva.
[65] Note 61 above.

Often waivers are granted to obligations under Part I of GATT (including schedules), so as, for instance, to allow a party to change tariff concessions pursuant to a revision of its customs tariff.[66] Article XXX, however, requires unanimity to amend Part I. Therefore, it has been argued, waivers should not be granted to Part I if they amount in effect to an amendment, unless the vote is unanimous. This argument has been rejected by the GATT contracting parties, partly because of the opening clause of Article XXX (which states: "Except where provision for modification is made elsewhere in this Agreement . . .") arguing that Article XXV is just such other provision for modification excepted from Article XXX.[67] The problem is, of course, that if the waiver power is unlimited[68] it could be used to produce an effect substantially the same as an amendment. In fact, at least two waivers[69] have been framed in general terms to apply to any contracting party who fulfilled the *criteria* just as an amendment would be. Most waivers apply to just one named contracting party, and often for a limited time.[70] At their eleventh session the Contracting Parties formulated a series of guidelines for the issuance of waivers, partly as a response to the "amendment" problem.[71]

The procedural difficulties that can result from Article XXX can be illustrated by the following hypothetical. Article XXV provides that most actions of the Contracting Parties be by majority vote. Suppose an amendment were adopted by two-thirds under Article XXX which changed Article XXV to require a majority of GATT members (not just those present and voting), and suppose nation A voted for the amendment but B did not. Article XXX provides that such amendment is effective "in respect of those contracting parties which accept it." Thus the amended Article XXV applies to A but not to B. B is governed by the prior Article XXV. Now consider a vote at a meeting of the Contracting Parties! How is it to be evaluated?[72]

---

[66] Waiver to Brazil of November 16, 1956, *Basic Instruments and Selected Documents*, 5th Supplement, 36. Recent waivers to obligations under Part I of GATT include a waiver to the United States (automotive products), *Basic Instruments and Selected Documents*, 14th Supplement, 37, December 20, 1956; and to Australia (preferences for less developed countries), March 28, 1966, *Basic Instruments and Selected Documents*, 14th Supplement, 23.

[67] L/403, September 7, 1955.

[68] Working Party report adopted by Contracting Parties on November 10, 1952, *Basic Instruments and Selected Documents*, 1st Supplement, 86.

[69] Decision of October 22, 1951 extending the time limit in Article XX, Part II, *Basic Instruments and Selected Documents*, vol. II, 28; decision of March 5, 1955 ("hard-core" decision relating to import restrictions), *Basic Instruments and Selected Documents*, 3rd Supplement, 38.

[70] See list of waivers at *Basic Instruments and Selected Documents*, 14th Supplement, 224–228.

[71] Procedures adopted November 1, 1956, *Basic Instruments and Selected Documents*, 5th Supplement, 25.

[72] *Basic Instruments and Selected Documents*, 13th Supplement, 108.

Article XXX's phrasing reflects ideas stemming from days when trade relations were primarily bilateral, and no obligations could be imposed on a nation without its consent.[73] In addition it fails to distinguish between the rules which are procedural in nature and those which are substantive. It is submitted that the idea that no international trade obligations should be imposed on a nation without its consent no longer deserves unwavering recognition. Such an idea was truly effective, if at all, for only a few large, powerful nations. For most countries, dependence on international trade is a fact of life and leaves them vulnerable to forces beyond their control including sometimes selfish and irresponsible actions of trading parties.[74] The very purpose of an international organization of trading relationships is to reduce the chance of such actions hurting other nations and thereby to increase the stability of international trading relations. A change in the amending Article of GATT seems in order. Even the 1955 amendment (not yet in effect) is probably inadequate for the future of GATT.

D.   *Membership and participation in GATT*

There are basically four ways to become a "contracting party" (loosely referred to as a "member") of GATT. Three involve accession by a government: by the Protocol of Provisional Application;[75] by subsequent protocol and agreement under Article XXXIII of GATT;[76] and by directly accepting the GATT itself under Article XXVI(2) (only one nation has accepted GATT in this manner and then only after acceding to GATT through a protocol).[77] These methods of accession are preceded by tariff negotiations, the "ticket of admission,"[78] and often these negotiations extend for several years, during which time, by special declaration (proto-

---

[73] See, for example, discussion at EPTC/TAC/PV15, as excerpted in GATT, *Analytical Index to the General Agreements* (2nd revision, 1966), 150.

[74] An analysis of the percentage ratio of exports to total GNP is one measure of dependence on international trade. For example, the percentage for Netherlands is 48 percent, for Switzerland 31 percent, for Canada 21 percent, whereas for the US only 5.7 percent (based on IMF, *International Financial Statistics* (1966)).

[75] 55 UNTS 308, October 30, 1947.

[76] A list can be found in GATT, *Analytical Index to the General Agreements* (2nd revision, 1966), 155–156. This includes the so-called "Annecy Protocol" and the "Torquay Protocol."

[77] The sole nation accepting the agreement pursuant to Article XXVI is Haiti, L/2375/Add. 1, 20.

[78] The second and third "rounds" of tariff negotiations, at Annecy in 1949 and Torquay in 1951, were in substantial part negotiations for the accession of groups of governments. Ten new contracting parties entered GATT by the Annecy Protocol, and six by the Torquay Protocol. See *Basic Instruments and Selected Documents*, vol. II, 33–35, and 62 UNTS 121, 142 UNTS 34.

col) the applicant government is given "provisional accession"[79] to GATT, or relations with GATT are established by other special arrangements.[80]

The fourth "route" to membership is open to "customs territories, in respect of which a contracting party has accepted this Agreement: when such territory "possesses or acquires full autonomy in the conduct of its external commercial relations . . ."[81] In 1957 GATT set forth a series of recommended procedures to guide this sponsorship route to membership,[82] which enabled a newly independent government to have *de facto* participation in GATT pending a final decision as to entry into GATT.[83] Since 1960 a large group of new members have entered GATT in this manner.[84] The "sponsored" government is deemed to step into the GATT legal relations and obligations of the sponsoring parent just as they were when sponsorship occurred.[85]

---

[79] GATT Doc. PROT/2, Rev. 2. For example, Declaration on Provisional Accession of Yugoslavia, November 13, 1962, *Basic Instruments and Selected Documents*, 11th Supplement, 50.

[80] GATT Doc. PROT/2/Rev. 2. For example, Declaration on Relations between Contracting Parties and the Government of Poland, November 9, 1959, *Basic Instruments and Selected Documents*, 8th Supplement, 12. See also L/2595.

[81] Article XXVI(5)(c) provides: "If any of the customs territories, in respect of which a contracting party has accepted this agreement, possesses or acquires full autonomy in the conduct of its external commercial relations and of the other matters provided for in this agreement, such territories shall, upon sponsorship through a declaration by the responsible contracting party establishing the above-mentioned fact, be deemed to be a contracting party." See Kunugi, "State Succession in the Framework of GATT" (1965) 59 *American Journal of International Law* 28.

[82] *Basic Instruments and Selected Documents*, 6th Supplement, 11.

[83] *Ibid.*, para. 2. "At their next ordinary session, the contracting parties, after consultation with the representatives of the responsible contracting party and of the territory in question, should set a reasonable period during which the contracting party should continue to apply *de facto* the agreement in their relations with that territory, provided that that territory also continues to apply *de facto* the agreement to them . . ." The latest report on GATT membership contained in GATT press release 973 of November 1, 1966 indicates that eight countries are now applying GATT *de facto* pending a decision as to their future commercial policy. These countries are Algeria, Botswana, Congo, the Democratic Republic of Lesotho, the Maldive Islands, Mali, Singapore, and Zambia.

[84] A list can be found at GATT, *Analytical Index to the General Agreements* (2nd revision, 1966), 140.

[85] Report adopted on December 7, 1961 by the Contracting Parties, *Basic Instruments and Selected Documents*, 10th Supplement, 73. "The working party . . . wishes to point out that there can be no doubt that a government becoming a contracting party under Article XXVI(5)(c) does so on the terms and conditions previously accepted by the metropolitan government on behalf of the territory in question." The report in which this paragraph is contained concerns the application by a country of Article XXXV against Japan so that the GATT would not apply between that country and Japan. Newly sponsored states were deemed to inherit the same position *vis-à-vis* Japan under Article XXV as the sponsoring contracting party. It is not entirely clear how far this principle will extend, however, particularly with reference to protocols and treaties relating to GATT. See note 19 above.

Conclusion

GATT has clearly worked better during the two decades of its existence than anyone had the right to expect at the time the ITO died. Despite an inadequate constitutional base, the GATT has pragmatically picked its way from obstacle to obstacle to the point where its achievements are generally recognized.

But the future is always uncertain, and the GATT as it presently exists has defects which could prove troublesome if not disastrous. The complex tangle of treaties and protocols that have resulted from cumbersome amending processes and nineteen years of groping have several inherent dangers:

1. it makes it more difficult for the public to understand GATT and therefore more difficult to build the base of popular support that is probably essential for such an international institution to survive the onslaught of local or narrow protectionist interests;
2. its potential for unnecessary misunderstandings among nations concerning their obligations; and
3. it makes it more difficult to adjust flexibly to new circumstances and adapt to new needs.

This inflexibility may prove particularly troublesome now that the homogeneity of GATT membership has been destroyed by the accession of a large number of less developed countries. The added diversity of interest and viewpoint introduced by this phenomenon, plus the greater diversity that may be introduced as more state trading countries (especially those of Eastern Europe) become interested and join, will impose greater needs for flexibility and change upon GATT.

On the other hand GATT has strong points worth preserving. The specific trade conduct rules have been tested and are beginning to have a context of experience that is invaluable for interpretation and appraisal. There is a basic core of delicately balanced obligations recognized as desirable by most nations, including the tariff bindings and concessions which few governments would want to lose. There is a procedure for almost daily consultation and study about international trade problems, that, however, probably needs strengthening by more secretariat and staff resources, and by a procedure for speedy confidential consultation and decisions in those cases where speed and secrecy are essential to forestall a trade or payments crisis.

Thus, it would seem that soon after the Kennedy Round, careful attention should be given to a new or revised legal structure for GATT. As indicated early in this article, at balance may not only be economic and material benefits, but the fabric and essential conditions of peace itself.

The fact that GATT has survived and actually achieved much in the course of its history to date should not lead to the conclusion that the same will occur in the future. The fact that GATT has developed in spite of legal and constitutional defects does not automatically mean that the forces now coming to bear on GATT are very different from those of much of its experience. The participation of less developed countries and of socialist state trading countries has been mentioned. Indeed some observers already note in GATT a more strident tone of debate, and an increasing degree of procedural maneuvering, centering on bloc politics, and a tendency to ignore or overlook GATT obligations whenever they get "in the way." These tactics are justified on the ground that without them some GATT members seem to overlook legitimate aspirations of less powerful nations. But these tactics can destroy whatever values that presently exist in the GATT unless the various conflicting aspirations are reconciled or compromised by formal (i.e., legal) undertakings, both procedural and substantive.

A further factor suggests the need for greater attention to the "law" of GATT. So far GATT has existed in a period of overall growth and growing prosperity. In such a period nations as well as individuals become confident and sometimes lax. Failure to develop legal institutions can, however, come back to haunt the world if a real crisis occurs and the structure begins to break apart. It may break apart anyway, of course, but it would be tragic if the destruction were aided by misunderstandings engendered by a lack of adequate legal craftsmanship, or by the absence of appropriate institutions worked out in advance and impossible to develop during the heat of a crisis.

The pieces of the GATT puzzle now need to be fitted together.

3   The birth of the GATT–MTN system: a constitutional appraisal*

Introduction

The Multilateral Trade Negotiation (MTN) has now been completed.[1] This is an impressive accomplishment because the MTN[2] was conducted during one of the most difficult periods of peacetime economic stress.[3] Although launched in September 1973, at a General Agreement on Tariffs and Trade (GATT)[4] ministerial-level meeting,[5] the MTN proceeded by fits and starts and suffered long periods of relative inactivity. The negotiations were targeted for substantial completion in the summer of 1978,[6] but the formal initialing of the Agreements actually occurred on April 12, 1979.[7] Neverthe-

---

* This chapter is based on John H. Jackson, "The Birth of the GATT–MTN System: A Constitutional Appraisal" (1980) 12 *Law and Policy in International Business* 21–58. During 1978–1979, I was legal consultant to the US Senate Finance Committee on matters relating to the implementation of the Multilateral Trade Negotiations Agreements. Substantial portions of this article were drawn from a report I made to the Senate Finance Committee.

[1] Agreements Reached in the Tokyo Round of the Multilateral Trade Negotiations, HR Doc. No. 153, 96th Cong., 1st Sess., Part 1 (1979) (hereinafter cited as MTA). Ministers from developed countries and some developing countries initialed the MTA in Geneva on April 12, 1979. S. Rep. No. 249, 96th Cong., 1st Sess., 4 (hereinafter cited as S. Rep. No. 249), reprinted in (1979) *US United States Code Congressional and Administrative News*, Part 6A, at 3, 12.

[2] The MTN is often called the "Tokyo Round" because it was launched in Tokyo. See notes 4–5 below and accompanying text.

[3] The groundwork for the MTN was begun in 1967. S. Rep. No. 249, 2.

[4] General Agreement on Tariffs and Trade, opened for signature October 30, 1947, 61 Stat. A3, TIAS No. 1700, 55 UNTS 187. The GATT has been modified in several respects since 1947. The current version of the Agreement is contained in General Agreement on Tariffs and Trade, *Basic Instruments and Selected Documents* (1969), vol. Iv. The GATT is a multilateral international agreement that is the principal instrument for the regulation of world trade. See generally J. Jackson, *World Trade and the Law of GATT* (1969). The ministerial level meeting in Tokyo began the seventh round of trade negotiations held under the auspices of the GATT since 1948. S. Rep. No. 249, 1.

[5] S. Rep No. 249, 1–2.   [6] *Ibid.*, 3.

[7] *Ibid.*, 4. A number of issues required further attention after the initialing. *Ibid.* One of the most important of these unfinished segments of the MTN concerns "safeguard" procedures that would allow a country to restrict imports found to be causing injury to competing domestic industries. Negotiations on a safeguards agreement continued into the summer of 1979, but as of this writing it appears an agreement will not be reached.

less, the international negotiations are now formally and substantially over, and the MTN results are entering the implementation phase.[8] Except for the original drafting of the GATT itself, the MTN results may well be the most far-reaching and substantively important product of the seven major trade negotiating rounds of the GATT. The immediate predecessor of the MTN, the Kennedy Round,[9] was very extensive and probably accomplished more in terms of tariff reductions.[10] Unfortunately, the Kennedy Round failed to achieve significant progress on the formulation of rules relating to nontariff barriers to trade (NTBs),[11] which have become increasingly troublesome.[12] The MTN was the first negotiating effort since the origin of the GATT to address significantly the problems of nontariff measures affecting international trade.[13] It produced an extensive series of international Agreements relating to nontariff measures,[14] including Agreements on:

1. subsidies and countervailing duties;[15]
2. antidumping duties;[16]
3. technical barriers to trade;[17]

[8] See note 14–23 below and accompanying text.

[9] See J. Evans, *The Kennedy Round in American Trade Policy* (1971), 183. The Kennedy Round of trade negotiations officially started in 1964 and lasted until 1967. S. Rep. No. 249, 1.

[10] The Kennedy Round centered primarily on tariff reductions, although some nontariff barriers were discussed. The MTN, on the other hand, focused primarily on the nontariff barriers. S. Rep. No. 249, 1–2. For example, the Kennedy Round achieved an average reduction of 35 percent on tariffs on manufactured products. W. Cline, N. Kawanabe, T. Kronsjö, and T. Williams, *Trade Negotiations in the Tokyo Round: A Quantitative Assessment* (1978), 9 See Subcommittee on International Trade of the Senate Committee on Finance, 96th Cong., 1st Sess., *MTN Studies: An Economic Analysis of the Effects of the Tokyo Round of Multilateral Trade Negotiations on the United States and Other Major Industrialized Countries* (Committee Print, 1979), vol. V, 34–37 (report prepared by A. Deardorff and R. Stern).

[11] For a discussion of NTBs and their underlying economic theories after the Kennedy Round, see Marks and Malmgren, "Negotiating Nontariff Distortions to Trade" (1975) 7 *Law and Policy of International Business* 327.

[12] Although the Kennedy Round did negotiate agreements on national antidumping laws and national customs valuation laws, Congress did not implement these two NTB agreements. S. Rep. No. 249, 1.

[13] *Ibid.*, 2.

[14] The Agreements are set out in the MTA. The word "Code" is used in this article to describe the separate Agreements emerging from the MTN. The structure and text of all Codes cited in this article comport with the rectified MTA text.

[15] Agreement on Interpretation and Application of Articles VI, XVI, and XXIII of the General Agreement on Tariffs and Trade, done April 12, 1979, MTN/NTM/W/236 (hereinafter cited as Subsidies and Countervailing Measures Agreement), reprinted in MTA, 257–307.

[16] Agreement on Implementation of Article VI of the General Agreement on Tariffs and Trade, done April 9, 1979, MTN/NTM/W/232 (hereinafter cited as Anti-Dumping Agreement), reprinted in MTA, 309–337.

[17] Agreement on Technical Barriers to Trade, done March 29, 1979, MTN/NTM/W/192/Rev. 5 (hereinafter cited as Technical Barriers to Trade Agreement), reprinted in MTA, 209–256.

4. government procurement;[18]
5. procedures for licensing of imports (when licensing is permitted);[19]
6. valuation for customs purposes;[20]
7. a framework of GATT (with subparts relating to developing country privileges and obligations, balance-of-payments measures and disputes settlement procedures);[21]
8. agricultural products;[22] and
9. trade in civil aircraft.[23]

The MTN results are particularly impressive in light of the enormous difficulties through which the international economic system has been passing for the past decade:[24] the economic impact of US military activity in Vietnam; the dramatic increases in oil prices; and slowing economies, high unemployment, and rampant inflation. All of this has occurred at a time of increasing economic interdependence (resulting partly at least from three decades of successful trade liberalization under GATT leadership and through the six rounds of GATT trade negotiations). At the same time, major political systems have had to operate on narrow parliamentary majorities – majorities that consequently had to respond to constituent complaints about harm caused by imports. It is little wonder that the MTN was difficult to complete or that it bears the scars and blemishes of the gauntlet it had to run.

Despite these obstacles, the MTN has produced a large variety of complex and technical Agreements. These Agreements should increase

[18] Agreement on Government Procurement, done April 11, 1979, MTN/NTM/W/211/Rev. 1 (hereinafter cited as Government Procurement Agreement), reprinted in MTA, 67–189.
[19] Agreement on Import Licensing Procedures, done April 10, 1979, MTN/NTM/W/231/Rev. 2 (hereinafter cited as Import Licensing Procedures Agreement), reprinted in MTA, 191–207.
[20] Agreement on Implementation of Article VII of the General Agreement on Tariffs and Trade, done April 12, 1979, MTN/NTM/W/229/Rev. 1 (hereinafter cited as Customs Valuation Agreement), reprinted in MTA, 3–65.
[21] Texts Concerning a Framework for the Conduct of World Trade, done April 12, 1979, MTN/FR/W/20/Rev. 2 (hereinafter cited as Framework for World Trade), reprinted in MTA, 619–661.
[22] International Dairy Agreement, done April 12, 1979, MTN/DP/8 (hereinafter cited as Dairy Arrangement), reprinted in MTA, 339–412; Arrangement Regarding Bovine Meat, done April 12, 1979, MTN/ME/8 (hereinafter cited as Meat Arrangement), reprinted in MTA, 583–595. In addition, the MTN contains a number of bilateral agreements on cheese, other dairy products, and meat. See MTA, 413–581.
[23] Agreement on Trade in Civil Aircraft, done June 12, 1979 (hereinafter cited as Civil Aircraft Agreement), reprinted in MTA, 597–618.
[24] See GATT, Press Release No. 1199, November 9, 1977, "The Future of World Trade" (address by Olivier Long, Director-General, General Agreement on Tariffs and Trade to the Zürich Economic Society), 9: "These negotiations have so far moved slowly, for various reasons which include the complexity of the issues, the influence of political factors in several of the leading participating countries, and the reluctance of governments to undertake major economic commitments at a time of recession."

considerably the international community's awareness of and surveillance over the activities of national governments that affect international economic relations. In short, the scope of the existing GATT system has been greatly broadened. We have witnessed no less than the birth of the GATT–MTN system for the international surveillance, consultation, and regulation of world trade.

It is very difficult at this early stage to appraise the MTN and its future impact. Some studies conducted before the completion of the negotiations used computer-modeling techniques to forecast the economic impact of those portions of the MTN that were relatively amenable to quantification (such as tariff reductions, quota liberalization, and even government procurement regulations).[25] A majority of the MTN results, however, concern matters not easily quantified. These matters are in the form of obligations that will have varying impacts, depending heavily on the manner in which these obligations are in fact *administered* at the national and international level.

Furthermore, important as the economic result of international trade obligations are, the political results are equally important. For example, will the system help nations resolve disputes more peacefully in the future? Will the system be perceived as fair, and will it therefore minimize international tensions that inevitably arise when one nation's economic policies cause economic distress in another country? Will the system permit a fair degree of national decision-making over internal priorities and goals (i.e., will it permit a fair degree of sovereignty)? Will the system facilitate the degree of international coordination and cooperation essential to general economic progress in the world? Will it enhance the ability of national leaders to cooperate in the resolution of persistent and potentially dangerous world economic problems: extreme poverty, economic welfare disparities, and uncertain resource supplies?

The purpose of this article is to formulate some very preliminary judgments – more in the nature of hypotheses – concerning these questions. The article assumes that some answers to these difficult questions will emerge from an examination of the "institutional–legal" structure – what might be called the "constitution" – of the new GATT–MTN international economic system. There are, of course, other factors that could be examined. The chosen scope of this article, however, is the new GATT–MTN constitution in light of the history, impact and effectiveness (weakness) of the preceding GATT constitution.

. . .

---

[25] See, e.g., Cline, Kawanabe, Kronsjö, and Williams, *Trade Negotiations in the Tokyo Round*; and *MTN Studies: An Economic Analysis of the Effects of the Tokyo Round.*

II.   The GATT constitution[26]

. . .

The developing weaknesses of the constitution

The GATT system overall has been enormously successful, reducing tariff barriers and promoting a surge in post-World War II international trade.[27] This increase in world trade, in turn, has created the problems attendant to growing international economic interdependence. During the last three decades, weaknesses have appeared in the GATT system. Some of these weaknesses can be termed "substantive" in that they involve rules that are substantively inadequate or out of date. For example, the GATT obligation of nondiscrimination[28] – the most-favored-nation (MFN) principle – has been eroded by expansive use (or abuse) of a series of exceptions in the GATT.[29] Similarly, the GATT lacked rules to apply to many newly important nontariff measures that influenced or distorted trade flows.[30] In addition, the GATT rules regarding trade in agricultural goods[31] and the tragic problems of developing countries[32] were not always adequate. Finally, in

---

[26] For a comprehensive treatment of the GATT, see generally Jackson, *World Trade*; and J. Jackson, *Legal Problems of International Economic Relations* (1977).

[27] See generally Hudec, "GATT or GABB? The Future Design of the General Agreement on Tariffs and Trade" (1971) 80 *Yale Law Journal* 1299 (1971).

[28] GATT Article I. Article I contains the major MFN obligation in the GATT. Jackson, *World Trade*, 255. Other articles, however, contain similar nondiscrimination language specific to the subject covered. *Ibid.* These provisions pertain to "cinema films, internal mixing requirements, transit of goods, marks of origin, quantitative restrictions, state trading, measures to assist economic development, and measures for goods in short supply." *Ibid.* (parentheticals omitted).

[29] See Jackson, *World Trade*, 264–272, for a discussion of the exceptions to GATT's MFN obligation.

[30] As tariffs decline, various nontariff measures become relatively more important in their impact on the restriction or distortion of world trade flows. See generally R. Galdwin, *Nontariff Distortions of International Trade* (1970). The whole area of standards gained increasing prominence, as countries exercised their legitimate governmental powers to impose on products various standards for the purposes of achieving consumer protection, environmental protection, safety requirements, etc. In promulgating many of these regulations, however, it was often conveniently easy to arrange the specifications of the regulations so that they would be most conveniently achieved by domestic producers, and often somewhat less conveniently achieved by foreign producers who were exporting to that market. See Sweeney, *Technical Analysis of the Technical Barriers to Trade Agreement*, 179–217. Other examples of the way the GATT rules became out of date, or at least difficult to apply because of their ambiguity, include the developments of various limiting devices such as the "import deposit" schemes of the United Kingdom or Italy which require the importer to deposit for periods of up to ninety days an amount equal to the value of the imported items. Although the deposit is returned at the end of the time period, the schemes represent an economic cost to the importer.

[31] See Houck, *US Agricultural Trade and the Tokyo Round*, 265–295.

[32] Jackson, *World Trade*, 663–671. "In several clauses in GATT, a distinction is made between primary products and industrial products. It can be argued that since less-developed countries tend to depend more upon primary commodities for export than upon industrial products, such a division operates to discriminate between less-developed and industrial

recent years, new "safeguards" techniques – ways to restrict imports that were injuring domestic producers – were developed that fell outside the discipline of the GATT rules.[33]

III.   The MTN response: appraising the GATT–MTN constitution

An overview

Upon reading the MTN Agreements, one is struck by their remarkable complexity, variety and far-reaching scope. The willingness of nations to yield "sovereignty" (if that is a meaningful concept) on such matters as government procurement is impressive. Yet the overall impact is perplexing. The variety of Agreements and the variety of approaches within the Agreements on both substantive and institutional questions reflect a somewhat fragmented method to the negotiation.

On a number of substantive issues, there seems to be a variety of approaches, probably reflecting the different objectives of national domestic interest groups who influenced different parts of the negotiations. (Of course, because of the complexity of many of these substantive issues, negotiations had to proceed in subgroups.) Thus, some of the Agreements seem tuned towards the direction of trade liberalization to increase the flow of trade;[34] others seem more trade-restricting.[35] Some seem to enhance MFN;[36] others seem to erode it further.[37]

nations." *Ibid.*, 666. See also Jackson, *Legal Problems of International Economic Relations*, 1009–1016.

[33] One of the more prominent techniques developed was the broader use of the so-called "voluntary restraint agreement" (VRA) or "orderly marketing agreement" (OMA). In a VRA, an exporting nation concerned that unilateral trade measures would otherwise be imposed against it by an importing country "voluntarily" agrees to restrain its exports to that country. See Smith, "Voluntary Export Quotas and US Trade Policy – A New Nontariff Barrier" (1973) 5 *Law and Policy of International Business* 10; and Jackson, *Legal Problems of International Economic Relations*, 668–678. It has been argued that these arrangements are technically illegal under the GATT, but in general these arguments have had little effect. One of the objectives in the MTN was to obtain a new safeguards code that would bring some measures of discipline to the use of VRAs or OMAs. A safeguards code ultimately was not agreed upon at the Tokyo Round.

[34] See, e.g., Technical Barriers to Trade Agreement, Article 2.1, reprinted in MTA, 216: "Parties shall ensure that technical regulations and standards are not prepared, adopted or applied with a view to creating obstacles to international trade." In the preamble to the Government Procurement Agreement, reprinted in MTA, 72, the parties to the Agreement recognized "the need to establish an agreed international framework of rights and obligations with respect to laws, regulations, procedures and practices regarding government procurement with a view to achieving greater liberalization and expansion of world trade." See also the preamble to the Customs Valuation Agreement, reprinted in MTA, 7.

[35] See, e.g., the Subsidies and Countervailing Measures Agreements.

[36] See, e.g., the Technical Barriers to Trade Agreement, Articles 5.1.1 and 7.2, reprinted in MTA, 221, 223; and the Import Licensing Agreement.

[37] See, e.g., Framework for World Trade, points 1 and 4, para. 1, reprinted in MTA, 622 ("Notwithstanding the provisions of Article I of the General Agreement, contracting

Generally, these substantive problems of international trade can be approached in two divergent ways, each resulting from a particular philosophy. On the one hand, there is the "freer trade" or nongovernmental approach, which attempts to create international rules designed generally to minimize government interference.[38] On the other hand, there is a more "managed" approach,[39] which encourages governments to cooperate and to manage or direct the type and amount of trade flow.[40] The original GATT reflected the views of the first approach;[41] whereas in the MTN Agreements, different Codes seem to take differing approaches. Some of the Agreements seem designed to establish new mechanisms through which governments and international bodies can manage trade. The creation of new "committees" in many of the Codes leans in this direction.[42] Portions of the subsidies Agreement suggest the same.[43] Other Agreements, however, appear to be more in tune with the first approach – that is, with the traditional GATT view – and thus seem designed to limit further governmental interference with international trade.[44]

It is also difficult to discover an overall consistent policy on the institutional and legal questions addressed by this article. The Agreements vary widely on such matters as dispute settlement, the degree of precision in rule statements, and the extent and nature of international decision-making authority.

With respect to the weaknesses of the GATT constitution discussed above, a number of the tougher questions unfortunately were avoided.[45]

parties may accord differential and more favorable treatment to developing countries, without according such treatment to other contracting parties."); and the Subsidies and Countervailing Measures Agreement, Part III, Article 14, reprinted in MTA, 284–285.

[38] See Subcommittee on International Trade of the Senate Committee on Finance, 96th Cong., 1st Sess., *MTN Studies: MTN and the Legal Institutions of International Trade* (Committee Print, 1979), vol. IV, 4–5 (report prepared by J. Jackson at the request of the Subcommittee on International Trade). See generally K. Dam, *The GATT: Law and International Economic Organization* (1970), 12–13.

[39] This approach is sometimes called "organized free trade" or "*dirigisme*." *MTN Studies: MTN and the Legal Institutions of International Trade*, 5.

[40] *Ibid.*   [41] Dam, *The GATT: Law and International Economic Organization*, 12–13.

[42] See, e.g., Dairy Arrangement, Part I, Articles II(2) and IV, reprinted in MTA, 344–346 (establishment of an International Dairy Products Council to evaluate "the situation in and outlook for the world market for dairy products" and to propose possible solutions for disequilibria in that market); and Meat Arrangement, Part II, Article V(1), reprinted in MTA, 593 (establishment of an International Meat Council to "carry out all the functions which are necessary to implement the provisions of the Arrangement").

[43] The Agreement, for example, establishes a procedure for consultation among signatories whose products are subject to an investigation. Subsidies and Countervailing Measures Agreement, Part I, Article 3; Part II, Article 12, reprinted in MTA, 266–267 and 282.

[44] See, e.g., Government Procurement Agreement; the Technical Barriers to Trade Agreement; and the Customs Valuation Agreement.

[45] The MTN, for example, failed to design a better system for amending the GATT or for

This is perhaps understandable; to achieve any agreement at all, it might have been necessary to avoid many tough issues that could have sidetracked the negotiations. Yet it must be recognized that many of these tough issues remain and are even more perplexing as a result of the MTN. Some of the comments later in this article illustrate this point.

Although the focus of this article is on legal–institutional questions, it should be noted that a number of substantive GATT problems also were avoided by the MTN. For example, the erosion of the MFN policy of nondiscrimination seems to perpetuate and extend important deviations from the MFN policy on behalf of developing countries.[46] The restriction of some Code benefits to signatories also makes inroads into the general concept of MFN.[47] These inroads do have some policy justifications. The question that must be asked, however, is whether the general policies favoring MFN have been weighed adequately against the particular desires in certain contexts to depart from MFN.

Another example of a difficult substantive problem relatively unresolved by the MTN is control of agricultural products. This tough question of how best to manage international trade in agricultural products seems largely unanswered, although some particular attempts to nudge agriculture into the general discipline of international trade rules can be found.[48]

Finally, some perplexing questions of developing country trade are handled primarily by a "legalization" of the currently tolerated noncompliance practices of those countries,[49] the extension of the legal opportuni-

making decisions for developing new rules in the GATT. It did not address many difficult questions of voting; indeed, it may have worsened the general voting question by the studied ambiguity contained in various Codes Committees and their procedures. In addition, the negotiations did not seriously address the issue of "grandfather rights," although certain specific rights, such as in the injury test in countervailing duty cases, were the subject of particular negotiations.

46 See, e.g., the Framework for World Trade, points 1 and 4 (Differential and More Favorable Treatment; Reciprocity and Fuller Participation of Developing Countries), reprinted in MTA, 622–625. Other portions of the Framework for World Trade have favorable conditions for developing nations as well. See, e.g., *ibid.*, point 2A, para. 2, reprinted in MTA, 627 (developed countries in applying restrictive import measures for balance-of-payments purposes must take account of "the export interests of the less-developed contracting parties and may exempt from its measures products of export interest to those contracting parties").

47 See, e.g., Subsidies and Countervailing Measures Agreement, Part II, Article 8(3), reprinted in MTA, 277 (mandating *signatories* "to avoid causing, through the use of any subsidy" injury, nullification or the impairment of benefits received by, or serious prejudice to the interests of, another signatory (emphasis added)). The Agreement implies that nonsignatories will be treated less favorably.

48 See, e.g., Trade Agreements Act of 1979, Pub. L. No. 96–39, § 101, 93 Stat. 144 (hereinafter cited as Trade Agreements Act), adding Title VII to the Tariff Act of 1930. See generally Houck, *US Agricultural Trade*.

49 See, e.g., Framework for World Trade, points 1 and 4, paras. 5–7, reprinted in MTA, 624–625.

ties of those countries to deviate from GATT rules,[50] and an expression of desire that developing countries will "graduate" to the more significant GATT and MTN rules of trade.[51]

Perfection, of course, cannot reasonably be expected in a negotiation among so many nations with so many divergent goals. The real and substantial gains made by the MTN on such matters as government procurement policy, valuation, and product standards may more than offset the failure meaningfully to address some problems, particularly when those problems have become almost perennial. A tidy world certainly is not the likely characteristic of any foreseeable trade policy. Yet the MTN bargaining process and the resulting Codes, which stand virtually alone as treaties in themselves, have an overall impact on the GATT legal system. The interrelationships between the various Codes and the GATT will become increasingly complex. Such complexity, in turn, will make it harder for the general public to understand the GATT–MTN system, perhaps resulting in less public support for that system over time. The complexity will hurt those countries that cannot devote additional governmental expertise to GATT representation problems. In addition, such complexity inevitably will give rise to a variety of legal disputes among GATT parties. Finally, it will contribute to the belief that the richer nations can control and can manipulate the GATT system for their own advantage.

It should be noted that many (maybe all) of these MTN-created technical and legal problems with the GATT may be fully justified as fulfilling important policy objectives in the face of the rigidity and unamendability of the GATT and in the face of the GATT's inadequate constitutional structure. In each such case, however, it must be recognized that there is a long-term cost to the usefulness of the GATT and its related agreements. That cost may be worth it. But what is suggested by this discussion and the discussion that follows is that there are still many important, unresolved issues that will require considerable efforts in the years ahead.

In the next sections, this article will examine more thoroughly several important constitutional institutions, including the dispute resolution mechanism, rule information,[52] and the role of national government processes in the GATT–MTN constitution.

---

[50] *Ibid.*, para. 7, reprinted in MTA, 625.

[51] As their economies progressively develop and their trade situations improve, developing countries are expected "to participate more fully in the framework of rights and obligations under the [GATT]." *Ibid.*

[52] See generally Jackson, "The Crumbling Institutions of the Liberal Trade System" (1978) 12 *Journal of World Trade Law* 93 for a more comprehensive treatment of the thesis.

Dispute resolution and rule application

. . .

National government processes and the GATT–MTN constitution

Although there is a tendency to divide an analysis of governmental institutions into two parts – the international institutions and the domestic or national institutions – the two are so inextricably interrelated, particularly in relation to economic affairs, that to talk about the constitution of the GATT System or the GATT–MTN System without discussing its relationship to national institutions would be a mistake. This article cannot go into this subject for many countries, not even for all the influential countries, but some interesting and potentially significant developments in the United States can be reviewed briefly.

The salient feature of the US conduct of its international economic policy is the constitutionally induced tension between the Executive and the Legislative branches of government. Congress is highly conscious of its explicit constitutional power to regulate interstate and foreign commerce.[53] But Congress cannot effectively negotiate foreign agreements and, as a result of the history outlined earlier, delegation and Executive assertion resulted in a substantial transfer of power from Congress to the President.

The Kennedy Round negotiations of 1967 ushered in a period of increased Congressional hostility towards US trade policy. The Congress, very disappointed with the Kennedy Round results, refused to approve those few subjects requiring action.[54] Indeed, Congress attempted to block US implementation of the Kennedy Round Anti-Dumping Code (one of only two agreements devoted to nontariff measures completed in that Round) even though Executive branch lawyers had argued that this agreement did not need Congressional approval.[55]

With this history in mind, those who participated in the drafting of the Bill that became the Trade Act of 1974[56] (which, *inter alia*, established the authority and conditions for US participation in the MTN)[57] sought to establish a procedure for meaningful Congressional participation and approval of nontariff barrier negotiations.[58] They also sought a procedure that would still give the Executive branch negotiating credibility and room

---

[53] US Constitution, Article I, sec. 8, cl. 3.   [54] See Evans, *The Kennedy Round*, 299–304.

[55] See Jackson, *Legal Problems of International Economic Relations*, 740–753.

[56] Pub. L. No. 93–618, 88 Stat. 1978 (1975) (codified at 19 USC §§ 2111–2487 (1976)).

[57] *Ibid.*, § 101 (codified at 19 USC § 2111 (1976)).

[58] S. Rep. No. 1298, 93rd Cong., 2nd Sess., 8 (hereinafter cited as S. Rep. No. 1298), reprinted in (1974) *US United States Code Congressional and Administrative News* 7186 at 7186–7187.

to maneuver so that a negotiation could be successful.[59] The procedure initially designed was one adapted from the familiar legislative veto process. In that process, the President lays a proposal (e.g., a government agency reorganization plan[60]) before Congress, and if Congress does nothing – i.e., fails to adopt a resolution of disapproval – the proposal becomes law.[61] In designing the procedure for approval of an international agreement, some modifications were necessary. One such modification was a provision for a ninety-day consultation period with Congress *before* the international agreement and proposed implementing legislation were laid before it.[62] The purpose of this provision was to allow Congressional (and citizen) comments and suggestions to be taken into account by the US representatives in their negotiations, so that the results would be more likely to achieve Congressional approval.[63]

During the 1973–1974 Congressional consideration of this NTB procedure, constitutional and other objections caused the abandonment of the legislative veto proposal.[64] As a substitute, a special Congressional procedure, often called the "fast-track" procedure, was designed, which retained the ninety-day consultation period.[65] The "fast-track" procedure, while following the normal constitutional statutory approval process (positive adoption by both Houses and signing by the President),[66] also retained three important attributes inherent in a "legislative veto" procedure: automatic discharge from a committee so a committee could not "bottle up" the legislation; prohibition of amendments; and limited debate on the floor of each House.[67] This approach ensured that the negotiation results would, within a reasonable time, be voted upon by Congress without amendment (important because amendments would likely make it necessary to reopen the international negotiations).

This process in fact worked in some unanticipated ways. The Executive branch duly notified the Congress, in early January 1979, of its intent to conclude agreements ninety days or more later.[68] The then current negotiating texts were in fact transmitted to all members of Congress (and soon became generally available to the interested public).[69] After the January

---

[59] S. Rep. No. 1298, 18.   [60] 5 USC § 906 (1976).
[61] Jackson, *Legal Problems of International Economic Relations*, 147–148, note 15 (list of US laws containing legislative veto provisions).
[62] S. Rep. No. 1298, 22.   [63] *Ibid.*   [64] See *ibid.*   [65] 19 USC § 2112(e) (1976).
[66] *Ibid.*, § 2112(d) and (e).   [67] *Ibid.*, § 2191 (1976). See S. Rep. No. 1298, 22.
[68] Memorandum of January 4, 1979, 44 Fed. Reg. 1933, 1934 (1979).
[69] This access represented unprecedented generosity with current negotiating information while an international economic negotiation was pending. In addition to this notification, the members of Congress were briefed frequently throughout the course of the negotiations, and key Congressional Committees (particularly Finance and Ways and Means) assigned several staff members each to devote full time to following the course of the negotiation. These staff members had broad access to negotiating information, made trips to Geneva and attended some negotiating sessions. S. Rep. No. 249, 5–6.

1979 notification, the key Congressional committees – especially the Finance Committee of the Senate and the Ways and Means Committee of the House – began consulting with Executive branch negotiators, holding public hearings and studying the negotiation results.[70] In fact, the Senate Finance Committee and the House Ways and Means Committee went further than expected and, in private sessions with Executive branch officials, actually began *drafting* the text of proposed legislation they would like to see introduced by the President.[71] The Committees even went so far as to hold a joint "conference" to resolve differences between the House and Senate versions – in essence duplicating the normal post-vote legislative process *before the Bill was even introduced.*[72]

The significant difficulty, however, was that the Bill finally introduced was an Executive branch Bill, which did not in all respects conform to the draft proposed by the consultation procedure.[73] Nevertheless, the careful consultation and bargaining between the Executive branch and Congress (occasionally resulting in US negotiations with foreign countries concerned) so that the international agreements would not diverge from domestic law, resulted in a product in which the Congress had great confidence. Thus, Congress gave the Bill an overwhelming vote of approval.[74] The process was so well accepted that Congress agreed to extend the life of the "fast-track" procedure by eight years (to January 3, 1988).[75]

Although it is hard to forecast the impact of this procedure, it raises some encouraging possibilities for economic diplomacy. Not everyone got all he wanted from the process. One persistent worry is that sensitivity to domestic pressure groups may have led Congress to force the Executive branch into yielding too much to statutory language that may make it easier to erode the liberal trade discipline of the international trade system. Only time will tell whether this perception is accurate. Finally, the US government is currently undertaking a process of reorganization that could substantially alter its techniques of conducting its trade policy. This too, could have substantial impact on the implementation of the MTN results, for better or worse.[76]

---

[70] See *ibid.*, 6.   [71] See *ibid.*   [72] *Ibid.*

[73] This author has not yet seen a complete textual analysis of the differences between the two drafts, but he was informed that there were only five or six differences between the Bill introduced by the Executive branch and that drafted by Congress in the consultation period. One example of such differences is section 1101 of the final draft of the joint "conference" print (on file at the offices of *Law and Policy in International Business*), which would have extended certain tariff negotiating authority. This was omitted entirely from the Executive branch version ultimately submitted and passed into law without amendment.

[74] 125 Cong. Rec. H5690–91 (daily edition, July 11, 1979) (House vote: 395 to 7); 125 Cong. Rec. S10340 (daily edition, July 23, 1979) (Senate vote: 90 to 4).

[75] Trade Agreements Act, § 1101 (amending 19 USC § 2112).

[76] See Presidential Reorganization Plan No. 3 of 1979, 44 Fed. Reg. 69273 (1979).

Conclusion

The MTN produced impressive results, but many of these results are understandably short-term oriented. Very little was accomplished in dealing with the long-term (and very real) problems of the institutional–legal structure of a workable and effective international system for economic relations. Indeed, the MTN Agreements could increase the difficulty of those institutional problems. The great expansion of the scope of this subject matter into government procurement, technical standards, subsidies, and other areas, the balkanization of institutions and dispute settlement procedures, and the lack of attention on the overall ability of the existing GATT system to shoulder these new responsibilities will cause a number of stresses on that system. Further inroads on the principles of MFN, the introduction of a series of rules that contain ambiguity and the failure to complete a new safeguards Code hold the potential for deterioration of the liberal trade discipline built up over the last three decades.

What we have witnessed is nothing less than the birth of a new system – the GATT–MTN system – which, similar to a newly born federal state, is still relatively formless, with many critical constitutional questions yet to be answered. The probable dangers to the new constitution are subtle: a dwindling faith in the system by private-enterprise decision-makers and the public at large, an increasing pressure on national governments to react or retaliate against perceived unfair actions taken abroad, and a slight but gradual spiraling down of the economic benefits from trade. The US Congress could become more assertive and surly on matters of trade. European national leaders could become more critical of a failure of US leadership and could move significantly towards "go it alone" policies. This in turn would anger the body politic in the US and elsewhere.

Fortunately, the risks and fears mentioned above are not inevitable. The MTN put in place a number of building blocks upon which an effective international trade system could be built. In the process of experimentation, some mistakes will undoubtedly occur. But if government leaders have in mind a general constitutional direction they wish to see the GATT–MTN system take, the system *can* be nudged in that direction. Some direction seems both feasible and advisable.

What should be that direction? Some ideas have been implicit in the previous sections of this article. Modest movement towards a more rule-oriented diplomatic system may seem unattainable to those accustomed to viewing governments through cynical eyes. There is doubt, for example, that government officials and diplomats *want* rules that can limit their own freedom of action and sense of power.[77] There is also particular doubt that the great economic powers really want to move away from the power-oriented system that seems to favor them so much.

Yet, there are important contrary indications. The largest economic powers of the GATT–MTN system today are modern democratic states. They do not have monolithic governments but are composed of a multitude of competing interest groups and political factions. These factions often distrust government (or at least the other party's government!) and thus often seek to limit executive discretion. One technique for such limiting is the development of rules and participatory procedures to accompany these rules. The litigiousness of US society may in fact be a necessary concomitant to real democracy (although many would dispute that idea and blame it on the lawyers!). Even more striking is the situation in those large democratic powers that have a federal structure. In such cases, where the "one-city" form of government proves impossible, there is a tendency to develop a rule-oriented approach. The emerging European "federal state" – the EC – seems to bear this out as one examines the work of the Luxembourg Court and the relations of the Brussels bureaucracy to member states and private citizens. This experience, of course, is not without exceptions. Counter-examples can be cited. But the EC strikes a foreign observer as remarkably "rule/court"-oriented even when compared with the governments of some of its member states.

In the United States, there seems to be considerable support in Congress for a better international system of trade rules. This support, no doubt, is influenced in part by distrust of the Executive branch and in part by a desire to reduce constituent pressure for measures that members of Congress secretly feel bear long-run dangers.

What other directions might the GATT–MTN system take? It is possible that the GATT could become viewed as a loose umbrella organization for a kaleidoscope of economic agreements with a variety of nation groups on a variety of subjects. Indeed, this could have a number of advantages. If the tight cohesiveness and the single code idea of the original GATT is abandoned, there is the possibility of a broader-based system – one accommodating a larger membership with a greater variety of economic structures. Such an organization could play a greater role in interfacing widely disparate economic philosophies in a world of increasing interdependence. For the essential discipline and predictability of rules governing trade among particular subsets of the broader member-

---

[77] The carefully crafted Treaty of Rome limitations on the powers of the EC institutions suggest, however, that government officials can be limited. See Treaty Establishing the European Economic Community, Articles 137–198, entered into force January 1, 1958, 298 UNTS 11.

ships, however, officials and the public would look to separate "codes" and even "subcodes," some of which have now sprung up in the context of the GATT.

The umbrella GATT–MTN system, then, can provide the essential logistical and procedural support for a variety of particular codes on particular areas, perhaps subjecting these codes to some overall minimum standards of world citizenship (for example, a modified MFN for nondiscrimination), and of procedural fairness (including a right for noncode members to be heard on particular code actions that might harm them). It is even possible, despite the initial balkanization of the dispute settlement process, to work towards a unified procedure through the development of secretariat services specializing in dispute settlement, and a model set of effective procedural rules that can be offered for adoption by various MTN dispute panels. In sum, the elements necessary to the development of a more effective system are present – if those elements are properly utilized.

That is the challenge of the next few years.

4   GATT machinery and the Tokyo Round agreements*

US Trade Representative William E. Brock stated before the US Senate Finance Committee on March 24, 1983:[1]

Our adherence to a free trade policy requires us to strictly enforce existing trade agreements. To strengthen our domestic trade laws to make them more useful and responsive to the needs of those they protect, and seek expanded coverage of trade issues under the mutually accepted international framework of the General Agreement on Tariffs and Trade. Four principles will guide our approach to any suggested legislature. First, it must be absolutely consistent with current obligations under the GATT and other international agreements . . .

On March 5, 1982, Arthur Dunkel, Director-General of GATT, stated in an address at Hamburg:[2]

Let me go further and say that international economic policy commitments, in the form of agreed rules, have far-reaching domestic effects, indeed effects so important that they are indispensable for democratic governance. They are the element which secures the ultimate coordination and mutual compatibility of the purely domestic economic policies. They form the basis from which the government can arbitrate and secure an equitable and efficient balance between the diverse domestic interests: producers vs. consumers, export industries vs. import-competing industries, between particular narrowly defined industries. Last but not least, only a firm commitment to international rules makes possible the all-important reconciliation, which I have already alluded to, of the necessary balance on the production side and on the financial side of the national economy. I am still convinced that it is in the national interest of every trading nation to abide by the rules, which were accepted as valid for good times and bad, and to frame their internal policies accordingly. One of the major benefits of international disciplines is that they offer equal opportunities and require comparable sacrifices from all the countries involved in international competition. Those who believe in the open trading system must recognize and accept the need to correct those rigidities in their economic and social systems which obstruct the process of continuing adjustments on which economic growth depends . . .

---

* This chapter is based on John H. Jackson, "GATT Machinery and the Tokyo Round Agreements" in William R. Cline (ed.), *Trade Policy in the 1980s* (Institute for International Economics, Washington, DC, 1983), chapter 5.
[1] Reprinted (1982) 121 *BNA International Trade Reports US Import Weekly*, March 31, 673.
[2] GATT Press Release No. 1312, March 5, 1982.

Introduction

For three-and-a-half decades, the institution of the General Agreement on Tariffs and Trade (GATT) has been the source of considerable worry among policy-makers, governmental officials, and scholars.[3] Since it was never intended to be an international organization, the GATT constitutional structure is not very well thought out. That structure, such as it is, contains only the barest outlines of necessary procedures and distribution of powers. Yet somehow the GATT seems to subsist, a tribute to the improvisation and ingenuity of the diplomats and particularly, the first Director-General of GATT.

An international institution, such as the GATT, which purports to regulate international economic relations among countries, needs a mechanism or framework for at least three essential functions:

1. discussion and exchange of views on policies and trends, including sufficient staff resources (national or international) to provide the necessary background information (these exchanges and discussions can themselves influence the course of events as embodied in national governmental policies);
2. the formulation of new rules that will keep abreast of changing international economic conditions; and
3. a system for both formal and informal resolution of differences or disputes between nations.

The critical questions

In examining the GATT–Multilateral Trade Negotiations (MTN) mechanism and constitutional structure, it is necessary to bear in mind these three essential functions, and to ask how well is the existing structure of GATT and its related agreements able to support these functions. In addition, for the United States (and certain other nations), there are some other important questions. Can the United States rely on the GATT as a central instrument and focal point of international economic regulation, to the extent it has in the past, and appears willing to rely in the future? More specifically, are the United States policy-makers wise in adhering to a firm

---

[3] The interested reader may want to consult one or more of the following: Robert E. Hudec, *The GATT Legal System and World Trade Diplomacy* (New York, Praeger, 1975); John H. Jackson, *World Trade and the Law of GATT* (New York, Bobbs Merrill, 1969); Jackson, "The Crumbling Institutions of the Liberal Trade System" (1978) 12 *Journal of World Trade Law*, No. 93; and Jackson, "The Birth of the GATT–MTN System: A Constitutional Appraisal" (1980) 12 *Journal of Law and Policy in International Business*, No. 21.

commitment not to break the rules of GATT? In pursuing many US complaints against foreign government actions concerning international trade in the GATT procedures for dispute resolution? For seeking to develop new rules in the GATT context to govern areas of international economic activities which are not now adequately governed? In short, is the United States well advised in placing so many of its "eggs" in the "GATT basket"? Can the GATT as an institution cope with the problems currently facing international economic relations in the near and not-so-near future?

There is no easy way to answer the questions posed above. First of all, the masses of details bearing on these questions are not easily assembled or understood. Secondly, much of this information is kept confidential by governments, or by the GATT itself, and therefore is not readily available. Thirdly, there is a judgmental aspect to conclusions based on that information which is available and which can be understood. It is much like the difference between a glass that is half full and one that is half empty. Given the same sets of facts and details, persons with different biases or different premises can come to apparently opposite conclusions. Among the details that are available, some can support considerable worry about the capacity of the GATT system to fulfill even minimally the roles that appear to be assigned to it. On the other hand, there are other details which support a proposition that the GATT system had achieved much and shows signs of continuing to achieve much.

In this chapter, some attempt will be made to point to some of the particular aspects of the GATT–MTN constitutional and legal system, as a mechanism for achieving a variety of goals that have been mentioned above. No attempt will be made to draw a "bottom line" conclusion, however, partly because it is premature to do so in light of the revolutionary overhauling to which the GATT was submitted during the Tokyo Round negotiation. In trying to point to some of the aspects that influence the subject of this paper, it is necessary to bear in mind that the GATT–MTN institutional framework must be evaluated in the context of its total legal system. This total legal system involves not only the GATT itself, as an international instrument and institution, but an interplay between that institution and a large number of national legal systems, including constitutional and governmental structures. This is particularly important with respect to the major "players" in the GATT scene, i.e. those governments which for one reason or another seem to have a major influential role in the GATT.

"Rule diplomacy" versus "power diplomacy"

...

The Tokyo Round of negotiations (MTN), from 1973 to 1979, was an extraordinary trade negotiation. For the first time important attention was given to nontariff barriers as well as to tariffs. The results of the Tokyo Round probably increased the jurisdictional competence (with the consequential complexity of institutional arrangements) of the GATT about fourfold or more. The following major agreements resulted from that Tokyo Round and are the subject of attention in the paper:[4]

1. Geneva (1979) protocol (tariffs);
2. Agreement on technical barriers to trade;
3. Agreement on government procurement;
4. Agreement on interpretation and application of Articles VI, XVI, and XXIII (countervailing duties and subsidies);
5. Arrangement regarding bovine meat;
6. International dairy arrangement;
7. Agreement on implementation of Article VII (customs valuation);
8. Agreement on import licensing procedures;
9. Agreement on trade in civil aircraft;
10. Agreement on implementation of Article VI (antidumping); and
11. "Framework" agreements.

National implementation of the Tokyo Round Agreements: legal aspects

The GATT–MTN constitutional system cannot be understood in isolation, as a sort of island set off somewhere in the ocean of international affairs. It can only be understood in the context of its interrelationship with the national governmental systems of the contracting parties to the GATT. However, it is not possible to develop this interrelationship for eighty-seven countries. In the Tokyo Round negotiation, there was a tendency for the United States and European Community (EC) officials to negotiate and consult together on important issues. Sometimes the representative from Japan was present, and these three participants constituted the major "power bloc" in the GATT. This section of this chapter examines briefly some of the important issues of national implementation of the Tokyo Round Agreements in these three areas, drawing heavily on a study to be

---

[4] The agreements are set forth in GATT, *Basic Instruments and Selected Documents*, 26th Supplement (1978–1979), Geneva, March 1980.

published soon, written by this author and two other professors (one from Japan and one from Belgium).[5]

In broad perspective, it can be said that the United States, the EC, and Japan have implemented all of the major international agreements resulting from the Tokyo Round negotiations. However, underneath the surface of this broad statement, there are a number of very difficult legal and constitutional questions about the implementation of the Tokyo Round Agreements.

At least three important subordinate issues can be raised in the case of national implementation of the Tokyo Round Agreements. The first of these is perhaps the easiest, namely, has the nation concerned accepted, as a matter of international legal obligation, the agreement at issue? The affirmative answer to this, as to all of the Tokyo Round Agreements and with respect to the three entities mentioned (United States, the EC, and Japan), is established by the international acts of signing and accepting the agreements, and evidenced by the current GATT list of acceptances of the agreements. It should be noted that the "Framework Agreements" are not international agreements, but instead are being "implemented," by virtue of a decision of the GATT contracting parties meeting in November 1979. With respect to the international obligatory nature of a nation's acceptance, it is often interesting to examine under what domestic constitutional procedure the acceptance was made, because different procedures may imply different levels of political as well as legal commitment to the international agreement.

A second important question concerning each of the international agreements with respect to the national procedures of implementation, is the degree to which the international agreement is "directly applied" in the domestic law of the nation, a question that in US law is sometimes called the "self-executing nature." If the particular agreement is not itself directly applicable or self-executing in the domestic law of the nation concerned, is it applied through some domestic statute or regulation which "transforms" the international norms of obligation into domestic legal rules? And if neither of these cases exists, is there some reason why the international rule does not need to be applied as part of the domestic law?

A third question with respect to the national implementation, is to examine the extent of the implementing mechanisms within the nation concerned. This has at least two possible aspects: first, the question of "hierarchy of norms," which refers to the issue of whether the norms of the

---

[5] The research by John H. Jackson (United States), Jean-Victor Louis (Belgium), and Mitsuo Matsushita (Japan) can be found in J. Jackson, J. Louis, and M. Matsushita, *Implementing the Tokyo Round: National Constitutions and International Economic Rules* (University of Michigan Press, 1984)

Tokyo Round Agreements have a higher legal status that other competing norms within the domestic legal system of the nation concerned. The second aspect of this, is the degree to which the international norms are being applied, elaborated upon, or otherwise implemented by domestic governmental regulations which have come into force.

A final question that should be asked, but cannot yet be answered in a very detailed sense, is the degree to which the national implementation of the Tokyo Round Agreements is in fact having results in changing national government, private enterprise or citizen actions with respect to international trade in a way that is consistent with the principles that underlie the Tokyo Round Agreements. This would involve a rather elaborate empirical examination of the various societies concerned, which is beyond the resources available to this author for the chapter. Some indication of an answer to this question can be seen in the international processes of dispute resolution and policy discussions occurring in the GATT–MTN system, however.

Information about these national implementing processes and their legal problems is, of course, of considerable relevance to possible future negotiations. Not only do the different processes have an influence on the negotiators and their negotiating tactics, but it could well be that there are certain asymmetries in the legal implementation of international economic negotiation results, in the various countries, which asymmetries could defeat some aspects of true reciprocity that the negotiating parties thought they were achieving, or could create certain difficulties or misunderstandings in future years of the operation of an agreement concluded internationally.

Now we will examine each of these three national systems briefly.

. . .

Part III
Trade policy fundamentals

The next part of this book turns from the "constitutional" or "institutional" view of the world trade system, to some of the substantive trade policies of that system. Obviously there are dozens of subjects which can and should be the subject of articles, and many of these are covered in the various books I have written (refer to the bibliography for full details). In this part, however, I have decided to include just four chapters embracing portions of four articles which deal with four different but fundamental trade policies issues, namely MFN or "Most Favored Nation" rules, voluntary restraint arrangements, subsidies and countervailing duties, and finally the question of "regionalism" as contrasted with "multilateralism." These were selected not only for their centrality to considerations about the international trade system, but because in some instances they deal in a targeted way with more detail and policy discussion than other parts of my writing, or elaborate on certain policy analyses in ways not commonly expressed by other authors or policy papers.

The first of these, chapter 5, explores the policy basis for the MFN principle, which is often described as the core of GATT rules and thus of the trade system. Why should MFN or the rule against discriminating between different countries be so central? Such supporting policies as lowering transaction costs, avoiding trade distortions, and generally lowering the probability of trade tensions among nations, are discussed. But it is also noted that there are important criticisms which can be leveled at the MFN norm, and some of the exceptions to the norm are discussed. The Uruguay Round texts continue this principle and indeed extend it also to trade in services, and to trade-related intellectual property rules, although in slightly different forms.

The next policy taken up is the question of "voluntary export arrangements," often called VERs or VRAs (voluntary restraint agreements or arrangements) and is discussed in chapter 6. These tempting devices have been extensively used by governments, often informally and secretively. The basic structure is for an importing country to indicate "distress" due to exports from another country, and for the latter to come to some arrangement to limit the amount of its exports to the importing country, possibly to avoid perceived potential worse treatment for its exports. The legal questions here are somewhat intricate and it is not easy to answer which VERs are "legal" and which not. The Uruguay Round result includes a very important text about "safeguards" which includes an obligation to avoid using VERs or VRAs, with some exceptions (as usual). Nevertheless there are still ways to engage in VERs, for instance to provide the equivalent as a "settlement" of an antidumping or countervailing duty action.

The third chapter of this part, chapter 7, examines some of the policies of countervailing duties as a response to subsidies enjoyed by goods exported by the subsidizing country. Subsidies generally are some of the most perplexing and complex of the trade policies. This relatively brief article deals almost solely with the countervailing duty, which many economists dislike. Here the argument is made that the countervailing duties may have a constructive effect on trading nations to inhibit them from using subsidies in a way that distorts market forces affecting trade and thus lowering world welfare. The Uruguay Round extensively revised the subsidy and countervailing duty rules of world trade and provided a new conceptual framework for dealing with these problems, so later developments will need to be watched to see how these new rules work out.

Finally, the fourth chapter of this part, chapter 8, examines the general problem of "regionalism." GATT, and now the WTO, have always been confronted with the tug-of-war juxtaposition of MFN and multilateralism on the one hand, and the policies leading to an exception on the other hand. This chapter discusses in a broad systemic context some of the policies on each side of this conflict, noting *inter alia* that some policies that are relevant are not "economic" policies, but instead more "political" or "good governance" policies. In recent years the world has seen a strong regionalist development, with a variety of new regional institutions and treaty frameworks such as NAFTA (North American Free Trade Agreement), Mercosur (Mercado Común del Sur – Common Market of the South), APEC (Asia Pacific Economic Cooperation agreement), etc. The WTO working party has inventoried well over 100 regional arrangements (not all of which are actively implemented), and some feel that these pose a severe threat to the broader principles of multilateralism embodied (arguably) in the WTO and GATT.

5   Equality and discrimination in international economic law: the General Agreement on Tariffs and Trade*

The history of nondiscrimination obligations concerning international economic matters extends back for centuries, but in recent decades it has become increasingly complex, and, in some eyes at least, increasingly "checkered." Although it has been argued that customary international law imposes a nondiscrimination obligation on nations in the conduct of their international trading relationships, the prevailing view seems to be that this is not so, that if such an obligation exists it does so by virtue of treaty agreements only.[1] For centuries, various treaties, especially FCN (Friendship, Commerce, and Navigation) treaties, have contained a variety of nondiscrimination clauses, but since World War II, the principal nondiscrimination norms are those which are included in the General Agreement on Tariffs and Trade (GATT). This article will focus on these norms as expressed in GATT.

Basically there are two types of nondiscrimination norms relating to international economic behavior. First there is the norm of "Most-Favored-Nation" (MFN) treatment. This norm requires nation A to give equal treatment to economic transactions originating in, or destined for, other countries entitled to the benefit of the norm. A second form of nondiscrimination requirements is the "National Treatment" obligation. This norm requires that a nation treat within its own borders, goods, services, persons, etc., originating from outside its borders, in the same manner that it treats those which are of domestic origin.

While the descriptions of these two types of "economic equality" norms

---

* This chapter is based on John H. Jackson, "Equality and Discrimination in International Economic Law: The General Agreement on Tariffs and Trade" in *The British Yearbook of World Affairs* 1983 (London Institute of World Affairs, 1983), 224–239.

[1] G. Schwarzenberg, "Equality and Discrimination in International Economic Law" in *The British Yearbook of World Affairs* 1971 (London Institute of World Affairs, 1971), 163–181; and J. N. Hazard, "Editorial Comment: Commercial Discrimination and International Law" (1958) 52 *American Journal of International Law* 495.

– MFN and National Treatment – have been stated broadly, to remind readers that they can apply to a variety of contexts (even to "human rights treatment"), nevertheless the GATT only applies to trade in goods.[2] It does not apply to trade in services such as insurance, banking, engineering or technology, nor does it apply to many other matters treated in FCN and other treaties, such as treatment of investment or capital flows, the right of "establishment," etc. The remainder of this article will focus on the GATT norms and thus be confined to the subject of international trade in *goods*.

In addition, this paper will be confined to the first of the two types of nondiscrimination mentioned above, namely the MFN obligation.

I.   The background of GATT and its obligation

. . .

II.   The most-favored-nation obligation

(A)   Background and history of the obligation

Most-Favored-Nation (MFN) clauses in international commercial matters came into use in the seventeenth and eighteenth centuries. They were used in bilateral treaties as a short-hand means of "incorporating by reference" benefits that had been granted in other agreements.[3] In many cases governments used a conditional MFN clause, by which concessions granted to one country are granted to another on an MFN basis only if that other country grants compensatory or reciprocal concessions. Gradually governments moved to an unconditional MFN. Starting with the Tariff Act of 1922, the United States has pursued a policy of granting MFN treatment on such an "unconditional" basis.[4]

The League of Nations Covenant included a reference to the goal of "equitable treatment for the commerce of all members." A 1936 League of Nations standard MFN clause formed the basis for the MFN clause included in an early draft of an ITO charter, and was an important influence on the MFN clause that was incorporated in the GATT.[5]

---

[2] See generally J. H. Jackson, *World Trade and the Law of GATT* (1969), chapter 20.
[3] *Ibid.*, 250.
[4] Executive Branch GATT Studies, No. 9, "The Most-Favored-Nation Provision," Committee on Finance, United States Senate, Subcommittee on International Trade, 93rd Cong., 2nd Sess., 134 (compilation of 1973 studies prepared by the Executive Branch, Committee Print, March 1974).
[5] League of Nations Economic Committee, Report on the Most-Favored-Nation Clause, LN Doc. C.379, M.250, 1936 II.B (Sales No. 1936 II.B.9).

(B)   GATT Article I and its application

Although there are several MFN or nondiscrimination clauses in the GATT, the most important MFN clause is that which appears in Article I, paragraph 1. It reads:

With respect to customs duties and charges of any kind imposed on or in connection with importation or exportation or imposed on the international transfer of payments for imports or exports, and with respect to the method of levying such duties and charges, and with respect to all rules and formalities in connection with importation and exportation, and with respect to all matters referred to in paragraphs 2 and 4 of Article III, any advantage, favor, privilege or immunity granted by any contracting party to any product originating in or destined for any other country shall be accorded immediately and unconditionally to the like product originating in or destined for the territories of all other contracting parties.

It will be noted that the application of the clause is limited to matters relating to the importation and exportation of *products*, and that the obligation of this clause is unconditional. Any concession granted by a contracting party to a product of another country "shall be accorded immediately and unconditionally to the like product originating in or destined for the territories of all other contracting parties." For example, if country A, a GATT contracting party, negotiates a bilateral agreement to reduce its tariff on widgets from 20 percent *ad valorem* to 10 percent, it must apply the new tariff rate to widgets originating in the territory of any GATT contracting party. The obligation to extend any bilaterally negotiated concession to all GATT contracting parties essentially leads members to negotiate tariff reductions on a multilateral basis.

Countries have developed means of avoiding some of the effect of MFN obligations. Tariff classifications can be narrowed so that a tariff rate will be applied only to the product of the country with which the reduction was negotiated. The classic example of such a narrow classification is that appearing in the Swiss–German Treaty of 1904 calling for a reduction of tariffs on "large dapple mountain cattle reared at a spot at least 300 meters above sea level and having at least one month grazing each year at a spot at least 800 meters above sea level."[6]

There are a number of interstitial interpretative questions of GATT Article I that can pose difficulties. For example, in applying a countervailing duty to offset a subsidy enjoyed by goods originating from a particular country, it is clear by practice and custom that the duty may be applied only to the goods from the country, without violating MFN obligations

---

[6] G. Curzon, *Multilateral Commercial Diplomacy: The General Agreement on Tariffs and Trade and Its Impact on National Commercial Policies and Techniques* (Michael Joseph, London, 1965), 60, note 1.

owed to that country[7] (GATT Article VI is relevant here). But can a nation consistently follow a policy which exempts subsidized goods from certain countries (e.g., less developed countries) from countervailing duty actions, while at the same time applying such duties to subsidized goods from other GATT members?[8]

Likewise it is not always clear what is a "like product" deserving most favorable treatment.[9] Furthermore, the phrase "originating in" can be troublesome.[10] Are goods assembled in B from parts produced in X to be considered goods of B or goods of X? Often a formula based on percentage of value added is utilized in these cases.

(C)   The policies of MFN

It is appropriate to ask what are the basic policies of an MFN obligation. A thorough answer will not be attempted here, but a few of the objectives of the MFN clause can be mentioned. Basically, it appears that there are two groups of arguments that buttress the policy of MFN: first, a group we can loosely call "economic reasons"; and, secondly, a group of political or "not-so-economic" arguments.

With respect to economic arguments for MFN, one can list several. First, a principle of nondiscrimination could have a salutary effect of minimizing distortions in the "market" principles that motivate some views of economic institutions. By applying government trade restrictions uniformly, without regard for the origin of goods, the market system of allocation of goods and production will have maximum effect. Widgets will tend not to be shipped half way around the world, when widgets just as good, for a comparable price, can be obtained from a neighboring country. If tariffs are applied more heavily to the neighboring goods, however, goods from afar may be purchased, and long shipments stimulated, incurring inefficient costs.

Another economic type argument for MFN links the MFN policy to a more general policy of freeing trade from as much government interference as possible. Since MFN has the effect of generalizing specific trade liberalizing practices, it is argued that more liberalization *overall* is obtained when MFN prevails than when it does not.

Finally, under this loose grouping of economic arguments, can be men-

---

[7] Practice clearly supports this, but in addition the basic purpose of countervailing duties or antidumping duties would be partially undermined if MFN application were required in each situation. See GATT Article VI.

[8] Recently this issue was involved in a complaint brought in GATT by India against the United States. This case was subsequently settled before a decision by the panel constituted to hear the case. Bureau of National Affairs, (1981) *US Import Weekly*, No. 97, 5.

[9] Jackson, *World Trade and the Law of GATT*, 259.   [10] *Ibid.*, 257 and 464.

tioned the value of minimizing transaction costs. If MFN were fully applied, customs officials would not need to bother with the "origin of goods" question, and customs procedures would be simplified.

A second group of policies stresses the "political" side of MFN. Without MFN, governments could form trade cliques and groupings more readily. These special groupings can cause rancor, misunderstanding, and disputes, as those countries "left out" of favors resent their inferior status. Since special preference "deals" between nations, as well as specifically targeted trade-restraining actions, are more easily implemented if MFN does not apply, a world trading system is basically a less stable economic environment. The risk ensues that tensions among nations will be more frequent. Such economic tensions have been instrumental in the past for escalating controversies that lead to military action or other breaches of the peace.

Consequently one can acknowledge some important policies which support an MFN principle, although clearly there may be countervailing policies that would suggest legitimate departures from MFN. The trend in recent years appears to be towards more departures.

(D)   *Exceptions to MFN in the GATT agreement*

The combination of the basic MFN clause in Article I, paragraph 1 and the other MFN clauses appearing in the GATT means that most GATT obligations are subject to the MFN obligation.[11] However, the GATT Agreement itself contains a number of exceptions, and actions taken within the context of GATT or outside of it also establish a number of departures from MFN. During the decades of GATT existence, there has allegedly been an erosion of the rigor of MFN, for one reason or another.[12]

In this and the next few sections will be discussed some of the exceptions to the MFN principle. Perhaps most significant are the exceptions for customs unions and free trade areas, and the exception for preferences for developing countries. Each of these will be taken up in later sections.

Article I itself contains exceptions to the MFN obligation, which were important historically. This Article allows exceptions for preferential arrangements listed in Annexes A to F of GATT, many of which arose out of colonial ties. For example, the British Commonwealth preferences are given some exemption from MFN under this exception. Over the decades

[11] MFN or similar obligations are found in GATT Articles I, IV, III(7), V(2), (5), and (6), IX(1), XIII(1), XVII(1), and XX(j). Jackson, *World Trade and the Law of GATT.*

[12] United States Tariff Commission, Report to the Committee on Finance of the United States and its Subcommittee on International Trade, Part I, "Trade Barriers: An Overview," TC Publ. 665 (1974), 110. Quoted in J. H. Jackson, *Legal Problems of International Economic Relations* (1977), 544.

of GATT existence, with the steady lowering of general MFN levels of tariffs through seven trade negotiation rounds, these historical preferences have tended to become gradually less significant. The formation and enlargement of the European Economic Community (a major "exception" itself) has further altered the meaning of the historical preferences of the GATT annexes. However the Yaoundé and Lomé conventions between the EEC and a number of developing countries,[13] many of which were former colonies of EEC member states, may in some cases be regarded as a form of continuation of these historical preferences, albeit without the explicit legal basis provided in the GATT Annexes.

At the First Session of the Contracting Parties, Article XXXIII of the GATT was amended to allow accession of new members to GATT on the vote of two-thirds of the contracting parties. One logical consequence of this action was to add Article XXXV to permit a contracting party to decide that the GATT will not apply as between it and another contracting party, if a decision to this effect is taken at the time either first joins GATT. This was designed to avoid forcing a country to enter an international trade agreement with another country against its will. The most extensive use of Article XXXV was in connection with Japan. Fifteen contracting parties invoked Article XXXV with respect to Japan at the time of Japan's accession to GATT in 1955, but subsequently most of these invocations have been lifted.[14]

Article XXV of GATT contains a general power of "waiver" by a special (two-thirds) majority of the contracting parties. Although it has been argued that this power should not be used to alter the effects of GATT Article I because amendments to that Article require unanimity,[15] nevertheless a number of waivers have been adopted granting exemption from MFN obligations. The most significant of these was the 1971 waiver for the preference system for trade of developing countries (discussed below). Waivers have also been granted for the United States for its part in the Canadian–United States Automotive Products Agreement (providing preferential free trade in auto products), and a number of other specific exemptions from MFN.[16]

Various other Articles provide potential exceptions from MFN. For example, Article XX contains exceptions to all GATT obligations for certain health and welfare-type government actions, although the Article

---

[13] See GATT Report, "The ACP–EEC Convention of Lomé" in *Basic Instruments and Selected Documents*, 23rd Supplement (1977), 46.
[14] Jackson, *World Trade and the Law of GATT*, 100; GATT, *Analytical Index to the General Agreements* (2nd revision, 1966), 160–162.
[15] GATT Document L/403 (1955).
[16] Jackson, *World Trade and the Law of GATT*, 549 (for a list of waivers). GATT, *Basic Instruments and Selected Documents*, 14th Supplement (1966), 37.

requires that actions "not be applied in a manner which would constitute an unjustified discrimination between countries." Article XXI provides an exception for national security reasons. Articles XII–XIV establish various exceptions to GATT obligations, when quotas are justifiable for balance-of-payments reasons, and these articles, especially Article XIV, can afford some limited exemption from the MFN obligations. Similarly Article XVIII offers some balance-of-payments exemptions for developing countries.

Although not made explicit, it is clear by practice and custom that antidumping duties or countervailing duties (GATT Article VI) can be applied to certain imports of certain origin, without a need to generalize such duties (which would partly defeat their purpose). It is not clear, as previously mentioned, whether a *policy* of applying such duties could be established which exempted certain countries.

Government procurement practices have traditionally been considered unreached by the language of GATT Article I, and the language of GATT Article III and the preparatory work of GATT seem to support this approach.[17]

The Article XXIII complaints and dispute procedures of GATT provide for the possibility of non-MFN actions in response to an offending nation's activity causing "nullification or impairment" of benefits under the Agreement. Although many cases have occurred under Article XXIII, only one went so far as to obtain the necessary Contracting Parties' approval for a retaliatory action. In that case Netherlands was authorized to apply a discriminatory quota against exports from the United States.[18]

Finally there are two GATT provisions which at least implicitly touch on the MFN question. First, under the escape clause of Article XIX of GATT, a country which finds that imports are causing serious injury to one of its competing domestic industries is sometimes allowed to restrain temporarily those imports. There is interpretative material suggesting that such import restraints must be imposed on an MFN basis, although this interpretation is disputed, and has been one cause of an impasse in the "safeguards" negotiation during the Tokyo Round.[19]

Secondly, Article XVII dealing with state trading enterprises has been interpreted by some to allow departure from MFN. The issue is not yet settled.[20]

---

[17] Jackson, *World Trade and the Law of GATT*, 254, 360; GATT Articles I and III(8).
[18] GATT, *Basic Instruments and Selected Documents*, 1st Supplement (1953), 32.
[19] Jackson, *World Trade and the Law of GATT*, 564; GATT, *The Tokyo Round of Multilateral Trade Negotiations* (report by the Director-General, 1979), 90.
[20] Jackson, *World Trade and the Law of GATT*, 346.

(E)   Customs unions and free trade areas: Article XXIV

Article XXIV allows an exception to the obligations of GATT for certain regional arrangements. The exception in Article XXIV applies to three types of arrangements: customs unions; free trade areas; and "an interim agreement necessary for the formation of a customs union or of a free trade area."

A free trade area is a group of customs territories in which customs duties and other restrictive regulations on "substantially all" products originating in the territory are eliminated. A customs union, like a free trade area, involves the elimination of customs duties between the member states. In addition, in a customs union, the members adopt a common schedule of tariffs and system of regulation of trade with respect to products from the territories of non-members.

The establishment of a customs union or free trade area requires a departure from the MFN principle. If there were no such exception to the MFN principle, the elimination of customs duties between the participants would have to be generalized to all contracting parties to GATT with no *quid pro quo.*

The policy underlying the Article XXIV exception as expressed in that Article is a recognition of "the desirability of increasing freedom of trade by the development, through voluntary agreements, of closer integration between the economies of the countries parties to such agreements." While the GATT makes an allowance for regional arrangements, Article XXIV, paragraph 5 provides that regional arrangements shall not have the effect of increasing restrictions on imports from third countries. For customs unions or interim agreements leading thereto, the common tariffs applied by the members of the arrangement to imports from third countries shall not be higher on the whole than the "general incidence" of such tariffs in the territories of the parties prior to the arrangement. Arrangements establishing or leading to the establishment of a free trade area shall not result in higher tariffs in the constituent territories than those existing prior to the arrangement.

Article XXIV allows an exception to MFN treatment for interim agreements leading to the formation of customs unions or free trade areas. Such agreements must contain a "plan and schedule for the formation of such a customs union or such a free trade area within a reasonable length of time." None of the arrangements notified to GATT have at the outset satisfied the definitions of a free trade area or a customs union contained in paragraph 8 of Article XXIV, although some evolved into one of these. A number of regional arrangements have been so loosely drawn as to draw into question whether they even fulfill the requirements for an "interim" agreement. The

GATT language is unfortunately ambiguous, and the GATT has allowed some very loose preferential arrangements to exist without effective challenge in the context of GATT. Article XXIV has become, some say, the most significant loophole to the MFN obligation.[21]

(F)   The generalized system of preferences

At the first session of the United Nations Conference on Trade and Development (UNCTAD) in 1964, the developing countries called for a generalized system of preferences (GSP) to be granted by the industrialized countries to all developing countries, partly to replace the mélange of then existing preferential arrangements based primarily on colonial ties. Discussions on the nature of GSP took place in the late 1960s in the contexts of UNCTAD and the Organization for Economic Cooperation and Development (OECD). The developed countries wanted a system which would allow each developed country to determine the beneficiaries, product coverage, amount of reduction and other aspects of the plan it was to implement.

In 1971, the Contracting Parties to GATT approved a waiver of MFN under Article XXV, paragraph 5 of GATT, for the purpose of instituting GSP. The waiver allows for a departure from Article I obligations for a period of ten years, but actions resulting from the Tokyo Round negotiation have effectively perpetuated this departure.[22] The waiver of the MFN obligation extends to all developed countries and is for the purpose of allowing them to extend preferential tariff treatment to developing countries without having to generalize such treatment to other GATT contracting parties.

The schemes adopted by the individual developed countries to implement GSP vary in their terms. The preference schemes vary in terms of the products covered, the countries benefiting from the schemes, the level of tariff cuts, rules of origin, and whether the products on which the preferences are granted are subject to nontariff barriers such as quotas or tariff quotas. In addition, all of the schemes include safeguard mechanisms such as escape clause provisions or quantitative limitations on trade under the preference schemes.[23]

---

[21] K. Dam, "Regional Economic Arrangements and the GATT: The Legacy of a Misconception" (1963) 30 *University of Chicago Law Review* 615; Jackson, *World Trade and the Law of GATT*, 575.

[22] GATT waiver (Decision of June 25, 1971), in GATT, *Basic Instruments and Selected Documents*, 18th Supplement (1972), 24; Tokyo Round Decision, GATT, *Basic Instruments and Selected Documents*, 26th Supplement (1980), 203.

[23] McCulloch, "United States Preferences: The Proposed System" (1974) 8 *Journal of World Trade Law* 216 at 217.

The United States was the last major developed country to institute a preference scheme, doing so almost four years after the GATT waiver. Congress delegated authority to the President to implement GSP in the Trade Act of 1974. The Congress provided guidelines for the selection of beneficiaries, expressly excluding certain countries (such as OPEC members), and establishing criteria for inclusion of specific products in the preference list. Such preference goods receive duty free treatment when imported into the United States from a "beneficiary country," unless certain conditions which lift the preference in some cases have occurred.[24]

Several of the codes of conduct negotiated in the Multilateral Trade Negotiations provide for special treatment for developing countries. At the Thirty-Fifth Session of the Contracting Parties to GATT in November 1979, the Contracting Parties adopted four decisions relating to the framework of international trade, which decisions were drafted in the Tokyo Round negotiations. One of these decisions, the Decision of November 28, 1979 on "Differential and More Favorable Treatment and Reciprocity and Fuller Participation of Developing Countries" allows an exception to the Article I obligations to "accord differential and more favorable treatment to developing countries" including preferential tariff treatment under the GSP. Unlike the 1971 waiver, this Decision does not have a time limit.[25]

(G)The "voluntary export restraint" problem

Voluntary export restraints (VERs) are becoming more frequently used by nations seeking to limit imports into their country. The importing country (or representatives of one of its industries) approaches an exporting country and seeks a formal or merely tacit "arrangement" whereby the exporters limit the amount of products they ship to the importing country. In some cases this practice is justified as an "escape clause" action, but in many other cases it has no legal basis, and often is a technical violation of GATT. Yet no country complains – the exporters fear worse measures if they do not comply; the importing country is hardly interested in complaining.[26] Since a VER can be targeted at a particular country, it operates as an important exception to MFN in practice.

---

[24] United States, Trade Act of 1974, Pub. L. No. 93-618, approved January 3, 1975, 19 USC §§2101–2487, 88 *Stat.* 1978, *Title V.*
[25] See note 22 above.
[26] S. D. Metzger, "Injury and Market Disruption from Imports" in *Papers Submitted to the Commission on International Trade and Investment Policy* (the "Williams Commission") (US Government, July 1971), vol. I, 168–173.

(H)The Tokyo Round Agreements and their effects on MFN

Other agreements reached in the Tokyo Round have broadened the GATT system governing international trade relations. The MTN codes provide new rules and new forums for consultation and dispute settlement, and several of these "codes" have a significant relationship to the MFN principle.

The MTN codes deal primarily with nontariff barriers to trade. Two of the codes, the Subsidies Code and the Government Procurement Code, allow a sort of conditional MFN approach in their substantive obligations. One effect of United States acceptance of the Subsidies Code was to require the introduction of an injury test in United States countervailing duty law. The United States had avoided the GATT obligation of an injury determination as a prerequisite to the imposition of a countervailing duty through the application of the "grandfather clause" of the Protocol of Provisional Application. The United States was unwilling to grant the concession of an injury test to countries that were not willing to make commitments contained in the Code to reduce the use of subsidies in international trade. Consequently the United States has taken the position that it will not grant the injury test to subsidized goods from countries which have not accepted the Code or comparable commitments. United States law requires the Executive to carry out this condition,[27] although the Code itself does not require it, and it has been argued that the United States position is contrary to United States obligations under GATT's MFN clause. This raises, *inter alia*, the issue (discussed above) whether a nation can discriminate in establishing its *policy* of applying countervailing duties.

The Government Procurement Code took a similar approach to MFN. Countries were not willing to grant national treatment for their government procurement practices to countries that were not willing to grant similar treatment reciprocally. In this case it can be argued that the GATT does not impose any MFN obligation.[28]

Another MTN code, the "Technical Barriers" or "Standards" Code, is also being implemented by the United States on a partly conditional basis. Only those countries willing to accept this code or its principles, will be accorded the full procedural advantages regarding information about and challenges to the development of certain product standards, under the United States law.[29]

---

[27] Trade Agreements Act of 1979, Pub. L. No. 96-39, approved July 26, 1979, 93 Stat. 144, sections 2 and 101.
[28] See note 17 above. [29] Trade Agreements Act of 1979, section 421.

Conclusions

Although overstatement should be avoided, nevertheless it seems fair to say that the principle of nondiscrimination in international trade, as embodied in GATT Article I, has been central to the post-World War II trading system. It is based upon policies that are both economic and political in nature, and which appear to remain valid for today and the future. Yet there clearly are countervailing policy considerations – the desire to aid developing countries and the desire to promote deeper trade liberalization by encouraging customs unions and free trade areas, among others. These countervailing considerations, plus the usual and frequent government motivations of expediency or special "deals," have led over the years to substantial and apparently growing departures from MFN. Whether the advantages of MFN treatment can be retained in the face of such trends, remains to be seen.

6   Consistency of export-restraint arrangements with the GATT*

Forty years of stressful history would challenge the capacity of any international agreement on trade and commerce to cope with new developments and practices not carefully enough contemplated by the original draftsman. The General Agreement on Tariffs and Trade (GATT)[1] is no exception.

Indeed, the lack of an adequate institutional structure for the GATT[2] renders it even more vulnerable than many agreements to the problem of "relevance" in a world now substantially different from the one which existed in the immediate post-World War II period. Yet few practices have posed as large a problem for the policy objectives and "rule" language of the GATT as those generally called "voluntary export restraints" (VERs), "voluntary restraint arrangements" (VRAs) or "orderly marketing arrangements" (OMAs). In spite of extensive economic and policy criticism suggesting that, as an instrument of trade policy, export-restraint arrangements are usually a fourth- or fifth-best choice[3] (or worse), these

---

* This chapter is based on John H. Jackson, "Consistency of Export-Restraint Arrangements with the GATT" (1988) 11 *World Economy* 4, 485–500. The author wishes to acknowledge the able assistance of Thijs Alexander and Ross Denton, both postgraduate students in law, from the Netherlands and the United Kingdom, at the University of Michigan during 1987–1988.
[1] General Agreement on Tariffs and Trade, October 30, 1947, reproduced in the following: 61 Stat., Parts 5 and 6; TIAS, No. 1700; 55 UNTS 194. See, generally, John H. Jackson, *World Trade and the Law of GATT* (Bobbs-Merrill, Indianapolis, 1969), and John H. Jackson and William Davey, *Legal Problems of International Economic Relations: Cases, Materials and Text* (2nd edn., West Publishing, St. Paul, MN, 1986), especially 609–621.
[2] Although the GATT does not provide much institutional structure, Article XXV provides for the contracting parties acting jointly. Moreover, Article XXX allows the GATT to be amended, but, because of the stringent voting and procedural requirements, the GATT is often deemed unamendable.
[3] Michel Kostecki, "Export-Restraint Arrangements and Trade Liberalization" (1987) *The World Economy* 425; David Greenaway and Brian Hindley, *What Britain Pays for Voluntary Export Restraints* (Thames Essay No. 43, Trade Policy Research Centre, London, 1985); Carl Hamilton, "Economic Aspects of Voluntary Export Restraints" in Greenaway (ed.), *Current Issues in International Trade* (Macmillan, London, 1985), 99; Kent Jones, "The

arrangements have proliferated to such an extent that it appears that some countries prefer them to all other trade-restricting devices.

Why this is so has been the subject of comment elsewhere.[4] Clearly it relates, *inter alia*, to the national constitutional structures of governments which inhibit the use of other measures (such as tariffs or quantitative import restrictions, which may sometimes require parliamentary action or prerequisites specified in legislative delegations of power). It also relates to international rules such as the GATT's Article XIX, its main "escape clause" (providing for emergency protection against sudden surges of imports of a particular product), which requires an import-restricting country to "compensate" exporting countries with new trade "concessions."

While economic and other policy considerations surrounding the use of export-restraint arrangements have been amply explored, there is remarkably little analytical examination of the related legal question of whether such arrangements are consistent with GATT obligations. Yet that legal question could have a considerable impact on the policy debate on, as well as on the negotiating context of, any attempt to revise the rules. It is the purpose of this article to analyze the legal question. Are export-restraint arrangements consistent with GATT obligations?

The answer turns out to be rather complex. There are a number of different types of export-restraint arrangement and the GATT consistency of some of them differs from that of others. In addition, certain circumstances offer legal escapes for the use of such arrangements, which in other situations may not be consistent with the GATT. In short, there is no simple overall answer. "It depends . . ." is the best that can be said.

First, it is necessary to explore, in the next section, some of the different characteristics of export-restraint arrangements. Then in the following section the analysis will turn to nongovernment measures largely escaping

Political Economy of Voluntary Export Restraint Agreements" (1984) 37 *Kyklos* (Basel) 82; Tracy Murray, Wilson Schmidt, and Ingo Walter, "On the Equivalence of Import Quotas and Voluntary Export Restraint" (1983) *Journal of International Economics* (Amsterdam) 191; Morris E. Morkre and David Tarr, *Staff Report on Effects of Restrictions on United States Imports: Five Case Studies and Theory* (Federal Trade Commission, Washington, DC, 1980); and Wendy E. Takacs. "The Non-Equivalence of Tariffs, Import Quotas and Voluntary Export Restraints" (1978) *Journal of International Economics* 565.

[4] See, for example, Hindley, "Voluntary Export Restraints and the GATT's Main Escape Clause" (1980) *The World Economy* 313; Ernst-Ulrich Petersmann, "Grey Area Policy and the Rule of Law" (1988) *Journal of World Trade* (Geneva), April, 23; Thomas Sauermilch, "Market Safeguards Against Import Competition: Article XIX of the General Agreement on Tariffs and Trade" (1982) *Case Western Reserve Journal of International Law* 83; Christopher W. Savage and Gary N. Horlick, "United States Voluntary Restraint Agreements: Practical Considerations and Policy Recommendations" (1985) *Stanford Journal of International Law* 281; January Tumlir, *Protectionism: Trade Policy in Democratic Society* (American Enterprise Institute, Washington, DC, 1985); and Jagdish N. Bhagwati, "VERs Quid Pro Quo DFI and VIEs: Political-Economy-Theoretic Analyses" (1987) *International Economic Journal* (Seoul), Spring, 1.

GATT discipline, after which there is a section on governmental measures. After that the most significant potential exception in the GATT, namely Article XIX, the "escape clause," will be explored, followed by a brief section on other exceptions and some concluding remarks.

In this discussion it will be assumed that all relevant participating governments are "contracting parties" to the GATT.

Export-restraint arrangements

A number of different types of measures, which can be considered under the overall concept of "export-restraint arrangements," impose restraints on exports from an exporting country. What is common to all of them is that the restraints are primarily imposed or regulated by, or within, the exporting country. In the terminology often used in international trade meetings in recent years, these are called "gray area" measures, suggesting that they may not always be clearly inconsistent with international rules (such would presumably be "black"), but that they do not live up to the basic policy goals of the international economic system.

The principal classification of importance is the distinction between those measures imposed by the *government* of the exporting country and those imposed or effected totally by an *industry* through an industry association or some other nongovernment entity.

Non government measures could include agreements, whether explicit or implicit (tacit), between industry groups in the exporting and importing countries. Various subtle approaches have also been observed, such as "predictions" of export trends.

Government measures can include explicit government-to-government agreements (usually, technically, in treaty form) in which the exporting government agrees to limit exports to the other country in certain ways. In the law of the United States, and in some other countries, these are termed "orderly marketing arrangements."[5] In some cases, a government on one side may explicitly agree with a nongovernment group on the other side (an industry association or group of firms) that exports should be restrained. The government might be that of the exporting country or it might be that of the importing country. In such cases the agreement is usually deemed "informal" and not legally binding.

With government measures that are informal or tacit, the usual pattern is for the government of the exporting country to make some sort of "statement," or explanation of intent, by which it will seek to ensure that exports of a particular product to another country will be kept below

[5] See, for example, section 203 of the United States Trade Act of 1974.

certain limits. The Japanese restraints on automobile exports to the American market are a prime example.[6]

Reasons for the use of export-restraint arrangements

Why are these measures so attractive to governments and their trade-policy officials? There are several reasons, to some of which there have already been allusions. Informal measures often escape various constraints in national or international law. Thus a government, which under its constitution or statutory law has no formal authority to enter into an explicit international agreement, may find it feasible and reasonably effective to have an implicit or informal arrangement for the foreign limitation of exports. This allows both governments concerned to avoid the necessity of implementing legislation or complicated procedures (which would often lead to delay as well as rigidities on the power to remove the measure in the future). Furthermore, the possibility of "negotiating" export-restraint arrangements on a selective, rather than a most-favored-nation (MFN), basis is sometimes felt to be politically useful.[7] Finally, it also tacitly allows avoidance of the "compensation requirement" under the GATT's main "escape clause."[8]

The government of the exporting country may cooperate in an export-restraint arrangement for various reasons. First, the government may expect that an arrangement of this kind, similar to an export cartel, will be "profitable." Economists have noted that the "monopoly rents" of export-restraint arrangements are often captured by the exporting country and may function partly as a replacement for the compensation requirement. Secondly, the exporting country can be coerced by the government of the importing country threatening other forms of trade restriction that would be more harmful to its interests. Finally, it can be persuaded, or coerced, to cooperate for nontrade policy reasons.[9]

Non government measures

If governments do not participate in an export-restraint arrangement there is very little exposure to a claim of inconsistency with GATT obligations. For example, if the measure is an explicit or tacit agreement or "arrange-

---

[6] See note 11 below.   [7] See the section below on "Selectivity and MFN in Article XIX."
[8] See the section below on "Compensation Requirement of Article XIX."
[9] An example of this may be the Japanese acceptance of the Arrangement Regarding International Trade in Textiles in exchange for the reversion of Okinawa. See, generally, David B. Yoffie, *Power and Protectionism: Strategies of the Newly Industrializing Countries* (Columbia University Press, New York, 1983), 135–138. On the issue of coercion, see also Hindley, "Voluntary Export Restraints," 331–332.

ment" by which the exporting firms in one country restrain their exports to a particular country – possibly at the request of competing industry groups in the potential importing country – arguably the GATT does not cover the arrangement. The GATT does not normally purport to regulate non-government behavior or the behavior of private firms.[10] The general purpose and thrust of the GATT is to restrain government interference in international trade, so as to leave private firms the maximum freedom of choice about business matters, thus conforming to market-oriented principles.

Non government activity, however, can create a great risk of exposure to the national laws of competition of an importing country. Without government involvement, there may be little or no opportunity to use, as a defense, an importing country's antitrust or competition law which would be allowed for "government compulsion" or "act of state."[11]

This is particularly so in respect of exports directed to the United States. The nongovernment arrangement restraining trade destined for the American man is very risky indeed.[12] As a matter of international law, however, there is little that constrains this behavior. Thus, for importing countries which do not have antitrust or other significant laws on competition, nongovernment export-restraint arrangements may escape the charge of inconsistency with GATT rules and with national laws.

This highlights an important lacuna in the current structure of international economic rules. Although the draft charter of the International Trade Organization (ITO), the Havana Charter,[13] contained a chapter devoted to the subject of inappropriate anticompetitive behavior of private firms, the charter never came into force.[14] In 1960, the Contracting Parties

[10] Apart from a provision covering official import monopolies (Article II(4)) and state trading companies (Article XVII(1)(b)), which can still be regarded as within the public domain, the only type of private behavior alluded to in the GATT is dumping. The GATT, however, does not prohibit dumping. It merely regulates the control of dumping by governments (Article VI).

[11] See, generally, Spencer Weber Waller, "Redefining the Foreign Compulsion Defense in US Antitrust Law: The Japanese Auto Restraints and Beyond" (1982) 14 *Law and Policy in International Business* 747; Michael William Lochmann, "The Japanese Voluntary Restraint on Automobile Exports: An Abandonment of the Free Trade Principles of the GATT and the Free Market Principles of United States Antitrust Laws" (1986) *Harvard International Law Journal* 99 and 141–149; Donald E. deKieffer, "Antitrust and the Japanese Auto Quotas" (1982) *Brooklyn Journal of International Law* 59; Mitsuo Matsushita and Lawrence Repeta, "Restricting the Supply of Japanese Automobiles: Sovereign Compulsion or Sovereign Collusion" (1982) *Case Western Reserve Journal of International Law* 47; and Barry Hawk, *United States, Common Market and International Antitrust: A Comparative Guide* (Prentice-Hall, New York, 1986), 300–306, 578–609, and 614–636.

[12] See, for example, *Consumers Union of US Inc. v. Kissinger*, 506 F. 2d 136 (Court of Appeals, DC Cir., 1974), cert. denied, 421 US 1004 (1975).

[13] Havana Charter, UN Doc. ICITO/1/4, New York, 1948, chapter V.

[14] On the history of the GATT, see Jackson, *World Trade and the Law of GATT*, chapter 23.

to the GATT made a determination that it would be inappropriate to try to bring under its authority this category of questions.[15] Since then, other international organizations have tried to develop international rules governing the behavior of private firms, but so far none of these operates with any binding character.[16]

Governmental export-restraint arrangements and GATT obligations

In respect of export-restraint arrangements that involve government action, two basic types of arrangement must be evaluated: those which impose quantitative restraints; and those which involve price controls or floors (similar to part of the agreement between the United States and Japan on trade in semi-conductors).

Quantitative restrictions of exports

There are two Articles in the GATT which deal with quantitative restrictions of exports – Article XI and Article XIII. These will be evaluated in turn.

Article XI

When the government acts explicitly to restrain exports to a particular country, then the risk of inconsistency with GATT rules is apparent. The most obvious provision of the GATT which relates to export-restraint measures is Article XI(1) which reads:

[15] The Contracting Parties adopted a report by a group of experts in which the majority considered that it would be unrealistic to recommend a multilateral agreement for the control of international restrictive business practices because "[t]he necessary consensus among countries upon which such an agreement could be based did not yet exist." See GATT, *Basic Instruments and Selected Documents*, 9th Supplement (GATT Secretariat, Geneva, 1961), 171. See, generally, *Restrictive Business Practices* (GATT Secretariat, Geneva, 1959). The majority of the group of experts felt, furthermore, that they, as experts on restrictive business practices rather than on the legal aspects of the GATT, were incompetent to judge whether these practice should be deemed to fall under any specific provisions of the GATT. See also Jackson, *World Trade and the Law of GATT*, section 14.1.

[16] The most important in this context are the codes of the Organization for Economic Cooperation and Development (OECD) and the United Nations Conference on Trade and Development (UNCTAD). See, generally, Hawk, *United States, Common Market and International Antitrust*, 786–802; Joel Davidow, "The Implementation of International Antitrust Principles" in Seymour J. Rubin and Gary C. Hufbauer (eds.), *Emerging Standards of International Trade and Investment* (Rowman and Allanheld, Totowa, NJ, 1984); and Norbert Horn (ed.), *Legal Problems of Codes of Conduct for Multinational Enterprises* (Kluwer, Deventer, 1980).

No prohibitions or restrictions other than duties, taxes or other charges, whether made effective through quotas, import or export licenses or other measures, shall be instituted or maintained by any contracting party on the importation . . . or on the exportation . . . of any product . . .

Most export-restraint arrangements constitute such restrictions and, therefore, appear to be contrary to this provision.

Difficulties may arise when some export-restraint arrangements, although nongovernmental in form, closely approximate to government action. A government may merely "encourage the voluntary restraint" of its exporting firms and argue that the measure is essentially nongovernmental in character. Some might argue that Japanese "administrative guidance" approaches this characterization. Other governmental approaches might tacitly condition certain government benefits (for example, access to capital, sympathetic "regulatory" decisions, and tax measures) on "patriotic compliance" with a request to restrain exports.

This, then, raises a troublesome question as to which government activity becomes a measure recognized by GATT rules as "governmental." Article XI of the GATT refers to "other measures" and thus has within it the potential, in a GATT or other dispute settlement panel having "creative inclinations," of a determination that informal governmental measures are nevertheless contrary to the GATT.

Another difficulty under Article XI may be the effects of export-restraint arrangements on competition. In 1950, the Contracting Parties unanimously approved a working party report on Article XI which concluded that, "where export restrictions were in fact intended for the purpose of avoiding competition among exporters and not for the purpose set out in the exception provisions of Articles XI and XX, such restrictions were inconsistent with the provisions of the [General] Agreement."[17] This early approach, however, must be viewed in the context of the GATT determination, already referred to, not to bring within the competence of the GATT questions of anticompetition policy. In 1950, there still remained a hope that an ITO charter would come into being, but in 1960 that hope had died.

Article XIII

Article XIII contains an obligation that the allocation of quotas should be nondiscriminatory, including those which are exempted from the general prohibition on the use of quantitative restrictions under Article XI.[18]

---

[17] *Use of Quantitative Restrictions for Protective and Other Commercial Purposes* (GATT Secretariat, Geneva, 1950), 9.
[18] It should be realized that the most-favored-nation (MFN) obligation of Article I is probably not broad enough to cover quotas. See Jackson, *World Trade and the Law of GATT*, 322.

Under this, product from all third countries, or the exportation of the like product to third countries, should be similarly prohibited or restricted, based on historical or "normal" patterns of trade allocation.[19]

Apart from the possibility that action is required only against exporting countries which have created particular difficulties because of a dynamic and unforeseen increase in exports, it seems likely that the importing country will seek to protect its domestic industry against all suppliers and that, therefore, it will have an incentive to act on a nondiscriminatory basis. An example of this may be the 1984–1985 VRAs on steel shipments to the United States which attempted to include all major suppliers. Nevertheless, several difficulties may arise.

First, it may be that certain exporting countries will not accept export-restraint arrangements. Secondly, it is possible that all the exporting countries are subject to such arrangements, but that the conditions in the separate bilateral agreements with the importing country differ significantly. Such differences may result in restraint arrangements that could be contrary to Article XIII.

There may also be some situations where the heavy hand of the importing country suggests that the export-restraint arrangements are not "voluntary." Discrimination will result from the actions of the importing countries, thus representing another challenge to GATT rules.

Other interpretations of Article XI

It has been argued that, although government-ordained export-restraint arrangements may fall under a literal reading of the prohibition of Article XI, these provisions, as far as export restrictions are concerned, may have been written merely in order to protect countries from export controls that would limit their supplies.[20] When the importing country to which the exports were directed itself instigates the restrictions in order to safeguard its domestic industry, it would not need such protection against limitations of its supplies. Under this line of reasoning, the prohibition in Article XI on the use of quotas to restrict exports should not apply to the case being examined here.[21]

There are few reasons to suppose though that the prohibition of export quotas in Article XI is as limited in scope as only to protect supplies of other countries. It is also possible that the Contracting Parties to the GATT did not link the prohibition of quotas to a specific purpose, but wanted to prohibit the use of quantitative restrictions in general irrespec-

[19] GATT Article XIII(2)(d). See Jackson, *World Trade and the Law of GATT*, 322–327.
[20] Kostecki, "Export-Restraint Arrangements and Trade Liberalization," 441; and Sauermilch, "Market Safeguards Against Import Competition," 116.
[21] *Ibid.*

tive of the possible purposes of the action, because quotas (i) are relatively nontransparent, (ii) create too much uncertainty for exporters, and (iii) cannot be "overcome" by greater efficiency by the producer-exporter. The 1960 GATT ruling already mentioned reinforces this view.[22]

Export-restraint arrangements establishing floor prices

A few export-restraint arrangements have been designed to prevent exports to one or more foreign markets below a certain floor price. Obviously, this would offer competitive benefits to importing-country producers, possibly even benefiting their exports to third markets or the competing down-stream industries (since parts would be just as costly to foreign downstream competitors). The "other measures" language assists the arguments that such arrangements (if not implemented with "duties, taxes or other charges") are inconsistent with GATT Article XI. Likewise, the nondiscrimination rules of Articles I and XIII could be invoked in the case of selective price-floor restraint arrangements.[23] Of course, as noted below, some of these arrangements may have a separate justification in the GATT. In particular, some of these arrangements may be justified as "settlement" agreements in proceedings dealing with unfair practices, as in dumping or subsidy cases, sometimes called "price undertakings."

Enforcement: who will complain?

The discussion above suggests that a government-imposed measure re-straining exports can be contrary to the GATT. In fact, there seems to be little doubt that (in spite of statements sometimes made in speeches or the literature) governmental export-restraint arrangements are often *prima facie* inconsistent with the GATT. Perhaps exceptions can be found to square the measures with GATT rules, but that is a separate question (discussed in other sections below). Thus the initial indication is that most voluntary restraint arrangements, orderly marketing arrangements, and so on are inconsistent with Article XI or other Articles of the GATT.

The problem comes, however, in exploring the consequences of such breaches of the GATT. Two aspects of this can be explored: (i) the rights

---

[22] See note 15 above. On the issue of whether the Contracting Parties intended to create a general elimination of quotas, see G. Curzon, *Multilateral Commercial Diplomacy: The General Agreement on Tariffs and Trade and Its Impact on National Commercial Policies and Techniques* (Michael Joseph, London, 1965), 130–135; and William Adams Brown, *The United States and the Restoration of World Trade* (Brookings Institution, Washington, DC, 1950), 75–78.

[23] While the MFN obligation of Article I arguably does not cover quotas, it may apply to measures establishing floor prices.

and obligations of the two countries which are "parties" to the export-restraint arrangement; and (ii) the rights and obligations of third parties.

Participants in arrangements

Who will complain? The government imposing the restraint is unlikely to complain in the GATT against its own activity. The government of the country to which the restrained exports are destined is very likely to have been the rule of the measures, requesting the restraints as a "safeguard" measure to alleviate "injury" to its own competing industry. Thus a dilemma of the GATT rule is the question of enforcement.

If the export-restraint arrangement is embodied in a legally binding instrument (which would be a "treaty" under international law) this agreement itself, as between its parties, may prevent any "GATT liability" of the parties towards each other. This is because the restraint agreement is later in time; and, as between the parties to both it and the GATT, the "later in time" rule prevails under traditional international treaty law.[24] It can be argued that, even if the later treaty was illegal because it was incompatible with the multilateral treaty, this would involve liability towards third parties only and not between the participants in the restraint arrangement.

But a counter-argument may exist. According to international law, parties cannot bilaterally derogate from a multilateral treaty, as such would be "incompatible with the effective execution of the object and purpose of the treaty as a whole."[25] The possibility of discriminating among countries through the use of export-restraint arrangements, or of concealing actions contrary to general multilateral policies of "transparence," could arguably cause such incompatibility.[26] The counter-counter-argument is that the GATT does not apply as long as there is no effect on third parties.[27]

It is possible that in some (probably very few) cases, the domestic law of either the exporting country or the importing country would be so structured as to allow challenge to the measures or government activity by some

---

[24] Of course, some of these agreements explicitly reserve rights under the GATT and this would still theoretically allow a party to bring a GATT complaint, but there is very likely to be little interest to either participant in the export-restraint arrangement to bring a GATT or other complaint.

[25] Article 41 of the 1969 Vienna Convention on the Law of Treaties states: "Two or more of the parties to a multilateral treaty may conclude an agreement to modify the treaty as between themselves alone if: (a) the possibility of such a modification is provided for by the treaty; or (b) the modification in question is not prohibited by the treaty and: (i) does not affect the enjoyment by the other parties of their rights under the treaty or the performance of their obligations; (ii) does not relate to a provision, derogation from which is incompatible with the effective execution of the object and purpose of the treaty as a whole."

[26] Petersmann, "Grey Area Policy and the Rule of Law."

[27] Hindley, "Voluntary Export Restraints," 329.

private party (such as an importing or exporting establishment) which argues that it has been harmed. This was nearly (but not quite) the situation in the *Consumers Unions* v. *Kissinger* case in the United States during the 1970s.[28]

Third-party complaints

A country (which is not a member of the GATT) which is not in any way a participant in any export-restraint arrangement could complain. It would have some hurdles to get over. For example, if it brought a complaint in the GATT under Article XXIII, it technically needs to show "that any benefit accruing to it . . . is being nullified or impaired or that the attainment of any objective of the [General] Agreement is being impeded." The mere inconsistency of an export-restraint arrangement with the GATT (for example, Article XI) only gives rise to the GATT legal theory of *"prima facie* nullification or impairment" (such that the burden would shift to the defending country to show that there was no nullification or impairment).[29] Likewise, even if a measure is not contrary to any specific provision of the GATT, a nullification or impairment of benefits accruing to a contracting party is technically possible under Article XXIII.

In general, the "harm" in this context is that the restraint measures between countries A and B harm country C either because they divert more exports (and competitive pressures) towards the market of country C or because they cause prices for the products to country C to be increased. These cases, however, are seldom brought and only one has succeeded.[30]

Third countries could furthermore be affected by an export-restraint arrangement when this implies a warning to their exporters that "unilateral

---

[28] See note 12 above. After the antitrust issue was dismissed, the case centered around the question of whether officials in the United States Department of State had acted *ultra vires* in seeking the export limitations. The Court held that such was not the case, since the action by the Executive was lacking any "legally binding effects." See also *Sneaker Circus Inc.* v. *Carter*, 457 F. Supp. 771 (District Court EDNY, 1978).

[29] If a panel of the GATT finds a *prima facie* nullification or impairment, for example in the case of a violation of a GATT obligation, it will normally recommend cessation of the measure complained against, unless the offending country is able to carry the burden of proof against the recommendation, including a burden of proof that no nullification or impairment has occurred. See, generally, Jackson and Davey, *Legal Problems of International Economic Relations*, 351. *Cf.* the report of the GATT panel on taxes on petroleum and certain imported substances levied by the United States under the Superfund Amendments and Reauthorization Act of 1986, *Basic Instruments and Selected Documents*, 34th Supplement (1988), especially 155–158.

[30] See, for example, the GATT panel report on the European Community's action against Japan over the United States–Japan semiconductor agreement, GATT Doc. L/6309, Geneva, 1988. See also the 1976 complaint (rejected) under the United States section 301 procedure in which United States steel interests complained against an export-restraint arrangement between the European Community and Japan. See Jackson and Davey, *Legal Problems of International Economic Relations*, 809.

action" may be taken against them if their exports surge above certain levels (and especially warnings not to try to take advantage of the established restraint arrangements with other countries). Such "warnings" may inhibit potential exporters even if, in fact, it is not very likely that the protectionist action will or can be taken.[31]

It is also possible that an export-restraint arrangement with a floor-price agreement may prevent other countries from making certain trade-policy choices. For example, if two countries, A and B, hold between them a large percentage of world trade in a product that has significant economies of scale and they agree that country B will undertake not to sell that product in country A below $1, then there is an incentive for country B to divert its products to a market where it can price more cheaply and keep its economies of scale. The effect of this will be to displace the products of country A from third markets. In this case, it will be to the advantage of country A to seek to have country B apply the discipline applying to the A market to products destined for third markets. In such a case, the third-market countries might argue that their rights and benefits have been impaired in that they cannot opt to receive lower-priced goods. This could be especially irritating when the exports of country B are important inputs to downstream production in the third market. This appears to be part of the basis for a complaint in the European Community in the GATT against the agreement on semi-conductors between the United States and Japan.[32]

International supervision or surveillance

Part of the analysis above has led some to argue that the only effective policing of these "gray area" measures must be through an international body such as the GATT. The Contracting Parties to the GATT have authorized, since 1982, a half-yearly survey of developments in the international trading system. As part of this, the GATT Secretariat now prepares a report twice a year which includes, *inter alia*, a list of "gray area" measures. The next question will be what should happen in the light of such reports. Perhaps the Uruguay Round negotiations on a safeguards code can address this question.

Exceptions to GATT obligations: Article XIX

The main Article of the GATT which might be invoked to justify export-restraint measures is Article XIX. Three aspects of this Article, in relation to export-restraint arrangements, are examined below.

---

[31] See, for example, the European Community's protest against United States warnings regarding imports of machine tools into the United States, *International Trade Reporter* (Bureau of National Affairs, Washington, DC), January 7, 1987, 12.

[32] See note 30 above.

Policies on safeguards

While liberal trade may benefit an importing country as a whole, it may also harm its domestic industry which produces similar or competing products. In order to give the domestic industry of the importing country time to adjust to the new situation, and also to release some of the political pressure against liberal trade, Article XIX of the GATT allows contracting parties to take safeguard measures temporarily to restrain imports of a particular product and to protect the corresponding domestic industry for a short period of time.[33]

GATT Article XIX includes language which, when a member country can show that Article XIX prerequisites are met (not too hard), allows a member country to "suspend" its obligations under the GATT if these have led to injury to the domestic industry. The rules of the GATT so suspended would include Article XI. Indeed, current practice amply confirms that import quotas are used under Article XIX, in spite of the prohibition contained in Article XI. Thus countries could also use "other measures" or export restraints. Since most export-restraint arrangements are probably imposed in the context of a claim for "safeguards" purposes – this is to restrain import competition affecting an injured competing domestic in-dustry – Article XIX could be the prime candidate to support an assertion that restraint arrangements are consistent with the GATT in spite of Article XI prohibitions.

The conceptual problem is that Article XIX allows the *importing* country to suspend its obligation and says nothing about the *exporting* country. At first sight it appears that Article XIX may not assist either participant in the export-restraint arrangement, for the action (that is, the need for the suspension of the GATT rule) is performed by the *exporting* country, not the importing country as Article XIX implies. The question then becomes one of whether the language of Article XIX in such circumstances could be interpreted as authorizing the exporting country to take such measures, at least when the importing country (alleging injury to its industry) has sought and asked for them (this problem is not confined to the exception of Article XIX, but may occur under other possible exceptions listed below).

Perhaps such an argument could be sustained. It might go as follows: if, in certain cases, a safeguard measure under Article XIX of the GATT would have been possible, but the countries involved prefer an export-restraint arrangement, such a measure should be allowed if it would not affect third parties.[34]

---

[33] See, generally, David Robertson, *Fail Safe Systems for Trade Liberalisation* (Thames Essay No. 12, Trade Policy Research Centre, London, 1977).
[34] See, for example, Hindley, "Voluntary Export Restraints," 328–332.

Selectivity and MFN in Article XIX

One of the important debates of recent years about Article XIX of the GATT is whether measures taken under this Article must be imposed in a manner consistent with the most-favored-nation principle.[35] The principal argument in favor of selective safeguard measures is that there is no explicit MFN requirement in Article XIX, so that this provision does not prevent the suspension of the MFN requirement of Article I as part of the "escape clause" authority. Supporters of a nondiscriminatory application of safeguards argue that Article XIX allows the suspension of an obligation in respect of a product, as opposed to a country. They refer to an interpretative note to Article 40 of the Havana Charter, equivalent to Article XIX of the GATT, which provides that safeguards "must not discriminate against imports from any member country." It is also argued that, as a matter of economic policy, the MFN requirement is much to be preferred. Clearly a specific export-restraint arrangement with just one exporting country (when more than one exists) would seem to contravene the MFN requirement of Article XIX. Thus, if Article XIX can be deemed to provide an exception for export-restraint measures, it may be argued that it does so only when a network of such measures is put in place, thereby closely approximating an MFN approach (if tariffs or quantitative import restrictions were used instead).

Compensation requirement of Article XIX

Article XIX(2) of the GATT provides for consultation between the country which wants to take safeguard action and "the contracting parties having a substantial interest as exporters of the product concerned." Since Article XIX(3) authorizes a retaliatory response for the affected parties, it is accepted that the parties entitled to consultation can accept compensatory "concessions" by the safeguard-acting country. Alternatively, the harmed country can implement compensatory trade restraints on the products of the safeguard-acting country. Providing protection for the domestic industry through the use of export-restraint arrangements may tacitly allow an avoidance of this compensation requirement.

Compensation is not always given in practice.[36] An explanation for this

---

[35] See M. C. E. J. Bronckers, *Selective Safeguard Measures in Multilateral Trade Relations: Issues of Protectionism in GATT, European Community and United States Law* (Kluwer, Deventer, 1985); Mark Koulen, "The Non-Discriminatory Interpretation of GATT Article XIX(1): A Reply" (1983) *Legal Issues of European Integration* 87; E.-U. Petersmann, "Economic, Legal and Political Functions of the Principle of Non-Discrimination" (1986) *The World Economy* 113; and Jackson and Davey, *Legal Problems of International Economic Relations*, 428–435.

[36] Robertson, *Fail Safe Systems for Trade Liberalisation*, 23.

may be the costs of a retaliatory withdrawal of concessions for countries depending on imports and the fact that, as a result of the already extensive tariff reductions made during successive GATT rounds of multilateral tariff negotiations, there is often very little left with which to compensate, particularly if the trade in the item on which safeguard action is being taken is very large, as is the case with steel or automobiles.[37]

As noted previously, however, economists have observed that an export-restraint arrangement may increase the profitability of the exporting firms. These "monopoly rents" thus function partly as a replacement for the "compensation requirement."

Recently, it has been suggested that auctioning the available import quotas would enable the importing country's government to capture these rents, thereby reducing the cost of the protection.[38] Since these monopoly rents can be an important inducement for the cooperation of the exporting countries, the use of such auctioned quotas may lead the exporting countries to refuse "voluntary" restriction of their exports. Moreover, since auctioned quotas would appear to be administered by the importing country, they would probably amount to "normal" quantitative import restrictions instead of an export-restraint arrangement.[39]

Other GATT exceptions

Obviously, in spite of Articles I, XI, and XIII, export-restraint arrangements may be legally justified under the GATT by other measures which provide exceptions. For example, the GATT Contracting Parties could always grant a waiver under Article XXV. Balance-of-payments exceptions

---

[37] See, for example, *Japanese Voluntary Restraints on Auto Exports to the United States*, Hearings Before the Subcommittee on Trade, House Committee on Ways and Means, 99th Cong., 1st Sess. (US Government Printing Office, Washington, DC, 1985), 17–18, statement by Michael B. Smith, Acting United States Trade Representative; and Hindley, "Voluntary Export Restraints," 327.

[38] See, for example, Hufbauer, *The Legacy of the Japanese Voluntary Export Restraints*, Hearing Before the Subcommittee on Trade, Productivity and Economic Growth, Joint Economic Committee, 99th Cong., 1st Sess. (US Government Printing Office, Washington, DC, 1985), 78–79; and C. Fred Bergsten, Kimberly Ann Elliott, Jeffrey J. Schott and Wendy E. Takacs, *Auction Quotas and United States Trade Policy* (Policy Analyses in International Economic No. 19, Institute for International Economics, Washington, DC, 1987). In the United States, section 1102 of the Trade Act of 1974 authorized the President to sell import licenses at public auction. This included *inter alia* section 201 procedures. Section 1401 of the Omnibus Trade and Competitiveness Act of 1988 amended section 203 to include, in section 203(a)(3)(F), the option of auctioning quotas as an explicit presidential remedy.

[39] Auctioned quotas may raise difficult problems with regard to several GATT provisions, particularly Articles II, VIII, and XIII, the GATT Licensing Code and even the "standstill" commitment of the Punta del Este Declaration. On the GATT consistency of auctioned quotas, see Bergsten, Elliott, Schott, and Takacs, *Auction Quotas and United States Trade Policy*, 125–145, and Laura Baughman, "Auctioning of Quotas: Lots of Pain for Little Gain" (1988) *The World Economy* 397.

in the GATT (including those for developing countries), under Article XII, might be extended to the actions of an exporting country at the request of an importing country troubled by balance-of-payments difficulties (subject to an analysis similar to that of the "escape clause" above). Developing countries might likewise use a similar argument quoting clauses in Article XVIII. In addition, it is theoretically possible that a country would be able to call on the GATT provision which enables member countries to maintain legislation which conflicts with the GATT if such legislation was in force on accession to the GATT (so-called "grandfather" rights). If these rights were applied to a particular export restraint on the grounds that it was in force prior to the country's entry into the GATT, it could escape challenge under Article XI or Article XIII[40] (grandfather rights do not apply to Article I).

A few more likely GATT exceptions (in addition to the "escape clause" previously discussed) are briefly explored below.

Price undertakings and settlements in unfair trade cases

The General Agreement itself and the GATT codes on dumping and subsidies explicitly allow governments or firms to establish "price undertakings" (that is assurances of minimum export prices) as a method of suspending or settling antidumping[41] or countervailing duty[42] proceedings in an importing country. In addition, there is arguably "implied" authority in the dumping and subsidy rules to enter into at least certain types of agreements to "settle" or to reach a compromise in such cases. A number of measures which might be included in the category of export-restraint arrangements may be "justified" under these international rules of exception. If so justified, relief from both the rules of Article XI and the principle of nondiscrimination in Articles I and XIII would be claimed. It is not clear just how far such authority for exceptions might extend to justify an export-restraint arrangement, but clearly this authority should not be deemed unlimited. More elaboration of this question, however, must await other works.

---

[40] Article 1(b) of the Protocol of Provisional Application of the General Agreement on Tariffs and Trade (55 UNTS 308 (1950)) exempts the contracting parties from certain obligations that are inconsistent with prior legislation.
[41] Article 7 of the Agreement on Implementation of Article VI of the General Agreement on Tariffs and Trade, reprinted in *Basic Instruments and Selected Documents*, 26th Supplement (1980), 171–188.
[42] Article 4 of the Agreement on Interpretation and Application of Articles VI, XVI and XXIII of the General Agreement on Tariffs and Trade, reprinted in *Basic Instruments and Selected Documents*, 26th Supplement (1980), 56–83.

Article XX (general exceptions)

Article XX of the GATT contains several general exceptions for the purpose of, for example, the protection of public morals and health. Generally speaking, the measures taken under this provision must be "necessary," so the exception does not apply if its purpose could be served by a less restrictive alternative. Moreover, the actions are subject to a "soft MFN clause." Although theoretically possible, it is not very likely that an otherwise illegal export-restraint arrangement would be justified by this Article.

Article XXI (security exceptions)

In practice, the exception of Article XXI, which is based on the national security interests of a country, may be more important. It can be argued, for example, that a strong steel or automobile industry is vital to these security interests.[43] If so, measures contrary to specific GATT obligations, taken to protect these interests, could qualify for this exception. Although Article XXI states that the measure must be "necessary" for a country's security interests, it is primarily left to the judgment of the national government whether there exists a less restrictive alternative. Again, it may be conceptually difficult to apply this exception to export-restraint arrangements and exempt the exporting country from its obligations under Article XI of the GATT on the basis of the security interests of the importing country. But since, under this provision, the importing country would be allowed to take almost any protective measure, the use of export-restraint arrangements could, in these cases, be defended as a less harmful action than the available alternatives.

Conclusions

It seems clear that, in many cases, export-restraint arrangements are not consistent with GATT rules, particularly those of Article XI. This is quite apart from a number of policy arguments showing that such arrangements have damaging economic consequences. Yet in analyzing the legal issues, it must be recognized that there are a number of legal justifications, which can be made under the exceptions to GATT rules, for certain export-restraint arrangements. The most significant such legal exception is that of

---

[43] See, for example, *Issues Relating to the Domestic Auto Industry*, Hearings Before the Subcommittee on International Trade, Senate Finance Committee, 97th Cong., 1st Sess. (US Government Printing Office, Washington, DC, 1981), 88, statement by Paul J. Fannin, former United States Senator; and Lochmann, "The Japanese Voluntary Restraint on Automobile Exports," 118–119.

Article XIX, the (main) "escape clause." Although it is not clear that Article XIX would legally justify a deviation from Article XI by an exporting country, there is at least a plausible argument that it would do so. Clearly export-restraint arrangements are an important part of the general "safeguards" subject. Once again, this points to the need for a negotiated rule discipline that will explicitly constrain the temptation to use export-restraint arrangements frequently as an instrument of trade policy.

7   Perspectives on countervailing duties*

Introduction

The article by Professor Richard Diamond entitled "A Search for Economic and Financial Principles in the Administration of US Countervailing Duty Law," is an intriguing presentation of certain economic principles applied to an area of international and national law that desperately needs such analysis. The subsidy rules of the General Agreement on Tariffs and Trade (GATT) system could substantially undermine the post-World War II Bretton Woods system as it applies to trade, unless these rules are refined and disciplined by current or future international trade negotiations. An expansive interpretation of subsidy and countervailing duty rules could result in the application of countervailing duties to almost any imported product. If this were to occur, the forty-year effort to liberalize border trade barriers could be largely nullified.

Thus far, the United States is the most extensive user of countervailing duties. Few other governments have applied countervailing duties, and have done so only in rare cases. Nevertheless, there is a fear that these other governments may follow the lead of the United States. In fact, it is thought, they may utilize principles of United States law and thereby not only disrupt trade, but disrupt exports from the United States. As a result, an attempt to develop a more rational international discipline for the use of countervailing duties, and for subsidized trade, became a priority item at the September 1986 GATT ministerial meeting held at Punta del Este, Uruguay, which launched the GATT Uruguay Round of trade negotiations.

The article by Professor Diamond is one of relatively few attempts to apply rigorously the principles of economics to the law of countervailing duties and subsidies and thus is a substantial contribution to the literature. It is my role to comment on that article, with some emphasis on GATT and the Uruguay Round.

This comment primarily reflects its author's reactions to the principal

* This chapter is based on John H. Jackson, "Perspectives on Countervailing Duties" (1990) 21 *Law and Policy in International Business* 739–756.

article. However, to some extent it also addresses a 1989 work by the principal author,[1] and a paper by Goetz, Granet and Schwartz,[2] to which Professor Diamond's 1989 paper replies. While this comment will raise some fundamental objections to the central thesis of the article, it also demonstrates an admiration for the analysis undertaken. That analysis, perhaps modified, can substantially contribute to the national and international debate on this subject.

The first issue this comment will discuss is the reasons underlying or justifying a nation's response to subsidized imports. It is important to explore that issue because, at least in theory, one possible response would be to do nothing except, as some economists have said, "send a thank you note."[3] In exploring why there should be a response to subsidized imports, we can begin to appreciate what some of the policy goals of the response system could be. These goals would shape the economic and other rules for disciplining that system.

A second problem that must be explored further, is whether or not the analysis of the author is "administrable." Although commendable in theoretical terms, the analysis may require a level of expertise and immunity from political or bureaucratic forces that is unattainable in the real world. The principal author's approach appears to require sophisticated economic analysis, and provides few of the clear, bright lines and categories that make a system administrable. On the other hand, the analysis might well provide a basis for evaluating certain bright lines, existing or proposed. This would be a considerable contribution.

In discussing this last point, this comment will briefly survey the current GATT system and suggest ways in which the principal author's analysis fits into the system (as used in this comment, the phrase "GATT system" refers not only to the international treaties, including the GATT and the 1979 Subsidies Code of the Tokyo Round, but also to national legal systems that apply to subsidized imports, namely the countervailing duty laws of national systems). The attached Appendix lists a number of practices that have been, or could be, considered subsidies. These demonstrate some of the conceptual problems of administering the current GATT system. Finally, this paper outlines several specific principles relating to the countervailing duty subsidy system, and discusses those in the light of the principal article and the previous parts of this comment.

[1] Diamond, "Economic Foundations of Countervailing Duty Law" (1989) 29 *Virginia Journal of International Law* 767.
[2] Goetz, Granet, and Schwartz, "The Meaning of 'Subsidy' and 'Injury' in the Countervailing Duty Law" (1986) 6 *International Review of Law and Economics* 17.
[3] See, e.g., Sykes, "Second-Best Countervailing Duty Policy: A Critique of the Entitlement Approach" (1990) 21 *Law and Policy of International Business* 699; Trebilcock, "Is the Game Worth the Candle?" (1990) 21 *Law and Policy of International Business* 723.

The policy objectives of the GATT system concerning subsidized products in international trade

Professor Diamond refers to tension between a distortion deterrent model and an entitlement model.[4] Application of the entitlement model would lead to the use of countervailing duties to neutralize the effects in the importing market of the subsidies in the exporting market – an elaborate fine tuning. This author does not agree, however, that the entitlement model is necessarily the best one, or for that matter that it is always necessary to choose between models. In fact, the international community appears to have adopted the rationale that primarily supports a deterrent to distortion,[5] even though specific treaty language may be ambiguous in that regard. Experiences in the agricultural sector strongly suggest to governments the need to deter and inhibit the use of subsidies that affect international trade.[6]

Furthermore, a focus solely on Congressional intent behind the US statutes is only partially adequate or revealing. Both the legislative history and the statutory language are often ambiguous. On the one hand, the reasonably clear legislative history for the 1979 Trade Agreements Act[7] (which established the current countervailing duty statute) indicates that Congress intended the Act to satisfy US obligations arising from the Tokyo Round agreements.[8] On the other hand, references to the earlier counter-vailing duty statute and definitions could lead to contrary implications, particularly if one believes that the earlier statute was merely protectionist.

Fundamentally, however, it is necessary to ask, before endorsing an entitlement model, why should there be any entitlement? What gives a US

---

[4] See Diamond, "A Search for Economic and Financial Principles in the Administration of US Countervailing Duty Law" (1990) 21 *Law and Policy of International Business* 507.

[5] The 1979 Subsidies Code includes language "[r]ecognizing also that subsidies may have harmful effects on trade and production." Agreement on Interpretation and Application of Articles VI, XVI, and XXIII of the General Agreement on Tariffs and Trade, done April 12, 1979, 31 UST 513 at 518; TIAS No. 9619 at 1; 1186 UNTS 204 at 204 (hereinafter the GATT Subsidies Code). See also Rivers and Greenwald, "The Negotiation of a Code on Subsidies and Countervailing Measures: Bridging Fundamental Policy Differences" (1979) 11 *Law and Policy of International Business* 1447 at 1448–1449; Baldwin, "Nontariff Distortions of International Trade" in *United States International Economic Policy in an Interdependent World: Compendium of Papers* (1971), vol. I, 641 at 646–647; and HR Rep. No. 317, 96th Cong., 2nd Sess. (1979), 8.

[6] See Winglee, "Agricultural Trade Policies of Industrial Countries" (1989) *Finance and Development*, March, 9; "The True Costs of Farm Support: Canada's Shame" *Economist*, March 31, 1990, 67; "USDA Undersecretary: Export Bonus a Success" *Journal of Commerce* August 1, 1989, 7A; Boaden, "Abolish Farm Export Subsidy" *Journal of Commerce*, July 20, 1989, 8A.

[7] 19 USC § 2501 (1982).

[8] See J. Jackson, J. Louis, and M. Matsushita, *Implementing the Tokyo Round: National Constitutions and International Economic Rules* (University of Michigan Press, 1984), 167.

industry sector the right to demand that its government offset or neutralize the effects of foreign subsidies on its business? Professor Diamond's answer refers generally to unfair actions, but does not explain why subsidies are unfair.

This author has previously considered the question of the policy underpinnings of countervailing duties and international subsidies rules.[9] What follows is a brief review of part of that discussion, starting with the question of why the GATT system should provide for any sort of response to the international trade of subsidized products.

Many have argued that subsidized imports represent a benefit to the importing country, which substantially exceeds the potential detriments (on a welfare basis), and thus that the best response would be a "thank you note" sent to the subsidizing government that exported the goods. Further, it has been argued that levying a countervailing duty in response to such a subsidy would have the same welfare damaging effects as any tariff. These arguments, however, seem inadequate. Since economists demonstrate persuasively that subsidies can have a considerable distorting effect, it seems clear from a global perspective that many subsidies in international trade reduce overall world welfare.

On the other hand, it can be argued that the principal welfare reduction occurs in the economy of the subsidizing government, and that, therefore, no retaliatory or recompensating response need be levied by the importing countries. This argument also is inadequate. There are a number of market and political factors which illustrate why governments may choose to respond. The unfettered use of subsidies in international trade can lead to counter-subsidies, and counter-counter-subsidies in an escalating progression, all of which can seriously damage world welfare. This has already been demonstrated in the agricultural sector. In some cases, the countries whose welfare is damaged can ill afford the costs. Thus, it can be argued there is a reason for the international system to intervene, and in some way to try to inhibit the use of subsidies generally. Game theorists, such as Robert Axelrod, would suggest that a "tit for tat" policy of counter-measure can have desirable effects in circumstances such as these.[10]

The GATT system provides two approaches for disciplining subsidies in international trade. The first, embodied in GATT Article VI[11] and in Track I of the 1979 Code,[12] is to permit countervailing duties by national govern-

---

[9] J. H. Jackson, *The World Trading System: Law and Policy of International Economic Relations* (1989).
[10] See R. Axelrod, *The Evolution of Cooperation* (1984), 27.
[11] General Agreement on Tariffs and Trade, opened for signature October 30, 1947, Article VI, 61 Stat. A3 at A23; TIAS No. 1700; 55 UNTS 187 at 212 (hereinafter GATT).
[12] GATT Subsidies Code, 31 UST at 523; TIAS No. 9619 at 6; 1186 UNTS at 212.

ments. The second, contained in GATT Article XVI[13] and in Track II of the Code,[14] is to provide substantive international law rules that prohibit certain kinds of government subsidies. Perhaps in a perfect world, only the second of these measures would be used, and countervailing duties would never be permitted because they can substantially distort the welfare in the importing country. International rules, however, often do not work satisfactorily.

Thus, an argument can be made for a fall-back or second best approach which would allow governments to utilize countervailing duties, in the general hope that the use of such countervailing duties will in the long run tend to discourage the use of subsidies, or at least those that affect internationally traded goods. This approach can be countenanced even though the motives of governments in applying countervailing duties are really not to maximize world welfare, but are instead to maximize the welfare of the producers who constitute important political constituencies within the country. Nevertheless, if the use of countervailing duties also has a beneficial effect on world welfare, then arguably such countervailing duties should be permitted.

This conclusion, of course, avoids the empirical question concerning whether or not countervailing duties do in fact tend to discourage the use of subsidies. A cursory study, primarily based on anecdotal evidence and some direct observations and discussions with officials, suggests that the use of countervailing duties by the United States has had some effect in discouraging the use of subsidies. Indeed, at the conference at which the articles contained in this publication were presented, private and government practitioners noted the decreasing frequency of complaints about foreign subsidies. Perhaps US countervailing duty actions have already had some impact.[15]

It is important to note, however, that only large countries are able to use countervailing duties to create such an impact. Small countries will generally be unable to use countervailing duties to change foreign governmental activity. Thus, there is an important asymmetry in the use of countervailing duties by the United States or other large countries. This may explain part of Canada's frustration with the GATT subsidies system.

There are several other policy arguments which support some sort of a GATT system response to subsidization.[16] A brief summary of these follows.

[13] GATT, Article XVI, 61 Stat. at A51; TIAS No. 1700; 55 UNTS at 250.
[14] GATT Subsidies Code, 31 UST at 530; TIAS No. 9619 at 13; 1186 UNTS at 220.
[15] The author has had personal discussions with foreign government officials who are planning to change their government subsidy programs due to pressure from exposure to US countervailing duty actions.
[16] Jackson, Louis, and Matsushita, *Implementing the Tokyo Round*, chapter 11.

First, it has been argued that short-term subsidies could have an "in and out adjustment cost," which could total more than the welfare benefit received from the subsidy. This is not likely. In addition, most subsidies tend to be much longer in duration (despite fiscal incentives of governments to get rid of them), so it would be unwise to rely too heavily on this argument.

A second argument is based on an analogy from antidumping law, namely "the risk of predation." Unlike antidumping law, where the predation argument would be based on the action of firms (dumping goods to achieve market share, and then capturing new monopoly rents), subsidy cases generally involve government action. It seems anomalous to argue that governments would engage in predatory trading activity with a view to capturing future monopoly rents.

On the other hand, it has been pointed out that governments so motivated are much more likely to succeed than individual firms, which would have difficulty policing a coalition of firms attempting to have such an impact. The governments are generally larger, and can influence more firms, and thus could predate. A government might want to predate for purposes of what is now commonly called targeting. That is, a government may want to encourage a certain industry sector to obtain a global market share so as to allow that sector in the future to obtain monopoly rents and thus increase the welfare of that government's society.

Again, whether or not this actually occurs is an empirical question that has been little studied. Furthermore, the declining cost curve, or "learning curve efficiency arguments," must be considered. If government subsidization merely enables industries more quickly to gain the economies of scale that allow them to continue to produce at considerably lower prices (and not necessarily to capture monopoly rents), perhaps the whole world benefits from such targeting.

Finally, it has been argued that governments and societies should be able to choose their own economic systems, without undue interference from foreign countries. Subsidies on goods exported to other countries to some extent interfere with the importing society's choice of an economic system. Such subsidies add a layer of risk to entrepreneurial decisions in the importing society and create a sense of unfairness at having to compete with foreign finance ministries. In some cases, such subsidies could lead to political pressure directed towards causing the government in the importing country to institute counter-subsidies.

This argument probably best supports the entitlement approach offered by Professor Diamond. However, this argument can be seen as a rationalization on the basis of a purely protectionist impulse – urging a government to reduce competition for domestic producers so that they will benefit at the expense of domestic consumers and of producers abroad who do not vote.

There is an additional policy that should be mentioned, which lurks behind all discussions of unfair trade practices in international trade.[17] This is the concept of interface, which suggests that even relatively minor differences between economic systems can, at certain times in the business cycle, cause uneven distress between trading partners. This distress can have a considerable political impact when specific groups in an importing country feel that their distress is due to unfair burden-sharing in the world trading system.

There are certainly policy grounds for arguing that a mechanism, presumably an international interface mechanism, should help ameliorate these political forces. To some extent, this argument suggests that a safeguard policy underlies or should underlie what has traditionally been analyzed as an unfair trade matter. In other words, it suggests that the unfair trade laws, including countervailing duty laws, may be substituted for inadequate safeguards, institutions, and policies, which have very little to do with a lack of fairness.

Having discussed the policy underpinnings of countervailing duty law, this comment now relates these policies to Professor Diamond's discussion in the principal article. If the policies outlined above constitute a plausible basis for the GATT system response to subsidies, it would seem to follow that the entitlement model is not fully supported. The policies outlined, it seems, tend to support the distortion model, and possibly a predation prevention model, and this latter model is related to targeting policies. Quite probably the policies are mixed – there are certain elements of all of the above policies reflected in the actual rules applied, or in the desires of negotiators to change those rules.

An important criticism of the distortion model made in the principal article is that the model fails to take into account externalities. This is a valuable contribution of the article. It does not follow from this, however, that the distortion model should be abandoned and the entitlement model preferred. Another approach would be to amend the distortion model to include measures designed to cope with externality problems – that is, to better tune the distortion model.

The GATT system for subsidy/countervailing duty actions

The GATT system, as it pertains to the subject matter of this comment, may be easily described in three parts. First, the GATT; secondly, the 1979 Subsidies Code from the Tokyo Round; and, thirdly, the current Uruguay Round negotiations.

[17] See *ibid.*, chapter 10 (discussing the interface principle in relation to antidumping duties).

For at least 100 years, international trade policy-makers have felt that at least certain kinds of subsidies were inappropriate and unfair. As noted above, the international system has responded with two different mechanisms for dealing with such situations: (i) permitting national governments to offset the subsidy element in imported goods by using countervailing duties; and (ii) providing international rules concerning the use of subsidies in international trade.

The original GATT Treaty document of 1947 contains both approaches.[18] Article VI of the GATT permitted the use of countervailing duties in the case of subsidized imports that caused material injury to the competing domestic industry. Article XVI in the original GATT contained a soft reporting requirement along with some admonitions concerning the use of subsidies in international trade. Basically, however, the original GATT had very little international rule discipline on the use of subsidies.

It was only in the 1955 amendment to GATT Article XVI that the first substantive international obligation against the use of certain kinds of subsidies (export subsidies) was included in the GATT. Even then, as stated in the Article XIV amendments, the discipline was very meager. First, for technical, treaty-amending reasons, it only applied to the industrial countries which were signatories to the GATT, and not to the developing countries.[19] Secondly, its obligation related only to export subsidies. Even in that case, certain technical clauses undercut the rigor of the obligation, particularly as to primary products.[20]

Thus, by the time of the Tokyo Round in 1973–1979, there was a strong desire, spearheaded by the US government, to develop additional international rules to discipline the use of subsidies in international trade. This became a major priority for the Tokyo Round negotiation. The resulting 1979 Subsidies Code follows the GATT two-track system. It further regulates the use of countervailing duties, although it does not provide a definition of "subsidy." In the second track, it lays down more stringent international rules which prohibited the use of export subsidies on non-primary goods.[21]

The second track has a number of provisions useful for defining "subsidy," including the important annex regarding export subsidies. However, some signatory countries believe that the definition of "subsidy" for Track II purposes does not necessarily apply to Track I. Operating on that

[18] See John H. Jackson and William Davey, *Legal Problems of International Economic Relations: Cases, Materials and Text* (2nd edn., West Publishing, St. Paul, MN, 1986), 727–728.
[19] Jackson, Louis, and Matsushita, *Implementing the Tokyo Round*, 256.
[20] See Rivers and Greenwald, "The Negotiation of a Code on Subsidies and Countervailing Measures," 1461.
[21] GATT Subsidies Code, 31 UST at 531; TIAS No. 9619 at 14; 1186 UNTS at 222.

assumption, national governments applying countervailing duties have considerable discretionary scope for defining "subsidy" – a risk for international trade policy.

An important new development in Track II of the GATT 1979 Subsidies Code is the provision of international rules on so-called "domestic subsidies." Article 11 of the Code discusses these. It notes that some subsidies are appropriate governmental measures but that they can have damaging impacts on importing countries. Signatories are obligated to seek to avoid causing such effects through the use of subsidies.[22]

Track I of the Code (concerning countervailing duties) does not have elaborate provisions concerning the calculation of the subsidy, or appropriate amounts of countervailing duties. Article 4 of the Code does limit countervailing duties to the "amount of the subsidy found to exist, calculated in terms of subsidization per unit."[23] In addition, Article 4 states that "it is desirable that the imposition be permissive,"[24] and "that the duty be less than the total amount of the subsidy if such lesser duty would be adequate to remove the injury to the domestic industry."[25] This lesser duty rule is not binding and US law prevents its use in US countervailing duty law.

Additional language in Article 4 (of Track I) of the Code provides that material injury must be found "through the effects of the subsidy."[26] This causal relationship has been the subject of some controversy in GATT unfair trade negotiations for several decades, but no resolution has been reached. Professor Diamond's analysis might very well provide a means to flesh out the causal relationships required in the Code.

When the Uruguay Round of GATT negotiations was launched at Punta del Este in September 1986, the negotiators felt that a priority subject for the new negotiation was revision of the subsidies rules. That is partly because many of the rules contained in the 1979 Code are ambiguous. The ambiguities that exist are in part attributable to a lack of substantive agreement among the negotiators in the Tokyo Round. One of fourteen of the Uruguay Round negotiating groups on trade in products (a fifteenth concerns trade in services) is devoted to revision of the subsidies rules.

One idea this negotiating group is considering is the so-called "three basket," or "red-green-yellow light" approach. This approach was initially suggested during the Tokyo Round, but was blocked by some of the negotiating partners so that it did not become the basis for the 1979 Code. One basic idea of this approach is to try to specify, directly in the treaty,

---

[22] GATT Subsidies Code, 31 UST at 530; TIAS No. 9619 at 13; 1186 UNTS at 224.
[23] GATT Subsidies Code, 31 UST at 523; TIAS No. 9619 at 6; 1186 UNTS at 212.
[24] *Ibid.*   [25] *Ibid.*
[26] GATT Subsidies Code, 31 UST at 524; TIAS No. 9619 at 7; 1186 UNTS at 212.

exactly which types of subsidy can result in countervailing duties, and which cannot.

A "green light" basket would list a series of subsidy practices which would always be permitted, and should not be grounds for countervailing duties. An example might include broad societal infrastructure activities, such as the building of schools and roads or the provisions of fire and police protection. A "red light" basket might include a list of subsidy practices that would either be forbidden under international law, and/or always subject to countervailing duties, perhaps even without the requirement of an injury test. Some suggest that export subsidies would fall into this category. In the field of antitrust law, the analogous provision would be a list of practices that would, as *per se* rule, occasion antitrust liability.

The middle basket, the "yellow light" basket, would consist of all other subsidy practices. Here, the injury test would be important. Countervailing duties would be allowed in the cases where these types of subsidies occurred, provided that they were causally related to the material injury of the competing industry in the importing country. As of this writing, it is not clear how much the negotiations will be able to achieve.

Professor Diamond's analysis provided in the principal article could be exceedingly useful in helping negotiators determine into which category certain subsidy practices would fall. On the other hand, it must be recognized that the results of the negotiations need to be administrable, with a minimum of administrative costs. Thus, the categories cannot be too finely tuned, or administration may become too difficult. The economic analysis of the principal article could be used to ascertain when certain broad categories of subsidies have, because of their effect on the marginal cost of the subsidy recipient, a causal relationship to material injury in the importing market. In addition, as discussed below, this analysis could reinforce the idea that unless a subsidy has some effect outside the subsidizing country, the GATT system should not allow counter-measures.

One way to test the analysis of the principal article is to determine how it might apply to different types of subsidies. Appendix A lists hypothetical subsidy situations useful for the purpose of testing some of the analysis.

Comments on several selected problems and applications

. . .

Conclusion

Professor Diamond's principal article offers some important insights and a mode of analysis that can help advance knowledge about the appropriate international response to subsidies that affect international trade. Nonetheless, it leaves many questions unanswered.

A policy analysis of this subject might more appropriately begin at a different starting point – inquiring as to the rationale for any response before considering what response is most effective. To this author, it seems clear that the "thank you note" approach (no response) is justified only with respect to the goal of national welfare, as opposed to world welfare. World experience, especially with respect to agricultural products (with the United States and the EEC in a virtual subsidy war) reinforces the need for this broader perspective. In fact, even many "thank you note" proponents recognize a need to address export subsidy problems, in contrast to domestic subsidies.

The argument in favor of countervailing duties, of course, is weakened by such economic analyses as those presented in the Sykes[27] and Trebilcock[28] papers, which show that countervailing duties have the welfare-limiting effects of any tariff. This leads some to emphasize a system of international rules as a way to control the world welfare damage of subsidies. It is interesting to note, for example, that in the current trade negotiations of the Uruguay Round, some proposals concerning services trade do not suggest countervailing duties, but do provide for international rules to discipline subsidies. Indeed, in some instances the international rule may be the only way to proceed. Such is the case when the goods are targeted to so-called third markets – neither the market of the subsidizing country nor the country complaining about subsidies.

Some feel, however, that a system of international rules is still a "second best" solution. There is much skepticism that the international rules can work adequately to achieve the discipline needed. Thus, countervailing duties and the various methods for measuring and applying them remain the primary subject of debate. Even though these duties may themselves cause welfare harms, future empirical exploration may indicate that they are effective, in the long term, in reducing the use of distorting subsidies. Many persons engaged in the study of subsidies and countervailing duties are of the opinion that such duties do influence governments to limit subsidies. It must be recognized, however, that the opportunity to make effective use of countervailing duties is not evenly spread among nations – countervailing duties utilized by a small market will not have much effect on large markets. Likewise, it must be recognized that pressures for more extensive use of countervailing duties normally come from competing producers in the importing country.

Nevertheless, as this author has stated elsewhere, if one believes that the

[27] See Sykes, "Second-Best Countervailing Duty Policy."
[28] See Trebilcock, "Is the Game Worth the Candle?"

world would be better off if there were a general reduction of the use by governments of subsidies relating to products that flow in international trade, one could argue that the US policies, motivated for entirely different reasons, may fortuitously or coincidentally be having a salutary effect on the world economy.[29]

If we reluctantly accept the usefulness of countervailing duties, and that appears to be a political certainty, then the question of how to prevent the abuse of such duties arises. That is the subject of Professor Diamond's article. However, it is questionable whether the entitlement model is the optimal basis upon which to build such an analysis. Doing so may only facilitate the protectionist or competition-limiting goals of competing domestic producers. Furthermore, the legislative history of the relevant statutes only provides limited insight into this issue.

Despite all this, however, the analysis targeting the marginal cost effects of subsidies is a worthwhile contribution. While it does not adequately contribute to several important subsidy policy questions (for example, the specificity test, or the problem of nonmarket economies), it may provide a very useful way to help contain or discipline the unwarranted use of countervailing duties. It can help identify some large categories of subsidies for which countervailing duties would be inappropriate (for example, certain regional aids or subsidies to assist downsizing or decommissioning), and could be used to analyze many of the subsidy-type practices listed in Appendix A. Furthermore, this analysis is potentially very useful in relation to the evolution of the injury test and its related concept of cause.

It is this general policy analysis that it is hoped will assist government officials and negotiators in the Uruguay Round, and contribute to a better understanding of the relevant issues. In the view of this author, this is more important than the marginal differences in duty that most likely would be calculated under the entitlement approach as compared with certain existing practices.

[29] Jackson, Louis, and Matsushita, *Implementing the Tokyo Round*, 255.

8   Regional trade blocs and the GATT*

1.   Introduction

International economic interdependence is now commonly recognized as a growing phenomenon. Economic events, whether caused by certain government decisions or otherwise, have impacts on neighboring nations, as well as on those on the other side of the globe, and these impacts often occur very swiftly and profoundly. This is leading to frustration on the part of national political leaders, who find it increasingly difficult to take action within their countries which can reasonably fulfill goals of constituencies. Certain kinds of tensions arise between nations because of this phenomenon, and those tensions can threaten to disrupt economic or even political relationships in a way that can be damaging to goals of increasing world welfare, or maintenance of the peace.

Since the early days after World War II, statesmen and political leaders have expressed the goal of developing an international economic institutional framework, which would prevent or inhibit some of the damaging economic characteristics which affected the world in the earlier part of this century. The Bretton Woods system, broadly defined to include not only the IMF and the World Bank, but also the GATT trading system (after the failure of an International Trade Organization Charter to come into effect), was one result of these policy goals. Subsequently, there developed major initiatives in various parts of the world towards regional trading blocs. Thus, there is now increasing attention given to the question of whether the world is better served with an overall multilateral system (such as a GATT/MTO system),[1] or by various trading blocs. There seems to be some trend towards a world with three major blocs: Europe, Western Hemisphere, and Pacific region. On the other hand, there is considerable con-

---

* This chapter is based on John H. Jackson, "Regional Trade Blocs and the GATT" (1993) 16 *World Economy* 2, 121–130. The original article was partially adapted from a paper delivered at a conference in Buenos Aires, Argentina, July 1992. Comments from an anonymous referee are gratefully acknowledged.

[1] See Draft Final Act Embodying the Results of the Uruguay Round of Multilateral Trade Negotiations ("the Dunkel Draft"), GATT Doc. MTN.TNC/W/FA, December 20, 1991.

cern that the development of such blocs could create the characteristics of tensions and conflict. Thus, the relationship of a broad multilateral system to the various actual or potential trade blocs is under discussion.[2] That relationship is the focus of this article.

Although the subject of this article deals primarily with economic matters, it must be recognized that there are various relationships to noneconomic policies. Of course, there are links between the rules of trading blocs and a multilateral trading system, with such subjects as investments, monetary policy, environmental quality, etc. But there are also clearly links to subjects such as human rights, democratization, demilitarization, and other political relationships, such as arms control.[3] These linkages cannot be totally ignored and indeed it has sometimes been said that economic integration, such as that experienced in some of the trading blocs (especially Europe), simply will not work satisfactorily even to achieve economic goals, unless there is a strong political goal motivating the economic integration. In Europe, this strong political goal was seen from the inception of the European economic integration institutions (the Coal and Steel Community of 1952 and the Treaty of Rome of 1957) as relating to the overwhelming objective of preventing World War III, and particularly preventing conflict between France and Germany.[4] In other regional blocs, political goals may not be so obvious, but they surely exist in the background.[5] Part of the attention we give to the issues of the relationship of a multilateral trading system with that of trade blocs must take cognizance of noneconomic goals.

In this article, I will discuss some of these issues in five further sections.

---

[2] Address by Mr. Arthur Dunkel. Director-General of GATT, to the Conference of the *International Herald Tribune* in association with the International Chamber of Commerce, Paris, France, April 2, 1992, reprinted in GATT Doc. GATT/1540, April 3, 1992.

[3] See P. Smith, "The Political Impact of Free Trade on Mexico" (1992) *Journal of Inter-American Studies and World Affairs*; address by President Bush to the Forum of the Americas, Washington, DC, April 23, 1992, excerpts reprinted in US State Department, *Dispatch*, May 4, 1992, 333; Round Table Discussion, "North America Free Trade Agreement: In Whose Best Interest?" Northwestern University School of Law, October 17, 1991, reprinted in (1992) 12 *Northwestern Journal of International Law and Business* 541–543, 549–550, and 568–570; P. Morici (1992) *Foreign Affairs* 101; A. Hurrell, "Latin America in the New World Order: A Regional Bloc of the Americas" (1992) *International Affairs* 68 at 131 and 134; and J. H. Jackson, "The European Communities and World Trade: The Commercial Policy Dimension" in W. J. Adams (ed.), *Singular Europe: Economy and Polity of the European Community After* 1992 (University of Michigan Press, 1992).

[4] See F. Fontaine, *The Schuman Plan and the ECSC* (1987); S. D'Oppuers, "The ECD, WEU, Messina, Val Duchesse, Rome" in *Europe, Dream, Adventure, Reality* (1987), 105–127; and Jackson, "The European Communities and World Trade."

[5] Statement of Robert B. Zoellick, Counselor of the State Department, before the Senate Foreign Relations Committee, April 11, 1991, reprinted in US State Department, *Dispatch*, April 15, 1991, 254–256.

Section 2 discusses the policies of the GATT/MTO trading system regarding regional trading blocs and the reasons for GATT exceptions to its broader policy of most-favored-nation. Section 3 discusses some of the specifics of the GATT rules and the experience under them. Most detail, however, will be left to other referenced works. Section 4 considers issues that go beyond the original notions of policy expressed in the GATT, and indeed relate to a series of new trade and economic issues which are faced by the multilateral trade system as well as trading blocs. Likewise, we will look briefly at some of the deepening questions of linkages to noneconomic goals and effects on matter such as cultural/political change.

Section 5 addresses particularly the Western Hemisphere and its possibilities with respect to regional integration; and, finally, section 6 discusses ways of reconciling the apparent tension between multilateral supervision of international economic actions and supervision within various trading blocs, drawing some conclusions and possibilities for future action.

2.   Policies

The starting point for considering policies relating to regional trade blocs and the multilateral trade system is the most-favored-nation (MFN) clause, particularly that in Article I of GATT. The policies regarding MFN are generally well known, but are reasonably complex. Particularly in a world where the multilateral system embraces MFN but includes more than 100 countries, there are a number of problems engendered by an MFN. These problems are characterized as "the free-rider," or "lowest common denominator" problems.[6] Nevertheless, the basic idea that trade in the world should proceed with the least possible amount of discrimination among countries, so as to facilitate trade, reduce the transaction costs (such as determining origin of goods), and reduce tensions, remains one of the central pillars of the multilateral system.

Even at the outset of this system, however, it was recognized that there would be exceptions to MFN. The most significant exception is that expressed in Article XXIV of GATT, which allows the creation of certain kinds of preferential trading blocs if certain criteria are met. The basic policy goal was to allow preferential trading arrangements if they constituted a genuine attempt to develop free trade within the bloc. This notion is expressed by the "substantially all" criterion, discussed in section

[6] John H. Jackson, "Equality and Discrimination in International Economic Law: The General Agreement on Tariffs and Trade" in *The British Yearbook of World Affairs* 1983 (London Institute of World Affairs, 1983); and J. H. Jackson, *The World Trading System: Law and Policy of International Relations* (MIT Press, Cambridge, MA, 1989).

3 below. Often, it has been stated that the goal of the exception of Article XXIV was "trade creating" rather than "trade diverting."[7]

With the development of preferential agreements among developing countries in the GATT, as represented in the GSP programs and later in the Tokyo Round "understanding" (often called the "enabling clause"[8]), a new policy was introduced about which there is some ambivalence. This policy expressed the desire to allow preferential systems which benefit developing countries, as part of a general trend at that time within the GATT to give special favors to developing countries. As some developing countries have become "newly industrializing," there has developed a trend to encourage or pressure such countries into a fuller acceptance of the rules of the GATT trading system. This has been strongly manifested in the negotiating documents and work of the Uruguay Round, and presumably will be a trend that will continue.

Although the policy goals of permitting preferential systems originally may have been expressed above, as decades passed it became clear that other objectives played a very prominent role in the desire of certain countries to develop preferential trading bloc systems. In particular, the uses or, some would say, misuses of the "unfair trade rules," such as antidumping or countervailing duties, have led some countries to seek some relief from the harsh application of those duties, particularly from the United States. Thus, Canada approached the United States for the development of a free trade system, with one of its most important objectives being to ameliorate the hazards of the US unfair trade laws.[9] Similar motivations can be detected in the Mexican request to the US for a preferential trading bloc.[10]

3.   The GATT rules and experiences

The GATT rules are primarily expressed in Article XXIV. It is not feasible or appropriate in this short work to try to accomplish a detailed analysis of

[7] J. H. Jackson, *World Trade and the Law of GATT* (New York, Bobbs Merrill, 1969), 580; Jackson, *The World Trading System*, 141; GATT, "Working Party Report – US–Canada Free Trade Agreement," GATT Doc. L/6927, November 12, 1991, reprinted in *Inside US Trade*, Special Report, November 29, 1991, S2; and K. Bradsher, "Negotiators Hope to Finish Free Trade Pact Today," *New York Times*, August 6, 1992, C1.

[8] See GATT, *Basic Instruments and Selected Documents*, 26th Supplement (1980), 203.

[9] See J. H. Bello and H. E. Moyer, *A Guide to the US–Canada Free Trade Agreement* (1990), 816–817; and J. McKinney, "Dispute Settlement Under the US–Canada Free Trade Agreement" (1991) 25 *Journal of World Trade* 118–120.

[10] "Mexico Said to Seek Relief from US Dumping and Countervailing Duty Law in FTA Negotiations" (1991) 8 *International Trade Reporter* (Bureau of National Affairs, Washington, DC), 809 (noting that in the early 1980s some 26 percent of all US trade actions were aimed at Mexico).

those rules. Interested readers can look elsewhere for those.[11] But a few major points should be emphasized.

There are four rules in particular which might be mentioned. These include the "substantially all" criteria; the "not on the whole higher" criterion for customs unions; the interim agreement plan and schedule; and the problem of notification and decision of the GATT.

The "substantially all" criterion is contained in the definition of the entities which are permitted to have the Article XXIV exception. This exception from MFN is granted to customs unions and free trade areas, providing that in each case the participating nations eliminate trade barriers with respect to "substantially all the trade between the constituent territories." This obviously is at the core of the policy compromise originally contemplated in GATT Article XXIV, whereby the advantages of a preferential agreement that went so far as to eliminate substantially all the barriers, would be deemed to outweigh the disadvantages of departure from MFN. Nevertheless, the phrase "substantially all" is troublesomely ambiguous. Likewise, the word "eliminate" poses problems.

For customs unions (which not only eliminate barriers between the members, but form a common external trade regulation system regarding imports from third countries) there is the additional requirement that the regulations and duties of the common external system shall "not on the whole be higher or more restrictive than the general incidence of the duties and regulations" applicable prior to the formation of the union. This language also has been troublesome. On the one hand, it is argued that essentially the new union need only "net out" the various advantages and disadvantages granted to third country trade to fulfill this requirement. On the other hand, there have been troublesome issues of negotiating the changes in external duties, particularly when they involve preexisting "bindings" by certain countries that became members of the broader preferential area.[12]

The Article XXIV privilege of MFN exception applies not only to free trade areas or customs unions, but also to a third category known as an "interim agreement," designed to lead to the formation of a customs union free trade area. This GATT provision pragmatically recognizes that a customs union free trade area cannot come into being overnight. There needs to be a period of adjustment and transition. Thus, the GATT

[11] Jackson, *World Trade and the Law of GATT*, chapter 24; and GATT, *Analytical Index* (1990).
[12] GATT, Working Party Report – Accession of Portugal and Spain to the European Community, GATT Doc. L/6405, *Basic Instruments and Selected Documents*, 35th Supplement, 300–301; and "European Community Foreign Ministers Sign Agreement Settling Trade Dispute, Averting Higher US Tariffs," *International Trade Reporter* (Bureau of National Affairs, Washington, DC), February 4, 1987, 122.

language about an interim agreement states that it shall "include a plan and schedule for the formation of such customs union or of such a free trade area within a reasonable length of time." Once again, this language has been troublesome, particularly the question of what is a "reasonable length of time."[13]

Finally, GATT Article XXIV provides some procedural rules regarding new preferential arrangements, requiring that they be notified to the Contracting Parties. Likewise, the language of Article XXIV(7) states that if, after studying the notification, the Contracting Parties find that an appropriate agreement is not likely to result within a period that is reasonable, the Contracting Parties shall make recommendations and the preference parties shall not maintain or put into force their agreement if they are not prepared to modify it in accordance with those recommendations. The interesting thing about this procedural language is that it does not require advance or later approval of the Contracting Parties of GATT. Instead, it places the initiative with the Contracting Parties to put forward recommendations for changes in the preferential agreement. This means that technically, once the agreement has been notified to the GATT, unless the Contracting Parties can somehow arrive at an agreed set of recommendations, the language of GATT permits the preference parties to go ahead. The presumption is thus in favor of the preferential arrangement. To the knowledge of this author, the Contracting Parties of GATT have never made an agreed set of recommendations to notifiers of preferential agreements. Thus, many such arrangements have been entered into and operated which arguably do not fully comply with the policy goals and the intent and spirit of Article XXIV of GATT.[14]

Furthermore, in applying Article XXIV over some decades, it has become increasingly clear that the language of Article XXIV is not adequate for the developing international economic practices of today. For example, neither the GATT generally, nor the language of Article XXIV, deal with the important question of "rules of origin" by which preferential parties

---

[13] See GATT, Working Party Report – EEC Agreement of Association with Malta, *Basic Instruments and Selected Documents*, 19th Supplement (1972), 92–93; GATT, Working Party Report – EEC Agreement of Association with Turkey, *Basic Instruments and Selected Documents*, 19th Supplement (1972), 102–105; and GATT, Working Party Report – Agreement Between European Community and Israel, *Basic Instruments and Selected Documents*, 23rd Supplement (1976), 63.

[14] See K. Dam, "Regional Economic Arrangements and the GATT: The Legacy of Misconception" (1963) 30 *University of Chicago Law Review* 615; GATT, Working Party Report Accession of Portugal and Spain to the European Community, GATT Doc. L/6405, *Basic Instruments and Selected Documents*, 35th Supplement, 300–301; and "European Community Foreign Ministers Sign Agreement Settling Trade Dispute, Averting Higher US Tariffs," *International Trade Reporter* (Bureau of National Affairs, Washington, DC), February 4, 1987, 122.

determine whether goods are entitled to receive the preference of their arrangement. Rules of origin can be very damaging to the trade of third parties if the rules are designed to strongly favor products and parts manufactured within the preferential area.[15] Likewise, certain other trade policy laws and rules are not clearly addressed in the GATT language. For example, how does a safeguard or escape clause measure operate? Can a preferential arrangement give preferences to its preference parties in the application of an escape clause? Arguably, the answer should be yes, since the preferential group should be treated more like a single trading entity. A similar argument or problem is raised by the unfair trade rules (antidumping and countervailing duties), but there is now a practice of tolerating preferential agreements which do not eliminate such unfair trade rules between the preference parties.[16]

Furthermore, there are a number of issues regarding the institutional structure of preferential arrangements, particularly those relating to dispute settlement. Since one of the motivations for preferential arrangements is a certain frustration with the GATT, it is not surprising to find different procedures in some arrangements. This might detract from the eligibility of such a system for the GATT Article XXIV exception.

Another area of considerable ambiguity, even with regard to the traditional subjects of the GATT, includes the application of certain other GATT exceptions, such as the general exceptions of Article XX (e.g., health regulations and competition) and the newly prominent issues of environmental regulation. The major new subjects of trade in services and intellectual property can also be a question, at least for future development of standards and policies relating to preferential areas.[17]

Indeed, there are so many variations and so many possible preferential arrangements, that nations entering them may find it necessary to develop a new type of "MFN" clause: a clause which will ensure to the preference parties, preference at least as favorable as those granted to other potential preferential parties when a nation belonging to one enters into similar arrangements!

[15] See E. A. Vermulst, J. Bourgeois, and P. Waer, *Rules of Origin in International Trade: A Comparative Study* (University of Michigan Press, 1994); and Jackson, *The World Trading System*, chapter 4.

[16] See US–Canada Free Trade Agreement, December 22, 1987 to January 2, 1988, Article 1902, HR Doc. No. 216, 100th Cong., 2nd Sess., 297, entered into force January 1, 1989, reprinted in 27 ILM 281 (1988); GATT Doc. L/6927, November 1991. Note, however, that the agreement also contemplates the two countries negotiating a substitute system of rules in both countries for antidumping and countervailing duties as applied to their bilateral trade. See US–Canada Free Trade Agreement, Articles 1906–1907.

[17] See, e.g., "Conference Explores Issues, Obstacles and Support for NAFTA Agreement," IMF Survey, August 3, 1992, at 242; and Round Table Discussion, "North America Free Trade Agreement: In Whose Best Interest?" See also note 16 above.

The GATT experience is extensive. In a list developed by the GATT Secretariat, there are almost eighty preferential arrangements which have been notified to the GATT or otherwise have GATT implications. In many cases, there have been doubts raised as to whether some of these arrangements comply with the criteria established by Article XXIV of GATT. Yet there has not yet been a concrete "turn down" by the GATT system. All this had led to discussion about the need to revise the GATT, or to establish more detailed interpretations for Article XXIV, discussion which has been resisted by some prominent trading countries in the GATT.[18]

4.   New subjects and the changing world: beyond Article XXIV

As indicated in section 2 above, the reasons today why various countries wish to enter into preferential trade and economic groupings go well beyond the rationale originally conceived in the GATT of the 1940s. During the course of the decades of GATT's experience, statesmen and political leaders have learned that a number of problems are affecting trade relations that were either not conceived at all, or hardly conceived, in the GATT. Prime examples include trade in services and intellectual property. In general, the focus has shifted from tariffs to nontariff barriers and the latter are myriad in number. As the bilateral discussions between the United States and Japan, entitled "SII – Structural Impediments Initiative," demonstrate,[19] trade relations now require consideration of matters formally thought to be well within national sovereignty and matters which are deeply embedded in societal structures and cultures. Thus, when small groups of nations decide to join together in a preferential system, there is the possibility (and indeed demonstrated temptation) for such groups to develop preferences which are effectuated through matters that not only are not mentioned by Article XXIV of GATT, but often not mentioned at all in the GATT. These might include a number of different kinds of regulatory standards which would address environmental concerns or prudential concerns in the area of financial services, or labor standards, or even human rights. One can foresee some preferential areas developing environmental rules that give advantages to the preference partners, while disadvantaging trade from third countries. The same might be true for a number of other subjects.

In some cases, these matters are dealt with in so-called "transition" or

---

[18] "Understanding on the Interpretation of Article XXIV of the General Agreement on Tariffs and Trade," Dunkel Draft, at U1–4. See also US–Israel Free Trade Agreement, April 2, 1985, 23 ILM 653 (1985).

[19] US Trade Representatives' Office, *Joint Report of the US–Japan Working Group on the Structural Impediments Initiative* (June 28, 1990); Japan Federation of Economic Organizations, *Interim Report on the Future of Japan–US Economic Relations and the Structural Impediments Initiative*, reprinted in *Inside US Trade*, Special Report, June 26, 1992, S5.

"phase-in" rules. Obviously, movements towards freer trade tend to require adjustment in the preference participants' societies, and there is often a desire to limit the scope of that adjustment by using transition rules that exclude advantages to trade from the third countries. In many cases, the treaty draftsmen are in uncharted waters, and the GATT does not provide an adequate discipline to prevent the preferential arrangement from undermining trade goals of the broader multilateral system in a way that was not contemplated in the language of Article XXIV.

Another dimension of these new issues is the questions about the impact of the preference system arrangement itself on a number of noneconomic aspects of the countries concerned. Thus, there is developing evidence and opinions that preferential arrangements can have a number of effects in the societies concerned, such as altering government structures, changing cultures, requiring new standards of governmental regulation (such as environmental and labor standards), etc.[20] In addition, participants in the preferential arrangement may want explicitly or implicitly to use the advantages of the preference system to induce certain kinds of noneconomic action on the part of participants or proposed new members. For example, the existing participants may require new entrants to develop stronger protection of human rights as a condition of such entry.[21]

5. The Western Hemisphere and its possibilities

One of the most intriguing possibilities for a new preferential arrangement is that which has been mentioned for the Western Hemisphere. Approximately a decade ago, the United States (after developing a preference on auto products with Canada and a more general program for the Caribbean) began to entertain petitions to enter into free trade areas. Israel was first[22] and then came Canada.[23] After that, Mexico requested a similar arrangement and, after an extraordinarily detailed negotiation, we now have a draft "NAFTA" (North American Free Trade Area).[24] There has

[20] See W. J. Adams (ed.), *Singular Europe: Economy and Polity of the European Community After 1992* (University of Michigan Press, 1992); and Belmont Policy Centre, *The New Treaty on European Union* (1991 and 1992).
[21] See J. M. Brown, "Threat to Turkish EC Deal," *Financial Times*, July 7, 1992, 3; and J. M. Brown, *Financial Times*, July 10, 1992, 6.   [22] See US–Israel Free Trade Agreement.
[23] See US–Canada Free Trade Agreement.
[24] Draft NAFTA texts on investment, rules of origin, agriculture, and textiles, February 21, 1992, reprinted in *Inside US Trade*, Special Report, March 27, 1992; and draft NAFTA texts on intellectual property rights, financial services, and land transportation, February 21, 1992, reprinted in *Inside US Trade*, Special Report, March 24, 1992. See also T. Golden, "Talks Resume to Complete North American Free Trade Pact," *New York Times*, July 26, 1992, 8; T. Golden, "Progress But No Agreements in Trade Talks," *New York Times*, July 27, 1992, C1; and Jackson, *The World Trading System*, chapter 4.

been a great deal of speculation about whether the NAFTA would be broadened, accepting other members from the Western Hemisphere, and indeed participants have mentioned this possibility. Thus there are those who contemplate that, during the course of some years, possibly the remainder of this decade, there could develop a free trade area consisting of most or all of the countries in this hemisphere.[25] Already, experience in the case of Canada and the anticipation of the NAFTA suggests that a broader Western Hemisphere arrangement could have staggering implications, mostly beneficial for the citizens of this hemisphere. Several points should be made.

First, it is reasonably clear, as suggested above, that although there is a very strong economic policy motivation for the development of a broader hemisphere free trade agreement (FTA), there are a number of non-economic policy objectives implicit or explicit in such an arrangement. This includes democratization, demilitarization, respect for human rights, development of environmental rules, amelioration of certain worker migration problems, etc. These are linked to the more explicit goals of a potential FTA to enhance world welfare through advantages of economics of scale and comparative advantage, and to enhance investment flow, protection of property rights, etc.

Secondly, just as there is talk about a "fortress Europe," there are grounds to be concerned about similar tendency in a Western Hemisphere FTA, a "fortress America." Thus, the question of a broader multilateral discipline for trading blocs, to keep them from fighting amongst themselves, is raised.

6.   Reconciling competing objectives: directions of potential

All these factors make it reasonably clear that the GATT and its Article XXIV, as well as the more ambiguous legal framework of the 1979 enabling clause, are woefully inadequate for the tasks required of a multilateral system to provide some sort of adequate supervision and discipline on certain of the more dangerous tendencies of trading blocs. GATT Article XXIV is out of date, and some would say fatally flawed from the outset (given its inability to impose some GATT discipline). This raises the question of what needs to be done in the future. The Dunkel Draft (December 1991 draft agreements in the context of the Uruguay Round)[26] includes a draft "Understanding on the Interpretation of Article XXIV," which

---

[25] Robert B. Zoellick, "The Soviet Economy: It's Always Darkest Before It's Pitch Black" (1991) 5 *International Economics* 17–23; and "Free Trade Free-For-All," *Economist*, January 4, 1992, 63.

[26] See note 18 above.

establishes some useful principles and benchmarks for providing rigor to the language of Article XXIV. For example, a "reasonable length of time" is said not to exceed ten years, except in exceptional cases. This draft agreement would undoubtedly be useful if adopted, and one can hope that it will become part of the Uruguay Round package. But it is clear that it leaves much open. The draft agreement on services also has a clause concerning "economic integration" or preferential agreements.[27] It is very important that services trade be brought under this type of discipline, and the draft Article of the services Dunkel draft text is a valuable start. Nevertheless, more will be needed. Some subjects for consideration in this regard might include:

1. Strengthened GATT/MTO review of new agreements, with strong emphasis on transparency. In many ways, the preferential agreements are justified (even in some cases when they do not meet the Article XXIV criteria). They provide an outlet for smaller groups of countries to go well beyond what the GATT seems able to design in the way of rules and disciplines for international trade relations, and this is often commendable. Likewise, they provide an opportunity for experimentation with various rules which can then later be assimilated into the broader multilateral system. But it can be argued that a more detailed report should be presented to the GATT and available to all Contracting Parties, an opportunity to comment (and in some cases, depending on specific rules such as those in the Dunkel text, to impose a requirement of change) be made available.
2. Regular periodic reviews should be strengthened. Periodic reviews of preferential trade blocs could be developed along the lines of the new TPRM (Trade Policy Review Mechanism) of the GATT.
3. GATT dispute settlement provisions should be available, as suggested by the Dunkel draft, to challenge "nullification or impairment" imposed on third parties by preference arrangements.
4. There should be an opportunity to develop some specific rules which would obligate the preference partners and the preference arrangement institutions, so as to provide the basis of a complaint under dispute settlement processes. These rules might require, for example, regulatory actions to be the "least trade restrictive" possible. The rules of origin provisions in the GATT Dunkel draft text[28] are also highly relevant and could be extremely important.

[27] Agreement on Trade in Services, Article V, in Dunkel Draft, Annex II, 9–11.
[28] Agreement on Rules of Origin, in Dunkel Draft, D1–4.

Part IV

Dispute settlement procedures

A central and, some would say, most important feature of both the GATT and the WTO are the dispute settlement procedures. Obviously these are vital to most of the questions one could ask in relation to international economic law. The GATT dispute procedure evolved from minimal treaty clauses, hampered by the "birth defects" of GATT, into a remarkably sophisticated institution which had much influence on the relative effectiveness of the implementation of the GATT treaty clauses. In this part of this book are gathered five excerpts from as many articles, treating various aspects and perspectives on these dispute settlement processes. The selection of articles for this part was particularly difficult, given the many facets which are treated by this author in many places. For more systematic "overview" approaches, readers are once again referred to relevant chapters of the author's books.

The first selection (chapter 9) is about one of the most complex cases ever treated by the GATT dispute procedures, and for the purposes here the article has been much abridged. Most of the intricate details of the DISC (Domestic International Sales Corporation) case have been omitted, but the passages presented are some of those which give some perspectives and judgments about the dispute procedures generally. Perhaps enough is presented here to stimulate some readers to seek out the full article (which is readily accessible in the *American Journal of International Law*). The full version of the article by this author is rather critical of the logic and findings of the panel (unusually consisting of five individuals rather than three, and including nongovernment experts). The logic and reasoning seem to me to be quite contrived in blurring over some important distinctions. Although a 1982 decision of the Council of the GATT Contracting Parties decided to "adopt" the panel report as to the US practices while rejecting those as to the US counter-claims against Belgium, France, and the Netherlands, the case has not entirely gone away. The US changed its law to transform the DISC into an FSC (foreign sales corporation), which was the US view as to what the panel report required. The US claimed that this change made its practice legally the same under GATT as the territorial tax practices of the counter-claim defendants. Recently, however, this issue has returned and the European Communities have launched a case in the WTO against the

US arguing that the FSC is still inconsistent with US WTO/GATT obligations.[1]

As the GATT dispute procedures evolved through trial and error, the practice became regularized to have panels report their findings to the GATT Council for adoption or other decision. A number of questions then gradually began to appear regarding the legal force or meaning of the Council action or inaction. Chapter 10 is a chapter for a 1994 Festschrift book to honor Professor Henry Schermers of Leiden University, in which this author takes up these questions and discusses some of the possible judgments about questions of legal meaning in the GATT context. The WTO procedures managed to improve the dispute procedures for the world trading system, but unfortunately left open (possibly on purpose) some of these "legal meaning" questions, which have perplexed scholars and political/diplomatic leaders and caused them to give diametrically opposite views. The fourth selection in this part, chapter 12, also turns to the topic of chapter 10, but this time in the context of the WTO. In a brief "editorial comment" for the *American Journal of International Law*, I outline my arguments as to why the adopted result of a panel or appeal process (and under WTO procedures the adoption is virtually automatic) casts an international law obligation on the party concerned to carry out the recommendations of the panel or appellate report.

The third selection for this part, chapter 11, turns to another fundamental question of the new WTO trading system. The title of the article republished here, "Standard of Review," only partly reveals what it is really about. The question here is the degree to which the dispute settlement procedures in the WTO context should defer to judgments of nation-states in their regulatory decisions about economic activities which cross national borders and the legal consistency of those regulatory decisions with the WTO rules. This is an issue that also exists at the nation-state level, often with regard to judicial review of regulatory decisions, and this issue was a hotly contested negotiating issue during the Uruguay Round. Jointly with a co-author, Professor Steven Croley, this author discusses the principles which should affect international dispute panel judgments and their relation to national-level decisions.

Finally in this part, chapter 13 steps back from some of the detail about the dispute settlement process and looks at it "constitutionally," in the sense of exploring its role in the institutional structure of the WTO and what might be some systemic constraints on that role. Again some topics here can draw on analogies from nation-state domestic legal structures, posing questions about how far can the dispute bodies reach into domains some might call law making rather than law applying, e.g. how "judicially activist" should the panels be.

[1] WTO Case No. DS108, filed November 18, 1997.

The jurisprudence of international trade: the
      DISC case in GATT*

. . .

All too often, however, international rules are drafted with little sensitivity
to their total context; indeed there is a certain naïveté about the "viability"
of rules. There are important differences between domestic legal rules – in
the context of legal systems involving elaborate procedural rules and a
monopoly of force – and international rules which are often unaccompan-
ied by enforcement or application procedures and which do not benefit
from a well-established "legal system." In a national setting there is often a
degree of public consensus on ethical and other philosophical values that
enables even vaguely formulated rules and procedures to operate effectively (e.g., the British "Constitution"), while on an international plane the
extraordinary differences of language, culture, religion, and political philosophy necessitate greater care in constructing the total "legal system"
needed for rules to be effective.

The naïveté at the international level extends to reliance on false analogies between national legal rules and international legal rules. National
court techniques of interpretation or construction, for example, may not
apply in the international consideration of a similar problem. The degree to
which courts will be trusted (and thus the leeway for "creative interpretation") is likely to be quite different in a national setting from that in an
international setting. The perception of a rule as an "ethical goal" as
opposed to a pragmatic description of consequences (the "ought" versus
the "is") will differ substantially in the two contexts.

One of the most interesting systems of international rules existing today
is that of the treaty called "GATT," the General Agreement on Tariffs and
Trade.[1] The GATT, formulated in the period 1946–1948, has been forced to
assume the role of the central regulatory institution for the great majority
of world trade, although it was not originally designed for that purpose. In

---

* This chapter is based on John H. Jackson, "The Jurisprudence of International Trade: The
  DISC Case in GATT" (1978) 72 *American Journal of International Law* 747–781.
[1] See generally Jackson, *World Trade and the Law of GATT – A Legal Analysis of the General
  Agreement on Tariffs and Trade* (1969).

the last decade the GATT has been heavily criticized for its inability to keep its rules abreast of changes in economic conditions. With the great increase and diversity of membership, it is generally felt to be impossible to amend GATT. In addition, although the original GATT draftsmen clearly had in mind binding precise rules,[2] and, although the procedures of GATT tended to reinforce that view during the first decades of its existence, in recent years the GATT has been increasingly criticized for its institutional inability to maintain compliance with the rules. Rule departures (breaches) have in some cases become so frequent and so tolerated that the rules are now simply traps for the unwary, inexpert, or naïve. The United States Congress, for example, has complained in official reports that[3] "Today, many GATT principles are observed more in the breach," and mandated the President to seek improvements in the procedures. Executive branch officials have also criticized this aspect of GATT and the Director-General of GATT has stated,[4] referring to the GATT rules: "The trouble is that governments do not always respect them, or tend to pay more attention to their letter than their spirit."

An extraordinarily complex but interesting dispute has been considered recently under GATT procedures. Because this case illustrates most of the difficulties and dilemmas of the GATT in today's interdependent economic world, I propose in this article to use this case as the basis for a number of comments on the "jurisprudence of international trade." My basic proposition is as follows. Agreed rules have great importance as a tool of modern diplomacy, particularly in international economic matters which are so complex and which engender difficult-to-control domestic political pressures that could be detrimental to world well-being. But these rules are incapable of playing their important role unless they are set in a framework of an effective "legal system," a system that provides for application of the rules to particular facts, objective methods of determining those facts, trusted interpretations of the rules, and methods by which these actions are kept consistent and reasonably predictable. In the GATT (and in world economic relations generally) this well-constructed system is missing. Thus the effectiveness of agreements on new substantive rules will be uncertain and future noncompliance could even engender further angry political pressures for policies damaging to the world economy.

---

[2] Jackson, "The General Agreement on Tariffs and Trade in United States Domestic Law" (1967) 66 *Michigan Law Review* 249 at 285 note 199. See UN Doc. EPCT/C.II/PV2 at 8 (1946).
[3] Senate Committee on Finance, Trade Reform Act of 1974, S. Rep. No. 93–1298, 93rd Cong., 2nd Sess., 83 (1974).
[4] Address by Mr. Oliver Long, Director-General of the General Agreement on Tariffs and Trade to the Zurich Economic Society, Zurich, November 9, 1977, GATT Press Release No. 1199 at 10.

The case to be examined here is the so-called "DISC" case, together with related counter-complaints.[5] These cases involved the single most difficult substantive problem of international trade today – the problem of "subsidies," namely, what are appropriate or inappropriate governmental measures which, incidentally or purposely, aid exports? This substantive problem is a high priority subject of the Geneva Tokyo Round negotiations, and one which has occasioned considerable near-bitter diplomatic activity in recent years. But apart from the substantive question (which will not be discussed in detail in this article), I wish to examine the procedures of the particular controversy, and to show failures at three stages: (i) the process of getting the procedures in motion; (ii) the reasoning of the "judges"; and (iii) the lack of implementation of the result. These failures are related to a lack of an effective legal system for the rules concerned. In Part I, I will describe the DISC case and will also briefly explain two other subjects as background necessary for an understanding of the analysis of this case and its counterparts, which follows in Part II. In Part III, I will state some conclusions.

I.   The DISC case and its context

. . .

III.   Some conclusions

. . .

The critical question is whether and how to draw the line between hundreds of governmental measures often taken for legitimate domestic policy reasons, and those measures which are to be deemed so "predatory" in nature that the international trading system cannot long tolerate them. This question is *not* now well regulated by GATT; it is far too complex for the existing rules, and it will take considerable knowledge and sophistication to design future appropriate rules. The tax practices alone will be an intricate and complex subject, probably requiring years of negotiation, if not the perpetual attention of some international body. Perhaps conscious

---

5 These cases are reported in a series of GATT documents, the most important of which are those giving the report of the various panels. For the DISC case, see GATT Doc. L/4422 of November 2, 1976, reprinted in *Basic Instruments and Selected Documents*, 23rd Supplement (1977), 98; for the Income Tax Practices Maintained by Belgium case, see GATT Doc. L/4424 of November 12, 1976, reprinted in *Basic Instruments and Selected Documents*, 23rd Supplement (1977), 127; for the Income Tax Practices Maintained by France case, see GATT Doc. L/4424 of November 12, 1976, reprinted in *Basic Instruments and Selected Documents*, 23rd Supplement (1977), 114; and for the Income Tax Practices Maintained by the Netherlands case, see GATT Doc. L/4425 of November 12, 1976, reprinted in *Basic Instruments and Selected Documents*, 23rd Supplement (1977), 114.

intent to favor exports (as discussed in Part II.C above) will become part of those rules.

More broadly, what do the DISC and related cases tell us about "the jurisprudence of international trade" and the GATT system? In this author's view they demonstrate the weakness of the GATT dispute resolution or rule-application-interpretation procedures, in several respects:

1. the procedures for getting the process under way are faulty and subject to delay and foot dragging;
2. the delay plays into the hands of a *fait accompli* approach to trade policy;
3. meager resources of personnel, and money, may contribute to inadequate consideration of the cases and faulty reasoning;
4. fact-finding resources and procedures are inadequate;
5. the role of the decision panel is not well defined;
6. the procedures for reopening a complex case that seems to have gone astray are inadequate;
7. the ambiguity of the "nullification or impairment criteria of Article XXIII" weakens the whole process;
8. the "*prima facie* nullification or impairment" doctrine in GATT, formulated to respond to the ambiguity of "nullification or impairment," can itself be abused and cause weighty consideration of trivia, undermining the traditional GATT notion of confining its dispute procedures to matters of real, and not just theoretical, importance; and
9. the implementation phases of the procedures are too loose, too ill defined, and too much subject to the criticism that they involve political forces and calculations that are inappropriate to an adjudicatory procedure that needs to develop confidence and trust.

One important question not adequately considered in the GATT dispute settlement process is the question of what issues can be appropriately handled by those procedures. In other words, when is a disputed issue so inextricably bound up in the need for "rule making" as opposed to "rule applying," that the dispute settlement mechanism of GATT ought not to be the technique for resolving the differences? This is a very complex and important issue, virtually unaddressed in GATT practice. In national government practice this issue is troublesome also, and in some jurisdictions courts have developed techniques to aid them in refusing to accept cases through concepts such as "nonjusticiability." An international dispute settlement mechanism must also address this question, or continuously run the risk of trying to perform tasks beyond its capacity. The DISC and related cases are a prime illustration of this problem.

These tax measure cases are the most complex ever to be considered under the GATT Article XXIII procedures, and the procedures failed. Thus these cases have set back the potential for evolutionary improvement of this process. Let us hope that the diplomats and government representatives can conceive of some amicable way to minimize the damage, to begin serious rule-formulation consideration on the complex tax issues involved, and, perhaps most important, to begin fundamental improvements in the GATT dispute settlement process[6] which is part of the larger "legal system" which, in turn, is vital to the usefulness and effectiveness of world economic rules.

[6] For some suggestions regarding improvements to the GATT dispute settlement process see the Report of the Panel on International Trade Policy Institutions of the American Society of International Law, *Remaking the System of World Trade: A Proposal for Institutional Reform* (Studies in Transnational Legal Policy No. 12, 1976); and Jackson, "The Crumbling Institutions of International Trade" (1978) 12 *Journal of World Trade Law* 93. See also the Trade Act of 1974, § 121; Robert E. Hudec, *The GATT Legal System and World Trade Diplomacy* (New York, Praeger, 1975); and ABA Summary of Action of the House of Delegates, Reports of Sections, No. 102 (February 1978).

10   The legal meaning of a GATT dispute settlement report: some reflections*

1.   Introduction

Perhaps it is true that probing questions about the legal and jurisprudential nature of international law norms and practices more often raise
perplexing questions about the ambiguity of law than would be the case for
such questions regarding domestic law. But in any event such questions
about the General Agreement on Tariffs and Trade (GATT) certainly do![1]
    One of the most interesting features of the checkered evolution of the
GATT during its forty-five years of history, has been its dispute settlement
process. In this brief "reflection article" I propose to discuss some fundamental jurisprudential questions about the portion of that process that lies
at the heart of the "law of GATT," but which has hardly been explored in
the scholarly literatures,[2] namely, what is the legal nature of a report by a
GATT Dispute Settlement Panel? In an international organization or
adjudication procedure better legally established (such as for the World
Court), treaty text often supplies fairly concrete answers to similar questions. Not so for the GATT, as we will see.
    It is not my intention here to consider the GATT procedures generally,
but instead to focus on just the one question posed in the title. Many other
interesting aspects of these procedures are left to other works, past and
future.

---

* This chapter is based on John H. Jackson, "The Legal Meaning of a GATT Dispute
  Settlement Report: Some Reflections" in Niels Blokker and Sam Muller (eds.), *Towards
  More Effective Supervision by International Organization: Essays in Honour of Henry G.
  Schermers* (Martinus Nijhoff Publishers, Dordrecht, Boston and London, 1994).
[1] See generally J. H. Jackson, *World Trade and the Law of GATT* (1969); J. H. Jackson and
  William Davey, *Legal Problems of International Economic Relations: Cases, Materials and
  Text* (2nd edn., West Publishing, St. Paul, MN, 1986); J. H. Jackson, *The World Trading
  System: Law and Policy of International Economic Relations* (1989); J. H. Jackson, J. V.
  Louis, and M. Matsushita, *Implementing the Tokyo Round: National Constitutions and
  International Economic Rules* (University of Michigan Press, 1984); and J. H. Jackson,
  Restructuring the GATT System (1990).
[2] See note 1 above; and R. E. Hudec, *GATT Legal System and World Trade Diplomacy* (2nd
  edn., 1990).

118

2.   The dispute over GATT dispute procedures

2.1.   *GATT and the ITO: a failed concept and its substitute*

As is widely known, the GATT was never originally intended to be an international organization. Rather the negotiators in the conferences of 1946, 1947, and 1948 contemplated the establishment of an ITO, an International Trade Organization, which would supply the institutional framework for world trade, as a complement to the other Bretton Woods institutions (the World Bank and the International Monetary Fund). The GATT was thought to be merely a reciprocal-tariff reduction agreement (with ancillary related clauses to make such reductions meaningful and to provide nondiscriminatory trade among participating nations). When the ITO failed to come into being (after the US Congress refused to approve US ratification), the GATT (which was applied provisionally by a Protocol of Provisional Application) gradually took over the function and role of the failed ITO as the principal international treaty and institution to provide the legal framework for international trade. Because of this history, the GATT treaty language itself has only very sketchy institutional clauses (including those regarding dispute settlement), and these "birth defects" have troubled world trade rules ever since.

2.2.   *The GATT procedures: historical perspectives*

The procedures for resolution of disputes are centered in Articles XXII and XXIII of GATT, although there are a number of other provisions sprinkled throughout the GATT that relate to resolution of disputes, or renegotiation or compensation of obligations.[3]

Article XXII of GATT merely provides for consultation, on any matter regarding GATT, when any contracting party requests it. It is a simple but sometimes very useful provision.

The core provisions of GATT concerning dispute settlement are contained in Article XXIII.[4] This Article is very brief by comparison to most international organization dispute settlement Articles, and it has some anomalies. For example, the basis of a "complaint" is not a "breach" of the legal obligations in the agreement, but is instead something called "nullification or impairment." This is a phrase that has always been rather ambiguous in GATT, although an early case in GATT suggested relating this to denial of benefits expected under negotiated concessions.[5]

---

[3] See Jackson, *World Trade and the Law of GATT*, chapter 8.
[4] Jackson, *The World Trading System*, chapter 4.
[5] GATT, "Australia – Subsidy on Ammonium Sulphate," GATT Doc. GATT/CP.4/39, *Basic Instruments and Selected Documents*, vol. II, 188 at 192–195 (working party report adopted April 3, 1950).

One of the striking features of GATT's forty-five-year history, however, is that it has evolved a rather elaborate dispute settlement procedure that has in recent years taken a fairly rigorous approach to the legal obligations of the GATT. In fact, an argument can be made that the GATT jurisprudence which now exists – almost 200 reported cases – is the largest significant body of case law experience developed for a major multilateral treaty of broad purpose and application. Among the many issues raised in this jurisprudence are those of institutional power distribution, treaty compliance, role of tribunals in settlement negotiations, use of prior reports as a sort of "precedent," legal authority of an organization to interpret its own charter, and third party interests in a procedure between two other disputants, to say nothing of the headline-grabbing questions such as those in the 1991 *Tuna–Dolphin* case mediating a clash between international trade and environment treaties.[6]

At the outset of GATT's history, one would have been hard pressed to predict the degree to which the GATT has evolved into a sophisticated organization, and particularly to predict the degree to which dispute settlement has become so central to the GATT process. Indeed, the relative success of the GATT dispute settlement procedure has attracted attention from various economic interest groups who desire to place one subject or another (intellectual property, services) under the discipline of the GATT, at least partly because of the attraction of a reasonably disciplined dispute settlement procedure.[7] Dispute settlement procedures are seen as a core measure for the effective enforcement of treaty obligations, as will be noted below.

2.3.   The core policies: rule orientation

Since its beginning GATT has experienced a policy controversy concerning dispute settlement. To over-generalize a bit, there were roughly two disputing camps: one group, which we can term "negotiation" or "diplomacy" oriented, held the view that dispute settlement procedures should not be juridical or "legalistic" in their approach, but should simply be procedures that would assist negotiators to resolve differences through negotiation and compromise. Another approach viewed the dispute settlement procedure as a relatively disciplined process by which an impartial

---

[6] Tuna/Dolphin case, GATT, DS21/R of September 3, 1991. J. H. Jackson, "Dolphins and Hormones: GATT and the Legal Environment for International Trade after the Uruguay Round" (1992) 14 *University of Arkansas at Little Rock Law Journal* 429–454.

[7] Ministerial Declaration of the Uruguay Round ("Punta del Este Declaration"), GATT Doc. GATT/1396, September 25, 1986.

panel could make objective rulings about whether certain activities were consistent with GATT obligations or not.

In the early years of GATT, disputes were generally heard before "working parties" which consisted of nation-states as members (each nation then designating who would represent it). Some time in the mid-1950s, under the leadership of the then Director-General, Eric Wyndham-White, the GATT procedure shifted to a panel process, whereby a panel of persons, named in their own right, would hear the disputing arguments and make findings about the legal issues. The panelists were deemed not to represent governments, and presumably should not take instruction from governments. Thus the procedure of GATT moved rather strikingly towards the "juridical" approach, although panelists would still declare that part of their responsibility was to encourage settlement of a dispute between disputing parties.[8]

In other works, this author has argued for what is termed a "rule-oriented approach."[9] In general we can contrast the "rule-oriented" approach to what might be called a "power-oriented" or "diplomacy" approach. This author has suggested that the rule-oriented approach, particularly as to international economic affairs, has much policy advantage. It is this approach that focuses the disputing parties' attention on the rule, and on predicting what an impartial tribunal is likely to conclude regarding whether the rule has been fulfilled. This, in turn, will lead parties to pay closer attention to the rules of the treaty system, and this can lead to greater certainty and predictability which is essential in international affairs, particularly *economic* affairs driven by market-oriented principles of decentralized decision-making, with participation by millions of entrepreneurs. Such entrepreneurs need a certain amount of predictability and guidance so that they can make the appropriate efficient investment and market development decisions.

Nevertheless, there still exists, even today, some tension between these different approaches to GATT dispute settlement.[10] By way of contrast,

---

[8] French Import Restrictions, *Basic Instruments and Selected Documents*, 11th Supplement, 94 (panel report adopted November 14, 1962); Paragraph 18, Understanding Regarding Notification, Consultation, Dispute Settlement, and Surveillance, adopted November 28, 1979, GATT Doc. L/4907, *Basic Instruments and Selected Documents*, 26th Supplement, 210; Jackson, *The World Trading System*, 92–93.

[9] Jackson, *The World Trading System*, chapter 4. See also J. H. Jackson, "Governmental Disputes in International Trade Relations: A Proposal in the Context of GATT" (1979) 13 *Journal of World Trade Law* 1.

[10] GATT Secretariat, Multilateral Trade Negotiations of the Uruguay Round Trade Negotiations Committee, "The Dunkel Draft," MTN.TNC/W/FA (1992); Understanding on Rules and Procedures Governing the Settlement of Disputes Under Article XXII and XXIII of the GATT, S1–S23; Elements of an Integrated Dispute Settlement System, T1–T6; Improvements to the GATT Dispute Settlement Rules and Procedures, Council Decision of April 12, 1989, GATT Doc. L/6488, *Basic Instruments and Selected Documents*, 36th Supplement, 61.

dispute settlement in most other international agreements, including economic agreements, tends to be rule-oriented. Furthermore, it can now be argued that the rule-orientation ideas have generally won out in the GATT, particularly after the history of the 1980s when panels became considerably more rigorous in their approach to legal issues, assisted by a newly established secretariat staff of lawyers. One result has been a flourishing of "business" for the dispute settlement procedures of GATT, with many more cases undertaken in the GATT.[11]

As mentioned before, the dispute procedures have attracted the attention of other economic interest groups such as those regarding intellectual property and services, as a desirable feature. In addition, when the United States and Canada negotiated their Free Trade Agreement, a rigorous rule-oriented approach was built into the dispute settlement procedures there, particularly those of chapter 19 regarding unfair trade laws (anti-dumping and countervailing duties).[12] It should also be noted that the European Community has a very rigorous rule-oriented constitution, with a Court of Justice (sitting at Luxembourg) which makes a number of very significant rulings that have influenced the constitutional development of the European Community.[13] This author has been told by distinguished Latin American diplomats that an important and rigorous dispute settlement procedure is often considered by the business community as the essence of a creditable free trade agreement. Only when such credibility is present will businesses (it is said) begin to base their longer term planning on the effective operation of the agreement.

2.4.   The dispute procedures of GATT

Under current procedures (as largely set out in a 1979 understanding, further modified and elaborated by actions through the 1980s and particularly at the Uruguay Round mid-term review in Montreal in December of 1988), the first step is consultation between the disputing parties

---

[11] See, e.g., GATT, Index – Conciliation, *Basic Instruments and Selected Documents*, 37th Supplement, 344–347 (1991). See also P. Pescatore, W. J. Davey, and A. F. Lowenfeld, *Handbook of GATT Dispute Settlement* (1991).

[12] See J. H. Bello, A. F. Holmer, and D. A. Kelly, "Midterm Report on Binational Dispute Settlement under the United States–Canada Free Trade Agreement" (1989) 26 *Stanford Journal of International Law* 153.

[13] Treaty Establishing the European Economic Community, signed March 25, 1957, 298 UNTS 11; Treaty Establishing the European Atomic Energy Community, signed March 25, 1957, 295 UNTS 259; Treaty Establishing the European Coal and Steel Community, signed April 18, 1951, 261 UNTS 140; all amended by the Single European Act, OJ L1969/1 (1987). See also the Treaty on European Union, signed February 7, 1992, Europe Doc. No. 1759/60 1993, approved on May 18, 1992 by Denmark (plebiscite) and on May 22, 1993 by the UK (Parliament).

(following the framework of GATT Article XXIII). When this does not result in agreement, then the complaining party can ask the GATT Contracting Parties (generally the Council) to establish a "panel" for undertaking an examination of the dispute. Sometimes the defending party will try to block the establishment of a panel, but generally that has not succeeded for long in recent years. A panel will usually consist of three (sometimes five) individuals acting in their own capacity, and in recent years those individuals have included nongovernment specialists, such as academicians, retired diplomats, or retired GATT secretariat officials. The parties must agree on the composition of the panel, although if an impasse is reached, there are provisions for the intervention of the Director-General.[14] Advocacy proceeds both orally and in writing, and sometimes Contracting Parties that are not disputants will be given an opportunity to give their views about the subject. The panel deliberates in secret, and produces a report which is transmitted to the GATT Council for adoption or approval.

One of the most significant difficulties with the existing GATT dispute settlement process has been the "blockage" opportunity that arises from the principle of "consensus decision-making." Although the GATT provides for a majority vote in decisions of the Contracting Parties, with "one nation, one vote," the GATT Contracting Parties for some years have endeavored to avoid strict voting and to adopt decisions by "consensus," which generally means extensive negotiation for a text to which all parties can agree. It is this idea of consensus that has been carried over into the dispute settlement procedure, such that it is deemed necessary to have a consensus decision of the Council to adopt a panel report. Although not entirely clear, the Contracting Parties have generally deferred to the idea that consensus means no dissent, or at least no significant dissent. Thus it has been the case that when the losing party of a dispute objects to the adoption by the Council (or other dispute committee), adoption is blocked. Thus the losing party to a panel procedure has had the ability to prevent the panel report from coming into force, and this blocking action has been used in a number of significant cases (particularly cases relating to subsidies). This has been a very troublesome defect of the procedure, and one for which there is determination to correct in the Uruguay Round, probably through the establishment of an appellate procedure. Since many of the 1979 Tokyo Round Agreements have their own dispute settlement procedures (which largely parallel the GATT procedure), technically there are a number of different dispute settlement procedures in the GATT system, most of them vulnerable to blocking.

[14] Article F(c)5 of the 1989 Decision, note 10 above.

3.   **Evolution of GATT jurisprudence: from nullification or impairment to breach of obligation**

Although the sketchy language of Article XXIII of GATT speaks of "nullification or impairment" and thus does not condition a complaint on an actual breach of GATT rules, the practice in GATT has developed in a somewhat different direction. In 1962 a panel made an epic decision that a breach of a GATT obligation would be considered "*prima facie* nullification or impairment,"[15] and since that time a number of other panels have repeated and applied that principle. As a result, panels and advocacy have focused attention much more on the legal principles of rule application. In a very interesting development a more recent panel (the 1987 *Oil "Superfund" Tax* case)[16] concluded that in certain kinds of cases (mostly those under national treatment obligations of Article III) the presumption of nullification or impairment created by the finding of breach of obligation would not be rebuttable! Thus, at least for certain kinds of cases (and perhaps the principle will spread to other cases), the GATT jurisprudence has come virtually full circle, bringing the actual practice back to the notion of "breach of obligation" which is found in so many other international organizations.

The legal status of GATT panel reports has raised a number of questions. The practice of GATT has been that unless the Council "adopts" the panel report, the report is not "binding." But even if the Council does adopt the report, as in almost all cases it has, there is still some legal question as to the legal impact of the panel rulings.[17]

When one surveys the historical evolution of the GATT procedures, it generally confirms the trend away from the "negotiating" model for those procedures, and towards a "rule-oriented" model. The shift from the working party process to panels with "objective" third party panelist experts supports that trend. Likewise, the shift away from "nullification or impairment" towards more precise evaluation of "breach of obligations" supports the trend, and if there develops a jurisprudence that does not allow rebuttal of the *prima facie* nullification or impairment, at least in some cases, this is even stronger support. Furthermore, when one reads the panel reports, one finds considerable reference to prior cases, utilizing them as a sort of "precedent." In addition, particularly during the 1980s it has become increasingly apparent that the interests in particular disputes are often

---

[15] GATT, Uruguayan Recourse to Article XXIII, GATT Doc. L/1923, *Basic Instruments and Selected Documents*, 11th Supplement, 95 at 100 (panel report adopted November 16, 1962).

[16] GATT, United States – Taxes on Petroleum and Certain Imported Substances, GATT Doc. L/6175, *Basic Instruments and Selected Documents*, 34th Supplement, 136 at 155–159 (panel report adopted June 17, 1987).

[17] See GATT, EEC – Restrictions on Imports of Dessert Apples – Complaint by Chile, GATT Doc. L/6491, *Basic Instruments and Selected Documents*, 36th Supplement, 93 at 127 (panel report adopted June 22, 1989).

much broader than the disputing parties themselves. Third parties, members of GATT, often ask to intervene and make statements about the case, because they recognize the influence of the case and a panel report towards the developing jurisprudence of the GATT generally. Likewise, there has been increasing emphasis on the notion of "transparency" in the dispute settlement process. Some of this emphasis has developed through the advocacy of environmental groups,[18] who worry considerably about the broader implications of results in specific disputes under the GATT procedures, and thus want more transparency and opportunity for policy and evidence inputs into the process. But that concern again supports a trend towards a philosophy of "rule orientation" in the procedure.

4.   International law effects of a GATT dispute panel report

Given this history, what can we say about the international legal effects of the result of the GATT dispute procedure? GATT Article XXIII itself is not very revealing. It does say that if disputing parties cannot reach a satisfactory adjustment between them, they can refer the matter to the Contracting Parties who:

shall promptly investigate any matter so referred to them and shall make appropriate recommendations to the Contracting Parties which they consider to be concerned, or give a ruling on the matter, as appropriate.

The Article also provides explicit authority for the Contracting Parties to authorize the suspension of concessions or other obligations under the agreement to offending Contracting Parties. But the Article does not explicitly say that there is an international law obligation to carry out the results of the dispute settlement process. Indeed, the Article does not even provide for such process, except referral to the Contracting Parties. As we have seen, however, there has evolved a fairly elaborate dispute settlement procedure with a process of written and oral advocacy before panels leading to a panel report. We have also seen that the panel report is not considered binding until the Contracting Parties (acting through the Council under current procedures) has "adopted" the report, or modified it and adopted it. Thus, an unadopted report under the practice does not have binding force (although it may have persuasive force as the opinion of experts).

Assuming that the process has resulted in an adopted panel report, however, what is its legal effect? Several possibilities come to mind:

1. merely a recommendation, possibly implying that failure to follow it could result in Contracting Parties' authorization of suspension of concessions;

[18] Green Groups' Position on NAFTA Environmental Pact, *Inside US Trade*, Special Report, May 7, 1993, S-2.

2. an obligation to obey, with some notion of precedent operating, so that the report has a legal and moral obligation on other nonparticipating Contracting Parties;
3. an obligation under international law for the disputants to obey in the instant case but with no precedential effect;
4. the possibility that the adoption by the Contracting Parties (or its Council) of a panel report is the equivalent of a "definitive" resolution by the Contracting Parties (as a governing body) interpreting the GATT, pursuant to authority of GATT Article XXV; and
5. "practice" under the treaty and the institution, such as to provide a basis for arguing for a particular interpretation consistent with the practice, as suggested by Article 31 of the Vienna Convention on the Law of Treaties.[19]

I will now briefly explore each of these possibilities. Basically I will argue that the most likely interpretation of the legal effect of the GATT panel report which is adopted, is a combination of alternatives three and five listed above.

4.1.   Mere recommendation

Sometimes it has been argued, referring to the structure of Article XXIII of GATT, that there is no obligation under GATT to obey the results of the dispute settlement process, or even "findings" of the GATT Contracting Parties. The argument supports this by reference to the possibility under Article XXIII of the Contracting Parties' authorization of the suspension of concessions. Thus the legal impact resulting from the dispute settlement process is in the form of a contingency: it can result in the authorization of suspension of concessions, but insofar as it does not, there is no further legal exposure to the losing party. The problem with this interpretation is the extensive practice that we now have in the GATT, which seems generally to confirm the view of the Contracting Parties that there is an obligation to carry out a dispute settlement result.[20]

4.2.   Precedent

Some might argue that not only does the practice of GATT suggest an interpretation that there is an obligation to obey the results of the dispute settlement process, but an adopted panel report would have a "precedent effect," and thus operate with a legal and moral obligation on nondisputant

---

[19] Vienna Convention on the Law of Treaties, signed May 23, 1969, 1155 UNTS 331.
[20] Jackson, *The World Trading System*, chapter 4.

Contracting Parties. There are several problems with this idea, however. First, generally under international law it is considered that dispute settlement procedures or tribunal opinions or decisions do not have a *stare decisis* effect.[21] In addition, there are several specific instances in the GATT jurisprudence, where panels have consciously decided to depart from the results of a prior panel, and the panel seemed to think that it was within its power to do so. This reinforces the notion that a strict "precedent effect" or *stare decisis* is not operating, even though panels often do cite prior panel reports to support their conclusions. However, there clearly is a *de facto* precedential effect operating, albeit not strictly.

4.3.   Obligating disputants only

Thus, it can be argued that the general effect of an adopted dispute settlement panel report has by practice (and possibly by implications of the GATT language) the effect of providing an international legal obligation for the disputants to obey the results and adopted report of the panel (sometimes as modified by the Council) for the facts of the particular case being reviewed. Arguably, there is no precedential effect for any future cases, including future cases between the same parties, although it would appear that a future panel could be strongly influenced by the result of the prior panel. There is considerable practice in the GATT to support this approach, although the next alternative suggests a possibly different conclusion.

4.4.   Definitive interpretation

It can be argued that the Council adoption of a panel report is the equivalent of a resolution or decision by the Contracting Parties (as the GATT governing body) definitively interpreting the GATT. Article XXV of the GATT treaty provides very broad authority for the Contracting Parties to act jointly:

for the purpose of giving effect to those provisions of this Agreement which involve joint action and, generally, with a view to facilitating the operation and furthering of the objectives of this Agreement.

This language would appear to support the notion that the Contracting Parties have the power to make a definitive interpretation by decision or resolution (adopted by majority vote, under "one nation, one vote" pro-

---

[21] I. Brownlie, *Principles of Public International Law* (4th edn., 1990), 21; Article 59 of the Statute of the ICJ, signed June 26, 1945, 59 Stat. 1055; TS 993.

cedures also established in Article XXV). A definitive interpretation is intended to mean a binding secondary treaty action which obligates all Contracting Parties to the GATT pursuant to their advance delegation of this authority under Article XXV. This concept of the adoption of a panel report would provide its strongest legal impact. In this case, the impact is stronger even than *stare decisis*. It is virtually as strong as the treaty language itself.

That the Contracting Parties have the authority to act in this manner seems supported by the practice in GATT. Sometimes these have been in the form of a chairman's ruling made without objection.[22] At other times, the Contracting Parties have adopted elaborate "understandings" concerning the implications of the GATT language. One such understanding adopted in 1979 at the end of the Tokyo Round provides many pages describing the procedures traditionally followed in disputes.[23] Although the form of this action by the Contracting Parties is somewhat ambiguous (probably deliberately so), it could be considered a definitive interpretation as well as elaboration of the GATT provisions in Article XXIII.

However, even if the Contracting Parties do have the authority to make a definitive interpretation (as this author would argue),[24] it is not clear that they *intend* their adoption of a panel report to have that effect. Indeed, it seems that their intention is quite the contrary. If delegates were asked when they voted to adopt a panel report whether they intended to make it binding as a matter of treaty law on all Contracting Parties, it is very doubtful that they would answer in the affirmative. Statements from time to time, as well as the practice evidenced in some panel reports of departing from prior panel reports, seem to confirm that the GATT Contracting Parties do not view their adoption of a panel report as a "definitive interpretation pursuant to authority of Article XXV."

There is an advantage to the GATT dispute settlement system in not taking this alternative approach to the legal effect of a panel ruling, but rather following the third approach mentioned. The advantage is that the Contracting Parties in accepting a dispute settlement report do not have to view it as locking in concrete all the reasoning and conclusions of the panel report. This leaves open the possibility in the future for the Council itself to take action (perhaps actually intending a definitive interpretation) which

[22] Jackson, *World Trade and the Law of GATT*, 411; GATT Doc. L/3149 (1968).
[23] Understanding Regarding Notification, Consultation, Dispute Settlement, and Surveillance, adopted November 28, 1979, GATT Doc. L/4907, *Basic Instruments and Selected Documents*, 26th Supplement, 210; Annex on Agreed Description of the Customary Practice of the GATT in the Field of Dispute Settlement (Article XXIII(2)), *Basic Instruments and Selected Documents*, 26th Supplement, 215.
[24] See Jackson, *The World Trading System*, chapter 4.

might be different from a previously adopted panel report. It also, of course, leaves open the possibility of future panels departing from prior panel reports, more consistent with general international law practice.

4.5.   Practice of states

Apart from the various approaches mentioned above, if a panel report is adopted, and results in the disputing parties conforming their practice to the conclusions and findings of the report, this is one piece of evidence of "practice under the agreement," as mentioned in the Vienna Convention of Law of Treaties as a ground for interpretation. The Vienna Convention Article 31 states that in interpreting a treaty:

> There shall be taken into account, together with the context . . . (b) any subsequent practice in the application of the treaty which establishes the agreement of the parties regarding its interpretation . . .

Thus there can be some controversy whether the practice has gone far enough to establish this "agreement of the parties." If later panels follow prior panels, this would add to the evidence of practice, and if there were no considered counter-examples in practice among the Contracting Parties, it is likely to be argued that the practice confirms the particular interpretation of the GATT treaty that has been set forth in the adopted panel reports. This is a more fluid approach than alternative three mentioned above, and also one that has considerable conceptual difficulties, particularly in what constitutes the "sufficient practice." Nevertheless, it can be a useful adjunct to the points made in alternative three.

5.   Effect of GATT panel reports on national laws (United States)

Another aspect of our inquiry relates to the domestic law effect (if any) of a panel report. Obviously this question will vary considerably from nation to nation, so the remarks here will be confined to a brief explanation of some aspects relating to United States law. The question to be discussed here then is the effect of an adopted dispute settlement report of GATT (or one of its ancillary bodies) on the domestic law of the United States.

In broad brush, it is probably safe to say that no legal institutions of the United States (courts or Congress or the Executive) will treat the results of even an adopted panel report as automatically incorporated into domestic jurisprudence in such a way as to be relied upon in that jurisprudence by litigants or others. The United States has often taken a position in the GATT Council that a GATT panel ruling that US practice is not consistent with its GATT obligations, will, when adopted, be followed by the US, but the implication is that the US will take a later action that will implement the result of the panel.

Nevertheless, some further exploration of this question is merited. In a more strictly theoretical approach, one could argue that if an international agreement itself has become directly applicable in United States jurisprudence ("self-executing"), then the domestic legal institutions of the United States are bound to treat it on a par with federal statutes (with the later-in-time rule prevailing). It can be argued then that the treaty to be applied in the United States, is the treaty as interpreted by international law principles (as long as those are clear and definitive). In such a case, if an adopted panel report interprets a particular clause of the GATT, and the GATT is deemed part of the US jurisprudence,[25] then it could be argued that the domestic courts and other legal institutions of the United States would be bound by the panel report. However, this author has not found a single instance in which this approach has been followed. Indeed, such an instance has been rarely if ever found in connection with other treaties (interpreted by an international body).[26] To some extent this casts some doubt on the whole idea of self-executing in the United States. Furthermore, as many US treaties are not self-executing, and as there has been developing more cases of Congressional or Senate approval of treaties with the express statement that the treaty should not be self-executing, this issue is possibly less likely to arise.

In several recent United States court cases, the courts have rejected the definitive application of GATT or GATT code dispute settlement panel results, and indeed have taken an approach that seems unduly antagonistic to such panel results.[27] Nevertheless, the *Restatement of Foreign Relations Law of the United States* strongly supports the notion that US courts in interpreting a statute, should do so (if they have the reasonable option through potential alternative interpretations) in a manner that would interpret the statute consistently with US international obligations.[28] This

---

[25] *Ibid.*, chapters 3 and 4; Jackson, *World Trade and the Law of GATT*; Jackson, *Legal Problems of International Economic Relations*, chapter 5; J. H. Jackson, "Status of Treaties in Domestic Legal Systems: A Policy Analysis" (1992) 86 *American Journal of International Law* 310–340; and R. E. Hudec, "The Legal Status of GATT in the Domestic Law of the United States" in M. Hilf, F. G. Jacobs, and E.-U. Petersmann (eds.), *The European Community and GATT* (Studies in Transnational Economic Law No. 4, 1986), 187–249.

[26] See *United States* v. *Palestine Liberation Organization* (SDNY, June 29, 1988), 27 ILM 1055 (1988). This case said that "the ultimate decision as to how the United States should honor its treaty obligations with the international community is one which has, for at least one hundred years, been left to the executive to decide." 27 ILM 1055 at 1069.

[27] *Suramerica de Aleaciones Laminadas CA* v. *United States*, 966 F. 2d 660 (Federal Cir. 1992); *Public Citizen, Office of the United States Trade Representative*, 804 F. Supp. 385 (DDC, 1992).

[28] *Restatement (Third) of Foreign Relations Law of the United States* (1987), § 114, comment a

Restatement clause is supported by extensive case precedent in the United States.[29] Thus, although a GATT panel report may not have "direct" effect,[30] it appears clear that a GATT panel does have a considerable role to play in the domestic jurisprudence of the United States. It should be part of the materials used to interpret the international obligations of the United States, and this in turn should influence the domestic court in its statutory interpretations. This is made even stronger in the case where the domestic statute has been described in its legislative history as designed to fulfill an international treaty, such as the case with the 1979 Trade Agreements Act implementing the Tokyo Round results of the GATT negotiations.[31] Even stronger are those situations where a US statute explicitly conditions certain statutory language or obligations on the results of the GATT dispute settlement procedure, such as the case in section 301 procedures.[32]

6.   Reforms and the future

At the time of this writing, the Uruguay Round negotiations (launched in September 1986) under the auspices of GATT have yet to be completed. Indeed, they have been prolonged much longer than was originally intended, and have from time to time been declared "dead." However, there seems to be some continuing momentum to conclude the Round. An important part of the Uruguay Round has been an objective to reform the dispute settlement procedures of GATT, and in a draft text for those procedures, a number of interesting reforms are contemplated. While this is not the place to explain those in detail, a few points can be mentioned.

First there is an intent to create a single unified dispute procedure. Secondly, there is a proposal to make it explicit that there is an international legal obligation upon disputing parties to carry out the adopted

---

(1987).
[29] *Lauritzen v. Larsen*, 345 US 571 at 578; 73 S. Ct. 921 at 926; 97 L. Ed. 1254 (1958); *Chew Heong v. US* 112 US 536 at 539–540; 5 S. Ct. 255 at 255–256; 28 L. Ed. 770 (1884); *Weinberger v. Rossi*, 456 US 25 at 33; 102 S. Ct. 1510 at 1516; 71 L. Ed. 2d 715 (1982); *Clark v. Allen*, 331 US 503; 67 S. Ct. 1431; 91 L. Ed. 1633 (1947); *Cook v. US*, 288 US 102; 53 S. Ct. 305; 77 L. Ed. 641 (1933).
[30] Jackson, *Status of Treaties in Domestic Legal Systems*.
[31] See Jackson, Louis, and Matsushita, *Implementing the Tokyo Round*, chapter 4, at 164; Jackson, *The World Trading System*, chapter 4.
[32] US Trade Act of 1974 (Title III), Relief from Unfair Trade Practices, Enforcement of US Rights under Trade Agreements and Response to Certain Foreign Trade Practices, Pub. L. No. 93-618, approved January 3, 1975, 19 USC 2411 at § 301, amended by Pub. L. No. 100-418, approved August 23, 1988.

results of a dispute settlement procedure.[33] Furthermore, there are proposals to prevent the "blockage" of panel reports. These proposals would
substitute an appellate procedure with an appellate tribunal to review
reports which are appealed, and then provide for a referral to the Contracting Parties in a manner that would make it difficult to prevent their
adoption. In addition, the draft procedures contemplate a distinction
between so-called "violation cases," and "nonviolation cases." This would
separate the notions of rule-oriented procedure whereby the focus is on the
consistency of a nation's practice with GATT obligations, from a more
general "nonviolation" process which undertakes to examine whether
"nullification or impairment" has occurred even if there has been no
violation. In the latter case, the draft provisions suggest that there is no
legal obligation to carry out the conclusions of a GATT dispute settlement
process, but there would exist an obligation to negotiate for "compensation."

In any event, it seems generally clear that a rule-orientation has now
largely prevailed in the GATT context. This brings the GATT into line
with most other international dispute settlement procedures, and appropriately focuses attention on the specific treaty obligations, rather than
general and arguable notions of "equity" or "nullification or impairment."
It will be interesting to follow these developments in the future, not only in
the context of GATT, but in the context of a number of developing free
trade and other economic treaties, to see whether these trends continue
despite a number of reservations, particularly in large powerful countries,
about binding nations to the result of international dispute settlement
procedures.

[33] GATT Secretariat, Multilateral Trade Negotiations of the Uruguay Round Trade Negoti-
ations Committee, "The Dunkel Draft," MTN.TNC/W/FA (1992); see Paragraph 19,
Understanding on Rules and Procedures Governing the Settlement of Disputes under
Article XXII and XXIII of the GATT, S1–S23.

11 WTO dispute procedures, standard of review, and deference to national governments*

I.   Introduction

Increasing international economic interdependence is obviously becoming a growing challenge to governments, which are frustrated by their limited capacities to regulate or control cross-border economic activities.[1] Many subjects trigger this frustration, including interest rates, various fraudulent or criminal activities, product standards, consumer protection, environmental issues, and prudential concerns for financial services.[2] Although it has been said that "all politics is local,"[3] it has also been said, with considerable justification, that "all economics is international."[4]

The Uruguay Round's result (including the Agreement Establishing the World Trade Organization (WTO)) is one important effort to face up to some of the problems associated with interdependent international economic activity. Central and vital to the WTO institutional structure is the dispute settlement procedure derived from decades of experiment and practice in the GATT, but now (for the first time) elaborately set forth in the new treaty text of the Dispute Settlement Understanding (DSU), as part of the WTO charter.[5]

* This chapter is based on Steven P. Croley and John H. Jackson, "WTO Dispute Procedures, Standard of Review, and Deference to National Governments" (1996) 90 *American Journal of International Law* 2, 193–213. This article was originally adapted from a chapter prepared for a symposium book edited by Professor Ulrich Petersmann, as part of a project by the International Trade Committee of the International Law Association.

[1] See, e.g., John H. Jackson, *The World Trading System: Law and Policy of International Economic Relations* (1989), 1.1; see also note 2 below.
[2] See John H. Jackson, "Alternative Approaches for Implementing Competition Rules in International Economic Relations" (1994) 2 *Swiss Review of International Economic Relations* 2 at 2–25 (1994); John H. Jackson, "Reflections on Problems of International Economic Relations" in Michael K. Young and Yuji Iwasa (eds.), *Trilateral Perspectives on International Legal Issues: Relevance of Domestic Law and Policy* (Proceedings of Trilateral Symposium on International Law, July 25–28, 1994) (forthcoming 1996), 307; John H. Jackson, "The Uruguay Round, World Trade Organization, and the Problem of Regulating International Economic Behavior" in *Policy Debates* (Centre for Trade Policy and Law, Ottawa, 1995).
[3] See Tip O'Neill and Gary Hymel, *All Politics is Local* (1994).
[4] Peter F. Drucker, "Trade Lessons from the World Economy" (1994) *Foreign Affairs* 99.
[5] Final Act Embodying the Results of the Uruguay Round of Multilateral Trade

Over the last fifteen years, many countries have come to recognize the crucial role that dispute settlement plays for any treaty system. It is particularly crucial for a treaty system designed to address today's myriad of complex economic questions of international relations and to facilitate the cooperation among nations that is essential to the peaceful and welfare-enhancing aspect of those relations.[6] Dispute settlement procedures assist in making rules effective, adding an essential measure of predictability and effectiveness to the operation of a rule-oriented system in the otherwise relatively weak realm of international norms.[7] Thus, the GATT contracting parties resolved at the 1986 launching meeting of the Uruguay Round (at Punta del Este) to deal with some of the defects and problems of existing dispute settlement rules. The result of that resolve was the new DSU.

Yet dispute settlement by an international body such as GATT or WTO panels treads on the delicate and confusing issue of national "sovereignty." Even if one recognizes that some concepts of "sovereignty" are out of date or unrealistic in today's interdependent world,[8] the word still raises important questions about the relationship of international rules and institutions to national governments, and about the appropriate roles of each in such matters as regulating economic behavior that crosses national borders. The GATT dispute settlement procedures have increasingly confronted these questions, including the degree to which, in a GATT (and now WTO) dispute settlement procedure, an international body should "second-guess" a decision of a national government agency concerning economic regulations that are allegedly inconsistent with an international rule.

To pose a concrete example, suppose that a government applies certain domestic product standards, perhaps for reasons of domestic environment policy, in a manner that causes some citizens (or foreign exporters) to argue that the government action is inconsistent with certain WTO norms (such as rules in the WTO Technical Barriers to Trade Agreement). Suppose also, however, that a national government agency (or court) deter-

Negotiations, April 15, 1994, 33 ILM 1140 (1994) (hereinafter the Final Act). The Final Act embodies, *inter alia*, the Agreement Establishing the World Trade Organization, opened for signature April 15, 1994, 33 ILM at 1144 (1994) (hereinafter the WTO Agreement). See primarily the part of that Final Act devoted to dispute settlement, Understanding on Rules and Procedures Governing the Settlement of Disputes, Annex 2 to the WTO Agreement, 33 ILM at 1226 (hereinafter the DSU); see also HR Doc. No. 316, 103rd Cong., 2nd Sess. (1994); and Hugo Paemen and Alexandra Bensch, *From the GATT to the WTO – The European Community in the Uruguay Round* (1995), 71.

6 See Jackson, "Uruguay Round."
7 See generally Paemen and Bensch, *From the GATT to the WTO*; and Jackson, *The World Trading System*, chapter 4.
8 See, e.g., Louis Henkin, "The Mythology of Sovereignty" *American Society of International Law Newsletter*, March–May 1993, 1.

mines that the national action is *not* consistent with WTO rules, and another nation decides to challenge that determination in a WTO proceeding. It would seem clear that the international agreement does not permit a national government's determination *always* to prevail (otherwise the international rules could be easily evaded or rendered ineffective). But should the international body approach the issues involved (including factual determinations) *de novo*, without any deference to the national government? Certainly, it has been argued in GATT proceedings (especially those relating to antidumping measures)[9] that panels should respect national government determinations, up to some point. That "point" is the crucial issue that has sometimes been labeled the "standard of review."[10]

This issue is not unique to GATT or the WTO of course; nor even to "economic affairs," as literature in the human rights arena indicates.[11] Even so, during the past several years the standard-of-review question has become something of a touchstone regarding the relationship of "sovereignty" concepts to the GATT/WTO rule system. Indeed, in the waning months of the Uruguay Round, the standard-of-review issue assumed such importance to some negotiators that it reached a place on the short list of problems called "deal breakers" – problems that could have caused the entire negotiations to fail. This was particularly odd, given that the issue was one that only a few persons understood, and that was virtually unnoticed by almost all the public or private policy-makers concerned with the negotiation. Clearly, certain economic interests were deeply concerned, most notably those in the United States who favored greater restraints on the capacity of the international body to overrule US government determinations on antidumping duties, and who were perceptive and economically endowed enough to carry their views deeply into the negotiating process.[12] And those views cannot be easily dismissed. In many ways they go to a central problem for the future of the trading system – how to reconcile competing views about the allocation of power between national governments and international institutions on matters of vital concern to many governments, as well as the domestic constituencies of some of those governments. They also raise important "constitutional" questions about international institutions and the potential need

9 See Part II below.
10 Agreement on Implementation of Article VI of the General Agreement on Tariffs and Trade 1994, Article 17.6, in Annex 1A to the WTO Agreement (hereinafter the Anti-Dumping Agreement).
11 R. St. J. Macdonald, "Margins of Appreciation" in R. St. J. Macdonald, Franz Matscher, and Herbert Petzold (eds.), *European System for the Protection of Human Rights* (1993), chapter 6; see also Thomas A. O'Donnell, "The Margin of Appreciation Doctrine: Standards in the Jurisprudence of the European Court of Human Rights" 4 (1982) *Human Rights Quarterly* 474.
12 Based on interviews by Professor Jackson.

for "checks and balances" against misuse or misallocation of power in and for those institutions.[13]

For immediate purposes, however, we want to focus on the more particular question of the proper standard of review for a WTO panel when it undertakes to examine a national government's actions or rulings that engage the issue of consistency with the various WTO Agreements and are subject to the WTO's DSU procedures. We will not here explore another interesting standard-of-review question – pertaining to the review by the new WTO Appellate Body established under the DSU of a report by a first-level panel acting under DSU. In this appeal procedure, the Appellate Body's review is limited to "issues of law covered in the panel report and legal interpretations developed by the panel."[14] The difficult question will be how to distinguish questions of law from other questions (fact?). But it seems clear that the standard of review of the first-level panel as it examines national government actions and determinations is a question of law, and so could very well come before the Appellate Body at some point, probably quite early in the evolution of the WTO.

Naturally, the standard-of-review issue is one that many legal systems face. Indeed, some negotiators drew on certain national-level legal doctrines for analogies to use in the GATT/WTO context. For example, the matter has been the subject of considerable litigation, and Supreme Court attention in the United States, and the European Union Court of Justice in Luxembourg has faced similar issues in its jurisprudence. In fact, one of the questions that interests us most is whether it is appropriate to draw an analogy from national-level jurisprudence – specifically, from US jurisprudence – for help in determining the scope or standard of review of an international body over national-level activity.

We proceed here, then, as follows. In Part II, we explore briefly the GATT context of the question, remembering that Article XVI(1) of the WTO Agreement mandates that GATT jurisprudence will "guide" the jurisprudence and practice of the WTO.[15] In Part III, we look at the new WTO Agreements relevant to the standard-of-review question, and consider their potential meaning against the backdrop of some of the history of the Uruguay Round negotiation. In Part IV, we turn to the jurisprudence of US administrative law, which has struggled for many decades with a somewhat similar standard-of-review question, associated in recent years with the US *Chevron* doctrine, explained in Part IV. In Part V, we explore some of the basic policies underlying the *Chevron* doctrine and argue that those policies do not find easy application in the context of an international proceeding. Finally, in Part VI we briefly draw some tentative conclusions

---

[13] See Jackson, "The Uruguay Round."   [14] See DSU, Article 17.6, 33 ILM at 1236.
[15] WTO Agreement, Article XVI(1).

and suggest some avenues that may be useful for considering the approach of the WTO panels.

II.   Background: illustrative GATT panel jurisprudence

Clearly, the desire of some negotiators to deal explicitly with this subject in the Uruguay Round was influenced by their reaction (or that of their constituencies) to some GATT panel cases, especially antidumping cases, in which observers felt the panels had over-reached their authority and been too intrusive in disagreeing with national government authorities. Thus, it is worth noting some of the GATT panel reports that addressed this question or topics related to it.[16]

In fact, a very early GATT working party discussed this subject in 1951 in a case involving a complaint by Czechoslovakia against a US escape clause action that had raised tariff barriers on the importation of "hatter's fur." The working party concluded in favor of the United States, reasoning as follows:

48. These members were satisfied that the United States authorities had investigated the matter thoroughly on the basis of the data available to them at the time of inquiry and had reached in good faith the conclusion that the proposed action fell within the terms of Article XIX as in their view it should be interpreted. Moreover, those differences of view on interpretation which emerged in the Working Party are not such as to affect the view of these members on the particular case under review. If they, in their appraisal of the facts, naturally gave what they consider to be appropriate weight to international factors and the effect of the action under Article XIX on the interests of exporting countries while the United States authorities would normally tend to give more weight to domestic factors, it must be recognized that any view on such a matter must be to a certain extent a matter of economic judgment and that it is natural that governments should on occasion be greatly influenced by social factors, such as local employment problems. It would not be proper to regard the consequent withdrawal of a tariff concession as *ipso facto* contrary to Article XIX unless the weight attached by the government concerned to such factors was clearly unreasonably great.[17]

By contrast, in a case brought by Finland against New Zealand's application of antidumping duties on imports of transformers, the panel ruled in 1985 that New Zealand authorities had not sufficiently established the

---

[16] We will not here analyze in detail the jurisprudence of the GATT panel reports regarding the standard of review. Rather, in this article, we focus on the policy arguments and the question of applying analogous national legal system rules about such a standard.

[17] GATT Dispute Settlement Panel, "Hatter's Fur Case," Report on the Withdrawal by the United States of a Tariff Concession under Article XIX of the GATT (1951), paras. 8–14, GATT Sales No. GATT/1951-3 (1951), portions reproduced in John H. Jackson and William Davey, *Legal Problems of International Economic Relations: Cases, Materials and Text* (2nd edn., West Publishing, St. Paul, MN, 1986), 556.

validity of a "material injury" determination,[18] a ruling that rejected New Zealand's contention that neither other contracting parties nor a GATT panel could challenge or scrutinize that determination. The panel said that to refuse such scrutiny "would lead to an unacceptable situation under the aspect of law and order in international trade relations as governed by the GATT."[19] The panel in this connection further noted that a similar point had been raised, and rejected, in the 1955 report of the panel on complaints relating to Swedish antidumping duties.[20] The 1985 panel shared the view expressed by the 1955 panel that "it was clear from the wording of Article VI that no antidumping duties should be levied until certain facts had been established." The 1985 panel further pointed out, again quoting the 1955 panel: "As this represented an obligation on the part of the contracting party imposing such duties, it would be reasonable to expect that contracting party should establish the existence of these facts when its action is challenged."[21]

To examine another example, in a case against Korea's antidumping duties on polyacetal resins, the United States challenged the Korean Government's determination of injury. Korea argued that "it was not the task of the Panel to second guess the KTC [Korean government body] . . . the Panel's job was not to conduct a *de novo* investigation, not to attach its own weights to the different factors."[22] Nevertheless, relying on language in the relevant GATT antidumping agreement, the panel decided that the KTC's injury determination before the panel did not meet the requirements of that treaty language.[23] Other cases have raised similar issues and, indeed, the criticism of the panel's approach in some cases is clearly what engendered the US effort to obtain some limitations on the "standard of review" in the Uruguay Round negotiations.

Some later cases, however, seemed to take a more restrained view of a panel's authority. In the 1994 case of US restrictions on imports of tuna, for instance, the panel noted:

The reasonableness inherent in the interpretation of "necessary" was not a test of what was reasonable for a government to do, but of what a reasonable govern-

---

[18] GATT Dispute Settlement Panel, New Zealand – Imports of Electrical Transformers from Finland, GATT, *Basic Instruments and Selected Documents*, 32nd Supplement (1985), 55, 69, para. 4(7) (hereinafter New Zealand Transformers).

[19] *Ibid.*, 67, para. 4(4).

[20] GATT Dispute Settlement Panel, Swedish Anti-Dumping Duties, *Basic Instruments and Selected Documents*, 3rd Supplement (1955), 81.

[21] New Zealand Transformers, 68, para. 4(4) (quoting the Swedish Anti-Dumping Duties case, 85–86, para. 15).

[22] GATT Dispute Settlement Panel, Korea – Anti-Dumping Duties on Imports of Polyacetal Resins from the United States, GATT Doc. ADP/92 (1993), para. 57 (hereinafter Korea Resins).

[23] *Ibid.*, paras. 208–213.

ment would or could do. In this way, the panel did not substitute its judgment for that of the government. The test of reasonableness was very close to the good faith criterion in international law. Such a standard, in different forms, was also applied in the administrative law of many contracting parties, including the EEC and its member states, and the United States. It was a standard of review of government actions which did not lead to a wholesale second guessing of such actions.[24]

Similarly, in the prominent cases of twin complaints by Norway against the US antidumping and countervailing duties on imports of Atlantic salmon, the panel in both cases ruled mostly in favor of the United States, finding that the US action was not inconsistent with its GATT obligations, and seemed quite cautiously restrained in its approach (too restrained, some argue). The Government of Norway wrote a letter criticizing the panel's approach, to which the panel replied, saying, *inter alia*, that "the panel found it inappropriate to make its own judgment as to the relative weight to be accorded to the facts before the USITC."[25]

Thus it can be seen that the standard-of-review question is recurring and delicate, and one that to some extent goes to the core of an international procedure that (in a rule-based system) must assess a national government's actions against treaty or other international norms. Indeed, a more detailed review of these and other cases would show that quite a few concepts invoked by panels over the years relate to the broader question of the appropriate actions.[26] With such broader questions in mind, we turn to

[24] GATT Dispute Settlement Panel, United States – Restrictions on Imports of Tuna, GATT Doc. DS29/R (1994), para. 373 (hereinafter Tuna II).

[25] GATT Dispute Settlement Panel, United States – Imposition of Anti-Dumping Duties on Imports of Fresh and Chilled Atlantic Salmon from Norway, GATT Doc. ADP/8 (1992), 232; and GATT Dispute Settlement Panel, United States – Imposition of Countervailing Duties on Imports of Fresh and Chilled Atlantic Salmon from Norway, GATT Doc. SCM/153 (1992), paras. 209–212. Many GATT panel cases discuss this question of "deference." See, e.g., United States – Section 337 of the Tariff Act of 1930, *Basic Instruments and Selected Documents*, 36th Supplement (1990), 345; Korea Resins, paras. 208–213; United States – Taxes on Automobiles, GATT Doc. DS31/R (1994), paras. 5.11–5.15; and United States – Imposition of Countervailing Duties on Imports of Fresh and Chilled Atlantic Salmon from Norway, GATT Doc. ADP/8 (1992), paras. 43–67.

[26] Many concepts struggle with drawing the appropriate line between overreaching intrusion by international panels and tribunals into sovereign national affairs, on the one hand, and the inevitable necessity for an effective rule-based system to accord such panels and tribunals the power to evaluate national government actions, on the other. These concepts include the question of exhaustion of national remedies as a prerequisite to an international case; questions of the leeway given to national governments under exceptions to GATT Article XX that require "necessary" criteria; questions relating to how a national authority should weigh different factors that could lead to an injury test in antidumping or countervailing duty cases, such as in the US challenge to the latitude granted by the Korean Government to national regulations as measured against the nondiscriminatory obligations of Article III (national treatment); and various questions relating to the burden of proof in a contentious proceeding between nations. Some of these are expressed in cases cited in note 25 above.

the more particular question of the appropriate standard of review for GATT/WTO panels, focusing especially on antidumping.

III.   The law and negotiating context of the WTO

Relevant texts

The Uruguay Round texts contain several different explicit or implied references to the standard-of-review question. The most prominent of these is found in the Anti-Dumping Agreement in Article 17.6. This provision, which applies *only* to antidumping measures, reads as follows:

In examining the matter referred to in paragraph 5:
(i) in its assessment of the facts of the matter, the panel shall determine whether the authorities' establishment of the facts was proper and whether their evaluation of those facts was unbiased and objective, even though the panel might have reached a different conclusion, the evaluation shall not be overturned;
(ii) the panel shall interpret the relevant provisions of the Agreement in accordance with customary rules of interpretation of public international law. Where the panel finds that a relevant provision of the Agreement admits of more than one permissible interpretation, the panel shall find the authorities' measure to be in conformity with the Agreement if it rests upon one of those permissible interpretations.[27]

Article 17.6 is not the only provision bearing on the standard of review. Also relevant are two Ministerial Decisions taken at the final Ministerial Conference of the Uruguay Round at Marrakesh, Morocco, in April 1994, and made part of the text of the Uruguay Round Final Act. These state, respectively:

Decision on review of Article 17.6 of the Agreement on Implementation of Article VI of the General Agreement on Tariffs and Trade 1994

Ministers decide as follows: The standard of review in paragraph 6 of Article 17 of the Agreement on Implementation of Article VI of GATT 1994 shall be reviewed after a period of three years with a view to considering the question of whether it is capable of general application.

Declaration on Dispute Settlement Pursuant to the Agreement on Implementation of Article VI of the General Agreement on Tariffs and Trade 1994 or Part V of the Agreement on Subsidies and Countervailing Measures

Ministers recognize, with respect to dispute settlement pursuant to the Agreement on Implementation of Article VI of GATT 1994 or Part V of the Agreement on

---

[27] Anti-Dumping Agreement.

Subsidies and Countervailing Measures, the need for the consistent resolution of disputes arising from antidumping and countervailing duty measures.[28]

As both of these passages suggest, the antidumping provisions were not uncontroversial, for the Ministerial Decisions seem both to limit the application of those provisions, and to raise questions about how they fit into the overall jurisprudence of the WTO. To understand the source of that controversy, one must read these texts, Article 17.6 in particular, in the light of their negotiating context and history. That history, as we understand it, was briefly as follows.[29]

Negotiating context

Some government representatives thought it would be wise to have language constraining the standard of review by a GATT or WTO panel, and believed that US administrative law jurisprudence provided a useful model for this constraint. As explained in more detail below, the US jurisprudence seemed to suggest an approach whereby the courts (absent definitive statutory language to the contrary) would show deference to administrative actions by the executive branch of government, if those actions were based on a "reasonable interpretation" of the statute. Thus, negotiators suggested that the international rules of procedure should restrain WTO panels from ruling against a nation if its approach or interpretation was "reasonable."

This suggestion provoked opposition from at least two quarters. First, it drew opposition from many nations that felt such a rule would overly constrain panels while giving too much leeway to national governments to act in a manner inconsistent with the purposes of the WTO Agreements. In addition, many believed that a "reasonable" standard would allow different nations to develop different approaches to the international rules of the WTO Agreements, thus reducing consistency and reciprocity, and potentially allowing many different national administrative versions of the same treaty language.

Secondly, the "reasonable" standard worried certain other interests who wanted to ensure the effectiveness of many rules of the WTO, particularly those in the intellectual property area. These interests also believed that the

---

[28] Ministerial Decisions, in the Final Act.
[29] These observations are based partly on interviews by Professor Jackson of negotiators and business observers of the negotiations, and on articles during 1993 in *Inside US Trade*. The reader should note that in reviewing this negotiating history, or *travaux préparatoires*, we are not arguing that it should necessarily be used by a panel interpreting the WTO texts, since, as we note below, that is a matter of controversy. We present it here to assist us as observers in better identifying the issues embedded in various competing approaches to interpretation.

"reasonableness criteria" would constrain panels too much, and make it difficult to successfully challenge objectionable practices that were inconsistent with various WTO rules.

In the tense moments of the final days of the negotiations, several compromises were reached. First, the text of Article 17.6 was reworded to use the word "permissible" rather than "reasonable" as justification for a national approach, *but* (a very big "but") this provision was preceded by the language of the first sentence in Article 17.6(ii), which we discuss below. No less important, the negotiators compromised so that the limiting language on standard of review would apply only to the antidumping text (which attracted the proposals in the first place), and not necessarily to other dispute settlement cases before the WTO panels. The Ministerial Decisions quoted above reflect the divisions of opinion on these issues by calling for consideration in three years of whether Article 17.6 "is capable of general application," and "recognizing" the "need for consistent resolution of disputes" with regard to "antidumping and countervailing duty measures."[30] As to the general approach for panels (outside the antidumping area), while there are no provisions in the DSU explicitly concerning the "standard of review" as such, some language may be construed as relevant. The most interesting, perhaps, is found in DSU Article 3.2: "Recommendations and rulings of the DSB [Dispute Settlement Body] cannot add to or diminish the rights and obligations provided in the covered agreements."[31] This language could be interpreted as a constraint on the standard of review, but possibly not to the extent of Article 17.6 of the Anti-Dumping Agreement.

The fruits of compromise

Now to focus on the structure of Article 17.6 of the Anti-Dumping Agreement itself. The key language is in paragraph 6(ii), quoted above.[32] This was the compromise language of the Uruguay Round negotiators. What does it mean? A better understanding of its meaning must await future panel

---

[30] See the text at note 28 above.   [31] DSU, 33 ILM at 1227.

[32] See the text at note 27 above. We will largely ignore Article 17.6(i), which suggests that panels should not redo national government fact determinations. Of course, the troublesome question of what is "fact" and what is "law" is involved, and much national jurisprudence addresses that question (in a different context, to be sure). See, e.g., Bernard Schwartz, *Administrative Law* (3rd edn., 1991), §10.5 (explaining judicial treatment of the law–fact distinction). As a practical matter, at least for some time, the WTO panels will likely not have the capacity to do much in the way of fact-gathering procedures. Moreover, the private parties concerned are often the real participants in national-level administrative procedures, while at the WTO panel the government is the party and the government may not have had any realistic chance to present facts at the national level. But we put these issues aside for the future.

decisions. (Thus, early cases may be enormously important in this regard.) But, at least on the face of it, subsection (ii) seems to establish a two-step process for panel review of interpretive questions. First, the panel must consider whether the provision of the agreement in question admits of more than one interpretation. If not, the panel must vindicate the provision's only permissible interpretation. If, on the other hand, the panel determines that the provision indeed admits of more than one interpretation, the panel shall proceed to the second step of the analysis and consider whether the national interpretation is within the set of "permissible" interpretations. If so, the panel must defer to the interpretation given to the provision by the national government.

Note that, in the first step of the analysis, subsection (ii) instructs the reviewing panel to consider the interpretive question, mindful of "the customary rules of interpretation of public international law." According to negotiators, this admonition is a direct, albeit implicit, invocation of the Vienna Convention on the Law of Treaties.[33] Interestingly, however, it is not clear in light of that Convention whether or how a panel could ever reach the conclusion that provisions of an agreement admit of more than one interpretation. This is true because the Vienna Convention provides a set of rules for the interpretation of treaties – defined as any "international agreement[s] concluded between States in written form and governed by international law" and thus clearly including the GATT/WTO[34] – aimed at resolving ambiguities in the text. Articles 31 and 32 of the Vienna Convention are particularly relevant here. Article 31, "General rule of interpretation," sets forth a set of rules guiding the interpretation of the text of a treaty.[35] Article 32, "Supplementary means of interpretation," provides

---

[33] This statement is based on interviews with negotiators and observers.
[34] Vienna Convention on the Law of Treaties, opened for signature May 23, 1969, Article 2(1)(a), 1155 UNTS 331, 8 ILM 679 (1969) (hereinafter Vienna Convention). Of course, the Vienna Convention does not bind countries that have not accepted it (including, as of 1995, the United States), but it is widely accepted that almost all of the Vienna Convention codifies customary international law, or has become later customary international law. See, e.g., Louis Henkin, Richard Crawford Pugh, Oscar Schachter and Hans Smit, *International Law: Cases and Materials* (3rd edn., 1993), 418. The position of the US Executive generally recognizing the Vienna Convention as an authoritative guide to customary international law regarding treaties is explained at the beginning of Part III (before § 301) of *Restatement (Third) of the Foreign Relations Law of the United States* (1987), vol. I, 145 (hereinafter *Restatement*). In particular, Articles 31 and 32 of the Vienna Convention, which cover the interpretation of treaties, are often considered to codify, or currently to represent, customary international law.
[35] Specifically, Article 31 provides that a treaty shall be interpreted in accordance with the ordinary meaning to be given its terms in their context and in light of the treaty's purposes, where context includes any "agreement relating to the treaty" and any "instrument in connection with the conclusion of the treaty." Furthermore, "any subsequent agreement . . . regarding the interpretation of the treaty or the application of its provisions" shall be taken into account together with the treaty's context. Vienna Convention, Article 31(1)–(3).

additional guidelines for any case in which application of the rules in Article 31 still leaves the meaning of a provision "ambiguous or obscure," or when it renders a provision "manifestly absurd or unreasonable."[36] Article 32 suggests, in other words, that the application of Article 31 should in many cases resolve ambiguities, and that where the application of Article 31 does not do so, Article 32's own rule – "[r]ecourse . . . to supplementary means of interpretation, including the preparatory work of the treaty and the circumstances of its conclusion" – will resolve any lingering ambiguities.

Thus, it is not clear what sort of ambiguity in an agreement's provision is sufficient to lead a reviewing panel to the second step of the analysis contemplated in Article 17.6(ii). Once a panel has invoked Articles 31 and 32 of the Vienna Convention, it presumably will have already settled on a nonambiguous, nonabsurd interpretation. Article 17.6 thus raises several questions about the relationship between it and Articles 31 and 32: Is any ambiguity whatsoever sufficient to move a panel to consider the range of permissible interpretations? Or does a provision admit of more than one interpretation for the purposes of Article 17.6(ii) after application of Article 31, but before application of Article 32? Or does a provision admit of more than one interpretation for the purposes of Article 17.6(ii) only after application of both Articles 31 and 32? In short, just what sort of ambiguity is sufficient to trigger a panel's deference? Without answering these questions, Article 17.6(ii) does, at least on the surface, suppose that a panel could somehow reach the conclusion that a provision admits of more than one permissible interpretation, for the second sentence of paragraph 6(ii) would otherwise never come into play. Indeed, some of the negotiators seem to feel that this is precisely the case: there never can be resort to the second sentence. Others, however, mostly proponents of the original "reasonable" language who desire more constraint on panels, argue the contrary.[37]

---

[36] Article 32 of the Vienna Convention reads as follows: "Recourse may be had to supplementary means of interpretation, including the preparatory work of the treaty and the circumstances of its conclusion, in order to confirm the meaning resulting from the application of article 31, or to determine the meaning when the interpretation according to article 31: (a) leaves the meaning ambiguous or obscure; or (b) leads to a result which is manifestly absurd or unreasonable."

[37] One of the most significant, but almost hidden, issues surrounding Article 17.6 is the potential for use of negotiating history (*travaux préparatoires*). The habitual technique for lawyers from some jurisdictions, such as the United States, is to turn readily and immediately to such history (often called "legislative history"), although even in the United States some members of the Supreme Court in recent years have disparaged this approach. See, e.g., *Gustafson v. Alloyd Co.*, 115A S. Ct. 1061 at 1071 (1995) (Kennedy J.); *United States v. Thompson/Center Arms Co.*, 504 US 505 at 521 (1992) (Scalia J., concurring). Some lawyer-negotiators with these legal habits may have important knowledge of the Uruguay Round negotiations, some having even been present in the midnight discussions and

IV.   The US jurisprudence: a valid source of analogy?

As already suggested, an apparently similar standard-of-review issue, rais-ing analogous questions, figures prominently in US administrative law (the same is probably true for other countries as well). In US law, that issue concerns the level of deference that federal courts reviewing decisions made by federal administrative agencies will exercise towards those decisions. Until fairly recently, and broadly speaking, reviewing courts exercised considerable deference with respect to agencies' "factual" determinations, and accorded less deference to agencies' "legal" decisions.[38] This two-tiered approach reflected a familiar division of function between the separate branches of government, according to which agencies were to handle the more or less "technical" aspects of statutory implementation, while courts were to ensure that agencies exercised their authority within the bound-aries of the law. This bifurcated approach also followed the US Adminis-trative Procedure Act's direction for courts to "decide all relevant ques-tions of law,"[39] which itself reflected traditional understandings of the proper roles of courts and agencies. Traditionally, judicial deference to agencies' legal determinations required special justification, whereas defer-ence to factual determinations did not. That general rule was altered, however, in 1984, when the US Supreme Court handed down its decision in

compromises, and thus may be eager to argue one way or another that this history should determine the meaning of Article 17.6 (and other clauses of the Anti-Dumping Agreement). Such an interpretive approach raises several problems. First of all, the approach under the Vienna Convention, now understood to be applicable to the interpretive deliberations of WTO panels, is generally considered to relegate preparatory history (Article 32) to a subsidiary role in interpretation, to be used only when the means specified in Article 31 do not resolve an interpretive problem. See e.g., the Tuna II case; and Ian Brownlie, *Principles of Public International Law* (4th edn., 1990), 630. Application of this approach could mean that the first sentence of Article 17.6(ii), by implicit incorporation of Articles 31 and 32, always resolves the interpretive issue in question, with no option to turn to Article 17.6(ii)'s second sentence. Of course, those with the "legislative history habit" might argue that Article 17.6's own such history clearly demonstrates a different intent. They might further argue that the Vienna Convention's approach is not favored by the structure and language of Article 17.6 itself. Yet there are important reasons to apply the "supplementary" or subsidiary approach to preparatory work, some of which can be briefly mentioned. For one thing, not all national negotiators were present at some of the tiny meetings used to resolve differences in the late nights at the end of the negotiations. For another, nations that did not participate at all in the negotiations but joined the WTO later will understandably not want to be bound by an uncertain and often unobtainable negotiating history. Indeed, the lack of documentation on much of this history reinforces the danger of relying on it, which leads to a third reason recommending the Vienna Convention's approach to preparatory work. In the past, negotiators who have left government to join the private practice of law have written articles or testified in various government proceedings about their own negotiating experiences as evidence of the negotiating history. In some cases, these persons have received fees for such testimony from a party in interest. Such testimony cannot always be given full credibility.

[38]   See, e.g., *FTC* v. *Gratz*, 253 US 421 at 427 (1920).   [39]   5 USC § 706 (1988).

Chevron USA Inc. v. *Natural Resources Defense Council Inc.*,[40] in which the Court articulated a new standard of review for agencies' interpretations of law – the *Chevron* doctrine.[41]

The Chevron doctrine

Courts applying the *Chevron* doctrine face two sequential questions, often referred to as "step one" and "step two" of *Chevron*. First, has Congress "directly spoken to the precise question at issue,"[42] or is the statute interpreted by the agency "silent or ambiguous"?[43] To answer this question, the reviewing court applies the "traditional tools of statutory construction."[44] If, upon applying those traditional tools, the reviewing court concludes that Congress has indeed spoken to the precise issue in question, then "that is the end of the matter";[45] the court will hold the agency faithful to Congress's will, as unambiguously expressed in the statute.[46]

If the court concludes instead that the statute is "silent or ambiguous"

[40] 467 US 837 (1984).

[41] While *Chevron* is widely and rightly considered an important change in administrative law jurisprudence, the case is more evolution than revolution. Its tenor and logic are traceable at least to *Gray* v. *Powell*, 314 US 402 at 411 (1941) (directing the lower courts to respect reasonable agency decisions). See also *NLRB* v. *Hearst Publications Inc.*, 322 US 111 at 130–131 (1944) (suggesting that appellate court should have deferred to an agency's interpretation since that interpretation had "a reasonable basis in law"). In the decades between 1941 and 1984, the Supreme Court sent widely varying signals with respect to the extent of judicial deference agency interpretations of statutes should enjoy. See generally Kenneth Culp Davis and Richard J. Pierce Jr., *Administrative Law Treatise* (3rd edn., 1994), § 3.1. *Chevron* aimed at settling some of the confusion born of these mixed signals. For analysis and commentary on the doctrine and its application (still a matter of some debate), see, e.g., Stephen Breyer, "Judicial Review of Questions of Law and Policy" (1986) 38 *Administrative Law Review* 363 at 372–382; Thomas W. Merrill, "Judicial Deference to Executive Precedent" (1992) 101 *Yale Law Journal* 969; Abner J. Mikva, "How Should the Courts Treat Administrative Agencies?" (1986) 36 *American University Law Review* 1; Antonin Scalia, "Judicial Deference to Administrative Interpretations of Law" (1989) *Duke Law Journal* 511; Peter Schuck and E. Donald Elliott, "To the Chevron Station: An Empirical Study of Federal Administrative Law" (1990) *Duke Law Journal* 984; Kenneth W. Starr, "Judicial Review in the Post-Chevron Era" (1986) 3 *Yale Journal on Regulation* 283; Cass Sunstein, "Law and Administration After Chevron" (1990) 90 *Columbia Law Review* 2071; and Russell L. Weaver, "Some Realism About Chevron" (1993) 58 *Minnesota Law Review* 129.

[42] *Chevron*, 467 US 837 at 842.   [43] *Ibid.*, 843.

[44] *Ibid.*, note 9. See also *Kmart Corp.* v. *Cartier Inc.*, 486 US 281 at 300 (1988) (Brennan J., concurring); *NLRB* v. *United Food and Commercial Workers Union, Local* 23, 484 US 112 at 123 (1987); and *INS* v. *Cardoza-Fonseca*, 480 US 421 at 446 (1987).

[45] *Chevron*, 467 US 837 at 842.

[46] For examples of lower courts' invocation of step one of the *Chevron* doctrine, see, e.g., *Skandalis* v. *Rowe*, 14 F. 3d 173 at 178–179 (2nd Cir. 1994); *Sweet Home Chapter of Communities for a Great Oregon* v. *Babbitt*, 17 F. 3d 1463 at 1464 (DC Cir. 1994), reversed on other grounds 115 S. Ct. 2407 (1995); *Satellite Broadcasting and Communications Association of American* v. *Oman*, 17 F. 3d 344 at 348 (11th Cir.), cert. denied 115 S. Ct. 88 (1994).

with respect to the interpretive question at issue, then the reviewing court proceeds to a second question. Step two asks: is the agency's interpretation of the statute a "reasonable" or "permissible" one?[47] If the court determines that the agency's interpretation is not reasonable, then the court will supply one. If, however, the court determines that the agency's interpretation is reasonable, the court will defer to the agency's interpretation, even if – and this is the bite of the *Chevron* doctrine – the agency's interpretation is not one the court itself would have adopted had it considered the question on its own.[48]

At least at first glance, then, the *Chevron* doctrine is straightforward: It instructs courts to defer to agencies' interpretations of law if and only if the statute in question is ambiguous and the agency's interpretation is reasonable. A close reading of *Chevron*, however, reveals that the doctrine itself is ambiguous, not least of all with respect to exactly how much interpretive ambiguity is necessary to proceed to step two.[49] Will any statutory ambiguity suffice, or must the provision in question be utterly ambiguous, after the reviewing court's application of the traditional tools of statutory construction, before the court will move on to address the reasonableness question? The best answer may be somewhere in between. What *is* clear is that *Chevron* provides sufficient leeway for courts to find ambiguities, or not, as they will.[50] Accordingly, while lower courts cite and apply *Chevron* and its progeny routinely, their decisions vary

[47] *Chevron*, 467 US 837 at 842–844.
[48] *Ibid.*, 843 note 11 ("The court need not conclude that the agency construction was the only one it permissibly could have adopted to uphold the construction, or even the reading the court would have reached if the question initially had arisen in a judicial proceeding") (citations omitted).
[49] *Chevron* also left open the question whether the deferential standard articulated in the case would apply only to agency rule-making, as in *Chevron* itself, or also to agency adjudication, the other main mode of agency decision-making. Some lower courts interpreted *Chevron* to apply to adjudicatory decisions, too. See, e.g., *National Fuel Gas Supply Corp. v. FERC*, 811 F. 2d 1563 at 1569–1571 (DC Cir. 1987). Eventually, the Supreme Court resolved this question. See *DeBartolo Corp. v. Florida Gulf Coast Building and Construction Trades Council*, 485 US 568 at 574 (1988) (applying *Chevron* to agency adjudication). Finally, *Chevron* was not crystal-clear about whether the standard of review articulated in that case applied to "pure" questions of statutory interpretation or, rather, only to agencies' application of law to particular facts. Supreme Court jurisprudence since the *Chevron* case has clarified that question somewhat. In *NLRB v. United Food and Commercial Workers Union, Local 23*, 484 US 112 at 123 (1987), the Supreme Court made clear that *Chevron* deference does indeed apply to "pure" questions of statutory construction, as well as to applications of legal standards to facts – notwithstanding suggestions to the contrary in earlier post-*Chevron* cases. See *INS v. Cardoza-Fonseca*, 480 US 421 at 446–448 (1987).
[50] Part of this confusion results from the open-endedness of the *Chevron* doctrine's essential concepts – "ambiguous," "precise," "reasonable." Part results from the fact that the traditional rules of statutory construction are themselves contradictory and thus easily subject to manipulation. And post-*Chevron* Supreme Court jurisprudence has shed little light on the matters. For a most helpful overview, see Thomas W. Merrill, "Textualism and the Future of the Chevron Doctrine" (1994) 72 *Washington University Law Quarterly* 351.

widely with respect to what constitutes sufficient ambiguity to trigger step two of the doctrine.

According to many US administrative law scholars, the *Chevron* doctrine constituted a significant shift of power from courts to agencies.[51] As explained shortly below, the shift is commonly justified by reference to some of the most important principles underlying US administrative government – expertise, accountability, and administrative efficiency. But, first, the important surface similarities between the *Chevron* doctrine in US administrative law, on the one hand, and the standard of review set forth in Article 17.6 of the Anti-Dumping Agreement, on the other, deserve careful attention.

Chevron and Article 17.6(ii)

For one thing, *Chevron* requires a federal court to defer to an agency's interpretation of an ambiguous statutory provision so long as that interpretation is "reasonable" or "permissible,"[52] even if the reviewing court would have interpreted the statute differently had it considered the question in the first instance. Similarly, Article 17.6 requires a GATT/WTO panel to defer to a party's interpretation of an ambiguous Agreement provision so long as that interpretation is "permissible,"[53] even if (by direct implication) the reviewing panel would have adopted an alternative interpretation had it considered the question originally. Secondly, the *Chevron* doctrine instructs courts to employ the "traditional tools of statutory construction" when determining whether the statutory provision in question is "ambiguous" in the first place.[54] Article 17.6, for its part, instructs panels to apply the "customary rules of interpretation of public international law" when determining whether the Agreement provision in question "admits of more than one permissible interpretation." Thirdly, as noted, the *Chevron* doctrine is somewhat unclear about the level of ambiguity that is required to trigger step two of the *Chevron* analysis and, accordingly, lower courts vary widely on their approach to this issue. Article 17.6, similarly, is unclear about how panels will ever get to "step two" of the Article 17.6 standard, given the section's implicit invocation of the interpretive rules set forth in the Vienna Convention on the Law of Treaties.

---

[51] See, e.g., Davis and Pierce, *Administrative Law Treatise*, § 3.3.

[52] See 467 US 837 at 843–844; see also *INS* v. *Cardoza-Fonseca*, 480 US at 454 (Scalia J., concurring); *Babbitt* v. *Sweet Home Chapter of Communities for a Great Oregon*, 115 S. Ct. 2407 at 2414–2416 (1995); *Reno* v. *Koray*, 115 S. Ct. 2021 at 2027 (1995); and *NationsBank* v. *Variable Annuity Life Insurance Co.*, 115 S. Ct. 810 at 813 (1995).

[53] Interestingly, as noted above, early drafts of Article 17.6 used the word "reasonable" instead of "permissible," but that formulation was ultimately rejected by negotiators.

[54] See, e.g., *Chevron*, 467 US 837 at 843 note 9.

Finally, and most fundamentally, both *Chevron* and the standard-of-review issue in Article 17.6 bear important implications about the distribution of legal and political authority. In the US administrative regime, *Chevron* spelled an important shift of interpretive power from federal courts to agencies (and, thus, to the President). According to the conventional wisdom, whereas courts previously had most of the authority to resolve ambiguities in legislation, now agencies have significant authority to determine what Congress meant. Unless agencies exercise that authority unreasonably, courts must go along.

While this wisdom is sound so far as it goes, *Chevron*'s allocation of power is probably more complicated and more subtle than the conventional view suggests. Because reviewing courts have significant leeway to find, or not to find, a step-one ambiguity, courts retain significant power to vindicate or invalidate agencies' interpretive decisions. This is true because where courts' *Chevron* analyses end at step one, agencies often lose, and where the analyses proceed to step two, agencies usually win.[55] Thus, courts retain an important check on agency authority, even though as a formal matter agencies and not courts have the authority to pass on the interpretive question initially. *Chevron* ties courts' hands only insofar as step one requires a court to defer to an interpretation it would have invalidated otherwise. *Chevron* shifts power *to* courts, however, insofar as step one allows a court to defer to what it considers a preferred interpretation of a statute that, under the pre-*Chevron* regime, the court would not have been able to support. In sum, *Chevron* comes with offsetting effects on judicial power: Reviewing federal courts "lose" in the sense that they must defer to unwelcome agency interpretations that, before *Chevron*, they could have invalidated; but they "gain" in the sense that they are permitted to vindicate welcome interpretations that, before *Chevron*, they would have been required to invalidate. What is more, courts hold the key to *Chevron*'s step two – given that the reviewing court itself decides at step one whether there is an ambiguity of sufficient proportions to proceed to step two.[56]

While *Chevron*'s (re)allocation of interpretive authority between agencies and courts is complex, Congress's power almost certainly was curtailed as a result. This is so because, after *Chevron*, there are more interpretations of statutory provisions that courts can potentially uphold; again, some interpretations that courts would have been required to invalidate before *Chevron* will now be upheld. As a result, Congress must now speak with

---

[55] See, e.g., Davis and Pierce, *Administrative Law Treatise*, § 3.6 at 129–130; Starr, "Judicial Review in the Post-Chevron Era," 298–299; and Sunstein, "Law and Administration After Chevron," 2104–2105.

[56] Indeed, as one author indicates, arguably the Supreme Court has not even followed the *Chevron* case in a number of its later decisions. See Merrill, "Judicial Deference to Executive Precedent," 980–990.

greater specificity, or run the risk that an agency will interpret a statute, with judicial blessing, in a manner that pre-*Chevron* courts would have said Congress did not intend.

Chevron-type deference and interpretive authority in the GATT/WTO context

In the GATT/WTO context, the standard-of-review question implicated a similar allocation of interpretive power – among countries that first interpret a disputed provision of the Anti-Dumping Agreement, GATT/WTO panels hearing disputes, and members party to the Anti-Dumping Agreement. Here, too, the issue is complex and subtle. On the one hand, if panels were to interpret Article 17.6 as requiring considerable deference to a member's interpretation of a provision, disputing members would enjoy greater authority *vis-à-vis* GATT/WTO panels. On the other hand, if panels were to interpret Article 17.6 as requiring considerable deference where a provision admits of more than one interpretation, *and* as providing them with considerable leeway to determine whether a provision does admit of more than one interpretation, then panels themselves would enjoy significant power both to invalidate interpretations (under step one of Article 17.6) they deemed undesirable and to vindicate interpretations (under step two of Article 17.6) they deemed desirable. What is more, the power of WTO members, analogously to the power of Congress, would be compromised under a *Chevron*-like application of Article 17.6. Some of the members' intentions – specifically, those that were ambiguously, but nevertheless ascertainably, expressed in the Agreement – would not necessarily be vindicated under a *Chevron*-like interpretive framework. Indeed, beneficiaries of antidumping duty orders probably sought a *Chevron*-like standard of review for precisely this reason – so that panels would be less powerful. As suggested above, such interests no doubt thought that a *Chevron*-type standard, by making it more difficult for panels to invalidate a party's interpretation as contrary to the intent of the GATT/WTO membership, would effectively allocate power to GATT/WTO disputants and away from the members collectively. But, to reiterate, since panels will decide what is ambiguous, the result of the standard could conversely shift more power *to panels*.

None of this is to suggest, however, that Article 17.6(ii) should be interpreted like the *Chevron* doctrine, whatever hopes may or may not have motivated certain negotiators. At least two important differences distinguish the standard of review embodied in Article 17.6 from *Chevron* deference. First, Article 17.6(ii) uses the word "permissible," which may not be identical in meaning to "reasonable" or "permissible" as construed in

US law.[57] In US law, the essential test for step two of the *Chevron* analysis is whether the agency's interpretation is "rational and consistent with the statute,"[58] a test that agencies can quite easily pass. Secondly, the "customary rules of interpretation of public international law" referred to in Article 17.6 certainly are by no means identical to the "traditional tools of statutory construction" in US domestic law, the latter being more quickly consulted and more open-ended than the former (especially, as indicated above, with regard to legislative history). As already explained, Articles 31 and 32 of the Vienna Convention aim at resolving any facial ambiguities in treaty text. In US law, in contrast, it is well understood that application of the traditional tools of statutory construction can exacerbate as much as eliminate statutory ambiguities.[59]

These important differences notwithstanding, at least some GATT/WTO disputants and negotiators[60] have recognized both the analogy between *Chevron* and the standard of review for international panels, and the specific doctrinal and theoretical similarities between *Chevron's* and Article 17.6's approaches to those analogous issues. In fact, the *Chevron* doctrine seems likely to shape the perspective of US disputants in particular, for whom it is such a familiar and influential doctrine in their home regime. Thus the question arises, and will arise in future panel cases, about how far the *Chevron* analogy can be sustained in the context of GATT/WTO panel review. Should future GATT/WTO panels exercise

[57] Indeed, it is at least possible that "reasonable" and "permissible" are not perfectly synonymous within *Chevron* jurisprudence, notwithstanding that in *Chevron* itself the Supreme Court repeatedly used both the word "reasonable" (see *Chevron*, 467 US 837 at 844, 845, and 865) and the word "permissible" (see *Chevron*, 467 US 837 at 843 note 11, and 866).

[58] *NLRB* v. *United Food and Commercial Workers Union, Local* 23, 484 US 112 at 123 (1987); accord *Sullivan* v. *Everhart*, 494 US 83 at 89 (1990); see also *Fall River Dyeing and Finishing Corp.* v. *NLRB*, 482 US 27 at 42 (1987).

[59] For a classic treatment of the point, see Karl N. Llewellyn, "Remarks on the Theory of Appellate Decision and the Rules or Canons About How Statutes Are To Be Construed" (1950) 3 *Vanderbilt Law Review* 395.

[60] See Part III above. Often GATT/WTO panels, just like US federal courts, consider interpretations supplied in the first instance by US administrative agencies, since under US domestic law the Commerce Department and the International Trade Commission carry out the administration of GATT implementing legislation. In an antidumping procedure under US antidumping legislation, a petitioner brings a case before the Commerce Department, which determines whether there was dumping – the "margin of dumping" question. If the Commerce Department concludes there was dumping, the case moves to the International Trade Commission, which determines the extent of the injury – the "material injury" question. (A closely analogous procedure, which assigns similar roles to the Commerce Department and the International Trade Commission, governs countervailing duties cases as well.) Both Commerce Department and International Trade Commission final decisions can be appealed to the US Court of International Trade. In any event, when the Commerce Department makes a ruling in an antidumping case, it does so by implicitly or explicitly interpreting the US statute in light of the US Uruguay Round implementing legislation and, thus, in light of the GATT/WTO Agreement itself. See note 67 below.

Chevron-like deference? Or should they instead interpret the word "permissible" rather narrowly and/or apply the Vienna Convention's rules governing treaty interpretation in such a manner as to be very reluctant ever to conclude that an agreement provision "admits of more than one interpretation"? Part V is a first attempt to consider this crucial question.

V.   Policy considerations: the limits of the Chevron analogy

Some common justifications for Chevron deference

One traditional justification for greater judicial deference to agencies on legal questions in the US administrative regime is that of agency expertise – the "expertise argument." This justification comports with traditional understandings about the respective roles of the different branches of government and agencies' place in modern government. Agencies, on this view, are the technical experts that put into operation the policy judgments made by legislators. Indeed, technical expertise is the *raison d'être* of agencies; by focusing on a particular regulatory field, or sector of the economy, agencies can do what Congress lacks the time and other institutional resources to do. *Chevron* itself, which presented the question whether the statutory term "stationary source" referred to an entire pollution-emitting plant or, rather, to every single smokestack within such a plant, supplies an apt example of when an agency's special technical expertise can aid statutory interpretation.[61] According to the expertise argument, agencies are deemed to understand even the legal ramifications of the problems agencies are created to work on. Admittedly, the dichotomy between legal and factual questions may at times be difficult to maintain, but that observation argues as much in favor of as it does against *Chevron* deference.

Agency expertise, however, is not the only common justification for *Chevron*-type deference. Sometimes the doctrine is justified also on demo-

---

[61] At issue in the case was the meaning of the term "stationary source" in the Clean Air Act Amendments of 1977. The amendments required states to develop permit systems to govern the construction and operation of new or modified major stationary sources of air pollution in regions of the nation that had not yet achieved national air quality standards. The permit systems were to impose stringent emissions requirements on such sources. The agency, the Environmental Protection Agency (EPA), sought to allow states to adopt a plant-wide definition of "stationary source" for the purposes of the permit programs. That way, a state could issue a permit allowing a plant to construct or modify one smokestack that did not meet the strict emission requirements, so long as the emissions of that entire plant (taking all of its smokestacks together) did not increase. According to *Chevron*, such a decision, involving complicated and technical trade-offs, is best left to the agency specifically delegated the responsibility of regulating air quality and administering the Clean Air Act and its amendments, rather than to judges, who "are not experts in the field." *Chevron*, 467 US 837 at 865.

cratic grounds. According to the argument from democracy, it is agencies, not courts, that are answerable to both the executive and legislative representatives of the citizenry. Because judges are not elected, while presidents and legislators are, and because agencies but not judges are accountable to the President and to Congress, judicial deference to agency decisions enhances the political legitimacy of the administrative regime.[62]

Finally, *Chevron* may be justified also in the name of administrative efficiency or coordination. Before *Chevron*, different federal courts in different jurisdictions could interpret the same statutory provision differently. Multiple interpretations by different federal courts would mean that the statute "said" different things in those different jurisdictions. Such confusion could be eliminated by appellate review, but agencies faced uncertainty pending review, and the possibility of different interpretations across different appellate circuits remained. Because multiple agencies do not typically interpret the same statutory language,[63] however, *Chevron* deference allows the agency charged with administering a statute to interpret that statute. One agency, rather than many federal courts, now resolves ambiguities in the statute that the agency in question is charged to administer. Such interpretive streamlining not only reduces uncertainty but also promotes regulatory coordination. Once an agency has settled on a reasonable interpretation, it can act on the basis of that interpretation nationally.

These three arguments are not offered here to supply an unassailable normative defense of the *Chevron* doctrine; whether *Chevron* was a welcome development in US administrative law is a debatable question beyond the scope of the present analysis. While these common justifications resonate with some of the most fundamental principles underlying administrative government, they do not necessarily exhaust the arguments that might be offered on behalf of *Chevron*. Each of the above justifications is subject to serious objection when applied to international review, however.

---

[62] This argument, too, finds expression in *Chevron* itself: "Judges . . . are not part of either political branch of Government. Courts must, in some cases, reconcile competing political interests, but not on the basis of the judges' personal policy preferences. In contrast, an agency to which Congress has delegated policymaking responsibilities may, within the limits of that delegation, properly rely upon the incumbent administration's views of wise policy to inform its judgments. While agencies are not directly accountable to the people, the Chief Executive is." *Ibid.*

[63] Rather, agencies enjoy *Chevron* deference with respect to their own statutes – their organic statutes and any other statutes that an agency is specifically charged with administering. See Peter L. Strauss, "One Hundred Fifty Cases Per Year: Some Implications of the Supreme Court's Limited Resources for Judicial Review of Agency Action" (1987) 87 *Columbia Law Review* 1093.

Chevron-type deference and GATT/WTO panels

Whatever the doctrine's ultimate merits or demerits, *Chevron*'s central concept of "reasonableness" has at the very least a surface appeal. In fact, across many substantive areas of US law, legal rules impose in one form or another requirements that are satisfied by reasonableness; where parties have acted in a reasonable way or have adopted reasonable positions, legal institutions and legal rules do not interfere. In the GATT/WTO context, the permissibility standard of Article 17.6 has a similar commonsense ring. The WTO Anti-Dumping Agreement will invariably raise many complicated interpretive questions involving a variety of underlying factual and legal issues. So long as a member's interpretation of the Agreement is permissible – within the realm of the plausible, in some general sense – deference on the part of reviewing panels may be sensible. After all members may reasonably disagree about the meaning of the Agreement's provisions, and, unless GATT/WTO panels have some privileged access to the meaning of the Agreement, there may be no reason to substitute a panel's interpretation for that of one authority. In addition, a deferential posture on the part of antidumping panels may help guard against panel activism more generally. Whatever the merits of *Chevron* in US administrative law, then, do not the doctrine's general justifications also argue for a *Chevron*-like standard of review in the context of the Anti-Dumping Agreement?

Return first to the expertise argument, which justifies a deferential standard of review on the grounds that agencies are experts within their respective statutory domains. In the GATT/WTO context, there is probably no analogous rationale, certainly not one as strong. That GATT/WTO members have superior information to GATT/WTO panels about the meaning or ultimate aim of the Agreement's provisions seems implausible. Nor is any particular GATT/WTO member an "expert" relative to any other. GATT/WTO members undoubtedly have their own incentives to become experts about the meaning of the Agreement, but none can plausibly claim expertise over any other.

Granted, disputing parties who have made decisions facing a GATT/WTO panel challenge almost surely have vastly more *factual* information than reviewing panels do. Because panels themselves lack many fact-gathering resources, they are ill-positioned to second-guess a party's factual determinations. Article 17.6(i), appropriately, reflects this reality by establishing a rather deferential standard of review of factual conclusions. That standard provides that panels shall ask only whether an authority's factual determinations were "proper" and whether an authority's evaluation of those facts was "unbiased and objective."[64] If these conditions hold,

---

[64] See Anti-Dumping Agreement, Article 17.6(i), quoted in the text at note 27 above.

a panel is to defer to the authority's view of the facts, "even though the panel might have reached a different conclusion."[65] But parties' technical superiority over factual matters does not justify a deferential standard of review for authorities' interpretation of the Agreement's provisions. National authorities probably do not bring to a dispute any specialized understanding that renders them specially qualified to ascertain the legal meaning of *international agreements*, in the same way that the EPA's specialized understanding of environmental regulatory issues arguably renders that agency specially qualified to ascertain the meaning of "stationary source."

This leads to a second and related distinction between the posture of agencies and GATT/WTO members. In stark contrast to administrative agencies, GATT/WTO members are not specifically charged with carrying out the GATT/WTO. To be sure, members are obligated to fulfill their responsibilities under the WTO Agreement. In that limited sense, GATT/WTO members are charged with administering the GATT/WTO. But no country or combination of countries was ever delegated the responsibility of implementing the WTO Agreement in the way that administrative agencies are charged with implementing their statutes. Countries party to an antidumping dispute are not delegates whose technical expertise specially qualifies them to make authoritative interpretive decisions. They are, rather, interested parties whose own (national) interests may not always sustain a necessary fidelity to the terms of international agreements. Thus, while there may well be reasons for panels to defer to an authority's permissible interpretation of the WTO Agreement, the expertise of parties to a panel dispute is probably not among them.

The same is true for the argument from democracy. Indeed, this argument cuts in the opposite direction from *Chevron*, once transplanted to the GATT/WTO context. Unlike agencies, national authorities that are parties to an antidumping dispute are not accountable to the GATT/WTO membership at large. GATT/WTO panels, not disputing parties, are the membership's delegates. Panels are delegated the authority to try to vindicate the political decisions – the compromises, the trade-offs – made by members as a whole. Therefore, while GATT/WTO panels resemble courts, and while they are asked to adjudicate claims between competing national parties, their interpretation of any WTO Agreement will *not* displace the interpretations of any body that is accountable to the membership – will not, in other words, displace interpretations by others who can

---

[65] *Ibid.* This standard of review of facts may appear similar to a long-standing "arbitrary and capricious" standard in US administrative law, but arguably the language of Article 17.6(i) gives an even greater obligation to the panels to evaluate the process of fact-finding. In addition, since antidumping cases are often very fact specific, requiring a series of decisions determining whether facts are "sufficient" for findings (*inter alia*) of dumping, causation, material injury, or retroactivity, the line between "fact" and "law" may be particularly fuzzy.

plausibly be said to be representatives of the GATT/WTO membership. The argument in *Chevron* that judges should defer to the interpretive decisions made by those accountable to the citizenry's representatives simply has no analogue in the GATT/WTO antidumping context.

The observation that national authorities, unlike agencies, are not accountable to the membership at large speaks to the very purpose of the dispute settlement process, indeed the GATT/WTO Agreement itself – an agreement that, at bottom, seeks to overcome the significant coordination or collective-action problems that its membership otherwise faces. Absent the Agreement (or one like it), individual members have an incentive to erect trade barriers that may "benefit" them individually, to the greater detriment of other members. Furthermore, absent some dispute settlement process for keeping members faithful to the Agreement, members have similar incentives to apply the Agreement in ways "advantageous" to them. Further still, absent a standard of review for legal questions that prohibits self-serving interpretations of the Agreement that are *arguably* but not *persuasively* faithful to the text, members have an incentive to erode the Agreement through interpretation. In this light, respecting the policy preferences and judgments of the GATT/WTO constituency argues against, not in favor of, a *Chevron*-like standard of review.

Indeed, the fundamental problem with attempting to transplant a *Chevron*-like national standard of review to the GATT/WTO context is that such an approach overlooks the basic fact that in an international proceeding the underlying legal problem is rather different: Whereas in a national procedure the court is reviewing a national administrative action or determination under the national law, such as a statute, the international body has the task of ascertaining the meaning and application of an international norm. The question before the international body generally is whether the interpretation of an agreement underlying a national government's action is actually consistent or inconsistent with that agreement. This is not necessarily the same question as that faced by the national courts, at least in some legal systems. Of course, the international rule may be the applicable national rule if the treaty has direct "statute like" application[66] (if, for example, the treaty is self-executing), and the international rule may also have a role in influencing national interpretations of national law.[67] But in many cases, at least in the United States, the courts are

---

[66] "Status of International Law and Agreements in United States Law" in *Restatement*, chapter 2; see also John H. Jackson, "Status of Treaties in Domestic Legal Systems: A Policy Analysis" (1992) 86 *American Journal of International Law* 310.

[67] *Restatement*, § 114, which reads "Where fairly possible, a United States statute is to be construed so as not to conflict with international law or with an international agreement of the United States" (citing, *inter alia*, *Murray* v. *The Schooner Charming Betsy*, 6 US (2 Cranch) 64 (1804)).

reviewing *national* law,[68] which is determinative of the outcome of the national case, even if that determination proves to be inconsistent with *international* obligations. The international body, on the other hand, is charged with interpreting and applying the international norms engaged by the case.[69] Accordingly, in almost all cases the parties to the dispute at the international process (nation-state governments) are different from the parties in the national case, which may be private firms, or subordinate parts of the government.

The efficiency argument fares no better in justifying a deferential standard of review. Whereas in the US administrative law setting there is typically little danger of multiple interpretations of the statutory language by several different agencies, in the GATT/WTO setting multiple interpretations of agreement provisions is precisely one of the problems that panel review is designed to ameliorate. For in the GATT/WTO context it is highly likely that multiple countries will confront interpretive questions about one and the same GATT/WTO provision. The danger of multiple interpretations of the same provision as a threat to reciprocity thus seems considerable; as already observed, the Agreement itself is a response to a serious international coordination problem. At the same time, there seems to be little threat that the new GATT/WTO panels will render multiple and incompatible interpretations of the same agreement provision. Even though GATT/WTO panels are composed (at least at the initial stage) on an *ad hoc* basis, and even though, strictly speaking, GATT/WTO cases do not constitute binding precedent on subsequent GATT/WTO panels, the jurisdiction of these panels (in contrast to that of US federal courts) is not confined to specific geographical regions. Moreover, while the principle of *stare decisis* does not govern GATT/WTO dispute settlement, panels very often make authoritative references to previous panels' consistent treatment of a given issue that over time can assume the force of a "practice" that guides panel interpretation of the Agreement. Here again, then, the GATT/WTO context presents an inverse situation as compared to US administrative law: Whereas in the US domestic context *Chevron* deference shifts interpretive power away from multiple courts and to one agency, similar deference in the antidumping context would shift interpretive

---

[68] On US law, see, e.g., *Restatement*, § 11 (non-self-executing treaties) and § 115 (later-in-time statute supersedes a self-executing treaty). See, e.g., *Suramerica de Aleaciones Laminadas CA* v. *United States*, 966 F. 2d 660 at 667–668 (Federal Cir. 1992). See also John H. Jackson, William Davey, and Alan O. Sykes, *International Economic Relations: Cases, Materials and Texts* (3rd edn., 1995), 321. The law in the European Union is not completely clear on this subject. The preamble to the document recommending approval of the Uruguay Round suggests that the Uruguay Round treaties will not be "directly applicable" in Europe. Commission of the European Communities, COM (94) 143 final.

[69] This point has also been made by David Palmeter, "United States Implementation of the Uruguay Round Anti-Dumping Code" (1995) *Journal of World Trade*, June, 39 and 76.

power away from one institution and to multiple and varied parties to the GATT/WTO, each with a different culture and legal institution. Of course, to argue that expertise, accountability and efficiency do not counsel in favor of a *Chevron*-like application of Article 17.6(ii) is not to argue that a *Chevron*-like approach is ultimately unjustifiable. Rather, the argument here is that some of the most common and most powerful justifications of the *Chevron* doctrine carry very little weight once transplanted to the context of GATT/WTO dispute settlement. To the extent that the *Chevron* doctrine influenced the drafting of Article 17.6, consideration of the appropriateness of that approach is in order. If Article 17.6 is to be applied in a *Chevron*-like way, its justification must come from outside the *Chevron* paradigm. We conclude with one possible justification.

VI.   Conclusion: sovereignty and standard of review in international law

While the analysis here has focused on the scope of review in the GATT/WTO antidumping context specifically, the basic question considered reaches beyond the process of GATT/WTO dispute resolution itself. The standard-of-review question is faced at least implicitly whenever sovereign members of a treaty yield interpretive and dispute settlement powers to international panels and tribunals. Moreover, as national economies become increasingly interdependent, and as the need for international cooperation and coordination accordingly becomes greater, the standard-of-review question will become more and more important. The difficulty is clear: On the one hand, effective international cooperation depends in part upon the willingness of sovereign states to constrain themselves by relinquishing to international tribunals at least minimum power to interpret treaties and articulate international obligations. Recognizing the necessity of such power does not lessen the importance at the national level of decision-making expertise, democratic accountability, or institutional efficiency. On the other hand, nations and their citizens – and particularly those particular interests within nation-states that are reasonably successful at influencing their national political actors – will want to maintain control of the government decisions.

Such parties may at times invoke the principle of national "sovereignty" to justify a deferential standard of review in the international context. At the same time, national authorities may also resist relinquishing interpretive power to GATT/WTO panels on the grounds that doing so compromises their sovereignty. Admittedly, the word "sovereignty" has been much abused and misused; nevertheless, if the term refers to policies and concepts that focus on an appropriate allocation of power between international and national governments, and if one is willing to recognize that nation-states *ought* still to retain powers for effective governing of national (or local) democratic constituencies in a variety of contexts and cultures – perhaps using theories of "subsidiarity" – then a case can be made for at least *some* international deference to national decisions, even decisions regarding interpretations of international agreements. After all, if the decisions and policy choices of national political and administrative bodies (such as the Commerce Department and the ITC in the United States)[70] are too severely constrained by panel interpretation of the Agreement, those bodies and their constituencies will understandably resist. Important sovereignty values, in short, will inevitably come into the conflict settlement process. And there is no *a priori* reason why coordination values must, in every case across *every* context, trump sovereignty values. Some trade-off is necessary.[71]

Yet merely identifying important sovereignty values does not by itself provide a persuasive argument justifying deferential panel review. Standing alone, the argument that deferential review is necessary to protect authorities' national sovereignty fails to acknowledge that some balance between authorities' interest in protecting their sovereignty, on the one side, and the broader interest in realizing the gains of international coordination, on the other, must be struck. The argument proves too much, in other words, as it unwittingly challenges the very rationale of the GATT/WTO itself.

We thus approach the end of our analysis by identifying a major problem without recommending any easy solution. The problem is how to formulate and articulate the necessary mediating principle or principles between the international policy values for which a dispute settlement is desired, on the one hand, and the remaining important policy values of preserving national "sovereign" authority both as a check and balance against centralized power, and as a means to facilitate good government decisions close to the constituencies affected, on the other hand. Our appeal is to the dual propositions that the national-level approach to the standard-of-review issue, specifically a *Chevron*-like approach, does not

---

[70] See note 60 above, explaining the roles of the ITC and the Commerce Department.

[71] Alan Sykes, "The (Limited) Role of Regulatory Harmonization in the International System," paper for the Conference on the Multilateral Trade Regime in the 21st Century: Structural Issues, Columbia Law School, November 3–4, 1995. See also Alan O. Sykes, *Product Standards for Internationally Integrated Goods Markets* (Brookings Institution, 1995). For one example, the treaty word "necessary" in text like that of GATT Article XX (which provides, *inter alia*, an exception from other GATT obligations for measures "necessary to protect human, animal or plant life or health") may need to be interpreted to recognize that governments should be authorized to have some choice among several government measures (not mandated to choose, e.g., the "least restrictive" measure), as long as the choice does not unduly detract from the basic broader policy goals of the treaty.

provide appropriate analogies for the international approach, but that there is nevertheless an important policy value in recognizing the need for some deference to national government decisions. A reasonable, nuanced approach by the WTO panels is important for the credibility of the WTO dispute settlement system, and such an approach will lessen the dangers of inappropriate unilateral reactions by governments and citizen constituencies of nation-state members of the WTO. It should be obvious that this approach is needed for virtually all types of cases and not just those in antidumping or other specified categories.

Of course, we do not here prescribe any particular standard of review for panels considering national governments' interpretations of treaty obligations. Time and experience with particular cases will likely clarify the appropriate standard, or standards (since these may vary with different subject matters). Indeed, perhaps all that is required is that panels (including appellate panels) perceive and show sensitivity towards the issues involved when an international body reviews the legal appropriateness of national government authorities' actions. In this connection, panels should keep the relevant purposes, strengths, and limitations of their institution in mind.

For example, panels should be cautious about adopting "activist" postures in the GATT/WTO context. For one thing, the international system and its dispute settlement procedures, in stark contrast to most national systems, depend heavily on voluntary compliance by participating members. Inappropriate panel "activism" could well alienate members, thus threatening the stability of the GATT/WTO dispute settlement procedure itself. Relatedly, panels should recognize that voluntary compliance with panel reports is grounded in the perception that panel decisions are fair, unbiased, and rationally articulated.

Quite apart from these concerns, panels would be well advised to be aware also of the potential shortcomings of the international procedures, shortcomings that sometimes relate to a shortage of resources, especially (but not only) resources for fact-finding, as well as to the need for a very broad multilateral consensus. Moreover, panels should also recognize that national governments often have legitimate reasons for the decisions they take. At times, for example, such governments can justifiably argue that an appropriate allocation of power should tilt in favor of the national governments that are closest to the constituencies most affected by a given decision. More generally, panels should keep in mind that a broad-based, multilateral, international institution must contend with a wide variety of legal, political, and cultural values, which counsel in favor of caution towards interpreting treaty obligations in a way that may be appropriate to one society but not to other participants.

Notwithstanding these (and other) reasons for "judicial restraint," panels must at the same time understand the central role that the GATT/WTO adjudicatory system plays in enhancing the implementation, effectiveness, and credibility of the elaborate sets of rules the WTO was created to maintain. Successful cooperation among national authorities to a large extent rests with the institutions given the responsibility to help carry out the WTO's dispute settlement procedures. Thus, when a particular national authority's activity or decision would undermine the effectiveness of WTO rules, or would establish a practice that could trigger damaging activities by other member countries, panels will undoubtedly show it less deference.

12   The WTO Dispute Settlement Understanding: misunderstandings on the nature of legal obligation*

The new World Trade Organization (WTO) has now been operating for two years, and there is little doubt that it has had a very successful launch. It has fortunately avoided two or three potholes in its roadway and is recognized to have a very large potential for future, but not trouble-free, development. One of the more interesting current aspects of the WTO is the focus on the new dispute settlement rules as established by the new Dispute Settlement Understanding (DSU), which is part of the extraordinarily broad agreement embodying the results of the Uruguay Round. Because of the implications of many of the legal obligations in the Uruguay Round texts, and because they were negotiated among more than 120 participating national governments, it is not surprising that one can find ambiguities, omissions, and other troublesome interpretive problems in this vast treaty. For this reason, the dispute settlement process becomes crucial, since it is one of the principal means for resolving the inevitable differences that arise about the various legal obligations of the world trading system.

   In an interesting and perceptive Editorial Comment in the July 1996 issue of this journal,[1] Judith H. Bello brings to bear not only her intellectual acumen, but her extensive experience both in and out of government concerning trade matters and subjects central to the new WTO, including its dispute settlement procedure. However, in my view, at one point in this Editorial Comment she makes a statement that is wrong, or at least misleading. This may have been largely inadvertent in the context of her general message, but I wish to suggest an alternative viewpoint concerning a very vital problem of the new dispute settlement procedure, a problem that has been getting increasing attention in diplomatic, political, and academic circles.

---

* This chapter is based on John H. Jackson, "The WTO Dispute Settlement Understanding – Misunderstandings on the Nature of Legal Obligation" (1997) 91 *American Journal of International Law*, 60–64.
[1] Judith Hippler Bello, "The WTO Dispute Settlement Understanding: Less Is More" (1996) 90 *American Journal of International Law* 416.

This problem is part of the broader question of the legal effect of a final ruling of the dispute settlement process (that is, a report of a dispute settlement panel, or of the appellate panel that judges an appeal from the first-level dispute settlement report). There is some controversy about the legal status of such a report when adopted (as it will almost automatically be under the new WTO procedures). The specific question here is whether the international law obligation deriving from such a report gives the option either to compensate with trade or other measures, or to fulfill the recommendation of the report mandating that the member bring its practices or law into consistency with the texts of the annexes to the WTO Agreement. In other words, does it give the choice to "compensate" or to obey? There has been some confusion about this, and some important leaders of major trading entities in the WTO have made statements that indicate this confusion or are misleading, and in some cases flatly wrong.

The alternative interpretation is that an adopted dispute settlement report establishes an international law obligation upon the member in question to change its practice to make it consistent with the rules of the WTO Agreement and its annexes. In this view, the "compensation" (or retaliation) approach is only a fallback in the event of noncompliance. This latter approach to the question I have posed above, I believe, is correct.

Mrs. Bello, in her Editorial Comment, states the following:

In view of the heat, if not light, being generated by economic nationalists in general, and the specific concerns resulting from some GATT dispute settlement rulings in particular, a review of WTO/GATT dispute settlement rules is overdue. Like the GATT rules that preceded them, the WTO rules are simply not "binding" in the traditional sense. When a panel established under the WTO Dispute Settlement Understanding issues a ruling adverse to a member, there is no prospect of incarceration, injunctive relief, damages for harm inflicted or police enforcement. The WTO has no jailhouse, no bail bondsmen, no blue helmets, no truncheons or tear gas. Rather, the WTO – essentially a confederation of sovereign national governments – relies upon voluntary compliance. The genius of the GATT/WTO system is the flexibility with which it accommodates the national exercise of sovereignty, yet promotes compliance with its trade rules through incentives.[2]

Although I agree with portions of the quoted text above (and also other parts of her Editorial Comment), I believe that the second sentence is particularly misleading and wrong as phrased. Of course, Mrs. Bello is trying to look at the "realpolitik" of the situation. But I think she is overlooking the traditional and historical meaning of general international law obligations and, in particular, obligations connected with trade rules.

[2] *Ibid.,* 416–417.

An international law obligation generally has some of the weaknesses that she mentions – no jailhouse, bail bondsmen, blue helmets, truncheons or tear gas. In other words, international law, as we all know and have struggled with, does not enjoy the kind of monopoly of force that many (but not all) of the "sovereign" states of the world enjoy.

International law, however, has very important real effects. In particular, the difference between the two approaches to the legal effect of a dispute settlement process in the WTO can have some important impacts. In some legal systems, the legal obligation may actually have "direct application," or at least fairly direct effects on the legal system. It is true that in other major jurisdictions, including the United States and the Commonwealth countries, this effect is much different. Arguably, in these latter places there is no "direct application" or "self-executing" effect; nevertheless, under long-established US court precedents[3] a court is bound to utilize international law obligations in its interpretation of national law (statutes, etc.). Likewise, if there is an international legal obligation upon a member state and that state refuses to comply with it, this has a number of "diplomatic ripples." Various responses, albeit often inadequate, are permitted under international law. In addition, there are informal pressures that can be applied. The United States, for example, found in the 1970s, when it refused to follow the results of the GATT DISC (Domestic International Sales Corporation) case relating to the subsidy rules, that it was having trouble capturing meaningful attention from other major trading entities with regard to their own subsidy rules, which the United States felt were quite inadequate. Other trading entities would simply note that the United States was not complying with its obligations, so why should they take US complaints against them seriously? This matter was finally resolved by an uneasy, complex, and somewhat contradictory settlement, but the point had nevertheless been made to the United States.[4] In another context, the Court of Justice of the European Communities (Luxembourg) has struggled with different questions concerning the GATT and its domestic application. If one concludes that under the WTO the result of a dispute settlement is not "binding," this will likely have an important effect on the jurisprudence of that Court.

Now what is the situation with respect to panel reports, under both the GATT and the WTO DSU? Under the GATT, the language of the dispute settlement provisions was very minimal and quite ambiguous on this (and

---

[3] See *Restatement (Third) of the Foreign Relations Law of the United States* (1987), chapter 2, especially § 114.
[4] GATT *Basic Instruments and Selected Documents*, 28th Supplement (1982), 114; John H. Jackson, William Davey and Alan O. Sykes, *International Economic Relations* (3rd edn., 1995), 777.

other) points.[5] At the outset of the GATT, there were various conflicting viewpoints about the appropriate direction and procedure of the dispute settlement process. However, as time passed, the GATT developed in the direction of "rule orientation," or a more "juridical" approach.[6] This development in itself, of course, does not resolve the interpretive question of the legal effect of a panel report. However, by the last two decades of the GATT's history, it seems quite clear to virtually any perceptive and close observer of GATT practice that the GATT contracting parties were treating the results of an adopted panel report as legally binding. These reports often "recommended" that a nation bring its practice into conformity with its legal obligations under the GATT. Indeed, the Tokyo Round "Understanding" on the dispute settlement process makes this somewhat clear.[7] When adopted, a panel report was treated as binding. A basic problem with the GATT procedure was the opportunity for nations to "block" a consensus vote on adoption, and thus keep a panel report in "legal limbo." It was generally agreed that an *unadopted* report did not have legally binding effect. The practice of the GATT is quite strong in this regard, and of course we all know that, under both customary international law and the Vienna Convention on the Law of Treaties, "practice under the agreement" is important interpretive material.[8]

What can we say about the new DSU? Unfortunately, the language of the DSU does not solidly "nail down" this issue. For example and contrasts, Article 94 of the United Nations Charter states: "Each Member of the United Nations undertakes to comply with the decision of the International Court of Justice in any case to which it is a party." Similarly, the Statute of the International Court of Justice, in Article 59, implies such an obligation, stating: "The decision of the Court has no binding force except between the parties and in respect of that particular case."

Some sort of comparable language for the WTO Agreement[9] and/or the

---

[5] General Agreement on Tariffs and Trade, October 30, 1947, Article XXIII, TIAS No. 1700 at 60, 55 UNTS 188 at 266. See also John H. Jackson, *The World Trading System* (1989), chapter 4.

[6] Jackson, *The World Trading System*, 85.

[7] Understanding Regarding Notification, Consultation, Dispute Settlement, and Surveillance, November 28, 1979, GATT, *Basic Instruments and Selected Documents*, 27th Supplement (1980), 210. See especially paras. 16, 21, 22, and Annex, para. 5.

[8] Vienna Convention on the Law of Treaties, May 23, 1969, Article 31(3)(b), 1155 UNTS 331 at 340.

[9] The WTO Agreement includes the following language, which could be relevant: "4. Each member shall ensure the conformity of its laws, regulations and administrative procedures with its obligations as provided in the annexed Agreements." Agreement Establishing the World Trade Organization, in Final Act Embodying the Results of the Uruguay Round of Multilateral Trade Negotiations (hereinafter the Final Act), April 15, 1994, Article XVI(4), 33 ILM 1125 at 1152 (1994). However, this language appears to beg the question, since it depends on a determination as to what the provided obligations are.

DSU would have been welcome. Oddly enough, some diplomats who assisted in the negotiation of the DSU told me that they thought they had nailed it down. But one does not find language of the UN/ICJ type in the DSU.

It is also true that the DSU for the first time explicitly establishes in a treaty text an implementing procedure for the result of panel reports. This procedure includes measures for possible "compensation" or retaliation. Thus, some people have argued that this is an option available to members as an alternative to obeying the mandate of the panel report. As I have indicated, however, several arguments point to a contrary view.

So what does the DSU language itself say? Here we can examine a good number of clauses, and I would suggest that the overall gist of those clauses, in the light of the practice of GATT, and perhaps supplemented by the preparatory work of the negotiators (unfortunately not well documented), strongly suggests that the legal effect of an adopted panel report[10] is the international law obligation to perform the recommendation of the panel report.

At least eleven of the DSU clauses are relevant.[11] In particular, it should be noted that the DSU clauses provide, *inter alia*:

[T]he first objective of the dispute settlement mechanism is usually to secure the withdrawal of the measures concerned . . . [C]ompensation should be resorted to only if the immediate withdrawal . . . is impracticable. (Article 3(7))

Where a panel or the Appellate Body concludes that a measure is inconsistent with a covered agreement, it shall recommend that the Member concerned bring the measure into conformity with that agreement. (Article 19(1))

Prompt compliance with recommendations or rulings of the DSB is essential in order to ensure effective resolution of disputes to the benefit of all Members. (Article 21(1))

Compensation and the suspension of concessions or other obligations are temporary measures available in the event that the recommendations and rulings are not implemented within a reasonable period of time. However, neither compensation nor the suspension of concessions or other obligations is preferred to full implementation of a recommendation to bring a measure into conformity with the covered agreements. (Article 22(1))

---

[10] Remember that under the new procedures there can be no blocking and therefore adoption is virtually automatic. Also remember that the report will almost always specify an obligation to bring the national practices and law into consistency with the international treaty clauses.

[11] See particularly the following Articles and paragraphs of the Dispute Settlement Understanding, in Annex 2 to the WTO Agreement, in the Final Act: Articles 3(4), 3(5), 3(7), 11, 19(1), 21(1), 21(6), 22(1), 22(2), 22(8) and 26(1)(b).

suspension of concessions or other obligations shall be temporary . . . [T]he DSB shall continue to keep under surveillance the implementation of adopted recommendations or rulings . . . [while] the recommendations to bring a measure into conformity with the covered agreements have not been implemented. (Article 22(8))

For "nonviolation complaints," the DSU specifies:

where a measure has been found to nullify or impair benefits under, or impede the attainment of objectives, of the relevant covered agreement without violation thereof, there is no obligation to withdraw the measure. (Article 26(1)(b))

Thus, the DSU clearly establishes a preference for an obligation to perform the recommendation; notes that the matter shall be kept under surveillance until performance has occurred; indicates that compensation shall be resorted to only if the immediate withdrawal of the measure is impracticable; and provides that in nonviolation cases, there is no obligation to withdraw an offending measure, which strongly implies that in violation cases there is an obligation to perform.

It is true that once the "binding" international law obligation to follow the recommendation of a panel report has been established, international law has a variety of ways of dealing with a breach of that obligation, and that, understandably, those methods are not always very effective.[12] However, that is a different issue from the question of whether the "WTO rules are . . . 'binding' in the traditional sense." Certainly they are binding in the traditional international law sense. In fact, for many national legal systems, they are also binding in the "traditional sense" domestically, although not always in a "statute like" sense. In the United States, it can be argued (and this author has so argued) that the WTO rules, and certainly therefore the results of a dispute settlement panel, do not *ipso facto* become part of the domestic jurisprudence that courts are bound to follow as a matter of judicial notice, etc. However, the international law "bindingness" of a report certainly can and should have an important effect in domestic US jurisprudence as in the jurisprudence of many other nation-states.

---

[12] I do not here address another interesting legal question of the WTO and the DSU, namely, whether the new text of the DSU imposes an obligation on states to refrain from all international law remedies for redress of a complaint other than those provided in the DSU.

13   Dispute settlement and the WTO: emerging problems*

Introduction[1]

On January 1, 1995, a new international economic organization came into being, resulting from the lengthy, extensive, and complex Uruguay Round trade negotiation in the context of the General Agreement on Tariffs and Trade (GATT). The Uruguay Round Agreement of the GATT/WTO has been described as "the most important event in recent economic history." In addition the WTO is described as the "central international economic institution,"[2] and nations are more and more engaged with the detailed processes of the WTO, especially its dispute settlement procedure. But the WTO Agreement, including all of its elaborate annexes, is probably fully understood by no nation which has accepted it, including some of the richest and most powerful trading nations that are members.

We now have more than three years' experience under the new organization and its "constitution." At this point in time, appraisals of the launch and early experience of the WTO are almost uniformly optimistic and approving. The new organization has had a successful launch, it has engaged in a number of different activities (not all of which have individually been successful), and it has put into practice a quite remarkable set of

---

* This chapter is based on John H. Jackson, "Dispute Settlement and the WTO: Emerging Problems" (1998) 1 *Journal of International Economic Law* 3, 329–351. This article was a revision and extension of a manuscript first presented at the WTO conference in Geneva on April 30, 1998, commemorating the fiftieth anniversary year of the GATT.
[1] Portions of this manuscript are partly drawn from several other recent works of this author, which may be of interest to the readers. See J. H. Jackson, "The Great 1994 Sovereignty Debate: United States Acceptance and Implementation of the Uruguay Round Results" (1997) 36 *Columbia Journal of Transnational Law* 157–188; and J. H. Jackson, *The World Trade Organization: Constitution and Jurisprudence* (Chatham House Papers, RIIA/Pinter, 1998). See also J. H. Jackson, "Global Economics and International Economic Law" (1998) 1 *Journal of International Economic Law* 1.
[2] L. Bierman *et al.*, "The General Agreement on Tariffs and Trade from a Market Perspective" (1996) 17 *University of Pennsylvania Journal of International Economic Law* 821 at 845.

new procedures for dispute settlement among nations concerning trade matters.

The purpose of this article is to put forward some generalizations or tentative hypotheses about the meaning and potential of these early years of experience. It will do this in four parts: first, it will discuss a brief overview of the history, background, and "landscape" of the new organization, illustrating not only the continuity from its predecessor the GATT, but also some of the major problems of the GATT and how the Uruguay Round negotiators approached those problems in developing the new organization and the extraordinarily extensive treaty text of the Uruguay Round.

Secondly, this article will examine the jurisprudence of the new organization during the early years up to the present (the present, as this is written, being May 1998). A brief overview of the dispute settlement cases will be presented, along with some indications of the potential meaning of those cases and some hypotheses about the directions of the new Appellate Body.

Thirdly, this article will discuss some of the emerging constitutional problems, particularly questions about allocation of power within the Organization, and between the Organization and the member states. Particular attention will be given to the potential ability or inability of the Organization to cope with some of the many problems of "globalization" which are emerging.

Finally, this article will, in section 4, suggest some possible solutions or partial solutions to some problems, and draw some conclusions and prognoses.

1.   Overview of the GATT history and the WTO

Looking back over the 1946–1994 history of the GATT allows one to reflect on how surprising it was that this relatively feeble institution with many "birth defects" managed to play such a significant role for almost five decades. It certainly was far more successful than could have been fairly predicted in the late 1940s.

World economic developments have pushed GATT to a central role during the past few decades. The growing economic interdependence of the world has been increasingly commented upon. Events that occur halfway around the world have a powerful influence on the other side of the globe. Armed conflict and social unrest in the Middle East affect the farmers in Iowa and France and the auto workers in Michigan and Germany. Interest rate decisions in Washington have a profound influence on the external debt of many countries of the world which, in turn, affects their ability to purchase goods made in industrial countries and their ability to provide economic advancement to their citizenry. Environmental problems have obvious cross-border effects. More and more frequently, government leaders find their freedom of action circumscribed because of the impact of external economic factors on their national economies.

One of the interesting and certainly more controversial aspects of the GATT as an institution was its dispute settlement mechanism. It is probably fair to say that this mechanism was unique. It was also flawed, due in part to the troubled beginnings of GATT. Yet these procedures worked better than might be expected, and some could argue that in fact they worked better than those of the World Court and many other international dispute procedures. A number of interesting policy questions are raised by the experience of the procedure, not the least of which is the question about what should be the fundamental objective of the system – to solve the instant dispute (by conciliation, obfuscation, power-threats, or otherwise), or to promote certain longer-term systemic goals such as predictability and stability of interpretations of treaty text.

Even though some argued that GATT dispute settlement was merely a facilitation of negotiations designed to reach a settlement, the original intention was for GATT to be placed in the institutional setting of the ITO, and the draft ITO Charter called for a rigorous dispute settlement procedure which contemplated effective use of arbitration (not always mandatory, however), and even appeal to the World Court in some circumstances.[3] Clair Wilcox, Vice-Chairman of the US Delegation to the Havana Conference, notes that the possibility of suspending trade concessions under this procedure was:

regarded as a method of restoring a balance of benefits and obligations that, for any reason, may have been disturbed. It is nowhere described as a penalty to be imposed on members who may violate their obligations or as a sanction to insure that these obligations will be observed. But even though it is not so regarded, it will operate in fact as a sanction and a penalty.

He further notes the procedure for obtaining a World Court opinion on the law involved in a dispute, and says: "A basis is thus provided for the development of a body of international law to govern trade relationships." Although the ITO Charter would have established a rather elaborate dispute settlement procedure, the GATT had only a few paragraphs devoted to this subject.[4]

---

[3] Havana Charter for an International Trade Organization, Articles 92–97 in UN Conference on Trade and Employment – Final Act and Related Documents, UN Doc. E/Conf. 2/78 (1948). See also C. Wilcox, *A Charter For World Trade* (1949), 159 at 305–308.

[4] J. H. Jackson, *World Trade and the Law of GATT* (Bobbs-Merrill, 1969), 167–171. Generally on the GATT dispute settlement procedure, see also W. J. Davey, "Dispute Settlement in GATT" (1987) 11 *Fordham International Law Journal* 51; Plank, "An Unofficial Description of How a GATT Panel Works and Does Not" (1987) 29 *Swiss Review of International Competition Law* 81.

Article XXIII was the centerpiece for dispute settlement in GATT. It also provided for consultation as a prerequisite to invoke the multilateral GATT processes. Three features of these processes can be stressed:

1. they were usually invocable on grounds of "nullification or impairment" of benefits expected under the Agreement, and did not depend on actual breach of legal obligation;
2. they established the power for the Contracting Parties not only to investigate and recommend action, but to "give a ruling on the matter"; and
3. they gave the Contracting Parties the power in appropriately serious cases to authorize "a contracting party or parties" to suspend GATT obligations to other Contracting Parties.

Each of these features has important interpretations and implications, and, although Article XXIII does not say much about them, the procedures followed to implement these principles have evolved over the four decades of practice into a rather elaborate process.[5]

Originally the key to invoking the GATT dispute settlement mechanism was almost always "nullification or impairment,"[6] an unfortunately ambiguous phrase, and one that might connote a "power" or "negotiation" oriented approach. It was neither sufficient nor necessary to find a "breach of obligation" under this language, although later practice has made doing so important, as we shall see. An early case in GATT[7] defined the nullification or impairment phrase as including actions by a Contracting Party which harmed the trade of another, and which "could not reasonably have been anticipated" by the other at the time it negotiated for a concession. Thus the concept of "reasonable expectations" was introduced, which is almost a "contract" type concept.[8] But even this elaboration is ambiguous.

---

[5] See, e.g., GATT, *Analytical Index* (1995) on Article XXIII of GATT.
[6] An action may also be brought under Article XXIII when the attainment of any objective of the agreement is being impeded.
[7] The Australian Subsidy on Ammonium Sulphate, April 3, 1950, GATT, *Basic Instruments and Selected Documents* (1952), vol. II, 188. This case is sometimes called the "*Marbury* v. *Madison*" of GATT. See R. E. Hudec, "Retaliation Against Unreasonable Foreign Trade Practices" (1975) 59 *Minnesota Law Review* 461; Robert E. Hudec, *The GATT Legal System and World Trade Diplomacy* (1975), 144–153; R. E. Hudec, "GATT or GABB? The Future Design of the General Agreement on Tariffs and Trade" (1971) 80 *Yale Law Journal* 1299 at 1341.
[8] The Australian Subsidy on Ammonium Sulphate case and the German Duty on Sardines case (October 31, 1952, GATT, *Basic Instruments and Selected Documents*, 1st Supplement (1953), 53) both endorsed the view that the GATT should be construed to protect the "reasonable expectations" of the Contracting Parties. See R. E. Hudec, *The GATT Legal System and World Trade Diplomacy* (1975), 144–153; and R. E. Hudec, "GATT or GABB? The Future Design of the General Agreement on Tariffs and Trade" (1971) 80 *Yale Law Journal* 1299 at 1341.

At the beginning of GATT's history, disputes were generally taken up by the diplomatic procedures. At first they were dealt with at semi-annual meetings of the Contracting Parties. Later they would be brought to an "intercessional committee" of the Contracting Parties, and even later were delegated to a working party set up to examine either all disputes, or only particular disputes brought to GATT.[9]

However, around 1955 a major shift in the procedure occurred, largely because of the influence of the then Director-General, Eric Wyndham-White.[10] It was decided that, rather than use a "working party" composed of nations (so that each nation could designate the person who would represent it, subject to that government's instructions), a dispute would be referred to a "panel" of experts. The three or five experts would be specifically named and were to act in their own capacities and not as representatives of any government. This development, it can be argued, represented a shift from primarily a "negotiating" atmosphere of multilateral diplomacy, to a more "arbitrational" or "judicial" procedure designed to arrive impartially at the truth of the facts and the best interpretation of the law. Almost all subsequent dispute procedures in GATT (and the new WTO) have contemplated the use of a panel in this fashion.[11]

Although under GATT Article XXIII the Contracting Parties were authorized (by majority vote) to suspend concessions (by way of retorsion, retaliation, or "re-balancing" of benefits – a term which is not and never has been clear), they have actually done so in only one case. That 1953 instance was the result of a complaint brought by the Netherlands against the US for the latter's use, contrary to GATT, of import restraints on imported dairy products from the Netherlands.[12] For seven years in a row, the Netherlands was authorized to utilize restraints against importation of US grain,[13] although it never acted on that authorization. This had no effect on US action, however. There have been other moves to seek authorization to

9 See R. E. Hudec, *The GATT Legal System and World Trade Diplomacy* (1975), 66–96.
10 Some of this information is developed from private conversations with senior GATT officials closely associated with the early development of GATT.
11 Understanding Regarding Notification, Consultation, Dispute Settlement, and Surveillance, November 28, 1979, GATT, *Basic Instruments and Selected Documents*, 26th Supplement (1980), 210, especially paras. 10–21 (hereinafter the Understanding).
12 Netherlands Measures of Suspension of Obligations to the United States, November 8, 1952, GATT, *Basic Instruments and Selected Documents*, 1st Supplement (1953), 32. This was one fallout result of the US Congress' enactment of section 22 of the Agriculture Act in 1951. See J. H. Jackson et al., *International Economic Relations* (West Publishing Company, 3rd edn., 1995), 956.
13 The Netherlands never enforced the quota, arguably because of its ineffectiveness in removing the US quota on dairy products. See R. E. Hudec, "Retaliation Against Unreasonable Foreign Trade Practices: The New Section 301 and GATT Nullification and Impairment" (1975) 59 *Minnesota Law Review* 461 at 507.

suspend obligations.[14] Also, the US has taken "retaliatory" measures without authorization.[15]

In 1962 an important case was brought by Uruguay, alleging that various practices of certain industrial countries were violations of the GATT obligations. The panel grappled with the language of Article XXIII which called for "nullification or impairment" as the basis of a complaint, but the panel decided to push the jurisprudence beyond the language, and determined in its report that any "violation" of the GATT would be considered a *"prima facie* nullification or impairment"[16] which required a defending Contracting Party to carry the burden of proving that nullification or impairment did not exist. This case, followed by many subsequent GATT dispute panels, reinforced a shift in the focus of GATT cases towards the treaty obligations of the GATT, i.e. in the direction of rule orientation. The panels still talked about the need to facilitate settlements and sometimes the panels acted like mediators. But in some cases occurring much later, panels which tried too much to "mediate" were criticized for not developing more precise and analytical "legal" approaches.[17]

---

[14] As a result of the panel decision in the so-called "Superfund" case, June 17, 1987, GATT, *Basic Instruments and Selected Documents*, 34th Supplement (1988), 136, the EC requested that the Contracting Parties authorize retaliation. "EC Superfund Tax Complaint" (1988) 5 *International Trade Reporter* (Bureau of National Affairs, Washington, DC), 681; "EC Superfund Complaint" (1988) 5 *International Trade Reporter* (Bureau of National Affairs, Washington, DC), 1303.

[15] For example, in the Citrus case, as a result of the failure of the EC to accept the findings of a 1985 GATT panel. Proclamation 5354, 50 Fed. Reg. 26 at 143 (1985). However, in the light of continuing discussion between the EC and the US, the President issued Proclamation 5363 of August 15, 1985, 50 Fed. Reg. 33 at 711 (1985), suspending the application of the duty until November 1, 1985. The duties became effective until August 21, 1986, when the President revoked the increased rates of duty due to a settlement of the Citrus case. 51 Fed. Reg. 30 at 146 (1986). However, it must be noted that trade in pasta between the US and the EC was itself a problem, and so retaliation against a problematic product may have had a certain added attraction.

[16] Uruguayan Recourse to Article XXIII, November 16, 1962, GATT, *Basic Instruments and Selected Documents*, 11th Supplement (1963), 95. In cases where there is a clear infringement of the provisions of the General Agreement, or, in other words, where measures are applied in conflict with the provisions of GATT and are not permitted under the terms of the relevant protocol under which the GATT is applied by the contracting party, the action would, *prima facie*, constitute a case of nullification or impairment and would *ipso facto* require consideration of whether the circumstances are serious enough to justify the authorization of suspension of concessions or obligations. *Ibid.*, 100. See also DISC – United States Tax Legislation, November 12, 1976, GATT, *Basic Instruments and Selected Documents*, 23rd Supplement (1977), 98 (*prima facie* violation of Article XVI); Japanese Measures on Imports of Leather, May 15–16, 1984, GATT, *Basic Instruments and Selected Documents*, 31st Supplement (1985), 94 (*prima facie* violation of Article XI). The *prima facie* concept was also applied in situations involving quotas or domestic subsidies on products subject to agreed-upon tariff limitations (i.e., tariffs bound under Article II). See generally J. H. Jackson, *World Trade and the Law of GATT* (1969), 182.

[17] See, e.g., French Assistance to Exports of Wheat and Wheat Flour, November 21, 1958, GATT, *Basic Instruments and Selected Documents*, 7th Supplement (1959), 46; Spain –

During the Tokyo Round negotiation, there was some initiative taken to improve the dispute settlement processes of the GATT. The so-called "Group Framework Committee" of the negotiation was given this task, among others. However, partly because of the strong objection of the EC to any changes in the existing procedures, this effort did not get very far. The result was a document entitled, "Understanding Regarding Notification, Consultation, Dispute Settlement and Surveillance," which was adopted by the Contracting Parties at their Thirty-Fifth Session in Geneva, November 1979.[18] Like that of the other "Understandings" resulting from the Tokyo Round, the precise legal status of this Understanding is not clear. Unlike the Tokyo Round Codes and other Agreements, it is not a stand-alone treaty. It is also not a waiver under Article XXV of GATT, but is presumably adopted under the general powers of Article XXV to "facilitate the operation and further the objectives" of GATT. This document was, nevertheless, very interesting and was also very influential, since it, along with its annex, consisted of a detailed description of the dispute settlement processes of GATT. It can be considered a "definitive" interpretation of the GATT Agreement, binding on all parties by a decision taken by consensus. It thus formed a sort of "constitutional framework" for these processes in the GATT after 1974 and prior to the WTO.

This Understanding described the procedures of the GATT dispute settlement, noting the requirement of consultation as the first step, and providing explicit recognition of a conciliation role for the GATT Director-General (almost never utilized). If these steps did not result in a settlement, then there was provision for a panel process (on decision of the Contracting Parties usually acting through their "Council"). There was some ambiguity whether the complaining party had a right to a panel process. If the process went forward, there was provision for oral and written advocacy from the disputants, and a written report by the panel. The Understanding reinforced the concept of the *prima facie* nullification or impairment and permitted the use of nongovernment persons for panels while stating a preference for government persons.

The procedure under GATT was for the panel to make its report and deliver it to the "Council" which was the standing body of the GATT, which met regularly and disposed of most of the business of GATT. (This body was not provided in the GATT text, but arose through practice and decision of the Contracting Parties.) The practice then became firmly

Measures Concerning Domestic Sale of Soybean Oil, June 17, 1981, GATT Doc. L/5142. See also GATT, *Analytical Index* (1995), 171 (explaining several Contracting Parties' criticism of the Spanish Oil Panel's conclusion that the term "like products" meant "more or less the same product").

[18] Understanding (note 11 above).

established that if the Council approved the report by consensus, it became "binding." If it did not approve, then the report would not have a binding status. The problem was "consensus." In effect, the procedure which relied on consensus meant that the nation which "lost" in the panel and might otherwise be obligated to follow the panel obligations, could block the council action by raising objections to the consensus. Thus, the losing party to the dispute could avoid the consequences of its loss. This "blocking" was deemed to be the most significant defect in the GATT process.

Subsequent to the 1979 Understanding, there was continued dissatisfaction in GATT about the dispute settlement procedures. At the 1982 Ministerial Meeting, a new attempt to improve them was made, again with modest success. The resulting resolution suggests the possibility of departing from the tradition of requiring a consensus to approve a panel report, so that the "losing" party could not block or delay that approval,[19] but subsequent practice did not seem much improved. Later, many GATT members continued to talk of the need for improving procedures, and this subject was included in the Punta del Este Declaration, establishing the framework for the eighth round of trade negotiations.[20]

In the 1980s, as the procedures became more legally precise and juridical in nature, there developed the idea that there were two types of cases in GATT: the violation cases (based on the *prima facie* concept); and certain "nonviolation cases," which were cases not involving a violation, but nevertheless alleging "nullification or impairment." In fact, the nonviolation cases have been relatively few in the history of GATT. One group of scholars has indicated that there are only from three to eight cases of this type in the history of GATT (out of several hundred total cases).[21] Nevertheless, some of these nonviolation cases have been quite important.[22]

Many of the treaty agreements resulting from the Tokyo Round negotiations included special procedures devoted to the settlement of disputes relating to a particular agreement. Some of these followed very closely the

---

[19] GATT, *Basic Instruments and Selected Documents*, 29th Supplement (1983), 13.
[20] See Ministerial Declaration, GATT, *Basic Instruments and Selected Documents*, 33rd Supplement (1987), 19 and 25; and Decision of January 28, 1987, GATT, *Basic Instruments and Selected Documents*, 33rd Supplement (1987), 31 and 44–45. See also, for example, Yeutter, "The GATT Must Be Repaired – And Fast!" (1987) *The International Economy*, March–April, 44–48; and address by Lamb, US Department of State, (1984) *Current Policy*, No. 585. Improvement of the dispute settlement procedures of GATT is also listed in the 1988 Trade Act (Omnibus Trade and Competitiveness Act of 1988, Pub. L. No. 100–418, section 1101(b)(1), 102 Stat. 1121) as a US objective under the Uruguay Round.
[21] Jackson *et al.*, *International Economic Relations*, 362.
[22] EC – Payments and Subsidies Paid to Processors and Producers of Oilseeds and Related Animal Feed Proteins, January 25, 1990, GATT, *Basic Instruments and Selected Documents*, 37th Supplement (1990), 37; and Jackson *et al.*, *International Economic Relations*, 357.

traditional GATT procedure, and unfortunately they utilized the language "nullification or impairment." In a few cases, special "expert" groups have been called into the process to handle highly technical problems involving such things as scientific judgments.[23]

A 1988 panel report pushed the *prima facie* concept even one step further. The case was a complaint (sometimes called the *Superfund* case) by the European Community, Mexico, and Canada against the US for the effects of the US 1986 tax legislation which taxed imported petroleum products. Since the tax on imported products was admittedly higher than that for domestic products, the US did not deny that the Article III national treatment obligation had been violated. But the US then prepared to prove that the small tax had not caused nullification or impairment, by using trade flow statistics to show that no effects on the flow occurred because of the tax. The panel refused to examine this proof. It noted that "there was no case in the history of the GATT in which a Contracting Party had successfully rebutted the presumption that a measure infringing obligations causes nullification and impairment." It then also noted "although the Contracting Parties had not explicitly decided whether the presumption ... could be rebutted, the presumption had in practice operated as an irrefutable presumption." The panel said that Article III(2), first sentence, "obliges the Contracting Parties to establish certain competitive conditions for imported products in relation to domestic products. Unlike some other provisions in the General Agreement, it does not refer to trade effects ... A change in the competitive relationship contrary to that provision must consequently be regarded *ipso facto* as a nullification or impairment of benefits accruing under the General Agreement." Therefore, the panel concluded, a demonstration that a measure was inconsistent with Article III(2), first sentence, and has no or insignificant effects would "in the view of the panel not be a sufficient demonstration that the benefits accruing under that provision had not been nullified or impaired even if such a rebuttal were in principle permitted."

The oil fee case may perhaps be a high water mark in this regard, since it arguably turns the treaty language "on its head," because by stating that a "*prima facie* case" cannot be rebutted, it makes the "presumption" of nullification or impairment derive *ipso facto* from a violation, thus almost discarding the nullification or impairment concept in favor of a focus on whether or not a "violation" or "breach" of obligation exists.

The GATT jurisprudence was thus brought almost full circle by the evolutionary case-by-case process of the procedure. However, before one accepts completely this conclusion, it must be said that it is not clear that the implications of the oil fee case – non-rebuttability – will be pursued in

---

[23] Agreement on Technical Barriers to Trade, GATT, *Basic Instruments and Selected Documents*, 26th Supplement (1980), 8.

the future. The language of the DSU[24] largely copied from the 1979 Understanding on Dispute Settlement[25] still states that the *prima facie* nullification or impairment creates a presumption so that then "it shall be up to the Member against whom the complaint has been brought to rebut the charge." This may lead panels to back away from some of the implications of the oil fee panel under GATT.

The GATT process still had a number of problems, mostly due to the "birth defects" resulting from the flawed GATT origins described earlier. These flaws included:

1. sparse language with little detail about goals or procedures;
2. imprecise power of the Contracting Parties concerning supervision of the dispute settlement process, leading to the practice of requiring consensus for many decisions which gave rise to two "blocking" defects, whereby a Contracting Party unwilling to submit the dispute procedure or unwilling to accept a panel report could block a decision by raising an objection which then prevented "consensus";
3. the potential for blocking: the first blocking potential could occur at the time of a request for a panel procedure by a complaining party; the defendant sometimes would block this decision, although by about the mid-1980s such a blocking vote became diplomatically very difficult to use;
4. a second and more serious blocking problem at the time the GATT Council (or a committee for one of the Tokyo Round agreement procedures) would be asked to "adopt" a panel report; as mentioned above, the losing party could object, defeat the consensus, and thus block the adoption of a report; during the 1980s various attempts to fix this problem were proposed, but none succeeded;
5. fragmented settlement procedures: because there were separate dispute settlement procedures in various Tokyo Round-specific "code" agreements, dispute settlement procedures were fragmented; also disputes would occur over which procedure to use; and
6. government intervention: there had been several unfortunate instances of a contracting party government interfering with potential panel decisions by inappropriately pressuring a particular panelist.

[24] Final Act Embodying the Results of the Uruguay Round of Multilateral Trade Negotiations, opened for signature April 15, 1994, Marrakesh, Morocco, 33 ILM 1140–1272 (1994), Annex 2, Understanding on Rules and Procedures Governing the Settlement of Disputes, Article 3(8), reprinted in Jackson *et al.*, *International Economic Relations* 368, states: "In cases where there is an infringement of the obligations assumed under a covered agreement, the action is considered *prima facie* to constitute a case of nullification or impairment. This means that there is normally a presumption that a breach of the rules has an adverse impact on other Members parties to that covered agreement, and in such cases, it shall be up to the Member against whom the complaint has been brought to rebut the charge."

[25] Understanding (note 12 above).

When one reflects on the almost fifty years of pre-WTO history of the GATT dispute settlement process, some generalizations seem both apparent and quite remarkable. With very meager treaty language as a start, plus divergent alternative views about the policy goals of the system, the GATT, like so many human institutions, took on a life of its own. Both as to the dispute procedures (a shift from "working parties" to "panels"), and as to the substantive focus of the system (a shift from general ambiguous ideas about "nullification or impairment," to more analytical or "legalistic" approaches to interpret rules of treaty obligation), the GATT panel procedure evolved towards more rule orientation.

The GATT dispute settlement process became admired enough that various trade policy interests sought to bring their subjects under it. This was one of the motivations which led both the intellectual property interests and the services trade interests to urge those subjects to be included in the Uruguay Round. The Uruguay Round results, of course, apply the new Dispute Settlement Understanding (DSU) procedures to those subjects.

Not all of the GATT problems have been solved, of course, but the DSU measurably improves the dispute procedures.

1. It establishes a unified dispute settlement system for all parts of the GATT/WTO system, including the new subjects of services and intellectual property. Thus, controversies over which procedure to use will not occur.
2. It clarifies that all parts of the Uruguay Round legal text relevant to the matter in issue and argued by the parties can be considered in a particular dispute case.
3. It reaffirms and clarifies the right of a complaining government to have a panel process initiated, preventing blocking at that stage.
4. It establishes a unique new appellate procedure which will substitute for some of the former procedures of Council approval of a panel report. Thus, a panel report will effectively be deemed adopted by the new Dispute Settlement Body (DSB), unless it is appealed by one of the parties to the dispute. If appealed, the dispute will go to an appellate panel. After the Appellate Body has ruled, its report will go to the DSB, but in this case it will be deemed adopted unless there is a consensus against adoption, and presumably that negative consensus can be defeated by any major objector. Thus the presumption is reversed, compared to the previous procedures, with the ultimate result that the appellate report will come into force as a matter of international law in virtually every case. The opportunity of a losing party to block adoption of a panel report will no longer be available.

The DSU is designed to provide a single unified dispute settlement procedure for almost all the Uruguay Round texts. However, there remain some potential disparities. Many of the separate documents entitled "agreements" including the GATT in Annex 1A and certain other texts such as the subsidies "code," or the textiles text, have clauses in them relating to dispute settlement. But the DSU Article 1 provides that the DSU rules and procedures shall apply to all disputes concerning "covered agreements" listed in a DSU appendix, so presumably this trumps most of the specific dispute settlement procedures. However, even the DSU provisions allow for some disparity. For example, parties to each of the plurilateral agreements (Annex 4) may make a decision regarding dispute settlement procedures and how the DSU shall apply (or not apply). In addition another DSU appendix specifies exceptions for certain listed texts. Thus the goal of uniformity of dispute settlement procedures may not be 100 percent achieved. Actual practice will determine to what degree this may be a problem.

2.   The jurisprudence of the WTO early years

The first years of the new WTO dispute settlement procedures

The WTO Secretariat listings of April 1, 1998 show that 122 cases have been brought under the new procedures. This is a remarkable increase, about fourfold, over the rate of cases under the GATT. Various conclusions can be made. Perhaps the numbers represent a great deal of confidence by the nation-state members of the WTO in the new procedure. Or perhaps they are testing it, trying it out by bringing cases. Or perhaps the new texts of the Uruguay Round Agreements have sufficient ambiguity (fairly typical at the beginning of practice under a treaty text) that they engender more cases. Finally, most likely it is a combination of all these factors.

One of the more optimistic indicia of the figures is the relatively large number of settlements that are apparently occurring. This could be an indication that the procedures are enhancing and inducing settlements, and that these settlements are consistent with the "rule orientation" principles of the procedures. Governments start a procedure, and then as the procedure advances more becomes known about the case. At some point, the jurisprudence will suggest to the participants the likely outcome of the case and this will induce settlement, consistent with the rules as interpreted in prior cases. Thus the jurisprudence contributes to predictability which assists the governments in coming to agreement about their case, consistent with the rules themselves.

Another optimistic indication is the general spirit of compliance with the result of the dispute settlement procedures. Even the major powers have indicated that they will comply with the mandates of the dispute settlement reports when they are finalized and formally adopted (which is virtually automatic). Of course there are grumblings and complaints, particularly by special interests within societies, about the rulings of the panels and the Appellate Body. Nevertheless, this observer has attended meetings where officials from the major participating members in the WTO have all indicated that their governments intend to comply with the results of holdings against their governments.[26] So far, there seems to be no exception to this spirit of compliance, although the question of what is appropriate "compliance" is controverted from time to time.[27]

There is also some controversy about whether a WTO member who is subject to a dispute panel report directing action to become consistent with WTO treaty rules is obligated as a matter of international law to comply (as this author has opined), or has the option merely to "compensate" by other trade measures.[28]

Another interesting facet of the cases brought so far is the much higher amount of participation by developing countries. Developing countries have brought a number of the cases themselves, even against some of the big industrial countries (with rather satisfying wins). In addition, for virtually the first time in GATT/WTO history, developing countries have brought cases against other developing countries.

Some tentative generalizations about the developing jurisprudence

The addition of the right to appeal to an Appellate Body made up of a permanent cadre (a roster of seven, sitting in divisions of three), in conjunction with the automatic approval of panel reports, has already had a very profound impact on the world trading system as embodied in the GATT and WTO. (The GATT continues as a treaty, although the WTO has taken over all of the organizational functions of what used to be the GATT.)

Some of these impacts will be discussed in the next subsection, but several aspects of the nine or ten reports that we now have from the

---

[26] Conference on WTO Dispute Settlement organized by the American Bar Association at Georgetown University Law Center, February 20, 1998.

[27] For several cases the new procedural rules (DSU) calling for an arbitrator to resolve a controversy over the reasonable time allowed to conform to a panel report were invoked. See "US Asks for Arbitrator in Fight with EU over WTO Banana Ruling," *Inside US Trade*, December 5, 1997; "US Requests Arbitration over Japan's Implementation of Liquor Panel," *Inside US Trade*, January 10, 1998; and "EU Asks for WTO Arbitration on Implementation of Hormone Panel," *Inside US Trade*, April 10, 1998. See also Japan – Taxes on Alcoholic Beverages: Arbitration under Article 21(3)(c) of the Understanding on Rules and Procedures Governing the Settlement of Disputes, WT/DS8/15, WT/DS/10/15, and WT/DS11/13, February 14, 1997; and EC – Measures Affecting Livestock and Meat (Hormones), WT/DS26 and 48/AB/R, January 16, 1998.

[28] See J. H. Jackson, "The WTO Dispute Settlement Understanding: Misunderstandings on the Nature of Legal Obligation" (1997) 91 *American Journal of International Law* 60 (editorial comment); *cf.* J. H. Hippler Bello, "The WTO Dispute Settlement Understanding: Less is More" (1996) 90 *American Journal of International Law* 416 (editorial comment).

Appellate Body divisions indicate characteristics and general approaches that are of considerable interest.

First, the Appellate Body has made it reasonably clear that general international law is relevant and applies in the case of the WTO and its treaty annexes, including the GATT. In the past there has been some question about this, with certain parties arguing that the GATT was a "separate regime," in some way insulated from the general body of international law. The Appellate Body has made it quite clear that this is not the case and has made reference to general international law principles, particularly as embodied in the Vienna Convention on the Law of Treaties, which the Appellate Body calls upon for principles of treaty interpretation.

The Appellate Body also has produced reports which, while arguably not entirely free of possible error, have been very carefully crafted, and give the strong impression of opinions that judicial institutions in many legal systems follow. The Appellate Body reasoning has been quite thorough, and generally careful (especially considering the very short time limits within which they have to operate). The Appellate Body has also been quite independent and impartial. I think it is fair to say that one cannot detect nationality influence on the Appellate Body. There is no indication of particular authorship of any part of an Appellate Body report and no provision for dissenting opinions. Thus an Appellate Body report is only attributed generally to the three members of the roster which sat in the division. One can also say that the Appellate Body work has been more "juridical," or some might say "legalistic," in tenor than before in the GATT, and indeed more so than in many if not most international tribunals.

Another characteristic that seems to be emerging from the jurisprudence with the Appellate Body is a more deferential attitude by the Appellate Body towards national government decisions (or in other words more deference to national "sovereignty"), than sometimes has been the case for the first-level panels or the panels under GATT.[29] In some sense, therefore,

---

[29] Examples of some attitudinal statements of this type (not necessarily supported by the "holding" of the case) include: USA – Standards for Reformulated and Conventional Gasoline, WT/DS2/AB/R, April 29, 1996, 30 ("WTO Members have a large measure of autonomy to determine their own policies on the environment (including its relationship with trade), their environmental objectives and the environmental legislation they enact and implement"); Japan – Taxes on Alcoholic Beverages, WT/DS8, 10, and 11/AB/R, October 4, 1996, 22 ("WTO rules are not so rigid or so inflexible as not to leave room for reasoned judgments in confronting the endless and ever-changing ebb and flow of real facts in real cases in the real world"); and EC – Measures Affecting Livestock and Meat (Hormones), WT/DS26 and 48/AB/R, January 16, 1998, especially para. 165 and the language used therein ("We cannot lightly assume that sovereign states intended to impose upon themselves the more onerous, rather than the less burdensome obligation by mandating conformity or compliance with such standards, guidelines and recommendations. To sustain such an assumption and to warrant such a far-reaching interpretation, treaty language far more specific and compelling than that found in Article 3 of the SPS Agreement would be necessary.").

the Appellate Body has been exercising more "judicial restraint" and has been more hesitant to develop new ideas of interpreting the treaty language than sometimes has been the case in the first-level panels themselves. It is not clear why this is so, but one can note that the Appellate Body roster contains relatively few GATT specialists; rather the Appellate Body, which generally is considered to have outstanding members, has members that are more "generalists" than one would typically find on the first-level panels or in the GATT panels in previous years. This could be a very good omen, because the care and appropriate deference to national decisions may be a significant factor in the long-run general acceptance of the work of the WTO Dispute Settlement Body among a great variety and large number of nations of the world.

Role of the WTO dispute settlement system in the new world trading framework

It has already been mentioned that the dispute settlement system under the new procedures is having a profound impact on the world trade system. In particular, diplomats find themselves in new territory. Rather than operating in what is thoroughly a "negotiating atmosphere," diplomats find themselves acting as lawyers, or relying on lawyers, much more heavily than before, and much more heavily than some of them would like. The dispute settlement procedure itself becomes part of the negotiating tactics for various dispute settlement attempts. One hears or sees in the media reference to "nation A" arguing against "nation B" measures, and "threatening to bring a case in the WTO" if it does not get the matter resolved.[30] The negotiations concerning potential and threatened US action against Japanese automobile imports is a case in point, where the option to bring the case in the WTO apparently worked in a way that was deemed by the Japanese appropriately favorable to their negotiating position.[31] In another case, Costa Rica, small as it is, brought a case against the giant of the north – the US – concerning import quotas in the US against the importation of cotton underwear and some other textile products.

---

[30] See, e.g., "US Threatens Canada with WTO Case, Hints at Mexico Challenge," *Inside US Trade*, April 3, 1998; J. Zarocostas, "US to Request a WTO Panel on Duty Hikes," *Journal of Commerce*, February 20, 1997, 2A; J. Zarocostas, "EU May Go to WTO over US Textiles Rules," *Journal of Commerce*, March 10, 1997, 3A; and "US Considering WTO Talks on Japanese Barriers to Apples," *Inside US Trade*, November 29, 1996.

[31] "Japan Files Case with Trade Body in Fight with US Over Auto Sanctions" (1995) 12 *International Trade Reporter* (Bureau of National Affairs, Washington, DC), 891; "Japan to Charge US in WTO with Violation of MFN, Bound Tariffs," *Inside US Trade*, May 17, 1995. See also statement by Ambassador Mickey Kantor, June 28, 1995 at http://www.ustr.gov/releases/1995/06/95–45, announcing the settlement of the dispute.

Costa Rica won the case, both at the first level and on appeal, and to some
this is quite an eye-opener.[32]
One interesting set of developments that has been evolving, first of all
under the GATT and now under the WTO, is the participation of private
attorneys who are retained by governments involved in the WTO dispute
settlement process. Small governments in particular often do not have
in-house expertise that is adequate to handle some of the complex cases (or
even some of the simple cases) which are finding their way into the WTO
dispute settlement arena. Such states are put at a substantial disadvantage
against large entities like the US or the European Community which have
such in-house expertise. These smaller states consequently have in some
circumstances been eager to retain the services of private attorneys, usually
Europeans or Americans. But there has been some objection made, most
often by the US, to the practice. During the course of the last year,
developments seem to have moved very substantially in the direction of
permitting this practice of governments retaining private attorneys, with
certain limitations. In their 1997 Bananas case report,[33] the Appellate Body
division indicated that there were little valid grounds for refusing the
participation of government-retained private counsel at the appellate proceeding, and this reasoning could very well apply to first-level panel
proceedings. Subsequently there have been indications that some first-level
panels have accepted the practice. I believe this is a welcome move, but it
will necessitate a certain amount of careful thinking about the role and
relationship of the private attorneys *vis-à-vis* their government clients, and
vis-à-vis the WTO system. It will be wise for the DSB or other appropriate
bodies to develop certain standards and ethical rules, perhaps including
conflict-of-interest rules as well as confidentiality rules, which would generally be recommended to governments as part of the contract they use to
retain attorneys. It is hoped this matter will receive appropriate attention
and the appropriate practices and documents will evolve.

3.   Emerging constitutional problems of the WTO

Perhaps almost every human institution has to face the task of how to
evolve and change in the face of conditions and circumstances not originally considered when the institution was set up. This is most certainly
true of the original GATT, and now of the WTO. With the fast-paced
change of a globalizing economy, the WTO will necessarily have to cope

[32] USA – Restrictions on Imports of Cotton and Man-Made Fibre Underwear,
WT/DS24/AB/R, February 25, 1997.
[33] EC – Regime for the Importation, Sale and Distribution of Bananas, WT/DS27/AB/R,
September 9, 1997, paras. 4–12, September 9, 1997.

with new factors, new policies, and new subject matters. If it fails to do that, it will sooner or later, faster or more gradually, be marginalized. This could be quite detrimental to its broader multilateral approach to international economic relations, pushing nations to solve their problems through regional arrangements, bilateral arrangements, and even unilateral actions. Although these alternatives can have an appropriate role and also can be constructive innovators for the world trading system, they also run considerable additional risks of ignoring key components and the diversity of societies and societal policies that exist in the world. In other words, they run a high risk of generating significant disputes and rancor among nations, which can inhibit or debilitate the advantages of cooperation otherwise hoped for under the multilateral system.

In addition, also perhaps inevitable with human institutions and particularly with treaty negotiations involving over 130 participating nations or entities, is the fact that in many places in the Uruguay Round and WTO treaty there are gaps, and considerable ambiguities. These are beginning to emerge in the discussions and dispute settlement proceedings of the new WTO. They seem to be particularly significant in the context of the new issue texts, namely GATS for services and TRIPS for intellectual property. However, even concerning the traditional GATT text itself, there are ongoing ambiguity problems that are calling for new approaches. We can see, for example, an evolution in thinking about the Article III national treatment obligations, as affected and perhaps embellished by other texts in the context of GATT in Annex 1A, such as the Agreement on the Application of Sanitary and Phytosanitary Measures, the Agreement on Technical Barriers to Trade, etc.[34]

Already a number of other newer subjects have been suggested for allocation to cooperative mechanisms in the WTO context. These include questions about competition policy, investment rules, human rights issues, environment in trade, labor standards issues, sanctions (unilateral or otherwise) to enforce some of these policies, and also questions of threats to peace and arms control. The inventory of potential new issues does not stop there.[35]

How will the WTO solve or attempt to solve some of these issues? The First Ministerial Meeting, held at Singapore in 1996, faced some of these questions. Many conclude that the results of that meeting did not suggest very innovative ways to cope with new issues. Obviously, the ministers felt

[34] See, e.g., Japan – Taxes on Alcoholic Beverages, WT/DS8, 10 and 11/AB/R, October 4, 1996; EC – Regime for the Importation, Sale and Distribution of Bananas, WT/DS27/AB/R, September 9, 1997; and EC – Measures Concerning Meat and Meat Products (Hormones), WT/DS26 and 48/AB/R, January 16, 1998.

[35] See J. H. Jackson, "Global Economics and International Economic Law" (1998) 1 *Journal of International Economic Law* 1.

both the legal constraints of the WTO "charter," and political as well as economic constraints of attitudes of constituents in a number of different societies.

The issues needing resolution could be broadly grouped into two categories:

1. substantively new issues (such as some of those discussed or listed above); but also
2. a number of procedural or arguably interstitial ("fine tuning") issues for the Organization.

It is clear, for example, that a variety of the procedures of the dispute settlement process (particularly relating to the text of the Dispute Settlement Understanding), as well as other procedures regarding decision-making, waivers, and new accessions, are being scrutinized and various suggestions for improvement are being put on the table. With respect to dispute settlement, most readers are aware that the treaty text itself calls for a review during the calendar year 1998, now ensuing.

How can these many issues be considered and dealt with in the current WTO institutional framework? First of all, it has to be recognized that there is a delicate interplay between the dispute settlement process on the one hand, and the possibilities or difficulties of negotiating new treaty texts or making decisions by the organization that are authorized by the Uruguay Round treaty text, on the other hand.

What are the possibilities of negotiating new texts or making decisions pursuant to explicit authority of the WTO "charter"? Clearly these possibilities are quite constrained. In the last months of the Uruguay Round negotiations, the diplomatic representatives at the negotiation felt it was important to build in a number of checks and balances in the WTO charter, to constrain decision-making by the international institution which would be too intrusive on sovereignty. Thus the decision-making clauses of Article IX and the amending clauses of Article X established a number of limitations on what the membership of the WTO can do. The amending procedures are probably at least as difficult as those that existed under the GATT (largely copied from the GATT, with the possible exception of certain nonsubstantive procedural amendments). Under the GATT, it was perceived by the time of the Tokyo Round in the 1970s that amendment was virtually impossible, so the Contracting Parties developed the technique of "side agreements." The theory of the WTO was to avoid this "GATT à la carte" approach and pursue a "single agreement" approach. Various attitudes towards that approach persist in the WTO.

Apart from formal amendments, one can look at the powers concerning decisions, waivers, and formal interpretations. But in each of these cases, there are substantial constraints. Decision-making (at least as a fallback from attempts to achieve consensus) is generally ruled by a majority-vote system, but there is language in the WTO (Article IX, paragraph 3) as well as the long practice under the GATT, that suggests that decisions cannot be used to impose new obligations on members.[36] Waivers were sometimes used in the GATT as ways to innovate and adjust to new circumstances, but that process fell into disrepute and caused the negotiators to develop Uruguay Round texts that quite constrained the use of waivers, particularly as to the duration of waivers and also by subjecting waivers to explicit revocation authorities. The GATT had no formal provision regarding interpretations, and thus the GATT panels probably had a bit more scope for setting forth interpretations that would ultimately become embedded in the GATT practice and even subsequent negotiated treaty language. However, the WTO addresses this issue of formal interpretations directly, imposing a very stringent voting requirement of three-fourths of the total membership. Since many people observe that often a quarter of the WTO membership is not present at key meetings, one can see that the formal interpretation process is not an easy one to achieve. Some observers feel, however, that in some contexts the technical requirements of consensus (not unanimity)[37] may not always be so difficult to fulfill.

Given these various constraints, it would be understandable if there was a temptation to try to use the dispute settlement process and the general conclusions of the panel reports regarding interpretation of many of the treaty clauses which have ambiguity or gaps. However, the Dispute Settlement Understanding itself in Article 3, paragraph 2, warns against proceeding in this direction too far, by saying "Recommendations and rulings of the DSB cannot add to or diminish the rights and obligations provided in the covered agreements." As suggested in Part II above, the emerging attitudes of the Appellate Body reports seem to reinforce a policy of considerable deference to national government decision-making, possibly as a matter of "judicial restraint" ideas such as that quoted from the DSU Article 3, and otherwise expressed by various countries who fear too much intrusion on "sovereignty" (whatever that means). The provision of an explicit power of "formal interpretation" with a super-majority requirement in the WTO charter also arguably constrains how far the dispute

---

[36] Final Act Embodying the Results of the Uruguay Round of Multilateral Trade Negotiations, opened for signature April 15, 1994, Marrakesh, Morocco, 33 ILM 1140–1272 (1994), Articles IX(2), X(3), X(4), and Annex 2, Dispute Settlement Understanding, Article 3(2).

[37] WTO Agreement Article IX, footnote 1, defines consensus as follows: "The body concerned shall be deemed to have decided by consensus on a matter submitted for consideration, if no Member, present at the meeting when the decision is taken, formally objects to the proposed decision."

settlement system can push the idea of its report rulings and recommendations becoming "definitive."

In short, there are indications that the dispute settlement system cannot and should not carry much of the weight of formulating new rules either by way of filling gaps in the existing agreements, or by setting forth norms which carry the organization into totally new territory such as competition policy or labor standards.

In addition, as noted above, there are many procedural questions. Some of the procedures under the Dispute Settlement Understanding are now being questioned. Various suggestions are coming forward, and some lists of proposals for change exceed sixty or eighty items or suggestions.[38] Many of these suggestions are reasonable "fine tuning," without dramatic consequence to the system, but even the fine tuning can be difficult to achieve given some of the constraints on decision-making. One of the geniuses of the GATT and its history was its ability to evolve partly through trial and error and practice. Indeed the dispute settlement under GATT evolved over four decades quite dramatically – with such concepts as *"prima facie nullification,"* or the use of panels instead of working parties, becoming gradually embedded in the process – and under the Tokyo Round Understanding on Dispute Settlement became "definitive" by consensus action of the Contracting Parties.

But the language of the DSU (as well as the WTO "charter") seems to constrain greatly some of this approach compared to the GATT. DSU Article 2, paragraph 4, states: "Where the rules and procedures of this understanding provide for the DSB to take a decision, it shall do so by consensus." The definition of consensus is then supplied in a footnote, and although not identical with "unanimity," provides that an objecting member can block consensus. Likewise, the WTO "charter" itself provides a consensus requirement for amendments to Annexes 2 and 3 of the WTO. It will be recalled that Annex 2 is the DSU and the dispute settlement procedures. Thus the opportunity to evolve by experiment and trial and error, plus practice over time, seems considerably more constrained under the WTO than was the case under the very loose and ambiguous language of the GATT, with its minimalist institutional language.

Thus we have a potential for stalemate, or potential for inability to cope with some of the problems that will be facing and are already facing the new WTO institution. That leads us to our final part of this article.

---

[38] The Decision on the Application and Review of the Understanding on Rules and Procedures Governing the Settlement of Disputes, reprinted in J. H. Jackson *et al.*, *International Economic Relations Documents Supplement* (West Publishing Company, 3rd edn., 1995), 956, calls for a "full review of the dispute settlement rules" of the WTO within four years of their entry into force, i.e. during 1998.

4.   Possible solutions and developing conclusions and prognosis for the future

Perhaps the WTO can develop somewhat better opportunities for explicit amendment, using the two-thirds (and three-fourths in substance cases) power of amendment in the WTO charter. Perhaps also, some of the decisions that are possible by the WTO membership at its ministerial meeting or various council meetings can "creep up on" some of the issues and decide them in such a way that certain small steps of reform can be taken. These decisions will become part of the "practice under the agreement" referred to in the Vienna Convention on the Law of Treaties. What are some other possibilities? With respect to the dispute settlement details and potential changes in procedures, it may be possible to work within the "consensus rule" to make some changes in Annex 2 (the DSU). It at least appears that this does not require national government member approvals of treaty text amendments, and thus avoids some of the elaborate procedures of national government ratification of treaties, etc. The question of such consensus relates to at least two different kinds of decisions: changes in the text of the DSU; and decisions by the DSB which could involve incidental or interstitial and ancillary procedural rules, assuming that they are not inconsistent with treaty provisions of the DSU. Again of course, the consensus rule apparently applies. There may be a few situations where basic small and relatively unimportant decisions can be made as a matter of practice of the administration of the dispute settlement system, such as decisions about how to interpret time deadlines, or the form of complaints that should be filed, or the development of a relatively uniform set of procedural rules about activities of panels and panel members, translations, documentation, etc. Even then, there is at least some likelihood that an objecting member could force an issue to go to the DSB and that member could dare to block consensus.

With respect to larger "new subjects" for WTO additions, subjects as significant for example as rules on investment, or competition policy, or even environmental rules, it appears that matters will be somewhat more difficult even than the procedural changes. If amendment of the agreements is not feasible, one could look at the WTO Annex 4 plurilateral agreements which are optional, and thus in the drafting process do not need to be subject to "consensus." However, to add a negotiated plurilateral agreement to Annex 4 of the WTO does require so-called "full consensus." Thus once again, that could be blocked, and clearly that blocking opportunity will translate back into the negotiating process about what can be negotiated to be placed in such a new potential plurilateral agreement.

Other legal and procedural innovations to accomplish change may develop. For example, implementation of the results of both the telecommunication services negotiation and the financial service negotiation rely heavily upon insertions into the individual service schedules of commitments by members.[39]

Thus it may be that the critical development for the WTO is to address "consensus" procedures and thus give attention to the meaning and practice of consensus.

It might be feasible to develop certain practices about consensus that would lead member nations of the WTO to restrain themselves from blocking a consensus in certain circumstances and under certain conditions. In other words, the General Council, or the DSB (the General Council acting with different hats) might develop a series of criteria about consensus concerning certain kinds of decisions, which would strongly suggest to member states that, if these criteria are fulfilled, they would normally refrain from blocking the consensus. Perhaps this could develop a bit like the practice in the European Community history and jurisprudence of the "Luxembourg Compromise," where it has been understood that governments would refrain from exercising their potential vote against a measure in certain circumstances, unless the measure involves something of "vital interest" to the nation member involved. While not pursuing the analogy too far, one might see something similar develop in the context of the WTO. A "vital national interest" declaration could be in practice a condition for blocking consensus, but a practice could develop to subject such declarations to inquiry, debate, and criticism.

Let us by way of a thought experiment consider what some of the conditions or circumstances might be to encourage nations to refrain from blocking a consensus on some of the more purely procedural reforms that might be desired, either in amending the DSU, or in decisions of the DSB. The following might be considered.

1. Clearly the major criterion is that a proposed measure be consistent with the fundamental principles of the WTO, including MFN, and perhaps some of the substantive requirements of treaty texts such as national treatment, or restraints on border measures. Procedural changes ought not normally to challenge those particular rules anyway.
2. In addition, perhaps there should be a super-majority threshold such as 70 or 90 percent of the members present, or some threshold percentage of total WTO membership trade represented by agreeing members (e.g.,

---

[39] From discussions with WTO officials and from WTO documents, Successful Conclusion of the WTO's Financial Services Negotiation, December 15, 1997, http://www.wto.org/wto/press/press86.htm; Basic Telecommunications Schedules of Commitments and Lists of Article II Exemptions, April 1997, http://www.wto.org/wto/press/gbtoff.htm.

90 percent WTO trade?). Some ideas about a "critical mass" threshold have already been discussed.[40]

3. In addition, perhaps the consideration of any new procedural measure should first be examined in depth by a special expert group appointed by the DSB or the WTO membership, which group would consist of considerable expertise on legal procedures being considered, and which group would be recognized as impartial and not prone to be pushing one reform or another for particular advantage to the nation concerned. It might be preferable that the members of the expert group should be, like panels, working and discussing in their own right and judgment and not on instruction of governments. Indeed, such an expert group might draw upon individuals who are not part of the diplomatic missions at Geneva, and in some cases not even government employees. The expert group could prepare certain recommendations or evaluate proposals that have otherwise been made, and then send them to the DSB, or to the WTO General Council, with a recommendation of adoption. Then if the other criteria mentioned above were fulfilled, again members would be strongly encouraged to refrain from blocking consensus, partly with the notion that in the future they may be supporting some other measures which likewise would benefit from restraint in using consensus-blocking techniques.

Turning to more substantial reforms which might be developed through plurilateral agreements as candidates for Annex 4, one might also develop a set of criteria which would be used to persuade nation members to refrain from exercising consensus-blocking techniques. For example, criteria for a new plurilateral agreement that would benefit from such a developing practice over time (informal and not part of the treaty, of course) could include the following.

The proposed agreement would not be inconsistent with any of the existing other rules of the WTO and its annexes, especially Annex 1 (GATT, GATS, and TRIPS). Thus MFN would be fulfilled where otherwise required by the rules of Annex 1. Other measures already embodied in the treaties would likewise be a requirement of consistency for the new treaty agreement. Of course, the new plurilateral agreement proposal would sometimes contain measures that would call for rules applying to those accepting the new protocol that differed from the other WTO rules. But there should be no impact on the non-members of the new protocol that would be considered detrimental.

[40] Address given by WTO Director-General Renato Ruggiero at the April 30, 1998, Fiftieth Anniversary Symposium (available on-line at http://www.wto.org/wto/new/symp-rem.htm).

The protocol or plurilateral agreement proposal should have among its proponents a substantial number of members of the WTO. What is "substantial"? It should be relatively clear that bilateral agreements would not be good candidates; beyond that, how many should be required? Perhaps ten or twenty? Or perhaps the minimum number would be left ambiguous, as long as it was not just a few members? It could also be noted that smaller groups of members can enter into regional trading arrangements, provided that these are not inconsistent with the other rules of the WTO, particularly including Article XXIV of GATT.

The proposed plurilateral agreement should be open to accession by any WTO member. Possibly this ability to accede to the plurilateral agreement should be unconditional. That would mean that the proposal for a plurilateral agreement would have within its text all the measures to be required, leaving nothing further to be negotiated for accession. There might be some exception for a "scheduling" type apparatus analogous to GATT tariff schedules or GATS service schedules.[41]

It could be required that a majority vote of the Council would recommend the addition of the plurilateral proposal to Annex 4. This majority vote could be something of a super-majority, such as two-thirds. Other formulas for the vote could be envisaged. Again, a vital national interest declaration could be used, however, to block consensus.

Since bringing a new plurilateral agreement under the WTO "umbrella" by adding it to Annex 4 might have some financial implications for the costs of the Secretariat and other assistance in enhancing and carrying out the plurilateral agreement, an additional principle to avoid consensus blocking could be that the financial costs of the additional activity created by the proposed plurilateral agreement would be carried entirely by the members who have acceded to the plurilateral agreement, under a special budget item in the WTO financial system.

Possibly with some approach like this to providing some constraint on blocking a developing consensus, the risk of the consensus requirement creating stalemate and an inability to evolve and cope with new problems in the global economy could be minimized. These criteria could be developed through resolutions of the General Council or the DSB, in the form of "recommendations to members" and might provide the relatively informal practice which nevertheless could be effective over time. If such practice was reasonably successful, it might achieve some of the best of several divergent policies, namely allowing measures to go forward short

---

[41] From discussions with WTO officials and from WTO documents, Successful Conclusion of the WTO's Financial Services Negotiation, December 15, 1997, http://www.wto.org/wto/press/press86.htm; Basic Telecommunications – Schedules of Commitments and Lists of Article II Exemptions, April 1997 http://www.wto.org/wto/press/gbtoff.htm.

of unanimity or total consensus, but at the same time protecting in some sort of ultimate and "vital sense" the right and power of every member of the WTO to object in (hopefully) only those very few cases where it felt it was so strongly important to its vital national interests that it would not refrain from blocking the consensus. Clearly this must develop as sort of a "gentlemen's agreement" over time, and the practice of this procedure in its formative period (perhaps several years) would be extraordinarily important.

Part V
GATT, international treaties, and national laws and constitutions

The context of any international treaty is an essential part of its "jurisprudence" and knowledge of the context is necessary for a well-founded understanding of the operation and effectiveness of the treaty. The GATT and the WTO are certainly not exceptions to this rule, and indeed the inter-relationship of these treaties and their ancillary and associated other treaty instruments to national laws of many nation-states is even more important than normal, given that the subject matter of these treaties often relates closely to national government powers and actions. Indeed, some of the international obligations of the WTO/GATT system provide constraints on national "sovereign activity" which even in recent decades would have appeared very surprising if not improper. The "sovereignty" argument is quite often heard in connection with policy considerations about this system, particularly at times when new treaty obligations are being fashioned and put to national government institutions for approval.

In this part of the book are collected six articles or excerpts which probe a number of different aspects of the relationship of GATT and WTO treaty instruments to national legal procedures and constitutions. Some of these articles are devoted to a broader context of treaty-making in a modern "globalized" world, taking up issues of treaty law which apply to all treaties, but noting the particular poignancy of such issues in the context of economic affairs. The works excerpted here, however, are not designed to present too much detail or a systematic overview of implementing the major GATT/WTO negotiating rounds. For those perspectives the reader is referred to several books authored or jointly edited and authored by this author and others, particularly this author's 1969 book, *World Trade and the Law of GATT*; J. Jackson, J. Louis, and M. Matsushita, *Implementing the Tokyo Round: National Constitutions and International Economic Rules* (University of Michigan Press, 1984); and John H. Jackson and Alan O. Sykes (eds.), *Implementing the Uruguay Round* (1997).

14   The General Agreement on Tariffs and Trade in United States domestic law*

I.   Introduction

The General Agreement on Tariffs and Trade (GATT)[1] is a multilateral international agreement which is today the principal instrument for the regulation of world trade. Over eighty nations, including the United States, participate in GATT and it has been estimated that about 80 percent of world trade is governed by this agreement.[2] With the recent completion of five agonizing years of "Kennedy Round"[3] tariff negotiations under GATT auspices, tariffs for many goods will be reduced to a point where they will no longer be effective barriers to world trade.[4] For this reason, nontariff

---

* This chapter is based on John H. Jackson, "The General Agreement on Tariffs and Trade in United States Domestic Law" (1967) 66 *Michigan Law Review* 249–316. I am indebted to Walter Hollis, Legal Advisor's Office, United States State Department, who generously read the manuscript of this article and made a number of useful suggestions. I am also indebted to members of the GATT Secretariat in Geneva for assisting my general research into GATT for this article.
[1] General Agreement on Tariffs and Trade, 61 Stat. Part 5, at A3 (1967); 55 UNTS 194 (1967) (hereinafter referred to as GATT). GATT has been extensively amended and modified, as can be seen from Appendix C. A more current version of GATT can be found in GATT, *Basic Instruments and Selected Documents* (revised edition, 1958), vol. III. Subsequent changes may be found in GATT Doc. IPRO/65–1 (1965) (which added Part IV) and GATT Doc INT (61) 34 (1961) (which modified Article XIV(1)). Although the full text of GATT is not being reprinted in this article, the general subject matter of each Article can be seen from the table in Appendix A. On GATT generally, see Jackson, "The Puzzle of GATT – Legal Aspects of a Surprising Institution" (1967) 1 *Journal of World Trade Law* 131 and the authorities cited therein. For an economist's view, see G. Curzon, *Multilateral Commercial Diplomacy: The General Agreement on Tariffs and Trade and Its Impact on National Commercial Policies and Techniques* (Michael Joseph, London, 1965). As to GATT documents in general and their availability, see GATT Docs. INF/121 and INF/122 (1966); Jackson, "The Puzzle of GATT," 131 note 2.
[2] Statement issued by the Director-General of GATT, GATT Press Release 990, reprinted in *New York Times*, May 16, 1967, 20, col. 3; GATT Press Release 973, November 1, 1966.
[3] See Farnsworth, "Kennedy Round Succeeds," *New York Times*, May 16, 1967, 1, col. 8. See also International Monetary Fund, "Kennedy Round Agreements" (1967) 19 *International Financial News Survey* 213.
[4] See statement by Eric Wyndham-White, Director-General of GATT, to the Deutsche Gesellschaft für Auswärtige Politik at Bad Godesberg, GATT Doc. INT (66) 567, October 27, 1967; address by Eric Wyndham-White at the meeting of the Trade Negotiating Committee at Geneva, GATT Press Release 993, 4, June 30, 1967; Chase Manhattan Bank, "Perspective on World Business" (1967) 7 *World Business*, July, 3.

trade barriers of wide variety and ingenuity[5] are now becoming relatively more significant.[6] In the United States, federal, state, and local legislators and officials, under pressure from special interest protectionists, have been experimenting with various types of barriers on foreign imports.[7] Since much of the general language of GATT concerns nontariff barriers, GATT's position in United States domestic law[8] may well take on increasing importance. However, determining the status of GATT in domestic law is a surprisingly complex problem, partly because of uncertainties that still lurk in our constitutional law relating to executive agreements,[9] and partly for reasons unique to GATT.[10]

GATT was negotiated at Geneva in 1947 at the same time that the final preliminary draft of the Charter for the International Trade Organization

[5] See, e.g., Lawrence, "State 'Buy US' Laws on Increase," *Journal of Commerce*, June 15, 1967, 1, col. 2. See also "Not for State Capitals," *Journal of Commerce*, July 25, 1967, 4, col. 1; Lawrence, "Anti-Dumping Code Foes Face Stiff Odds," *Journal of Commerce*, July 5, 1967, 1, col. 1; Lawrence, "No US Push on Non-Tariff Walls Likely," *Journal of Commerce*, July 3, 1967, 1, col. 7; "Revised Wool Import Testing Rule Reviewed," *Journal of Commerce*, June 28, 1967, 11, col. 4; Milche, "Buy US Laws: Are They Legal," *New York Times*, July 23, 1967, 1F, col. 1; and Reed, "President Orders a Slash in Imports of Dairy Products," *New York Times*, July 1, 1967, 1, col. 3.

[6] There have been over 100 Bills introduced in the current session of Congress relating to nontariff import restrictions of one kind or another. See *CCH Congressional Index* for the 90th Congress under the subject headings, "Dairies and Dairy Products, Imports and Importation" and "Meat and Meat Products."

[7] See cases cited in notes 261–264 below; the articles cited in note 5 above; and the discussion in the text at Part II.B below. In August 1967 the Pennsylvania legislature passed a Bill which would have required all state-financed projects in Pennsylvania to use only steel produced in the United States. The Bill was vetoed, however, in response to State Department opposition. Walker, "Steel Bill Vetoed in Pennsylvania," *New York Times*, August 11, 1967, 41, col. 1.

[8] Often the term "municipal law" is used by international lawyers to describe the law of one country as distinguished from international law. See I. Brownlie, *Principles of Public International Law* (1966), 29. The term "national law" is also used. See W. Bishop, "General Course of Public International Law" in Academy of International Law, *Recueil des Cours* (1965), vol. II, 191. In this article the term "domestic law" is used synonymously with "municipal law" and "national law" and unless the context indicates otherwise will refer to United States domestic law. "Domestic law" seems to be more understandable to the American lawyer and is the term used in the American Law Institute, *Restatement (Second) of the Law, Foreign Relations Law of the United States* (1965) (hereinafter cited as *Restatement*).

[9] See, e.g., E. Byrd, *Treaties and Executive Agreements in the United States* (1960); W. McClure, *International Executive or Presidential Agreements* (1941); MacDougal and Lans, "Treaties and Congressional-Executive or Presidential Agreements: Interchangeable Instruments of National Policy" (1945) 54 *Yale Law Journal* 181 and 534; "Comment, Presidential Amendment and Termination of Treaties: The Case of the Warsaw Convention" (1967) 34 *University of Chicago Law Review* 580; Note, (1961) 61 *Columbia Law Review* 505.

[10] In particular, the Protocol of Provisional Application and Article XXIV(12) of GATT introduce complexities. See the discussion in the text at Part III, especially Parts III.A.2 and III.B.2.

(ITO) was being prepared.[11] GATT was intended to embody concrete tariff commitments within the framework of the ITO when the latter came into existence.[12] The United States failed to accept the ITO Charter, however, and the ITO consequently failed to materialize;[13] thus, GATT became, by default, the general regulatory institution for world trade, filling the gap left by the demise of the ITO. This misdirected beginning, the political sensitivity and trade protectionism in the United States in the 1940s, and the shifting of the power over foreign economic affairs from the legislative to the executive branch in this country[14] all caused GATT to be established in a halting "provisional" manner that continues to make it an anomaly among major international institutions.[15]

This article will undertake a two-step analysis. First, in Part II, the question whether GATT is legally a part of United States domestic law will be examined. Then, assuming GATT is part of this law, Part III will examine the extent of GATT's domestic law effect and its general relationship to other law, both federal and state. The chosen focus of this article thus excludes treatment of substantive obligations under specific GATT clauses.[16] It also excludes intensive development of the myriad details of

[11] The relationship of the preparatory work for the International Trade Organization (ITO) and that for GATT is described in Jackson, "The Puzzle of GATT," 134. Four international conferences were held to draft the ITO Charter. The first three of these conferences were officially titled Meetings of the Preparatory Committee, and were held in London from October 15 to November 26, 1946; in Lake Success, New York, from January 29 to February 25, 1947; and in Geneva from April 10 to October 30, 1947. Most of the GATT was actually negotiated at Geneva, but portions of the preparatory work at the previous two meeting are also relevant.

[12] For instance, GATT Article XXIX(2) states: "Part II of this agreement shall be suspended on the day on which the Havana charter enters into force."

[13] The Administration had repeatedly stated to Congress that, while GATT was being negotiated pursuant to authority which the Executive already possessed, the ITO would be submitted to Congress for approval. S. Rep. No. 107, 81st Cong., 1st Sess., Part II, 4 (1949) (minority report); Hearings on House Joint Resolution 236 Providing for Membership and Participation by the US in the ITO Before the House Committee on Foreign Affairs, 81st Cong., 2nd Sess. (1950); Hearings Before the Senate Finance Committee, 81st Cong., 1st Sess., 549–550 (1949); Hearings Before the House Committee on Ways and Means, 80th Cong., 1st Sess., 11 (1947); and Hearings Before the Senate Committee on Finance, 80th Cong., 1st Sess., 2 (1947). Finally, however, the Executive branch decided not to resubmit the ITO to Congress, State Department Press Release, December 6, 1950, reprinted in (1950) 23 Department of State Bulletin 977; and Hearings Before the Senate Finance Committee, 82nd Cong., 1st Sess., 13, 1247 (1951). For a further description of the causes behind the decision not to submit the ITO, see Gardner, Sterling–Dollar Diplomacy (Clarendon Press, Oxford, 1956); and Diebold, The End of the ITO (Princeton Essays in International Finance No. 16, 1952).

[14] See the text accompanying notes 27 and 135 below.

[15] See the discussion in the text at Part III.A.2 below; and Jackson, "The Puzzle of GATT." Provisional application means, among other things, that a nation may withdraw upon only sixty days" notice. Protocol of Provisional Application, 61 Stat. Part 6, at A2051 (1947); 55 UNTS 308 (1950).

[16] Examination of certain of the clauses may be found in Jackson, "The Puzzle of GATT."

the scope of executive authority to negotiate particular trade concessions under legislation such as the Trade Expansion Act of 1962,[17] especially since the extent of this authority is perhaps more heavily dependent upon executive-Congressional political relationships than upon legal notions.

II. GATT as United States domestic law

Even though GATT is binding on the United States under international law,[18] it could fail to be effective as domestic law if either the agreement were not validly entered into under United States constitutional law or, though validly entered into and recognized by this country as an international legal obligation, it were not under its own terms or for United States constitutional reasons, domestic law.[19]

A. Authority for United States participation in GATT

It is generally settled that under our Constitution international "treaty"[20] obligations can be established in any of the following ways:

1. an agreement negotiated by the President, with advice and consent by a two-thirds vote in the Senate; and
2. an executive agreement of the President, acting under authority delegated by an act of Congress; and
3. an executive agreement of the President, acting under his constitutional power to conduct foreign affairs.[21]

---

[17] See the list of statutes in Appendix D. The US Tariff Schedules in GATT contain literally tens of thousands of items, and the question can be raised as to executive authority to negotiate any one of them. There are a number of especially interesting cases, many of which do not appear on the record and are known only to government officials who have spent lifetimes dealing with the subject.

[18] It is accepted, by some at least, that a nation may be bound under international law to a treaty, even though it has not followed its own internal constitutional or domestic law in accepting the treaty. See International Law Commission of the United Nations, *Draft Articles on the Law of Treaties and Commentaries*, UN Doc. A/6309/Rev. 1, reproduced in (1967) 61 *American Journal of International Law* 248 at 291 (comment 9 to Article II); *Restatement*, § 123. GATT was made effective by the Protocol of Provisional Application, which was signed by the requisite number of states to bring it into effect, including the signature of the United States representative with full powers. 55 UNTS 308 at 312 (1950). See also Hearings Before the Senate Finance Committee, 81st Cong., 1st Sess., 1092 (1949).

[19] *Restatement*, § 141; and Bishop, "General Course of Public International Law," 201.

[20] The term "treaty" has two senses. On the one hand, it is a generic term referring to all international agreements. See International Law Commission, *Draft Articles on the Law of Treaties and Commentaries*, comment 2 to Article 2. This is the sense used in the text above. On the other hand, in the United States constitutional law sense the word "treaty" refers only to those international agreements to which the Senate must and does give its "advice and consent." Thus the US can enter into "treaty" obligations in the international sense without Senate consent. See *Restatement*, § 123 (comment).

[21] See *Restatement*, §§ 130 and 131; and MacDougal and Lans, "Treaties and Congressional-Executive or Presidential Agreements."

The adherence of the United States to GATT rests upon the so-called "Protocol of Provisional Application," which was signed in Geneva on October 30, 1947.[22] GATT has never been submitted to the Senate; in fact, there was never even a plan to do so.[23] Thus the authority for American participation in GATT must stem from one of the two types of executive agreement mentioned above. Representatives of the executive branch have not always displayed certainty as to the true legal basis for GATT: some have stated that the executive agreement was based entirely upon Congressional authorization;[24] others have said that the basis, at least in part, was the independent constitutional power of the President to conduct foreign affairs.[25]

1.   Congressional delegation of authority to the President
The United States Constitution provides in Article I that "[t]he Congress shall have Power to lay and collect Taxes, Duties, Imports and Excises [and] ... To regulate Commerce with foreign Nations ...".[26] Thus, it seems clear that Congressional participation is essential for entry into any broad and detailed international trade agreement, such as GATT. But, although Congress at one time legislated tariff matters in great detail, this, as its own members have stated, proved to be unsatisfactory. Not only was it unduly burdensome, but the results by any fair appraisal were abominable. As one Senator put it in 1934:

[O]ur experience in writing tariff legislation . . . has been discouraging. Trading between groups and sections is inevitable. Log-rolling is inevitable, and in its most pernicious form. We do not write a national tariff law. We jam together, through various unholy alliances and combinations a potpourri or hodgepodge of

---

[22] 61 Stat. Part 6, at A2051 (1947); 55 UNTS 308 (1950). The Protocol was signed on behalf of the United States by Winthrop Brown, then Chief of the Division of Commercial Policy, Department of State, who acted with full powers.

[23] See State Department Press Release, December 13, 1945, reprinted in (1945) 13 *Department of State Bulletin* 970, announcing that invitations had been sent to a group of countries for negotiations on trade matters, and stating: "The latter agreements, so far as the United States is concerned, would be negotiated under the Reciprocal Trade Agreements Act." See also statements made by Executive branch spokesmen in Hearings on the International Trade Organization Before the Senate Committee on Finance, 80th Cong., 1st Sess., 70–74 (1947); and Hearings on the Reciprocal Trade Agreement Program Before the House Committee on Ways and Means, 80th Cong., 1st Sess., 11 (1947).

[24] 94 Cong. Rec. 12662 (1949).

[25] See HR Rep. No. 2007, 84th Cong., 2nd Sess., 113 (1955); Hearings on Extension of the Trade Agreements Act Before the Senate Finance Committee, 82nd Cong., 1st Sess., 1153 (1951); Hearings on the Extension of Reciprocal Trade Agreements Act Before the Senate Finance Committee, 81st Cong., 1st Sess., 1051 (1949); and Statement by the Legal Advisor to the State Department, reprinted in Hearings of the Senate Finance Committee on the ITO, 80th Cong., 1st Sess., 173–176 (1947). See also Appendix B for the State Department analysis of authority for entry into GATT on an Article-by-Article basis.

[26] US Constitution, Article I, § 8.

section and local tariff rates, which often add to our troubles and increase world misery.[27]

Consequently, in the last three decades, there has been an accelerating shift of power over foreign economic affairs from Congress to the executive. Moreover, because of GATT's unusual and unexpected origin, Congress has played a relatively minor role in the development of our relationship with GATT as an instrument of United States policy.[28] While admittedly these factors must be distinguished from the legal questions involved, their presence must also be noted since it colors those legal questions and influences the advocates of differing legal positions.

The basic Congressional delegation of power relied upon by the President in accepting the GATT Protocol of Provisional Application is contained in the Reciprocal Trade Agreements Act as amended and extended for three years in 1945.[29] The acceptance by the United States of subse-

[27] 78 Cong. Rec. 10379 (1934) (remarks of Senator Cooper), quoted in S. Rep. No. 258, 78th Cong., 1st Sess., 49 (1943).

[28] Congressional complaints about this can be found sprinkled throughout the large number of hearings on extensions of the Trade Agreements Acts from 1947 down to the present. For some particularly salient examples, see HR Rep. No. 2007, 84th Cong., 2nd Sess., 34 (1956) (supplemental views of Representative Thomas B. Curtis); Hearings on the Extension of the Trade Agreements Act Before the Senate Finance Committee, 82nd Cong., 1st Sess., 1096 (1951); and Hearings on the Extension of the Reciprocal Trade Agreements Act Before the Senate Finance Committee, 81st Cong., 1st Sess., 1253 (1949).

[29] 59 Stat. 410 (1945). See Appendix D for a complete listing of the citations to the successive Trade Agreements Acts. The basic trade agreements authority delegated by the 1945 statute was set out in section 350 in the following terms:

> (a) For the purpose of expanding foreign markets for the products of the United States (as a means of assisting in the present emergency in restoring the American standard of living, in overcoming domestic unemployment and the present economic depression, in increasing the purchasing power of the American public, and in establishing and maintaining a better relationship among various branches of American agriculture, industry, mining, and commerce) by regulating the admission of foreign goods into the United States in accordance with the characteristics and needs of various branches of American production so that foreign markets will be made available to those branches of American production which require and are capable of developing such outlets by affording corresponding market opportunities for foreign products in the United States, the President, whenever he finds as a fact that any existing duties or other import restrictions of the United States or any foreign country are unduly burdening and restricting the foreign trade of the United States and that the purpose above declared will be promoted by that means hereinafter specified, is authorized from time to time (1) To enter into foreign trade agreements with foreign governments or instrumentalities thereof; and (2) To proclaim such modifications of existing duties and other import restrictions, or such additional import restrictions, or such continuance, and for such minimum periods, of existing customs or excise treatment of any article covered by foreign trade agreement that the President has entered into hereunder. No proclamation shall be made increasing or decreasing by more than 50 per centum any rate of duty, however established, existing on January 1, 1945 (even though temporarily suspended by Act of Congress), or transferring any article between the dutiable and free lists. The proclaimed duties and other import restrictions shall apply to articles the growth, produce, or manufacture of all

quent amendments to GATT depends on later versions of this Act, and will be discussed below.[30] The question before us at this point, then, is whether this 1945 statute authorized the President to bind the United States to GATT, which at the time consisted of approximately 45,000[31] tariff concessions (commitments as to maximum tariffs on items listed) and thirty-four (later thirty-five) Articles obligating the signatory governments on such matters as most-favored-nation treatment, nondiscrimination in internal taxation, quantitative restrictions on imports, duties of consultation with other signatories, and duties to act "jointly" with other parties to GATT in certain situations.[32] If this question is answered in the negative, then the

> foreign countries, whether imported directly or indirectly: *Provided*, That the President may suspend the application to articles the growth, produce, or manufacture of any country because of discriminatory treatment of American commerce or because of other acts including the operation of international cartels or policies which in his opinion tend to defeat the purposes set forth in this section; and the proclaimed duties and other import restrictions shall be in effect from and after such time as is specified in the proclamation. The President may at any time terminate any such proclamation in whole or in part.
>
> (b) Nothing in this section shall be construed to prevent the application, with respect to rates of duty established under this section pursuant to agreements with countries other than Cuba, of the provisions of the treaty of commercial reciprocity concluded between the United States and the Republic of Cuba on December 11, 1902, or to preclude giving effect to an exclusive agreement with Cuba concluded under this section, modifying the existing preferential customs treatment of any article the growth, produce, or manufacture of Cuba: *Provided*, That the duties on such an article shall in no case be increased or decreased by more than 50 per centum of the duties, however established, existing on January 1, 1945 (even though temporarily suspended by Act of Congress).
>
> (c) As used in this section, the term "duties and other import restrictions" includes (1) rate and form of import duties and classification of articles, and (2) limitations, prohibitions, charges, and exactions other than duties, imposed on importation or imposed for the regulation of imports.
>
> (d) (1) When any rate of duty has been increased or decreased for the duration of war or an emergency, by agreement or otherwise, any further increase or decrease shall be computed upon the basis of the post-war or post-emergency rate carried in such agreement or otherwise. (2) Where under a foreign trade agreement the United States has reserved the unqualified right to withdraw or modify, after the termination of war or an emergency, a rate on a specific commodity, the rate on such commodity to be considered as "existing on January 1, 1945" for the purpose of this section shall be the rate which would have existed if the agreement had not been entered into. (3) No proclamation shall be made pursuant to this section for the purpose of carrying out any foreign trade agreement the proclamation with respect to which has been terminated in whole by the President prior to the date this subsection is enacted.

[30] See the discussion in the text at Part II.A.3.
[31] See HR Rep. No. 2009, 80th Cong., 2nd Sess., 12 (1948).
[32] See Appendix A for a list of the GATT Articles and their general subject matter. See also note 1 above. The strongest legal battles over the validity of GATT have been fought not in the courts, but in the Congressional hearings. See the list of renewal Acts and related House and Senate reports in Appendix D. See also Hearing on the ITO Before the House Foreign Affairs Committee, 1st Sess. (1947); and Hearings on the Operation of the Trade Agreements Act and the Proposed ITO Before the Senate Finance Committee, 80th Cong., 1st Sess. (1947).

source of authority must be sought in the President's independent constitutional powers or in other legislation.[33]

Legal attacks on the argument that our adherence to GATT is properly based upon this statute have usually been on two fronts:

1. the statute unconstitutionally delegated legislative power;[34] and
2. an agreement such as GATT is beyond the scope of the authority delegated by the statute.

At least one court has upheld this statute in the face of the constitutional argument.[35] Indeed, the history of similar delegations, which goes back almost to the beginning of the Republic,[36] and several Supreme Court opinions[37] rendered on similar statutes confirm the many memoranda[38] contained in the Congressional committee reports on the Reciprocal Trade Agreements Act and its extensions which conclude that the statute is not challengeable for unconstitutionality.

The second line of attack, that GATT goes beyond the authority delegated by the statute, is more complex. The arguments that the statute does not delegate such power can be sorted into three groups:

1. GATT is a multilateral agreement, whereas the Act authorized only bilateral agreements;

[33] See the discussion in the text at Part II.A.2.
[34] See Hearings on the Extension of the Trade Agreements Act Before the Senate Finance Committee, 78th Cong., 1st Sess., 143 (1943); Hearings on the Extension of the Reciprocal Trade Agreements Act Before the Senate Finance Committee, 76th Cong., 3rd Sess., 698 (1940); and Hearings on the Reciprocal Trade Agreements Act Before the Senate Finance Committee, 73rd Cong., 2nd Sess., 60 (1934).
[35] *Starkist Foods Inc.* v. *United States*, 47 CCPA 52 (1959). See also Note, (1961) 61 *Columbia Law Review* 505.
[36] See S. Rep. No. 1297, 76th Cong., 3rd Sess., 5 (1940); Hearings on Extension of Reciprocal Trade Agreements Act Before the Senate Finance Committee, 81st Cong., 1st Sess., 1095 (1949); memorandum of the State Department entitled "Congressional Legislation and Reciprocal Executive Agreements Concerning Tariff and Related Matters," reprinted in Hearings on Reciprocal Trade Agreements Before the Senate Finance Committee, 73rd Cong., 2nd Sess., 82 (1934). The effect of practice over a period of time was succinctly stated by Secretary Dulles when, in reference to the Trade Agreements Acts, he said: "I don't believe that this law which has remained on the books 21 years unchallenged is unconstitutional." Hearings on the Trade Agreements Extension Before the Senate Finance Committee, 84th Cong., 1st Sess., 1252 (1955).
[37] *Hampton and Co.* v. *United States*, 276 US 394 (1928); *Field* v. *Clark*, 143 US 649 (1892).
[38] See HR Rep. No. 2007, 84th Cong., 2nd Sess., Appendix G, 113 (1956); Hearings on Extension of the Trade Agreements Act Before the Senate Finance Committee, 81st Cong., 1st Sess., 1059 (1949); Hearings on Extension of the Trade Agreements Act Before the Senate Finance Committee, 80th Cong., 2nd Sess., 470–471 (1948); Hearings on Extension of Reciprocal Trade Agreements Act Before the Senate Finance Committee, 76th Cong., 3rd Sess., 729 (1940); and State and Justice Departments memoranda reprinted in Hearings on Reciprocal Trade Agreements Act Before the Senate Finance Committee, 73rd Cong., 2nd Sess., 82 (1934). See also Note, (1961) 61 *Columbia Law Review* 505.

2. various specific substantive clauses of GATT go beyond the statutory authorization (for example, provisions on quantitative restrictions, national treatment of imported goods, dumping, and customs valuation); and

3. GATT is an international organization, with voting and other administrative clauses, and the United States executive was given no authority to enter such an organization.

Let us deal first with the multilateral question. By the time the trade agreements authority was renewed in 1945, this country had entered into thirty-two separate trade agreements under the Reciprocal Trade Agreements Act and its extensions since the original Act was adopted in 1934.[39] Except for an agreement with the Belgo-Luxembourg Economic Union,[40] these agreements were all bilateral. A search of the legislative history for the 1945 Act, as well as that for the predecessor enactments in 1934, 1937, 1940, and 1943, reveals no explicit mention of the possibility of a multilateral agreement pursuant to the authority delegated, although one statement spoke of the agreements being "reciprocal rather than bilateral."[41] On the other hand, several statements in the 1945 legislative history refer to the Act as one of several postwar economic policy building blocks, side by side with such others as the Bretton Woods Agreements, which did set up two multilateral organizations.[42] In addition, some of the early Congressional criticism of the trade agreements program was directed at the most-favored-nation policy, which allowed some nations to reap the benefits of bilateral negotiations between the United States and third countries.[43] The logical way to prevent these "free rides" was to develop some sort of multilateral procedure for negotiation.[44] All things considered, however, it

[39] These agreements are listed in Hearings on the Extension of the Reciprocal Trade Agreements Act Before the House Committee on Ways and Means, 79th Cong., 1st Sess., 932 (1945).
[40] Agreement between the United States of America and the Belgo-Luxembourg Union. 49 Stat. 3680 (1935).
[41] 91 Cong. Rec. 5049 (1945). See Appendix D for a list of the Acts and some of their legislative history.
[42] Hearings on the Extension of the Reciprocal Trade Agreements Act Before the House Committee on Ways and Means, 79th Cong., 1st Sess., 45–46, 819 (1945); 91 Cong. Rec. 4885, 6019 (1945).
[43] HR Rep. No. 594, 79th Cong., 1st Sess., 49 (1945); Hearings of the House Ways and Means Committee, 79th Cong., 1st Sess., 41, 432, 819, and 837 (1945); and 91 Cong. Rec. 4979, 5049, 5086, 5089, 5100, 5142, and 6210 (1945).
[44] The policy of unconditional most-favored-nation application of foreign trade agreements was adopted by the United States in 1923 (91 Cong. Rec. 4979 (1945)), and enacted into law as § 350(a)(2) of the Reciprocal Trade Agreements Act of 1934, 48 Stat. 943. The statute provides: "The proclaimed duties and other import restrictions shall apply to articles the growth, produce, or manufacture of all foreign countries, whether imported directly or indirectly." The most-favored-nation clause was typically worded like that in the United States–Mexico Reciprocal Trade Agreement of 1942 (57 Stat. 833) which read: "With

is understandable that Congress was surprised when, less than six months after it extended the Trade Agreements Act without discussion of the possibility of a multilateral trade agreement, it learned that the executive branch had called on fifteen other nations to join with it in multilateral tariff negotiations.[45]

From examining the text of the statute,[46] one can see that it places no *explicit* hurdle against multilateral trade agreements. Furthermore, it was stressed in testimony before the Congressional committee[47] that the 1947 GATT negotiations would in reality be "bilateral," as before, with the results of the many bilateral negotiations simply drawn together in one instrument, for the sake of convenience. Even an opposing Congressman commented that merely because the result was one instrument signed by all, did not in itself mean that the President had exceeded his statutory authority.[48] Thus, one can conclude that GATT does not go beyond the statutory authority merely because of its multilateral nature.

respect to customs duties . . . [etc.] any advantage, favor, privilege, or immunity which has been or may hereafter be granted by the United States of America or the United Mexican States to any article originating in or destined for any third country shall be accorded immediately and unconditionally to the like article originating in or destined for the United Mexican States or the United States of America, respectively." *Ibid.*, 835. Thus, if the United States agreed with Great Britain that it would limit the amount of tariff on widgets to 10 percent, it was committed by the MFN clause in various other treaties to limit its tariff on widgets to the same amount when those widgets were imported from those other countries. If the United States negotiated with Great Britain for the lowering of widget tariffs, it would usually receive some benefit or concession in return from Great Britain. But if the percentage of its total imports of widgets which originated in Great Britain were 50 percent, then another 50 percent of widget imports would come in under the same duty reduction, without anything having been received in compensation to the United States. The rationale or justification for this type of policy is that, when all trading partners apply it, then the United States also reaps the benefit of negotiated concessions between other countries. Nevertheless, there is the danger of the free ride by third parties whenever the United States negotiates a tariff concession with another country. One way to prevent this is to develop multilateral negotiations (as was done in GATT), so that a tentative concession could be arranged between country A and country B, and then the importing country could go to its other trading partners who exported the same item and ask for compensatory concessions for the advantage they would receive by the lower tariff on those items. Thus if country B and C each exported 50 percent of the imports of widgets into A, and A negotiated a tentative tariff concession with B, A could then go to C during the multilateral negotiations and ask for some compensatory concession for the advantage C would receive by the lowering of the tariff on the widget.

[45] State Department Press Release, December 16, 1945, reproduced in (1945) 13 *Department of State Bulletin* 970. See also Hearings on the Operation of the Trade Agreements Act and the Proposed International Trade Organization Before the House Foreign Affairs Committee, 80th Cong., 1st Sess., Part 1, 6 (1947).

[46] See note 29 above.

[47] Hearings on Operation of the Trade Agreements Act and Proposed ITO Before the House Ways and Means Committee, 80th Cong., 1st Sess., 191–195 and 235 (1947).

[48] *Ibid.*, 235. The author has been informed that United States participation in the multilateral Universal Postal Union is also based on statutes which had been drafted with bilateral agreements in mind. This could be a precedent for GATT participation.

A more serious statutory assault on GATT is the argument that specific provisions of GATT exceed the authority delegated to the President by the Trade Agreements Act. Careful analysis is required to evaluate this argument, but to discuss each clause of GATT here would be tedious and lengthy. Appendix A outlines the sources, if the reader wishes to pursue the matter as to any specific article of GATT. Without reference to specific GATT provisions, however, the arguments for the statutory validity of our adherence to GATT can be summarized as follows:

1. the language of the statute can be read to permit United States entry into GATT, since it authorizes "trade agreements" either without explicit limitation or with limitations that can be interpreted not to preclude an agreement such as GATT;
2. the legislative history shows that provisions such as those in GATT were contemplated by Congress;
3. prior trade agreements known to Congress had provisions like those of GATT, thus further evidencing Congressional intent;
4. later actions of Congress can be taken as recognizing or accepting GATT; and
5. several court cases, while not directly litigating the validity of GATT, have resulted in decisions and opinions that necessarily imply its validity.

In a very real sense, one of the most telling arguments is simply the passage of time. The practice today of all three branches of our government recognizes the legal existence of GATT;[49] to disown GATT at this point would be a jolt to this nation's foreign policy and, indeed, to the stability of international economic relations throughout most of the world. While the political arms of the government might administer such a jolt, one can only conclude that, in any imaginable test of GATT's legality in American courts, the agreement as a whole will continue to be upheld. The legal arguments, however, can directly influence the future scope and extent of the impact of GATT. Additionally, legal arguments illustrate aspects of the Congressional–Executive relationship concerning GATT which have already affected GATT to a great extent and which will continue to do so.

---

[49] As to the effect of the passage of time on the legal issue, see note 36 above. The Executive branch initiated GATT and has, of course, continuously argued for its validity. When faced with a GATT question, the judiciary has assumed the valid existence of GATT. See notes 108 and 109 below and the accompanying text. As for Congress, even it today recognizes and relies on the validity of GATT; for example, legislation authorizing the Kennedy Round would make little sense unless the background of GATT existed. See note 108 below and the accompanying text.

THE STATUTORY LANGUAGE

The language of the statute is curiously bifurcated in form: it makes two grants of power to the President:[50] first, to "enter into foreign trade agreements"; and, secondly, "to proclaim such modifications of existing duties and other import restrictions . . . as are required or appropriate to carry out any foreign trade agreement." Then follow certain *limitations* on the power to proclaim.[51]

It has been argued[52] that the first clause is unlimited: the President is given the power to enter into any "foreign trade agreement," the only limitation on this power being implicit in the definition of "foreign trade agreement." This does not necessarily mean that the President could *carry out* all parts of such an agreement (for instance, domestic legal action might be necessary to do so), but merely that he has the authority to obligate the United States in the international sense to anything that can reasonably be called a "foreign trade agreement." If this be the case, it is possible to test the validity of GATT as an international obligation by checking each of its parts to see if it appropriately belongs in a "foreign trade agreement." Historical examples would help define "trade agreement," and the analysis below as to prior trade agreements known to Congress[53] would certainly be relevant, although not determinative. The broadest scope that can be argued for the statute is that anything that affects foreign trade (and, as nations are learning, there is little that does not)[54] is appropriate in a foreign trade agreement. The provisions of GATT would fall easily within this definition.

Arguably, the definition of "trade agreement" is much more restricted: it is possible to read the limiting language in the second clause, relating to the proclamation power, as also attaching to the grant of power in the first clause. The propriety of this reading is reinforced by the notion that it is idle (or worse, bad policy) to authorize the President to commit the United States internationally without giving him sufficient means to carry out this

---

[50] See § 350(a) of the Trade Agreements Extension Act of 1945, quoted in note 29 above.
[51] *Ibid.*
[52] Memorandum of the Department of State, printed in HR Rep. No. 2007, 84th Cong., 2nd Sess., 113 (1956).
[53] See the text following note 72 below.
[54] Even interest rates in the respective countries are now becoming a subject of international understanding or agreement. See Cowan, "US and 4 Nations Join To Seek Cuts in Interest Rates," *New York Times*, January 23, 1967, 1, col. 8. The potential broad reach of this argument was recognized in the 1949 Senate Finance Committee Hearings, 81st Cong., 1st Sess., 1156 (Senator Millikin: "I think you gave us a measuring stick a while ago that gave us, as I see it, a glimpse of your philosophy. Is it your contention that you can take any economic situation, any place, and say that this puts a hindrance upon trade, or puts up a hurdle to trade, export or import, and that if you find that to be a fact you can make an agreement of any nature that in our [*sic*] opinion will remove or tend to remove that hurdle?" Mr. Brown: "No, sir.").

commitment; such would be the case if the powers of implementation were restricted in a way that the power to agree was not. This interpretation would result in limiting the President's authority to enter into "trade agreements" to those agreements concerned with "duties and import restrictions." An examination of GATT provisions, however, reveals that most of the general Articles[55] can be justified as embraced within the term "import restriction."[56] Of the remaining Articles, some merely contain exceptions to commitments against tariff or nontariff barriers and thus are within the statutory language.[57] The articles which deal with administrative matters, such as consultation over disputes, accession of new parties, "waivers," amendments, and withdrawal, however, are the hardest to bring within the statutory language. Clearly, some of these provisions may be implicitly authorized as essentially concomitant to any foreign agreement, especially a foreign trade agreement.[58]

The scope of executive authority might also be limited by statutes other than the Trade Agreements Act. However, most such problems were avoided when Part II of GATT, the "trade conduct code" containing most of the questionable Articles, was made subject to "existing legislation."[59] Likewise, the President might turn to other statutes to expand the scope of his authority to enter trade agreements, as appears necessary to support the GATT clauses that deal with *export* controls.[60]

---

[55] The original General Agreement, as drafted at Geneva in 1947 and implemented on January 1, 1948, contained thirty-four Articles. As a result of some changes made in 1948, a new Article, Article XXXV, was added to GATT. Since this Article was added so soon after the origin of GATT, it is generally considered that GATT has always had thirty-five Articles. Today, of course, due to the addition of Part IV to GATT, which came into force in June 1966, GATT has a total of thirty-eight Articles. See note 160 below. In addition, there are the various annexes and bulky schedules of tariff concessions which are incorporated by reference.

[56] The general subject matter of each Article is stated in Appendix A, which also indicates a Congressional justification or precedent for each Article. As to the limits of tariff-cutting authority, see Department of State, *Analysis of General Agreement on Tariffs and Trade* (Commercial Policy Series 109, Pub. No. 2983, 1947), which states that the limits on Executive negotiating power as to tariff rates were observed.

[57] If authority exists to negotiate on a subject, such authority would seem usually to extend to negotiating exceptions to commitments regarding the subject.

[58] See the discussion in the text at Part III.A.2; note 56 above; and the text following note 111 below.

[59] See the discussion in the text at Part III.A.2; and the lists on "inconsistent legislation" cited in notes 250 and 251 below.

[60] GATT Articles which mention "exports" are Articles I(1), VI(1), VI(5), VI(6)(b), VI(7)(a), VIII(1) and (4), IX(2), XI(1), XIII(1), XVI(B), and XX(i). At the time GATT was negotiated, the President had authority to govern exports under § 6(d) of the Act of July 2, 1940, 54 Stat. 714, as amended by 56 Stat. 463 (1942) and 61 Stat. 946 (1947). A thorough study of United States export controls can be found in Bermann and Garson, "United States Export Controls – Past, Present, and Future" (1967) 67 *Columbia Law Review* 791. See also Appendix A. President Truman's 1947 Proclamation of GATT relies not only on § 350 of the Tariff Act (19 USC § 1351 (1964)), but also upon § 304(3) (19 USC § 1304 (1964)) which embodied a 1938 amendment relating to marking requirements.

In sum, looking only at the explicit language of the statutory delegation, the argument that GATT is within its scope as a "trade agreement" appears persuasive. But even if one chooses to apply other limiting language in the statute to the scope of authority to enter agreements, most of GATT can be justified under the express language.

LEGISLATIVE HISTORY

It is clear from the legislative proceedings in 1945 that Congress contemplated that provisions in trade agreements authorized under the statute would go considerably beyond tariff concessions. Not only did Congress have before it previously negotiated trade agreements with extensive nontariff provisions,[61] but criticisms of these agreements as well as other statements made in committee hearings show clearly that Congress was cognizant of the importance of nontariff concessions being effectively nullified by import quotas, currency devaluations, and other ingenious devices.[62] One Congressman listed twenty-nine trade barriers that he claimed had been used against the United States.[63] To have concluded a foreign trade agreement without provisions to protect the value of tariff concessions would have run counter to Congressional intent; indeed, American negotiators at Geneva in 1947 refused to enter into tariff commitments without the protection of the general provisions which were included in the GATT agreement.[64] Likewise, there was considerable discussion in Congress about the most-favored-nation clause[65] and about the "escape clause"[66] (including an informal commitment by the Adminis-

[61] See the text accompanying note 72 below.

[62] HR Rep. No. 594, 79th Cong., 1st Sess., 43, 51 (1945); 92 Cong. Rec. 4876 (remarks of Congressman Knutson), 4886 (remarks of Congressman Robertson), 4998–4999 (remarks of Congressman Reed), and 5070 (remarks of Congressman Curtis) (1945); Hearings on the Extension of the Reciprocal Trade Agreements Act Before the Senate Committee on Finance, 79th Cong., 1st Sess., 41–42, 83, and 92 (1945); and Hearing on the Extension of the Reciprocal Trade Agreements Act Before the House Ways and Means Committee, 79th Cong., 1st Sess., 63, 194, 226, 307, 309, 409, 576, 2337, and 2339 (1945).

[63] 91 Cong. Rec. 4999 (1945) (remarks of Congressman Reed).

[64] Meeting of the Trade Agreement Committee in Geneva, UN Doc. E/PC/T/-TAC/PV/3, at 17–19 (1947). Preparatory materials for drafting GATT, which were prepared in 1946–1947 under the auspices of the United Nations, bear the document identification UN Doc. E/PC/T. For purposes of simplification, these documents will be cited as EPCT/.

[65] HR Rep. No. 594, 79th Cong., 1st Sess., 49 (1945); 91 Cong. Rec. 4979 (remarks of Congressman Cooper), 5049 (remarks of Congressman Mills), 5086 (remarks of Congressman Hale), and 6210 (remarks of Congressman Thomas) (1945); and Hearings on the Extension of the Reciprocal Trade Agreements Act Before the House Committee on Ways and Means, 79th Cong., 1st Sess., 41, 432, 819, and 837 (1945).

[66] HR Rep. No. 954, 79th Cong., 1st Sess., 8 (1945); 91 Cong. Rec. 4872 and 4891 (1945); Hearings on the Extension of the Reciprocal Trade Agreements Act Before the Senate Finance Committee, 79th Cong., 1st Sess., 84, 86, 90, and 459 (1945); and Hearings on the Extension of the Reciprocal Trade Agreements Act Before the House Committee on Ways and Means, 79th Cong., 1st Sess., 273 (1945).

tration to include the escape clause in all future trade agreements).[67] In fact, most of the individual provisions of GATT, when matched against pertinent legislative history, relate to specific discussions in the latter (see Appendix A). The clauses which do not so relate are of three types:

1. those concerned with administrative matters;[68]
2. those which deal with import barriers not specifically mentioned in the legislative history, but similar to barriers expressly mentioned, and thus arguably within the scope of the general authority to protect the value of tariff concessions against nontariff barriers;[69] and
3. two clauses which except economic development arrangements[70] and regional trading blocks[71] from the application of the agreement.

PREVIOUS FOREIGN TRADE AGREEMENTS

During the 1945 debate, Congress had before it the previous thirty-two trade agreements negotiated under the authority of the Trade Agreements Acts.[72] It is logical to conclude that, as Congress extended the authority to enter into "foreign trade agreements," it intended to grant authority which at least encompassed subjects dealt with in prior agreements. Consequently, it is useful to compare the subject matter of some of these previous agreements with that of GATT, to see in what respects, if any, GATT departs from precedent and tradition.[73] It may be noted that the GATT negotiators at Geneva expressed the view on several occasions that GATT was to take merely the "usual form of trade agreements," and should include only clauses which were normally found in such agreements[74] and which were essential to safeguard the value of the tariff concessions negotiated.[75]

An analysis comparing GATT with certain of these prior agreements is also contained in Appendix A. It shows that almost the entire range of GATT's substantive subject matter had been dealt with in one or more

[67] 91 Cong. Rec. 4872 (1945) (remarks of Congressman Doughton). Later the President issued an executive order providing that an escape clause similar to that found in the Mexican treaty would be included in all future trade agreements. See Executive Order No. 9832 of February 25, 1947. 3 CFR 1943–1948 Comp. 624.
[68] GATT Articles XXII to XXXV and specific portions of other Articles.
[69] See Appendix A.   [70] GATT Article XVIII.   [71] GATT Article XXIV.
[72] See the list of the agreements reproduced in the Hearings on Extension of the Trade Agreements Act Before the House Committee on Ways and Means, 79th Cong., 1st Sess., 38, 636, and 932 (1948). A list of US agreements with most-favored-nation clauses appears at page 837 of these hearings. A full reprint of the agreement with Mexico, which is representative, may also be found at page 237.
[73] See Appendix A.
[74] Report of the Tariff Negotiation Working Party – General Agreement on Tariffs and Trade, UN Doc. EPCT/135, para. 6, 2 (1947); UN Doc. EPCT/TAC/PV.3, 19 (1947).
[75] Report of the First Session of the Preparatory Committee of the UN Conference on Trade and Employment, 50 (October 1946); UN Doc. EPCT/TAC/PV.2, 19 (1947).

prior United States trade agreements, including the regulation of exports. (The only exceptions to this are films and export or import-reduction subsidies.) Of course, the GATT administrative provisions are different from those of prior agreements due to the multilateral nature of GATT, but many of these provisions are simply multilateral parallels to bilateral provisions in prior agreements.[76] Given the complexity and comprehensiveness of United States trade agreements prior to the 1945 Act, and allowing for GATT's multilateral nature, it is hard to conclude that GATT was a radical or even a substantial departure from the pattern of prior agreements. Arguably, then, the general subjects of GATT were within the contemplation of Congress when it extended the authority to the President to enter "trade agreements." This, however, is a conclusion as to the then-existing intent; it may well be that Congress did not envision the resultant vast extension of power by the President. Particularly, GATT may have resulted in an unforeseen extension of executive power, simply because the same provision may have a greater impact in a multilateral context than in the context of bilateral relations.

CONGRESSIONAL RATIFICATION

The GATT provisions have never been formally submitted to Congress. The theory of the executive branch has been that GATT was authorized by a combination of existing statutes and presidential power, and that therefore there was no need to submit it to Congress.[77] It was intended that the ITO agreement be submitted to Congress;[78] this would have given Congress a formal opportunity to review provisions many of which are identically worded in GATT. The ITO was abandoned, however, so that, while the GATT provisions were extensively discussed in committee,[79] Congress has never formally approved them.

Congress has been acutely aware of GATT over the two decades of GATT's existence. Each time it extended the Trade Agreements Act, GATT was debated.[80] In 1955, the Draft Charter for the Organization for

[76] For an example of administrative provisions in a bilateral trade agreement, see clauses VI and X of the agreement between the United States and the Netherlands regarding, *inter alia*, "sympathetic consideration" and the appointment of a committee to handle certain disputes. 50 Stat. 1504 (1935).
[77] State Department Press Release, December 13, 1945, reprinted in (1945) 8 *Department of State Bulletin* 970; Hearings on ITO Before the State Finance Committee, 80th Cong., 1st Sess., 71 (1947); and Hearings on ITO Before the House Committee on Ways and Means, 80th Cong., 1st Sess., 11 (1947).
[78] Hearings on ITO Before the House Foreign Affairs Committee, 81st Cong., 2nd Sess. (1950); and Hearings on the Operation of the Trade Agreements Act and the Proposed ITO Before the House Committee on Ways and Means, 80th Cong., 1st Sess., 11 (1947).
[79] Hearings on the Trade Agreements Extension Act of 1951 Before the Senate Finance Committee, 82nd Cong., 1st Sess., 1142 (1951).
[80] See Appendix D; and note 78 above.

Trade Cooperation, which was prepared at GATT meetings and which would have set up a formal international organization to oversee GATT, was submitted to Congress,[81] but Congress did not approve it.[82] Arguments for and against the legality of GATT have continued in Congressional proceedings at least up to the end of the 1950s.[83]

Congressional enactments have mentioned GATT explicitly only a few times. The first of these was in the 1950 amendment to section 22 of the Agricultural Adjustment Act of 1933.[84] This section concerns import quotas on agricultural goods, a subject to which Article XI of GATT is intimately related. In 1948, just after GATT came into being, Congress had amended section 22(f) to read:

No proclamation under this section shall be enforced in contravention of any treaty or other international agreement to which the United States is or hereafter becomes a party.[85]

In 1950, certain Senators had attempted to reverse this order of precedence by proposing the following amendment:

No international agreement hereafter shall be entered into by the United States, or renewed, extended or allowed to extend beyond its permissible terminating date in contravention of this section.[86]

Instead Congress enacted the following amending language:

No proclamation under this section shall be enforced in contravention of any treaty or other international agreement to which the United States is or hereafter becomes a party; but no international agreement or amendment to an existing international agreement shall hereafter be entered into which does not permit the enforcement of this section with respect to the Articles and countries to which such agreement or amendment is applicable to the full extent that the General Agreement on Tariffs and Trade, as heretofore entered into by the United States, permit such enforcement with respect to the Articles and countries to which such general agreement is applicable.[87]

This was the first explicit statutory reference to GATT,[88] and, it may be

[81] HR Rep. No. 2007, 84th Cong., 2nd Sess. (1956).
[82] A check of the index to volume 102 of the *Congressional Record* and the *CCH Congressional Index* for the 84th Congress show that HR 5550 never came to a vote. After being reported to the House in HR Rep. No. 2007, 84th Cong., 2nd Sess. (1956), it was given to the Committee of the Whole House on the State of the Union. No further Congressional action was ever taken.
[83] Hearings on Extension of the Reciprocal Trade Agreements Act Before the Senate Finance Committee, 85th Cong., 2nd Sess., 155, 1355 (1958).
[84] 64 Stat. 261 (1950).   [85] 62 Stat. 1248 (1948).
[86] S. Rep. No. 1375, 81st Cong., 2nd Sess., 9 (1950); S. Rep. No. 1326, 81st Cong., 2nd Sess., 5 (1950).
[87] 64 Stat. 261 (1950).
[88] Based on the extensive search through federal statutes and reading of the legislative history for the various Reciprocal Trade Agreements Acts. See note 91 below.

argued, was express recognition by Congress of the existence and validity of GATT.

In 1948 and 1949, Congress extended the Trade Agreements Act for the fifth[89] and sixth[90] times. Although neither extension mentioned GATT, it was discussed in the legislative history; thus, arguably, this reenactment of the statutory authority under which the President claimed to enter GATT comprises a "ratification" of GATT.[91] The extensions, however, were for one year and two years respectively, instead of the usual three years, reflecting the uncertainty over foreign economic policy which existed in Congress at that time.[92] Administration officials testifying before Congress in 1951 refused to raise the ratification argument.[93]

The fortunes of politics change, however, and the 82nd Congress had other ideas about GATT. The Trade Agreements Extension Act of 1951 provides, in section 10, the second explicit statutory reference to GATT.[94]

The enactment of this Act shall not be construed to determine or indicate the approval by the Congress of the Executive Agreement known as the General Agreement on Tariffs and Trade.

This provision was repeated in the 1953, 1954, 1955, and 1958 extensions of the trade agreements authority.[95] Furthermore, in 1951 Congress amended the Defense Production Act of 1950 by adding a section which required import quotas on fats, oils, and certain dairy products in contravention of GATT.[96] In addition, that year Congress once again amended section 22(f) of the Agricultural Adjustment Act of 1933, this time to read:

[89] 62 Stat. 1053 (1948).   [90] 63 Stat. 697 (1949).
[91] This argument is implicit in an affidavit of Williard L. Thorp of the State Department made before the District Court of the United States for the District of Columbia in *Rodes* v. *Acheson*, Civil No. 3756–49 (1949): "The justification for discriminations by a country in balance of payments difficulties under certain circumstances is recognized by the United States and the 22 other parties to the General Agreement on Tariffs and Trade (*Treaties and Other International Acts Series* 1700). The authority to negotiate for the excession additional countries to this agreement has recently been extended by Congress without qualification (Public Law 307, 81st Congress), following hearings in which the provisions of the agreement, including those as to discriminations (Article XIV) were examined in detail (Finance Committee, Senate, Extension of Reciprocal Trade Agreements Act Hearings, vol. 2, 1250*ff*.)." This affidavit was disapprovingly noted by Senator Millikin in Hearings on Extension of the Reciprocal Trade Agreements Act Before the Senate Finance Committee, 82nd Cong., 1st Sess., 1191 (1951).
[92] In *Territory* v. *Ho*, 41 Hawaii 565 at 567 (1957), the court noted with respect to the Trade Agreements Act and GATT that: "The constitutionality of the grant of such authority has been repeatedly questioned in and out of Congress. Nevertheless, Congress has extended from time to time the period during which the President may exercise such authority."
[93] Hearings on Extension of the Trade Agreements Act Before the Senate Finance Committee, 82nd Cong., 1st Sess., 1191–1192 (1951).
[94] 65 Stat. 72 (1951).
[95] 72 Stat. 673 (1958); 69 Stat. 162 (1955); 68 Stat. 360 (1954); 67 Stat. 472 (1953).
[96] 65 Stat. 131, 132 (1951).

No trade agreement or other international agreement heretofore or hereafter entered into by the United States shall be applied in a manner inconsistent with the requirements of this section.[97]

This was done despite Congressional recognition that this might require the United States to breach GATT,[98] and, in fact, forced the President to obtain a GATT waiver to avoid such a breach.[99]

These actions illustrated Congressional hostility towards GATT, and caused the Randall Commission on Foreign Economic Policy to state in 1954:

The General Agreement on Tariffs and Trade has never been reviewed and approved by the Congress. Indeed, questions concerning the constitutionality of some aspects of the United States participation in the General Agreement have been raised in the Congress. This has created uncertainty about the future role of the United States in the General Agreement.[100]

When the Organization for Trade Cooperation was submitted to Congress in 1956, Congressmen again complained that they had not had an opportunity to review GATT, since the Administration carefully avoided submitting it to them.[101]

As a practical matter today, however, GATT is recognized by Congress as well as the executive branch as an important cornerstone of United States policy. The Kennedy Round of tariff negotiations authorized by the Trade Expansion Act of 1962,[102] makes very little sense without GATT. The evidence of Congressional ratification of GATT is thus equivocal. Immediately after GATT came into being Congress seemed to go along, at least until the ITO was scuttled. Then Congress backpedaled. Yet GATT has been so central to Western foreign economic policies that Congress has as a practical matter recognized and accepted its existence.

[97] 65 Stat. 75 (1951).
[98] Congress recognized the possibility that this statutory provision would be inconsistent with GATT. See S. Rep. No. 299, 82nd Cong., 1st Sess., 7 (1951); and Hearings on the Trade Agreements Extension Act of 1951 Before the Senate Committee on Finance, 82nd Cong., 1st Sess., 11 (1951). See also Waiver Granted to the United States in Connection with Import Restrictions Imposed under Section 22 of the United States Agricultural Adjustment Act of 1933, as amended, *Basic Instruments and Selected Documents*, 3rd Supplement (1955), 32.
[99] Decision of the Contracting Parties of GATT of March 5, 1955, GATT, *Basic Instruments and Selected Documents*, 3rd Supplement (1955), 32.
[100] Commission on Foreign Economic Policy, *Report to the President and the Congress* (1954), 49.
[101] HR Rep. No. 2007, 84th Cong., 2nd Sess., 34 (supplemental views of Honorable Thomas B. Curtis) and 46 (minority views).
[102] 19 USC § 1821 (1964). See Hearings on the Trade Expansion Act of 1962 Before the House Committee on Ways and Means, 87th Cong., 2nd Sess., 240 (1962) (memorandum on negotiating procedures under GATT). Compare 19 USC § 1882 (1964), with GATT Article XXIII.

214   GATT, international treaties, and national laws

COURT OPINIONS

Another factor that reinforces the argument for the validity of GATT is that it has been recognized by both federal and state (including territorial) courts. The specific issue of GATT's validity was raised in only one case, but that case was dismissed on other grounds.[103] However, a number of other cases have resulted in decisions necessarily implying the validity of GATT – particularly in tariff cases before the Customs Court and the Court of Customs and Patent Appeals.[104] In fact, since tariff concessions embodied in GATT are so extensive, the majority of cases in those courts now involve tariff rates proclaimed by the President pursuant to GATT or amending protocols.[105] Other than in these courts, only seven American cases, and three opinions of the California Attorney General,[106] have been found which explicitly cite or mention GATT.[107] Of these four were in state or territorial courts[108] and three in federal courts.[109] In each case GATT's validity was

[103] *Morgantown Glasswork Guild v. Humphrey*, 236 F. 2d 670 (DC Cir. 1956).
[104] See, e.g., *Bercut-Vandervoort v. United States*, 151 F. Supp. 942 (CCPA 1957); *George E. Bardwil and Sons v. United States*, 42 CCPA 118 (1955).
[105] Examination of any current volume of these courts' reports reveals that the vast majority of the cases cite a presidential proclamation which effectuates a GATT agreement. For instance, in volume 44 only twelve out of fifty-three fully reported decisions do not cite such a proclamation. See Appendix C for presidential proclamation citations for various GATT agreements.
[106] The California Attorney-General's opinions are 59–164, 34 Cal. AG 302; 60–141, 36 Cal. AG 147; 62–165, 40 Cal. AG 65.
[107] The Shepard citators for all states and territories of the United States and for all federal courts of the United States were searched since 1947 to the most currently available supplement in June of 1967 for all cases which cite 61 Stat. Parts 5 and 6, at A3. Since GATT is sometimes cited without using the "Stat." reference, it is possible that persons who prepare the citator could have missed some cases if they did not translate a different citation into the statutory citation. In addition to searching the citators, various attorneys both in and out of government were contacted who might have knowledge of other cases.
[108] *Baldwin-Lima-Hamilton Corp. v. Superior Court*, 208 Cal. App. 2d 803, 25 Cal. Reptr. 798 (1962), hearing denied December 19, 1962 (California "Buy American" Act held to be unenforceable because violative of GATT); *Bethlehem Steel Corp. v. Board of Commissioners*, Civil Nos. 899165 and 897591 (Super. Ct., County of Los Angeles 1966) (also challenged the California "Buy American" Act); *Territory v. Ho*, 41 Hawaii 565 (1957) (struck down as unconstitutional and contrary to GATT a territorial law requiring retailers selling imported eggs to advertise that fact); *Texas Association of Steel Importers v. Texas Highway Commissioner*, 364 SW 2d 749 (Tex. Ct. App. 1963) (administrative ruling of the highway commission requiring the use of domestic steel in highway projects challenged as contrary to state law, the Constitution, and GATT – disposed of on state law grounds). The *Bethlehem Steel* case held that *Baldwin-Lima-Hamilton* was controlling and that the plaintiffs had an adequate remedy at law and therefore denied a petition for a preliminary injunction. On May 2, 1967, the defendant's motion to dismiss was granted. The author has been informed that the case has been appealed. See note 286 below. See also Comment, "GATT, the California Buy American Act, and the Continuing Struggle Between Free Trade and Protectionism" (1964) 52 *California Law Review* 335; Note, (1964) 17 *Stanford Law Review* 119.
[109] *Talbot v. Atlantic Steel*, 275 F. 2d 4 (DC Cir. 1960); *Morgantown Glassware Guild v. Humphrey*, 236 F. 2d 670 (DC Cir. 1956); and *C. Tennant, Sons and Co. v. Dill*, 158 F. Supp. 63 (SDNY 1957).

either assumed, upheld, or not decided. No opinion citing or mentioning GATT has yet been rendered by the United States Supreme Court.

It is appropriate now to turn to the third question as to the statutory validity of GATT mentioned at the outset of this subsection: whether the administrative provisions[110] of GATT constituted it an international organization which the President did not have the statutory power to join. Most previous United States trade agreements had provisions in them for certain types of administrative functions,[111] such as arrangements for consulting[112] or agreeing on changes in tariff commitments.[113] Early in GATT's drafting history it was recognized that some of these administrative functions would be necessary to implement GATT.[114] It was hoped that the ITO would eventually assume these functions, but until that time a GATT mechanism was required.[115] Early GATT drafts consequently provided for an "Interim Trade Committee."[116]

Soon after these early drafts, and before negotiations opened at Geneva in the spring of 1947, House and Senate committees held extensive hearings on the proposed ITO and GATT negotiations.[117] Some members of Congress challenged the authority of the President to enter into GATT on the specific ground that he was not authorized to join an international "provisional organization."[118] At subsequent GATT drafting sessions in Geneva, the term "Interim Trade Committee" was omitted and instead the term "Contracting Parties" was used.[119] The expressed purpose of this change

---

[110] These provisions are found in GATT Articles XXII to XXXV. See Appendix A; and the text accompanying note 58 above.

[111] See Appendix A for illustrative prior trade agreement provisions that correspond to various Articles of GATT.

[112] E.g., Article XI of the Reciprocal Trade Agreement with Canada, 49 Stat. 3960 (1935); and Article XIV of the Trade Agreement with Mexico, 57 Stat. 833 (1943).

[113] E.g., Article XIV of the Reciprocal Trade Agreement with Canada, 49 Stat. 3960 (1935).

[114] Report of the First Session of the Preparatory Committee of the UN Conference on Trade and Employment, Annexure 10, § I, at 51 (October 1946).

[115] Ibid.

[116] Draft of GATT Article XX in UN Doc. EPCT/C.6/W.58 (1947); draft of GATT Article XXII in EPCT/C.6/85 (1947); draft of GATT Article XXII in Report of the Drafting Committee on the Preparatory Committee of the UN Conference on Trade and Employment, EPCT/34, at 78 (1947).

[117] Hearings on the Trade Agreements Acts and the Proposed ITO Before the House Ways and Means Committee, 80th Cong., 1st Sess. (1947); and Hearings on Operation of the Trade Agreements Acts and Proposed ITO Before the Senate Finance Committee, 80th Cong., 1st Sess. (1947).

[118] Hearings on the Operation on the Trade Agreements Act and the Proposed ITO Before the House Ways and Means Committee, 80th Cong., 1st Sess., 191–195 (1947); and Hearings on the Trade Agreements Act and the Proposed ITO Before the Senate Finance Committee, 80th Cong., 1st Sess., 74, 202, and 335 (1947).

[119] See draft of GATT Article XXIII, Joint Action by the Contracting Parties, in EPCT/135 (1947); draft of GATT Article XXIII, Joint Action by the Contracting Parties, in EPCT/189 (1947); and GATT Article XXV.

was to remove any connotation of formal organization.[120] The Administration has tried to maintain this fiction that GATT is not an organization[121] – going so far, in the 1955 Senate hearings, as to characterize GATT as merely a "forum."[122] Consistently, our contributions to GATT have been drawn from the State Department "Conferences and Contingency Fund" with the accounting entry listing GATT as a "provisional organization."[123] Furthermore, GATT has never been designated as an "international organization" for purposes of the Privileges and Immunities Act.[124]

Despite this fiction, GATT has all the essential characteristics of an "international organization" – it utilizes a secretariat,[125] it "contracts" with states,[126] and it makes decisions which bind

[120] UN Doc. EPCT/TAC/PV/12, at 3 (1947). See also GATT, *Analytical Index to the General Agreements* (2nd revision, 1966), 133.

[121] See Hearings on Extension of the Reciprocal Trade Agreements Act Before the Senate Finance Committee, 81st Cong., 1st Sess., 1080, 1456–1457 (1949).

[122] Hearings on HR 1 Before the Senate Finance Committee, 84th Cong., 1st Sess., 1254 (1955). In testifying further, however, Secretary Dulles did refer to GATT as an organization, "where representatives of some thirty-odd countries subscribed to certain, what you might call, good business principles, and it provides primarily a forum or a place for carrying on multilateral negotiations." See also HR Rep. No. 2007, 84th Cong., 2nd Sess., 9 (1956).

[123] For fiscal year 1967, for example, the United States" contribution to GATT (US$420,000) is listed on page 764 of the appendix to the budget, and is contained in the Department of State, Justice, Commerce and the Judiciary Appropriation Act for fiscal year 1967 under the general heading "International Organizations and Conferences," and the specific heading "International Conferences and Contingencies." For previous years, the fiscal year and the page on which the GATT appropriation can be found are as follows: for fiscal year 1966, see pages 690–691 of the Appendix; for fiscal year 1965, see pages 628–629 of the Appendix; for fiscal year 1964, see pages 642–643 of the Appendix; for fiscal year 1963, see pages 608–609 of the Appendix; for fiscal year 1962, see pages 862–863 of the Appendix; for fiscal year 1961, see pages 788–789 of the Appendix; for fiscal year 1960, see pages 819–820 of the budget; for fiscal year 1959, see page 769 of the budget; for fiscal year 1958, see page 872 of the budget; for fiscal year 1957, see pages 891–892 of the budget; for fiscal year 1956, see page 901 of the budget; for fiscal year 1955, see page 874 of the budget; for fiscal year 1954, see page 858 of the budget; for fiscal year 1953, see page 907 of the budget; for fiscal year 1952, see page 767 of the budget; and for fiscal year 1951, see page 985 of the budget. The 1951 fiscal budge appendix shows that GATT contributions were made as far back as 1949, but prior to the 1951 fiscal year report the budget item was not broken down to show the contribution of GATT.

[124] 22 USC § 288 (1964). Organizations are designated by executive order, and the 1967 supplement to USCA does not list GATT among the organizations so designated.

[125] Technically, GATT does not have a secretariat, but it contracts for such services from the Interim Commission for the International Trade Organization (ICITO). See rule 15 of the GATT Rules of Procedure, printed in GATT, *Basic Instruments and Selected Documents*, 5th Supplement (1957), 11. This technical distinction is one of form and not substance as the Secretariat concerned performs functions only for GATT and is generally recognized as the GATT Secretariat. See Jackson, "The Puzzle of GATT," 131 note 3.

[126] Article XXXIII of GATT provides that non-member governments may accede to GATT "on terms to be agreed between such government and the contracting parties." In practice, when a decision is made by the contracting parties to admit a new member (e.g., GATT, *Basic Instruments and Selected Documents*, 14th Supplement (1966), 13), a protocol with that new member is opened for signature by all contracting parties. However, the protocol sometimes states that it will come into effect as soon as the new member signs it, which suggests that it is in essence a contract between the GATT contracting parties acting

members.[127] This latter function is accomplished by the "Contracting Parties acting jointly,"[128] but this seems to be a distinction without substantive difference. In fact, Article XXV of GATT relating to such joint action is remarkably broad in scope:

1. Representatives of the contracting parties shall meet from time to time for the purpose of giving effect to those provisions of this agreement which involve joint action and, generally, with a view to facilitating the operation and furthering the objectives of this agreement. Wherever reference is made in this agreement to the contracting parties acting jointly they are designated as the CONTRACTING PARTIES.
2. Each contracting party shall be entitled to have one vote at all meetings of the CONTRACTING PARTIES.
3. Except as otherwise provided for in this agreement, decisions of the CONTRACTING PARTIES shall be taken by a majority of the votes cast.

In early years, GATT was very cautious in developing useful institutions to carry out its work.[129] But as the years passed, a series of committees gradually evolved into an institutional scheme.[130] GATT also broadened the scope of its attention and became a policy-making body for a wide variety of subjects touching on international economics and trade.[131] Is or

jointly, and the new member nation. See, e.g., the protocol for the accession of Switzerland, GATT, *Basic Instruments and Selected Documents*, 14th Supplement (1966), 6. In addition, GATT has, through its host country (Switzerland), for loans for construction of headquarters space, and pursuant to Article XV, entered into "Special Exchange Agreements" with several countries.

[127] Although Executive branch officials of the United States try to play down this aspect of GATT (e.g., Secretary Dulles in the Hearings on Extension of the Reciprocal Trade Agreements Act Before the Senate Finance Committee, 84th Cong., 1st Sess., 1239–1267 (1955)), Article XXV certainly contemplates actions which must be considered to be "binding" as an international obligation on contracting parties. The principal such action is a waiver.

[128] GATT Article XXV.

[129] See Report Adopted by the Contracting Parties on December 16, 1950, GATT Doc. CP.5/49, reprinted in GATT, *Basic Instruments and Selected Documents* (1952), vol. II, 194; and the discussions at the Fifth Session of the Contracting Parties to GATT concerning intercessional arrangements for continuing administration, GATT Docs. CP.5/SR 17, SR 18 and SR 25 (1950).

[130] The Council is perhaps the most significant of the GATT institutions and one of the most interesting in development. See GATT, *Basic Instruments and Selected Documents*, 9th Supplement (1961), 7. Other GATT standing committees include the Balance of Payments Committee, *Basic Instruments and Selected Documents*, 7th Supplement (1959), 10; and the Trade and Development Committee, *Basic Instruments and Selected Documents*, 13th Supplement (1965), 75.

[131] See GATT, *GATT: What It Is, What It Does, How It Works* (1966). Current GATT activities include administering the General Agreement itself, sponsoring tariff negotiations such as those in the Kennedy Round, undertaking studies of economic problems of less developed countries (e.g., Report of the Working Party of Economic Problems of Chad, GATT Doc. COM.TD/44 (1967)), and preparing studies of various aspects of international trade (e.g., the so-called Haberler Report, *Trends in International Trade*, GATT Sales No. GATT/1958–3; and *Restrictive Business Practice*, GATT Sales No. GATT/1959/-2).

was this aspect of GATT authorized? The administrative clauses of previous bilateral trade agreements furnish precedent and legislative history to show such authorization.[132] Additionally, authority to enter "trade agreements" arguably implies authority to agree to necessary administrative provisions.[133] Finally, it should be remembered that presidential powers may be the source of the requisite authority.[134]

Even conceding that the President was authorized to join GATT as it was constituted at its outset, it can be argued that there is no such authorization to adhere to the institution into which GATT has evolved. This is a difficult argument, however, and illustrates the problem of "static legalisms" in a dynamic world. The very practice which GATT developed, step by step, in a sense furnishes its own precedent. Gradually, acceptance of changes in a viable institution leads after some years to acceptance of an institution radically different than its origins would have suggested. GATT is not the first such phenomenon – it does, however, warrant special interest since it occurred in the international arena and has constitutional implications.

Thus, in answer to the question whether the President had statutory authority to enter GATT, it seems clear that he did. The working of the statute, legislative history, and the known precedents of prior trade agreements at the time of the 1945 Act combine to show a delegation of authority to enter into all particular portions of GATT, subject to "existing legislation" under the Protocol of Provisional Application, with the possible exception of some of the "administrative" clauses of GATT. Even agreement to these provisions can be justified as implicit in the basic authority to enter trade and principles previously established in the bilateral context.

Nevertheless, the development of GATT has brought with it some important policy questions. Even assuming that GATT is valid as a matter of United States domestic law, it is clear that the circumstances of its history have resulted in a considerable shift of power to the executive

---

[132] Examples of administrative provisions in previous bilateral trade agreements can be seen from the chart in Appendix A, provisions that correspond to Articles XXII to XXXV of GATT. The fact that these trade agreements were known to Congress supports the argument that Congress contemplated such administrative provisions in the trade agreements which it was authorizing.

[133] The argument was made in Congressional hearings: Hearings on Extension of the Reciprocal Trade Agreements Act Before the Senate Finance Committee, 81st Cong., 1st Sess., 1282 (1949); and Hearings on Extending Authority to Negotiate Trade Agreements Before the Senate Finance Committee, 80th Cong., 2nd Sess., 469, 471 (1948).

[134] The State Department has, in part, relied upon this source. See HR Rep. No. 2007, 84th Cong., 2nd Sess., 113 (1956); Hearings on the Trade Agreements Extension Act of 1951 Before the Senate Finance Committee, 82nd Cong., 1st Sess., 1153 (1951); and Hearings on Extension of the Reciprocal Trade Agreements Act Before the Senate Finance Committee, 81st Cong., 1st Sess., 1051 (1949), partially reproduced in Appendix B.

branch without the statutory framework which defines executive–legislative relations in connection with our participation in other international institutions, such as the International Monetary Fund, the International Bank for Reconstruction and Development, and the United Nations.[135] Lack of meaningful Congressional participation in foreign affairs is a problem not unique to the economic sphere.[136] Nevertheless, the regular renewal of the Trade Agreements Acts[137] does provide one opportunity for Congressional review of trade policy, and informal and formal participation of Congressmen at GATT negotiations provides other opportunities.[138] Whether or not this limited role delegated to the Congress in economic policy-making through GATT is adequate, either from a policy or constitutional standpoint, may yet be legitimately questioned.

2.   Constitutional powers of the President

The executive branch, in justifying our adherence to GATT, has usually relied, at least in part, upon the constitutional powers of the President to conduct foreign affairs.[139] A State Department memorandum, submitted during the 1949 Senate committee hearings on the Trade Agreements Act, noted precedents for presidential agreements relating to foreign commerce.[140] This memorandum further specified the sources of authority for this country's agreement to each Article of GATT, relying in a number of places, particularly as to the administrative provisions, on the President's constitutional authority. Arguments based on presidential authority are, however, weakened by a federal court of appeals case[141] which held that the President overstepped his delegated powers when he entered into an agreement with Canada which regulated trade. The court's statement on this issue was unmistakable:

---

[135] See, e.g., United Nations Participation Act, 22 USC § 287 (1964); Bretton Woods Agreement Act, 22 USC § 286 (1964).
[136] E.g., Senator Fulbright's remarks reported in Kenworthy, "Fulbright Sees Senate Influencing Policy Again," *New York Times*, July 20, 1967, 5, col.1.
[137] See Appendix D.
[138] Congressmen have participated informally in major GATT negotiations since the mid-1950s. This practice was formalized in the Kennedy Round. See Trade Expansion Act of 1962, § 1873 (1964); 111 Cong. Rec. 12348 (1965). The delegation included Representative Thomas B. Curtis, Representative Cecil King, Senator John Williams, Senator Herman Talmadge, and alternates Senator Frank Carlson and Senator Abraham Ribicoff. For reports on these negotiations see 113 Cong. Rec. 3819, 4128, and 4891 (1967).
[139] See Appendix B.
[140] Hearings on the Extension of the Reciprocal Trade Agreements Act Before the Senate Finance Committee, 81st Cong., 1st Sess., 1051–1055 (1949).
[141] *United States* v. *Guy W. Capps Inc.*, 204 F. 2d 655 (4th Cir. 1953), affirmed on other grounds 348 US 296 (1954).

The power to regulate foreign commerce is vested in Congress, not the executive or the courts; and the executive may not exercise the power by entering into executive agreements and suing in the courts.[142]

The earlier discussion concerning statutory authority, however, demonstrates that it is probably unnecessary to rely upon independent presidential authority for GATT, but to be able to do so would reinforce the basic proposition that United States participation in GATT is valid.

3.   Later GATT agreements
Heretofore, for purposes of clarity and simplicity, I have spoken of GATT largely as if it were a single agreement coming into force at one point of time. This is not the case – in fact, over 100 international agreements (listed in Appendix C), some not yet in force, can officially be termed "GATT agreements."[143] In order completely to present the picture of GATT in United States domestic law, it would be necessary to analyze many of these later agreements with respect to the President's power to enter into them. This would, of course, be unduly cumbersome, and for that reason, will not be attempted. However, some generalizations can be made.

In the first place, from 1945 down to the present except for several short gaps, there has been a statute in force with basic authorizing language similar to that of the 1945 Trade Agreements Extension Act.[144] Consequently, the analysis of the statutory language of the 1945 Act as a source of presidential authority will apply to these amendments and protocols, subject to some different limiting clauses in the subsequent Acts.[145] Secondly, all such protocols and agreements which affect the general language of GATT, except for the later agreement adding Part IV and certain recent agreements resulting from the Kennedy Round (which I shall discuss below), have concerned subject matter sufficiently close to the original

---

[142] 204 F. 2d at 658.
[143] The definition of an "official" GATT agreement must be somewhat arbitrary, but it is convenient to include all those GATT agreements which were deposited with the United Nations prior to 1955 (and listed in UN Doc. ST/LEG/3/Rev. 1 (1963)), and all those which have been deposited with the Executive Secretary of GATT since 1955 (and listed in *Status of Multilateral Protocols of Which the Executive Secretary Acts as Depository*, GATT Doc. PROT/2/Rev. 2 (1966) or in more recent GATT documents).
[144] Appendix D contains a chart of each of these statutes with their respective time spans. In each statute, there is authority to "enter into foreign trade agreements" and to "proclaim such modifications" subject to certain limitations. See note 29 above.
[145] These limiting clauses related primarily to the allowable percentage cuts in tariff rates and, in some of the statutes, to certain other negotiating limits (e.g., peril point or escape clauses). No instance of violation of negotiating limits has been found by this writer, but the subject is vast and technical since tens of thousands of items are involved. See note 56 above. This author has been told that some specific minor portions of the proclamations for the original GATT agreement arguably exceed some of these limits.

GATT that the conclusions based on legislative history and other arguments as to the scope of authority under the 1945 Act should be applicable in the case of these later protocols.[146] (This is especially so when it is remembered that Part II, the "safeguarding provisions," is subject to "existing legislation.")[147] Thirdly, some of these subsequent protocols and agreements could as well be based on presidential power alone.[148] For example, protocols of rectification are arguably within the executive's implicit power to continue to administer prior agreements.[149]

At the close of the Kennedy Round negotiations on June 30, 1967, a series of protocols and agreements were completed,[150] four of which related to accession of new members,[151] while four others embodied other results of the negotiations.[152] Two of these latter agreements are admittedly not authorized by the Trade Expansion Act of 1962, which is the current trade agreements legislation. Of these two, the Administration will probably ask Congress to pass legislation authorizing one, but argues that it has authority to carry out the other under existing statutes.[153]

[146] This is the judgment of the author. To analyze each clause of each amendment and protocol in detail would be too cumbersome to include in this article. Nevertheless, the reader can see from the chart of amendments and protocols in Appendix C the general nature of those amendments and protocols.

[147] The general practice within GATT has been to assume that protocols amending Part II are subject to the Protocol of Provisional Application by which GATT was originally applied. One could argue that the subsequent protocols and amendments stand upon their own feet and thus circumvent the Protocol of Provisional Application. A more appropriate analysis seems to be that technically the subsequent protocols or amendments are amendments to the Protocol of Provisional Application, which in turn incorporates by reference the General Agreement on Tariffs and Trade including the amending Article, which Article provides the authority for amending the Protocol of Provisional Application.

[148] See the discussion in the text at Part II.A.2.

[149] These protocols merely correct mistakes in prior protocols. See Appendix C.

[150] Final Act Authenticating the Results of the 1964–67 Trade Conference Held under the Auspices of the Contracting Parties to the General Agreement on Tariffs and Trade, GATT Doc. L/2813 (1967).

[151] Argentina, Iceland, Ireland, and Poland. See Appendix C.

[152] Geneva (1967) Protocol to the General Agreement on Tariffs and Trade; Agreement Relating Principally to Chemicals, Supplementary to the Geneva (1967) Protocol to the General Agreement on Tariffs and Trade; Memorandum of Agreement on Basic Elements for the Negotiation of a World Grains Arrangement; and Agreement on Implementation of Article VI of the General Agreement on Tariffs and Trade. See Appendix C.

[153] The Chemicals Agreements, note 152 above, provides that the United States will eliminate the "American Selling Price" (ASP) method of valuing certain goods (primarily benzenoid chemicals) which is contrary to GATT Article VII but was "existing legislation" in 1947 when GATT was signed and therefore not contrary to GATT as applied by the Protocol of Provisional Application. The Administration will likely ask Congress to accept the ASP changes, but argues that it can implement the antidumping provisions under Article VI of GATT without further legislative authority. See the discussion in the text at Part II.B.2. See also Dale, "Details Emerge on Tariff Accord," *New York Times*, July 8, 1967, 29, col. 1; Lawrence, "Single Trade Bill in '67 Seen Likely," *Journal of Commerce*, July 12, 1967, 1, col. 1; and GATT Doc. L/2375/Add. 1 at 17 (1965).

There is one problem as to these and other GATT amendments, how-ever, that is not only potentially troublesome in the GATT context but could come up in relation to other international agreements. This problem is posed by the inclusion of a power to amend in the agreement itself. Even if a procedure for adopting future amendments (Article XXX in GATT) were built into the original agreement, a question exists as to the scope of the President's power to agree to new amendments. It was argued above that the amending clause of GATT, like the other administrative provi-sions, can be justified as within the Congressional delegation of power either as a necessary and implicit concomitant to the trade agreement power, or by analogy to prior bilateral trade agreement provisions known to Congress.[154] But as worded in GATT Article XXX, there are no subject matter limits at all to this amending power.[155] Can the President then argue that, since Congress delegated to him the power to agree to amend GATT, any amendment he now desires to agree to is authorized by the Congres-sional delegation? This bootstrap argument must be answered in the negative. If the amending clause were indeed that broad, it can simply be argued that it was not originally authorized and so is itself *ultra vires*. A better approach, however, would be to assume that the amending power itself is valid, but then to construe the President's authority to agree to amendments as limited in the same way as his power to enter into a trade agreement independent of the amending clause of GATT.[156] In this connec-tion, it is interesting to note that both the Bretton Woods Agreement Act[157] – which governs our participation in the International Monetary Fund and in the International Bank for Reconstruction and Development – and the

[154] See the discussion in the text at Part II.A.1.

[155] GATT Article XXX reads: "1. Except where provision for modification is made elsewhere in this agreement amendments to the provisions of Part I of this agreement or to the provisions of Article XXIX or of this Article shall become effective upon acceptance by all the contracting parties, and other amendments to this agreement shall become effective, in respect of those contracting parties which accept them, upon acceptance by two-thirds of the contracting parties and thereafter for each other contracting party upon acceptance by it."

[156] There is at this point another argument which could give some trouble, namely, that since the amending Article was agreed to under the 1945 statute, that that statute gives the scope and limitation to the amending Article for all future time. Following this analysis, later statutes of the United States which amend the Trade Agreements Act could not expand or contract the authority to amend Article XXX of GATT. This argument must be rejected, however, since not only is it impractical and unduly rigid, but the intent of Congress in delegating authority to enter into an agreement with an amending provision must have been that the amending provision would take on the scope of authority of future Congres-sional Acts. Alternatively, it can be argued that each subsequent statutory amendment is an authorization to the Executive branch to continue to participate in GATT and the amending authority would take on the scope and extent of the then current statutory authority of the Executive.

[157] 22 USC § 286 (1964).

United Nations Participation Act[158] impose explicit limits on the presidential power to agree to amendments to the relevant international agreements. An argument could be made in favor of Congressional action to regularize United States participation in GATT on the pragmatic ground that such an act would afford an opportunity to spell out explicitly the limits on the power of the executive to agree to amendments of GATT, thus obtaining greater Congressional participation in any future major shift in GATT policy.[159]

The "Part IV amendments" to GATT, entitled "Trade and Development,"[160] require separate analysis. These consist of three Articles which detail matters relating to the use of trade to promote the economic development of less developed countries. The Articles "commit" those members who are deemed developed countries to "accord high priority to the reduction . . . of barriers to products . . . of . . . export interest to less-developed contracting parties" to refrain from fiscal measures that would hamper imports from less-developed countries, and to "make every effort," "give active consideration," and "have special regard" for certain similar policies that affect the economic development of less developed countries. The commitments are qualified by exceptions for "compelling reasons, which may include legal reasons."

Part IV was completed on February 8, 1965, and signed on that day by a number of nations. Some countries also agreed to apply Part IV *de facto* pending its entry into force on June 27, 1966.[161] At this time, the statutory authority for the United States to enter trade agreements was the Trade Expansion Act of 1962 which contained the standard language already discussed,[162] authorizing "entry into trade agreements" and proclamation of duty modifications.

Can the President's acceptance of Part IV be justified on the authority

---

[158] 22 USC § 287 (1964).

[159] The arguments contained in this subsection concerning Article XXX apply also to the authority for joint action contained in Article XXV, including the authority to grant a waiver, and possibly certain other "joint action" provisions. Of course, for Congress to impose a tight rein on the President in connection with joint action of the contracting parties would be a mistake, since a certain amount of flexibility is essential. Congress might appropriately require specific reports of United States votes at GATT meetings, however, so that the interested Congressional committee could have an opportunity to appraise the Executive branch activities on a continuing basis.

[160] The text of Part IV of GATT can be found in GATT Doc. IPRO/65–1 (1965) and in (1964) 51 *Department of State Bulletin* 922.

[161] GATT Doc. IPRO/65–1 (1965). See also, GATT Press Release 962, June 28, 1966.

[162] 19 USC § 1821(a) (1964): "(1) after June 30, 1962, and before July 1, 1967, enter into trade agreements with foreign countries or instrumentalities thereof; and (2) proclaim such modification on continuance of any existing duty on other import restrictions such continuance of existing duty-free or excise treatment, or such additional import restrictions, as he determines to be required or appropriate to carry out any such trade agreements."

of this statute? Two arguments can be made. First, we can reiterate the argument that separates the first clause from the limitations of the second clause and thereby authorizes any "trade agreement."[163] Part IV deals with trade and so is arguably authorized. Secondly, insofar as Part IV clauses relate to other GATT clauses, all the arguments made for the validity of GATT in 1947 apply to urge the validity of Part IV.[164] However, Part IV is a most radical departure from prior GATT language. True, the "old GATT" included Article XVIII which contains elaborate provisions regarding economic development of less developed countries. But these provisions are exceptions to, or escapes from, the other GATT commitments. No additional obligations, other than to consult and report, are imposed by Article XVIII. Part IV, on the other hand, commits developed countries to "refrain from introducing" barriers on products from less developed countries (whether subject to tariff schedule concessions in GATT or not),[165] to refrain from new fiscal measures that would hamper exports from these countries,[166] and so forth. It further provides that GATT shall establish institutional arrangements to accomplish the purposes of Part IV.[167] These commitments have purposes which arguably go beyond anything contemplated by the Trade Agreements Act of 1945.[168] Does the 1945 statutory language reenacted in 1962 have a new and expanded meaning? There is some basis for the argument that it does.[169] However, the failure of Congress to approve the Organization for Trade Cooperation in 1956 argues against an expanding interpretation of the trade agreements authority.[170] Consequently, to justify United States entry into the Part IV amendments, it may be necessary for the President to rely on his executive powers. Since the commitments in Part IV are carefully hedged and expressly subject to contrary "compelling reasons, which may include legal reasons,"[171] it is possible to argue that Part IV entry was within the presidential power even without statutory authority. If anything, the entry into Part IV demonstrates the anomaly of United States participation in GATT without a statutory framework for Con-

[163] See the text accompanying notes 50–54 above.
[164] See the discussion in the text at Part II.A.1; and Appendix A.
[165] GATT Article XXXVII(1)(b).   [166] GATT Article XXXVII(1)(c).
[167] GATT Article XXXVIII(1) and (2)(f).
[168] Article XXXV(2), for instance, states as a principal objective the "need for a rapid and sustained expansion of the export earnings of the less developed contracting parties."
[169] The Trade Expansion Act of 1962 contains some recognition of the problems of less developed countries by providing for the possibility of free entry of tropical, agricultural, and forestry commodities. See 19 USC § 1833 (1964). An early proposed version of this statute listed as one purpose, "to assist in the progress of countries in the earlier stages of economic development." HR Rep. No. 2518, 87th Cong., 2nd Sess., 5 (1962). This was omitted at a later stage.
[170] See the text accompanying note 101 above.   [171] GATT Article XXXVII(1).

gressional participation, and shows to what extent foreign commerce matters have come under the control of the executive branch of the government.

B.   Is GATT "law" in the United States?

A question separate from the validity of GATT as an international agreement of the United States is the "domestic law" effect of GATT within this country. To put it another way, the United States may have validly entered GATT, but it may only obligate the United States internationally, without being directly applicable in domestic courts or proceedings. In this section will be examined the general question of whether GATT has a domestic law effect in the United States, leaving for Part III the discussion of the extent and nature of that effect, if it does exist.

First, some general propositions about international agreements under constitutional law must be reviewed. The reader will recall the established rule that treaties, submitted only to the Senate, can be domestic law just as if the treaty were enacted by both houses as legislation.[172] This is true, so the doctrine goes, if the treaty is "self-executing," which, in turn, is ascertained by examining the language of the treaty (does it give direct rights to a litigant?) and the intent of its draftsmen.[173] This rule contrasts with the law of many nations, particularly the Commonwealth and Scandinavian countries, where no international treaty or agreement has a domestic law effect.[174] The doctrine for "treaties" also applies to executive agreements, both those entered pursuant to an act of Congress and those entered pursuant to the President's powers,[175] as the well-known Belmont[176] and Pink[177] cases illustrate.

These propositions seem simple enough, and there is an extensive literature concerning them,[178] but the application of these rules can be very difficult, and specific situations give rise to analytical difficulties that lurk behind the generalities.

---

[172] Bishop, "General Course of Public International Law," 201; Byrd, *Treaties and Executive Agreements*, chapter 5; and *Restatement*, § 141.

[173] Bishop, "General Course of Public International Law," 201; and *Restatement*, § 141 (comment and illustrations).

[174] Bishop, "General Course of Public International Law," 201; Brownlie, *Principles of Public International Law*, 43; and Buergenthal, "The Domestic Status of the European Commission of Human Rights: A Second Look" (1966) 7 *Journal of the International Commission of Jurists* 55 (the author discusses the domestic law effect of treaties in a synoptic fashion for a number of European countries in relation to the European Convention on Human Rights).

[175] *Restatement*, §§ 142, 143, and 144.

[176] *United States* v. *Belmont*, 301 US 324 (1937). Of course, the extent of that domestic effect may differ.

[177] *United States* v. *Pink*, 315 US 203 (1941).   [178] See notes 172–174 above.

1.   An agreement authorized by Congress

Examination of the domestic law effect of GATT in this country must begin with the Trade Agreements Act as it existed in 1945. Once again we meet the interesting bifurcated power delegation to the President:

(1) To enter into foreign trade agreements . . .
(2) To proclaim such modification of existing duties and other import restrictions
     . . . [etc.] . . . as are required or appropriate to carry out any foreign trade
     agreement.[179]

This language seems to indicate that only clause (2) authorizes a domestic law effect. To express it another way, this statute appears to distinguish the authority to obligate the United States internationally in clause (1) from the authority to make domestic law in clause (2).[180] On this view, then, only the President's proclamation and not the trade agreement, as such, has a domestic law effect.

This hypothesis will now be tested by examining the statutory language, the legislative history of the statute, the GATT language and preparatory work, judicial decisions, and the presidential pact regarding proclamations.

THE STATUTORY LANGUAGE

The bifurcated power delegation noted above does not necessarily lead to the conclusion stated by the hypothesis. One can argue that the word "proclaim" refers simply to a convenient symbolic act, a mere "announcement," in order that the public can take cognizance of the international agreement.[181] The notes to the *Restatement* (*Second*) *of Foreign Relations Law* provide some support for this view by indicating that "[e]xecutive [a]greements are not usually proclaimed by the President unless they modify tariff schedules."[182] Also, sometimes an international agreement will itself provide that it becomes effective upon "proclamation,"[183] simply because this is a convenient act to use as the "starting gun." Furthermore, the executive branch might be hesitant to accept the proposition that the

---

[179] See note 29 above for the full text of § 350.
[180] See State Department memorandum reprinted in HR Rep. No. 2007, 84th Cong., 2nd Sess., 113 (1956).
[181] For instance, Article XV of the Reciprocal Trade Agreement Between the United States and Canada, 49 Stat. 3960 (1935) states: "The present agreement shall be proclaimed by the President of the United States of America and shall be ratified by His Majesty the King of Great Britain . . . in respect of the Dominion of Canada . . . The entire agreement shall come into force on the day of the exchange of the proclamation and ratification at Ottawa."
[182] *Restatement*, § 131 (Reporter's Note). The Reporter's Note to § 130 concerning treaties notes the use by the President of a proclamation to establish the entry into effect of a treaty.
[183] See note 181 above.

domestic law effect of trade agreements stems only from the "proclaiming power," since, as argued above, the "trade agreements" power might well be broader than the power to proclaim.

The word "proclaim" is an interesting one in United States law, and seems to defy precise or narrow definition. A perusal of presidential proclamations[184] demonstrates that most are used to establish ceremonial days, or weeks, and holidays. But a sprinkling of other types exist.[185] Proclamations have in the past, for instance, been used to establish the legal effect of statehood for new states.[186] The language of the particular statute involved here seems to use the word "proclaim" in a more significant sense than a mere signal, and the legislative history bears this out.

LEGISLATIVE HISTORY

The language of the statute, including the bifurcated power approach, was probably chosen for the original 1934 Act more as a result of tradition and precedent than for any calculated purpose. As early as 1798, an Act empowered the President to undertake commercial intercourse with a foreign country (France) and "to make proclamation thereof."[187] This terminology was followed in a series of other international trade statutes during the ensuing century. The 1897 Tariff Act, for example, gave the President power to enter into "commercial agreements" with foreign governments, and separately to suspend duties on products subject to the agreement "by proclamation to that effect."[188] The Supreme Court, in

[184] Many presidential proclamations are printed in the *Federal Register* and the *Code of Federal Regulations* as well as in the weekly compilation of Presidential Documents. The proclamations are gathered each year in the *United States Code and Congressional Service*. See 1 CFR §§ 7.1–7.6 (1966) as to the preparation of presidential proclamation and executive orders, excluding those proclaiming treaties or international agreements. In *Texas Association of Steel Importers* v. *Texas Highway Commission*, 364 SW 2d 749, 750 (Tex. Civ. App. 1963), the Texas court used the term "proclamation" in connection with state laws and regulations as follows: Articles 6665 and 6666 provide for the "organization of the Commission and for the establishment and public proclamation of all rules and regulations." This usage suggests that "proclamation" can be used almost synonymously with "issuing a regulation."
[185] See, e.g., Presidential Proclamation No. 3754, 3 CFR 1966 Comp. 90 (effectuating the Florence Agreement on importation of educational, scientific, and cultural materials); and Presidential Proclamation No. 3681, 3 CFR 1964–1965 Comp. 139 (giving Australian military courts jurisdiction over offenses committed in the United States by Australian servicemen).
[186] Enabling Acts set forth the conditions which the state must meet to be admitted and, when those conditions were met, authorize the President to proclaim statehood. See, e.g., Act of March 3, 1875, chapter 139, 18 Stat. 474 (Colorado); and Act of June 16, 1906, chapter 3335, 34 Stat. 267 (Oklahoma). See also J. Sax, *Water Law: Cases and Materials* (1965), 355, 355 note 24.
[187] Act of June 13, 1798, chapter 53, 1 Stat. 565, 566. See Hearings on the Reciprocal Trade Agreements Act Before the Senate Finance Committee, 73rd Cong., 2nd Sess., 82 (1934).
[188] Act of July 24, 1897, chapter 11, §3, 30 Stat. 151, 203.

passing on the constitutionality of the delegation of power to the President under the Tariff Act of 1890, held that no "legislative power" was delegated because the President could only issue a proclamation based on particular findings of fact specified in the statute.[189] Later tariff statutes reinforced this practice of establishing a proclamation power as the normal means for the President to implement tariff changes.[190]

The 1934 legislative history does indicate, however, that the two powers delegated in the statute were considered separate and distinct. Both the Senate Finance Committee and the executive branch witnesses in the 1934 hearings appear to have recognized this separation, relying on the case of *Field* v. *Clark*[191] to establish that neither delegation was unconstitutional.[192] The 1934 House Report also stated:

> Former enactments have delegated to the President the power to fix tariff rates and have also delegated to the President the power to enter into executive agreements concerning tariff rates.[193]

The Report went on to note that these enactments had not been held unconstitutional by the courts.

The distinction was perhaps even more forcefully presented by Senator George speaking for the 1934 Act on the floor of the Senate. Although certain of his premises were either overboard or need modification in the light of *Belmont* and *Pink*, his statement is certainly significant evidence of Congressional intent:

> The well-recognized distinction between an executive agreement and a treaty is that the former cannot alter the existing law and must conform to all prior statutory enactments, whereas a treaty, if ratified by and with the advice and consent of two-thirds of the Senate itself becomes the supreme law of the land and takes precedence over any prior statutory enactment. If the contemplated agreements to be effective should require Senate's ratification, there would be no need for the proposed legislation, inasmuch as the President would then simply negotiate a treaty which, if ratified by the Senate, would itself have the effect of changing the tariff rates. However, in the present Bill, the Congress proposes to change the prevailing tariff law so that the proposed executive agreements may be made in harmony with the revised law. This is a fundamental distinction and answers the question as to why the Bill is here. A mere executive agreement can be made by the President without the consent of Congress. It is equally true – and the fact demonstrates beyond all question the real nature of the agreements – that the agreements contemplated in the present Bill could not be made effective by the President without prior Congressional authorization.[194]

---

[189] *Field* v. *Clark*, 143 US 649, 681 (1892).
[190] See Hearings on the Reciprocal Trade Agreements Act Before the Senate Finance Committee, 73rd Cong., 2nd Sess., 82–95 (1934).
[191] 143 US 649 (1892).
[192] See Hearings on the Reciprocal Trade Agreements Act Before the Senate Finance Committee, 73rd Cong., 2nd Sess., 59, 60 (1934).
[193] HR Rep. No. 1000, 73rd Cong., 2nd Sess., 11 (1934).   [194] 78 Cong. Rec. 10072 (1934).

The Senate and House Reports at the time of the Act's extension in 1943 reinforce this position. The Senate Report, for instance, stated:

Under the Trade Agreements Act changes in our tariff rates are made, so far as our domestic law is concerned, by the President's proclamation under the authority of the Trade Agreements Act. Changes in the tariff rates are not made by the agreements, *per se* . . . It is precisely the same procedural principle as that on which the Interstate Commerce Commission is authorized by Congress to fix fair and reasonable railroad rates.[195]

The Congressional meaning of "proclaim" in the trade agreements context, then, is not the simple ceremonial signal involved in a Thanksgiving Day proclamation, but rather is the means by which bargains struck with foreign trading nations are carried into law at home by the President.

GATT LANGUAGE AND PREPARATORY WORK

Even if, contrary to the view propounded above, the President was delegated the authority under the Act to enter a self-executing trade agreement, if he did not choose to enter this type of agreement (and the language of the agreement reflects this choice), then it would not be domestic law *per se*.[196] An examination of the 1947 trade agreement and its preparatory work is thus necessary in order to ascertain if that agreement purported to be self-executing or non-self-executing. It can be argued that the latter is the better interpretation, although the evidence is at least equivocal.

Many clauses of GATT read as though they were meant to be directly applicable as domestic law.[197] Moreover, several of these clauses were drawn from those portions of the ITO Draft Charter[198] which were intended to be applied in a self-executing manner.[199] However, it will be

---

[195] S. Rep. No. 258, 78th Cong., 1st Sess., 47, 48 (1943).
[196] *Restatement*, § 143 (comment).
[197] For instance, Article VI(3) of GATT begins: "No contravailing duty shall be levied on any product of the territory of another contracting party in excess of . . ."
[198] The general provisions of GATT are drawn mostly from what became chapter IV ("Commercial Policy") of the charter for the ITO. See Final Act, United Nations Conference on Trade and Employment (1947–1948), reprinted in UN Doc. ICITO/1/4 (1948). In previous drafts of the ITO Charter this chapter was chapter V. See UN Doc. EPCT/34 (1947). The draft of GATT contained in UN Doc. EPCT/34, at 65 (1947) includes notes relating the GATT Articles to Articles in the then draft ITO Charter. GATT, *Analytical Index to the General Agreements* (2nd revision, 1966), also gives corresponding numbers of the Havana Charter to the related GATT Article.
[199] At the London meeting of the Preparatory Committee of the United Nations Conference on Trade and Employment, Harry Hawkins, representing the United States, said: "This charter would deal with the subjects which the Preparatory Committee has assigned to its five working committees. It should deal with these subjects in precise detail so that the obligations of member governments would be clear and unambiguous. Most of these subjects readily lend themselves to such treatment. Provisions on such subjects, once agreed upon, would be self-executing and could be applied by the governments concerned without further elaboration or international actions." UN Doc. EPCT/C.II/PV2, at 8 (1946).

remembered that GATT itself has never technically come into force:[200] it is applied by the United States and other original parties only by virtue of the Protocol of Provisional Application. The language of this Protocol is that of commitment to apply GATT, not language of immediate application.[201] Moreover, there are other indications that the draftsmen of the Protocol did not intend a self-executing effect.[202] For example, at one point the American delegate spoke as follows:

[P]rovided there is simultaneous publication and entry into force of the document, there would be no objection if there were differences in the actual time at which they were put provisionally into force, provided there was a date before which that must be done.[203]

Since by definition a self-executing agreement requires no further steps to be put into force, this language is evidence of a non-self-executing intent.

COURT APPLICATION

Once again the American court treatment of GATT can be discussed in two parts. The Customs Court and the Court of Customs and Patent Appeals uniformly refer to GATT by citing the relevant presidential proclamation as reprinted in the *Treasury Decision* series.[204] In these courts,

[200] See the introduction to Part II of the text.
[201] 61 Stat. Part 6, at A2051 (1947); 55 UNTS 308 (1950):

    1. The Government of . . . [eight named nations including the United States] . . . *undertake*, provided that this Protocol shall have been signed on behalf of all the foregoing Governments not later than November 15, 1947, to *apply* provisionally on and after January 1, 1948:
        (a) Parts I and III of the General Agreement on Tariffs and Trade, and
        (b) Part II of the agreement to the fullest extent not inconsistent with the existing legislation.
    2. The foregoing governments shall make effective such provisional application of the General Agreement, in respect of any of their territories other than their metropolitan territories, on or after January 1, 1948, upon the expiration of 30 days from the day on which notice of such application is received by the Secretary-General of the United Nations.
    3. Any other government signatory to this protocol shall make effective such provisional application of the General Agreement, on or after January 1, 1948, upon the expiration of 30 days from the day of signature of this protocol on behalf of such government.

    Emphasis added. Compare the discussion of self-executing treaties in W. Bishop, *International Law Cases and Materials* (2nd edn., 1962), 146–149. In particular, the case of *Robertson* v. *General Electric Co.*, 32 F. 2d 495 (4th Cir. 1929) which, in holding a treaty provision non-self-executing, noted that the language of the statute provided that a patent period "extension shall be made, not by the instrument itself, but by each of the high contracting parties."
[202] See UN Doc. EPCT/TAC/PV.4 at 15, 19, and 22 (1947).
[203] UN Doc. EPCT/TAC/PV.4 at 22 (1947).
[204] See note 105 above. Although the chances are that at least some Customs Court or Court of Customs and Patent Appeals opinions fail to cite the proclamation reference when

then, at least in tariff matters, it can be assumed that it is the proclamation which is the "law," not the executive agreement.

In other courts, usage is less clear. Apparently, only three federal court cases have cited GATT.[205] Although the courts in these cases mentioned GATT only by its name, or by the *Statutes at Large* reference[206] (which does not contain the proclamation), the issues were such that GATT was not directly applied. In the only four state and territorial court decisions which mention GATT, the situation differs. One of these was decided without ruling on the legal effect of GATT,[207] but the other three purported to rely, at least in part, directly on GATT.[208] In each of these latter cases GATT was treated as a "treaty," and applied as law without citing its proclamation,[209] although one court mentioned generally that such agreements were proclaimed.[210] In three California Attorney General's opinions that involve GATT,[211] there was also no mention of the proclamation.

Yet in each of these seven cases and opinions, the provision of GATT involved was one which had in fact been proclaimed.[212] So the distinction

relying on GATT, no such opinion has been found and it is clear that the usual practice is to cite the Treasury Decision which incorporates the proclamation.

[205] See note 109 above.

[206] *Morgantown Glassware Guild Inc.* v. *Humphrey*, 236 F. 2d 670 (DC Cir. 1956), simply mentions "General Agreement on Tariffs and Trade, Geneva, 1947." *Talbot* v. *Atlantic Steel Co.*, 275 F. 2d 4 (DC Cir. 1960) also merely uses the title of the agreement. *C. Tennant, Sons and Co.* v. *Dill*, 158 F. Supp. 63, 66 (SDNY 1957), refers to "General Agreement on Tariffs and Trade, commonly known as GATT, 61 Stat., Part 5, pp. A3, A7 et seq."

[207] *Texas Association of Steel Importers* v. *Texas Highway Commission*, 364 SW 2d 749 (Tex. Civ. App. 1963).

[208] *Territory* v. *Ho*, 41 Hawaii 565 (1967); *Baldwin-Lima-Hamilton Corp.* v. *Superior Court*, 208 Cal. App. 2d 803, 25 Cal. Reptr. 798 (1962) (hearing denied December 19, 1962); and *Bethlehem Steel Corp.* v. *Board of Commissioners*, Civil No. 899165, 897591 (Super. Ct. County of Los Angeles 1966).

[209] For an example of this sort of judicial treatment of GATT when applied as law, see *Territory* v. *Ho*, 41 Hawaii 565 at 568 (1967): "This case poses the question: Is an executive agreement, such as the General Agreement on Tariffs and Trade, a treaty within the meaning of this constitutional provision [the Supremacy Clause of Article VI, section 2] so that it has the same efficacy as a treaty made by the President by and with the advice and consent of the Senate? We think it is, under the decisions of the Supreme Court of the United States in *United States* v. *Belmont* . . . and *United States* v. *Pink*."

[210] *Baldwin-Lima-Hamilton Corp.* v. *Superior Court*, 208 Cal. App. 2d 803, 820, 25 Cal. Reptr. 798, 820 (1962) (hearing denied December 19, 1962).

[211] See note 106 above.

[212] The *Ho* case invoked Article III(1) and (4) and Article XX of GATT. These provisions were proclaimed in the United States by Presidential Proclamation No. 2761A (3 CFR 1943–1948 Comp. 139) and subsequent amendments to these provisions were also proclaimed by Presidential Proclamations Nos. 279 (3 CFR 1943–1948 Comp. 204), 3513 (3 CFR 1959–1963 Comp. 246), and 2829 (3 CFR 1949–1953 Comp. 7). See Appendix C. The *Baldwin-Lima* case invoked Article III(2) and (5) of GATT which were proclaimed by Presidential Proclamation No. 2761A (3 CFR 2829 1943–1948 Comp. 139) and subsequently amended by Presidential Proclamation No. 2829 (3 CFR 1949–1953 Comp. 7). The *Bethlehem Steel* case relied on *Baldwin-Lima* and, insofar as it depended upon GATT, involved the same Articles. See note 286 below.

between the court's approach and that being propounded in this article would not have led to a difference in result in this cases that have so far arisen. The careful attorney must, however, beware of possible pitfalls in the distinction between a trade agreement proclaimed and one unproclaimed, particularly as to those portions of GATT, or agreements concerning GATT obligations, which have not been proclaimed.

THE PRESIDENTIAL PRACTICE OF PROCLAMATION

Appendix C contains a detailed analysis of the GATT agreements and protocols, including whether or not each has been proclaimed in whole or in part. This chart reveals an apparently bewildering diversity of treatment. Up to the time of this writing, there have been over 100 international agreements of various labels which have been opened for signature to GATT contracting parties, and deposited either at the United Nations (up to 1955) or at GATT headquarters (after 1955). About four-fifths of these have come into force. The United States has signed most of the GATT agreements, and proclaimed a large number of those signed but some which it signed and which are in force have not been proclaimed, whereas some which it signed but which are not yet in force have been proclaimed.[213]

Despite the apparent diversity of treatment, however, there is a discernible pattern in the proclamation practice. First, whenever a United States tariff rate is changed by an agreement, it has been proclaimed.[214] At times, for convenience, the proclamation may precede the effective date of the agreement, in which case the proclamation specifies the condition subsequent which effectuates the changes.[215] Secondly, a number of GATT agreements or parts of agreements which affect only tariff schedules of other countries have not been proclaimed by the United States.[216] Since these are obligations running to this country, there is no need for a domestic law effect here, and it is reasonable to omit proclaiming them. In fact, in some of these cases the United States is not even a party to the agreements.[217] Thirdly, some of the unproclaimed agreements are short-term temporary measures or are confined to administrative matters for which it is difficult to see why domestic legal consequences would or should occur.[218]

Most of the original GATT agreement was proclaimed, of course, as well as almost all of the modifications to the general Articles,[219] except for the recently added Part IV which apparently is not intended to be domestic

---

[213] See, e.g., Agreements Nos. 30 and 52 in Appendix C.
[214] See Agreements Nos. 41, 52, 57, and 83 in Appendix C.
[215] See Agreement No. 57 in Appendix C.
[216] See, e.g., Agreements Nos. 18, 19, 29, and 30 in Appendix C.
[217] See, e.g., Agreement No. 48 in Appendix C.
[218] See, e.g., Agreements Nos. 4 and 36 in Appendix C.   [219] See Appendix C.

law.[220] However, certain agreements which affect basic GATT obligations, but which do not actually modify the text, have been proclaimed.[221] In addition, some agreements providing for provisional accession of new members to GATT have not been proclaimed, although it could be argued that such proclamation is unnecessary.[222]

Sometimes there is a considerable time gap between entry into force of a particular GATT agreement and its proclamation in this country. This may be due more to the political complexion of the executive branch than to the operation of any legal theory. Thus, during the mid-1950s, GATT agreements tended not to get proclaimed at all. It is difficult to ascertain from published sources whether this state of affairs was due to antagonism to GATT and GATT policy on the part of certain governmental officials, or to the Bricker Amendment[223] "scare" which may have prompted the Republican Administration to avoid using executive agreements to generate domestic law whenever possible. These political factors might also explain the State Department position, taken in its letter to the Hawaii court,[224] that GATT has no legal effect on state law. In late 1962, with a new administration in office, there were several massive presidential proclamations which incorporated a number of early previously unproclaimed GATT agreements.[225]

The presidential proclamation practice, then, supports the hypothesis that it is the proclamation which is domestic law. This is clearest when domestic tariff schedules are concerned. Whether it is also true when the general clauses of GATT are involved cannot, perhaps, be inductively proved from the record.

2.   *Presidential power to give domestic legal effect to trade agreements*

Although it is clear that the President can, in some contexts, enter into an executive agreement which will itself have domestic legal consequences,[226] there has been no assertion of this power in connection with GATT.[227] Insofar as the President makes agreements pursuant to the power delegated to him by the various trade agreements acts, it seems

---

[220] See Agreement No. 98 in Appendix C.
[221] See Agreement No. 59 in Appendix C. But see Agreement No. 78 in Appendix C.
[222] See, e.g., Agreements Nos. 87 and 92 in Appendix C.
[223] See Bishop, *International Law, Cases and Materials*, 104–105; and P. Kauper, *Constitutional Law, Cases and Materials* (3rd edn., 1966), 265.
[224] See note 288 below.
[225] Presidential Proclamation No. 3513, 3 CFR 1959–1963 Comp. 246. See Appendix C.
[226] E.g., *United States* v. *Pink*, 315 US 203 (1942); *United States* v. *Belmont*, 301 US 324 (1937); and *Restatement*, § 144.
[227] This statement is limited to the GATT agreements listed in Appendix C.

very dubious that he can give them domestic legal effect without proclaiming them.

The courts of appeals opinion in the *Capps* case, mentioned earlier,[228] while holding that the executive agreement there involved was *ultra vires* and void, announced another reason for not enforcing a contract which was made pursuant to the agreement:

> There was no pretense of complying with the requirements of this statute. The President did not cause an investigation to be made by the Tariff Commission, the Commission did not conduct an investigation or make findings or recommendations, and the President made no findings of fact and issued no proclamation.[229]

Although the Supreme Court did not discuss this aspect while affirming on different grounds, the *Capps* case suggests that where regulation of foreign commerce is involved, the statutory scheme must be followed. If this suggestion were accepted, few if any trade agreements could have domestic law validity through the exercise of presidential powers. The statutory scheme would need to be followed, and, as argued above, proclamation would be essential for domestic law validity. It may be noted that the government's petition for *certiorari* in the *Capps* case took a less restrictive view of the executive's power.[230]

C.   Summary

To summarize the analysis of GATT's place in United States domestic law, it seems that insofar as GATT (including all its related protocols) is entered into by the President pursuant to the Trade Agreements Acts, it becomes domestic law only by virtue of a "proclamation." Both the statutory language and the legislative history lead to this conclusion. The practice of the courts and the presidential proclamation practice have not, at least, been inconsistent with this proposition. Moreover, this method of handling the domestic law effect of executive agreements has many admirable features from a policy viewpoint. One of the difficulties in determining the domestic legal effect of treaties and international agreements is the question of whether they are self-executing or not.[231] In the case of executive agreements, this difficulty can be largely overcome if a domestic legal effect results only from a proclamation or other domestic law-giving action. Not only are some

---

[228] See *United States* v. *Guy W. Capps Inc.*, 204 F. 2d 655 (4th Cir. 1953), affirmed on other grounds 348 US 296 (1954); and the text accompanying note 141 above.

[229] *United States* v. *Guy W. Capps Inc.*, 204 F. 2d 655 at 658 (4th Cir. 1953), affirmed on other grounds 348 US 296 (1954).

[230] *Petition for Writ of Certiorari to the United States Court of Appeals for the Fourth Circuit,* *United States* v. *Guy W. Capps Inc.*, 204 F. 2d 655 (4th Cir. 1953), affirmed on other grounds, 348 US 296 (1954).

[231] See *Restatement*, §§ 141 (comment) and 142 (comment).

ambiguities resolved by this methodology, but in certain circumstances this technique adds flexibility to the conduct of foreign relations. For example, the effectiveness or domestic application of an international agreement can be conditioned upon factual or other conditions precedent, with the proclamation being the certification of the meeting of the conditions. Additionally, and speaking pragmatically, this technique gives the President affirmative control over the domestic legal effect which he may need to exercise in some cases, even if it means a breach of obligation. It also gives Congress greater flexibility and control since Congress can prescribe limits to the power to proclaim, just as it may prescribe limits to the power to enter into agreements, and the extent of the two powers need not always coincide.

On the other hand, requiring a presidential proclamation is cumbersome and, because of the technical nature of the subject, may lead to error.[232] A court confronted with a case where the proclamation deviated from the trade agreement for no apparent reason would probably find a way to follow the trade agreement language,[233] either by "construing" the proclamation to be consistent with the agreement, or by concluding, in the face of the arguments to the contrary, that the agreement had a direct legal effect on domestic law. Perhaps an appropriate solution in future trade agreement legislation would be to abandon the old two-part formula, which, it will be remembered, stemmed from a period when fear of Supreme Court invalidation on grounds of delegation of legislative power were greater, and when (prior to *Belmont* and *Pink*) executive agreements were even less understood than they are today. The advantages of the old formula, mentioned above, could be retained and some of the disadvantages discarded if a regulation procedure were adopted authorizing the President or his delegate to take action which would give domestic legal effect to a trade agreement to the extent desired by the President and within his power as delegated by Congress.

III.   The extent of GATT's domestic law effect in the United States

Part II dealt with the question whether GATT has any domestic law effect in the United States. The conclusion reached was that to the extent GATT

---

[232] See, e.g., Presidential Proclamation No. 2865 (recital No. 10), 3 CFR 1949–1953 Comp. 38; Presidential Proclamation No. 3190 (recital No. 13), 3 CFR 1954–1958 Comp. 118; Proclamation No. 3562, 3 CFR 1959–1963 Comp. 315; and Presidential Proclamation No. 3597, 33 CFR 1964 Supp. 51. As to the formalistic nature of the recitals, see HR Rep. 1761, 85th Cong., 2nd Sess., 72 (1958) (minority views).

[233] Of course, if the differential were substantial or based on substantive reasons, the proclamation would be followed as domestic law. An example of a proclamation deviating from the related GATT agreement is Presidential Proclamation No. 3040 (para. 8 relating to Uruguayan accession to GATT), 3 CFR 1949–1953 Comp. 211.

and subsequent protocols have been "proclaimed" by the President they have a domestic law effect. It was suggested that it was very dubious that GATT agreements and protocols would have domestic legal effect in the United States *per se*, that is, without proclamation. Since the original GATT agreement and many amending protocols have, in fact, been proclaimed,[234] the next question concerns the relationship of this GATT "law" to both federal and state law in the United States. To put it another way, assuming GATT is "law" in the United States, at least to the extent that it has been proclaimed, is that law superior or inferior to other federal or state laws?

Two GATT provisions have a profound influence on this question; consequently, much of this part of the article is concerned with interpreting these two clauses. First, and most significant, is the clause in the Protocol of Provisional Application (through which GATT is applied) which states that governments will apply "Part II of that Agreement to the fullest extent not inconsistent with existing legislation."[235] Secondly, of concern only to the relation of GATT to state or territorial law, is paragraph 12 of Article XXIV which states:

Each contracting party shall take such reasonable measures as may be available to it to ensure observance of the provisions of this Agreement by the regional and local governments and authorities within its territory.[236]

A.   *GATT and federal law*

The general principles of American law concerning executive agreements which have domestic law effect are typically stated as follows:

1. executive agreements pursuant to acts of Congress supersede prior inconsistent legislation and are superseded (as domestic law) by subsequent inconsistent legislation;
2. executive agreements pursuant only to the President's independent authority do not supersede inconsistent legislation, whether prior or subsequent.[237]

For this purpose GATT would probably be considered an executive agreement by most lawyers and officials, but since it derives its domestic law effect from the presidential proclamations, it is technically more precise to analyze these proclamations as if they were regulations issued by the

---

[234] See Appendix C, and the text accompanying note 105 above.
[235] 61 Stat. Part 6, at A2051 (1947); 55 UNTS 308 (1950).
[236] GATT Article XXIV(12). Originally this was Article XXIV(6) of GATT, but the amendments contained in the "Special Protocol Relating to Article XXIV" (see Appendix C, Agreement No. 7) renumbered the paragraphs.
[237] *Restatement*, §§ 142, 143, and 144. See the authorities cited in note 172 above.

executive.[238] As regulations, however, they apparently have the same impact on prior and subsequent legislation as executive agreements: if pursuant to Congressional authority, the later in time prevails; if not, the legislation prevails.[239]

Analysis of GATT *vis-à-vis* federal law must give separate treatment to Part II, which alone is subject to the "existing legislation" clause of the Protocol of Provisional Application. The others – Parts I, III, and IV – may be treated as ordinary executive agreements.

1. Parts I, III and IV of GATT

Parts I and III were part of the original GATT and were proclaimed by the President.[240] The more recent addition, Part IV, has not been proclaimed,[241] and therefore probably has no domestic law effect.[242] In any case its provisions are such as to make it unlikely that a concrete case could come up in domestic law,[243] and its language strongly suggests that it was not intended to be self-executing.[244]

Part I, containing the most-favored-nations and tariff concession provisions, and Part II, consisting mostly of administrative provisions, as proclaimed, appear to supersede *prior* inconsistent federal legislation.[245] This

[238] See the discussion in the text at Part II.B.

[239] Of course, if a court were faced with such a case, an attempt would be made to construe so as to avoid inconsistency. Also, a regulation would probably yield even to prior legislation unless the legislation authorizing that regulation clearly manifested an intent to override prior legislation. See, e.g., *United States* v. *Mersky*, 361 US 431 (1960). However, it has been the general practice of the courts to give precedence to the tariff proclamation (a form of regulation) over such prior inconsistent legislation as the Tariff Act of 1930. See the authorities cited in notes 104 and 105 above.

[240] See Appendix C.

[241] The text of Part IV of GATT is contained in GATT Doc. IPRO/65–1 (1965), and at (1964) 51 *Department of State Bulletin* 922. Part IV entered into force for the countries which had signed it on June 27, 1966. GATT Press Release 962, June 28, 1966.

[242] As contended in the text, a proclamation is probably necessary for domestic law effect. It could be argued, however, that Part IV was entered into pursuant to presidential constitutional powers and not pursuant to authority delegated by the Trade Agreements Act: thus, no proclamation would be needed to give domestic law effect. Indeed, as indicated in the discussion in the text at Part II.B, there may be some difficulty in tying United States entry into Part IV to authority under the Trade Agreements Act. On the other hand, the language of Part IV can also be read as non-self-executing. I have intentionally set out the alternatives in a qualified and tentative manner to illustrate the ambiguous position that Part IV has in United States law.

[243] See the discussion in the text at Part II.A.3. Part IV consists primarily of general principles and objectives, or procedures for consultation. The Article involving commitments, Article XXXVII, is qualified by the language "to the fullest extent possible," or phrases such as "make every effort" or "give active consideration."

[244] The qualifying language mentioned in the previous footnote also suggests that Part IV is not self-executing.

[245] Unless specific exception for prior legislation is made in a particular clause, such as that in Article II(1)(b).

is clearly the case where domestic tariff rates are involved; the courts have uniformly held the latest GATT protocols to be the current law.[246] Indeed, no case holding a pre-GATT federal law superior to Part I or Part III of GATT has been found. Subsequent federal legislation would, of course prevail under the "later in time" rule.[247]

2.   Part II of GATT and the "existing legislation" clause

The major example of subsequent United States legislation inconsistent with Part II of GATT is the 1951 amendment to the Agricultural Adjustment Act of 1933[248] requiring certain agriculture import quotas to be imposed irrespective of GATT commitments contained in Article XI, Part II of GATT. This example confirms the superiority of later federal legislation over GATT in United States domestic law.

More interesting, however, is the case of pre-GATT legislation. Because the Protocol of Provisional Application applies Part II of GATT subject to "existing legislation,"[249] the usual rule making executive agreements superior to prior inconsistent legislation is reversed. Although the Administration has undertaken to furnish Congress[250] and, later, GATT headquarters[251] with a listing of such prior inconsistent legislation, there are

---

[246] See the text accompanying note 104 above.

[247] In a 1951 statute, for example, Congress stipulated as follows: "As soon as practicable, the President shall take such action as is necessary to suspend, withdraw or prevent the application of any reduction in any rate of duty, or binding of any existing customs or excise treatment, or other concession contained in any trade agreement entered into under authority of section 350 of the Tariff Act of 1930, as amended and extended, [the Reciprocal Trade Agreements provisions] to imports from the Union of Soviet Socialist Republics and to imports from any nation or area dominated or controlled by the foreign government or foreign organization controlling the world communist movement." At that time Czechoslovakia was the only communist country which was party to GATT, and the President withdrew GATT "application" from that country. Presidential Proclamation No. 2935, 3 CFR 1949–1953 Comp. 121, carried out by letter to the Secretary of the Treasury (reproduced in TD 52837). This action may have been inconsistent with GATT, although the United States obtained a "declaration" from GATT which "took note" of the United States action and may constitute a waiver under Article XXV of GATT, *Basic Instruments and Selected Documents*, vol. II, 36. See also Jackson, "The Puzzle of GATT," 153. In other post-GATT statutes, "escape clause" language was adopted that did not coincide with the relevant GATT clause in Article XIV. 65 Stat. 73 (1951); 69 Stat. 166 (1955). The United States Executive, however, apparently took the position that the 1951 statute was consistent with Article XIX. Report on Trade-Agreement Escape Clauses. Message from the President, HR Doc. No. 328, 82nd Cong., 2nd Sess. (1952). But *cf.* S. Metzger, *Trade Agreements and the Kennedy Round* (1964), 47.

[248] See the text accompanying note 87 above.

[249] 61 Stat. Part 6, at A2051 (1947); 55 UNTS 308 (1950).

[250] Hearings on Trade Agreements Extension Act of 1951 Before the Senate Finance Committee, 82nd Cong., 1st Sess., 1195 (1951). See also Note, (1961) 61 *Columbia Law Review* 505.

[251] See GATT Doc. L/2375/Add. l, at 17 (1965), which reproduces information submitted by governments in January 1955 and previously included in GATT Doc. L/309/Add. 1 and 2. This list, and that cited in note 250 above, may not be all inclusive – see the language used to introduce those lists.

several interpretative difficulties relating to the terms "existing" and "inconsistent" in the Protocol.

As to "existing," the question naturally arises: "existing when?" This ambiguity was considered in an early GATT session and was resolved there when the Contracting Parties "accepted" a ruling by their chairman that "existing legislation" refers "to legislation existing on October 30, 1947, the date of the Protocol as written at the end of its last paragraph."[252] The argument that the relevant point of time is the date on which a given nation signed the protocol was not adopted.[253] Another puzzle relating to the meaning of "existing" is the treatment of amendments to Part II. For example, a sequence such as the following could occur:

1. October 30, 1947, the Protocol of Provisional Application is signed agreeing to apply GATT;
2. in 1950, United States legislation consistent with the existing GATT is enacted; and
3. in 1955, a protocol amending GATT enters into force, and this protocol is inconsistent with the 1950 statute.

What would be the status of the 1950 legislation? Technically, the later in time would prevail, which here is the GATT protocol. Since the GATT amending provision[254] states that amendments are applicable only to those nations which accept them, the President can always refuse to accept an amendment which is inconsistent with domestic law if he desires to avoid the inconsistency.[255]

---

[252] Ruling by the chairman on August. 11, 1949, GATT, *Basic Instruments and Selected Documents* (1952), vol. II, 35; GATT Doc. CP.3/SR.40, at 4–7 (1949). See Jackson, "The Puzzle of GATT," 139.

[253] Protocols that involved accession of new contracting parties under Article XXXIII of GATT, subsequent to the Protocol of Provisional Application, have been more explicit as to the date of "existing legislation." See, e.g., the Annecy Protocol of Terms of Accession of Switzerland, GATT, *Basic Instruments and Selected Documents*, 14th Supplement (1966), 6. As to countries which became GATT contracting parties through sponsorship under Article XXVI, it is not clear what is the relevant date for "existing legislation," although technically it is probably that date which was the relevant date for the sponsoring contracting party. This would be consistent with the view that the sponsored government accepts GATT on the terms and conditions "previously accepted by the metropolitan government on behalf of the territory in question." See Report adopted on December 7, 1961 by the Contracting Parties, GATT, *Basic Instruments and Selected Documents*, 10th Supplement (1962), 69, 73. Jackson, "The Puzzle of GATT," 144.

[254] GATT Article XXX.

[255] The President could, if he had the trade agreements authority to do so, always enter a trade agreement which was inconsistent with GATT, but refuse to proclaim it. In this event, the agreement would not have a domestic law effect, and would not override the domestic law. The United States would be in a technical breach of its international obligation, but the President might decide to do things in this manner in the hope that a change in the legislation could ultimately be obtained to bring it into conformity with the international obligation. Of course, a more desirable procedure might be to sign the international agreement *ad referendum* and then seek Congressional approval.

An interpretative difficulty also turns on the word "inconsistent." The following hypotheticals will assist in forming the issues:

A. Legislation at the time the United States entered GATT *authorized* the President to impose quotas on widgets, and previously the President had imposed such a quota.

B. Similar legislation existed when the United States entered GATT, but the President only later imposed the widget quota.

C. Existing legislation *required* the President to impose the quota whenever he found fact X, and the President had previously found that fact and imposed the quota.

D. Similar legislation existed when GATT was entered, but only later did the President find fact X and impose the quota.

Under interpretations developed in the practice of GATT, cases A and B would not be "inconsistent" and would be violations by the United States of its *international obligation* if the quotas were permitted to continue. Cases C and D, however, are "inconsistent" and would not be such violations. The GATT interpretation is that measures are within the "existing legislation" clause, provided that the legislation on which it is based is by its terms or expressed intent of a mandatory character – that is, it imposes on the executive action.[256] This interpretation is supported by statements in the preparatory work of GATT which will be discussed below.[257]

But what is the domestic law effect of cases A through D? Where the legislation, although inconsistent with Part II of GATT, is not deemed a violation of the international obligation pursuant to the "inconsistent legislation" clause (cases C and D), it would seem clear that it should be considered superior to GATT as domestic law even though GATT is subsequent.[258] This puts the domestic interpretation of the "inconsistent

---

[256] Report approved by the Contracting Parties on August 10, 1949, GATT Doc. CP.3/60/Rev. 1, para. 99, reprinted in GATT, *Basic Instruments and Selected Documents* (1952), vol. II, 49, 62. See the discussion of GATT preparatory work contained in text at Part II.B.1; and Jackson, "The Puzzle of GATT," 140. See also the GATT documents reproduced in GATT, *Basic Instruments and Selected Documents*, 7th Supplement (1959), 104–107; *Basic Instruments and Selected Documents*, 6th Supplement (1958), 60–61; *Basic Instruments and Selected Documents*, 3rd Supplement (1955), 249; and *Basic Instruments and Selected Documents*, 1st Supplement (1953), 61.

[257] See the text accompanying note 277 below.

[258] There is a logical circularity involved in cases C and D in a nation like the United States where an executive agreement pursuant to legislative authority can override previous legislation. Since the Protocol of Provisional Application clause on "existing legislation" was intended to make GATT apply to the fullest extent of executive authority, if the executive has the authority to enter into and proclaim an international agreement which then has the domestic law effect of overriding previous legislation, it could be argued that GATT, even if applied by the Protocol of Provisional Application, should override

legislation" clause in line with the international obligation, and recognizes the superiority of the domestic law.

In case B, the quota imposed, being subsequent to GATT, would prevail in domestic law under the "later in time" rule, even though this would be a clear violation of the international obligation.[259] Case A, however, is more difficult. If for domestic law purposes an inconsistency is found, then the "later in time" rule would provide that the previously established quota was abrogated automatically when GATT became domestic law. But the scope of the President's proclamation should be determinative of this question as to domestic law, and the impact on the previous inconsistent quota would depend on the tenor and interpretation of the subsequent GATT proclamation.

B. GATT and state law

When GATT is considered in relation to inconsistent state law, both of the "problem" clauses of GATT, the "existing legislation" clause already discussed and the "local governments" clause, are involved. Additionally, an important constitutional problem is presented: whether federal control of "foreign commerce" is exclusive and precludes any state regulation of foreign imports or exports. The classic case, of course, was *Brown* v. *Maryland* in 1827,[260] holding invalid a state law requiring an importer of foreign goods to obtain a state license for a fee. In recent years, several cases involving various types of local government regulation of imports[261] – for example, labeling regulations[262] and state agency purchasing

previous legislation, if this country is to fulfill its international obligations. However, the whole gist of the preparatory work of GATT, and the representation made by the Executive branch to Congress, is to the effect that existing legislation would not be affected by GATT without further action by Congress. Thus, despite the fact that to apply GATT to the fullest extent of executive authority would be to override previous federal legislation, it is clear that that was not the intent of the GATT draftsmen.

[259] See the authorities cited in note 237 above. [260] 25 US (12 Wheat.) 419 (1827).

[261] The four state and territorial cases involving GATT cited in note 108 above are among those cases. In addition, there have been several such which do not make any reference to GATT. These include, for example, *Ness Produce Co.* v. *Short*, 263 F. Supp. 586 (D. Ore. 1966), affirmed 385 US 537 (1967) (holding that a meat-labeling law which was based on country of origin, not quality, was not a valid exercise of police power); *Tuppman Thurlow Co. Inc.* v. *Moss*, 252 F. Supp. 641 (MD Tenn. 1966) (holding invalid a Tennessee meat-labeling statute); *Tuppman Thurlow Co. Inc.* v. *Todd*, 230 F. Supp. 230 (MD Ala. 1964) (holding invalid an Alabama meat-inspection law which had resulted in seizure of meat imports); *Cunard SS Co.* v. *Lucci*, 94 NJ Super. 440 (Super. Ct. 1966) (holding unconstitutional a state statute requiring that every advertisement for maritime passage indicate the flag of registry of the vessel); *City of Columbus* v. *Miqdadi*, 25 Ohio Op. 2d 337, 195 NE 2d 923 (Mun. Ct. 1963); and *City of Columbus* v. *McGuire*, 25 Ohio Op. 2d 331, 195 NE 2d 916 (Mun. Ct. 1963).

[262] The Tennessee *Tuppman-Thurlow* and *Ness* cases cited in note 261 above involved labeling statutes.

preferences[263] – have been decided, including one Supreme Court case concerning a tax which discriminated against imports.[264] It is not my intention here to deviate from the purpose of this article to examine this constitutional question in detail. I do want to draw the reader's attention to the issue, however, and note that it can be used as an alternative argument for the invalidity of state law in virtually every case involving a conflict between GATT and state law.[265]

1.   The "existing legislation" clause

In the four state or territorial cases found which cite GATT,[266] Part II clauses have been invoked to override a state law. Some of these laws existed prior to the signing of the Protocol on October 30, 1947,[267] the relevant date for the "existing inconsistent legislation" exemption.[268] There is some question whether this clause was meant to apply to local as well as federal legislation. Three sources of interpretive evidence relating to this question will be examined: the GATT preparatory work, GATT practice, and United States government interpretations and practice.

The first several drafts of GATT did not mention an exception for "existing legislation" for any part of GATT.[269] After tariff negotiations had begun at Geneva, however, all participating delegations were asked

---

[263] The *Baldwin-Lima* and *Bethlehem Steel* cases (see note 108 above), as well as the California Attorney-General's opinions (see note 106 above), involved state "buy American" statutes. The opinion in the *Bethlehem Steel* case suggests that even this type of statute is unconstitutional under the federal Constitution. See note 286 below. This view is propounded by Note, (1960) 12 *Stanford Law Review* 355.

[264] *Department of Revenue* v. *James B. Beam Distilling Co.*, 377 US 341 (1964).

[265] Since GATT is entirely concerned with the question of international trade within the definition of "foreign commerce" in the United States Constitution, it can be seen that every portion of GATT in relation to state laws involves this constitutional issue. Presumably, the federal power over foreign commerce, even if it is exclusive and preempts state regulation of foreign commerce, would have to be balanced against the police power of the state and necessary state regulation for the health, welfare, and morals of its citizenry. GATT Article XX excepts from the application of GATT measures "necessary to protect public morals," "necessary to protect human, animal, or plant life or health," and similar purposes, provided that "such measures are not applied in a manner which would constitute a means of arbitrary or unjustifiable discrimination between countries where the same conditions prevail, or a disguised restriction on international trade." It is possible that, as the cases and United States constitutional law develop, this Article of GATT may play a part in defining the borderline between federal preemption in matters of foreign commerce, and state regulation for the protection of the health, welfare, and morals of its citizens.

[266] See note 108 above.

[267] This is true for this California statute invoked in the California cases and in the California Attorney General's opinions.

[268] See the text accompanying note 252 above.

[269] The latest of these early drafts is contained in Report of the Drafting Committee of the Preparatory Committee of the United Nations Conference on Trade and Employment, UN Doc. EPCT/34, at 65, March 5, 1967.

whether their respective governments could put GATT into effect at the end of the conference.[270] From the answers received, it was learned that a number of governments, while having authority to agree to lower tariffs, could not, without parliamentary approval, agree to those portions of GATT which dealt with nontariff barriers and other general matters, most of which were contained in Part II of GATT.[271] Some delegates, therefore, urged postponing GATT's entry into force until the end of the Havana Conference (when the ITO Charter would be complete),[272] but others feared that such a postponement would be dangerous, since the momentum of the tariff negotiations would be lost, leaks in information might occur, political opposition to the tariff concessions might develop, and disruption in international trade could result.[273] The alternative of putting the tariff concessions into effect without any general nontariff provisions was unacceptable to some representatives, who felt that the tariff commitments could be too easily evaded without the additional protective clauses of Part II.[274] Consequently, when a working party reported a full draft of GATT, its recommendation was to include, as an Article of GATT, a clause similar to the "existing legislation" language ultimately adopted in the Protocol of Provisional Application. The working party's explanation was as follows:

It will be noted that application of Part II is to take place "to the fullest extent not inconsistent with existing legislation." The position of governments unable to put Part II of the Agreement fully into force on a provisional basis without changes in existing legislation is, therefore, covered.[275]

Later, this clause was taken out of the Agreement itself, and put into the separate Protocol.[276]

Explanations of the "existing legislation" clause were made on several occasions. A committee, reporting on the countries that would be able to give provisional application to GATT, stated that "provisional application is interpreted as meaning that action in accordance with Article XXXII which can be taken by executive action."[277] At another point in the deliberations, an American delegate explained the clause as follows:

I think the intent is that it should be what the executive authority can do – in other words, the administration would be required to give effect to the general provisions to the extent that it could do so without either (1) changing existing legislation or (2)

270 UN Doc. EPCT/100, June 18, 1947.   271 UN Doc. EPCT/135, July 24, 1947.
272 UN Doc. EPCT/TAC/PV/4, at 8, August 20, 1947.
273 UN Doc. EPCT/TAC/PV/1, at 3, August 5, 1947.
274 UN Doc. EPCT/TAC/PV/1, at 24, August 5, 1947.
275 UN Doc. EPCT/135, at 9, July 24, 1947.
276 UN Doc. EPCT/196, September 13, 1947.
277 UN Doc. EPCT/W/301, at 7, August 15, 1947.

violating existing legislation. If a particular administrative regulation is necessary
to carry out the law, I should think that the regulation would, of course, have to
stand; but to the extent that the administration had the authority within the
framework of existing laws to carry out these provisions, it would be required to do
so.[278]

Thus the purpose of the "existing legislation" clause is clear: it was to
enable governments which would not otherwise be legally able to do so, to
put GATT into provisional effect soon after the Geneva Conference closed.
Additionally it was realized that the Havana Conference might result in
some changes to portions of the GATT agreement, in particular Part II,[279]
and it seemed reasonable to allow countries with inconsistent legislation to
wait until the results of that conference were known before taking legislative action. In any event, it appears that the clause thus excepted from
GATT only those laws that could not be affected by executive action
without the help of the legislature.

As previously indicated, the Administration in 1951 presented to Congress a list of legislation it deemed inconsistent with GATT.[280] No state
legislation was contained in this list. This could be taken as evidence that it
was felt that the "existing legislation" clause was not intended to exempt
state legislation. A counter-argument, however, would be that the Administration did not believe it was necessary to bring state legislation under the
"existing legislation" clause because, under Article XXIV(12), it was not
affected anyway. More likely, the Administration simply was not aware of
this problem when the list was compiled.

As to the practice of GATT, a thorough search for relevant documents
turned up only one instance when the issue of the relating of the "existing
legislation" clause to state legislation was recognized. This was in the
report of India in response to a request for a list of "existing legislation"
from each GATT party:

At the outset it is necessary to point out that in India the powers to legislate over
matters affecting trade and commerce vest not only in the Indian Parliament but
also in the Legislatures of the States (formerly Provinces of British India and Indian
States). Within the time given, no attempt whatsoever could be made to examine
the legislation of the various States and no idea can, therefore, be formed at this
stage of the possible scope of the Government of India's obligation under paragraph 12 of Article XXIV.[281]

What, then, can one conclude about state "existing legislation" and
GATT? I suggest that, based on the preparatory works of GATT, the

[278] UN Doc. EPCT/TAC/PV/5, at 20 (1947). See also UN Doc. EPCT/TAC/PV/23, at 15–16
(1947).
[279] See GATT Article XXIX(2).   [280] See note 250 above.
[281] GATT Doc. L/2375/Add. l, at 11 (1965), reproducing GATT Doc. L/309 (1955).

purpose of the "existing legislation" clause was to require a country to apply GATT to the fullest extent of its "executive power." In the context of the preparatory meetings, "executive" meant federal executive. Following this line of reasoning, the question depends on whether the federal executive authority can override state legislation. In the United States it is settled that a valid executive agreement is superior to state law.[282] Additionally, a President's valid proclamation or regulation is, under the supremacy clause, superior to state legislation.[283] Thus, it can be concluded that state legislation "existing" at the time of GATT was not within the meaning of the exception in the Protocol of Provisional Application.

This position can also be supported as a matter of policy. The need for federal control over matters affecting foreign commerce, recognized in the Constitution, should tip the scales in favor of federal law. This rationale has, as was discussed above, led a number of courts to negate state laws affecting foreign commerce without relying on GATT at all. Where federal law on the subject exists, there is even more reason to hold that the states cannot regulate.

2.   The "local government" clause

Even if state law is not excepted from GATT superiority by other provisions of the agreement, it has been argued[284] that it is made so exempt by the language of Article XXIV(12):

Each contracting party shall take such reasonable measures as may be available to it to ensure observance of the provisions of this Agreement by the regional and local governments and authorities within its territory.[285]

Simple and straightforward as it appears, this language contains an ambiguity that has an important impact on the domestic law application of GATT. The opposing interpretations can be expressed as follows:

1. The language does not change the binding application of GATT to political subdivisions, but it recognizes that in a federal system certain matters are legally within the power of subdivisions and beyond the

---

[282] See the cases cited in note 226 above; and *Restatement*, §§ 141–144 (1965).

[283] *Pennsylvania Railroad v. Illinois Brick Co.*, 297 US 477 (1936) (holding regulations of the Interstate Commerce Commission superior to state law). Consequently, insofar as the President's order is pursuant to delegation of Congress, this case supports the proposition in the text.

[284] *Brief for Petitioner, Bethlehem Steel v. Board of Commissioners*, Civil Nos. 899165, 897591 (Super Ct. County of Los Angeles 1966). The argument is discussed in 36 *California Attorney-General's Opinions* 147 at 148–149 (1960).

[285] This paragraph was originally numbered 6 of Article XXIV, 55 UNTS 194 (1950). Subsequently, amendments to Article XXIV (see the authorities cited in note 236 above) changed the number to 12.

control of the central government. In such a case, the central government is not in breach of its international obligations when a subdivision violates GATT, as long as the central government does everything *within its power* to ensure local observance of GATT.

2. On the contrary, this language indicates that GATT was not intended to apply as a matter of law against local subdivisions at all, and even when the central government has legal power to require local observance of GATT, it is not obligated under GATT to do so, but merely to take "reasonable measures."

If the second interpretation is correct, then GATT cannot be invoked as a matter of law in any state proceeding involving state law. This precise issue has arisen in several cases, including a very recent California case.[286] The unanimous conclusion of the courts thus far has been that GATT does apply to and override state or territorial law.[287] However, the State Department took the contrary position in a letter to the Hawaii Territorial Supreme Court in the earliest of these cases. This letter,[288] signed by the then State Department Legal Advisor, Herman Phleger, referring to Article XXIV(12), states:

This provision . . . has always been interpreted as preventing the General Agreement from overriding legislation of political subdivisions of contracting parties inconsistent with the provisions of the Agreement; by placing upon contracting parties the obligation to take reasonable measures to obtain observance of the

---

[286] *Bethlehem Steel* v. *Board of Commissioners*, Civil Nos. 899165, 897591 (Super. Ct. County of Los Angeles 1966). The court, while finding that the *Baldwin-Lima* case (see note 108 above) was controlling, indicated that, if the case were one of first impression, it would hold that "the Buy American Act is a violation of the commerce clause of the United States Constitution." Further, relying on the imposts and duties clause of the Constitution (Article I, § 10), the court stated that a state could not constitutionally impose such a "complete embargo" as results from the Buy American Act. The court did not undertake to examine the bases of GATT in United States law, but accepted it as superior to state legislation without discussion, while denying the injunction petition on the grounds of the existence of an adequate remedy at law. Oral Opinion of the Court, *Bethlehem Steel Corp.* v. *Board of Commissioners*, Judge Charles A. Loring, rendered December 22, 1966. Copy on file at the *Michigan Law Review* office. On May 2, 1967, the court granted the defendant's motion for summary judgment. Letter from Kenneth W. Downey, Deputy City Attorney of Los Angeles, dated May 9, 1967; copy on file at the *Michigan Law Review* office. It is understood that the decision is being appealed.

[287] The Texas case turned on another legal issue, but the remaining state and territorial cases (see the cases cited in note 108 above) so applied GATT.

[288] Letter from Herman Phleger, Legal Advisor of the Department of State, to Mr. Sharpless, Acting Attorney-General of Hawaii, February 26, 1957. This letter is on file in the Department of the Attorney-General of Hawaii, as contained and certified in an affidavit of April 5, 1967, by Burt T. Kobayashi, Attorney-General of the State of Hawaii. It was filed by the attorneys for the plaintiff in *Bethlehem Steel Corporation* v. *Board of Commissioners*, Civil Nos. 899591 (Super. Ct. County of Los Angeles 1965). Portions of this letter are also quoted in Ebb, *Regulation and Protection of International Business, Cases, Comments and Materials* (1964), 763.

Agreement by such subdivisions, the parties indicated that as a matter of law the General Agreement did not override such laws . . . In light of the provisions of paragraph 12 of Article XXIV . . . the reliance by the Supreme Court of the Territory on Article VI, clause 2 of the United States Constitution to invalidate the legislation would appear to have been based on a misconception of the General Agreement and of its effect on the legislation of the parties to it . . . it is suggested that you might desire to request a rehearing of the case on the basis that the particular constitutional grounds relied on are not appropriate in view of paragraph 12 of Article XXIV.

This letter is consistent with the testimony of a State Department official in hearings before a Senate Committee in 1949, one-and-one-half years after GATT was signed. Referring to article XXIV(12), the colloquy was as follows:

SENATOR MILLIKIN: Well, with reference to that, what can we do about it? Supposing any of our States, within their proper constitutional authority, put up a tax that is inconsistent with the provisions of this article which we have been discussing? What is our obligation?

MR. BROWN: I do not think we could do anything about it, Senator.

SENATOR MILLIKIN: Have we promised, or held out an implied promise, to do something that we could do anything about?

MR. BROWN: I don't think so.

SENATOR MILLIKIN: Let us read that.

MR. BROWN: Let me just check. The only commitment that we have taken, on that point, Senator, is in the last paragraph of Article XXIV, page 82.

SENATOR MILLIKIN: Article XXIV of GATT?

MR. BROWN: Article XXIV of the general agreement; yes. Because it was recognized that the Federal Government did not have the power to compel action by the local government. It only had powers of persuasion.

SENATOR MILLIKIN: Well, can we accept it as beyond "if's," "but's," "maybe's" that it is not intended that the Federal Government shall attempt to conform State laws by any method whatsoever, to the provisions of this agreement?

MR. BROWN: That may be taken categorically, but that does not mean that the Federal Government might not get in touch with a governor and suggest to him that he consider that a course of action which the State is following has certain effects. But that would be simply a matter of persuasion and consultation.

. . .

SENATOR MILLIKIN: Would the provisions of this Article or any other part of GATT impose upon the Federal Government any duties to do anything as to local State laws or movements, which are intended to promote State products, such as "Buy Georgia peaches," "Buy Colorado cantaloupes," state advertising campaigns out of public funds to promote those local buying movements?

MR. BROWN: No, sir.

SENATOR MILLIKIN: Is there anything in this agreement any place that imposes any obligation on the Federal Government to stop anything of that sort?

MR. BROWN: I don't think so, sir.

SENATOR MILLIKIN: Is there any question about it?
MR. BROWN: No; I don't know of anything. It was not intended.[289]

The actual drafting history of GATT, however, leaves one with a somewhat different impression. The language of Article XXIV(12) was drawn directly from an identical provision that was in the draft ITO Charter[290] at the time the GATT draft was formulated.[291] A later attempt to delete this language from GATT was rebuffed at Geneva, with the United States delegate explaining:

> Mr. Chairman, this particular paragraph was drawn from the Charter and I think some rather careful consideration went into its framing. I believe it is necessary to distinguish between central or federal governments, which undertake these obligations in a firm way, and local authorities, which are not strictly bound, so to speak, by the provisions of the Agreement, depending of course on the constitutional procedure of the country concerned. I think it really would be preferable to retain this language; it has some relationship with references in other parts of the Agreement dealing with action taken by governments. I am afraid that if we change the language of Paragraph 7 we shall probably disturb some of the interpretations and understandings that have been arrived at with respect to other parts of the agreement, as well as raising questions with regard to the Charter when we get to Havana. Therefore I should be rather inclined to take the present draft.[292]

A previous attempt to transfer the clause to Part II of GATT, so that it would be subject to "existing legislation," also failed.[293]

In working back into the history of this language as it developed in the ITO Charter, it appears that the question of treaty application to federal subdivisions came up very soon after the start of the first preparatory meeting in London in 1946. In connection with a draft commitment to prevent internal tax and regulatory discrimination against imported goods (compare Article III of GATT), Australia noted:

> Where the matter is one solely of action by a state, and our "external powers" laws do not give the Commonwealth authority to act, we would agree to use our best

[289] Hearings on HR 1211, Extension of Reciprocal Trade Agreements Act, Before the Senate Committee on Finance, 81st Cong., 1st Sess., Part 2, at 1161–1162 (1949).
[290] This so-called Geneva draft of the ITO Charter, the result of the Geneva meeting, is contained in the Report of the Second Session of the Preparatory Committee of the United Nations Conference on Trade and Employment, UN Doc. EPCT/186 (1947). Article 99(3) of this draft is the language identical to the present Article XXIV(12) of GATT, except for minor changes reflecting the difference in the instruments in which the language is located. Earlier GATT drafts likewise had included ITO Charter versions of this same clause.
[291] The earliest Geneva draft of GATT, following the fairly complete redraft of the ITO Charter, is contained in EPCT/135 (1947). At this point the local government clause was in Article XXII of GATT. Subsequent drafts of GATT carried this language forward without change. See Article XXII of UN Doc. EPCT/189 (1947); Article XXIV of UN Doc. EPCT/196 (1947); and Article XXIV of UN Doc. EPCT/214 (1947).
[292] UN Doc. EPCT/TAC/PV/19, at 32–33 (1947).
[293] UN Doc. EPCT/TAC PV/11, at 43–46 (1947).

efforts to secure modification or elimination of any practice regarded as discrimina-tory.[294]

And, at a later point, a United States delegate noted:

The obligation to accord fair and equitable treatment in awarding contracts applied to both central and local government where the central government was traditionally or constitutionally able to control the local government. Although he could not speak decisively, he thought that the United States Government would be able to control actions of states in this matter.[295]

A subcommittee later reported as follows:

Several countries emphasized that central governments could not in many cases control subsidiary governments in this regard, but agree that all should take such measures as might be open to them to ensure the objective.[296]

Therefore, the subcommittee proposed the addition of a new clause which read:

Each member agrees that it will take all measures open to it to assure that the objectives of this Article are not impaired in any way by taxes, charges, laws, regulations or requirements of subsidiary governments within the territory of the member governments.[297]

This language, as a part of the "national treatment Article," was carried over to the next preparatory meeting in New York in early 1947. At this meeting, the clause was changed to read:

Each accepting government shall take such reasonable measures as may be avail-able to it to assure observance of the provisions of this Charter by subsidiary governments within its territory.[298]

It was further pointed out that this problem of federal–state power alloca-tion also applied to other parts of the draft charter. The clause was then transferred from the Article on national treatment to a general miscellan-eous Article.[299] It was in this form that the clause first found its way into the draft GATT,[300] only to be changed later to accord with the draft ITO Charter changes as they occurred.[301]

---

[294] UN Doc. EPCT/13, at 1 (1946). See also UN Doc. EPCT/C.II/7 (1946).
[295] UN Doc. EPCT/C.11/27, at 1 (1946).
[296] UN Doc. EPCT/C.II/54, at 4 (1946). See also UN Doc. EPCT/C.II/64, at 3 (1946).
[297] UN Doc. EPCT/C.II/54, at 6 (1946).
[298] UN Doc. EPCT/34, at 52 (Article 88(5) of the Geneva draft of the ITO Charter) and 79 (Article XXV(5) of the then GATT draft) (1947).
[299] UN Doc. EPCT/C.6/6, at 3 (1947); UN Doc. EPCT/C.6/55 at 5–6 (1947).
[300] UN Doc. EPCT/C.6/W.58 (Article XXII(5)) (1947).
[301] See note 290 above. Ultimately, the "Havana Charter," the final version of the ITO Charter as drafted at Havana in the early part of 1948, included the local government clause as Article 104(3). UN Doc. ICITO/1/4 (1948).

Before drawing some conclusions from this history, one complicating factor must be mentioned. An interpretative note in Annex I to GATT, relating to paragraph 1 of Article III, states:

The application of paragraph 1 to internal taxes imposed by local governments and authorities within the territory of a contracting party is subject to the provisions of the final paragraph of Article XXIV. The term "reasonable measures" in the last mentioned paragraph would not require, for example, the repeal of existing national legislation authorizing local governments to impose internal taxes which, although technically inconsistent with the letter of Article III, are not in fact inconsistent with its spirit if its repeal would result in a serious financial hardship for the local governments or authorities concerned. With regard to taxation by local governments or authorities which is inconsistent with both the letter and spirit of Article III, the term "reasonable measures" would permit a contracting party to eliminate the inconsistent taxation gradually over a transition period, if abrupt action would create serious administrative and financial difficulties.

This note was explained in the 1949 Senate hearing:

SENATOR MILLIKIN: Well, is it understood that this does not apply to the United States?
MR. BROWN: Yes, sir, because it applies only to a national law, and we don't have any.[302]

It can be argued that the interpretative note indicates that GATT was not intended to apply to state law, since it interprets "reasonable measures" not to require immediate overriding of a state law. One could argue, however, that this note applies only to *national* legislation. A look at the history of this troublesome note may help elucidate its meaning.

The note was drafted at the Havana Conference on the ITO Charter in early 1948, some months after GATT was signed.[303] In September 1948, at the Second Session of the Contracting Parties of GATT, protocols were drafted to amend some specific portions of GATT to take account of changes made at Havana in the corresponding ITO Articles.[304] Among the changes made to GATT were those that tightened up Article III, dealing with "national treatment."[305] Since the Havana Conference had added an interpretative note to the Charter when it changed the corresponding

---

[302] Hearings on HR 1211, Extension of Reciprocal Trade Agreements Act Before the Senate Finance Committee, 81st Cong., 1st Sess., Part 2, at 1162 (1949).

[303] Final Act and Related Documents of the United Nations Conference on Trade and Employment, Havana, Cuba (1947–1948), UN Doc. ICITO/1/4, at 62 (1948). This interpretive note was in the ITO Charter at Annex P, Article 18(1).

[304] See GATT Doc. CP.2/SR.1–25 (1948); Report Adopted by the Contracting Parties (1948), GATT Doc. CP.2/22/Rev. 1, reprinted at GATT, *Basic Instruments and Selected Documents* (1952), vol. II, 39; GATT, *Basic Instruments and Selected Documents* (1952), vol. II, para. 32, at 45.

[305] GATT, *Basic Instruments and Selected Documents* (1952), vol. II, 40.

provision, the same note was carried over into GATT when the changes were made to Article III.[306] Reports of the Havana Conference[307] suggest that the interpretative note was a result of a compromise and a desire to accommodate several countries who feared the political and administrative consequences, including the revenue loss to subsidiary government, of immediate revocation of discriminatory internal taxes.[308] The solution agreed upon was to permit the gradual elimination of such taxes, but it was thought easier to handle this in an interpretative note than in the text of the Article itself.[309] It seems doubtful that this note was intended to affect the language in Article XXIV(12) at all. Its placement as a note to the "national treatment" Article confirms this view.[310]

What, then, can be concluded from the preparatory history of Article XXIV(12)? The fragments of that history which were recorded suggest that this clause was intended to apply only to the situation in which the central government did not have the constitutional power to control the subsidiary governments. Australia and other countries made reference to this situation. The United States delegate did likewise, adding his tentative judgment that the United States did not find itself in this circumstance. Thus, it can be argued that interpretation (A) which was presented at the outset of this section is the correct one, despite the opposing view expressed in the 1949 Senate Finance Committee hearings. It should be added that the witness at that hearing may have been suffering under a misunderstanding of United States law at the time of his testimony. He said that "it was recognized that the Federal Government did not have the power to compel action by the local government,"[311] but the supremacy clause of the Constitution seems to belie that statement. Furthermore, this hearing was held at a time when political opposition to ITO and GATT was apparently growing, and several of the Senators at the hearing were obviously hostile and were challenging the validity of GATT in its entirety. Under these circumstances, it is natural that the Administration spokesman would desire to play down the scope of GATT.[312]

---

[306] See the authorities cited in notes 303 and 304 above.
[307] UN Conference on Trade and Employment, Reports of Committee and Principal Subcommittee, UN Doc. ICITO/1/8, at 62 (Report of Subcommittee A of the 3rd Committee on Articles 16, 17, 18, and 19, UN Doc. E/CONF.2/C.3/59, at para. 38) (1948).
[308] UN Conference on Trade and Employment, UN Doc. E/CONF.2/C.3/A/W.30, 31–35, 47, and 52 (1948); UN Doc. E/CONF.2/C.3/SR.40, at 2 (1948).
[309] UN Doc. E/CONF.2/C.3/A/W.30, at 1 (1948); UN Doc. E/CONF.2/C.3/A/W.50, at 3 (1948).
[310] UN Doc. E/CONF.2/C.3/A/W.50, at 3 (1948).
[311] Hearings on HR 1211, Extension of Reciprocal Trade Agreements Act, Before the Senate Committee on Finance, 81st Cong., 1st Sess., Part 2, at 1161 (1949).
[312] See the authorities cited in note 223 above and the accompanying text.

One can, of course, also raise the question of the comparative relevance to GATT legal questions of the GATT preparatory work as against United States Senate hearings. Theoretically, the preparatory work should weigh more heavily.[313] Indeed, the legislative hearings that occurred after GATT was in force are arguably irrelevant, although, in practice, they are accepted as having some value.[314] Yet the practical problem in attempting to ascribe any meaning at all to certain GATT provisions has been the difficulty of finding and obtaining access to any GATT interpretative materials. The legislative hearings are relatively easy to find and read, whereas GATT preparatory work is just the opposite. For a number of years, the preparatory work material was restricted and unavailable for public use – even now, only a few libraries or locations have a reasonable collection.[315] Moreover, the sheer volume is so great[316] and indexing so poor (or nonexistent)[317] that even with access the attorney needs a wealthy and willing client to be able to undertake the necessary search. There is something of an anomaly in fact that an instrument can have legal force in domestic law while important interpretative material relating to that instrument is, as a practical matter, unavailable to the domestic lawyer or court. The anomaly is even more difficult to accept when these materials are available only to government attorneys. This situation is not unique to foreign trade matters; indeed, it is pervasive. Such a situation can have the practical effect of giving the administering

---

313 The *Restatement*'s "criteria for interpretation" of treaties and executive agreements include "the circumstances attending the negotiation of the agreement," and "drafts and other documents submitted for consideration, action taken on them, and the official record of the deliberations during the course of the negotiation." *Restatement*, § 147.

314 *Ibid.* This section does not consider legislative discussion of an international agreement subsequent to the time the agreement enters into force to be relevant, although subsequent practice of one party, if the other party or parties knew or had reason to know of it, is relevant. *Ibid.*, § 147(f). As a matter of practice, legislative materials of a major member of an international organization tend to be regarded as significant in interpreting the agreement, even by the international staff. See Gold, "Interpretation by the International Monetary Fund of Its Articles of Agreement" (1967) 16 *International and Comparative Law Quarterly* 289 at 296. The Supreme Court of the United States has recognized the relevance of administrative interpretations of international agreements by the department charged with its negotiation and enforcement. *Kolovrat* v. *Oregon*, 366 US 187 (1961); and *Factor* v. *Laubenheimer*, 290 US 276 (1933).

315 GATT headquarters in Geneva, of course, has a very complete collection. In the United States, fairly complete collections exist at the United Nations headquarters library, at the State Department offices in Washington, and at the International Monetary Fund offices in Washington. The situation has improved, however, as most of the preparatory work is now available on microfilm. Also GATT has recently liberalized its restrictive policy as to current documents. See GATT Docs. INF/121 and INF/122.

316 I would estimate that the volume of materials comprising the preparatory work for GATT and ITO (which is intermingled) amounts to something on the order of 27,000 pages – about 100 volumes.

317 A very small number of references to the preparatory work can be found in GATT, *Analytical Index to the General Agreements* (2nd revision, 1966).

government agency undue influence on the ultimate interpretation of important domestic laws.[318] Interestingly enough, however, in the one clear case in which a government agency has tried to influence a state court's interpretation of GATT, the agency's position has so far not been followed.[319]

Since there are these problems in using the preparatory work or United States legislative history concerning GATT, and since these materials are contradictory, it is worthwhile to note briefly some policy arguments relating to GATT's position *vis-à-vis* state or local law. There are two broad policy groupings that any state court will face in the appraisal of the significance of GATT to state law. The first group will consist of the policies of the particular state law being compared with GATT, whether explicitly admitted by the court or not. If the court feels, for example, that a state "Buy American" statute is based on weak or faulty premises, it will be more likely to apply GATT to override this statute, particularly if it feels the legislature is not likely to correct defects in the law. The second policy group involves basic questions of constitutional law and the powers of the federal government to control foreign commerce. Various nontariff trade barriers can be even more inhibiting to international trade than tariffs. This fact has clearly been recognized by both the legislative and executive branches of the federal government.[320] Local government actions are certainly capable of frustrating international trade almost as significantly as federal government actions.[321] Therefore, meaningful international agreement on trade matters must regulate local government actions. In this country, the Constitution gives the federal government power so to affect local actions.[322]

But such general statements do not answer the GATT question: is there any reason peculiar to GATT for interpreting it (or not) to override directly state law? The policies already expressed seem to indicate that in case of doubt GATT should be so applied. But countering this are the following arguments:

---

[318] These interpretations are likely to be influenced by current policy positions of the government agency, which in turn usually reflect current political conditions. It is fundamental to an independent judiciary that there be free access to relevant interpretive materials in order to formulate its conclusions independently of the administration, even though the final result may be the same.

[319] See the text accompanying note 288 above.

[320] See the authorities cited in note 62 above.

[321] See note 261 above and the accompanying text. See also excerpts from the memorandum of the United States as *amicus curiae* in *Tuppman-Thurlow Co.* v. *Moss*, 252 F. Supp. 641 (MD Tenn. 1966), reproduced at 5 ILM 483 (1966).

[322] US Constitution, Article VI (the Supremacy Clause); Article I, § 8 ('to regulate commerce with foreign nations'); Article I, § 10 ('no state shall, without the consent of the Congress, lay any imposts or duties on imports or exports').

1. to interpret Article XXIV(12) of GATT in this manner means that GATT will apply to different countries in different ways depending on their constitutional structure; and

2. United States constitutional uncertainty and controversy regarding executive agreements should lead courts to be cautious in applying such agreements to override state law.

In reply to the first argument, it may be said that uniformity of application is not essential, especially when the mechanism for registering complaints and urging corrective action exists within GATT.[323] Moreover, the "existing legislation" clause of the Protocol of Provisional Application clearly already allows nonuniformity depending on constitutional structure.[324] Indeed, it can be argued that such international recognition and allowance for individual national constitutional differences is salutary and analogous to the policies of federalism within nations. As to the second argument, while self-restraint by the federal legislative and executive branches is well received in many contexts, once the executive agreement has become effective the courts should not be deterred by this argument from giving full force under the supremacy clause to such agreements when other policies urge such effect. Both the supremacy clause and the foreign commerce clause of the Constitution should, in the context of GATT, lead to a presumption that federal law, including proclaimed executive agreements on trade, supersedes state law.

Furthermore, this country is likely to have future occasion to protest the use of foreign regional and local laws to restrict our exports. In such a case, the United States, an exporting nation, will be in a stronger position to use diplomatic means to obtain revocation of those laws, if, within this country, state and local laws are automatically subject to GATT.

IV.   Conclusion

The legal position of GATT in United States domestic law turns out to be surprisingly complex. This may be only a natural result – GATT itself was a highly intricate and perplexing instrument when born. Years of amendments and subtle changes in practice have made it even more difficult to understand fully. It appears, however, that the following generalizations can be made about the domestic legal position of GATT:

1. GATT is a valid executive agreement, entered into by the United States pursuant to authority of Congressional legislation.[325]

---

[323] GATT Articles XXII and XXIII (nullification and impairment, and the complaint procedure); GATT Article XXV (waivers and joint action).
[324] See the discussion in the text at Part III.B.1.
[325] See the discussion in the text at Part II.A.1.

2. To the extent entry into GATT is pursuant to Congressional authority, its domestic legal effect is probably achieved only through "proclamation." Not all parts of GATT have been proclaimed, but proclaimed parts do include all changes to United States tariff schedules and notes, as well as the original full text of GATT's general provisions, but not some subsequent textual amendments.[326]
3. Part II of GATT is expressly subject to pre-GATT federal legislation, pursuant to the Protocol of Provisional Application (which was proclaimed). It is inferior to subsequent federal legislation by virtue of the usual legal principles concerning executive agreements. Thus, Part II of GATT is inferior to any inconsistent federal legislation. Parts I and III are superior to pre-GATT legislation, and Part IV is probably not domestic law in the United States.[327]
4. It is this author's opinion that GATT is directly applicable to state and local governments in the United States, and supersedes state or local law even when that law is not automatically preempted by federal law, and even when such law existed prior to GATT.[328]

Appendix A Analysis of GATT in relation to 1945 United States statutory authority, Congressional history, and prior trade agreements

The following chart briefly presents for each Article of GATT: (1) its general subject matter; (2) its statutory basis; (3) the relevant Congressional history; and (4) similar provisions in various trade agreements entered into by the United States prior to the 1945 Trade Agreements Extension Act. It should be noted that the Congressional history on any clause is often extensive, and that only one illustrative reference may have been selected for inclusion in this chart. This analysis does not purport to show that explicit Congressional approval existed for any specific clause, but merely that the general subject matter of each GATT Article was mentioned in the Congressional history, and thus is arguably within the intended scope of the legislative delegation of power. It should also be noted that, even though unmentioned in the legislative history or prior precedents, clauses which are similar to subject matter already so mentioned, such as Article IV, can be justified as within the general overall scope of negotiating authority.

[326] See the discussion in the text at Part II.B; and Appendix C.
[327] See the discussion in the text at Part III.A.
[328] See the discussion in the text at Part III.B.

| | | | | Prior US trade agreements | | |
GATT Article	General subject	Statute	Congressional history	Mexico 1942	Uruguay 1942	Other trade agreement precedents
Part I						
I	Most-favored-nation clause	TAEA	CR-5071	I	I	
II	Commitment on maximum tariffs	TAEA	HH-274	VII, VIII	VII, VIII	
Part II	Safeguarding provisions	IR (note 1)	HR-8			
III	Internal taxation and regulations	TAEA	CR-4999	III, IX	II	Canada (1938), V
IV	Cinematograph films	IR, EXC				
V	Freedom of transit	IR	CR-4999	XIII		
VI	Antidumping	IR	CR-5071			Costa Rica (1936), XI; and El Salvador (1937), XI
VII	Customs valuation	IR	HH-274	XII	X	
VIII	Customs fees and formalities	TAEA(c)	CR-4999	VI		
IX	Marks of origin	IR	Canada (1938), IX			
X	Publications/administration, customs regulations quantitative restrictions	TAEA(c)	HH-274	VI	VI	
XI	Quantitative restrictions (BOP exception)	TAEA	HR-8	III, X	XI	
XII	Quantitative restrictions (MFN)	TAEA(c), EXC	HR-8	III, X		
XIII	Quantitative restrictions (BOP exception)	TAEA(c)	HR-8	III, X		
XIV	Currency manipulations and BOP	TAEA(c), EXC	HR-8	III, X	III	See Peru (1942), III

XV	Subsidies on exports or to reduce imports	IR	CR-4886	IV	IV
XVI	State trading and state monopolies	IR	CR-5070	V	V
XVII	Assisting economic development	IR	CR-5071		
XVIII	Escape clause	EXC		XI	
XIX	Health and morals regulations	EXC	HR-8	XVII	XV
XX	National security exceptions	IR, EXC	CR-4999	XVII	XV
XXI	Consultation	EXC	CR-5070	XIV	XII
XXII	Nullification (sanction)	IMP	HH-274	XIV	XII
XXIII		IMP	HH-409		
Part III	Administrative				
XXIV	Territorial, application/regional blocs	EXC		XV, XVI	XIII, XIV
XXV	Voting, decisions, waivers	note 2		XVII	XII
XXVI	Acceptance, entry in force	IMP		note 7	
XXVII	Withholding concessions to nonmembers				
XVIII	Negotiating and modifying tariff concessions	IMP		XVIII	XVIII
XXIX	Relations to ITO	TAEA	HH-275	note 7	note 7
XXX	Amending GATT	note 3		note 7	note 7
XXXI	Withdrawal from GATT	note 4	HH-274	XVIII	XVIII
XXXII	Contracting parties defined	IMP		note 8	note 8
XXXIII	Accession of new members	IMP		note 7	note 7
XXXIV	Annexes incorporated by reference	note 5		note 8	note 8
XXXV	Withholding application of GATT	IMP		note 7	note 7
	to new members	note 5			

GATT Article	General subject	Statute	Congressional history	Prior US trade agreements		
				Mexico 1942	Uruguay 1942	Other trade agreement precedents
Part IV	Trade and development	note 9				
Annexes	Relate to specific GATT Articles	IMP				
Schedules	Contain tariff concessions and relate to Article II	TAEA				
Some special clauses						
	Exports	note 6		III	III	
	Principal Supplier Rule in tariff negotiations		CR-5050			Canada (1938), XVIII
	Provisional Application of the Protocol					Canada (1938), XVIII
	Local Governments (Article XXIV(12))			XV(2)		

Key:

CR 91 Cong. Rec. (1945). The number which follows is the page.

EXC "Exception" (meaning the Article can be justified under the statute as being merely an exception to commitments otherwise authorized).

HH Hearings on the Extension of the Reciprocal Trade Agreements Act Before the House Ways and Means Committee, 79th Cong., 1st Sess. (1945). The number which follows is the page.

HR HR Rep. No. 594, 79th Cong., 1st Sess. (1945). The number which follows is the page.

IMP "Implied" (suggesting that the Article is an administrative provision that can be justified as impliedly authorized by the statute as a necessary measure to carry out the other commitments).

IR "Import Restrictions" (referring to this language in the Trade Agreements Extension Act).

SH Hearings on the Extension of the Reciprocal Trade Agreements Act Before the Senate Finance Committee, 79th Cong., 1st Sess. (1945). The number which follows is the page.

TAEA   §§ 350 of the Tariff Act of 1930 as amended by the Reciprocal Trade Agreements Act of 1934 and extended by the Trade Agreements Extension Act of 1945 (19 USC § 1351 (1964)). If a small letter follows, it refers to a subsection of § 350. If a number follows, it refers to another section of the same Act.

Notes:

1 Part II is subject to "existing legislation." See the discussion in the text at II.B.1.

2 The joint action provisions of Article XXV can also be justified as administrative provisions necessarily implied in the authority delegated to enter GATT. The language of Article XXV, however, is very broad on its face; it may well be argued that it should be limited by the scope of GATT itself or at least that United States representatives should be subject to some limitations in voting to exercise joint action.

3 Since the ITO was intended to be submitted to Congress, it can be argued that a provision governing the relationship to the ITO was not beyond the scope of the trade agreements delegation. Some provisions of Article XXIV, however, provide positive commitments, themselves. Paragraph 1 commits parties to observe chapters I to VI and IX of the ITO Charter "to the fullest extent of their executive authority," thereby ducking the *ultra vires* problem. Paragraph 6 provides that GATT parties "shall not invoke the provisions" of GATT to prevent the operation of any provision of the Havana Charter, but this seems merely an exception to GATT, not an additional commitment. In practice, the ITO Charter has apparently become a dead letter, other than as a generalized statement of principle.

4 The amending Article, like Article XXV, is probably justified as a necessary administrative clause. This Article is discussed in more detail in the text at II.A.3.

5 Articles XXXIII (new members) and XXV (withholding the application of GATT to a new member) must be read together. Article XXXV simply gives an option to new or old parties of GATT not to apply GATT to each other. This is analogous to a refusal to enter a bilateral trade agreement, and is a remnant of bilateralism in GATT.

6 At the time GATT was negotiated, the President had other statutory authority over exports (see note 60 to the text). Even if that authority would not expressly support the clauses in GATT, it is evidence that the President had general authority to negotiate on export matters. In addition, prior trade agreements dealt with exports.

7 These provisions of GATT are not needed in a bilateral agreement because the same purposes could be effectuated by bilateral negotiations.

8 Definitional clauses or incorporating clauses do not need authorization.

9 Part IV was added in 1965–1966. Its basis in United States law is discussed in the text following note 160 above.

15 United States–EEC trade relations: constitutional problems of economic interdependence[*]

I. Introduction

It is likely that there is no more important trade relationship in the world today than that between the United States and the European Economic Community. The combined economies of these two trading partners represent 11.8 percent of the world population, but over 50 percent of the non-Communist world international trade (not counting intra-EEC trade). Neither of these partners depends primarily on the other for its trade, but the percentage of US exports going to the Common Market is 21.5 percent; and the percentage of EEC exports going to the US is 10.6 percent. Because the well-being of these two partners can have such a large impact on the rest of the world, and because the health of the trade and economic relations between these two partners can have such a large impact on the economy of each, the importance of these trade relations to world well-being can be easily seen.[1]

These economic realities are verified when one examines the variety of institutional relationships which the two partners share, and their respective and joint roles in them. Both the United States and member nations of the EEC were instrumental founders of the "Bretton Woods system" for regulating international economic relations, which rests on the two pillars of the International Monetary Fund and the GATT.[2] In both of these

[*] This chapter is based on John H. Jackson, "United States–EEC Trade Relations: Constitutional Problems of Economic Interdependence" (1979) 16 *Common Market Law Review* 453–478. During 1975–1976 I was a Rockefeller Research Fellow, residing in Brussels, Belgium, for the purpose of observing the legal affairs of the European Economic Community related to external relations, and I wish to express my appreciation to the Rockefeller Foundation for that assistance.

[1] Eurostat, *Basic Statistics of the Community* 1977 (1977), 11, 116–119, 125, and 129 (based on 1975 data); and Staff of Senate Committee on Finance, 93rd Cong., 2nd Sess., *US Trade and Balance of Payments* (Committee Print, 1974), 38.

[2] With respect to the General Agreement of Tariffs and Trade (hereinafter cited as GATT), see generally J. Jackson, *World Trade and the Law of GATT* (1969), especially chapter 2. With respect to the International Monetary Fund (IMF), see generally J. Gold, *Membership and*

institutions the two partners together now enjoy a nearly predominant position of power and influence (after the waning of United States hegemony in the 1960s) and when working together the two partners probably enjoy the power on many issues to effectuate proposals, while each separately probably enjoys an effective "blocking veto." Thus the US–EEC relationship enjoys the pivotal role in the world's economic system.

Yet despite centuries of close economic, political, and cultural ties between these partners of the "transatlantic alliance," and despite the growth in trade and economic relations between them, tensions and acrimony stemming from these economic relations seem in recent years to be rising. Indeed it may be *because* of the growth in economic interdependence that these tensions develop. Because of the central role of the transatlantic alliance, however, these tensions have an important "spill-over" effect on the rest of the world. Therefore the US and the EEC carry a special responsibility, even in their bilateral dealings with each other.

Undoubtedly there are a number of reasons for the tensions between the transatlantic partners. Some of these may stem from healthy competition. Others may simply be the language and cultural differences (small though they may be when compared to other parts of the world) which have traditionally caused misunderstandings between nations. What I propose to do in this article, however, is to focus particularly on the *legal* and *constitutional* structures and philosophy of the two partners, as these bear on their *trade relations*, to see if within a comparison of that legal structure and the attendant "methods of governing" trade policy matters we can identify and better understand some of the causes or potential causes of economic tensions between the United States and the European Economic Community to some comparative observations as seen through the eyes of a United States scholar, participant, and observer.

Most people are familiar with the long agenda of "trade disputes" (current and recent past) between the US and the EEC: the chicken war, the cheese war, the tensions about the common agricultural policy, minimum import pricing, milk powder mixing requirements, questions of subsidies, countervailing duties and the "injury test," and many other issues negotiated in the Geneva talks ("multilateral trade negotiations" or MTN).[3] I do

Nonmembership (1974); and J. Horsefield, *The International Monetary Fund 1945–1965* (1969), vol. I.

[3] The trade negotiations entitled the "MTN–Multilateral Trade Negotiations," under the sponsorship of GATT, were launched by a ministerial meeting in the fall of 1973 in Tokyo, and therefore are sometimes called the "Tokyo Round." With respect to disputes between the United States and the EEC on trade matters, a number of these have resulted in proceedings in the GATT, and can be seen in GATT documents. See e.g., GATT, *Basic Instruments and Selected Documents*, 12th Supplement (1964), 65 (chicken war); GATT Doc. L/1910 of November 13, 1962 (Common Agricultural Policy); and GATT Doc. L/2389 of March 13, 1965 (Common Agricultural Policy). Others are briefly described in Jackson,

not propose here to try to catalogue or systematically examine these many issues. But I will draw upon those issues insofar as it is useful to do so, in order to illustrate my propositions regarding the impact of the legal and constitutional structure.

Several general preliminary observations can be made: first, it is striking to one who has recently spent considerable time on both sides of the Atlantic, how much misperception there exists on each side about the other. Each side seems to feel (as expressed *inter alia* by official government statements) that its economy is the most open and unrestricted for imports in the world. Each side feels that the other is basically protectionist. Furthermore, each side expresses dismay about the alleged "lawlessness" of the other as measured by the international trade rules of the GATT or the IMF, while believing its own actions to be basically "law-abiding."[4]

World Trade and the Law of GATT, 739 (Common Agricultural Policy); Staff of Senate Subcommittee on International Trade, Committee on Finance, 93rd Cong., 2nd. Sess., *The Common Agricultural Policy of the European Community* (Executive Branch GATT Studies No. 12, compilation of 1973 studies prepared by the Executive Branch, Committee Print, March 1974), portions reprinted in J. Jackson, *Legal Problems of International Economic Relations: Cases, Materials and Text*, 991 (Common Agricultural Policy); letter from Senator Hubert Humphry to the President of the United States, March 23, 1976, reprinted in Jackson, *Legal Problems of International Economic Relations*, 994 (milk powder); European Community Restrictions on Imports of United States Specialty Agricultural Products: Hearings on HR 238 and HR 320 Before the Subcommittee on Trade of the House Committee on Ways and Means, 95th Cong., 1st Sess. (1977) (minimum import pricing) GATT, *Basic Instruments and Selected Documents*, 23rd Supplement (1977), 98 (United States DISC tax legislation).

4 A sampling of the American perception includes the following. European Community Restrictions on Imports of United States Specialty Agricultural Products, Hearings on HR 238 and HR 320 Before the Subcommittee on Trade of the House Committee on Ways and Means, 95th Cong., 1st Sess., 9 (1977) (statement of Representative John McFall):

> [House Resolutions 238 and 320] are intended to demonstrate the support of the House for free trade and to draw attention to the need to eliminate the onerous EEC import regulations that are thwarting the free exchange of agricultural products from this country to Europe. It is vitally important that the United States Government, through both its executive and legislative branches, make a clear statement to the EEC and the rest of the world that restrictive trade mechanisms such as the EEC regulations will be adamantly opposed.

Sector Negotiations: Executive Hearings on the Trade Act of 1974 Before the Senate Committee on Finance, 93rd Cong., 2nd Sess., 11 (1974) (statement of Mr. Bell):

> And this leads us to the reason why we have concern about the sector-by-sector negotiations. If you look at our trade barriers on agricultural commodities coming into the United States, you see they are very low. Our duties are only in the vicinity of 5 to 20 percent on most of the agricultural imports, and we have very few nontariff barriers. In fact, about the only one that we have left today is the import quotas on dairy products, which is used to support the price support system for milk . . . If we are going to be put into a position of having to negotiate only on a sector-by-sector basis, we feel that there can be very little to come out of any trade negotiation for agriculture because we have very little to give.

Secondly, we must recognize that there are considerable differences in economic theory which divide the two sides of the Atlantic. These differences, while not necessarily fundamental, may be engendering serious problems of inconsistent governmental actions as the transatlantic partners become more interdependent. These differences can be oversimplified as the division between those who desire an economic system to become more "decentralized" and governed by the free market and price mechanisms on the one hand (as reflected in movements in the United States to deregulate airlines, trucking, and to avoid when possible government planning such as "industrial policies"), as compared on the other hand to those who welcome government intervention to alter or channel the market forces (as reflected in at least some countries of Europe, which emphasize national-

The opposing view held by Europeans was expressed in Agence Internationale d'Information pour la Presse, No. 2038 (NS), August 25–26, 1976 at 10 (report of August 1976 speech of Mr. Lardinois before the US National Soybean Association):

> We have been excluded from your market for dairy products by a rigid system of quotas and are now being expelled from your market for canned yams. You have taken measures against our exports of alcohol. New sanitary regulations constantly menace diverse minor products. We have the impression that the United States deliberately considers agriculture exchanges as a stream in one direction. You preach free trade as long as it concerns the interior market of others, but you enforce a rigid protection at home. For us Europeans, America has become the most protected agricultural market of the world.

See also M. Limouzy, Rapporteur, Rapport fait au nom de la Commission d'enquete parlementaire chargee d'examiner les conditions dans lesquelles ont lieu des importations sauvage de diverses categories de marchandises, No. 3230, Assemblée Nationale, Première Session Ordinaire de 1977/1978, November 18, 1977, at 140–141:

> Il faut noter que, dans le concert des nations, ceux qui se font les défenseurs les plus ardents de la necéssité du libéralisme dans les relations commerciales ne s'imposent pas toujours, pour ce qui les concerne, les disciplines les plus contraignantes. C'est le cas du Japon, qui reste – par l'organisation même de son système de production et de commerce – un marché d'accès très difficile pour les exportateurs. C'est le cas surtout des Etats-Unis, où les forces protectionnistes disposent traditionnellement d'un puissant arsenal de moyens de défense commerciale qui s'est encore enrichi dans la période récente à l'approche de la négociation du Tokyo round, notamment avec l'adoption du Trade Reform Act du 3 janvier 1975. Votre commission, par son object, n'a pas reçu mandat d'analyser la resurgence des protectionnismes dans le monde, et notamment les manifestations nombreuses qui ont pu être relevées dans le monde, et notamment les manifestations nombreuses qui ont pu être relevées dans la politique commerciale récente des Etats-Unis. Nul doute cependant que l'effet de domination exercée par l'économie américaine soit un des éléments importants qui expliquent la montée de l'agressivité – souvent insupportable – des nouveaux exportateurs. La politique restrictive aux importations, qui s'est concretisée par la conclusion d'un nombre important d'accords d'autolimitation acceptés par les partenaires des Etats-Unis, fait inévitablement refluer sur les autres marchés solvables–et d'abord les marchés européens–la plus grande part des marchandises provenant des pays en voie d'industrialisation.

ized industries, heavy subsidies to prevent plant failure unemployment, the cartelization of the steel industry, and notions of "organized free trade").

One example of how these divergent economic philosophies can create international tensions in an interdependent world is the problem of subsidies and countervailing duties. Government activity in one country, pursued for legitimate domestic policy purposes (such as investment tax credits, or regional aid) may have the effect of a "subsidy" enabling products to be exported and sold abroad at a price that is less than it would be without the government help. The competing producers in the importing country may then argue that the prices are "unfair" because of the different governmental attitude towards market intervention which exists in their own country. This leads to tensions between the systems, and raises difficult policy questions which are now ineptly handled by GATT rules.[5]

II.   United States constitutional and legal system relating to US international trade relations

Because of its predominant economic position in the immediate post-World War II era, the United States naturally had a decisive influence on the structure of the international economic institutions that were formed at that time (the IMF and GATT in particular). Thus it is not surprising to discover that the *constitutional structure* of the United States in turn has had an important influence on those institutions. The GATT, for example, plays the role it has today largely because of the failure of the ITO (International Trade Organization) to come into being, after the GATT was created. These phenomena in turn can be traced back to the US constitutional and legal system which required Congressional approval of the ITO (which Congress refused), whereas the GATT was accepted by the United States as an "Executive Agreement" under prior statutory authority of the President without need for further approval of the Congress.[6] It is this type of relationship that leads us now to look more closely at the US constitutional and legal system.

1.   The US Constitution

Several important characteristics of the United States Constitution have had considerable influence on the US international economic relations.

---

[5] Jackson, *World Trade and the Law of GATT*, chapter 15; Barcelo, "Subsidies and Countervailing Duties – Analysis and a Proposal" (1977) 9 *Law and Policy in International Business* 779.

[6] Jackson, *World Trade and the Law of GATT*, chapter 2; Jackson, "The General Agreement on Tariffs and Trade in US Domestic Law" (1967) 66 *Michigan Law Review* 249.

First, it is common knowledge that the US operates under a written constitution buttressed by a system of formal court review, and that this has an important influence on all US government affairs. Secondly, and again commonly known, the US government is based on a "separation of powers" structure, so that the three major divisions of government (the Congress, the Executive (Presidency) and the judiciary) each have certain powers, some of which operate to impose limits and checks on other divisions. These two characteristics are common to all governmental action in the United States as related to many subjects, including international economic affairs. These characteristics have resulted in a constant tension or power struggle between the Congress and the President, with the Supreme Court stepping in occasionally as arbitrator.

A third characteristic of the US Constitution is more particularly related to international economics. The Constitution makes the President the "Commander-in-Chief" of the military, and also grants to the President powers (such as power to receive ambassadors and powers to carry out the laws) which have been construed to give the President a broad authority over foreign relations generally (an authority which recently has been much challenged and somewhat limited). Of course international *agreements* negotiated by the President must be approved either by the Senate or by legislation requiring Congressional action (both Houses), unless the agreement is one of those few that can be said to be within the President's sole authority under the Constitution or unless legislation has previously delegated such authority to the President.[7] But the President not only has considerable delegated authority under prior legislation, but also has important scope for action and decision short of formal international agreements. Thus it has been suggested that the President has a specially predominant role in foreign affairs.

As to international economic affairs, however, the Constitution tilts the "balance of power" towards the Congress rather than the President. This is because express clauses of the Constitution specify that the Congress has the power "to regulate Commerce with foreign nations," as well as the power to tax.[8]

Thus even at times when vast presidential power over most foreign political or military affairs has been conceded by Congress, the Congress has jealously guarded its "special prerogative" over international commerce. This special prerogative is continuously asserted, as Congressional reports and legislation manifest.[9]

---

[7] See generally Jackson, *Legal Problems of International Economic Relations*, chapters 4–5; and L. Henkin, *Foreign Affairs and the Constitution* (1972).
[8] US Constitution, Article I, § 8, clauses 1 and 3.
[9] House Committee on Ways and Means, Trade Reform Act of 1973, HR Rep. No. 93–571, 93rd Cong., 1st Sess., 4 (1973).

In particular, since tariffs were once a major revenue source, they are still considered to fall within the "taxing" power and thus Congressional action is required for permanent changes in them. Only reluctantly, over a period of eighty years, has the Congress gradually loosened its tight grip on tariffs. Since so much of international trade policy has tended to concern tariffs, Congress's role in trade policy was often more vital than in other subject areas of international affairs. Likewise, as international trade and interdependence grew, a larger portion of the public was affected (jobs, sales, consumer choice, investment, tourism). It was natural that those citizens affected would take their complaints to their elected representatives in Congress, which thus has found a political need to exercise its special prerogatives.

2.   *Delegations of power to the President*

Despite its central constitutional role for "international commerce," the US Congress has historically found it difficult to carry out this responsibility. Too often the parochial constituent interest of particular Congressmen or Senators has lead them to pursue policies damaging to overall national interest, often by combining with other representatives whose parochial constituent interest could be traded ("You vote for my high tariff and I will vote for yours"). These interests led to the disastrous Smoot–Hawley Tariff Act of 1930, and the subsequent realization by the Congress that it was not able to develop wise legislation dealing with specific tariffs.[10]
. . .
Several propositions can be stated to describe the legal and constitutional structure of the conduct of the US international trade relations. First, these affairs operate in a milieu of legalisms, depending on constitutional and statutory interpretations, often made by the courts. Among other results of this situation is the tendency for these matters to be brought into public view, to be scrutinized by a variety of opposing interests, and often to be tested by court procedures with public oral and written argument. Private "deals" are very hard to make.

Secondly, the constant power struggle between branches of government,

[10] Jackson, "The General Agreement on Tariffs and Trade in US Domestic Law," 254. Smoot–Hawley Tariff Act, Act of June 17, 1930, Pub. L. No. 71–361, 46 Stat. 590 (1930). In the 1934 Congressional debates on the Trade Agreement Act, one Senator said: "[O]ur experience in writing tariff legislation . . . has been discouraging. Trading between groups and sections is inevitable. Log-rolling is inevitable, and in its most pernicious form. We do not write a national tariff law. We jam together, through various unholy alliances and combinations a potpourri or hodgepodge of section and local tariff rates, which often add to our troubles and increase world misery." See Jackson, "The General Agreement on Tariffs and Trade in US Domestic Law," 254.

particularly Congress and the Executive, reinforces the tendencies just mentioned above. Any private interest disadvantaged by a presidential trade decision will have access to its elected representatives in Congress and the natural suspicion of Congress about presidential powers will often lead to Congressional activity such as that mentioned earlier in this article.

Thirdly, while presidential powers generally, including those related to international trade, greatly increased in the crisis of the 1930s and 1940s, and carried into the 1960s, it is generally considered that presidential powers have weakened in the last decade and that the Congress has been reasserting itself. Whether this is a long-term trend or not is uncertain. Nevertheless, these trends have important implications for US trade policy and for its trade relationship with the European Common Market. It does not necessarily portend negative implications. But if presidential power is now to be permanently less impressive in relation to Congressional power, at the very least it implies that the older "diplomatic" techniques of conducting trade policy (sometimes characterized as "secrecy and deals") will have to be revised.

Fourthly, the Constitutional struggle built into the US system, while in broad perspective wise, does have some distorting influences. It tends, among other things, to encourage Executive branch policy-makers to respond to international economic problems in those ways which least call upon the powers of the rival branch. Thus the US Executive (probably similar to executives everywhere, including those in the EC and governments of the member states) will try to achieve a policy response within the framework of the Executive branch's constitutional and existing statutory powers. Thus an informal "handshake" or "gentlemen's agreement" (for instance, on export credit terms) will be preferred to a formal agreement that may require Congressional approval; an international "anti-dumping code" will be drafted in such a way as to avoid the need for Congressional approval; and an antidumping "trigger price mechanism" for steel imports will be devised that will rely exclusively on existing statutory authority.

III.   Trade policy on operation

In order better to illustrate the relationship between the US constitutional and legal structure and the realities of international trade between the US and the EEC, I propose in this section to examine several concrete situations. Perhaps the most important current problem of trade relations generally, also important to transatlantic trade relations, is that of subsidies and countervailing duties. It so happens that this subject is deeply influenced by the US legal structure and the GATT rules related to (and influenced by) that legal structure. Therefore we begin with the subsidy–countervailing issue. In addition, however, a brief description of three other trade policy situations will be used to help illustrate the principles of Part I of this article, namely the general structure of US "escape clause" actions; the 1967 Anti-Dumping Code; and the 1978 US "Trigger Price Mechanism."

1.   Subsidies and countervailing duties

For most of this century, international trade policy rules as formulated and implemented by trading nations have recognized the dangers to an importing country of foreign subsidies which benefit the goods imported. These rules were carried into the GATT which contains two approaches to the problem. First, GATT Article XVI prohibits (for those GATT countries which have accepted all of Article XVI) certain "export subsidies," that is subsidies granted for the exportation of good. This rule, like most in GATT, is enforced only through the rather weak dispute settlement and "nullification or impairment" procedures of GATT (principally Article XXII).

Secondly, however, GATT Article VI allows an importing nation to depart from its other GATT obligations so as unilaterally (without prior GATT approval) to impose "countervailing duties" on any imported goods to the extent that those goods benefit from the foreign "bounty or subsidy." To utilize this response, however, the importing nation must be able to establish that the subsidized goods are causing "material injury" to the domestic competing industry. The type of subsidy qualifying for countervailing duty response, however, is much broader than those which are prohibited under Article XVI; it does not have to be an "export subsidy."[11]
. . .

The GATT was forced to assume the central institutional role for international trade. It is still to this day, however, applied only through the Protocol of Provisional Application, and thus subject to this "grandfather rights" exception for prior legislation.

The US countervailing duty statute dates from 1897, and thus qualifies as "existing legislation." This statute requires no showing of "injury." Instead it merely states that the Secretary of the Treasury *shall* apply countervailing duties whenever imports have benefited "directly or indirectly" from "any bounty or grant upon the manufacture or production or export."[12] Thus the US benefits from "grandfather rights" under GATT

---

[11] Jackson, *World Trade and the Law of GATT*, §§ 15.4–15.5.

[12] The statute reads as follows: "§ 1303. Countervailing duties. Whenever any country, dependency, colony, province, or other political subdivision of government, person, partnership, association, cartel, or corporation shall pay or bestow, directly or indirectly, any bounty or grant upon the manufacture or production or export of any article or merchandise manufactured or produced in such country, dependency, colony, province, or other

and is not legally required to have an injury test for countervailing duties. This has been a source of considerable rancor between the US and its trading partners, including the EEC. It was a major subject of negotiation in the MTN Geneva talks. Europeans have argued that the US should "live up to its obligations in GATT" while the US argued that it has no legal obligation to yield its grandfather rights, but was willing to do so if it obtained reciprocal benefits in return.

In passage of the Trade Act of 1974, Congress, long critical of the Executive branch handling of countervailing duties, incorporated in the statute a series of procedural reforms which have the effect of substantially reducing the degree of latitude, which the Executive had exercised in implementing the countervailing duty statute.[13] This in turn has made it more certain that US policy would clash with that of other governments, including those of the EEC, and has engendered an important law suit testing the Executive's authority under the new statutes.[14]

2.   *The escape clause in US law*

The "escape clause" in United States trade law (revised in the 1974 Trade Act) has been one of the traditional "fields of contest" in the power struggle between the Executive and Congress. Consequently it is not surprising to find the current law not only intricate but delicately balanced in its allocation of power between these two branches of government. In the consideration of the 1974 Trade Act in Congress, the specifics of the escape clause were among the prominently contested provisions.

The escape clause, it will be recalled, under both GATT Article XIX and United States law provides that, when imports are increasing to such an extent as to cause "serious injury" to a domestic competing industry, a

political subdivision of government, and such article or merchandise is dutiable under the provisions of this chapter, then upon the importation of any such article or merchandise into the United States, whether the same shall be imported directly from the country of production or has been changed in condition by remanufacture or otherwise, there shall be levied and paid, in all such cases, in addition to the duties otherwise imposed by this chapter, an additional duty equal to the net amount of such bounty or grant, however the same be paid or bestowed. The Secretary of the Treasury shall from time to time ascertain and determine, or estimate, the net amount of such bounty or grant, and shall declare the net amount so determined or estimated. The Secretary of the Treasury shall make all regulations he deems necessary for the identification of such articles and merchandise and for the assessment and collection of such additional duties." 19 USC § 1303.

[13] Trade Act of 1974, § 331; Senate Committee on Finance, Trade Reform Act of 1974, S. Rep. No. 93–1298, 93rd Cong., 2nd Sess., 183–193 (1974).

[14] *US v. Zenith*, 562 F. 2d 1209 (CCPA 1977), affirmed 46 USLW 4752 (June 20, 1978), 457 US 443. The Supreme Court and Court of Customs and Patent Appeals upheld a US Treasury ruling that Japanese remission of an internal indirect tax did not constitute a bounty or grant which would require countervailing duties.

nation may take temporary action to restrain such imports to allow the domestic industry time to "adjust." The GATT rules are relatively broad and vague. With one possible exception, the US legal criteria for escape clause action have been much more stringent, i.e. harder to fulfill, than those of the GATT.[15]

Under the US law an escape clause proceeding begins with a complaint which is made to the US "International Trade Commission" (formerly the "Tariff Commission"). This body is a six-member independent regulatory commission charged with a variety of responsibilities relating to international trade. Like many regulatory commissions under the US law, members are appointed for staggered terms by the President and confirmed by the Senate. The committee in the Senate which initially passes on these appointments is the powerful Senate Finance Committee, which has general jurisdiction over international trade matters as well as tax and a variety of social welfare measures. This confirmation power gives this Committee, and the Senate generally, leverage over appointments, and it has sometimes been alleged that the ITC gives special political deference in its work to the concerns of Congress or the Senate. In recent years a number of Senate or Congressional aides have been appointed to this Commission.[16] The Commission is charged with the task of determining whether the criteria for an escape clause action exist, that is, whether imports are increasing and if so whether they are causing serious injury to a domestic industry. If the ITC determination is affirmative, then it formulates a recommendation of government response, which may be import restraints (higher tariffs, or quotas etc.) or adjustment assistance. The ITC formulation or remedy, however, is only a recommendation.

After an ITC affirmation determination, the matter is sent to the President. After his aides have reviewed the case, the President has the authority to make his own remedy determinations. He may or may not follow the ITC recommendations. He may agree that "serious injury" has been caused, but may alter the remedy, or provide no remedy.

If, however, the President does not follow the recommendation of the

---

[15] The GATT Article XIX criteria are described in Jackson, *World Trade and the Law of GATT*, chapter 23. The US law on escape clauses is analyzed in Jackson, *Legal Problems of International Economic Relations*, chapter 11, § 11.3. The 1974 Trade Act escape clause criteria are in § 201. For the first time, the US statutory escape clause omits any "causal link" to international obligations, and this is arguably a departure from the GATT requirements under Article XIX, although a counter-argument is that in all escape clause cases actually to be decided under the United States procedure, the very soft GATT "causal link" criteria are fulfilled.

[16] See § 172 of the Trade Act of 1974; Senate Committee on Finance, Trade Reform Act of 1974, S. Rep. No. 93–1298, 93rd Cong., 2nd Sess., at 115 (1974); Lawrence, "Trade Panel May Get More Clout This Year," *Journal of Commerce*, July 6, 1976, 1.

ITC then the matter is subject to a "Congressional veto" action.[17] If both Houses of Congress, within ninety legislative days after a President's decision in the escape clause case, adopt a resolution disapproving the President's decision, then the ITC recommendation must be implemented. Up to the time of this writing, no Congressional veto has rejected a presidential escape clause finding, but the President has sometimes been quite sensitive to the *potential* of such a veto in framing his decision in an escape clause case.

It can be seen that this process represents an uneasy compromise between delegation of authority to the President and retention of power by Congress, utilizing an "in-between" agency – the ITC – as a partial buffer. The delicacy of the balance is even more apparent, however, when one studies the legislative process leading to the adoption of the 1974 Trade Act. For example, the prior law also contained a "two-house" legislative veto in escape clause cases, but the disapproval resolution required a "majority of the authorized membership of each house." The 1974 Act changed this to the requirement of a "majority of the members of each House present and voting," which is slightly easier to achieve. In this way proposals to amend the law to make it even easier for Congress to override (e.g., by a vote of *either* House) were compromised to language which slightly increased the pressure on the President to follow the ITC recommendations.[18] At the same time the Congress took action to bring the ITC somewhat more under its own influence than before.

Several other examples of the delicate balance of the escape clause can also be mentioned. At one stage, for instance, there was a legislative attempt to require the President to provide "import relief" (restraints on imports) if the ITC made an affirmative determination. The House Bill stated that the President "may" provide import relief in such case. The Senate changed this to "shall." In conference, a compromise formula was agreed that retained "shall" but added "unless he determines that provision of such relief is not in the national economic interest of the United States."[19]

---

[17] Trade Act of 1974, § 203(c).

[18] Trade Expansion Act of 1962, § 351(a)(2)(B). The legislative history of the Trade Act of 1974 includes the following Congressional reports: House Committee on Ways and Means, Trade Reform Act of 1973, HR Rep. No. 93–571, 93rd Cong., 1st Sess. (1973); Senate Committee on Finance, Trade Reform Act of 1974, S. Rep. No. 93–1298, 93rd Cong., 2nd Sess. (1974); and House (Conference) Report No. 93–1644, 93rd Cong., 2nd Sess. (1974), reprinted in (1974) *US United States Code Congressional and Administrative News* 7367.

[19] See § 202 of the Trade Act of 1974, as proposed by the Executive branch; as adopted by the House of Representatives; as adopted by the Senate, and as finally compromised in the final Act. See Senate Committee on Finance, Trade Reform Act of 1974, S. Rep. No. 93–1298, 93rd Cong., 2nd Sess., at 124 (1974); and House (Conference) Report No. 93–1644, 93rd Cong., 2nd Sess., 34 (1974), reprinted in (1974) *US United States Code Congressional and Administrative News* 7367.

3.   *The Anti-Dumping Code*

. . .

4.   *The Trigger Price Mechanism*

. . .

IV.   Some EEC comparisons

It would be impossible within the scope of this article, and probably presumptuous besides, to present much detail here about facets of the EEC legal structure comparable to those of the United States. Nevertheless, a few tentative generalizations might be stated, partly designed to provoke those more immersed in European law to reflect on the comparisons and their meaning for international trading relationships.

It is particularly surprising to an American legal scholar to view the EEC constitutional development in the light of contrasting member state national legal systems. For example, the EEC Treaty of Rome structure as applied by the Luxembourg Court seems to be a highly "constitutional" or "legalistic" system, much more like that of the United States than is the case of the national systems of a number of the member countries. Not only is there an EEC "written constitution" but there is a carefully constructed "supreme court" to preside over it and ensure its observance. Effective "judicial review" over other branches of the EEC "government" now appears established, and an elaborate procedure for citizen court challenge of both EEC government actions and member state actions contravening the EEC "constitution" has been provided.[20]

In sum, one of the characteristics of the United States constitutional system can also be seen developing in the EEC. It seems fair to expect that this constitutional characteristic will also have its influence on the trade relationships between the transatlantic partners, as indeed it has.

An analogy to a second characteristic of the United States system can also be seen in the EEC, namely the "separation of power" and struggle for power among various branches of government. European law scholars are familiar with the struggle for jurisdiction and control between the EEC Commission and the EEC Council. Furthermore, both of these "govern-

---

[20] Treaty Establishing the European Economic Community (Treaty of Rome), in force March 25, 1997, Articles 164–192, 298 UNTS 3 (1958) (Article 173(2) specifically deals with private party standing); D. Lasok and J. Bridge, *Introduction to the Law and Institutions of the European Communities* (1973), 153–169; P. Mathijsen, *A Guide to European Community Law* (1975), 196–221.

ment branches" can be seen in struggle with the authority remaining in the member states.[21]

While these analogies between the US and the EEC government systems, particularly as related to transatlantic international trade matters, cannot, of course, be pushed too far (the systems certainly are not identical, and there is no certainty that they will further converge), nevertheless one can note several more analogous characteristics. For example, European observers have argued that Commission authority has diminished in recent years *vis-à-vis* the EEC Council and member states. Does this bear some analogy to the diminution of US Executive branch authority? The European Parliament is being strengthened by direct election, possibly recognizing the need for "legitimation" of the EEC through the broadening of participatory democracy. Does this have some analogy to US Congressional assertions of power? Will a future European Parliament play a stronger role in developing EEC international trade policy?

More particularly, now, it is likely that the EEC constitutional and legal structure can be shown to shape and constrain the possible trade policy choices, just as is the case in the United States. For example, the EEC has clear authority under its "constitution" (the Treaty of Rome) for commercial policy matters. EEC authority on financial and monetary matters is less clear, the member states claiming that competence on this subject largely remains with them. When international negotiations touch on monetary (or balance of payments) matters, how then are such negotiations to be managed?[22]

Certain ambiguities of the EEC system of concluding international agreements led to particular procedures such as "mixed" agreements, including approval of member states, which may in turn require approval of member states' parliaments.[23] Is it not likely, therefore, that such "formal" international agreements will be avoided by policy-makers?

The matter of "local cost" limits in an export credit international agree-

---

[21] Treaty of Rome, Articles 164–192; *Commission v. Council*, Court of Justice of the European Communities, Case 22/70, March 31, 1971, [1971] ECR 263; [1971] CMLR 355; and Lasok and Bridge, *Introduction to the Law and Institutions of the European Communities*, 159. Another example of this type of struggle is that which has centered on the question of how much competence remains in individual member states of the EEC to conclude so-called "Economic Cooperation Agreements" relating to the trade and economic matters, particularly with East European countries. See, e.g., *Eighth General Report on the Activities of the European Communities* (1974), 262.

[22] Compare the Treaty of Rome provisions Articles 104–109. Lasok and Bridge, *Introduction to the Law and Institutions of the European Communities*, 286.

[23] Lasok and Bridge, *Introduction to the Law and Institutions of the European Communities*, 176–187; Mathijsen, *A Guide to European Community Law*, 10–28; and Reaux and Flaesch-Mougin, "Les Accords Externes de la CEE" (1975) 11 *Revue trimestrielle du droit européen* 227.

ment is illustrative of some of these problems.[24] Likewise, the more general international "gentlemen's" agreement to refrain from competitive use of favorable government credits for export promotion raises the issue of the competition for competence between the EEC institutions and the member states.[25] Furthermore, there has been some suggestion that the important international trade issue of subsidies and countervailing duties is complicated by the question of whether the EEC institutions have competence to include restrictions on the permissible use of general subsidies (not just export subsidies), since general subsidies are found so deeply embedded in domestic laws and policies (including taxation) that they may not come within the "commercial policy" competence of the EEC.[26]

On the other hand, there are important differences between the EEC legal system of negotiating international trade agreements (e.g., in GATT) and that of the US. For example, the EEC Council, upon recommendation of the Commission and the "Article 113 Committee" of the Council, approves a "mandate" for the negotiation which sets forth the guidelines and limitations that the EEC expects its negotiators to follow.[27] Yet the negotiators realize that it is reasonably possible to obtain a revision of these guidelines at the last stages of an international negotiation, since the Council can act fairly quickly. In the US, the "mandate" is legislation tortuously guided through two years of Congressional debate. Thus revision is more difficult, and would open the Executive to a series of bargaining demands from Congress.

V.   Some conclusions

National constitutional and legal structures shape international economic and trade policies. These structures may constrain policy choices and require selection of second or third best options. In a system of growing

---

[24] See the opinion of the Court of Justice of the European Communities on "OECD Understanding on a Local Cost Standard," Advisory Opinion No. 1/75, November 11, 1975, [1975] ECR 1355. The Court held that the competence of the EEC institutions extended to the draft agreement concerning officially supported contracts related to exports on credit terms. Despite the opinion, there has apparently been some reluctance on the part of the member states to yield to the EEC institutions on the matter. See Agence Europe No. 2020 (NS) of July 9, 1976 and Agence Europe No. 2009 of June 24, 1976. See also the *Ninth General Report on the Activities of the EC* (1975), 279.

[25] US Department of Treasury, "New International Arrangement on Officially Supported Export Credits," Press Release, February 22, 1978, at 1.

[26] These suggestions have been made in some private discussions between government officials and the author.

[27] Memorandum from the Commission to the Council forwarded on April 9, 1973 and amended on May 22, 1973, "Development of an Overall Approach to Trade in View of the Coming Multilateral Negotiations in GATT," reprinted in *Bulletin of the EC*, Supplement 2/73.

economic interdependence, such as that experienced between the United States and Europe, independence to pursue national or domestic goals is diminished. Thus the ability of the two entities to consult and compromise divergent policy directions becomes increasingly important. But it may be that the constraints imposed by the national constitutional and legal structures will inhibit on one part or the other the selection of the "sensible compromise" among competing sets of policy options. More knowledge by each side of the other's structural constraints becomes necessary in order to understand the sources of some of the tensions that appear to be arising between them.

In summarizing some of the "constraining" characteristic of the two entities (the United States on one side, the European Common Market along with its member state governments on the other side), one can draw several conclusions. First, there is in the US a high degree of "legalism" or felt need to be able to defend in court the source and scope of authority (constitutional or statutory) on which the Executive relies in international dealings. In this respect there may be strong developing parallels in the EEC. Secondly, there is a "distribution" or "separation" of powers in the US and in the EEC, attended by a natural power struggle among divisions within those governments, which tends both to reinforce the "legalistic" approach and to engender some confusion and ambiguity as to where competence over particular issues lies. Thirdly, on both sides of the Atlantic there are important issues needing negotiation and compromise, for which there is considerable obscurity where power lies to negotiate and subsequently to implement a compromise. Fourthly, there is a growing demand for public or private citizen participation in international economic policy formation, accompanied by increasing pursuit of citizen complaints of harm through court and other challenges of the implementation of international economic policy. This too appears on both sides of the Atlantic. Finally, in the US one can see a general inclination in the Executive to avoid selecting policy options which require the consent of Congress, and often this means avoiding formal changes in international agreements or the preference to utilize informal arrangements internationally. These inclinations may also have parallels in the EEC.

These conclusions clearly have important implications, not only for the US–EEC trade relationship (which is perhaps the most advanced as well as the most important) but for general trade and economic relations in the world. The constraining influences imposed by domestic governmental structures which lead governments to pursue "informal" international mechanisms, for example, probably tend to emphasize short-run solutions, and generally involve unenforceable obligations which can (and do) break down. The break-down of "gentlemen's agreement" (why should we assume that governments act in a gentlemanly way anyhow?) in turn can exacerbate tensions and ill-will. When domestic political forces pressure national governments to pursue an action which only violates an "informal" obligation, the government has little in the way of argument based on international obligation to interpose and resist the pressure. The other country then feels betrayed when the agreement or even its "spirit" is violated.

Likewise the failure to implement the results of international negotiations, caused by the lack of Executive power and sometimes the lack of Congressional, parliamentary, or citizen participation in a negotiated compromise, creates added tensions among trading partners.

All of this suggests that it may no longer be possible to carry on modern economic international relations by traditional or habitual diplomatic techniques.[28] Diplomats no longer carry the power necessary to bind their governments, and the techniques of gentlemanly private negotiations do not lend themselves to a longer range of fundamental developments which will be accepted by the widely varied constituencies and implemented by fragmented power structures. This in turn suggests the need for considerably more attention to both the international and the national institutional structure of international economic relations, and the interaction of these two levels. Perhaps what is needed is to develop national structures which allow citizen participation and consensus building on international trade policy *in conjunction with* counterpart constituencies and citizens from other nations. In any event the *national* institutions – parliaments, courts, citizen litigation, open hearings, advisory committees – must be reconsidered and recognized as part of the international economic process, which they are. Thus *international* institutions also need revision in the light of a better appreciation of the practical possibilities that exist for international action as constrained by the national systems. Simply more short-run "informal" techniques will not suffice; they are already proving inadequate. Better international dispute settlement mechanisms, for example, accompanied by a better and continuous system of negotiation for consensus on rules to diminish the clash of national economic policies, could assist, if designed carefully, to dampen rather than exaggerate the inevitable international tensions of US–EEC growing economic interdependence. Those procedures, however, must take account of the national legal structures and must incorporate the national institutions. The subject matter can no longer be compartmentalized between "national" and "international."

---

[28] The reader may be interested generally in another article by this author relating to current problems of international trade relations, and including some suggestions. See Jackson, "The Crumbling Institutions of World Trade" (1978) 12 *Journal of World Trade Law* 93.

16 Perspectives on the jurisprudence of international trade: costs and benefits of legal procedures in the United States*

The question of how to implement worthy governmental policies is always important – and often neglected. Much attention goes towards the study and formulation of policies, but frequently the question of implementing the policy is relatively ignored or left to "technicians." Yet in connection with many subjects, certainly including international trade, major difficulties and perplexities are encountered in carrying out a policy. An important dimension of international economic policy consists of the legal processes, both international and national, that are connected with implementing those policies.[1]

Both in the United States and abroad the US legal system has been strongly criticized for its handling of international trade regulation.[2] Some of this criticism parallels general statements made about the United States as a litigious society, with too many lawyers and too much attention to "legalism." Despite their serious data faults and some serious misconceptions about comparing the role of a lawyer in the United States to false counterparts in other countries, I feel that it is worthwhile to examine these criticisms more systematically.

It is said, for example, that the US legalistic system of regulating trade is costly, is itself a "nontariff barrier" to trade, and lends itself to manipulative use by special domestic interests. Some of this may be true, but a systematic appraisal must examine at least three questions:

---

* This chapter is based on John H. Jackson, "Perspectives on the Jurisprudence of International Trade: Costs and Benefits of Legal Procedures in the United States" (1984) 82 *Michigan Law Review* 1570–1587. A preliminary and summary version of this article was presented by invitation at a panel chaired by Professor Robert Baldwin of the University of Wisconsin, at the annual meeting of the American Economic Association in San Francisco, December 27, 1983.
[1] See generally J. Jackson, *World Trade and the Law of GATT* (1969); and J. Jackson, *Legal Problems of International Economic Relations* (1977).
[2] See Green, "The New Protectionism" (1981) 3 *Northwestern Journal of International Law and Business* 1; and Advisory Council on Japan–US Economic Relations, *Japan–US Businessmen's Conference, Agenda for Action* (July 1983), 35–39.

1. What are the real costs of the system?
2. What are the benefits of the system?
3. What alternatives to the system exist or are feasible, and what are their costs and benefits?

In this brief article I will confine myself to an analysis of the US legal system pertaining to the regulation of imports, deferring to other works an exploration of similar questions relating to the regulation of exports or other international economic activities. First, however, I wish to touch on policies related to the legal structure of international rules for trade. This will help put the subject of this article in broader perspective, and, although I will focus on US domestic law measures, it will readily be seen that the international system depends greatly on national legal systems for its efficacy, and that to a lesser extent the national legal system likewise depends on the international system. Most policies of each category of system can apply almost equally in the other category. That is, many of the reasons for a "rule-oriented" approach in the international legal system also apply to a national system, and *vice versa*. The following sections discuss separately the three questions mentioned above, along with some policy and historical matters, in the context of US import regulation.

I.   Rule orientation versus power orientation for the procedures of international economic relations

I have written elsewhere about the distinction between "power-oriented" and "rule-oriented" diplomacy.[3] Roughly categorizing diplomatic techniques into these two groups is an oversimplification, of course, but it is a useful one in describing a certain difference in technique and spirit that is involved in international discourse. Particularly when it comes to international affairs, these distinctions can have considerable importance.

Power-oriented techniques suggest a diplomat asserting, subtly or otherwise, the power of the nation he or she represents. Often diplomats of the more powerful nations prefer negotiation as a method of settling matters because they can bring to bear that power to win advantage in the particular negotiation. The "bargaining chips" involved could be promised aid, trade concessions, movement of an aircraft carrier, influence on exchange rates, and the like.

A rule-oriented approach, by way of contrast, would be designed to help institutions which would ensure the highest possible degree of adher-

[3] See, e.g., Jackson, "The Crumbling Institutions of the Liberal Trade System" (1978) 12 *Journal of World Trade Law* 93 at 98.

ence and conformity to a set of rules. The rules themselves would be formulated in advance and would presumably make broad policy sense for the benefit of the world and the parties concerned. Of course, the process of formulating the rules will involve, to a certain extent, power-oriented techniques.

In negotiations for the settlement of disputes between countries, both techniques will be used in varying degrees. If a power orientation prevails, however, the dispute is likely to be settled more from the point of view of which party has the greater power. By contrast, if a rule-oriented approach prevails, the negotiation would resolve the dispute by reference to what the participants expect an international body would conclude about the application of preexisting international obligations.

Although to a large extent all government activity involves a mixture of these two techniques, and indeed to a large degree the history of civilization may be described as a gradual evolution from a power-oriented approach towards a rule-oriented approach, nevertheless the present state of international affairs tips the scales heavily in favor of the power orientation. Yet a strong argument can be made that the same evolution must occur in international affairs and that, as to international economic affairs particularly, there are strong arguments for pursuing evenhandedly, and with a fixed direction, progress in international procedures towards a rule-oriented approach. Several advantages accrue generally to international affairs through a rule-oriented approach, such as: (1) less reliance on raw power and the temptation to exercise it; (2) fairer treatment of the small countries, or at least a perception of greater fairness; and (3) the development of agreed procedures to achieve the necessary compromises. In economic affairs there are additional reasons for a rule-oriented approach.

Economic affairs tend (at least in peace time) to affect more citizens directly than do political and military affairs. As the world becomes more economically interdependent, private citizens increasingly find their jobs, their businesses, and their quality of life affected, if not controlled, by forces from outside their country's boundaries. Thus, they are more affected by the international economic negotiations pursued by their own country on their behalf. A rule-oriented approach allows citizens a greater opportunity to give their "input" into the processes, and also allows decentralized decision-makers (such as entrepreneurs in market-oriented economies) a greater opportunity to plan and to base action on more predictable and stable governmental policies.

II.   Historical overview of the US system of regulating imports

. . .

III.   The policy goals of the US government institutions and procedures for regulating imports

The details of substantive policy goals for US import policy are beyond the scope of this paper, which will instead focus on procedures. However, the first obvious policy goal of any system is to arrive in specific cases at the "right decision." What is the right decision in cases of import regulation is almost never easy to ascertain. Perhaps it is to permit the greatest liberality for imports coming into the United States that can be accomplished without causing undue harm to the US economy, without being too unjust to particular segments of the US economy, and without upsetting important international relations of the United States with foreign countries. As so stated, this is virtually a shibboleth. However, specific cases are very complex and they often pose dilemmas between contradictory goals, such as between the goals of permitting maximum imports yet preventing unfair hardship on particular small segments of the US economy. It is difficult to know and to decide what is right in each case, but that is the essence of government.

Having given due obeisance to substantive policy, most of the remaining policies that I will mention could be categorized as "procedural." These are the policies that underlie the way that institutions and procedures have been shaped within the United States. Unfortunately, many of these policies are overlooked by important critics of the system. Perhaps it will be easiest for the reader if I enumerate them briefly:

1. The procedure should maximize the opportunity of government officials to receive all relevant information, arguments, and perspectives. Thus, a procedure that allows all interested parties to present evidence and arguments would enhance the realization of this goal.
2. The procedure should prevent corruption and ethical *mala fides*, even when the latter fall short of corruption and illegal activity. Another way to express this is that an important policy goal of the procedure is to prevent "back room political deals" that favor special or particular interests while defeating broader policy objectives of the US government.
3. The procedure should enhance the perception of all parties who will be affected by a decision that they have had their chance to present information and arguments, i.e. that they have had their "day in court." This is an important policy objective, particularly for democratic socie-

ties; affected parties must have some confidence in the decision-making process, even when the decision goes against them.

4. The procedure should be perceived by the citizens at large as fair and tending to maximize the chances for a correct decision. A sense of fairness will include a desire that even weaker interests in a society be treated fairly, i.e. that the ability to get a favorable decision will not depend only on money, political power, status, or other elements deemed unfair.

5. The procedure should be reasonably efficient, that is, it should allow reasonably quick government decisions and minimize the cost both to government and to private parties of arriving at those decisions. It is this policy goal that is most questioned by the criticisms of the American "legalistic" procedures.

6. The procedure should tend to maximize the likelihood that a decision will be made on a general national basis (or international basis), not catering particularly to special interests. In other words, the procedure should be designed so that government officials can realistically be assisted in "fending off" special interests that conflict with the general good of the nation.

7. The procedure must fit into the overall constitutional system of the society concerned and be consistent with policy goals underpinning the constitutional system. For the United States, as stated above, an important policy underpinning the Constitution is the prevention of power monopolies within our society. The system of checks and balances thus creates a constant tension between various branches of the government, which may often appear messy, costly, and inefficient, but which is based on fundamental constitutional principles.

8. Predictability and stability of decisions are important values. Predictability of decisions, whether based on precedent, statutory formulas, or something else, enables private parties and their counselors (lawyers, economists, and politicians) to calculate generally the potential or lack of potential for a favorable decision under each of a variety of different regulatory schemes. The greater the predictability, the more likely that cases will be brought only if they have a good chance to succeed. The private lawyer often experiences the situation wherein he counsels clients in the privacy of his office in such a way that the client will use her best judgment to decide not to bring a case.

I make no claim that the list of policy objectives enumerated above is exhaustive; I am certain that others can be considered. Likewise, as stated earlier, the policy goals mentioned tend to be related to national procedures rather than to international procedures. However, many of these goals also apply, sometimes with modified weight, to international institutions and procedures.

IV.   Costs of the US system: quantifiable and non-quantifiable

I want to turn now to an attempt to appraise the costs to US society of the US government system of regulating imports. Again, I am only looking at the import side (export regulations could be taken up separately). Furthermore, I am attempting to evaluate the costs of the "legalistic system." There are certain costs that would be incurred no matter what type of import regulation system a government operated, whether it was a system of broad government discretion or a more legalistic system with hearings, statutory criteria, and judicial review.

The costs can be roughly divided into two types: those that are quantifiable, and those that are difficult, if not impossible, to quantify. I will take up each of these types in turn.

I should also note that the concept of "legalistic" is relative. Even in the US import regulation system, often deemed the most "legalistic" in the world, there are many possibilities for flexibility, executive discretion, and (less fortunately) "deal making."

A.   Quantifiable costs of the US import regulation system

As a rather simplistic exercise, I have tried to evaluate the quantifiable costs in dollars of the US method of regulating imports. A careful evaluation would involve a rather elaborate survey research study, and I have not so far had the resources to undertake that. Furthermore, I am not certain that such a study would be likely to produce results that are meaningfully better than my "rough and dirty" techniques.[4]

The quantifiable costs can be divided into three categories:

1. the budgetary costs of the US government agencies concerned;
2. the costs of private attorneys and external consultants who handle such cases; and
3. the in-house costs of the firms that are engaged in such cases.

---

[4] The available data for this simplistic exercise are limited, although a much more extensive project could probably refine them somewhat. In general I have tried to overstate rather than understate the costs. However, even when data are available, there are dozens of different ways to "array" or present the data, and I am sure many disputes can be generated by these techniques. My goal here is not to develop precise quantities, but to make "order of magnitude" guesses, to help point in the direction of policy conclusions. If nothing else, this exercise may suggest that the important considerations are not quantifiable. Nevertheless, I hope this article might stimulate some other scholar to undertake a more careful appraisal of the costs examined here.

There may be a few other costs that do not easily fall into these three categories, but they are likely to be very small. In evaluating these quantifiable costs I have attempted to exclude, to the extent feasible, the governmental and other costs that would be incurred regardless of the type of regulatory system involved. Thus, I exclude the governmental costs of the Customs Bureau, on the ground that the operation of a general tariff and customs system for imports is virtually universal among governments and does not depend on the type of import regulation. One can, of course, challenge this assumption since there are clearly some minor aspects of the Customs Bureau operations that relate to the "legalistic" regulation of imports. Nevertheless, this seems to be a plausible rough dividing line for the purposes of this article.

1. Governmental costs

Governmental costs are probably the easiest to identify. One simply takes the annual budgetary costs for the agencies involved in the regulation of imports and adds them together. Needless to say, some of the agencies are involved in both exports and imports, as well as some other international economic activities, and to be precise one should disaggregate the activities within an agency. I have found this too difficult, so I have simply included the total budget amount for the several agencies or agency parts that are most concerned with imports, recognizing that my figure in the end will likely be an overstatement of costs.[5] The agencies or parts thereof included were the Office of the US Trade Representative, the import regulation portion of the International Trade Administration (Commerce Department), the State Department Bureau of Economic and Business Affairs, and the International Trade Commission. The total costs estimated for these agencies is approximately $44 million per year.

It is possible on the one hand to try to identify a few positions in a number of other agencies, such as Treasury, Labor, Defense, Agriculture, and a few Congressional staff positions, which are concerned with the import processes of the United States, but on the other hand the inclusion of the entire agencies discussed in the preceding paragraph would certainly more than offset the costs in other parts of government, and if anything the total above will overstate the total US regulatory costs for imports.

2. Identifiable attorney and consultant costs

It is much more difficult to identify and evaluate the nongovernmental costs of the system. Indeed, the figures in this subsection and the next

[5] See Appendix B.

subsection are little more than guesses, although they are educated guesses. For attorneys' fees, I have had the benefit of confidential information from attorney friends who deal in these subjects daily, which has given me some sort of idea of the costs of the various different kinds of trade procedures. When these costs are multiplied by the number of such procedures that are brought in any given year and modified by the number of cases that go on to later procedural steps including judicial review, one can begin to develop a sense of the order of magnitude of the figures that are involved. The types of regulatory processes are numerous,[6] but essentially only five of these (as outlined in Appendix A) have a significant number of annual proceedings and also can be described as part of the "legalistic" trade system.

Using this technique, I have been able to establish that a reasonable (somewhat overstated) estimate of costs for all attorneys' fees for normal trade import actions during 1983 is likely to be about $97 million. There is one important caveat to this: certain major cases tend to have considerably higher costs. For example, the 1982 countervailing duty cases concerning carbon steel imports probably involved attorneys' fees approaching the total attorneys' fees estimated for all countervailing duty cases in one normal year.[7] In other words, there is a bulge in the statistics. Likewise, the Canadian lumber countervailing duty case involved significant attorneys' fees that would be above the average because of the enormous amount of trade covered ($2 billion) and the complexity of the case.[8] However, even with these payments in mind, it still seems fair to evaluate the rough average annual current costs for attorneys and private consultants engaged in various import trade actions of the United States at about the amount stated. This includes the representation for both importers and domestic industry, and would include, where relevant, the costs of representation when they are incurred by foreign governments.

3.   *Costs internal to the firms involved in the proceedings*
I have no sound basis for estimating this figure. It has been suggested to me, however, and I have accepted for present purposes, that the internal firm costs (executives' time, in-house lawyers, clerical time in marshaling evidence and data, etc.) are roughly the same as the external firm and consultant costs.

---

[6] See Appendix A.
[7] The final determination in the carbon steel countervailing duty cases is published in 47 Fed. Reg. 39,304 (1982).
[8] The final determination of the Canadian lumber case is at 48 Fed. Reg. 24,159 (1983).

4.   Combining the various figures

One can easily see that the figures under the three parts above would total approximately $238 million for 1983. To give due allowance to the imprecision of the estimates, we can expand that figure and say that the probability is very high that the total is less than $250 million.

With what can we compare this figure? One obvious comparison is the total value of imports during the year, which for 1983 is estimated to be $254 billion. The result is that the costs of the US import regulation system is 0.0009, or approximately 1/10th of 1 percent of the total annual value of imports. One could conclude that this figure is reasonably insignificant, if it were considered as a sort of "transaction cost" for a regulatory system that had other benefits. It is perhaps not entirely fair, however, to measure or evaluate the cost of the system by dividing those quantifiable costs by the total value of imports. A better cost-benefit approach would be to look at the regulatory system's welfare benefit to society, and I return to that question in the next section of this article. It should also be recognized that this aggregate approach does not answer all relevant questions. For example, the distribution of costs can vary enormously, and may in fact be very unfair (imposing, for example, substantial burdens on certain sectors of the economy, and few burdens on other sectors). Finally, we must remember that there are a number of nonquantifiable costs that need to be weighed in the balance.

B.   Nonquantifiable costs of the import regulatory system

To focus only on the quantifiable dollar costs of the system would be a major mistake. Some of the most important costs may in fact be nonquantifiable. A few of these should be mentioned.

1.   Foreign policy rigidity

A system that depends on statutory criteria and procedures, allows citizen access, and establishes predictability, will inherently diminish the discretion and flexibility of government officials. Indeed, that is exactly what it is designed to do. However, certain types of foreign policy activities may be inhibited by such a system. Secret negotiations are much more difficult and quick decisions are sometimes almost impossible under a "legalistic" system. Indeed, as we demonstrated in the recent countervailing duty case concerning Chinese textiles, as well as in certain portions of the 1982 carbon steel countervailing duty cases, a "legalistic system" tends to give citizen complainants a considerable amount of control over their cases, which in turn risks giving those particular citizens undue advantage to the detriment of broader US foreign policy considerations.[9]

2.   Manipulation or harassment

The legalistic type of system that exists in the United States also lends itself to some abuse by special interests that manipulate the system for their own advantage in ways not necessarily contemplated by the Congress when it enacted the relevant statutes. For example, a complainant may be tempted to initiate a proceeding knowing that the procedure will present considerable opportunity to create mischief and difficulty for US foreign policy while the real motive for using the procedure is to negotiate with the government towards some solution that is not contemplated within the statutory or regulatory procedure set up by Congress. A complainant may really desire certain tax benefits or cartel-like quotas dividing up the US market and ensuring domestic interests of a certain portion of that market. It may bring a trade proceeding that contemplates relief through imposition of a certain amount of tariff-like duties at the border solely to try to get the US government to negotiate in a way that would achieve the complainant's true objective of quota-like restraints. In addition, it has been alleged in some commentary and by some foreign observers that the US system tends to result in "multiple harassment," by which domestic industry complainants can bring one procedure after another even though they know that they probably will not succeed in such procedures. The running battle of domestic television interests against imported television sets is often cited as one instance of multiple harassment. The mere institution of such procedures creates considerable uncertainty in the market for the imports and creates costs for the importing firms concerned. Both factors tend to reduce the importation of such challenged goods initially and to increase importers' general costs of penetrating the US market, with attendant effects upon their later price structure and competitiveness in the US market. Although appraisal of the "multiple harassment" charge is not easy, there appear to be few instances in which it can actually be established that such action has occurred.[10] Even the threat of such activity, however, may itself be somewhat inhibiting to foreign exporters who are eyeing the potential of the US market.

[9] Lawrence, "Chinese Textile Case Rocks Global Trade Scene," *Journal of Commerce*, December 22, 1983, 4A; Pine, "US Delays Decision on Penalty Duties on Chinese Textile Imports Until December 16," *Wall Street Journal*, December 7, 1983, 8.

[10] Several colleagues and I recently examined trade cases in four or five different legal procedures of the United States going back several decades to search for instances in which a US industry had complained under more than one of those laws against the same foreign producer or importer within a span of five years. We discovered approximately twenty such cases.

3. *Wrong law rigidity*

One of the results of the US "legalistic" system of regulating imports is that criteria tend to be embodied in statutes enacted by Congress and then become very hard to change. Because Congress distrusts executive discretion, it tends to establish rather elaborate detail in statutory criteria. But on some occasions the statutory formulas prove later to be inappropriate from a policy or economic point of view.[11] Or an international proceeding will find that the US law violates US international obligations.[12] In these cases it has proved very difficult to get the Congress to change the law, because a variety of special interests tend to be able to block such change. Consequently, the result is that the system has a certain amount of "wrong law rigidity" built into it.

4. *Special interest influence on the formulation of the statutory criteria*

The processes by which the Congress writes the statutory criteria and formulates the law are reasonably well known. The system sometimes lends itself to manipulation by special economic interests in the United States that can foresee the results of certain statutory wordings on their potential cases in the future. Thus, an important economic sector can sometimes influence the Congress in developing criteria that will later prove to be very beneficial to it in particular cases, even though such criteria may not be in the overall best interests of the United States. In this respect, however, the process is no different from that of any domestic subject matter. It is perhaps a price one pays for an open democratic system.

5. *Big cases mishandled*

One of the allegations often made is that the United States' elaborately legalistic system of import regulation may operate with reasonable satisfaction only as to the little cases that are generally unimportant in themselves. But when it comes to very big cases that have a broad influence in major sectors of the economy (such as autos, textiles, agriculture, and

---

[11] For example, some of the intricate criteria of finding foreign "subsidies" for the purposes of the countervailing duty law can, with the advantage of hindsight, be considered inappropriate in terms of economic and other policies. Yet it is thought to be virtually impossible to get Congress to change the law.

[12] The famous "DISC" case (Domestic International Sales Corporation), in which there is a GATT finding that the US law contravenes US international obligations, is one example. US administrations have announced that they will try to get Congress to change the law, but the statute remains unchanged. For a discussion of the DISC case, see Jackson, "The Jurisprudence of International Trade: The DISC Case in GATT" (1978) 72 *American Journal of International Law* 747.

steel),[13] it is said that the system breaks down and in fact returns, by one subterfuge or another, to a "non-rule system" of extensive executive discretion and "back-room bargaining."

6.   *The dilemma of a legalistic system*

As one can begin to surmise from analyzing these various costs, both quantifiable and nonquantifiable, there is to a certain extent a dilemma involved in designing any institutional system for regulating imports. The dilemma is not unique to this subject and is involved in a number of other areas of governmental endeavor also. This dilemma is that the more one maximizes the goals of a legalistic system (predictability, transparency, and elimination of corruption and political back-room deals), the more one sacrifices other desirable goals such as flexibility and the ability of government officials to make determinations in the broad national interest as opposed to catering to specific special interests.

V.   The benefits of the system

The benefits of the legalistic system may be considerable, but they are perhaps harder to appraise. I will discuss them under two categories.

A.   *Procedural benefits of the system*

Apart from costs and delays, the legalistic system responds well to many of the goals and objectives set out in section III above. Clearly, the more extensive and detailed are the statutory criteria, the public proceedings, the opportunity for judicial review and the like, the more likely that the system will be predictable, corruption-proof, and devoid of back-room political deals. An exception to this might be the "big case" question: If the system becomes too rigid, the big cases – those involving considerable political power – will tend to make "end runs" around the system, and thus will not be channeled by the rules and will perhaps be even more vulnerable to flexible executive official discretion than would be the case if

---

[13] The escape clause action against the importation of automobiles resulted in a negative determination by the International Trade Commission. Nevertheless, political forces were such as to induce the United States to encourage the government of Japan voluntarily to restrain exports of automobiles to the United States. The carbon steel countervailing duty cases in 1982 resulted in a settlement agreement which, although heavily influenced by the legal procedures, nevertheless were not, at least explicitly, contemplated by those procedures. The autumn 1983 complaint against Chinese textile imports into the United States resulted in a withdrawal of the complaint at the last minute, after negotiations between the US government and the textile industry during which the government agreed to certain of the industry's import limitation demands. See note 4 above.

the formal procedures were less rigid and could better accommodate the big cases.

B.   Substantive benefits

One of the critical questions, and perhaps the most critical question, is whether this legalistic system, given its costs, in fact provides a substantial measure of benefits (benefits that exceed the costs) to the general welfare of the United States. Here it is necessary to indulge in some assumptions, and to recognize that conclusions are only tentative, in the form of hypotheses that need further testing.

The basic assumption that may be required to justify the legalistic system is that it in fact allows a higher degree of liberal trade access for imports into the US economy. This assumption itself is premised on the assumption that such trade liberalization provides a benefit to the US economy. Most economists believe that trade liberalization does provide such a benefit, and my colleagues at the University of Michigan Department of Economics, Alan Deardorff and Robert Stern, have used their very large international trade model to compute some of the welfare benefits of liberal trade.[14] For example, they conclude that a 50 percent reduction across the board in pre-Tokyo Round tariff levels (from an average of about 8 percent to half that), would result in an additional welfare benefit to the US economy of approximately US$1 billion. There is some indication by them and others that this welfare benefit amount is understated, but we can accept it provisionally, for purposes of comparison.

If we can believe (and although it is essentially a "judgment call" many people do believe it) that the US legalistic system – cumbersome, rigid, and costly as it is – in fact provides for an economy more open to imports than virtually any other major industrial economy in the world, then we could count this as a benefit. But measuring that benefit is obviously very difficult. We are measuring it against an unknown – namely, what would be the degree of import restraint in the US economy if the US system were not so legalistic and were more "discretion prone." Morici and Megna of the National Planning Association have tried to evaluate the current costs of all the various nontariff barriers in the United States, and they arrived at an amount of less than 1 percent tariff equivalent.[15] The current import restraints, they report, are fairly modest in comparison with those of other

---

[14] Deardorff and Stern, "The Structure and Sample Results of the Michigan Computational Model of World Production and Trade" (unpublished manuscript, December 5, 1983) (for presentation at the Symposium on General Equilibrium Trade Policy Modeling, Columbia University, April 5–6, 1984).

[15] Morici and Megna, *US Economic Policies Affecting Industrial Trade – A Quantitative Assessment* (National Planning Association Report No. 200, 1983), 47.

economies, so one might well imagine that the tariff equivalent of import restraints unfettered by a legalistic system might be considerably more restrictive. Another way to say it is that overall import restraint tariff equivalents could increase by 50 percent over pre-Tokyo Round US tariff levels (in the Deardorff–Stern model). Thus the Deardorff–Stern welfare benefit amount of about US$1 billion might be one "ballpark" measure of the more quantifiable of the economic benefits of the trade regulatory system. This compares quite favorably to the quantifiable costs mentioned above (and in Appendix B), although this comparison depends on much-hedged assumptions.

One must not forget, however, that there are also a number of nonquantifiable benefits to the system – greater confidence of the citizenry in the operation of its government in this subject matter, the business planning advantage of a higher degree of stability in governmental actions, reduction of corruption, etc.

VI.   Some concluding remarks and perspectives

What I have tried to do in this brief article is to approach the question of whether the US legalistic and procedural system of regulating imports, despite its considerable costs, has advantages that outweigh those costs. This is, to my knowledge, a first attempt to be somewhat concrete and even quasi-quantifiable in answering this question. Nevertheless, it is very difficult to be too precise, even as to the quantifiable aspects. One could conceive of a more elaborate research study that might gain greater precision in this matter, but one can also doubt that the additional effort of such study would really tell us very much. Even indulging in an overestimation of quantifiable costs and a possible underestimation of quantifiable benefits, one can see that the benefits appear to be very substantial compared to the costs. However, the most important part of the subject may indeed be the nonquantifiable parts, and on those one is likely to receive many different opinions from a variety of knowledgeable observers. In short, the matter seems to be very much "judgmental." People will bring to that judgment their own personal experiences, often involving specific cases, which cases may not be generally representative of the system as a whole.

One thing is clear, however: those who would criticize the existing system must bear the responsibility of weighing that system against viable alternative systems. It is not enough simply to describe in great detail all the horrors, or detriments, of the existing system. It is necessary to weigh in the balance the advantages of the system *and* to do that in comparison with viable alternative systems. Is there any viable alternative system that is likely to be more satisfactory than or even as satisfactory as the existing system? What are the possible alternative systems? The principal one that comes to mind is one that would involve a considerably higher degree of government officials' discretion. We can witness such systems in other major industrial countries with considerable imports. Such observation does not lead one to be confident about those alternatives to the US system. The dangers of corruption are high; the dangers of political manipulation and back-room deals are also high; and often the weaker segments of the domestic economy (frequently including consumers) are the ones who must pay for the resulting decisions that are made for the benefit of the more powerful producing interests. The legalistic system permits well-intentioned governmental officials to fend off certain types of particularistic pressures (but, of course, no system will fend off all such pressures).

Sometimes governmental officials, past, present or future, express considerable impatience with the US legalistic system and yearn for a simpler structure. Often they are simply expressing a bias that can frequently be perceived in government officials, that whatever system exists should leave to those government officials as much discretion and elbow room as possible to make the necessary decisions because those officials inherently feel that they will make the best decisions possible. Others of us may not have such a high degree of confidence in government officialdom.

Appendix A   Major US import regulations

The first five procedures have been analyzed for costs since they involve legalistic procedures and significant private party initiated proceedings each year. As explained in the text, normal customs procedures are omitted. Numbers 6 and 8 have averaged less than one case per year. The column headings refer to explicit statutory or regulatory procedures, but there are also implicit possibilities (such as constitutional challenges in court) that may occur in some cases.

1. *The escape clause*: this law (Trade Act of 1974, § 201, 12 USC § 2251 (1982)) provides that, when increasing imports are the substantial cause of serious injury to a competing US industry, the President can proclaim certain limitations regarding those imports for a temporary period not to exceed five years.
2. *Antidumping*: this law (Trade Agreements Act of 1979, § 101, 19 USC §§ 1673–1677 (1982)) provides that, if imports into the United States are priced at a level that is below the price at which those goods are sold in the market of the producer, then the difference (after adjusting for a number of different circumstances) can be offset with an additional tariff duty at the border of the United States.

Type	Statutory reference (as amended)	Agencies involved	Is there a statutory time limit?	Can citizens initiate complaints?	Is there a public hearing?	Reasoned determination to be published?	Judicial review provided by statute?
1 Escape clause	Trade Act of 1974, §201	International Trade Commission/President	yes	yes	yes	yes	no
2 Antidumping	Trade Agreements Act of 1979, §101	International Trade Administration (Department of Commerce)/International Trade Commission	yes	yes	yes	yes	yes
3 Countervailing duties	Trade Agreements Act of 1979, §101	International Trade Administration (Department of Commerce)/International Trade Commission	yes	yes	yes	yes	yes
4 Complaints against foreign government actions	Trade Act of 1974, §301	US Trade Representative/President	yes	yes	yes	yes	no
5 Unfair trade practices	Trade Act of 1974, §341 (Tariff Act of 1930, §337)	International Trade Commission/President	yes	yes	yes	yes	yes
6 Nonmarket economy safeguards	Trade Act of 1974, §406	International Trade Commission/President	yes	yes	yes	yes	no
7 Textiles	Agricultural Act of 1956, §22	President	no	no	yes	yes	no
8 National security	Trade Expansion Act of 1962, §232	Commerce Department/President	yes	yes	yes ("if it is appropriate")	yes	no

9	Dairy products	Agricultural Adjustment Act of 1933, § 22	Agriculture Department/International Trade Commission/President	no	no	yes	yes	no
10	Meat	Meat Import Act of 1979, § 1	President	no	no	yes (public comment)	yes	no
11	Tax measures (Houdaille)	Internal Revenue Code, § 103(a)(7)(D)	President	no	no	no	no	no
12	Generalized system of preferences	Trade Act of 1974, Title V	President	yes	no	no	yes	no
13	Voluntary restraint agreements	Trade Expansion Act of 1962, § 352	President	yes	no	no	no	no
14	General customs (tariffs)	Tariff Act of 1930, § 516	Treasury	yes	yes	yes	yes	yes

3. *Countervailing duties* (Trade Agreement Act of 1979, § 101, 19 USC §§ 1671–1672, 1675–1677 (1982)): these duties can be assessed at the border of the United States in addition to normal duties to offset any subsidies that the imported goods enjoy.

4. *Complaints against foreign government actions*: the Trade Act of 1974, § 301, as amended by the Trade Agreements Act of 1979, 19 USC §§ 2411–2416 (1982), sets forth a procedure by which US firms and citizens can complain to the US government about foreign government practices affecting US exports or other trading actions. The United States is obliged to study the complaint and if it finds the complaint meritorious, to undertake negotiations and other actions to persuade the foreign government to change its practices. Ultimately it gives authority to the President to retaliate by various measures.

5. *Unfair trade practices* (Tariff Act of 1930, § 337, as amended by the Trade Act of 1974, § 341, 19 USC § 1337 (1982)): this is a very generalized "unfair trade practices" provision, by which US companies can complain to the International Trade Commission that imports are involved in unfair trade practices such as patent or copyright infringement, monopolization, etc. If the ITC finds the complaint meritorious, it can order a ban on all imports of those goods, subject to a presidential override.

7. *Textile import barriers* (Agricultural Act of 1956, § 204, as amended by 7 USC § 1854): the United States, like many other textile-importing countries, takes advantage of the International Multifiber Agreement in the context of GATT, Agreement Regarding International Trade in Textiles, December 20, 1973, 25 UST 1001, TIAS No. 7840, to negotiate a series of bilateral export restraint arrangements with textile-supplying countries.

8. *National security*: A US statute (the Trade Expansion Act of 1962, § 232, as amended by Trade Act of 1974, § 127, 19 USC §§ 1862–1863 (1982)) provides that complaints can be made to the US government that imports are harming a US industry to the extent that would endanger national security. This requires an investigation of the matter by the Commerce Department and a report to the President. The President is authorized to take import-restraining measures if he finds them justified for national security purposes. Only petroleum products have actually benefited from import-restraint action, although a number of other complaints have been made and turned down (complaints average less than one per year).

9. *Dairy product import restraints* (Agricultural Adjustment Act of 1933, § 22, 7 USC § 624 (1982)): originally § 22 of the Agricultural Adjustment Act of 1933 provided for quota-type restraints on a number of agricul-

tural products. For the most part the quota restraints that remain are those involving diary products such as cheese.

10. *Meat imports* (Meat Import Act of 1979, § 1, 19 USC § 1202 (1982)): these can be restrained under provisions of agricultural legislation that try to set limits on the imports of meat based on projections of domestic supply and demand.

11. *Tax measures* (*Houdaille* 47 Fed. Reg. 20411 (1982) (discussion of complaint)): an unusual complaint was brought several years ago by domestic machine tool companies against imports from Japan, arguing that the imports have been favored with various unfair Japanese government practices, including subsidies, and that therefore under the Internal Revenue Act of 1971, § 103, 26 USC § 48(a)(7)(D) (1982), certain tax advantages to US companies for purchasing such imported machines should be denied. The complaint was turned down.

12. *Generalized system of preferences*: under Title V of the Trade Act of 1974, 19 USC §§ 2461–2465 (1982), many goods from most developing countries can be imported tariff-free into the United States. The list of goods, as well as the list of countries that can benefit, can be changed from time to time by the President.

13. *Voluntary restraint agreements* (e.g., Trade Expansion Act of 1962, § 352, 19 USC § 1982 (1982), Agricultural Act of 1956 § 204, 7 USC § 1854 and others): occasionally governments that are exporting to the US will be willing "voluntarily" to restrain the level of those exports. In general, US law prevents the US government from entering into agreements about this (the exceptions are textiles and agricultural goods), but sometimes foreign governments will restrain themselves without an explicit agreement with the US government, although generally with a favorable nod from the US government.

14. *General customs tariffs* (Tariff Act of 1930, as amended, § 516, 19 USC subtitle I (1982)): the United States, like other countries, has a general customs tariff law that requires an entry form to be made for each import. The tariff charge varies from item to item, according to an elaborate tariff schedule. Most tariffs have been reduced significantly under the various negotiating rounds of GATT.

Appendix B   Cost estimates of US import regulation

US Government costs[a]	1982 budget (US$m)	1983 budget (US$m)	Annual estimate (US$m)
International Trade Commission	17.6	19.8	20
International Trade Administration (Commerce, Import regulation)	8.1	n/a	10
Office of US Trade Representative	9.2	10.5	11
Bureau of Economics and Business Affairs, Department of State	n/a	2.23	2.5
Annual total	34.9	32.53	43.5

Private costs: extra-firm (attorneys, etc.)[b]	Approx.[c] number per year	Approx.[c] total cost (US$m)
Escape clause (201–203)	9	4.125
Antidumping: new	50	23.750
Antidumping: annual reviews	109	13.625
Countervailing duty: new	40	16.300
Countervailing duty: annual reviews	81	10.125
Section 337	40	28.000
Section 301	6	1.050
Total	335	96.975

Private costs: intra-firm[d]	96.975
Overall total annual estimate of costs	US$237.450m
Total value of imports, 1983	US$254bn
Costs as a percent of imports	0.0935 per cent
Costs as a fraction of imports	0.000935

Notes:

[a] Estimates are overstated since little attempt has been made to disaggregate for various functions within a unit. On the other hand, as explained in the text, agencies with a very small amount of activities in this area are omitted.

[b] Estimates of total costs are not simply a multiple of cases times average cost per case, but involve estimates of the number of cases which are appealed, go on for further procedures (injury test), etc.

[c] Based largely on 1983 filings, with averages of prior years used to estimate an annual number if 1983 figures seemed unrepresentative.

[d] Guess based on extra-firm costs.

17   The effect of treaties in domestic law in the United States*

Introduction

The law regarding application of treaties in the domestic law of the United States is remarkably complex, for at least two reasons.[1] First, the United States is a mixed or partly dualist legal system with respect to international treaties, so in the case of each treaty, the question must be asked whether it applies as part of the United States domestic law or not. Secondly, under United States constitutional principles, there are at least five different types of international agreements which must be analyzed, even though all of these instruments are "treaties" under international law.

In this study, we will explain the United States law regarding the implementation and application of treaties in its municipal law. We will not, however, be examining the processes of entering into a treaty, nor the legal rules by which it may be determined that an agreement is a valid treaty from either the point of view of United States law, or international law. Likewise we will not here be examining the international application of a United States treaty.

We will take up our subject in two basic parts, corresponding to the outline posed by the organizers of this conference, namely:

I. the effect of treaties in domestic law of the United States; and
II. the interpretation of international agreements by US domestic courts.

---

* This chapter is based on John H. Jackson, "United States" in Francis G. Jacobs and Shelley Roberts (United Kingdom National Committee of Comparative Law) (eds.), *The Effect of Treaties in Domestic Law* (Sweet & Maxwell, London, 1987), chapter 8. I wish to acknowledge the able assistance of Mr. P. Van den Bossche, a graduate student in the law from Belgium, in the preparation of this paper and the documentary support of its text.
[1] Note 27 below lists some of the extensive literature on this subject.

I.   Effect of treaties in domestic law of the United States

A.   *The types of international agreements under United States law*

The United States Constitution mentions only one type of international agreement, termed a "treaty," and provides for one method of approval for the United States. This method is the well-known "advice and consent" by a two-thirds vote of the Senate, following which the President may ratify. However, from the very beginning of United States history[2] a practice developed for alternative types of international agreements in United States law called "Executive Agreements." Although not mentioned explicitly in the United States Constitution, this practice developed and grew until the Executive Agreement (several types exist, as we shall discuss below) became the most numerous form of international agreement into which the United States entered.[3] Supreme Court cases[4] and numerous scholarly works[5] have approved this alternate form of international agreement under United States Constitutional law, although not entirely without challenge.[6]

Although there are various ways one can classify the "Executive Agreements" under United States law, it seems useful to do so by dividing them into four categories. This means there are five categories of international agreements under United States law, all of which, of course, fall within the

[2] For an historical analysis of the use of Executive Agreements, see E. Byrd, *Treaties and Executive Agreements in the US* (1960), 148–179.

[3] As of June 1, 1983, the United States was a party to 906 treaties and 6,571 Executive Agreements. See Treaties and International Agreements: The Role of the United States Senate, S. Rep. 205, 98th Cong., 2nd Sess., 38 (1984).

[4] For a recent example, see *Dames and Moore* v. *Regan*, 453 US 654 (1981), in which the Supreme Court upheld the validity of President Carter's Hostage Release Agreement with Iran. See also, e.g., *Altman and Co.* v. *United States*, 224 US 583 (1912), concerning Congressional Executive Agreements; *United States* v. *Belmont*, 301 US 324 (1937); and *United States* v. *Pink*, 315 US 203 (1942), concerning Presidential Executive Agreements; *Wilson* v. *Girard*, 354 US 524 (1957), concerning authorized Executive Agreements.

[5] E. Borchard, "Shall the Executive Agreement Replace the Treaty?" (1944) 53 *Yale Law Journal* 664; M. McDougal and A. Lans, "Treaties and Congressional-Executive or Presidential Agreements: Interchangeable Agreements: Interchangeable Instruments of National Policy" (1945) 54 *Yale Law Journal* 181; and L. Henkin, *Foreign Affairs and the Constitution* (1970), 173–176.

[6] Some scholars argue that the Framers had the intention to withhold the treaty-making power from the President and do not see any place for Executive Agreements. See R. Berger, "The Presidential Monopoly of Foreign Relations" (1972) 71 *Michigan Law Review* 39–40. Equally critical with regard to Executive Agreements and illustrative of the occasional Congressional attacks on this sort of agreement was the position of Senator Dole in *Dole* v. *Carter*, 444 F. Supp. 1065 (D. Kansas 1977).

single *international law category* of "treaty."[7] These categories can be described as follows.

1.   Treaty

The constitutional word, referring to an instrument which for United States ratification will be submitted to the United States Senate by the President, and, if the Senate gives its advice and consent with a two-thirds vote,[8] the President may ratify.[9]

2.   Congressional previously authorized Executive Agreement

Under well-established practice, confirmed by the courts, the United States Congress, by normal legislation, may delegate to the President the authority to enter into ("ratify") a future international agreement.[10]

3.   Congressional subsequently approved Executive Agreement

Similar to the previous type mentioned (and some classifications would lump these two together[11]) the President may first negotiate an international agreement and then submit it to the Congress (not just the Senate!) for its approval by a normal statute. The statute will specify the international agreement and authorize the President to enter into it on behalf of the United States Government.[12]

4.   Presidential Executive Agreement

In certain circumstances (often controversial), the President can claim direct authority under the Constitution to enter into an international

---

[7] The US Department of State in its internal *Foreign Affairs Manual* uses a four-part classification. Circular 175, *Foreign Affairs Manual*, vol. XI, chapter 700, reprinted in US Department of State, *Digest of United States Practice in International Law* (1974), 199, distinguishes between treaties, agreements pursuant to a treaty, agreements pursuant to legislation, and agreements pursuant to the constitutional authority of the President.

[8] Article II, section 2, clause (2) of the Constitution reads: "[The President] shall have Power, by and with the advice and Consent of the Senate to make Treaties, provided two thirds of the Senators present concur."

[9] But he does not have to ratify; instances exist where the Senate has given advice and consent, but the President later decided not to ratify.

[10] See, e.g., *Cotzhausen* v. *Nazro*, 107 US 215 (1882); and *B. Altmann and Co.* v. *United States*, 224 US 583 (1912). See also "Note, Congressional Authorization and Oversight of International Fishery Agreements under the Fishery Conservation and Management Act of 1976" (1977) 52 *Washington Law Review* 495–511.

[11] E.g., Henkin, *Foreign Affairs*, 173–176.

[12] E.g., the Trade Agreements Act of 1979, section 2(a) (Approval of Agreements): "In accordance with the provisions of section 102 and 151 of the Trade Act of 1974 . . . the Congress approves the trade agreements described in subsection (c) submitted to the Congress on June 19, 1979."

agreement *without any participation* of the Congress (or the Senate).[13] The borderlines of this power (not the subject of this paper[14]) are not entirely clear. the President's choice of procedure and type of agreement to use will be based upon his appraisal of various factors, including the political feasibility of alternative approaches. As a rule the President will, however, adhere to the customs and usages concerning form which have evolved in United States Government practices.[15]

5.   *Treaty-authorized Executive Agreement*
In some cases a fully approved and ratified treaty may itself contain clauses contemplating that the contracting parties to the treaty (nations) can later settle certain lacunae or develop specific applications by entering into a later agreement, which might be viewed as a "subordinate" agreement. Often these agreements are detailed and "ministerial" in nature, without significant broad policy implications and without the input of much official discretion.[16]

---

[13] Compare the Crown prerogative in the UK (Professor Higgins, "United Kingdom" in Jacobs and Roberts, *The Effect of Treaties in Domestic Law*, 124).

[14] See, e.g., McClure, *International Executive Agreements* (1941); C. Mathews, "The Constitutional Power of the President to Conclude International Agreements" (1955) 64 *Yale Law Journal* 345; G. Wright, "The US and International Agreements" (1944) 38 *American Journal of International Law* 341; A. Dean, "Amending the Treaty Power" (1954) 6 *Stanford Law Review* 589; J. Moore, "Contemporary Issues in an Ongoing Debate: The Roles of Congress and the President in Foreign Affairs" (1973) 7 *International Law* 733; "Note, Executive Agreements in the Aftermath of Weinberger v. Rossi: Undermining the Constitutional Treaty-Making Power" (1982–1983) 6 *Fordham International Law Journal* 636–657; "Note, Dames and Moore and Moore v. Regan: The Iranian Settlement Agreements, Supreme Court Acquiescence to Broad Presidential Discretion" (1982) 31 *Catholic University Law Review* 565–590; Wendel, "Constitutional Authority for Executive Agreements Pertaining to the Armed Forces" (1978) 20 *Armed Forces Law Review* 71–86; J. Sparkman, "Checks and Balances in the American Foreign Policy" (1977) 52 *Indiana Law Journal* 433–447; Glennon, "Treaty Process Reform: Saving Constitutionalism Without Destroying Diplomacy" (1983) 52 *University of Cincinnati Law Review* 84–107; and P. Fitzgerald, "Executive Agreements and the Intent Behind the Treaty Power" (1975) 2 *Hastings Constitutional Law Quarterly* 757–771.

[15] US Department of State, *Digest of United States Practice in International Law* (1975), 321.

[16] Examples might be agreements working out the details of a treaty for policy cooperation, or for the status of forces located on foreign soil, etc. In most of these situations, the treaty language can be interpreted, from the viewpoint of US law, as granting the power to enter into these subordinate agreements to the President without further reference to the Senate. The Senate's initial advice and consent to the underlying treaty can be deemed to be a delegation of power by the Senate to the President to carry out the terms of the treaty. Likewise, a similar analysis could be made for cases in which a Congressionally authorized Executive Agreement contains within it the contemplation that contracting parties will enter into later implementing and application agreements. These could be catalogued as a separate "type" or more efficiently simply included under categories 2 or 3 above.

Each of these types of agreement can pose major questions about the validity and correct procedure for entering into or ratifying the agreement, but those questions will not be taken up in this paper. For our purposes, the important questions concern how each of these types of agreements can become part of domestic United States law, and, if so, how we can answer other important questions such as the hierarchy of norms when a particular agreement's rules come into conflict with other rules of the United States legal system. In many situations, as we shall see, the answers to these questions are the same for most and maybe all of the types of agreements listed above. But in some cases the answers differ.

B.   *The key questions of applying international agreements in domestic law*

What is it that we mean when we speak of the domestic application of international agreements? This question is neither easy nor obvious. In fact, there are at least three related but separate questions concerning the domestic law application of each international agreement (in addition to an initial question of "validity," not here discussed).[17] In this section we discuss what each of these three questions is, and how they relate to one another. In the next three sections, we take up details of each of these three questions.

In our analysis of these questions we focus on courts or judges as the "actors" in the domestic legal system, but a more lengthy work could also take up, in a comparable fashion, the role of other branches of government, such as the Executive and its officers, and probably even the legislative branches, not to mention subordinate units of the government, particularly in a federal state. For example, when the President of the United States undertakes to issue a regulation or otherwise act in a way to alter legal rights and duties of persons within the jurisdiction of the United States, many of the same issues which face courts, regarding the domestic application of an international agreement, may need to be considered. For reasons of time and space, however, in this paper we will normally only mention action by courts. This is also a reasonable approach since, at least in the United States, it is usually the courts which are the ultimate arbitrators of these issues.

1.   *Direct application: international agreements as "statute-like law"*

The logical first question is whether a valid international agreement is deemed by the courts of a municipal system to be "law" such that courts

---

[17] Professor Higgins, "United Kingdom," 131*ff*, draws a similar differentiation.

must apply it, similar to "law" found in domestic statutes or other sources. The courts are established under the domestic or national government (written or unwritten) constitution, and therefore it is generally acknowledged that such courts must give their allegiance and obedience to that government constitution. Of course, such a constitution may explicitly command that courts give a certain status to international agreements.[18] But if it does not, the courts may be commanded by implicit direction of the constitution, possibly derived in the context of practice and other sources of interpretation.

If the courts are under the obligation always to apply the international agreement as if it were domestic law (such as a statute), then the courts can go on to the other questions posed below. If, on the other hand, the courts are obligated *never* to utilize an international agreement directly as "statute-like law" in their judgments, the matter is quite different. In a certain sense, the other questions posed below are then irrelevant. However, even when not "directly applicable" or, as often (unfortunately) termed in the United States, "self-executing," international agreements may have an influence or important role in the judicial process. For example, the courts may still be admonished to endeavor to interpret domestic law so as to be consistent with international agreement obligations. This is *not* what we mean by "direct applicability" or "self-executing" in this paper, however.

In the United States, the law on this question is mixed. Courts do not have an easy command either never or always to apply international agreements as domestic law. Instead, as we note in Part I.C below, the courts must explore this questions in each case, to determine whether a particular international agreement, or *even a part* of such agreement, is "self-executing" so that it must be considered as "statute-like" domestic law.

2.   Invocability

Now we come to one of the most confusing concepts regarding the domestic application of international agreements. Even if a particular international agreement, or part thereof, be deemed to play a role in the domestic juridical system similar to that of statute-like law, there is nevertheless an

---

[18] E.g., Article 25 of the German Basic Law (i.e., the Constitution) reads "The general rules of international law shall form part of federal law. They shall take precedence over the laws and create rights and duties for the inhabitants of the federal territory." Thus, treaty provisions would take precedence over domestic law to the extent that they embody "general rules of international law." Articles 65 and 66 of the Netherlands Constitution read: "Clauses of international agreements by whose content everybody is bound shall acquire binding force upon their publication . . ." and "Legislative provisions in force within the Kingdom shall not be applied in cases in which an application would be incompatible with clauses by which everybody is bound contained in agreements which have been concluded either before or after the entry into force of such provisions."

important additional question. This is the question whether a *particular party* before the court in the case being considered has the right to invoke a provision of the international agreement on his own or another's behalf. This question often seems to be discussed as part of the previous question outlined above. In many United States court opinions, for example,[19] the court does not distinguish between these two concepts (sometimes because it does not really need to, in order to come to a correct decision).

Sprinkled through some of the literature on the domestic application of international agreements is reference to some sort of distinction such as that outlined in the previous paragraph. For example, there is a small but undeveloped reference to this distinction in the new *Restatement of the United States Law of Foreign Relations*.[20] Other eminent scholars have mentioned this distinction.[21] Some of the discussion of this distinction, however, seems to confuse some attributes of the concept. For example, it has been suggested that the "self-executing" question is one of domestic law, while the other concept (whatever terminology is used) is one of international law. In fact, there are aspects of both of these questions which can be regarded as subject to domestic law, while other aspects are subject to international law. We will explore these issues further in subparts below.

3.   Hierarchy of norms

If a particular norm of an international agreement is directly applicable (self-executing) *and* it is invocable by a participant in a specific case, it may occur that there are alternative norms in the legal system which seem to be contradictory. If such be the case, then the actor (court) must ascertain which norm shall prevail, i.e. must decide on the hierarchy of competing norms in the particular case.

The first inquiry, of course, should be whether any of the norms are in fact invalid. In such a case, if only one norm is found to be valid, obviously it should prevail. It should be noted that we are talking here about *domestic law* validity. In the United States, for example, it may be that a particular international agreement is unconstitutional (e.g., in a case where the President has exceeded his authority by entering into the agreement), but still valid as an international treaty.[22] (In other systems, it may be that the law

---

[19] See note 29 below.
[20] American Law Institute, *Restatement of the Law, Foreign Relations Law of the US (Revised)* (1986 draft), section 131, note 9 (hereinafter cited as the draft revised *Restatement*).
[21] See note 67 below.
[22] Article 46 of the Vienna Convention on the Law of the Treaties reads: "A state may not invoke the fact that its consent to be bound by a treaty has been expressed in violation of a provision of its internal law regarding competence to conclude treaties as invalidating its consent unless that violation was manifest and concerned a rule of its internal law of fundamental importance."

commands that the question of domestic validity be determined by international law validity of an international agreement, but the essential issue is still the *domestic law* validity of the norm concerned.) For this reason, in many cases it will be necessary to explore the *domestic law* validity of international agreements. However, as previously noted, this topic is not a subject for this paper. In United States law this can, as the reader surely surmises by now, be very complex, requiring a fairly lengthy examination.

When two norms are found to be contradictory and both applicable to a particular case, and by assumption therefore these competing norms cannot be reconciled or "adjusted" to co-exist, the court is faced with the difficult issue of which norm to apply. It is at this point in United States jurisprudence that the analysis of the five different types of international agreements becomes most important. In addition, for purposes of analysis, one must recognize that competing norms could include other international agreements, prior or subsequent regulations at both federal and state levels, and, of course, the Constitution of the United States itself. Part I.E below will take up these "norms conflict" cases.

C.   The self-executing question

In United States jurisprudence, the term "self-executing" is often used to describe the issue of the question analyzed in Part B.1 above, namely, whether all or part of an international agreement can be applied by a court of law in the same manner that it would apply a domestic valid statute (thus we have used the term "statute-like").

1.   The basic approach of United States courts: "self-executing" and its meaning

The United States Constitution mentions the word "treaties" four times. First, in Article I, section 10, clause (1), depriving the states of the treaty-making power.[23] Secondly, in Article II, section 2, clause (2), which provides for presidential negotiation of treaties, then advice and consent of the Senate, and finally the ratification by the President. Thirdly, in Article III, section 2, clause (1), which stipulates that the judicial power shall extend to all cases arising under treaties made by the United States. Fourthly and finally, in Article VI, section 2, in which the Constitution simply states: "This Constitution and the laws of the United States which shall be made in pursuance thereof; and all Treaties made, or which shall

---

[23] *Cf.* Belgian Councils (Professor Maresceau, "Belgium" in Jacobs and Roberts, *The Effect of Treaties in Domestic Law*, 5) and German Länder (Professor Frowein, "Federal Republic of Germany" in Jacobs and Roberts, *The Effect of Treaties in Domestic Law*, 64).

be made, under the Authority of the United States, shall be the supreme Law of the Land . . ."

Referring to the language of this last provision, Chief Justice Marshall, in addressing the issue of a treaty's domestic law effect in the 1829 case of *Foster* v. *Neilson*[24] (still the leading United States Supreme Court case on the issue), stated:

> Our Constitution declares a treaty to be the law of the land. It is, consequently, to be regarded in the courts of justice as equivalent to an act of the legislature, whenever it operates of itself, without the aid of any legislative provision. But when the terms of the stipulation import a contract, when either of the parties engages to perform a particular act, the treaty addresses itself to the political, not to the judicial department, and the legislature must execute the contract before it can become a rule for the court.

The later *Head Money* cases[25] embellished this approach with the following language:

> A treaty . . . is a law of the land as an act of Congress is, whenever its provisions prescribe a rule by which the rights of the private citizen or subject may be determined. And when such rights are of a nature to be enforced in a court of justice, that court resorts to the treaty for a rule of decision for the case before it as it would to a statute.

Unfortunately, neither these nor later cases have prevented considerable confusion about the question of "self-executing." In a 1970 internal State Department memorandum, Attorney Advisor Diven observed that: "An examination of adjudicated cases and of some of the law reviews has failed to disclose a clear definition of the term 'Self-executing treaty.'"[26] The substantial volume of scholarly writing on this issue has not resolved the confusion[27] and the Court of Appeals of the Fifth Circuit stated in *United*

---

[24] 2 Pet. 253 (US 1829).   [25] 112 US 580 (1884).

[26] See Whiteman, *Digest of International Law* (1970), vol. XIV, 304.

[27] There is an impressive amount of scholarly writing, some of which reflects the confusion about the question of "self-executing." For a very recent and impressive article, see Y. Iwasawa, "The Doctrine of Self-Executing Treaties in the United States: A Critical Analysis" (1986) 26 *Virginia Journal of International Law* 627. See also A. Evans, "Self-Executing Treaties in the United States of America" (1953) 30 *British Yearbook of International Law* 178; A. Evans, "Some Aspects of the Problem of Self-Executing Treaties" (1951) 45 *Proceedings of the American Society of International Law* 66; Whiteman, *Digest of International Law* (1970), vol. XIV, 304; L. Preuss, "On Amending the Treaty-Making Power: A Comparative Study of the Problem of Self-Executing Treaties" (1953) 51 *Michigan Law Review* 1117; L. Preuss, "The Execution of the Treaty Obligations Through Internal Law: System of the United States and Some Other Countries" (1951) 45 *Proceedings of the American Society of International Law* 82; E. Feo, "Self-Execution of United Nations Security Resolutions under United States Law" (1976) 27 *UCLA Law Review* 387; L. Henkin, "The Treaty Makers and the Law Makers: The Niagara Reservation" (1956) 56 *Columbia Law Review* 1151; Henkin, *Foreign Affairs*; L. Wildhaber, *Treaty-Making Power and Constitutions: An International and Comparative Study* (1971); E. Dickinson, "Are the

States v. *Postal*, "the self-executing question is perhaps one of the most confounding in treaty law."[28]

In recent cases[29] it seems clear that the courts are sometimes speaking about the separate concept of "invocability" rather than speaking about the concept of "self-executing," but in some cases the courts do not clearly distinguish between these concepts.[30]

It is clear, however, that some international agreements become as much a part of the "law of the land" in United States courts as a federal statute approved by the Congress and the President.[31] On the other hand, courts have expressed the view that certain types of treaty obligations can *never* be "self-executing," because the Constitution reserves certain powers, such as

Liquor Treaties Self-Executing?" (1926) 20 *American Journal of International Law* 444; L. Henry, "When is a Treaty Self-Executing?" (1929) 27 *Michigan Law Review* 776; J. Jackson, "The General Agreement on Tariffs and Trade in United States Domestic Law" (1967) 66 *Michigan Law Review* 250; H. Reiff; "The Enforcement of Multipartite Administrative Treaties in the United States" (1940) 34 *American Journal of International Law* 661; S. Riesenfeld, "The Doctrine of Self-Executing Treaties and US v. Postal: Win at Any Price?" (1980) 74 *American Journal of International Law* 892; S. Riesenfeld, "The Doctrine of Self-Executing Treaties and Community Law: A Pioneer Decision of the Court of Justice of the European Treaties and Community" (1973) 67 *American Journal of International Law* 504; S. Riesenfeld, "The Doctrine of Self-Executing Treaties and GATT: A Notable German Judgment" (1971) 65 *American Journal of International Law* 548; C. Stotter, "Self-Executing Treaties and Human Rights Provisions of the United Nations Charter: A Separation of Powers Problem" (1976) 25 *Buffalo Law Review* 773; O. Schachter, "The Charter and the Constitution: The Human Rights Provisions in American Law" (1951) 4 *Vanderbilt Law Review* 643; B Schlüter, "The Domestic Status of Human Rights Clauses of the United Nations Charter" (1973) 61 *California Law Review* 110; E. Stein, "When is An International Agreement Self-Executing in American Law, Report Prepared for the Sixth International Congress of Comparative Law," reprinted in E. Stein and P. Hay, *Law and Institutions in the Atlantic Area* (1963); B. Cohen, "Self-Executing Agreements" (1974) 24 *Buffalo Law Review* 137; "Note, When Are Treaties Self-Executing?" (1952) 31 *Nebraska Law Review* 463; R. Brandt, "Security Council Resolutions: When Do They Give Rise to Enforceable Legal Rights? The United States Charter, the Byrd Amendment and a Self-Executing Treaty Analysis" (1976) 9 *Cornell International Law Journal* 298; Q. Wright, "National Courts and Human Rights – The Fujii Case" (1951) 45 *American Journal of International Law* 62; Q. Wright, "Treaties as Law in National Courts: The United States" (1956) 16 *Louisiana Law Review* 755; J. Jewett, "Self-Executing Agreements – Trusteeship Agreements" (1974) 10 *Texas International Law Journal* 138; C. Dearborn, "The Domestic Legal Effect of Declarations That Treaty Provisions Are Not Self-Executing" (1979) 57 *Texas Law Review* 233; D. Weissbrodt, "United States Ratification of the Human Rights Covenants" (1978) 63 *Minnesota Law Review* 35; and A. D'Amato, "What Does Tel-Oren Tell Lawyers?" (1985) 73 *American Yearbook of International Law* 92 at 98–99.
28 589 F. 2d 862 at 876 (1979).
29 See e.g., *Dreyfus* v. *Von Finck*, 534 F. 2d 24 (2nd Cir. 1976).
30 See, e.g., in *Mannington Mills Inc.* v. *Congoleum Corp.*, 595 F. 2d 1287 (3rd Cir. 1979) at 1298 in which the Court of Appeals stated: "Mannington has pointed to neither self-executing provisions of the treaty nor implementing legislation. On examining Article 17 of the Paris Convention, however, we find an expression contrary to the concept of a private right of action."
31 See note 27 above.

the power to appropriate funds,[32] or the power to declare war,[33] to the Congress. Likewise, courts have said that constitutional requirements prevent any treaty obligation purporting to define a crime, from being self-executing.[34]

In some cases there is controversy about whether a treaty can constitutionally be "self-executing," as in the celebrated case involving the 1978 treaty between the United States and Panama regarding the Canal, in which the court[35] held: "It appears from the very language used in the property clause [of the Constitution] that this provision was not intended to preclude the availability of self-executing applicable treaties as means for disposing of United States property."[36]

2.   *How to determine whether a treaty norm is "self-executing"*

In addressing the question whether a treaty obligation is self-executing, authors have noted that "there is no sure method for determining" an answer to this question.[37] Nevertheless, the courts have generally said that an obligation to take further legislative or administrative action is not capable of judicial enforcement and therefore not self-executing. On the other hand, courts have stated that if "the obligation is to enforce individual rights specified in the instrument, then rules are prescribed by which the rights of the private citizens or subjects may be determined and thus are of a nature which can be enforced by a court, i.e. self-executing."[38] Despite what courts and scholars sometimes say, however, a treaty can be directly applied ("self-executing") without necessarily creating individual rights. For example, an agreement which addresses only government officials, perhaps providing a basis for certain domestic constitutional powers,[39] may have a "direct effect" in the domestic law, but not create any "private rights."

---

[32] Article I, section 9 of the Constitution stipulates that: "No Money shall be drawn from the Treasury, but in Consequence of Appropriation made by Law." See *Turner* v. *American Baptist Missionary Union*, 24 F. Cas. 344 (No. 14251) (CC Mich. 1852).

[33] See Henkin, *Foreign Affairs*, 159–160.

[34] E.g., *The Over the Top Case*, 5 F. 2d 838 at 845 (D. Conn. 1925). See also Henkin, *Foreign Affairs*, 159–160.

[35] *Edwards* v. *Carter*, 580 F. 2d 1055 (DC Cir. 1978); and US Department of State, *Digest of United States Practice in International Law* (1977), 350.

[36] *Edwards* v. *Carter*, 580 F. 2d 1055 at 1059 (DC Cir. 1978).

[37] Stotter, "Self-Executing Treaties and Human Rights Provisions," 779.

[38] See, e.g., *Head Money Cases*, 112 US 580 at 598–599 (1884); *United States* v. *Bent-Santana*, 74 F. 2d 1545 at 1550 (11th Cir. 1985); *Dreyfus* v. *Von Finck*, 534 F. 2d 24 at 30 (2nd Cir. 1976); *Digges* v. *Richardson*, 555 F. 2d 848 at 850–851 (DC Cir. 1976); and *Re Alien Children Education Litigation*, 501 F. Supp. 544 at 590 (SD Tex. 1980). See also draft revised *Restatement*, § 131(4) and Note 5: Riesenfeld, "The Doctrine of Self-Executing Treaties and GATT," 550; Henry, "When is a Treaty Self-Executing?," 776; Stein, "When is An International Agreement Self-Executing in American Law," 12; and Jewett, "Self-Executing Agreements," 141.   [39] E.g., *Missouri* v. *Holland*, 252 US 416 (1920).

The courts seem to focus on "intent" as the crucial determinant of direct application.[40] For example, the court in *Sei Fujii* v. *State* stated that: "In determining whether a treaty is self-executing courts look to the intent of the signatory parties . . ."[41]

Let us explore these following concepts:

HYPOTHETICAL CASE NO. 1

A treaty between the United States and Nation X states: "It is expressly stipulated that this treaty is not intended to be self-executing nor to become a part of the domestic law of any contracting parties unless implemented by domestic legislation." It is quite clear that a treaty with this or a similar clause will not be self-executing.[42]

HYPOTHETICAL CASE NO. 2

A treaty between the United States and Nation X states: "Each contracting party agrees to enact implementing legislation to effectuate the purposes of this agreement within one year." Here it seems clear that some additional governmental act is contemplated before a measure can become domestic law.

HYPOTHETICAL CASE NO. 3

A treaty between the United States and Nation X provides that government representatives of X residing in the United States shall be authorized to drive vehicles with only a valid X driver's license. Here it seems plausible that the treaty contemplates direct "law of the land" effect and is self-executing. There are, however, unfortunately many in-between cases.[43] In

---

[40] We explore below, "whose intent."

[41] 38 Cal. 2d 718 at 721 (1952); See also *Frolova* v. *USSR*, 761 F. 2d 370 at 373 (7th Cir. 1985); *Cardenas* v. *Smith*, 733 F. 2d 909 at 918 (DC Cir. 1984); and *Tel-Oren* v. *Libyan Arab Republic*, 726 F. 2d 774 at 778 and 808 (DC Cir. 1984). See also Whiteman, *Digest of International Law* (1970), vol. XIV, 309–310; Henry, "When is a Treaty Self-Executing?," 777; Stein, "When is An International Agreement Self-Executing in American Law," 19; and M. McDougal, "The Impact of International Law upon National Law: A Policy-Oriented Perspective" (1959) 4 *South Dakota Law Review* 25 at 77.

[42] Iwasawa, "The Doctrine of Self-Executing Treaties," 657.

[43] In *Mannington Mills Inc.* v. *Congoleum Corporation*, 595 F. 2d 1287 (3rd Cir. 1979), the plaintiff alleged the Paris Convention of 1883 and the Pan-American Convention of 1910 were violated by the defendant. The Court of Appeals examined Article 17 of the Paris Convention ("Every country party to this Convention undertakes to adopt, in accordance with its constitution, the measures necessary to insure the application of this Convention . . . It is understood that at the time an instrument of ratification or accession is deposited on behalf of a country, such country will be in a position under its domestic law to give effect to the provisions of this Convention.") and Article IX of the Pan American Convention ("Persons who incur civil or criminal liability, because of injuries or damages to the rights of inventors, shall be prosecuted and punished, in accordance with the law of the countries wherein the offense has been committed or the damages occasioned.") and

addition, the language of some court opinions speaks not of intent but of the "nature of the obligation imposed by the agreement."[44] To some extent these may mean the same thing, but one could foresee the following case.

HYPOTHETICAL CASE NO. 4

A treaty between the United States and Nation X states in clause 1: "The contracting parties deem the obligations of this treaty to be supremely important and therefore directly applicable in their respective legal systems." And in clause 29: "The contracting parties shall respect the freedom of speech of all citizens of either party." In such a case, would the "intent" or the "nature" of the obligation prevail? It would seem unlikely that clause 29 could be applied as "self-executing" by a court. Possibly a court in the United States might have refuge to some other domestic legal concept, such as "justiciability" or "political question doctrine," to avoid deciding a case based on clause 29.

Commentators[45] have suggested that a list of various factors are used by the courts in these determinations, including:

1. the language of the agreement;[46]
2. the circumstances surrounding the execution of the agreement;[47]

concluded that neither of the treaties were self-executing. In *Demarines* v. *KLM Royal Dutch Airlines*, 580 F. 2d 1193 (1978), the plaintiff invoked the Warsaw Convention. Article 1(1) of the Convention reads: "This convention shall apply to all international transportation of persons, baggage, or goods performed by aircraft for hire." Article 17 of the Convention reads: "The carrier shall be liable for damage sustained in the event of the death or wounding of a passenger or any other bodily injury suffered by a passenger, if the accident which caused the damage so sustained took place on board the aircraft or in the course of any of the operations of embarking or disembarking." The parties and the court agreed on the self-executing nature of the relevant provisions of the Convention. In *People of Saipan* v. *United States Department of the Interior*, 502 F. 2d 90 (9th Cir. 1974), the plaintiff asserted that the action of the governmental defendants at issue was *inter alia* in violation of the Trusteeship Agreement, especially Article 6 thereof. Article 6 requires the United States to "promote the economic advancement and self-sufficiency of the inhabitants, and to this end . . . regulate the use of natural resources" and to "protect the inhabitants against the loss of their lands and resources." The District Court had held the Trusteeship Agreement not self-executing. The Court of Appeals reversed this decision.

[44] *Frolova* v. *USSR*, 761 F. 2d 370 (7th Cir. 1985). See also Jewett, "Self-Executing Agreements," 141.

[45] Weissbrodt, "United States Ratification of the Human Rights Covenants," 68; Wildhaber, *Treaty-Making Power and Constitutions*, 201–202; and Evans, "Some Aspects," 74.

[46] E.g., *Sei Fujii* v. *State*, 38 Cal. 2d 718 (1952); *Frolova* v. *USSR*, 761 F. 2d 370 (7th Cir. 1985); *Diggs* v. *Richardson*, 555 F. 2d 848 (DC Cir. 1976); and *Rice* v. *Sioux City Memorial Park Cemetery*, 349 US 70 (1955). See also Riesenfeld, "The Doctrine of Self-Executing Treaties and GATT," 548; and Schachter, "The Charter and the Constitution," 655.

[47] E.g., *Sei Fujii* v. *State*, 38 Cal. 2d 718 (1952); *People of Saipan* v. *United States Department of Interior*, 502 F. 2d 90 (9th Cir. 1974); *Rocca* v. *Thompson*, 223 US 332 (1912); and *Eck* v. *United Arab Airlines Inc.*, 14 NY 2d 53 (1964).

3. the class of the agreement;[48]
4. the subject matter of the agreement;[49]
5. the history of the agreement;[50]
6. the historical purpose of the agreement;[51] and
7. the parties' own "practical construction" of the treaty, that is, how it has been applied by the parties.[52]

The often-cited 1974 case of *People of Saipan* v. *United States Department of Interior*[53] suggested the following four factors:

1. the purpose of the treaty and the objectives of its creators;
2. the existence of domestic procedures and institutions appropriate for direct implementation;
3. the availability and feasibility of alternative enforcement methods; and
4. the immediate and long-range social consequences of self- or non-self-execution.

In the 1985 case *Frolova* v. *USSR*,[54] the Court of Appeals for the Seventh Circuit considered the following six factors:

1. the language and the purpose of the agreement as a whole;
2. the circumstances surrounding its execution;
3. the nature of the obligations imposed by the agreement;
4. the availability and feasibility of alternative enforcement mechanisms;
5. the implications of permitting a private right of action; and
6. the capacity of the judiciary to resolve the dispute.

3.   *What law determines whether a treaty norm is "self-executing"?*
When a United States court faces a question whether a certain treaty obligation is "self-executing," the question can be raised as to what law, domestic or international, governs this question. In Europe some authors

---

[48] E.g., *Santovicenzo* v. *Egan*, 284 US 30 (1931), which concerns the class of the consular treaties.

[49] E.g., agreements dealing with patents would never be self-executing, *Vanity Fair Mills Inc.* v. *T. Eaton Co.*, 234 F. 2d 633 (DC Cir. 1925); and *Master* v. *Cribben and Sexton Co.*, 202 F. 2d 779 (CCPA 1953); while FCN treaties and especially the provisions conferring rights on foreign nationals are on the contrary often assumed to be self-executing, *Clark* v. *Allen*, 331 US 503 (1947); *Kolovrat* v. *Oregon*, 366 US 187 (1961); and *Askura* v. *Seattle*, 225 US 332 (1924). See also Whiteman, *Digest of International Law* (1970), vol. XIV, 305; Evans, "Some Aspects," 74; and draft revised *Restatement*, § 131, Note 5a.

[50] E.g., *Arizona* v. *California*, 373 US 546 (1963); *Arizona* v. *California*, 292 US 341 (1934); and *Cook* v. *United States*, 288 US 102 (1932).

[51] E.g., *Bacardi* v. *Domenech*, 311 US 150 (1940); *Wright* v. *Henkel*, 190 US 40 (1902); and *Eck* v. *United Arab Airlines Inc.*, 15 NY 2d 53 (1964).

[52] E.g., *Factor* v. *Laubenheimer*, 290 US 276 (1933).   [53] 505 F. 2d 90 (9th Cir. 1974).

[54] 761 F. 2d 370 (7th Cir. 1985).

contend that international law determines whether a treaty is self-executing.[55] In the United States on the contrary, it is generally believed that domestic law determines whether a treaty is self-executing.[56] In a certain sense of course, it is always the "domestic" law which governs, since it is the domestic court which is making the determination. But further analysis is required. Is it possible that the court is bound by the "international law" (if there be any) on this subject? The courts have rarely, if ever, explored this question, simply formulating their legal conclusions and stating them, apparently as domestic law. The question of "whose intent" is sought when "intent" governs the issue is closely related, of course (see below).

As noted in the preceding Part B, however, it is this author's view that the issue of self-executing can involve both domestic and international law. Perhaps only a hypothetical case can clarify this problem. However, it should first be noted that in some systems it could be the case that the domestic law *requires* the courts (and others) to follow the international law (if it exists) on the problem. This seems clearly to be the case in the United States, and the possibility arises that a United States court could come to a conclusion contrary to that of international law, and that such a court decision would cause a breach of United States international obligations.

HYPOTHETICAL CASE NO. 5

A United States and Nation X treaty states: "The parties agree that this treaty shall be 'self-executing' in the domestic law of the United States . . ." (and *vice versa*, if reciprocity is followed in the treaty).

Although it has often been said that international law imposes no obligation on a nation as to *how* it implements an international obligation,[57] this statement is surely too broad. What is undoubtedly meant is that there is no *customary* international law norm on the question of how a nation implements its obligations. But neither is there any customary international law norm which prevents treaty parties from making an explicit agreement on this subject. Why should they want to? In modern diplomacy, diplomats and officials have become more sophisticated about the issues of implementation and about the internal constitutional process of opposing nations. It could well be that such officials feel, through experience or other observation, that the chances of effective implementa-

[55] See Iwasawa, "The Doctrine of Self-Executing Treaties," 650.

[56] See *Aerovias Interamericanas de Panama* v. *Board of County Commissioners*, 197 F. Supp. 230 at 245 (SD Fla. 1961); Preuss, "On Amending the Treaty-Making Power," 1137; Henkin, *Foreign Affairs*, 158; and Evans, "Self-Executing Treaties," 193–194.

[57] J. Winter, "Direct Applicability and Direct Effect, Two Distinct and Different Concepts in Community Law" (1972) 9 *Common Market Law Review* 425 at 426; P. de Visscher, "Les tendances internationales des Constitutions modernes" (1952) 80 *Recueil des cours* 511 at 555.

tion are greatly enhanced by a certain type of procedure. Indeed, it has been argued that "direct application" of treaty norms should be preferred because it may provide for more effective implementation. Thus, for this or other reasons, national negotiators may well desire to specify some modes of domestic implementation as a treaty obligation.

If our case is like that of number 5 above, then it seems clear that there is an *international* obligation on the United States to give self-executing status to the treaty, and that this obliges the courts as well as other government agencies. Yet there may be a domestic rule that prevents such effect, such as a constitutional rule (e.g., regarding appropriation of money). In such a case the domestic court will be bound to follow the domestic rule, and there will be a breach of the international obligation (or possibly the agreement is "invalid"). But our task in this paper is to ascertain the domestic law result.

From this analysis it seems clear that "what law" means domestic law. But it can be seen that there also exists an international law question on the issue of direct application, which in some cases may be inconsistent with the domestic rule. That, of course, is not a unique occurrence.

4.   *If intent is the test, whose intent is meant?*
Finally, for the purposes of this subsection, there remains a particularly troublesome question, namely the question of *whose* intent is relevant. Of course, a first approach of a court should probably be influenced by the general rule that courts should attempt to reconcile potential differences between domestic law and international obligations. Thus, if there is any discernible international obligation on the issue, the United States courts should attempt to apply the treaty norm in a way which is consistent with that obligation. (The United States Constitution may prevent this, of course, as noted above.) Often the international treaty is silent, or nearly so, as to any intent about the existence of an obligation regarding direct application, although the words of the treaty itself may imply to a United States court that a norm is or is not "self-executing," as we have seen above. The intent of a *treaty norm* on this issue was previously discussed as part of the question "what law." That is not what we are now concerned with. The question here is, as a matter of *domestic law* of the United States, whose intent controls?

Many courts have considered the Executive's intent as most relevant in determining whether a treaty is directly applicable. In *Frolova* v. *USSR*,[58] for example, the Court of Appeals for the Seventh Circuit considered President Ford's statement at the time of signature[59] as particularly rel-

---

[58] 761 F. 2d 370 at 373 (7th Cir. 1985).
[59] "[T]he document I will sign is neither a treaty nor is it legally binding on any particular state."

evant for its decision on the direct applicability of the Helsinki Accords. In another recent case, *Cardenas* v. *Smith*,[60] the Court of Appeals for the District of Columbia considered the report of the United States delegate in determining the self-executing nature of the treaty in question.[61] The view of the Executive is, however, not binding[62] and courts have on occasion rejected the Executive's view.[63]

HYPOTHETICAL CASE NO. 6

A United States treaty with Nation X contains a clause which says: "Product standards shall not be used in such a way as to make the sale of goods imported from one of the parties more difficult to sell in the other." When the treaty is presented to the Senate for advice and consent (or to the Congress for authorization to ratify), the Senate report specifies that the treaty shall *not* be self-executing. The President ratifies without further communication on this issue.

Some courts have looked at the Congressional intent.[64] Thus, if in the context of the advice and consent procedure, the Senate passes a resolution that the treaty in question is not self-executing," the courts will apparently follow that formally expressed view. If the view is less formally expressed, e.g. a matter of "legislative history," the issue is less clear.[65]

D.   *The issue of invocability*

Invocability, or something similar,[66] has been mentioned in the literature and court opinions.[67] Not unlike the concept of "self-executing," the analy-

---

[60] 733 F. 2d 909 at 918 (DC Cir. 1984).

[61] This case law found its reflection in the draft revised *Restatement*, § 131, comment h.

[62] E.g., *United States* v. *Postal*, 589 F. 2d 862 at 876 (5th Cir. 1979), cert. denied 444 US 832 (1979). See also Henkin, *Foreign Affairs*, 158.

[63] E.g., *Warren* v. *United States*, 340 US 523 (1951).

[64] E.g., *Re Demjanjuk* v. *Meese*, 784 F. 2d 1114 at 1116 (DC Cir. 1986); and *Bertrand* v. *Sava*, 684 F. 2d 204 at 218–219 (2nd Cir. 1982).

[65] See Henkin, *Foreign Affairs*, 135. The latter, however, is far from generally accepted. See Riesenfeld, "The Doctrine of Self-Executing Treaties and US v. Postal," 901 note 47. It was one of the big points of discussion during the debate on the Senate approval of the four international human rights treaties. See International Human Rights Treaties: Hearings Before the Senate Committee on Foreign Relations, 96th Cong., 1st Sess. (1979); and Iwasawa, "The Doctrine of Self-Executing Treaties," 669–670.

[66] I.e., the concept of creating a "right of action" or a "cause of action" or the concept of "standing."

[67] See, e.g., *Dreyfus* v. *Von Vinck*, 534 F. 2d 24 at 30 (2nd Cir. 1976). See also using the concept "right/cause of action," *Frolova* v. *USSR*, 761 F. 2d 370 at 373–376 (7th Cir. 1985); *Tel-Oren* v. *Libyan Arab Republic*, 726 F. 2d 774 at 808–810 (DC Cir. 1979); using the concept of "standing," *United States* v. *Bent-Santana*, 774 F. 2d 1545 at 1550 (11th Cir. 1985); *Puerto Rico* v. *Muskie*, 507 F. Supp. 1035 at 1064 (DPR 1981); and *Pauling* v. *McElroy*, 164 F. Supp. 390 at 392–393 (DDC 1958). L. Henkin *et al.*, *International Law, Cases and Materials* (1980), 161, suggests, without any elaboration and merely referring to

sis of this concept of "invocability" has been anything but clear. One writer has even stated that, while the issue of "self-executing" is a domestic (municipal) law question, that of "invocability" is an international law question.[68] We must respectfully disagree.

Under our analysis (Part B), we use the phrase "invocability" to indicate the question whether, *even though* a rule of an international agreement is directly applied, a particular party can rely on this rule as "law" in his particular case. This, as we noted, is very much akin to the question of "standing" in United States and other law, but does not need to be equated to it. (In particular, it is necessary to distinguish "standing to sue" from "standing to invoke a particular rule.")

It will be noted that this issue often involves the definition of a class of persons (or, in mathematical terms, a "set"). This could be defined as "all persons," "all citizens," "all officials," etc.

To try to act under the skin of this concept, we will examine some hypothetical cases, in several subsections below. In what follows, we will first deal with the question whether invocability is a domestic or an international law issue, then we will examine the United States jurisprudence.

1.   Is invocability a domestic or international law issue?

Our contention is that it can be both.

HYPOTHETICAL CASE NO. 7

Let us take, for example, an international agreement between Nations A and B, which provides that A and B agree "that this agreement shall be directly invocable by citizens of either in the domestic legal systems of either nation." This agreement creates an international law obligation

the *Dreyfus* case, that self-execution and invocability are two distinct concepts. D'Amato, "What Does Tel-Oren Tell Lawyers?," 98–99, criticizes the link between the concept of "cause of action" and treaties that are "self-executing" made by Judge Bork in his *Tel-Oren* decision. Riesenfeld, "The Doctrine of Self-Executing Treaties and US v. Postal," 896–897, distinguishes between what he calls two aspects of the concept of self-execution: a domestic constitutional aspect dealing with our first question, the "being part of the law of the land" issue; and an international aspect dealing with our second question, the invocability issue. Winter, "Direct Applicability and Direct Effect," 427–428, argues, pointing at the confusion regarding the concept of self-execution in the US, that one should distinguish between the issue of "becoming part of the law of the land" and the issue of "being enforceable by courts." See also L. Ferrari-Bravo, "International and Municipal Law: The Complementarity of Legal Systems" in R. MacDonald and J. Jonston, *The Structure and Process of International Law* (1983), 715. The draft revised *Restatement*, § 131, note 4, makes an "undeveloped reference" to the distinction: "Treaties and other international agreements sometimes confer rights that would support a cause of action by private parties . . . although many that may ultimately benefit individual interests do not give them justiciable legal rights."

[68] Riesenfeld, "The Doctrine of Self-Executing Treaties and US v. Postal," 896–897.

which commits these nations with respect to both questions 1 and 2 in our analysis, because in order to invoke, the agreement must also be directly applied by a court or other actor.

This commitment, incidentally, should be distinguished from the case where the international agreement purports to allow private (nongovernment) individuals *direct access* to an *international* process, as in the European Convention on Human Rights.[69] When an international agreement provides for such direct access to an international procedure or tribunal, it is doing this under international law. It can be a different case from that in which an international agreement obligates a nation to provide access or invocability to individuals of a certain class.

Now examine some other cases.

HYPOTHETICAL CASE NO. 8

Suppose the international agreement between Nations A and B merely states: "Each citizen of either nation shall have the right to own property in the territory of both." In this case the question of implementation has not been explicitly addressed, and thus presumptively has been left to each nation to determine.[70] Nation A might have a legal system like that of the United States, in which the obligation stated in the international agreement could be deemed "self-executing" and furthermore might provide that this rule is invocable by any citizen of either A or B. That would be a domestic law question. Nation B might enact a statute implementing the norm.

Suppose we have the international commitment expressed in the former hypothetical situation. What is the legal relationship of that to domestic law in one of the nations which agreed? (We discussed a similar situation in Part C on the self-executing concept.[71]) If the domestic courts or other actors in, say, Nation A provide for invocability, the domestic law complies with the international law. But if the domestic actor in A does not provide for invocability then Nation A is in violation of its international law obligation. The *domestic law*, however, does not provide the "invocability." Thus we see that, like "self-executing," the issue of invocability can have both an international law and a domestic law dimension. Incidentally, one should note that in addition to the general question of whether a rule is "invocable" in domestic law by members of some class, there is the question

---

[69] Article 25 reads: "The Commission may receive petitions addressed to the Secretary-General of the Council of Europe from any person . . . claiming to be the victim of a violation by one of the High Contracting Parties of the Rights set forth in this convention, provided that the High Contracting Party against which the complaint is lodged had declared that it recognized the competence of the Commission to receive such petitions." M. Miehsler and H. Petzold, *The European Convention on Human Rights, Text and Documents* (1982).

[70] Note 57 above.   [71] Notes 26–27 above.

of how to define the class. Once again, this may have both an international law and a domestic law dimension, and the domestic law determination, if it does not at least fulfill the international law obligation, could result in a breach of the international law obligation.

2.   United States jurisprudence

An analysis of the relevant case law reveals that United States courts quite often discuss invocability in a context where this concept is not carefully distinguished from, and is even confused with, that of self-executing.[72] Nevertheless in some cases the courts have clearly been addressing these two concepts as separate issues. For example, in *Smith* v. *Canadian Pacific Airways Ltd*,[73] the court denied access of a particular party's Warsaw Convention lawsuit to the federal courts on "jurisdictional" grounds, although it clearly and explicitly recognized (as federal courts dealing with the issue have done consistently) that the Warsaw Convention is "self-executing." The problem with this case was that the court felt that the particular circumstances did not give rise to the necessary claim needed to invoke the Convention.[74] In a more recent case *Dreyfus* v. *Von Vinck*, the court also very clearly distinguishes between on the one hand the question of self-execution and on the other hand the question of invocability.[75]

E.   Hierarchy of norms

1.   Analysis of the problem[76]

Assuming both that an international agreement norm is "self-executing" so as to become directly applicable in the domestic jurisprudence of an

---

[72] See, e.g., *Sumitomo Shoji America Inc.*, v. *Avagliano*, 102 S. Ct. 2374 (1982); *Frolova* v. *USSR*, 761 F. 2d 370 at 373–376 (7th Cir. 1985); *Tel-Oren* v. *Libyan Arab Republic*, 726 F. 2d 774 at 808–810 (DC Cir. 1984); *Mannington Mills Inc.* v. *Congoleum Corp.*, 595 F. 2d 1287 at 1298 (3rd Cir. 1979); *United States* v. *Bent-Santana*, 774 F. 2d 1545 at 1550 (11th Cir. 1985); *Puerto Rico* v. *Muskie*, 507 F. Supp. 1035 at 1064 (DPR 1981); and *Pauling* v. *McElroy*, 164 F. Supp. 390 at 392–393 (DDC 1958).
[73] 452 F. 2d 798 at 802 (2nd Cir. 1971).
[74] The plaintiff invoked the Warsaw Convention to recover for injuries suffered during a flight from Canada to Japan. The Court of Appeals for the Second Circuit, however, dismissed the complaint for lack of treaty jurisdiction. It was not contested that the Warsaw Convention was self-executing, needing no Congressional implementation to make it and its provisions creating a rebuttable presumption of liability (Article 17) and limitations thereon (Article 25) constitutionally enforceable. Article 28 of the Convention, however, set forth four forums as the only places in which a suit could be brought: the domicile of the carrier (Canada), the principal place of business of the carrier (Canada), the place of destination of the flight (Japan), and the place of business through which the contract has been made (Canada). Every phase of the activity involved in this case occurred outside the United States, a fact that places the appellant outside the boundaries of Article 28(1) and makes the Convention non-invocable before a US court.
[75] 534 F. 2d 24 (2nd Cir. 1976).   [76] See the Appendix to this article.

obligated state and that it is "invocable" so that it becomes relevant in a specific case before a national legal system court, then inevitably there will arise the question of conflict with other norms of that legal system. As indicated in Part B above there may be several "escapes" from the need to decide which of several conflicting norms shall prevail in a particular case:

1. First analysis may show that only one of the conflicting norms is a valid norm for the purposes of the domestic legal system. It must be stressed that the issue here is *not* the international legal validity of an international agreement, but the domestic legal validity. If a domestic statute, a domestic regulation, and a self-executing invocable international agreement all conflict, and it can be shown that the statute and the regulation are invalid (perhaps unconstitutional, or *ultra vires*), then there is no problem: the international agreement prevails. If, on the other hand, the statute or the regulation is valid in domestic law, the issue of the validity of the international agreement arises. This is the domestic law issue. For example, it may be established that a treaty was improperly entered into, or that the President has exceeded his authority under prior Congressional authorization for an Executive Agreement. In such a case the international agreement may be *invalid* under domestic law, although it is still possible for it to remain a binding international law obligation on the nation.[77]

2. Secondly, it may be possible to reconcile the divergences between the potentially conflicting norms. When the diverging norms are both international agreement norms, the courts may be guided by normal interpretive rules to try, as they would with two potentially conflicting domestic statutes, to interpret the two in such a way as to avoid conflict. If only one of the potentially conflicting rules is that of an international agreement, however, the courts in the United States have a long-standing rule of interpretation[78] which calls upon them to seek to avoid conflict with international obligations by interpreting the domestic norm so as to avoid conflict with the international norm.[79] If neither of these escapes is possible, nor the escape of "non-self-executing" or "non-

---

[77] See note 23 above. In Italy, the validity of treaties may also be questioned judicially (Professor Gaja, "Italy" in Jacobs and Roberts, *The Effect of Treaties in Domestic Law*, 101). Elsewhere, courts are often prohibited from questioning validity (Professor Higgins, "United Kingdom," 124; Professor de la Rochère, "France" in Jacobs and Roberts, *The Effect of Treaties in Domestic Law*, 42; and Professor Schermers, "Netherlands" in Jacobs and Roberts, *The Effect of Treaties in Domestic Law*, 111).

[78] This is a common rule (see also Professor Frowein, "Federal Republic of Germany," 691; Professor Higgins, "United Kingdom," 135 and 137; Professor Gulman, "Denmark" in Jacobs and Roberts, *The Effect of Treaties in Domestic Law*, 33; Professor Gaja, "Italy," 100; and Professor de la Rochère, "France," 60).

[79] Draft revised *Restatement*, § 123.

invocable," then the court faces the question of which of equally valid and applicable norms shall prevail.

We have seen at the outset of this paper that under United States domestic law there are five different types of international agreements.[80] Any one of these can come into conflict with a variety of domestic legal norms, including norms of the United States Constitution, federal statutes and regulations (prior and subsequent), similar state laws, and possibly even other "legal creatures." Again it must be stressed that, to find that any of these domestic norms prevail over a norm of an international agreement, does not determine whether such international norm continues to obligate the United States as a matter of international law. If such norm does continue to obligate, then a court action giving precedence to the domestic norm will almost always result in a breach by the United States of its international obligations, subjecting it to such international remedies as may be available to some foreign offended state.

2.   *International agreements and the common law*
No provision of the Constitution explicitly regulates the hierarchical place of self-executing international agreements among the federal legal norms. Quite early on, however, it was derived from the Supremacy Clause, Article VI, section 2, that international agreements and federal statutes are of equal authority.[81] Since statutes prevail over common law, so must international agreements.

3.   *Federal versus state law*
The relation between international agreements and state law[82] is explicitly regulated by Article VI, section 2 of the Constitution. This Article stipulates that treaties, similar to the Constitution and federal statutes, are part of the supreme law of the land. Therefore they are superior to state law.[83] Whereas the Constitution in fact only refers to "treaties" this term has been interpreted to cover all international agreements, even a Presidential Executive Agreement.[84] Moreover, an international agreement may prevail over the power of a state even with respect to matters which usually fall within the control of the state. In *Missouri* v. *Holland*,[85] Mr. Justice Holmes said: "It is

---

[80] See the Appendix to this article.
[81] See, e.g., *Head Money Cases*, 112 US 580 (1884); and *The Chinese Exclusion Case*, 130 US 581 (1899).
[82] I.e., the state constitution, state statutes, and state regulations.
[83] This is comparable with the situation in Germany and in Italy (Professor Frowein, "Federal Republic of Germany," 67; and Professor Gaja, "Italy," 95).
[84] See, e.g., *United States* v. *Belmont*, 301 US 324 (1937); *United States* v. *Pink*, 315 US 203 (1942); *Calnetics* v. *Volkswagen of America Inc.*, 353 F. Supp. 1219 (DC Cal. 1973); and *De Geofroy* v. *Riggs*, 133 US 258 (1890).   [85] 252 US 416 (1920).

obvious that there may be matters of the sharpest exigency for the national well-being that an act of Congress could not deal with but that a treaty by such an act could . . .''[86] This then raises the question whether anything residual exists in state-reserved powers, but we cannot go into that here.[87]

4.   Supremacy of the US Constitution

What happens if an individual invokes in court a norm of an international agreement which is clearly self-executing and invocable but which violates a Constitutional provision? Article VI, section 2 of the Constitution states: "This Constitution, and the law of the United States which shall be made in Pursuance thereof; and all Treaties, made or which shall be made under the Authority of the United States, shall be the Supreme Law of the Land."

For years, this language created some confusion since it seemed to imply that treaties, unlike laws, do not have to be in pursuance of the Constitution but merely have to be concluded under the authority of the United States. The Supreme Court itself was far from clear with regard to the relation between the Constitution and international agreements.

It was only in 1957 that the issue seemed finally to be laid to rest. In *Reid* v. *Covert*,[88] the Supreme Court ruled that:

no agreement with a foreign nation can confer power on Congress, or on any other branch of Government, which is free from the restraints of the Constitution . . . The prohibitions of the Constitution were designed to apply to all branches of the National Government and they cannot be nullified by the Executive or the Executive and the Senate combined.

The supremacy of the Constitution over treaties is now a firmly established rule.[89]

5.   United States law and the later-in-time principle

As pointed out above, courts have, on the basis of the Supremacy Clause, established that federal statutes and self-executing treaties are of equal status in United States law. Consequently, in case of inconsistency between a treaty and a statute, it will be the later-in-time which will prevail.[90] This

[86] 252 US 416 at 433 (1920).
[87] See J. Jackson, J.-V. Louis, and M. Matsushita, *Implementing the Tokyo Round, National Constitutions and International Economic Rules* (University of Michigan Press, 1984), 142–145.
[88] 354 US 1 (1957).   [89] Draft revised *Restatement*, § 131, comment a.
[90] Draft revised *Restatement*, § 135, comment a and note 1. See also, e.g., *The Chinese Exclusion Case*, 130 US 581 (1899); *Head Money Cases*, 112 US 580 (1884); *The Cherokee Tobacco*, 78 US (11 Wall.) 616 (1871); *Cook* v. *United States*, 288 US 102 (1933); *Whitney* v. *Robertson*, 124 US 190 (1887); *La Abra Silver Mining Co.* v. *United States*, 175 US 123 (1899); *Thomas* v. *Gay*, 169 US 261 (1898); *Fong Yue Ting* v. *United States*, 149 US 698 (1893); and *Botiller* v. *Dominguez*, 130 US 238 (1898).

later-in-time rule has been followed virtually universally by the United States courts. It has been criticized by a few writers, however.[91] The greater problem is the question of whether the later-in-time rule also applies in a conflict between a Congressional act and an Executive Agreement, especially a Presidential Executive Agreement.

6.   Remaining "toughest" cases

THE EXECUTIVE AGREEMENT AND PRIOR FEDERAL
STATUTE

In *United States* v. *Guy Capps Inc.*[92] The Court of Appeals held that an Executive Agreement could not prevail against an earlier act of Congress. The Supreme Court affirmed the case, though on other grounds, and refused to consider the question of hierarchy, thus weakening the *Guy Capps* precedential effect.[93] Under the 1965 *Restatement* an Executive Agreement concluded pursuant to the constitutional authority of the President "does not supersede inconsistent provisions of earlier acts of Congress."[94] Some commentators shared this position.[95] There have, however, always been dissenters.[96] This issue is particularly delicate and unresolved. The current draft *Restatement*[97] says:

The effect in domestic law of an executive agreement made by the President under his own constitutional authority (§ 303(4)) in respect of an earlier treaty or federal statute has not been established. See Reporters' Note 5.

Reporters' Note 5 states:

5. *Sole executive agreement inconsistent with State or federal law.* A sole executive agreement made by the President on his own constitutional authority, is the law of

---

[91] P. Potter, "Relative Authority of International Law and National Law in the US" (1925) 19 *American Journal of International Law* 315 (1925); and Howard Tolley Jr., "The Domestic Applicability of International Treaties in the United States: A 'Treaty Priority' Alternative to the 'Last-in-Time' Rule" (1983) 17 *Revista Juridica de la Universidad Ineramericana de Puerto Rico* 403.
[92] 204 F. 2d 655 (4th Cir., 1953).
[93] See *South Puerto Rico Sugar Co. Trading Corp.* v. *United States*, 334 F. 2d 622 (Ct. Cl. 1964). For a critical analysis of *Capps*, see Mathews, "The Constitutional Power of the President."
[94] *Restatement of the Law (Second), Foreign Relations Law of the United States* (1965), § 144(1)(b), note 10.
[95] McClure, *International Executive Agreements*, 344; Dean, "Amending the Treaty Power," 607; Borchard, "Shall the Executive Agreement Replace the Treaty?," 671; and McDougal and Lans, "Treaties and Congressional-Executive or Presidential Agreements," 317.
[96] Mathews, "The Constitutional Power of the President," 381; Moore, "Contemporary Issues in an Ongoing Debate," 741; and Henkin, *Foreign Affairs*, 186.
[97] *Restatement*, § 135, comment c.

the land and supreme to State law. *United States* v. *Belmont*, 301 US 324 (1937); *United States* v. *Pink*, 315 US 203 (1942). It has been held, however, that such an agreement cannot supersede an earlier treaty or act of Congress. *United States* v. *Guy W. Capps Inc.*, 204 F.2d 655 (4th Cir. 1953), affirmed on other grounds, 348 US 296 (1955) (executive agreement by-passing procedures prescribed by Congress for limiting imports); *Swearingen* v. *United States*, 556 F. Supp. 1019 (D. Colo. 1983). That view has been supported by the suggestion that the act of a single person, even the President, cannot repeal an act of Congress. On the other hand, it has been argued that a sole executive agreement within the President's constitutional authority is federal law, and United States jurisprudence has not known federal law of different status under the Constitution. "All Constitutional acts of power, whether in the executive or in the judicial department, have as much legal validity and obligation as if they proceeded from the legislature." *The Federalist* No. 64 (Jay), cited in *United States* v. *Pink*, 315 US 203, 230 (1942). See Henkin, *Foreign Affairs and the Constitution* 186, 432–433 (1972). Of course, even if a sole executive agreement were held to supersede a statute, Congress could proceed to reenact the statute and thereby supersede the intervening executive agreement as domestic law. In *Dames & Moore* v. *Regan*, 453 US 654 (1981), the Supreme Court upheld President action pursuant to a sole executive agreement that was claimed to be inconsistent with an earlier act of Congress, the Foreign Sovereign Immunities Act (see §§ 451*ff*). The Court upheld the agreement, in large part because Congress had historically accepted and had repeatedly acquiesced in the power of the President to make such agreements. It also found no inconsistency between the agreement and the Foreign Sovereign Immunities Act. See §.303, Reporters' Note 7.

Professor L. Henkin (the *Restatement* chief reporter), argues in his *Foreign Affairs and the Constitution* that later Executive Agreements prevail:[98]

If one sees the Treaty Power as basically a Presidential Power (albeit subject to checks by the Senate) there is no compelling reason for giving less effect to agreements which he has authority to make without the Senate. If one accepts Presidential primacy in foreign affairs in relation to Congress, one might allow his agreements to prevail even in the face of earlier Congressional legislation.[99]

It is interesting to note, however, that the Executive branch itself has apparently accepted that Presidential Executive Agreements do not always prevail over prior Congressional acts.[100]

---

[98] Henkin, *Foreign Affairs*.
[99] Henkin, *Foreign Affairs*, 186. Henkin cites only one judicial decision in support of his position, *Etlimar Société Anonyme of Casablanca* v. *United States*, 106 F. Supp. 191 (Ct. Cl. 1952). He fails to mention that *Etlimar* was expressly overruled by *Seery* v. *United States* 127 F. Supp. 601 (Ct. Cl. 1955).
[100] See P. Lesser, "Superseding Statutory Law by Sole Executive Agreement: An Analysis of the American Law Institute's Shift in Position" (1983) 23 *Virginia Journal of International Law* 671 at 692–694; and Whiteman, *Digest of International Law* (1970), vol. XIV, 227.

DOMESTIC LAW CONFLICT BETWEEN TWO INTERNATIONAL
AGREEMENTS

A problem may arise when two international agreements, both self-executing and invocable, are in conflict. The basic rule here is: the later-in-time
prevails. A later agreement supersedes or impliedly repeals a former agreement where it covers the subject matter of the former treaty.[101] Whether
this is also the case when a later Executive Agreement conflicts with an
earlier treaty remains unclear.[102]

II.   Interpretation of international agreements by United States
       domestic courts

A.   Introduction

There still seems to be an amazing lack of awareness of the fact that the
interpretation of international agreements by domestic courts is far more
common and in many cases more important than the interpretation by
international tribunals. In this part of the paper, we attempt to give a
general overview of the interpretation of treaties by United States courts.
Because of the restrictions on length, we focus on the questions posed by
the organizers. The study of the interpretation of international agreements
by courts in the United States is of special interest since the latter mode of
interpretation is allegedly somewhat different from the approach
commonly taken by the courts of many other countries.[103]

B.   The main characteristics of the United States courts' approach to
      interpretation

The courts of most countries interpret international agreements in accordance with the ordinary meaning of the text of the agreement; the object and
purpose of the agreement is merely ancillary, casting light on the ordinary
meaning.

The courts of the United States, however, have a distinctly different
approach to interpretation. The ordinary meaning of the words is for
American courts merely one of the factors to be taken into account in the

---

[101] *Fotochrome Inc.* v. *Copal Co. Ltd.*, 517 F. 2d 512 (2nd Cir. 1975); *Behring International Inc.*
v. *Imperial Iranian Air Force*, 175 F. Supp. 383 (DCNJ 1979); *République Française* v.
Schultz, 57 F. 37 (CCNY 1893); and *Junkers* v. *Chemical Foundation*, 287 F. 597 (DCNY
1922).
[102] Draft revised *Restatement*, § 135, note 5: "it has been held, however, that such agreements
cannot supersede an earlier treaty"; the draft revised *Restatement*, § 135, comment d, calls it
"uncertain."
[103] Draft revised *Restatement*, § 325, comment h and note 5.

interpretation process. The prime objective of interpretation by American courts is to ascertain the meaning intended by the contracting parties.[104] There is a strong tendency to reject literal-minded interpretation, a tendency that is not dominant in many other countries.[105] Even a very hasty analysis of the relevant case law reveals that American courts heavily rely on the intention of the parties. Characteristic are statements such as: "Treaties must receive a fair interpretation according to the intention of the contracting parties."[106]

The prevalence of the intent of the parties over the language of the agreement has been repeatedly sanctioned by the Supreme Court. In *Sumitomo Shoji America Inc.* v. *Avagliano* it was held that the clear import of the treaty language controls *unless* application of the words of the treaty according to their obvious meaning effects a result inconsistent with the intent or expectations of its signatories.[107] In another case, *Clark* v. *Pigeon River*, it was ruled that the intention of the parties as evidenced by the whole of a particular provision will govern, notwithstanding that as a matter of grammatical construction a different conclusion may be indicated.[108] In some cases the taking of the intention of the contracting parties as the governing principle of interpretation was expressly based on the presumptive identity of the rules governing the interpretation of both treaties and contracts.[109]

Apart from the importance given to the intention of the contracting parties, the American approach to interpretation is also characterized by the "rule of liberal interpretation." Courts are to interpret international agreements liberally so as to effect the apparent intention of the parties. This rule of liberal interpretation was first formulated in *Shanks* v. *Dupont*,[110] where the court rhetorically asked: "If the treaty admits of two interpretations, and one is limited, and the other liberal; one which furthers and the other which excludes private rights, why should not the most liberal exposition be adopted?"

---

[104] *United States* v. *Conners*, 606 F. 2d 269 (CA Colo. 1979); *Great-West Life Assurance Co.* v. *United States*, 678 F. 2d 180 (Ct. Cl. 1982); *Re Anschuetz and Co.*, 754 F. 2d 602 (CA 5th Cir. 1985); and *Wickes* v. *Olympic Airways*, 745 F. 2d 363 (CA 6th Cir. 1984).

[105] Draft revised *Restatement*, § 325, note 5. As noted there, the difference in result between the "international" and the American approaches to interpretation is perhaps not that big and should certainly not be exaggerated. The difference may be more a difference in emphasis and presentation.

[106] *Wright* v. *Henkel*, 190 US 40 at 57 (1903).

[107] *Sumitomo Shoji America* v. *Avagliano*, 457 US 176 (1982). See also *Maximov* v. *United States*, 373 US 49 (1963); and *Harris* v. *United States*, 768 F. 2d 1240 (11th Cir. 1985).

[108] *Clark* v. *Pigeon River Improvement Slide and Boom Co.* v. *Charles W. Cox*, 291 US 138 (1934).

[109] C. Scheuer, "The Interpretation of Treaties by Domestic Courts, *British Yearbook of International Law* (1971), 255 at 277.

[110] 3 Pet. 242 (1830).

C.   Factors to be taken into account in the interpretive process

In interpreting international agreements, American courts will take account of various factors. First, courts take account of the words of the agreement, but in addition they will have recourse to *travaux préparatoires*, "foreign" judicial decisions, state practice and a number of other factors in order to shed some light on the meaning of an international agreement.

1.   Travaux

The Supreme Court has ruled on several occasions that, in construing a treaty, recourse may be had to the negotiations. In a recent case, *Air France* v. *Saks*,[111] the Court ruled that, in interpreting a treaty, it is proper to refer to records of its drafting and negotiation.[112] The draft revised *Restatement* notes that whereas the Vienna Convention, reflecting the position of many countries, is quite reluctant in permitting the use of *travaux préparatoires*, American courts are not.[113]

2.   "Foreign" judicial decisions

While the interpretation of agreements by the courts of other nations will be given due weight, such "foreign" interpretations are ordinarily not binding on the United States as a matter of international law and therefore not binding on American courts.[114] The same is true for the interpretation of agreements by international tribunals in cases to which the United States is not a party. The interpretation of an agreement by an international body authorized by the agreement to interpret, however, is binding on the United States and its courts.[115]

3.   State practice

American courts, in interpreting international agreements, will take into account the subsequent practice of the contracting parties.[116] The construction which has been placed on an international agreement by the parties themselves, as reflected in state practice, is an important factor in

---

[111] 105 S. Ct. 1338 (1985).
[112] Other examples are *Nielson* v. *Johnson*, 279 US 47 (1929); *State of Arizona* v. *State of California*, 292 US 341 (1934); *Factor* v. *Laubenheimer*, 290 US 276 (1933); and *Cook* v. *United States*, 288 US 102 (1933).
[113] Draft revised *Restatement*, § 325, comment f.
[114] Draft revised *Restatement*, § 325, note 5.
[115] Draft revised *Restatement*, § 325, note 5 refers to *Matter of International Bank for Reconstruction and Development*, 17 FCC 450 at 461 (1953).
[116] Draft revised *Restatement*, § 325, comment d.

the interpretation by American courts.[117] To establish that state practice recourse may be had, for example, to diplomatic correspondence subsequent to the treaty.[118] The difficulty here is, however, that few countries publish a digest of their international practice, including diplomatic notes and other actions reflecting treaty interpretation. For most countries there are no systematic reports of practice available. Furthermore, those countries that do publish a digest, such as the United States,[119] often publish only after considerable time.[120]

4.   Other factors

1. US courts will give great weight to an interpretation made by the Executive.[121] Sometimes the State Department will file an *amicus curiae* brief in order to present the views of the government. Occasionally, courts have asked the State Department to do so. It is clear, however, that the interpretation given by the Executive is not binding.[122] Nevertheless, it has been noted that courts generally follow the Executive's interpretation. On occasion, however, courts have rejected the interpretation of the Executive. In the recent case of *Sumitomo Shoji American America* v. *Avagliano*, the District Court and the Court of Appeals did not follow the State Department's interpretation while the Supreme Court did so. It has been noted that courts are more likely to defer to an Executive interpretation already made in diplomatic negotiations with the other contracting parties than to one adopted by the Executive in relation to a case before the courts, especially where individual rights are involved.[123] It is noteworthy that, while the Senate plays no formal part in the carrying out of a treaty, the courts feel bound to respect understandings expressed by the Senate in the process of its advice and consent.[124] The meaning of a treaty will, however, not be controlled by a later Senate resolution purporting to clarify a treaty to which it had already given its consent.[125]

---

[117] *Pigeon River Improvement Slide and Boom Co.* v. *Charles W. Cox*, 291 US 138 (1934); *Sumitomo Shoji America* v. *Avagliano*, 457 US 176 (1982); and *United States* v. *Decker*, 600 F. 2d 733 (9th Cir. 1979).

[118] *United States* v. *Pink*, 315 US 203 (1942); and *Terrace* v. *Thompson*, 236 US 197 (1923).

[119] The digests edited by Wharton Moore, Hackworth and Whiteman and the more recent annual digests.

[120] Draft revised *Restatement*, § 325, note 4.

[121] *Factor* v. *Laubenheimer*, 290 US 276 (1933); *Kolovrat* v. *Oregon*, 366 US 187 (1961); *Zschernig* v. *Miller*, 389 US 429 (1968); *Sumitomo Shoji America* v. *Avagliano*, 457 US 176 (1982); and *Denjanjuk* v. *Petrovsky*, 776 F. 2d 571 (CA 6th Cir. 1985).

[122] *Galanis* v. *Pallanck*, 568 F. 2d 234 (2nd Cir. 1977).

[123] *TWA* v. *Franklin Mint Corp.*, 466 US 243 (2nd Cir. 1984).

[124] Draft revised *Restatement*, § 326, comment a.

[125] *14 Diamond Rings* v. *United States*, 183 US 176 at 180 (1901).

2. US courts seem to view the object and the purpose underlying an international agreement as an important factor to take into account in the interpretation process.[126] United States courts have repeatedly refused to choose interpretations of an international agreement which were inconsistent with the general purpose and object of that agreement.[127]

3. US courts will take into account the consequences of a particular interpretation. They must give effect to the clear and unambiguous provisions of a valid treaty notwithstanding resultant inconvenience but, in ascertaining the meaning of provisions which are not free from doubt, they may take into consideration the results which would follow a particular construction.[128]

D.   *The interpretation of international agreements in the light of a nation's own legal concepts*

When the interpretation of a term used in an international agreement after the exhaustion of all international law sources of interpretation is still impossible and no information about the intention of the parties is forthcoming, American courts will have recourse to the corresponding domestic legal term. Normally, however, resort to *lex fori* is rejected.[129] Words in an international agreement are to be given their natural and ordinary meaning as understood in the public law of nations.[130]

The application of American law concepts of interpretation is a different matter, however. The use of contract law concepts of interpretation has developed into a well-established rule. In *Sullivan et al.* v. *Kidd*,[131] the Supreme Court remarked that: "Writers of authority agree that treaties are to be interpreted upon the principles which govern the interpretation of contracts in writing between individuals."[132] More recently, it was ruled that: "the meaning of a treaty is to be ascertained by the same rules of construction and reasoning which apply to interpretation of private contracts."[133]

---

[126] *Wright* v. *Henkel*, 190 US 40 at 57 (1903); *Ross* v. *McIntyre*, 140 US 453 at 457 (1891); *Ford* v. *United States*, 273 US 593 at 618 (1927) *Todok et al.* v. *Union State Bank of Harvard, Nebraska et al.*, 281 US 449 at 454 (1930); *Santorincenzo* v. *Egan*, 284 US 30 at 37 (1931); *Warren* v. *United States*, 340 US 523 at 527 (1951); and *Maximov* v. *United States*, 373 US 49 at 55 (1962).

[127] *Sullivan et al.* v. *Kidd*, 254 US 433 at 440 (1921).

[128] *Chryssikos* v. *Demarco*, 107 A. 358, 134 Md. 533; *Matter of D'Adamo*, 106 NE 81, 212 NY 214.

[129] *Geofroy* v. *Riggs*, 133 US 258 (1890).

[130] *Watson* v. *Hoey*, 59 F. Supp. 197 (SDNY 1943); they should not be given any special or artificial meaning impressed on such words by local law in absence of a clear intention to the contrary.

[131] 254 US 433 (1921).   [132] 254 US 433 at 439 (1921).

[133] *United States* v. *Kember*, 685 F. 2d 451 (CADC 1982).

Appendix   Issues of hierarchy of norms

International law ⟶

Domestic law ⟶

	treaty	Congressional-Executive agreement		Presidential agreement	Treaty authority
		pre-	post-		
Customary international law	1	2	3	4	5
A. Common law					
B. Federal State "Statute-like"					
C. Constitution					
D. Federal statutes prior					
E. Subsequent					
F. Federal regulations prior					
G. Subsequent					
H. International agreements (five types)					
I. State statute (prior/subsequent)					
J. State regulations					

18   Status of treaties in domestic legal systems: a policy analysis*

Introduction: direct application and self-executing nature of treaties

The degree to which an international treaty is "directly applied" or "self-executing"[1] in a national (municipal)[2] legal system, i.e. to what extent the treaty norms are treated directly as norms of domestic law ("statute-like

* This chapter is based on John H. Jackson, "Status of Treaties in Domestic Legal Systems: A Policy Analysis" (1992) 86 *American Journal of International Law* 2, 310–340. I was General Counsel for the Office of the US Trade Representative in the mid-1970s. Some of the arguments and reflections in this article are derived from this and similar experience. I would like to express gratitude for the counsel and advice on various drafts of this article from Professors William Davey, Francis Jacobs, Richard Lauwaars, Meinhard Hilf, Marc Maresceau, Mitsuo Matsushita, Henry Schermers, Eric Stein, and Pieter van Dijk. In addition, I would like to express my gratitude for information received from Carlos Bernal of Mexico; Thomas Cottier of the Government of Switzerland; Professor Yuji Iwasawa of Osaka City University, Japan; Professor Autar K. Koul of the University of Delhi, India; and Matthew Schaefer (regarding Australia). I would also like to recognize the able research assistance of Yves Renouf and Daniel Nelson, students at the University of Michigan Law School.
1 The terms may not always be used identically, but "self-executing" is very similar to "direct application." "Direct application" will be the preferred term here, since it seems more effectively to express the notion that the international treaty will be a part of the domestic legal system, very similar to a "statute." As used here, "direct application" expresses the notion that the international treaty instrument has a "direct" statute-like role in the domestic legal system, but it is not meant to differentiate between different kinds of such direct roles. Thus, the term "direct application" will not be limited to situations in which private parties can sue on the basis of the treaty norm, but will also cover situations in which governments, or different levels of government, might utilize the treaty norm as part of domestic jurisprudence. It is therefore quite likely that the term "direct application," as used in the European Community's jurisprudence, is not the same in all respects as "direct application" in this article. Furthermore, this usage by the Community is probably not identical to the US use of the term "self-executing." Nevertheless, for most purposes, these differences should not prove troublesome, and the term "direct application" seems better to express the notions explored in this article. The reader should notice the distinction made below between "direct application" and "invocability." See the text at note 36 below.
2 International law practitioners and scholars often speak of "municipal law" in referring to the domestic laws of a particular nation-state and contrasting them with international law. In this article, the terms "municipal law," "national law," and "domestic law" will be used interchangeably.

law") without a further "act of transformation,"[3] has been debated in an extensive literature for more than a century. This subject is now receiving increased recognition as part of a broader trend acknowledging that understanding an international legal system necessitates understanding the relationship of national legal and political systems to that international system.[4] In connection with treaties, the basic concepts of "monism" and "dualism" have long been used to explain some of the relationships of treaty law to domestic law.[5]

This article explores some of the *policy* considerations relating to the effect of an international treaty in domestic law. Many excellent works

[3] When an international treaty is not directly applicable in the domestic law system but requires the provision of domestic rules to be carried out, such rules can often be provided by an "act of transformation." See the text at note 20 below; see also note 1 above. The phrase "act of transformation" is not precisely defined. In some cases, a statute may simply "implement" a treaty norm, such as by appropriating money for an award under a treaty. Such "implementation" probably can be distinguished from "transformation." Thus, "transformation" seems to be a term that is reserved for placing a general treaty norm into the domestic jurisprudence. In some cases, the treaty language would be altered by the act of transformation, and at some point the alteration will be so great as no longer to be transformation but, instead, implementation. Some scholars and practitioners also use terms such as "incorporation," "reception," and "adoption." See M. Hilf, "General Problems of Relations Between Constitutional Law and International Law" in Christian Starck (ed.), *Right, Institutions, and Impact of International Law According to the German Basic Law: The Contributions of the Federal Republic of Germany to the Second World Congress of the International Association of Constitutional Law* (1987), 177–195; van Dijk, "Domestic Status of Human-Rights Treaties and the Attitude of the Judiciary – The Dutch Case" in *Festschrift für Felix Ermacora* (1988), 631; and Seidl-Hohenveldern, "Transformation or Adoption of International Law into Municipal Law" (1963) 12 *International and Comparative Law Quarterly* 88. It is not entirely clear how these terms are distinguished among themselves, or from "transformation." Presumably, they refer to the transfer of the treaty language into domestic jurisprudence largely without alteration, or at least much alteration. There is also a concept of "publication," which would apply even in the case of direct application. Thus, it can be argued that, even though a treaty has direct application, it will not be "received" in the domestic jurisprudence until "published," in the same manner as for other laws.
[4] The importance of this relationship is recognized (although with substantial differences in opinion) in such works as M. S. McDougal and W. M. Reisman, *International Law in Contemporary Perspective: The Public Order of the World Community: Cases and Materials* (1981); McDougal, "The Impact of International Law upon National Law: A Policy-Oriented Perspective" (1959) 4 *South Dakota Law Review* 25 (1959); L. Henkin, *Foreign Affairs and the Constitution* (1972); L. Henkin, *Constitutionalism, Democracy and Foreign Affairs* (1990); L. Henkin, R. Pugh, O. Schachter, and H. Smit, *International Law Cases and Materials* (2nd edn., 1987), chapter 3; J. Jackson, *The World Trading System: Law and Policy of International Economic Relations* (1989); E.-U. Petersmann, *Constitutional Functions and Constitutional Problems of International Economic Law* (1991); and Trimble, "International Law, World Order, and Critical Legal Studies" (1990) 42 *Stanford Law Review* 811 at 812.
[5] See, e.g., I. Brownlie, *Principles of Public International Law* (4th edn., 1990); Sasse, "The Common Market: Between International and Municipal Law" (1966) 75 *Yale Law Journal* 695; and "Introduction" in Francis G. Jacobs and Shelley Roberts (United Kingdom National Committee of Comparative Law) (eds.), *The Effect of Treaties in Domestic Law* (1987), vol. VII, xxiv.

have endeavored to explain the complex and often-confusing legal effects of this relationship.[6] Often these works have taken the legal status of those effects, in one national system or another, as relatively given, perhaps by a constitutional rule. Sometimes, however, their legal status has been hotly disputed, or even deemed to change over time within the same country.[7] Some commentators have extensively debated the theoretical underpinnings of a rule on the domestic legal effects of treaties relating them to views about the nature of law and the basis of international law.[8] (In practice, in certain nations that do have such a rule, the courts and other institutions have seemed to find ways to evade applying it.) Rarely has a systematic attempt been made to explore the *policy* grounds for the contending positions, on the basis of empirical and pragmatic considerations.[9]

Currently, a great deal of "constitution making" is taking place in the world, as nations in Eastern and Central Europe reconstitute their governments, the actual and potential member states of the European Community continue the demanding, but exciting, process of developing a European constitution,[10] and other regional groupings of nation-states explore closer trade and treaty relations.[11] Some of this activity entails

---

[6] Jacobs and Roberts, *The Effect of Treaties in Domestic Law* is the most recent broad survey. See also M. Waelbroeck, *Traités internationales et juridictions internes dans les pays du Marché Commun* (1969); K. Holloway, *Modern Trends in Treaty Law* (1967); and H. Schermers and D. Waelbroeck, *Judicial Protection in the European Communities* (4th edn., 1987). For discussion of several special treaty types, which, however, has relevance to other treaties, see, e.g., on the ILO, V. Leary, *International Labour Conventions and National Law: The Effectiveness of the Automatic Incorporation of Treaties in National Legal Systems* (1982); on the Genocide Convention in US law, see E. Potter, *Freedom of Association, the Right to Organize and Collective Bargaining – The Impact on US Law and Practice of Ratification of ILO Conventions No. 87 and No. 98* (1984); and on the European Convention on Human Rights, see A. H. Robertson (ed.), *Human Rights in National and International Law* (Proceedings of the Second International Conference on the European Convention on Human Rights, 1965) (1968).
[7] See the interesting account of the ILO Conventions in Leary, *International Labour Conventions and National Law*, particularly at 154–155, noting (*inter alia*) that "governments themselves may erroneously report their national constitutional law, or the constitutional law may change." See also Robertson, *Human Rights in National and International Law*.
[8] See the works cited in notes 4, 5, 6, and 7 above.
[9] Among the works that discuss policy issues are McDougal, "The Impact of International Law upon National Law"; Sasse, "The Common Market"; Leary, *International Labour Conventions and National Law*; and Robertson, *Human Rights in National and International Law*.
[10] For a recent discussion of some of these questions in the European context, see "Symposium, Approaching Democracy: A New Legal Order for Eastern Europe" (1991) 58 *Chicago Law Review* 439.
[11] Prominent among these actual, or potential, regional groupings are the US–Canada Free Trade Agreement of 1988, and the negotiations that began in 1991 towards a broader "North American Free Trade Agreement" including the United States, Canada, and Mexico.

consideration of rules regarding the making of treaties and their status in domestic law. In addition, since within some existing constitutional systems the legal status of international treaties is not entirely clear, courts and other bodies still have room to influence this status in differing directions.[12] Thus, the *policies* concerning choices among different types of status for international treaties in domestic law are very important. These policies may relate to the pros and cons of the direct application of treaties. They may also suggest intermediate positions: only certain treaties or certain parts of treaties would have direct application, or treaties might have certain direct effects but not others, or such issues might be influenced or determined by the way certain clauses in the treaty itself or its preparatory work are drafted.[13]

Furthermore, a crucial issue raised by the direct application of treaties involves the hierarchical status of the treaty norms in the domestic legal system. In some jurisdictions, when there is a clash between a directly applied treaty norm and another norm (such as a statute, even a later-enacted statute), the treaty norm may prevail. This "trumping" effect obviously can affect the desirability of direct application, and also relates to (or derives from) the constitutional processes of treaty-making (such as the parliamentary or other democratic contribution to the process).

One of the basic conclusions of this article is that there are sound policy reasons for a national legal system with typical democratic institutions to avoid the combination of direct domestic law application of treaties and higher status for those treaty norms than later-enacted statutory law. This conclusion depends greatly on the relative degree to which constitution drafters trust international institutions and treaty-making processes compared with national institutions and legislative processes. But, in any event, the premise here is that these relationships and policies are too little understood and that gaining an understanding of them can have vital

---

[12] Although some feel that the legal situation in the European Community has now been established by decisions of the Court of Justice, others note that, while the Court has considered the matter, its actual decisions have not definitively ruled on some matters such as higher status for directly applicable treaties. See Stein, "External Relations of the European Community: Structure and Process" in *Course of the Academy of European Law* (1991), 13; Hilf, "The Single European Act and 1992: Legal Implications for Third Countries" (1990) 1 *European Journal of International Law* 89, especially at 94 and note 17; and note 124 below. The application of some of these rules in other countries such as Japan reveals considerable ambiguity. See the text below at note 121. There is even some debate in the United States, as well as recent court opinion (see note 118 below), that raises some interesting questions. Bodies that could influence the issue other than courts might include legislatures (which might specify their intent or control) or certain administrative bodies. See Reisman, "An International Farce: The Sad Case of the PLO Mission" (1989) 14 *Yale Journal of International Law* 412; and the text at notes 137–138 below.

[13] See Part IV below.

consequences both with national systems and beyond.[14] It should be quickly noted that even if a treaty norm does not prevail as a matter of domestic law, it will likely still be "in force" as a matter of international legal obligation. Furthermore, as we shall note below, it can have certain "internal effects" other than "statute-like direct application."

Thus, this article treats two questions: the status of treaties in national legal systems, that is, the question of "direct application"; and the hierarchical status in national legal systems when directly applied treaty norms clash with other norms of the same system. Although these two questions most often are visible in the action of courts, they can also be manifested in the working of other institutions.

It may not always please some readers' sense of style, but it is convenient and sometimes promotes precision to use acronyms for key concepts. Consequently, "direct application" of a treaty in response to Question 1 is sometimes abbreviated below as DA, and the according of higher status as HS. When both direct application and higher status are provided, the abbreviations may be merged to DAHS. Obviously, alternatives to DAHS include the lack of direct application (requiring an act of transformation, as discussed below) and, in cases where direct application has occurred, a status for the treaty that is not higher than that of other norms such as subsequent legislation.

It should be noted that the analogous and important issue of the status of *customary* international law in national legal systems is *not* treated in this article. Some (but not all) of the policy issues are similar, but that subject is left for other works.[15]

I.   The legal setting: understanding the alternatives

Monism and dualism

For those who have not had contact with the literature and practice on treaty effects in domestic law, let us first examine the broad outlines of the

[14] Obviously, the approach of this article is pragmatic, policy-oriented and empirical rather than "theoretical," and this is possibly controversial to those who are otherwise inclined, including those who argue that there is a "trend" towards direct application of treaties or that there is an international obligation to apply treaties directly. In addition, this article is not premised on the *a priori* superiority of international law, conventional or otherwise, but suggests that experience and observations about international norms by policy-makers will count heavily in their weighing of the relevant arguments in particular contexts. Clearly, these are issues that theorists or holders of contrary opinions should tackle.

[15] See, on that subject, Henkin, *Foreign Affairs*, especially chapter VIII; Henkin, "International Law as Law in the United States" (1984) 82 *Michigan Law Review* 1555; *Restatement (Third) of the Foreign Relations Law of the United States* (1987), chapter 2; Henkin, "Lexical Priority or 'Political Question': A Response" (1987) 101 *Harvard Law Review* 524.

existing international situation with respect to the direct applicability of a treaty, using a simple paradigmatic hypothetical to illustrate it. Suppose nations M and D have entered into a treaty[16] that includes the following obligation:

With respect to the right to own property within the territory of either contracting party [nation M or D], the citizens of the other contracting party shall have equal nondiscriminatory treatment as compared to treatment received by the citizens of that contracting party within which the property is located.

The intent of this language is to equalize the property ownership rights of both countries' citizens within the territory of each contracting party, a traditional expression of "national treatment" obligations found in many bilateral and multilateral[17] treaties, although the subject of the obligation may differ widely.

In traditional explanations of the effect of treaties (going back a century or more), a distinction is made between "monist" and "dualist" states.[18] This terminology has been criticized, and clearly it is too "dichotomous" in flavor, since there are various degrees of direct application of treaties, to say nothing of the considerable confusion about it. Nevertheless, even though not precise, these terms are used and may help to demonstrate the major alternative approaches.

Let us assume that state M is considered "monist" and state D is considered "dualist," and in each state a citizen of the other has been refused rights to own property by the national government even though that state's citizens possess those rights. What is the *national* legal situation?

Traditionally, the "monist" state's legal system is considered to include international treaties to which M is obligated. Thus, a citizen of D can sue

16 The terms "treaty" and "international agreement" are used here in the manner defined and described in the Vienna Convention on the Law of Treaties, opened for signature May 23, 1969, Article 2, 1155 UNTS 3311, reprinted in 8 ILM 697 (1969) (entered into force January 27, 1980). We will have occasion below to cite this Convention as a convenient reference on the rules of international law, or those governing treaties, even though various nations are not bound (not parties, such as the United States) and the Vienna Convention technically does not apply to some treaties (e.g., those which preceded the Convention).
17 For example, the General Agreement on Tariffs and Trade (GATT), Article III; and many treaties of friendship, commerce and navigation. John H. Jackson and William Davey, *Legal Problems of International Economic Relations: Cases, Materials and Text* (2nd edn., West Publishing, St. Paul, MN, 1986), chapter 8, and 266.
18 See note 5 above and the accompanying text. The author is aware that some writers tend to play down this terminology, or feel that it is unnecessary. See, e.g., the descriptions of such views in McDougal, "The Impact of International Law upon National Law," 28 and 31. Nevertheless, as a matter of empirical observation, court opinions, national officials, and authors do use this terminology, at least in some jurisdictions. See, e.g., Brownlie, *Principles of Public International Law*, chapter II; and Hilf, "Rights, Institutions and Impact of International Law."

as an individual in the courts of M to require that he be treated in accordance with the treaty standard.[19]

On the other hand, the term "dualist" has been used to describe the contrary result in state D. In a dualist state, international treaties are part of a separate legal system from that of the domestic law (hence a "dual" system). Therefore, a treaty is not part of the domestic law, at least not directly. Without further facts, a citizen of M who is refused the property ownership privilege in D that D's citizen has there, has no way to sue in the courts of D because those courts apply the law of D, which does not include the rule expressed in the treaty (at least not yet). The citizen of M's only recourse is to persuade his own government to use diplomatic means to encourage D to honor its obligation and assure him equal property owner-ship rights.

It is generally said that for the treaty rule to operate in the domestic legal system of a dualist state, there must be an "act of transformation," that is, a government action by that state incorporating the treaty norm into its domestic law.[20] This may be a statute duly enacted by the parliament that uses all or part of the treaty language and incorporates it as a statutory matter into domestic law.[21] Sometimes such a statute may paraphrase the treaty language, or "clarify" or elaborate on the treaty language. In all these cases, the domestic law is that of the act of transformation, but the treaty language usually has "relevance" in interpreting the statutory language, under various theories of domestic jurisprudence.[22] Other legal instru-ments can also serve as an act of transformation, including a regulation of an administrative body (if its authority so permits), and possibly even an action or decision of a court or tribunal (again, depending on the authority of the tribunal).[23] Like other concepts discussed here, "act of transform-

---

[19] It is assumed in this article that aliens or citizens of the relevant foreign nation have access to the courts of a domestic legal system.

[20] See Brownlie, *Principles of Public International Law*, the references in note 6 above, and the description in note 3 above.

[21] In many cases, the statute that operates as the act of transformation also authorizes the appropriate government officials to "accept" or ratify the treaty itself. For example, see the US Trade Agreements Act of 1979, Pub. L. No. 96–39, 93 Stat. 144, especially § 3, Relationship of Trade Agreements to United States Law, and relevant legislative history. See Jackson, *The World Trading System*, 76; Frowein, "Federal Republic of Germany" in Jacobs and Roberts, *The Effect of Treaties in Domestic Law*, 63 and 66.

[22] E.g., *Restatement*, § 114 (which reads: "Where fairly possible, a United States statute is to be construed so as not to conflict with international law, or with an international agreement of the United States"). See also Jackson, *The World Trading System*, 75; J. Jackson, J.-V. Louis, and M. Matsushita, *Implementing the Tokyo Round: National Constitutions and International Economic Rules* (University of Michigan Press, 1984), 167. See generally Jacobs and Roberts, *The Effect of Treaties in Domestic Law*.

[23] For example (although probably rare), a court might be delegated authority to issue a device that would apply a treaty, perhaps on a petition for *mandamus*. This situation is to be distinguished from a court's deciding that a treaty is directly applicable in a particular case.

ation" is not uniformly defined, and there are several other terms that compete with, or may (in the view of some) be subsumed within, this phrase, such as "incorporation," "adoption," "reception," and similar terms. Likewise, the term "implementation" of treaties must be contrasted with, and in some cases embraces, the "act of transformation," as well as "direct applicability."[24]

Issues of treaty application

The direct application of treaties is only one of a series of legal/constitutional issues relating to treaties and national legal systems. In this article we do not deal with all these issues, but an appreciation of the existence and relationships of some of them – in other words, the "landscape" or setting of the subject – may enhance understanding of direct application. Indeed, the issue of treaty-making, that is, how treaty-making powers are allocated among national government institutions and the procedures required for entering into a treaty, is closely related to policies concerning direct application. For instance, if a constitutional treaty-making procedure does not provide for "democratic participation" such as parliamentary approval, it would not be surprising to find reluctance to have the treaty affect domestic law until a parliament has acted (as we see in England and some Commonwealth countries[25]). The parliamentary act can be the act of transformation, and its requirement as part of the domestic law-making system can substitute in part for the direct participation in treaty-making of parliaments in other constitutional systems.[26]

This "landscape" of legal/constitutional issues regarding treaties in domestic law certainly includes the following (and perhaps more):

1. the power to negotiate;
2. the power to "sign" (usually *ad referendum*, only to certify the text);[27]
3. the power to "accept" the treaty as a binding international law obligation;
4. the "validity" of the treaty under national constitutional law (closely related to (3));
5. the power to implement the treaty obligations;

---

[24] See note 3 above.
[25] See Holloway, *Modern Trends in Treaty Law*, 193*ff*; and Sawyer, "Australian Constitutional Law in Relation to International Relations and International Law" (1984) *International Law in Australia* 35, especially at 47*ff*. Sawyer notes that "owing to the dominant position of Parliament in systems of British origin this corollary [that international agreements should be part of domestic law] is not accepted." *Ibid.*, 48.
[26] See Higgins, "United Kingdom" in Jacobs and Roberts, *The Effect of Treaties in Domestic Law*, 123; and Frowein, "Federal Republic of Germany."
[27] See Vienna Convention, Articles 9 and 10.

6. direct applicability of the treaty in domestic law;
7. invocability in municipal law (contrasted with direct applicability);
8. a hierarchy of norms in domestic law when treaty norms conflict with norms of that law; and
9. the power to administer the treaty, which includes a series of issues, such as the procedure for formal "ratification"; the power to interpret the treaty for domestic application and as a matter of international law; the power to represent the country in institutional procedures relating to the treaty (e.g., bilateral or multilateral meetings); the power to "vote" in such procedures; the power to amend the treaty; and the power to terminate the treaty (on various grounds, including the exercise of a termination clause).[28]

A complete description of each of these powers is not feasible here, but a brief comment on a few selected issues will illustrate the broader setting of the subject of this article.[29]

The first[30] and second[31] issues need not detain us, although they can be problems in certain circumstances.

The third issue, the power to "accept" the treaty, is more significant. Whether a nation is bound by a treaty, as a matter of international law, by virtue of having accepted it has substantial bearing on the *international* law determination of whether the treaty is "valid," in contrast to the *domestic* law question of validity.[32]

Fourthly, whether the treaty is "valid" under domestic law (usually constitutional law) can be a very difficult question in some constitutional systems (including that of the United States).[33] A treaty that is valid and binding under international law may nevertheless be *invalid* under the constitutional law of one of the participants, perhaps because that nation's

---

[28] Jackson, "United States of America" in Jacobs and Roberts, *The Effect of Treaties in Domestic Law*, 141.

[29] See also *ibid.*

[30] The power to negotiate refers to the power of a nation's representatives to negotiate with a view to forming a treaty. National systems differ in the extent to which this power is implied or always rests in an executive. The US President has this power under the Constitution, but in some other systems there must be a preliminary "mandate" or "direction" adopted by a law-making process before representatives are authorized (at least formally) to open discussions that might lead to a treaty. See, e.g., Stein, "Towards a European Foreign Policy? The European Foreign Affairs System from the Perspective of the United States Constitution" in Cappelletti, Seccombe, and Weiler (eds.), *Integration Through Law* (1986), vol. I, book 3, at 3.

[31] The power to "sign" refers to the concept in the Vienna Convention of signing to authenticate a treaty draft. Generally, today, this will not be the same as "acceptance." Signing is often *ad referendum*. See Vienna Convention, Article 10.

[32] *Ibid.*, Articles 11–15 and 46.

[33] Regarding US law, see Henkin, *Foreign Affairs*; Henkin, *Constitutionalism*; and Jackson, "United States of America."

representatives acted *ultra vires*, or (similarly) because the treaty is inconsistent with a provision of the domestic constitution. Generally speaking, domestic invalidity does not itself preclude the validity of a treaty under international law.[34] This issue may relate to the prior issues listed; for example, *ultra vires* actions of officials in undertaking negotiations could in some systems taint the subsequent domestic validity of the treaty thus "concluded."[35]

Fifthly, even though a treaty may be validly entered into by a nation's representatives, there may be a question of the power to fulfill or carry out the resulting obligations. In some cases, this capability may require (under a national constitution) an act of the parliamentary body (e.g., to appropriate money). Sometimes other constitutional bodies must act. Indeed, an "act of transformation" may achieve partial or full implementation.

Sixthly, we have one of the questions posed by this article, whether the treaty is "directly applicable" or, more generally, what role the treaty plays in the domestic legal system of a state party. Obviously, if a treaty is "invalid" under either international law or national law, this issue would usually never be reached. In some circumstances, direct application of a treaty might be one form of "implementation" of certain types of treaties. Here again, we refer to "statute-like" application, and note that there may be other types of internal effects of treaties that are not directly applicable.

Seventhly, comes the important, but often misunderstood, question that can be called "invocability."[36] This term can refer to a group of concepts, one of which is similar, but not necessarily identical, to "standing": even though a treaty is directly applicable in the domestic legal system, in a specific case a determination may need to be made as to *who* is entitled to invoke or rely on the treaty norms. In some jurisdictions this concept may be expressed as "partial direct application" or may be governed by the idea that a treaty is directly applicable for some purposes but not others. For example, a treaty might be directly applicable in disputes between different units or levels of government, or between the government and a private person ("vertically"), but not between private citizens or enterprises ("hori-

---

[34] Vienna Convention, Article 46; Henkin, "Lexical Priority."
[35] See Jackson, "United States of America." And note the case of *United States* v. *Guy W. Capps Inc.*, 204 F. 2d 655 (4th Cir. 1953), as discussed in Jackson and Davey, *Legal Problems of International Economic Relations*, 88.
[36] Jackson, "United States of America"; and Riesenfeld, "International Agreements" (1989) 14 *Yale Journal of International Law* 455 at 462. Riesenfeld is surely correct when (referring to Jackson, "United States of America") he notes that the concept of "invocability" embraces several ideas, perhaps intertwined. However, "invocability" can be a useful generic term to embrace a small inventory of means of judicial control over the use in a particular lawsuit of the direct applicability of a treaty. See note 134 below and the accompanying text.

zontally").[37] One way to analyze this is to conclude that the treaty as such is directly applicable, that is, becomes part of the domestic jurisprudence. Then the applying institution (e.g., the courts) must determine which parties/entities are entitled to "invoke" or rely on the treaty norms. Alternatively, it may be determined that only portions of a treaty are directly applicable (sometimes depending on the precision and other attributes of the language of specific portions), while the rest of the treaty is not.

In some cases courts or governments have confused (or fused) these two questions (numbers 6 and 7), judging "direct application" or "self-executing" partly by reference to whether a party may invoke the treaty. This author believes that it is analytically preferable (to avoid confusion and potential error) to separate these concepts, particularly since the policies that relate to each one differ considerably. For example, direct application may primarily be a question of intent of one or more of the treaty parties, while invocability may depend on the precision of the language, definitions of categories of persons (e.g., "citizen," "adult male"), or concepts of justiciability or "political question."[38]

The eighth issue, hierarchy of norms, relates closely to the two previous questions, and it is therefore these three issues (numbers 6, 7, and 8) that are central to this article.[39] Hierarchy of norms refers to the questions that arise when a directly applicable and invocable treaty norm is unavoidably inconsistent[40] with other norms in the national legal system. Those other norms may include the constitution, prior national-level statutes, subsequent national-level statutes, various regulatory acts, and laws of subordinate governmental units (states in a federal system) and, among other things, may be either prior or subsequent to the treaty.[41] In fact, a fairly elaborate matrix of possible clashes can be worked out,[42] and the answers for each "cell" can differ in different legal systems. With only one or two

[37] See note 38 below and the accompanying text.
[38] See note 39 below and the accompanying text and note 96 below and the accompanying text. The author also wishes to acknowledge the thinking of Professor Lauwaars (of the Netherlands) on this issue. Sometimes the terminology "horizontal application" and "vertical application" is used, the former to describe a case between private parties, the latter a case between a private party and a government entity.
[39] See generally Robertson, *Human Rights in National and International Law.* In chapter I of this book, Max Sørensen, in his "Report" at 11, 22, presents an interesting analysis of four general types of treaties with differing relevance to domestic law. Roughly paraphrased, these are: (1) treaties with purpose and substance outside the sphere of national law, such as alliances and the peaceful settlement of international disputes; (2) treaties affecting the administrative sphere of rights and duties of various public authorities, and not relating to individuals; (3) treaties relevant to relations between public authorities and individuals; and (4) treaties concerned with relations between individuals or other subjects of private law.
[40] Courts and other institutions will often try hard to avoid the inconsistency of norms by reconciling the different legal instruments when feasible. See, e.g., Higgins, "United Kingdom," 137; Jackson, "United States of America," 160; and *Restatement,* § 114.
[41] See, e.g., Jackson, "United States of America"; and *Restatement,* § 115.
[42] Jackson, "United States of America," 169.

exceptions, constitutions generally are deemed superior to treaties, but a key question is usually the status of a treaty norm that clashes with a later national legislative enactment.[43] In the United States, the later in time prevails. In some other countries, the treaty will prevail even over such later enactments, and this is the crux of the most important policy issue (in the view of this author) concerning direct application.

It should be noted that for this issue (number 8) to arise, a few other issues must be determined. That is, the treaty must be valid both internationally and domestically, it must be applied directly, and it must be invocable. Unless all these conditions are met, hierarchy of norms does not arise as a matter of domestic law. Of course, issues remain under both international law and internal law. For example, a treaty may be internationally and domestically valid but not directly applied, and thus a domestic system may perform a legal act or make a legal determination that violates the treaty. In that case the acting nation is still "liable," as a matter of *international law*, to the contracting parties of the treaty. However, international processes would have to be invoked to "enforce" the treaty obligation. Furthermore, the treaty (even though not directly applicable) may still have a variety of internal law effects, such as influencing the interpretation of municipal statutes and laws, operating through a statutory provision that makes reference to "international law" or a treaty standard, or influencing an appraisal of "public policy."[44]

Finally, the ninth issue subsumes several matters relating to the administration of treaties, which this article cannot practically discuss.[45] Among the more important administrative topics is interpretation of the treaty. Both who within a country has the authority to interpret a treaty and which techniques of interpretation will apply can be serious issues, and are sometimes heavily contested (as in the United States in the controversy over the Anti-Ballistic Missile Treaty).[46] As suggested above, an important internal effect of a treaty may be its bearing on interpretation of a municipal law, and in such a case it may also be necessary to interpret the treaty.[47]

---

[43] See the references in notes 5 and 6 above. See also Henkin, "Lexical Priority"; Westen, "The Place of Foreign Treaties in the Courts of the United States: A Reply to Louis Henkin" (1987) 101 *Harvard Law Review* 511.

[44] See, e.g., Brownlie, *Principles of Public International Law*, chapter II; and Ganshof van der Meersch, "Report" in Robertson, *Human Rights in National and International Law*, 97; *Restatement*, chapter 2; see also note 62 below; and Robertson, *Human Rights in National and International Law*, 101–102.

[45] See *Restatement*, § 115; Henkin, *Constitutionalism*, chapter II; and Henkin, "Litigating the President's Power to Terminate Treaties" (1979) 73 *American Journal of International Law* 647.

[46] There is considerable literature on this controversy, but the short reference in Henkin, *Constitutionalism*, 56, is a good starting point for the interested reader.

[47] See note 44 above, and particularly *Restatement*, § 114.

The approach of various countries

This article does not propose to describe the various national systems of treaty application. Many important works, published both recently – the 1987 volume edited by Francis Jacobs and Shelley Roberts is an outstanding example[48] – and earlier,[49] deal with the subject, as well as with topics affected by it, such as ILO Conventions[50] and the European Convention on Human Rights.[51] Nevertheless, a few brief descriptions may provide background for some of the policy issues to be discussed.

The United Kingdom is generally considered the prime example of a dualist system.[52] Treaties never have direct "statute-like" application in the United Kingdom, but of course may have other internal effects.[53] Many national systems derived from that of the United Kingdom, such as the Canadian and Australian systems, follow similar approaches.[54] The legislature may enact laws that incorporate ("transform") treaties or treaty norms into domestic law, but, interestingly, the UK Parliament does not have a formal role in treaty *making*. Treaties are entered into by the "Crown" (today, obviously with the counsel of ministers). Sometimes (such as with the UK European Communities Act of 1972) a parliament can make provision for the "transformation" in advance.[55] Variations on this approach are found in many other countries, for example, Germany and Italy.[56]

At the other extreme, perhaps, is the Constitution of the Netherlands, which could generally be called "monist" since it expressly provides that certain treaties are directly applied and that in such cases these treaties are deemed superior to all laws, including constitutional norms![57] The 1958

---

[48] Jacobs and Roberts, *The Effect of Treaties in Domestic Law.*

[49] See the other references in notes 5 and 6 above; and see notes 51 and 54 below.

[50] See Leary, *International Labour Conventions and National Law.*

[51] See Robertson, *Human Rights in National and International Law.*   [52] See *ibid.*

[53] F. A. Mann, *Foreign Affairs in English Courts* (1986), chapter 5; and Higgins, "United Kingdom."

[54] See Holloway, *Modern Trends in Treaty Law*, 193ff; and Sawyer, "Australian Constitutional Law," especially at 47.

[55] European Communities Act of the United Kingdom 1972, chapter 68. Section 2 states that the rights, powers, etc., provided under the treaties "as in accordance with the Treaties are without further enactment to be given legal effect or used in the United Kingdom" and "shall be recognised and available in law, and be enforced, allowed and followed accordingly." See also Maresceau, The Effect of Community Agreements in the UK" (1979) 28 *International and Comparative Law Quarterly* 241 (1979). See generally L. Collins, *European Community Law in the United Kingdom* (3rd edn., 1984).

[56] Frowein, "Federal Republic of Germany"; and Gaja, "Italy" in Jacobs and Roberts, *The Effect of Treaties in Domestic Law*, 87.

[57] Schermers, "Netherlands" in Jacobs and Roberts, *The Effect of Treaties in Domestic Law*, 109; Schermers and Waelbroeck, *Judicial Protection in the European Communities*, 109; van Dijk, "Domestic Status of Human-Rights Treaties"; Schermers, "Some Recent Cases Delaying the Direct Effect of International Treaties in Dutch Law" (1989) 10 *Michigan Journal of International Law* 266.

Constitution of France also calls for direct application and a higher status for treaties than later legislation.[58] With a variety of nuances, such provisions are found in the Constitutions of Belgium, Switzerland, Japan and other nations.[59]

The United States stands somewhere in between. Under US jurisprudence, some treaties can be found to be self-executing in which case they will be directly applied. To determine "self-executing," US courts look at a series of factors, but (it seems) primarily at the intent of the drafters,[60] including intent implied or expressed in the treaty itself. When the language is sufficiently precise and indicates that no further government action is needed to apply the treaty norms, a US court will be willing to conclude that the treaty is self-executing. However, under a long string of precedents over 100 years, US courts have ruled that a directly applied treaty has the same status as federal laws (statutes, etc.) and that the latest in time therefore prevails.[61] Thus, for internal law purposes, a later US statute will prevail over the international agreement (which sometimes causes the United States to violate its international obligations).[62]

The situation in the European Community is more difficult to describe, and is apparently still evolving. The details and arguments must be left to other authors,[63] but broadly it can be said that the Community has

[58] De la Rochère, "France" in Jacobs and Roberts, *The Effect of Treaties in Domestic Law*, 39. Article 55 of the 1958 French Constitution establishes a higher status for treaties than for even later-in-time legislation, subject, however, "for each separate agreement or treaty, to reciprocal application by the other party." *Ibid.*, 42. This reciprocity provision introduces a considerable amount of ambiguity, but also provides some measure of remedy for the asymmetry problem discussed in the text at note 89 below.

[59] On Belgium and Switzerland, see Jacobs and Roberts, *The Effect of Treaties in Domestic Law*. On Japan, see Matsushita, "Japan and the Implementation of the Tokyo Round Results" in Jackson, Louis, and Matsushita, *Implementing the Tokyo Round*, chapter 3, at 77.

[60] *Restatement*, § 111(4); Jackson, "United States of America"; and Henkin, *Constitutionalism*, 62. In an interesting and stimulating article, Professor Jordan Paust argues against the well-established approach of courts and the *Restatement* of distinguishing self-executing and non-self-executing treaties, and apparently (not too clearly) urges that all treaties be the "supreme law of the land." Paust, "Self-Executing Treaties" (1988) 82 *American Journal of International Law* 760.

[61] *Restatement*, § 115; and Jackson, "United States of America."

[62] Several GATT dispute panel reports have concluded that the implementation of US statutes enacted later than GATT caused the United States to be in contravention of its GATT treaty obligations. See, e.g., United States Manufacturing Clause, GATT, *Basic Instruments and Selected Documents*, 31st Supplement (1985), 74 (regarding copyright); and US Section 337 of the Tariff Act of 1930, GATT, *Basic Instruments and Selected Documents*, 36th Supplement (1988), 345.

[63] Pescatore, "Treaty-Making by the European Communities" in Jacobs and Roberts, *The Effect of Treaties in Domestic Law*, 171; Schermers and Waelbroeck, *Judicial Protection in the European Communities*; J. Schwarze (ed.), *The External Relations of the European Community*, in Particular EC–US Relations (1989); Stein, "External Relations of the European Community"; Hilf, "The Single European Act and 1992"; and E. L. M. Volker and J. Steenbergen, *Leading Cases and Materials on the External Relations Law of the European Community* (1985), chapter 2.

struggled with these problems in two contexts: the application of *EC law* (the basic treaties, regulations, directives, etc.) within the member states; and the application of external treaties between the Community (sometimes with member state participation) and "third countries" (i.e., non-EC nations) in EC jurisprudence, including the national legal systems of the member states. Although there is some tendency in the opinions and literature to equate these two categories of problems, the policies relating to them can substantially differ. Regarding the application of EC law in the member states, it can be argued that direct application (and trumping) is essential to developing the internal cohesion and coherence that will achieve the goals of a true customs union and (perhaps) federal system. Regarding the application of external treaties, those with third countries, direct application may be much less significant (although arguments can be made both ways). In any event, this article relates primarily to the latter category of problems: the effect of EC–third country treaties on the internal law of the community (including that of member states).

With these brief, but complex, descriptions of the setting of our problems, we now turn to the policies relating to the two questions: (1) the direct application of treaties; and (2) their hierarchical status when so applied.

II.   Policies relating to direct application of treaties

What does it mean in practice to "directly apply" a treaty in a domestic legal system? The concept was outlined in the paradigmatic hypothetical discussed in the previous section.[64] Although the answer to this question may vary, depending on the legal system involved, "direct application of a treaty" generally seems to mean that courts in the system (as well as all other government bodies) will look to the treaty language itself as a source of law, analogously to the way they look at constitutions, statutes or certain other instruments of domestic law. The language of the treaty (for example, by constituting "judicial notice" and thus obviating the necessity of "proof") will be a required source for the court to examine so as to determine the legal rules applicable to particular cases.[65] It therefore seems convenient to refer to the result of direct application as statute-like status, even though considerations of the hierarchy of norms (Question 2) may suggest in some cases that the treaty enjoys higher status than statutes.[66]

[64] See the text at note 16 above.
[65] The concept of "judicial notice" in US and other countries' jurisprudence generally refers to a court's acceptance of the probity of documents and legal instruments, such as statutes, constitutions, or calendars, which it may do on its own motion and without requiring proof. This is contrasted with use of elements that need proof at a trial, such as most facts of a case and foreign law. See, e.g., *Restatement*, § 113.
[66] Jackson, "United States of America."

We now turn to the various policies that favor or oppose direct application of treaties.

Policies favoring direct application

Why should treaties ever be given this statute-like status in domestic law? Some writers respond by taking a theoretical approach, suggesting that all laws are part of one system (monism), so that international law is automatically part of all national systems; indeed, many of these writers see international law as a higher form of the world legal system and thus as having, *a priori*, a higher status than domestic law.[67] The latter point, in touching on the hierarchy question (Question 2), illustrates the close relationship between these two questions. Apart from this theoretical approach, which has not been accepted by many important nations and evokes skepticism in many quarters, including theorists and scholars,[68] we can ask further if there are any significant practical reasons advanced for the direct application of treaties.

One such argument stresses enhancing the effectiveness of international law; giving direct application to treaties (and maybe also to customary international law) increases their importance and weight and decreases the likelihood that national authorities will refuse or neglect to provide for transforming the treaty norms into domestic law.[69] Direct reliance on treaties by citizens may also add to treaty effectiveness (although it can be countered that acts of transformation are much more likely to be found and utilized by the domestic legal institutions).[70]

Another related argument suggests that direct application better assures the other parties that all parties will carry out their obligations under the treaty. It has even been suggested that customary international law should

---

[67] See Pescatore, "Conclusion" in Jacobs and Roberts, *The Effect of Treaties in Domestic Law*, 273; and the discussion and description by Sasse, "The Common Market" and McDougal, "The Impact of International Law upon National Law."

[68] See generally Jacobs and Roberts, *The Effect of Treaties in Domestic Law*; Brownlie, *Principles of Public International Law*, chapter II; Henkin, *Constitutionalism*, 63; and McDougal, "The Impact of International Law upon National Law."

[69] See, e.g., Henkin, *Constitutionalism*, 63; and *Restatement*, § 111; see also Schermers and Waelbroeck, *Judicial Protection in the European Communities*; and Henkin, "Lexical Priority."

[70] See, e.g., Henkin, "Lexical Priority"; and Henkin, "The Constitution and United States Sovereignty: A Century of Chinese Exclusion and Its Progeny" (1987) 100 *Harvard Law Review* 853 at 886. An interesting conversation in mid-1991 with a Latin American lawyer-diplomat tends to support the statement in the text. He noted that the question of direct application did not come up often in his national jurisprudence (even though it was possible), because lawyers were not used to searching for or finding treaties as part of their cases. In fact, he commented that many of his country's treaties were negotiated by the Ministry of Foreign Affairs, and when approved (by the Parliament) were "locked in a cabinet and almost never looked at thereafter."

impose a good faith obligation to give treaties direct application.[71] How-ever, this proposition is hard to sustain, since state practice is so contrary. Not only do many states not give direct effect to treaties, but many important states (as noted above)[72] *cannot* do so under their constitutions. Nevertheless, this inability does not prevent parties from *expressly* obligat-ing themselves in a treaty to its direct application (some states would obviously avoid making such impossible commitments).[73]

Yet another argument for direct application is that it better assures the rights of individuals in the legal system when a treaty contains norms designed to apply to those individuals. The individuals can thus base claims on the treaty norm without the need for government intervention or an act of transformation. An act of transformation, it can be argued, gives too much temptation to governments to depart from the precise wording of the treaty and therefore to "transform" a norm that does not accord with the treaty norm itself.[74]

These various arguments for the utility of direct application also rein-force another, more general contention – that disrespect for international law is increased when international norms are not effective. Since, it is argued, direct applicability will enhance the effectiveness of international norms, it will also generally enhance the respect for and general prestige of international law, to the benefit of world order.[75]

Some arguments for direct applicability depend on the coexistence of a principle of higher status (Question 2) for the directly effective treaty norms. This point is easily illustrated by internal laws of a federal system (such as that of the United States and the developing EC structure, which some view as "federal"). When governments desire a federal system to be closer knit, more responsive to the federal level of authority, it makes sense

---

[71] See the text at note 69 above. See also Pescatore, "Conclusion," 275, where he appears to argue that the good faith requirement to implement treaties implies direct application, that is, "incorporation" without an act of transformation. He concludes (*ibid.*, 282):

> Incorporation procedures and methods based on "transformation" are therefore by their very essence incompatible with good faith in international relations. By ratification a state promises unqualified implementation of a treaty . . . while by using the "transformation" method for incorporation the same state retains the possibility of not implementing a treaty at all, or of implementing only part of it, or of altering its effect unilaterally.

See Vienna Convention, Article 26 ("good faith"); see also W. Bishop Jr., *International Law: Cases and Materials* (3rd edn., 1971), 80 (quoting Sprout, "International Law in the Federal Courts of the United States" (1932) 26 *American Journal of International Law* 280), and Sasse, "The Common Market," 712 ("Only a few outsiders maintain . . ." etc.).

[72] See notes 52–54 above and the accompanying text; and Jacobs and Roberts, *The Effect of Treaties in Domestic Law.*

[73] Note 66 above.   [74] See the counter-argument in text at note 81 below.

[75] See note 69 above and the accompanying text; and Pescatore, "Conclusion."

for federal law to be both directly effective and trumping, as is made explicit in the US Constitution, and as is evolving by judicial treaty interpretation in the European Community. Moving from this sphere to the international level, however, does not automatically imply that the same principles should prevail, as we will see below.

Policies opposing direct application

Still putting aside Question 2 ("higher status?"), we find that various arguments are made against the direct applicability of treaties. On the theoretical side, commentators have argued for a century that international law is a separate legal system from national legal systems (dualism) and that, consequently, there is no *a priori* reason that an international treaty norm should automatically be part of national legal systems.[76] Perhaps closely related to this argument is a notion that builds on concepts of national "sovereignty": that when a nation undertakes an international obligation, that nation is entitled to determine for itself its method of implementing or fulfilling that obligation, so long as it does so in good faith.[77] Indeed, it is sometimes argued that urging the direct application of treaties is tantamount to "interference in the internal affairs" of a sovereign state.

Perhaps more significant, however, are the functional arguments that can be advanced to oppose direct applicability. One of these concerns the procedures for treaty-making. Some constitutions provide for very little democratic participation in the treaty-making process; for example, by giving no formal role to parliaments[78] or structuring the government so that control over foreign relations is held by certain elites.[79] In such cases, it

[76] Sasse, "The Common Market," 712–713, outlines these theories and some of their proponents, writers at the turn of the century (such as Triepel (1899), Anzilotti (1905), and Kelsen (1920)). This part of Sasse's text is quoted in Henkin, Pugh, Schachter, and Smit, *International Law Cases and Materials*, 141.

[77] Henkin, *Constitutionalism*, 62:

> There is, then, a binding obligation on the parties to a treaty to carry out their undertakings, but how a state does so is ordinarily not a concern of international law; the status of treaties in the domestic law of any country is a constitutional, not an international, question. All states have incorporated international law into their legal system to some extent in some ways, but states differ both as to extent and as to ways. States differ also as to what – if anything – is necessary to make a treaty part of national law and what are the jurisprudential consequences.

[78] See note 3 above and the accompanying text and note 24 above and the accompanying text.
[79] See the sources cited in notes 5 and 6 above. Apart from formal and explicit governmental structures (such as the power of the Crown to enter into treaties), a "foreign policy establishment" can be found in certain governments and the criticism has been made that such elites are not in tune with the political will of the nation. The reader will have to appraise these arguments on the basis of his or her own country's experience. An articulate, but perhaps somewhat extreme, manifestation of the concern about international policy elites was recently expressed in a popular journal. The author criticizes:

is argued, the need to obtain parliamentary approval (or approval by some other democratic law-making process) of the act of transformation serves as an important democratic check on the treaty-making process. The importance of this safeguard can be multiplied many times if (Question 2 again) the directly applied treaty would have a higher status than many other types of law.

Another consideration militating against direct application is that legis-latures may wish to tailor the act of transformation[80] in certain ways, perhaps by rewording the treaty to match domestic circumstances. The most obvious example would be those agreements (usually multilateral treaties) whose official language is not the (legal) language of the implemen-ting nation. But even when the language is the same, certain nuances of usage may differ and legislatures may wish to express the norms in accord-ance with local usage. The legislators may also wish to elaborate on the treaty provisions, which they may view as ambiguous. (In the United

> the small, privileged caste of government officials, former government officials, professors, think-tank denizens, and journalists whose dreamy agenda has long dominated foreign-policy decision-making in America. For surely American foreign policy has been conducted with utter disregard for the home front largely because it has been made by people whose lives and needs have almost nothing in common with those of the mass of their countrymen.

Tonelson, "What is the National Interest?" *Atlantic*, July 1991, at 35, 37.
[80] A prime example can be found in the US Trade Agreements Act of 1979, in which Congress made it abundantly clear that the Tokyo Round agreements would not be self-executing, and then incorporated into this Act its version of the international agreements to be applied domestically. See Jackson, Louis, and Matsushita, *Implementing the Tokyo Round*, 196; and S. Rep. No. 249, 96th Cong., 1st Sess., 36 (1979). The Senate Report stated:

> The relationship between the trade agreements and United States law is among the most sensitive issues in the Bill. As stated in the statement of proposed administrative action, the trade agreements can only be achieved as is provided in the Trade Act of 1974.

The 1974 Act provided for statutory enactment, pursuant to a "fast-track" procedure. For a similar approach to the US–Canada Free Trade Agreement, see Communication from the President of the United States Transmitting the US–Canada Free Trade Agreement, July 26, 1988, HR Doc. No. 216, 100th Cong., 2nd Sess., 167 (1988) (Statement of Administrative Action). The statement said:

> Section 102(a) provides that a provision of the FTA will not be given effect as a matter of domestic law to the extent such provision is in conflict with federal law . . . [T]he section reflects the Congressional view that necessary changes in federal statutes should be specifically enacted rather than provided for in a blanket preemption of federal statutes by the trade agreement.

Quoted in Jackson, *The World Trading System*, 75. The word "legislatures" in this sentence of the text can be understood broadly to include other kinds of law-makers as well. It is frequently very difficult to achieve precision in multilateral treaties, since so many countries – often with different legal cultures – must agree, and there is a tendency for language to express the lowest common denominator of the negotiating approaches. At the same time, multilateral treaties are becoming more common and more important.

States, for example, the ambiguity of some treaty language has caused concern that its direct application to individuals might violate constitutional standards of due process.[81]) Language in the act of transformation may clarify some ambiguities (for use by domestic courts and other applications), or specify policy choices left open (implicitly or expressly) under the terms of the treaty. All of these eventualities may occur in the context of a good faith effort fully to apply the treaty norms.

Legislatures may also have other policies in mind. They may desire to place their interpretation of the treaty norm on record. Perhaps the treaty is ambiguous or leaves room for interpretation. The act of transformation can be used to impose an interpretation for domestic law. Such an act (and the domestic action under it) will constitute "practice" of a treaty party and may then become relevant[82] to later international interpretation of the treaty. In some cases, however, the domestic interpretation may concern domestic law only, such as by indicating the allocation within a country of authority to make certain decisions or to take certain actions in connection with the implementation of the treaty.[83] Indeed, the act of transformation sometimes becomes part of a purely *internal* power struggle, and may be used by certain governmental institutions to enhance their powers *vis-à-vis* other governmental entities.[84] (*Per contra*, advocates of direct application may have similar motives, viewing it as a way to forestall the adoption of alternative policies or allocations of power, or as a way to have them determined in accordance with their preferences.) Some constitutions may require a form of law-making that is circumvented by direct application of a treaty. In these circumstances, one might conclude that this should be a matter for national decision and that direct application should generally be avoided.

Legislatures may have still other motives in opposing direct application. For example, they may wish to limit direct application to portions of the

[81] Fiedlander, "Should the US Constitution's Treaty-Making Power Be Used as the Basis for Enactment of Domestic Legislation? Implications of the Senate-Approved Genocide Convention" (1986) 18 *Case Western Reserve Journal of International Law* 267 at 268.

[82] Vienna Convention, Article 31 (when the subsequent practice "establishes the agreement of the parties regarding" interpretation).

[83] One example of this is *Power Authority of New York v. Federal Power Commission*, 247 F. 2d 538 (DC Cir. 1957), which interpreted a "reservation" attached by the United States to a treaty with Canada to have only domestic concern, and therefore no domestic law effect as part of the treaty. See Jackson and Davey, *Legal Problems of International Economic Relations*, 125; and Henkin, Pugh, Schachter, and Smit, *International Law Cases and Materials*, 183; see also note 84 below.

[84] See Problem VIII, on the International Coffee Agreement, in A. Chayes, T. Ehrlich, and A. Lowenfeld, *International Legal Process: Materials for an Introductory Course* (1968), 588; on the Panama Treaty, see Bell and Foy, "The President, the Congress, and the Panama Canal: An Essay on the Powers of the Executive and Legislative Branches in the Field of Foreign Affairs" (1986) 16 *Georgia Journal of International and Comparative Law* 607 at 641 (executive branch pushed for a self-executing treaty).

treaty, or to apply it in ways that may not fully conform to the international obligation. Or a legislature may find it politic to delay application to allow internal consensus and acceptance to develop (or to wait out an imminent election!). Some of these examples suggest less than full "good faith application" – and even, perhaps, that the legislature desires to preserve the *option to breach* the treaty in its method of application. Is this approach to policy-making desirable or valid? Certainly, traditional internationalists will frown on it. Yet national sovereigns often have prerogatives enabling them to breach treaties; why (say some) take away one particular mode? Moreover, some breaches may be "minor" and therefore preferable to the alternative of refusing to join the treaty altogether.

These considerations move the discourse further into the general jurisprudence of international law and the question of treaty compliance. Is the international system better off if it relies on general democratic acceptance of treaty norms as the major technique of promoting effectiveness, rather than on sanction or legal constructs such as direct application? These questions are not easily answered.[85] For individuals, including statesmen and scholars, the response may depend somewhat on their degree of faith in the international system as compared to their national system. It has been maintained in the literature that some breaches of international norms may be desirable.[86] The relative status of directly applied treaties (Question 2) accentuates some of these arguments.[87]

A related consideration is that national officials may fear that direct application will result in court determinations that their government is acting in violation of the treaty. Such findings could embarrass that government and undercut its effectiveness if it should participate in an international proceeding where it is charged with breach of the treaty obligation. For this reason, it has been said that some domestic courts tend to avoid determining that their government has breached an international treaty.[88]

Another argument is based on the diversity of national constitutional systems regarding treaty application. The fact that some nations *never*

---

[85] See Robertson, *Human Rights in National and International Law*, and the works cited in note 5 above; see also Ress, "The European Convention on Human Rights and State Parties: The Legal Effect of the Judgments of the European Court of Human Rights on the Internal Law and Before Domestic Courts of the Contracting States" in I. Maier (ed.), *Protection of Human Rights in Europe*, 209 at 227.

[86] Hudec, "Thinking About the New Section 301: Beyond Good and Evil" in J. Bhagwati and H. T. Patrick (eds.), *Aggressive Unilateralism: America's 301 Trade Policy and the World Trading System* (1990), 113.

[87] Under some constitutions, the directly applied and higher-status treaty may be quite difficult to breach. Obviously, for some this is an argument in favor of this approach. See the text in Part III below.

[88] Schermers, "Some Recent Cases."

permit direct application may make governments or citizens of nations that require it feel that the asymmetry of the system is unfair. Where direct application is constitutionally permissible, this asymmetry may argue[89] in favor of avoiding its implementation. Sometimes direct application may expressly be conditioned on reciprocity.[90] (Counter to this is the view that what other governments do is not relevant; what matters is how the acting nation best lives up to its obligations.[91])

Still another argument for avoiding direct application is much stronger if higher status (Question 2) is given to the applied norm, and therefore will be discussed below. In those circumstances, direct application may inhibit national authorities from entering into international agreements that would otherwise be desirable.[92]

Direct application also prompts an interesting question about interpretation. If a treaty is directly applicable, it can be argued that an international body's interpretation of a question of international law is definitive in domestic law as well. According to this view, since the domestic law consists of the international treaty applied directly, the international interpretations are binding on the domestic legal institutions, including the courts. In contrast, an act of transformation is an act of the domestic legal system, and thus can be interpreted by that system's institutions, including the courts, just as the courts would interpret other legislation or domestic legal acts. However, even in the case of a directly applicable treaty norm, domestic courts may believe that they have the power of interpretation. They certainly have that power preliminarily until a definitive interpretation under international law is set forth. The interesting question is: what happens when an international interpretation of the treaty norm clashes with an interpretation by a domestic legal institution, in a case where the treaty norm is directly applicable? There is at least a suspicion, or hint, that the domestic legal institutions will

[89] The statement by Ehlermann could be interpreted to include this nuance. Ehlermann, "Application of GATT Rules in the European Community" in M. Hilf, F. G. Jacobs, and E.-U. Petersmann (eds.), *The European Community and GATT* (Studies in Transnational Economic Law No. 4, 1986), 127, reporting conferences held towards the end of 1984. See also discussion in E.-U. Petersmann, "Application of GATT by the Court of Justice of the European Communities" (1983) 20 *Common Market Law Review* 397 at 424–425.

[90] The French constitutional provision, quoted and discussed in note 58 above, is an example.

[91] See note 77 above.

[92] See the end of Part III below. The argument can be made that this consideration has restrained the United States from entering into ILO conventions and some human rights conventions. In the United States a solution is possible; namely, the clear, expressed intent by the relevant authority (Congress usually) that the treaty not be self-executing. See notes 80 and 81 above. See also The United States and the International Labor Organization: Hearing Before the Senate Committee on Labor and Human Resources, 99th Cong., 1st Sess. (1985); and Message of the President Transmitting Four Treaties Pertaining to Human Rights, S. Exec. Docs. C, D, E, and F, 95th Cong., 2nd Sess. (1978).

"strain" to apply their own interpretation, through one or another legal technique.[93]

These considerations also suggest that the attitude of national policy-makers towards direct application of treaties could be influenced by their view on the relative merit of national judges as compared to international judges. Since application of the law requires its interpretation, a key question will always be which institutions should hold the power to interpret the municipal law being applied. Should a nation rely primarily on its own courts? Or does it believe that the international tribunals will do a superior job?

Who decides and on what basis?

In legal systems with some form of direct application (including the US self-executing mode), there are a variety of possible approaches to the question of which domestic institution decides whether a treaty norm will be directly applied. Moreover, in actuality, a variety of countries seem to utilize virtually every approach. One policy would be to adopt a seemingly simple and firm rule providing for direct application of all treaties, leaving flexibility to the concept of "invocability," discussed earlier. However, even the so-called monist countries probably do not take this approach. For example, the Netherlands directly applies a certain category of treaties, but not necessarily all treaties.[94] Other countries may distinguish between treaties that are approved by a parliamentary body and other treaties (sometimes called "executive agreements").[95]

Even when the rule of direct application covers most, or theoretically all, treaties or certain broad categories of treaties, courts will find ways to avoid applying the treaty norm in particular cases,[96] perhaps by relying on one or another concept that can be lumped under the rubric of invocability (e.g., standing), or by holding that the treaty norm is designed to constrain or assist certain government agencies and not private litigants. Or the court may refuse to apply a treaty directly because it is not "specific and precise" enough for that purpose, a concept akin to "justiciability." Other disqualifying concepts may also be employed.[97]

---

[93] Henkin, *Constitutionalism*, 63. The cases are not clear or possibly not candid. There has been considerable debate about the relevance of the GATT and other dispute settlement reports to US courts' interpretation of domestic statutes implementing treaties. The cases discussed at the end of Part III below also "psychologically support" this suspicion.

[94] See Schermers, "Netherlands."

[95] See Holloway, *Modern Trends in Treaty Law*, sections on Japan, at 198, and Mexico, at 231.

[96] See the end of Part III below; see also Schermers and Waelbroeck, *Judicial Protection in the European Communities*; and van Dijk, "Domestic Status of Human-Rights Treaties."

[97] The "specific and precise" requirement can be used in two different modes of analysis: as an absolute "requirement" for direct applicability, part of a threshold examination whether a

In other systems, domestic legal institutions may be given greater latitude in determining whether a treaty is directly applicable. In the United States, for example, the courts have said that whether treaties are self-executing depends heavily on the intent of the treaty-makers. Direct and precise language in the treaty enters into the evaluation of this intent. In addition, a treaty may call for implementing action by the state, which will lead a US court to conclude that the treaty was not intended to be directly applicable.[98]

Two important questions will give some leeway to the system making this type of analysis. The first is: who decides? Often that is a court because the issue may come up in the context of litigation.[99] The second question is: what are the criteria this decision-maker or court uses?

As noted, the US courts speak of intent that the treaty be directly applicable, but it is not entirely clear whose intent is key. Although some courts speak of "mutual intent" manifested in the treaty, or possibly also in the preparatory work, or negotiating history, of the treaty, the argument can be made that the controlling intent in some systems, such as that of the United States, is the *unilateral* intent of the treaty-making officials or government entities in the state applying the treaty.[100]

This approach is supported by the fact that, under some national constitutions, direct application *cannot* occur. Thus, the unilateral approach of those constitutions has determined the domestic courts' approach to direct application. Likewise, in nations such as the United States where the matter is not predetermined, the issue arguably is one of domestic constitutional, or legislative policy, law and need not involve (as a matter of domestic law) the intent of other parties to the treaty. Of course, the other parties could express their desire or view, and the treaty could even include

particular treaty is to be directly applicable; or as part of the "invocability" concept explained above in this text (see notes 36 and 38 above and the accompanying text). It is this author's view that the second approach is analytically superior.

[98] See Part I, "Issues of Treaty Application" above. See also note 38 above on "horizontal direct effect" and "vertical direct effect."

[99] In the United States, for example, there is a fairly extensive jurisprudence of the courts. See, e.g., Jackson, "United States of America" (and the footnoted references therein); see also *Restatement*, § 111 and notes. Alternatives are conceivable and have been observed. For example, arguments between branches of a government about allocation of power, or policies to apply in relation to the treaty, are not unknown. In some cases, depending on whom the treaty addresses (and the question of invocability), the issue of direct application may only arise when a certain body of government decides to act as if the treaty were, or were not, directly applied.

[100] See Jackson, "United States of America"; Henkin, *Constitutionalism*, 63; and Iwasawa, "The Doctrine of Self-Executing Treaties in the United States: A Critical Analysis" (1986) 26 *Virginia Journal of International Law* 627. *Jurisdiction of the Courts of Danzig*, 1928 PCIJ (Ser. B) No. 15 (Advisory Opinion of March 3), is sometimes cited to support the view that direct application is an international law question, not one of domestic law. However, there is considerable practice to the contrary.

an *international obligation* of direct applicability – but that would not necessarily control whether, as a matter of *domestic* law, the treaty should be directly applied.

At this point, the arguments become more complex. A general concept of international law holds that an international obligation binds all of a nation's governmental institutions,[101] so that departure from the norm by any governmental unit (court, legislature, executive, subordinate units such as states and localities, etc.) engages the international responsibility of the state. Thus, in a national system that allows some leeway on the issue, a court that is determining whether to apply an international treaty directly, when the treaty itself so mandates, might find itself bound to uphold the international obligation so that it will not cause the nation to breach that obligation. This rationale, however, is analytically distinguishable from a determination that the national constitution requires direct application. Indeed, the propriety of such reasoning depends on the power of the domestic court. If the court is entitled to carry out the international obligation of direct application, it arguably should do so in these circumstances to avoid the breach of the international norm. In some circumstances, however, this power would not vest in the local court (for instance, in the dualist nations, such as the United Kingdom).

During the last several decades, the United States has seen an exercise of Congressional authority regarding direct applicability. Congress (sometimes as a whole, and sometimes the Senate acting to give its advice and consent) participates in most of the treaty-making of the United States Government.[102] Congress in some important cases[103] has expressed the intent, either in its statutory approval of a treaty or in the legislative history of that statute, that the treaty should not be directly applied. Thus, the domestic US law implementing the treaty is the law of the statute as passed by the Congress, i.e. the act of transformation. To the knowledge of this author, there has been no indication that the courts, or other institutions of the US Government, would try to contravene this expression of Congressional intent. It seems safe to conclude that the US constitutional practice and status is that the treaty-making officials, as a unilateral matter, will control the determination of "self-executing" in the domestic legal system. This is probably, on balance, a wise constitutional solution. It enables the democratic parliament to control some of the

---

[101] Brownlie, *Principles of Public International Law*, 446.
[102] There are some exceptions. See generally Henkin, *Foreign Affairs*; and Jackson, "United States of America."
[103] Examples include the Trade Agreements Act of 1979, and implementation of the Canada–US Free Trade Agreement. See note 80 above. The contrary is argued in Dearborn, "The Domestic Legal Effect of Declarations That Treaty Provisions Are Not Self-Executing" (1979) 57 *Texas Law Review* 233.

problems posed by direct applicability that were discussed in previous subsections of this article.

Overall, what can be said about the policy advisability of direct application of treaties? It is probably not feasible or accurate to over-generalize and say "never" or "always." Clearly, the situations and the criteria for direct applicability differ from country to country, as do the circumstances. Likewise, who makes the final decision about direct applicability differs from country to country. However, there are enough negative policy considerations to suggest considerable caution in embracing direct application. Perhaps if various circumstances are favorable (e.g., democratic input in treaty-making, a preference for international over national institutions), a presumption of direct application (controllable by the legislature) could be adopted. On the other hand, more serious problems stemming from "higher status" are revealed in the next section. Rather than a presumption of direct application, a national system might prefer a standard "act of transformation" as an expression of both parliamentary approval and incorporation/implementation in domestic law.

III.   The policies relating to higher status of directly applied norms

When we move to Question 2, that is, whether a directly applied treaty norm has a higher hierarchical status than most other laws, many of the above policy considerations are not only implicated but accentuated. To use a paradigmatic hypothetical, suppose the legal system of nation M requires direct application of treaty norms, and its constitution provides that such norms will trump all other laws except the constitution,[104] even laws enacted later at the highest legislative level. Suppose further that M is party to a treaty that imposes the type of "national treatment" obligation hypothesized in Part I above.[105] Ten years after M's accession to the treaty, its legislature, citizenry, and government leaders wish to enact a special rule giving M's poor citizens preferential property ownership rights (but they argue that to give these rights to non-citizens would attract an influx of poor persons from other countries who would exploit the rule and make it unacceptably expensive). The envisioned rule may accord purchasing preference to poor citizens when the government disposes of property it owns or has validly seized or repossessed. Yet the treaty norm (sometimes unexpectedly) may seem to preclude this act or be determined internationally to prevent it. Since the domestic application of the norm trumps later legislation, the government's hands are tied. It must either renegotiate the treaty (or terminate it) or refrain from enacting the desired legislation.

[104] See the text at notes 41–43 above.   [105] See the text at notes 16–17 above.

For the purposes of our discussion, we will assume that at least some treaty norms are directly applied, since it makes no sense to be concerned about higher status in domestic law unless the norm is part of domestic law. We now consider whether it is wise policy for treaty norms to be both directly applied and given higher status in domestic legal systems than most other laws.

Higher status as "constitutionalization"

In essence, DAHS (the acronym for "directly applicable with higher status," described in the introduction) means that a treaty norm has been "constitutionalized," or given a sort of "constitutional status" almost equivalent to the nation's own constitution.[106] It occurs through a procedure that often falls short of the rigor or democracy of constitutional amending procedures, which may surprise certain interest groups that did not focus on the treaty issues years ago. In these circumstances, what are some of the policy considerations?

One is immediately struck by how many of the arguments in Part II are accentuated by higher status. In the absence of higher status, a later statute or other law might correct some of the problems raised in Part II (e.g., a legislative desire to "interpret" the treaty or to reallocate internal decision-making power), albeit perhaps with some additional trouble and shifting of the political burden of taking the necessary initiative.[107] When higher status is added, however, the problems become much more difficult. For example, the asymmetrical situation noted above, in which some nations do not directly apply treaty norms while others do, is even more anomalous when some that do, do so with a higher status. Those nations find themselves more locked into the norms than the other parties.

Once again, the issue of the "democratic deficit" arises, but more acutely. If the procedures for treaty-making do not permit adequate democratic participation, the DAHS treaty norm can be criticized as imposing an elite's vision of control on a society (or worse, that of a special interest group). Indeed, it can be seriously doubted whether such a norm would be truly effective; governmental units, including courts, would struggle to attenuate the norm or avoid it altogether.[108]

Usually, this is not an either/or question, for the degree of democratic input varies and in many cases may be said to be sufficient, even for a "constitutionalized" norm like a DAHS. Yet a series of other concerns can

---

[106] Lecture by Walter Van Gerven, Free University of Brussels, February 1990.
[107] The burden of taking an initiative may be significant. Those who can rely on the *status quo* may have a considerable advantage.
[108] See the discussion at the end of Part III below.

be raised that should at least be understood by policy-makers who wish to oppose or to accept the DAHS idea. The most significant of these was noted in the hypothetical above, that the DAHS norm imposes considerable rigidity (almost equal to a constitutional rule) on future government action. Arguably, a constitution should generally contain norms deemed so essential to government that they *need* to impose rigidity: norms that preserve human rights, allocate power among governmental branches or entities, specify the rules for democratic governance (elections, terms of office) and the like. To constitutionalize the whole body of potential treaty relations is quite another matter. A government with DAHS would need to be *very* restrained in accepting treaty obligations, or it could find itself hamstrung at many turns by thousands or tens of thousands of treaty norms (especially on economic subjects).

Treaty-making, incidentally, can also mean the development of "secondary" treaty rules, i.e. regulations or decisions by international bodies pursuant to treaty authorization.[109] Thus, a nation with DAHS could find its legal system bound both by rules that only a few of its own diplomats (maybe instructed by an elite or small group within the executive part of their government) participated in drafting, and by the majoritarian or other (sometimes defective) voting procedures of multilateral bodies. A nation in that position could refuse to accept such treaties, or it might work towards building international institutions that avoid secondary norm making, but this approach could substantially inhibit the progress of the world legal system.

International institutions and rules

A serious problem is the weakness or inadequacy of international institutions (especially multilateral ones) that engage in treaty-making. Even if we assume that international institutions can adequately (and democratically) create new rules, many find it difficult to change, amend or improve treaty or secondary rules. Sometimes nations have the unenviable choice of living with rigid and/or out-of-date rules, terminating (withdrawing from) their treaty obligation entirely, or breaching it. If it were easier to change treaty norms, a DAHS nation might more easily tolerate them, obtaining modification at the international level when needed, but that very difficulty adds to the risk of DAHS.[110]

---

[109] E.g., GATT, the International Monetary Fund, the Organization for Economic Cooperation and Development, the International Civil Aviation Organization, the Food and Agriculture Organization and the ILO. On "elites," see note 79 above.

[110] It is often very difficult to amend a multilateral treaty "charter" with broad membership; for example, GATT, which requires a two-thirds vote of acceptance. See J. Jackson, *World Trade and the Law of GATT* (1969), 73; and Jackson, *The World Trading System* 51.

Thus, a DAHS approach can lead governments to be wary of accepting international norms.[111] That may be good (some argue that many international norms are not carefully drafted or wisely adopted), but it also may not be so good. As the world becomes "smaller" and more interdependent, accelerated international coordination is needed to prevent disputes and misunderstandings, and to allow enterprises to make plans and maximize economic welfare and development. This activity could be greatly inhibited by DAHS.

The amount of confidence that policy-makers have in international institutions relative to their national institutions has important influence on their thinking about these issues. Government officials and citizens who look upon their national institutions as having endured for a long time and as seeming to protect citizens' rights, sound economic policy, and democratic procedures will be inclined to trust those institutions. If at the same time they doubt the wisdom or durability of international institutions, they may reject a DAHS approach.

On the other hand, if government officials and citizens have a higher degree of trust in the international institutions and treaties than they do in their own governmental structure, they will probably prefer DAHS as a conscious or implicit check on their government. Thus, it is entirely understandable that some persons in recently autocratic countries might favor an international regime to protect human rights. The European Convention on Human Rights can be a convenient reference point, as well as a *constitutional check on participating national governments*, and this role will be enhanced by DAHS – the direct application of the treaty and even higher status for its norms than for subsequent legislation. In other countries, persons who have seen a recent shift from socialism or state planning towards market-oriented economic principles might feel more secure about the permanence of that shift if their nation accepted international treaty norms (such as in a customs union or free trade area agreement) that would directly apply with higher status – again, as a *check on their own government and any subsequent decisions* (even by democratic elections) that might alter the new market orientation.[112] Indeed, the DAHS principles might effectively introduce "judicial review and protection" of either human rights or economic structures in situations where they would never be assured by the national constitution.[113]

---

[111] See notes 89 and 84 above and the accompanying text; and the text below.

[112] Of course in some cases, the DAHS principle is simply older, adopted at a time before some of these policies were perceived, perhaps for the more theoretical reasons mentioned in the discussion above.

[113] Analogously, see the Constitution (Grundgesetz) of the Federal Republic of Germany, Article 25 (regarding customary international law). See also Petersmann, *Constitutional Functions and Constitutional Problems of International Economic Law*, 220.

Implications of differing constitutions

The ease with which the national constitution can be amended will also influence the choice of protection by international norms rather than national norms, or possibly even constitutional norms. An easily amended constitution[114] will facilitate the rectification of DAHS problems (as long as the higher status does not trump the constitution) through constitutional changes. Although in this case the difficulties of DAHS are less worrisome, the DAHS principle is less effective in protecting against or restraining national government actions contrary to treaties.[115]

As with direct application, higher status also presents the question of what domestic legal institution will decide which clashing norm prevails. If the treaty norm has higher hierarchical status, however, the domestic court is likely to have less discretion or leeway; that is, the question facing the court is much more likely to be a "constitutional" one. Of course, such an issue may be left to the court to determine on the basis of, say, the drafters' intent, or other criteria. Nevertheless, as surveys of constitutional practice suggest,[116] the issue is more often deemed to turn on a constitutional rule. For example, United States courts for many decades have accepted the rule that the "later in time prevails," basing it on early court opinions interpreting the Constitution itself.[117] The rule has been criticized, and in at least one odd recent case it may have been somewhat softened,[118] but it generally seems to be accepted as a constitutional requirement. Still, in some constitutional systems the issue has not been completely resolved, and some opportunity may remain for the courts to make that determination on the basis of various considerations, including some of those expressed in this article.

---

[114] Some constitutions seem to be easily and frequently amended, and require only a referendum or a national legislative act for the purpose. See the constitutions of Switzerland (Article 121) and Mexico. Within the United States, the constitution of California (Article 18) might be noted in this regard.

[115] See note 114 above.   [116] See note 6 above.

[117] Jackson, "United States of America," 162 note 88.

[118] In a 1988 case of the US Federal District Court in New York, *United States v. Palestine Liberation Organization,* 695 F. Supp. 1456 (SDNY 1988), the court held that a US statute requiring the closing of all offices of terrorist organizations, including the PLO, did not clearly enough indicate an intent to contravene US international obligations under the United Nations Headquarters Agreement. Consequently, the court ruled that the PLO office housing its UN Mission was not required by that statute to close. The case was not appealed, possibly because the US Executive branch had not favored the statute in the first place. The statutory language and legislative history seemed rather strongly to suggest an intent to close PLO offices, even the one at the United Nations; the court's requirement of explicit Congressional intent to act inconsistently with US international obligations is therefore interesting and controversial. See, e.g., Reisman, "An International Farce."

Several cases

Various specific cases and practices suggest that courts will often strive to seek a "way out" from the rigidities and other policy problems they face when a DAHS rule exists in a legal system. An example is the jurisprudence of the European Court of Justice;[119] the Court early refused to grant direct application to the GATT treaty (General Agreement on Tariffs and Trade), for reasons that have been criticized.[120] On the other hand, if the EC Court at that time was worried that a directly applicable norm might also have a higher status (i.e., the potential for a DAHS system), one can readily see why a court and all other policy-makers in the Community would have been nervous about directly applying the GATT. Thus, if the court has some leeway regarding direct applicability, but worries that it may not have such leeway regarding higher status, it would be highly tempted to discover an appropriate way to refuse direct application.

A 1990 Japanese Supreme Court case had some similar characteristics. Once again the GATT was invoked. The case was brought by Japanese necktie producers, who argued that their Government's restraints on the importation of silk for neckties (to protect domestic silk producers) violated rules of the GATT. The complainants claimed that the GATT was directly applicable and that, under the Japanese Constitution (Article 98), directly applicable norms were endowed with a higher status than legislation or other legal norms. The lower courts (in 1984 and 1987) concluded that the GATT did not apply to the situation, but their reasoning (or lack thereof) has been criticized, and on appeal the Supreme Court of Japan merely affirmed with very little analysis.[121] It can again be surmised that a court would find great difficulty in directly applying the GATT, with its many elaborate constraints on national government actions in international trade, in circumstances where those GATT norms would also have a higher status than even later in time legislation or other acts. Thus, it comes as no surprise when a court somehow manages to evade this consequence.

---

[119] See Schermers and Waelbroeck, *Judicial Protection in the European Communities*, § 746; and Pescatore, "Treaty-Making by the European Communities."

[120] Petersmann, "Application of GATT by the Court of Justice of the European Communities," 424*ff.*

[121] The so-called *Necktie* case, decided by the Kyoto District Court in 1984, affirmed by the Osaka High Court (1987) and by the Japanese Supreme Court in 1990 (with an extremely brief and uninformative opinion). See William J. Davey and A. O. Sykes (eds.), *Legal Problems of International Economic Relations: Cases, Materials, and Text on the National and International Regulation of Transnational Economic Relations* (3rd edn., West Publishing Co., 1995). Also discussed by Professor Yuji Iwasawa in "Implementation of International Trade Agreements in Japan" (paper delivered at Third Bielefeld Conference, September 1990).

The Netherlands, in the view of some, may be the most monist legal system in the world, but even there, according to eminent commentators, courts have ways to avoid the direct application of treaty norms that would take precedence not only over later legislation, but also over the Constitution itself.[122] The empirical observation that national courts in systems with DAHS try to avoid its logical consequences suggests that legal systems that have not yet fully decided the question should exercise great caution before embracing DAHS.[123]

A DAHS system can also significantly inhibit a national government's willingness to enter into international treaties. A recent example occurred in the European Communities. Although there may be an argument that Community level law has not yet been fully determined to be a DAHS system,[124] the apprehension that it would be apparently influenced the negotiations between the Community and the Government of Switzerland concerning a treaty on international trade in insurance services. The Community side feared that if it entered into such a treaty, and it became both directly applicable (as many desire) and superior to even later EC legislation, the Community would be greatly hampered in its ability to develop harmonization of national law and other regulatory principles on insurance in the future. The solution chosen by the negotiators was a fairly elaborate clause in the draft treaty permitting a contracting party to opt out of some provisions in certain circumstances.[125]

IV.   Applications and policy implementation

Some national legal systems have largely determined the internal rules about direct application of treaties and the hierarchical status of such norms, but in other systems the issues may still be evolving or completely open (e.g., if a constitution has yet to be completed). In the latter cases, the policies discussed in the previous sections should be carefully considered by the constitutional drafters, officials or judges responsible for the further development of the question. Even when the issues are ostensibly "settled," we have seen that judicial and other institutions have ways to evade the full

---

[122] See generally Schermers and Waelbroeck, *Judicial Protection in the European Communities*; and van Dijk, "Domestic Status of Human-Rights Treaties."

[123] See the text above; and also notes 97–101 above and the works cited therein; see also de la Rochère, "France."

[124] Stein, "External Relations of the European Community," 71, notes that in practice the European Court of Justice has never invalidated a Community law as contrary to a Community agreement with a third state. See also Hilf, "The Single European Act and 1992."

[125] Discussions with negotiators (1991); and Agreement Between the European Economic Community and the Swiss Confederation on Direct Insurance Other Than Life Assurance, October 10, 1989, Articles 39 and 40, 34 OJ L205 (1991), 3 at 12–13.

logical consequences of a DAHS system. In this section we discuss some variations in implementation, and the techniques of applying the rules so as to realize the policies selected from those discussed previously.

In broad brush strokes, we can consider three different circumstances:

1. the constitution is still being written;
2. the constitution is still evolving through practice or court decisions; and
3. the treaty or its implementing language can play an important or even decisive role in how a national legal system handles treaty norms internally.

In the first case, when the constitution is still being written, close attention to the questions of direct applicability and higher status seem merited. Of course, failure to spell out the pertinent constitutional principles may leave the issues open for later elaboration by the national legal system, which may be precisely what the constitution makers wish (perhaps as a compromise to a standoff). However, the various policies discussed suggest the value of normally avoiding a full DAHS system. Direct application combined with a later in time principle[126] at least affords the national government some relief from the rigidities of a full DAHS system, and is less likely to inhibit that nation's willingness to enter into international treaties. Rejection of direct application altogether would go even further in this regard.

In certain circumstances, however, the constitution makers and their democratic constituencies may strongly desire to constrain their government. As mentioned above, two subjects in particular have been noted in this connection: the protection of human rights and the preservation of a market-oriented economic system. Discussions in newly forming democracies such as those in Eastern Europe, as well as in countries in other parts of the world, demonstrate that their officials and citizens sometimes trust an *international treaty* to protect human rights more than their own governments. This consideration would have to be weighed against the policies that do not favor DAHS. The extent and specificity of the international treaties that are candidates for DAHS treatment must also be weighed. A treaty that is not overly broad in its reach and is reasonably precise and unambiguous would seem a better candidate for DAHS treatment than treaties with contrary characteristics.[127]

Similarly, in the flurry of privatization and evolving market-oriented economies that the world is currently witnessing, some national leaders

---

[126] Such as in the United States. See Jackson, "United States of America."

[127] Compare, for example, the two principal UN covenants on human rights, the International Covenant on Civil and Political Rights, December 16, 1966, 999 UNTS 171; and the International Covenant on Economic, Social and Cultural Rights, December 16, 1966, 993 UNTS 3.

and citizens see an advantage in international obligations that would restrain later domestic political attempts to overturn or erode the market mechanisms put in place. Membership in a treaty system such as the European Communities, or similar regional groupings elsewhere,[128] may be understood as playing an important constitutional role in this regard. This constitutional role will be stronger in a DAHS system.

Often these policy considerations are only dimly perceived and not articulated (at least with candor). They obviously suggest that the participants place a relatively *higher* trust in the international institutions than in their national constitutional institutions, and historical observation sometimes indicates that they have good reason to do so. In that case, is there any way to avoid some of the negative policy implications of a DAHS system? Several possibilities can be suggested.

First, a new constitutional provision[129] could treat different treaty subjects differently. It is certainly possible for a constitutional clause to give DAHS treatment only to "human rights" treaties, although the definitional problems would require great care.[130] Similarly, a constitutional provision may give DAHS treatment only to specifically named treaties (allowing future constitutional amendments to add to the list). It is even conceivable for a DAHS provision in a constitution to be limited in time, e.g. to operate for x years and then cease (perhaps in the questionable optimistic belief that national institutions will develop sufficient strength and credibility that overriding international protection will no longer be needed).

DAHS treatment might also be given to membership in an international (regional?) economic treaty organization. In some cases, a constitutional amendment could provide for this treatment (or otherwise secure the treaty norms). Some constitutions may now require this approach.[131] A new constitution might refer to this possibility and leave it to be implemented in the future by an amendment. It could even provide for a special amending procedure (perhaps one that is easier to execute than that for ordinary amendments) to incorporate international norms for the human rights or market-structure cases.

The second situation, where the constitution is still evolving, may require different approaches. Of course, if the evolution is achieved by

---

[128] Possibly a North American Free Trade Agreement (NAFTA).

[129] Amendment of an older constitution could do the same.

[130] What is a "human rights" treaty? Is it an economic, social, right to work or family law treaty? Austria is arguably an example of a nation that has applied only certain international treaties as directly applicable with "constitutional status," by amending the Constitution. See A. Drzemczewski, *European Human Rights Convention in Domestic Law: A Comparative Study* (1983), 93–95.

[131] For example, that of Switzerland.

amendment or changes in the constituent "treaty,"[132] the choices may be varied and considerations mentioned above could come into play. However, if the evolution is produced by judicial decision (or other practice of national legal institutions), the choices may be more limited. For example, if higher status for directly applied treaty norms already seems to be embedded in the legal system, the court or officials may wish to stress ways to avoid direct application, arguing that it requires either an overwhelming expression of intent or the framing of the norm in precise and direct language, or both. To rule against direct application would enable national officials to implement the treaty by means of an act of transformation.[133] Even with direct application, courts could employ various judicial doctrines used to "duck" issues, such as nonjusticiability, lack of definiteness, mootness, political question, standing, and ripeness.[134]

Alternatively, the question of higher status may not have been finally and firmly determined.[135] In that case, national judicial or other officials might still have the option to avoid conferring such status on treaty norms, which would make it easier to accept direct applicability (and to enter into treaties in the first place).

In the third case, where the treaty or implementing language can play a major role, it is assumed that this constitutional process gives great or decisive weight to the intent expressed in the treaty, in its preparatory work, or by national negotiators. For example, a treaty could incorporate such a clause: "It is intended that this treaty shall not have direct application in either [or one listed] party." Would the national judiciary or officials act accordingly? In many countries (including the United States), they probably would. One could envisage a sort of boilerplate clause that a nation's officials would *always* include in treaties, with some carefully considered exceptions, so as to clarify this question and avoid the policy pitfalls of either direct application or higher status.

Although strong evidence of this type of intent might be stated (or discovered by a court) in the preparatory work of a treaty, such an expression might be considered more ambiguous and could give greater leeway to the inclinations of the national legal system's courts or officials.[136]

---

[132] The situations of Switzerland, eastern Europe and even the European Community (Treaty of Rome amendments) come to mind.

[133] In an analogy to the European Community, the treaty would be more like a "directive" than a "regulation."

[134] See L. Tribe, *American Constitutional Law* (1978), chapter 3, §§ 10–17; see also note 36 above.

[135] Again, eastern Europe comes to mind, and this may also (arguably) be the case for the European Community.

[136] See note 80 above.

Finally, somewhat more removed and raising certain other issues would be a unilateral statement precluding direct application by the officials of one of the parties, during the negotiation of the treaty or the national constitutional process of its approval. The prime examples are probably found in the United States when the Senate gives advice to the President allowing him to ratify a treaty, but only if it is not self-executing,[137] and when Congress authorizes the President to ratify a treaty but specifies in the enabling statute or the legislative history that the treaty shall not be self-executing.[138] The President alone may even issue such a statement, and it is likely to be followed by the US courts.[139]

Expressions of intent are less likely to be used to govern the question of higher status when treaty norms are directly applicable. Although it is theoretically possible, this author knows of no such cases. Moreover, higher status is more likely to be considered a type of "constitutional" or judicial issue that only the courts can decide in a particular society.[140] Of course, a constitution could determine who decides, perhaps by relegating it to an executive or to a parliamentary vote.

V.   Conclusions

The questions of the direct application of treaties into national legal systems and the hierarchical status of the norms so applied are extraordinarily complex and vary from country to country, depending on constitutional and other municipal rules. The various answers to these questions can have enormous impact – as great as that of some constitutional norms. Although these answers are supported by assorted theoretical and functional arguments, many of the policies (some deriving from empirical observation of national practices) are often overlooked or not explored when decisions about these matters are made. In this article we have

---

[137] See note 84 above.   [138] See note 80 above.

[139] This could occur when the President alone enters into an agreement (without the participation of Congress), or even when Congress has participated but has not explicitly, or implicitly, stated its intent with regard to self-execution. Although it is not entirely clear how US courts respond to this type of intent language, there certainly are hints that they would follow an intent so expressed, and there are no cases to the contrary. A more difficult case might arise if Congress participated in the treaty-making and expressed its intent that the treaty be (or not be) self-executing, while the President expressed a contrary intent. In some such cases, it can be argued that the President would not have the authority to ratify the agreement if the ratification meant that he would implement the agreement contrary to the Congressional intent. By Congressional intent, I mean to include Senate intent when the treaty-making process relies solely on the Senate. See also Henkin, *Constitutionalism*, 71 and 77.

[140] Although decided only by a lower federal court, the PLO case, *United States* v. *Palestine Liberation Organization*, 695 F. Supp. 1456 (SDNY 1988), might be interpreted as emphasizing court control of this issue.

attempted, by referring to a variety of country practices, to explore the policy pros and cons of direct application, or higher status, or both. Obviously, "theory" has been relatively ignored, and we have not assumed that international law is always better than national law.

In general, it can reasonably be said that both direct application and higher status of treaty norms involve enough policy difficulties to suggest caution in introducing them into a national legal system. When a system includes both rules, even more significant policy difficulties are presented, such as rigid treaty constraints on future government action, the possible avoidance of democratic procedures for rule making, and inhibition of further treaty-making. Sometimes these difficulties are offset by policy preferences, as when national officials and citizens feel the international constraints to protect human rights or market economic mechanisms may be more effective than national constitutional constraints. In addition, some of these difficulties may be ameliorated by certain approaches of the courts or officials in national systems, or by the language in treaties or their preparatory work.

In sum, however, it behooves national officials to understand the various policy arguments and difficulties before making some of the policy choices that may be available to them. Where constitutions call for approval of a legislature to accept a treaty, the best approach may often be for the enactment of approval to provide as well (in a dual role) for an "act of transformation" of the treaty itself by incorporating it into the statute. This procedure usually affords domestic lawyers easy and noticeable access to the treaty text, while preserving certain legislative checks against some of the drawbacks of direct application and/or higher status. (The procedure is apparently common in the German system, and is sometimes used in the US and other systems. It is obviously available to the dualist systems, where direct effect is not possible.)[141]

Sometimes the relatively abstract concepts expressed in this article are more easily grasped when a concrete case or circumstance illustrates the application or policy problems of the subject. Several such cases have been mentioned in the text and footnotes above,[142] but many more could be inventoried. Let me suggest the following, by way of summarizing and integrating some of the considerations discussed here.

It is this author's opinion and observation (shared by others) that treaty rule making already has an important bearing on economic activity in a shrinking world and interdependent global economy and is very likely to become even more important – furnishing by far the largest number of

---

[141] See note 80 above; and see generally Jacobs and Roberts, *The Effect of Treaties in Domestic Law*.

[142] See particularly the end of Part III above.

international norms with which national societies will have to contend. Competition policy (antitrust), regulation of banks, insurance, the sale of securities, investment flows, the mobility of labor and professional services, protection of the environment and consumer protection are only a few of the many subjects the global economy must deal with. Many subjects involve difficult compromises and trade-offs between the desire for greater economic efficiency and legitimate social goals, such as protection of consumers, workers, the poor, and the environment, as well as numerous other legitimate governmental objectives, including prudential policies for banks, insurance companies, and brokerages, among others.

Some national societies have much more experience with such regulation than many others, and certainly more than any international institutions. The regulations are often the result of tortured compromises among many different interests, and are also evolving in the light of experience with the regulations. Moreover, different societies adopt different approaches, some using a legalistic or punitive approach, while others prefer the less formal avenues of societal pressure or moral admonitions. Societies also take different governmental approaches to rule making, democracy, elites, religion, and special interests. Thus, it can be very difficult to obtain an international consensus on treaty rules that are precise or "permanent." Yet the option of drafting treaties to deal with problems of cooperation and coordination across societies must be available and reasonably effective. The teachings of economists and game theorists (e.g., the analysis of the prisoner's dilemma) reinforce this conclusion.[143]

Now let us examine one particular subject, a prominent feature of recent news accounts,[144] regulation of the sale of corporate securities to the public. There are huge differences among the regulatory practices of similar societies (e.g., the major industrial societies), to say nothing of those among disparate societies (e.g., developing countries, state-trading countries, raw-materials producers). As the market for corporate securities (and investment funds) rushes to become global, multilateral regulation (through treaty rules) will obviously increase in importance. Yet it is also obvious that agreement of the various countries to many details of the rules will be hard to achieve.

Several implications of these facts can be noticed. Nations with some confidence in their own regulatory systems will be much more reluctant to enter into the relatively unknown territory of international treaty obligations if those obligations will suddenly be directly applicable, superseding (where conflict exists) their domestic regulation. This reluctance will be

---

[143] See, e.g., R. Axelrod, *The Evolution of Cooperation* (1984).
[144] See Henriques, "In World Markets, Loose Regulation," *New York Times*, July 23, 1991, D1, col. 3 (Mid-West edition).

heightened if the treaty rules not only are directly applied, but prevail over domestic later-in-time rules. Of course, treaties can be drafted to permit national flexibility and allow for other problems of direct application and higher status. But like all human endeavor, and perhaps all national legislation, many treaty rules will not be perfect. Indeed, chances are that treaties will be more ambiguous than national laws (because of the difficulty of reaching consensus), and that vague treaty norms will therefore be used to challenge national regulations. Also, vague treaty norms may later be interpreted by international institutions in ways that undermine municipal regulations. In addition, multilateral treaties generally are much more difficult to change so as to evolve in tandem with economic and societal circumstances.[145] And democratic nations that have achieved a (possibly uneasy) compromise of interests to construct a regulatory system will be interested in minimizing actions that might upset those compromises.

In these circumstances, in my view, prudent national political officials or statesmen would be reluctant to embrace a DAHS system for treaties, and if already constrained by a DAHS system, or even a DA system, they would be well advised to avoid the treaty process altogether for many endeavors. Without the rigidity of DAHS, nations might well find the treaty process useful and effective (if not perfect, of course) in furthering vitally needed international cooperation for handling the problems of a shrinking world. If this flexibility results in an occasional misfit between treaty obligations and national legal norms, is that not a worthwhile price? Would it not be better to devote efforts and attention to making treaty norms more effective, by devising processes for dispute settlement and for ensuring the democratic participation of each party's citizens in accepting the treaty norms, than to rely too heavily on the notions of direct applicability and higher status?

---

[145] The traditional doctrines, such as *rebus sic stantibus* (Vienna Convention, Article 62), do not begin to accommodate the type of evolution, innovation, and step-by-step change of circumstances that must be addressed by both national and international "legislation."

Sovereignty, strictly, is the locus of ultimate legitimate authority in a political society, once the Prince or "the Crown," later parliament or the people.

Sovereignty, a conception deriving from the relations between a prince and his/her subjects, is not a necessary or appropriate external attribute for the abstraction we call a state ... For international relations, surely for international law, it is a term largely unnecessary and better avoided.

For legal purposes at least, we might do well to relegate the term sovereignty to the shelf of history as a relic from an earlier era. To this end, it is necessary to analyze, "decompose," the concept; to identify the elements that have been deemed to be inherent in, or to derive from, "sovereignty;" in a system of states at the turn of the twenty-first century.[1]

I.   Introduction

It is a privilege and an honor to be invited to contribute to this *festschrift* volume for so distinguished an international law scholar and teacher as Louis Henkin. Indeed it is a formidable challenge – what can one say that could rise to even the shadow of the standard that Professor Henkin represents. The way that I have chosen to *try* to reach that shadow, however, is to address one of the many issues on which Professor Henkin has written and that seems to be of great interest to him.[2] For this reason I have chosen to comment on the concept of "sovereignty," which puzzles many of us toiling in the international legal vineyards. I must confess that I also chose this subject because it intrigues me too, and because recently I

---

* This chapter is based on John H. Jackson, "The Great 1994 Sovereignty Debate: United States Acceptance and Implementation of the Uruguay Round Results" (1997) 36 *Columbia Journal of Transnational Law* 157–188.
[1] Louis Henkin, *International Law: Politics and Values* (1995), 9–10.   [2] See *ibid.*

have had the experience of participating in some major policy debates which engage this concept, namely the 1994 debate in Congress (and other forums) about whether the United States should ratify the treaty embodying the results of the massive decade-long trade negotiation known as the Uruguay Round. This means, of course, that the reader must be aware that I speak at least partly as a "participant observer,"[3] hopefully in the best sense of that empirical technique. Thus, the reader is entitled to appraise my judgments accordingly. Professor Henkin himself has written from experiences and will understand the approach.

This brief contribution is designed to complement some of Professor Henkin's thoughts on the subject of sovereignty, and to build on them such as is known to me from his writings. The approach I will take here is to examine one particular "case" – the 1994 Uruguay Round debate – to explore how the concept (or, more appropriately, the concepts) of sovereignty played a role in various policy discussions. Through the examination of this specific case, I will illustrate how the concepts of sovereignty were used (differently in different contexts) and point out the more specific and disaggregated policy issues to which they were linked. In some sort of nominal sense, my views may appear to be somewhat contrary to parts of Professor Henkin's views, especially in those instances when he speaks of relegating "the term sovereignty to the shelf of history as a relic from an earlier era"[4] or doing away with the "S word."[5] Yet behind and beyond this "nominal sense," it should be clear that I am using the word "sovereignty" in a different context than Professor Henkin. Indeed, Professor Henkin himself notes that it is necessary to "decompose" the word, and to identify which elements of the concept are

---

[3] See Results of the Uruguay Round Trade Negotiations: Hearings Before the Senate Finance Committee, 103rd Cong., 114 (1994) (March 23, 1994, testimony of John H. Jackson, Hessel E. Yntema Professor of Law, University of Michigan); The World Trade Organization and US Sovereignty: Hearings Before the Senate Committee on Foreign Relations, 103rd Cong. (1994) (June 14, 1994, testimony of John H. Jackson, Hessel E. Yntema Professor of Law, University of Michigan), available in 1994 WL 14188767. Uruguay Round Agreements Act. Pub. L. No. 103–465. In addition to the above, the reader may be interested in some of the articles published about the Uruguay Round legislative debate, including the following: William J. Aceves, "Lost Sovereignty? The Implications of the Uruguay Round Agreements" (1995) 19 *Fordham International Law Journal* 427; Claudio Cocuzza and Andrea Forabosco, "Are States Relinquishing Their Sovereign Rights? The GATT Dispute Settlement Process in a Globalized Economy" (1996) 4 *Tulane Journal of International and Comparative Law* 161; Julie Long, "Note, Ratcheting up Federalism: A Supremacy Clause Analysis of NAFTA and the Uruguay Round Agreements" (1995) 80 *Minnesota Law Review* 231; and Samuel C. Straight, "Note, GATT and NAFTA: Marrying Effective Dispute Settlement and the Sovereignty of the Fifty States" (1995) 45 *Duke Law Journal* 216.

[4] Henkin, *International Law*, 10.

[5] Louis Henkin, "The Mythology of Sovereignty," *American Society of International Law Newsletter*, March–May 1993, 1.

"appropriate and desirable for a state in a system of states at the turn of the twenty-first century."[6]

I could, of course, fashion a new word (or, perhaps more modernly, a new phrase with a catchy acronym), but the observable fact is that the word "sovereignty" is still being used widely, often in different settings which imply different "submeanings." Consequently, I cling to the word and will use it, knowing that most of my readers should understand it. As I use the word it will not always (indeed almost never) signify the more "antiquated" definition (that is also ambiguous and multi-definitional). In broad brush I see the "antiquated" definition of "sovereignty" that should be "relegated" as something like the notion of a nation-state's supreme absolute power and authority over its subjects and territory, unfettered by any higher law or rule (except perhaps ethical or religious standards) unless the nation-state consents in an individual and meaningful way. It could be character-ized as the nation-state's power (embodied in the Prince?) to violate virgins, chop off heads, arbitrarily confiscate property, and all sorts of other excessive and inappropriate actions.

No sensible person would agree that such an antiquated version of sovereignty exists at all in today's world. A multitude of treaties and customary international law norms impose international legal constraints (at least) that circumscribe extreme forms of arbitrary actions on even a sovereign's own citizens. Of course some theories can explain these con-straints as having been "consented to" by sovereigns, but these explana-tions cannot always explain the observable phenomena of modern-day international law applications. Furthermore, policy advocates and politi-cal representatives make the argument that their government should de-cline to accept a treaty because it takes away the nation's sovereignty *even when* it consents. Indeed, in this sense *all* treaties "take away sover-eignty," and so the argument of some would seem to deny the validity of *any* treaty acceptance. Let us indeed "relegate" or abolish such use of the "S" word.

But then what does "sovereignty," as practically used today, signify? I will suggest a tentative hypothesis: most (but not all) of the time when "sovereignty" is used in current policy debates, it really refers to questions about the allocation of power; this is normally government decision-mak-ing power. I would argue that most of the sovereignty objections to joining an international treaty are arguments about the allocation of power among different levels of different human institutions, mostly governmental. That is, when a party argues that the US should not accept a treaty because it takes away US sovereignty to do so, what that party most often really

---

[6] Henkin, *International Law*, 10.

means is that he or she believes a certain set of decisions should, as a matter of good government policy, be made at the nation-state (US) level and not at an international level. Often this is not articulated and the objection to a treaty is stated in generic and opaque terms, sometimes with "religious fervor," so that the argument seems easy to dismiss. When stated so broadly, opaquely, and categorically, the sovereign argument frequently appears unrealistic. It assumes a degree of independent action for a nation-state that in a "real" sense hardly exists anyway. When viewed as a question of allocation of power, however, the debate only begins with the "sovereignty" objection; it must continue with an analysis demonstrating why it is better or worse for such a power shift to occur in certain circumstances.[7] As discussed below, this is rarely done, but ought to be done if the argument is to be persuasive.

I suggest that the allocation of power issue, as often embraced by an invocation of the "sovereignty" argument, is part of a very complex and vast landscape of issues relating to allocation of power for all types of government (and nongovernment) decisions in our world today. First, there is a question of "vertical" allocation of power: at what level should a decision or armed intervention be made? An international body? A national body (federal level)? A subfederal entity? A local neighborhood? Where should a decision about which potholes to fill, which streets to repair, be made? For contrast, where should a decision about standards for products moving in international trade be made? What are the elements for deciding such questions? Secondly, there are also "horizontal" power allocation questions. Should a certain decision be under the control of the legislature, the executive, the judiciary, another government entity, or even a non-government (such as private business) entity?[8]

When sovereignty objection arguments are "decomposed" and examined for underlying reasons, it becomes clear that there is merit to scrutinize closely what is at stake for a nation in accepting the constraints of an international treaty.[9] Clearly what is at stake will differ with the size,

---

[7] The concept of "subsidiarity," currently very heavily debated in Europe, is clearly closely related to this discussion. I do not intend here, however, to get into the middle of the European debate on this subject.

[8] Market economics obviously has much to say about the last in this list. See generally, Richard G. Lipsey and Paul N. Courant, *Microeconomics* (8th edn., 1994).

[9] See The World Trade Organization and US Sovereignty: Hearings Before the Senate Committee on Foreign Relations, 103rd Cong., 3–4 (1994) (June 14, 1994, testimony of John H. Jackson, Hessel E. Yntema Professor of Law, University of Michigan), available in 1994 WL 14188767. This does not mean that it is frivolous to carefully study the question, as this hearing is designed to do. It is important to assure ourselves that if there develops the rare situation when an international body or rule system operates in a manner to abuse the rules or abuse the procedures of an organization so as to threaten the vital interests of the United States, that the US will still retain the tools to take appropriate counter-measures. In the

power, population, economic circumstances, etc., of the nation-state. A large and powerful state would more likely be hesitant to accept obligations to an international decision-making procedure that would most probably result in decisions contrary to the national goals of such a powerful state. This might be because of a "one nation, one vote" decision-making structure with a large membership of mini-states whose national goals are inconsistent with those of the large states. Consequently, what often becomes important is the actual "constitutional" structure of the international institutions put in place by the treaty.[10]

By way of contrast, small countries might find that membership in certain types of treaty-based international institutions actually "enhance sovereignty" in certain real senses. By such membership, they may feel less threatened by other nations that are much larger and more powerful. For example, a dispute settlement mechanism might, in the view of a small country, redress some of the imbalance of power when it comes to handling disputes or sources of tension about the way either nation has been applying its international economic policies (such as trade barriers).

Part of the challenge for international law and international relations is to analyze the "decomposed" arguments. This may help nations with divergent perspectives to consider the broader and longer-term perspectives of both national policy and international policy objectives, and to understand better the risks of developing international institutions as weighed against the advantages of such development.

In looking behind the surface of the Uruguay Round Treaty debate in the United States in 1994, we can readily see many issues stirred together. This is why I believe much of this 1994 activity can be termed the "Great Sovereignty Debate" of this decade. It may not have been much noticed in this context. That is partly because the debate occurred in many different forms. These included several committees of the US Congress, the floor of the House and the Senate, and many forms of the media (e.g., radio, television, newspapers, journals, etc.). Yet if one follows the threads of the debate about the US accepting the Uruguay Round results, one constantly discovers references to "sovereignty" as addressing essentially power-allo

---

case of the WTO, I believe that the US and other nations are protected in that respect. Among other protections, the WTO Charter allows for withdrawal with a brief six month notice. It is also the case that this Congress is likely to specify in the implementing legislation that the WTO Charter and the Uruguay Round rules are not "self-executing," so again in the rare case of serious abuse of international procedures the US would maintain its own constitutional freedom to act even if inconsistent with international rules. In such a case, of course, the US could be in breach of its international legal obligations and might face counter-measures.

[10] See *ibid.*

cation issues.[11] These include my own statements responding to the arguments of others.[12]

Consequently, in the three remaining sections of this paper, I will explore the 1994 debate. In Part II, I will outline the background context of the debate and some of the specific parts of it. In Part III, I will discuss in somewhat greater detail the various ways the "sovereignty argument" was used in the debate over whether the United States should accept the Uruguay Round negotiation results. This will be the core of my analysis, and will suggest a number of different contexts and, therefore, different meanings of the "sovereignty objection." In Part IV, I will draw some tentative conclusions or perspectives from the material addressed in Part III.

What are some of the different issues discussed? Even in Part III, I will not attempt in this short space to provide a complete and exhaustive inventory of all the different possible "decomposed" policy questions to which sovereignty arguments were addressed in the 1994 debate. However, to illustrate some of the specific issues, I will discuss sovereignty issues in four broad categories, including elements of the World Trade Organization (WTO) decision-making procedures, the structure of the new WTO dispute settlement process, and some questions about the constitutional and other arguments regarding US internal law and procedures and how they would be affected by US acceptance of the Uruguay Round results. Many particular issues are thus discussed below. These include: the implications and risks of the WTO treaty text regarding potential decisions of the WTO affecting national economic regulation; the effect of the WTO dispute processes on domestic environmental standards; and the interrelationship between the US constitutional federal structure and the effects of the WTO institutional procedures.

II.   GATT, the Uruguay Round and the WTO: the background for the 1994 debate

A.   *The General Agreement on Tariffs and Trade: a half-century trade treaty*

Looking back over the 1946–1996 history of the General Agreement on Tariffs and Trade (GATT) allows one to reflect on how surprising it was that this relatively feeble institution with many "birth defects" managed to

---

[11] For relevant hearings, see Bernard D. Reams Jr. and Jon S. Schultz (eds.), *Uruguay Round Agreements Act: A Legislative History of Public Law No. 103–465* (1995).

[12] See The World Trade Organization and US Sovereignty: Hearings Before the Senate Committee on Foreign Relations, 103rd Cong. (1994) (June 14, 1994, testimony of John H. Jackson, Hessel E. Yntema Professor of Law, University of Michigan), available in 1994 WL 14188767.

play such a significant role for almost five decades. It certainly was far more successful than one might have predicted in the late 1940s.

The GATT, often described as the major trade organization and the principal treaty for trade relations, was technically neither. As a treaty, it never itself came into force. It was always applied "provisionally" by the Protocol of Provisional Application (PPA).[13] In addition, technically the GATT was not intended to be an organization. The negotiators in the drafting conferences in 1946 (New York), 1947 (Geneva), and 1948 (Havana) expected the International Trade Organization (ITO), created by their draft treaty-charter, to be the institutional framework to which the GATT (an agreement among "contracting parties" to liberalize trade restrictions) would be attached. When the US Congress refused to approve the ITO Charter, declared dead by 1951, the GATT, which came into (provisional) force in 1948 by the terms of the PPA, became the focus of attention as a possible institution where nations could solve some of their trade problems. An attempt in 1955 to create a small mini-organization to solve institutional problems also failed. Yet the GATT, through a series of major trade rounds designed to gradually reduce tariffs and other trade barriers (culminating in the Uruguay Round which was the eighth round) along with an increasingly important set of relatively precise (and complex) rules, was able to achieve an astonishing amount of world trade liberalization.

The relative lack of treaty clauses that could serve as a basis for a trade institution, and the ambiguity of those that were contained in the GATT, became increasingly troublesome as the GATT grew in scope and detail in order to cope with a fascinating set of concrete problems of international economic relations. While most of this story has been told elsewhere[14] and need not occupy us here, several institutional problems in particular relate to the general notion of "sovereignty" and deserve mention.

One of these problems was embedded ambiguously in GATT Article XXV regarding decisions of the "Contracting Parties" acting jointly.[15] The treaty language was extraordinarily broad due to the historical context that expected an ITO charter to oversee and supervise what could be done. Article XXV stated that the contracting parties would meet from time to

---

[13] Protocol of Provisional Application to the General Agreement on Tariffs and Trade, signed October 30, 1947, 61 Stat. A2051; 55 UNTS 308.
[14] See, e.g., John H. Jackson, *World Trade and the Law of GATT: A Legal Analysis of the General Agreement on Tariffs and Trade* (1969); John H. Jackson, "The World Trade Organization: Watershed Innovation or Cautious Small Step Forward?" (1995) *The World Economy* 11; John H. Jackson, "The Uruguay Round and the Launch of the WTO – Significance and Challenges" in Terence P. Stewart (ed.), *The World Trade Organization: The Multilateral Trade Framework for the 21st Century and US Implementing Legislation* (1996), 5; and John H. Jackson, *The World Trading System: Economic Relations* (2nd edn., MIT Press, 1997).
[15] Note that the terms "member" or "membership" were not used.

time "for the purpose of giving effect" to the agreement, and "with a view to facilitating the operation and furthering the objectives of this Agreement." The procedure was mostly "one nation, one vote," with decisions taken by a majority of votes cast. Despite the generality of the language, however, it is fair to say it was not used to its limit; indeed the contracting parties appeared cautious and arguably never used this authority to impose any new substantive obligation on any nation-state. Instead a powerful practice developed of taking major decisions by "consensus," which, although not itself defined, generally appeared to require at least the absence of objections from any Contracting Party.[16] When we discuss the "sovereignty" arguments about membership in the new WTO described below, it should be remembered that most of the nations concerned were already previously committed to the broad GATT language.

A second major problem concerned the dispute settlement procedures of the GATT. With only the sparse GATT treaty text to look to, an extraordinarily elaborate (and some argue very successful) dispute settlement procedure was developed in reliance on several decades of GATT practice. During its existence, the GATT procedure handled over 233 formal disputes (and was the background for many more that were settled or abandoned).[17] As practice developed, disputes were considered by a panel of experts (usually three but sometimes five individuals) not to be guided by any government. A report of this panel was sent to a "Council" of the GATT Contracting Parties (again not a treaty body but one constituted by practice and a resolution of the Contracting Parties). If the Council "adopted" the report, it was considered binding on the parties. But the decision to adopt the report had to be by "consensus." Thus, the Contracting Party that "lost" the panel proceeding (as indicated in the report) could "block" the adoption, leaving matters in limbo. Increasingly this was recognized as an anomaly for an effective dispute settlement procedure, and during the 1980s the Contracting Parties, and panels, struggled with ways to overcome this and other similar "birth defects." The Uruguay Round results contain important provisions on this issue, and instigate further "sovereignty" arguments, as we shall see.

---

[16] The Agreement Establishing the World Trade Organization contains a definition of the "consensus" decision-making procedure: "The body concerned shall be deemed to have decided by consensus on a matter submitted for its consideration, if no member, present at the meeting when the decision is taken, formally objects to the proposed decision." The Agreement Establishing the World Trade Organization, opened for signature April 15, 1994, Article IX note 1, 33 ILM 1144 at 1148 (1994). See also John H. Jackson, *The World Trading System: Law and Policy of International Economic Relations* (1997), 49–50.

[17] See Jackson, *The World Trading System*, 99; Robert E. Hudec, *Enforcing International Trade Law: The Evolution of the Modern GATT Legal System* (1993), 287; and Robert E. Hudec, *The GATT Legal System and World Trade Diplomacy* (2nd edn., 1990).

B.   *The Uruguay Round negotiations 1986–1994*

Almost as soon as the seventh trade round, the "Tokyo Round" of 1973–1979, was at an end, some planning began for a next round. The Tokyo Round was the first to address extensively nontariff barriers, using the treaty technique (to avoid the difficulties of amending the GATT) of proposing a series of about ten stand-alone "side agreements" or "codes" on various subjects. Contracting Parties could then pick and choose which ones they would accept.

The eighth round was launched formally at Punta del Este, Uruguay, in September 1986 with an incredibly ambitious agenda. The Uruguay Round agenda called for further work on the "goods" or "product" rules of trade, with attention to revisions of the Tokyo Round codes and some new measures. But even more formidable was the Uruguay Round participants' ambition to bring into the GATT trading system new subjects such as trade in services (potentially embracing 155 or more specific service sectors such as transport, tourism, financial services, and professional services (accountants, lawyers, engineers, etc.)), and also to develop rules for "trade-related intellectual property" (TRIPS) questions. It was not surprising that the original goal of completing this round at a Brussels ministerial meeting in December 1990 was not achieved. After the "Brussels Impasse," negotiations continued. They were largely concluded by December 15, 1993 (after intensive negotiations during the last half of 1993), and formally concluded at the final ministerial meeting at Marrakesh, Morocco, on April 15, 1994. These dates were primarily controlled by the provisions of the United States "fast-track" legislation that specified the procedure by which the US Congress would consider its approval of the Uruguay Round results.

A key element of the Uruguay Round negotiation approach was the "single package" ideal by which every nation would have to accept the whole Uruguay Round results as one entire package, or stay out of the Uruguay Round treaty system. This was in contrast to the "GATT à la carte" approach, as the Tokyo Round results were called. This Uruguay Round approach also established an entirely new treaty for nations to join, thus avoiding the troublesome amendment requirements of the GATT. The GATT, after a transition period, was to be formally abandoned (with some nations exercising the formal right under the GATT and PPA language to withdraw from those treaties upon sufficient but brief notice).

In the Uruguay Round package two very important institutional structures are established:

1. the new World Trade Organization as a formal international organization; and

2. a new twenty-seven-Article Dispute Settlement Understanding (DSU) of twenty-five pages that specify and control the dispute settlement procedure while correcting some of the "birth defects," especially the "blocking" problem.

The WTO Agreement provides, for the first time, a formal international trade organization charter and structure. The "charter" is quite short – about fifteen pages. But it embraces four annexes which include altogether about 16,000 pages of text, schedule commitments, and other matters. Undoubtedly this treaty is a record for its length. With the breadth of subject matter it is also extraordinarily complex and loaded with potential impacts as well as with ambiguities (inevitable when drafting involves 130 or more participating nations). The WTO charter becomes a sort of "umbrella" for this whole single package, with only a few "optional" texts ("plurilateral agreements" in Annex 4) included as part of the single package.

The DSU, which is contained in Annex 2, is strikingly significant – as the history of the first two years of the WTO already demonstrates. Over three times the prior GATT annual rate of dispute process initiations occurred during that time.[18] One of the most interesting features of the DSU is the creation for the first time of an "appellate procedure," plus the virtual "automatic adoption" of panel and appeal reports.[19] No longer will a "sovereign state" be able to block consensus adoption of a dispute report. This obviously gives rise to sovereignty arguments.

When negotiators struggle with the concepts of "sovereignty" as implying ultimate choice for the nation-state, the "realism" of such a choice was certainly difficult for many. The Uruguay Round package is incredibly far-reaching, and certainly, as a matter of treaty law, imposes a number of constraints on nation-state members. Of course, the argument is that the members accepted these constraints. But looking at this history realistically, one can see some qualifications about "acceptance." Major players, such as the United States and the European Union took many months to complete elaborate domestic constitutional procedures, with extensive debates about various aspects. The parliament of a country like Costa Rica, however, took less than one hour! For many small countries (Costa Rica, one might add, is not atypical), the choices were not very extensive. To stay

---

[18] See World Trade Organization, Overview of the State-of-Play of WTO Disputes, constantly updated at the following website, http://www.wto.org/wto/dispute/bulletin.htm. By mid-1997, over eighty-eight disputes were documented. During the 1950s there were fifty-three complaints; in the 1960s, there were seven complaints; in the 1970s, there were thirty-two complaints; and in the 1980s, there were 115 complaints. See Hudec, *Enforcing International Trade Law*, 287.

[19] See Understanding on Rules and Procedures Governing the Settlement of Disputes (hereinafter DSU), Annex 2 of WTO Agreement, Articles 16–17, 33 ILM 1226 at 1235–1237 (1994). See Part III.C below.

out of the new trade system could put whole economies in jeopardy, give up "rule-based" leverage that the new procedures might afford small nations, and prevent participation in the development of new rules, as well as the elaboration and interpretation of the extensive Uruguay Round texts.[20]

C.   United States acceptance of the Uruguay Round results: the Uruguay Round Trade Agreements Act of 1994

Since the Trade Agreements Act of 1974, the United States Congress has considered approval of all major trade agreements (GATT rounds and free trade agreements such as the NAFTA) under a procedure known as the "fast-track". While somewhat intricate and based on an interesting history, the fast-track is essentially a "statutory" treaty approval procedure designed for what in US domestic law are called "Executive Congressional Agreements." This contrasts with the constitutional requirement of Senate approval by a two-thirds vote.[21]

Under the fast-track process, the US Congress approves a statute (usually proposed by the President after treaty negotiations with foreign states) that authorizes ("delegates power to") the President (sometimes with certain conditions) to accept a proposed treaty. After both Houses of the US Congress approve such a statute and the President signs it, this law is the basis for further presidential action "ratifying" or accepting the proposed treaty. The US Congress usually also includes in the statute the measures that it wishes to enact into domestic law so as to implement the treaty. Whether the treaty itself becomes part of US domestic law is a separate question which depends on the US doctrine of self-executing treaties. However, as to the trade treaties of 1979 and subsequently, statutory phrases and legislative history provide that these treaties are not self-executing, with some possible minor exceptions.[22]

---

[20] See John H. Jackson and Alan O. Sykes (eds.), *Implementing the Uruguay Round* (1997), 399, a volume of works by thirteen authors including analysis of eleven different countries' implementation processes.

[21] It should be noted that the term "executive agreement" used in United States domestic law to contrast with "treaties" for which a separate constitutional procedure exists is confusing. Clearly both of these categories of international agreement are, under international law, "treaties."

[22] See John H. Jackson *et al.*, *Legal Problems of International Economic Relations* (3rd edn., 1995), 147; Jackson, *The World Trading System*, 75; John H. Jackson *et al.*, *Implementing The Tokyo Round: National Constitutions and International Economic Rules* (1984), 169–170; Statement of Administrative Action for the North American Free Trade Agreement, Title I, Section 101, HR Doc. No. 103–59, at 10 (1993); and Statement of Administrative Action for the Uruguay Round Trade Agreements, Title I, Section 101, HR Doc. No. 103–316, at 12 (1994). See also Statement of Administrative Action for the North American Free Trade Agreement, Section 102(b), HR Doc. No. 103–59, at 13 (discussing the relationship of the agreement to state law).

The fast-track adds several features to the standard Congressional procedure (as embodied in the rules of the House and the Senate). First, the proposed statute may not be amended once it is introduced. Secondly, once introduced the Bill must be considered and discharged from committees of the US Congress within specified time periods. Finally, the floor debate in both houses on this Bill is strictly limited. The whole procedure is designed to take a maximum period of 90 to 120 days (depending on some technicalities), and to ensure that the US Congress will vote ("up or down") on the whole proposed Bill to accept the treaty that has been negotiated. Thus, foreign countries should be assured that at least the US Congress will consider the results negotiated, and will not (at this step) "reopen the negotiations" through a variety of amendments to the domestic statute, etc.

Other features of the fast-track include various deadlines for submission of the near-final negotiation results to the Congress, and for the signing of the agreement (subject to national approval procedures, i.e. a referendum). In addition, the fast-track provides for extensive consultation with the Congress throughout a negotiation, and the practice has developed that during the specified Congressional consultation period (recently 120 days) before the treaty is signed, key Congressional committees will work extensively with Administration officials to prepare the draft proposed legislation. The fast-track process is eagerly sought by foreign nations who begin a trade negotiation with the US. But this procedure has also been criticized by opponents of trade treaty legislation as "undemocratic" or "unconstitutional," or possibly as another track towards "infringement on US sovereignty."[23]

The Uruguay Round results were "signed" on April 15, 1994. During the ensuing months the US Trade Representative's office and its officials worked with the Congress to develop a proposed statute. For various reasons (and some miscalculations) the proposed Bill was not sent to the Congress until September 27, 1994. Consequently, the timing restrictions of the fast-track procedures did not call for a final vote until after the November 1994 Congressional elections – at a "lame duck" special session. In fact, the votes were held in the House of Representatives on November 29, 1994, with approval by a vote of 288 to 146. The Senate vote took place on December 1, 1994, with approval by a vote of 76 to 24. During 1994, many Congressional hearings in a large number of different committees were held on the Uruguay Round results and the proposed statute (including some ancillary issues). In a number of these hearings the issue of sovereignty was an important focus in one way or another. Com-

[23] The World Trade Organization and US Sovereignty: Hearings Before the Senate Committee on Foreign Relations, 103rd Cong. (1994) (testimony of Ralph Nader, Center for Responsive Law), available in 1994 WL 14188790.

bined with a general public debate in all the various media, as well as many academic, business, and other public forums, 1994 was a year for a truly major and historical US debate about questions of this nation's economic treaty participation and its relation to various concepts of sovereignty.[24]

III.   The Uruguay Round Implementing Act: decomposing the sovereignty arguments

With the background outlined above in mind, we now look more closely and specifically at some of the various issues discussed in the Great 1994 Sovereignty Debate. There will be no attempt here to present an exhaustive inventory of all the varied arguments relating to sovereignty; this would require a much longer work to accommodate. Rather, we will examine certain sets of related arguments in four parts (A to D below). The basic question is, what did the opponents of the Uruguay Round mean when they argued that the US should not accept the Uruguay Round results because it "detracts from or takes away US sovereignty"? And what did the proponents mean when they said that such arguments did not lead to the opponents' conclusions?

It should be immediately noted that, although the conclusion (to accept or not to accept) is basically bipolar, the arguments are not necessarily so. Specific sovereignty considerations may add up to a conclusion one way or the other, but merely because a small bit of sovereignty is taken away does not mean that no treaty should be accepted. Offsetting policies may make it appropriate to "give up some sovereignty" in order to achieve some important policy results. A classic situation is represented by the "prisoner's dilemma," in which independent actions by a group of players can result in worsening the situation for all but cooperation can prevent such a result.[25] Likewise it should be noted that sovereignty "loss" can have a number of different meanings, which different persons weigh differently in their policy advocacy. For example, loss of sovereignty could mean:

1. any diminution of a nation's right/power to pursue certain domestic

---

[24] See, generally, Reams and Schultz, *Uruguay Round Agreements Act*. Four hearings, in particular, are useful in trying to understand the discussion in this article. See Uruguay Round of Multilateral Trade Negotiations: Hearing Before the Senate Finance Committee, 103rd Cong. (1994); Trade Agreements Resulting from the Uruguay Round of Multilateral Trade Negotiations: Hearings Before the Committee on Ways and Means and its Subcommittee on Trade in the House of Representatives, 103rd Cong. (1994); The World Trade Organization and US Sovereignty: Hearings Before the Committee on Foreign Relations, 103rd Cong. (1994); S.2467, GATT Implementing Legislation: Hearings Before the Committee on Commerce, Science and Transportation in the Senate, 103rd Cong. (1994).

[25] This is a classical trade policy argument. See, e.g., Jackson *et al.*, *Legal Problems*, 33; and Peter B. Kenen, *The International Economy* (2nd edn., 1989), 125.

policies without, for example, interference by notions of international law constraints, regardless of whether these operate effectively or whether they cause domestic law changes which in turn pose practical or "real" constraints (e.g., because of international economic interdependence); or interference by international law institutions in a manner that changes domestic law and the constraints it offers; or constraints of international treaty law norms which, although ignorable, can result in retaliation, compensation, or other counter-actions by other nations or players;

2. treaty acceptance might cause external influences on domestic policy in certain ways disadvantageous to the opponent of the treaty: for example, an opponent may fear that certain domestic special interests (e.g., large corporations) may have greater abilities than most groups to influence the international body; thus, they might be able to achieve results by the remote pressure of international decisions or norms that could not otherwise be achieved at the national government level.[26]

A.   General implications of accepting substantive treaty norms

Some of the sovereignty arguments of Uruguay Round opponents are aimed at the mere fact of accepting treaty obligations for certain subjects. Other objections may relate to the implications of becoming part of the treaty institutions. This subpart will explore the former. Later subparts will deal with institutional questions.

Focus for the moment on the question of acceptance of a treaty with various substantive norms, but with no institutions – for example, no joint decision-making powers or dispute settlement procedures – contained in the treaty. In other words, consider in the abstract only the fact of accepting a series of substantive treaty norms. When an opponent to such acceptance argues that the treaty "takes away sovereignty," what is he or she likely to mean?

Clearly, acceptance of *any* treaty in some sense reduces the freedom of scope of national government actions. At the very least, certain types of actions inconsistent with the treaty norms would give rise to an international law violation. The amount of constraint might then vary not only with the institutional mechanisms for enforcement, but also with the national domestic government structure or political attitude towards international norms. Some skeptics might dismiss an international norm as ineffective and, thus, not constraining. But if a treaty norm were self-

---

[26] For different subjects, this can operate in different directions, so it is not impossible to find a particular domestic interest opposing some treaties and favoring others, even though both "diminish national sovereignty."

executing or directly applicable in a domestic legal system, it could have a greater constraining effect. Even without those effects, a treaty can have important domestic legal effects, such as influencing how domestic courts interpret domestic legislation.[27] Beyond that, a treaty norm even without domestic legal effect can have weight in some domestic policy debates where some advocates will stress that positions contrary to their views would raise serious international or treaty concerns. Thus, the sovereignty objection can be directed more to the question of where a decision should be made, and what influences on that decision should be permitted.

It can also be observed that the lack of direct effect of a treaty in domestic law is considered a possible protection against sovereignty diminution. This is because, without direct effect, a nation normally can decide how to respond to a complaint that its actions have breached international law, and one possible response is to ignore the complaint and live with the breach. This may not be particularly admirable but it can act as a sort of a buffering process, or safety valve, against international action that might be deemed overreaching or otherwise inappropriate.[28]

Finally, it should be noted that the legal ability to withdraw with a reasonable period of notice arguably reduces the concern about infringement on sovereignty. This option seemed to be interesting to some of those worried about the sovereignty arguments. The Uruguay Round treaty provisions allow withdrawal upon six months' notice. Whether this is a realistic option for nations today, in the light of their considerable dependence on international trade and the trade system of the GATT/WTO, is a somewhat different question that can also be considered.[29]

Related to the considerations mentioned above, some general objections to a treaty are driven by the substance of particular issues. Many environmental advocates and groups in the 1994 debate were concerned that specific treaty clauses would "trump" US environmental law, or even state laws, such as California's, and would harmonize downward the more stringent US law about which the environmentalists were justifiably proud. Thus, important questions were raised about the legal and practical effect of the WTO and Uruguay Round treaty norms on particular subjects, and sovereignty objections became objections to the substance of the international norms, at least to the extent that those norms appeared not to give enough leeway to domestic US political institutions to adopt more appropriate higher standards.

---

[27] *Restatement (Third) of the Foreign Relations Law of the United States*, § 114 (1990).
[28] See John H. Jackson, "Status of Treaties in Domestic Legal Systems: A Policy Analysis" (1992) 86 *American Journal of International Law* 310.
[29] See WTO Agreement, Article XV(2), 33 ILM at 1152.

B.   *WTO decision-making procedures: risk to sovereignty*

Some of the sovereignty objections in the 1994 debate were targeted towards the institution of the WTO. Various opponents to the treaty argued that the WTO posed risks to US sovereignty because decisions could be made in the WTO that would override US law. This objection engages a number of particular clauses of the WTO, as well as the legal effect of potential WTO decisions on US domestic law. As to the latter, testimony pointed out that WTO decisions did not have self-executing or direct legal effect in US law. Consequently, once again there was an element of buffering protection which in realistic terms gave the national government some opportunity to resist inappropriate international decisions.[30]

But more significant, perhaps, is the fact that the decision-making procedures of the WTO have been significantly circumscribed by negotiated treaty text. In fact, by comparison to the loose language of the GATT – which would have remained in effect if the WTO had failed to emerge – the WTO had many more protections for national sovereignty. These protections were significantly enhanced in the treaty drafting that went on during the fall of 1993, spurred by the US negotiators and other countries who worried about some of the general treaty text of the previous Uruguay Round drafts.

To be more specific, but without going into these matters in depth,[31] an examination of a series of specific decision-making powers for the WTO general bodies shows protections such as super-majorities (often three-fourths requirement of all the members, not just those voting – a very difficult target to achieve) and prohibitions against changing the substantive rights and obligations of the members without more difficult amending or treaty negotiation procedures. In addition, an emphasis on consensus decision-making is manifested in a number of provisions, sometimes with fallbacks to voting only after providing a period of time for an attempt to achieve consensus. Indeed, some of these provisions could be seen to give a "*de facto* veto" power to a few of the most powerful trading entities. These features can be seen in the texts relating to:

1. amending the WTO and subsidiary agreements (Article X);
2. adopting a formal "interpretation" (Article IX(2));

[30] See The World Trade Organization and US Sovereignty: Hearings Before the Senate Committee on Foreign Relations, 103rd Cong. (1994) (testimony by Rufus Yerxa, Deputy US Trade Representative), available in 1994 WL 14188843.

[31] See Jackson, *The World Trade Organization*; Jackson, "The Uruguay Round"; see also The World Trade Organization and US Sovereignty: Hearings Before the Senate Committee on Foreign Relations, 103rd Cong. (1994) (June 14, 1994, testimony of John H. Jackson, Hessel E. Yntema Professor of Law, University of Michigan), available in 1994 WL 14188767; and Results of the Uruguay Round Trade Negotiations: Hearings Before the Senate Finance Committee, 103rd Cong., 114 (1994) (March 23, 1994, testimony of John H. Jackson, Hessel E. Yntema Professor of Law, University of Michigan).

3. adopting waivers (Article IX(3) and (4));
4. adding plurilateral agreements (optional agreements) to Annex 4 (Article X(9)); and
5. changing the Dispute Settlement Understanding in Annex 2 (Article X(8)).

Most sovereignty objections clearly were aimed at power allocation. Members of the Congress were concerned whether the allocation of power regarding WTO decision-making was an inappropriate infringement on US sovereign decision-making. Certainly, this allocation was more protective of national government decision-making than either the GATT or many other international organizations in today's world (although few of those organizations have such an extensive impact on national economies). It was clear in the Uruguay Round negotiation that there was no possibility of achieving any formal weighted voting (such as in the International Monetary Fund or International Bank for Reconstruction and Development), or even a small special body with added power like vetoes or special competence (such as the United Nations Security Council). Thus, the negotiators greatly restricted the decision-making powers of the WTO bodies, even to the point of concern that the WTO will be hamstrung by inaction derived from its "consensus" culture.

C.   WTO dispute settlement process and the sovereignty arguments

The issue of a nation-state's participation in an international dispute settlement procedure poses sovereignty questions of a different sort. If a nation has consented to a treaty and the norms it contains, why should it object to an external process that could rule on the consistency of that nation's actions with the treaty norms? It might be argued that such objections manifest a lack of intent to follow the norms – sort of accepting the treaty with fingers crossed behind the back. Indeed, there may be some elements of this thinking in this context. It could also be suggested, however, that a nervousness about international dispute settlement procedures reflects a government's desire to have some flexibility to resist future strict conformity to norms in certain special circumstances, particularly circumstances that could pose great danger to essential national objectives. This sort of an "escape clause" idea would allow a nation to accept norms with sincere intent to follow them except in the most severe and egregious cases of danger to the nation or to its political system.[32]

Apart from these escape clause notions, however, there is also an institutional concern that the dispute settlement procedures may not be objective,

---

[32] Candidly, though, it may also be noted that danger to the political fortunes of the ruling party in such nation may take on great weight in these considerations.

may be subject to procedural irregularities and overreaching, or may have other important defects that even other nations would recognize but that are not addressed by the treaty or its institutional structure. This danger, either at the outset or developing at some later time, could legitimately constrain a nation's willingness to enter into stringent commitments to a dispute settlement procedure.

Clearly some of these considerations played a part in the US Great 1994 Sovereignty Debate. The objections raised to dispute settlement procedures may, thus, not be objections to the substance of the rules discussed in the previous subpart, but may be objections to the nature, stringency, or automaticity of the enforcement mechanisms for those rules. Since international institutions are generally less sophisticated or elaborate than most national institutions, various problems can be feared. These might include the difficulty of changing treaties and treaty norms that may become seriously out of date, or the methods of filling in the details of seriously ambiguous texts (a problem often associated with treaties drafted by many countries). The text of the WTO charter may contain some of these problems. An example is the super-majority procedure included in that text for decisions on "formal interpretations." Likewise, the Dispute Settlement Understanding (DSU) contains a number of hedges that reflect concerns about international dispute settlement.

The DSU continues some of the GATT dispute procedures as developed through practice over forty years, but it now includes an elaborate treaty text to govern this practice and adds a number of new features. As in the GATT, a dispute is initiated by a request for consultations by a disputant (or group of complainants), and the consultation period is a prerequisite for further procedures. If no settlement is achieved, then the DSU now makes clear that the complainant is entitled to a panel procedure, and rules spell out the process for forming a panel (usually three impartial individuals). The rules correct some problems seen in GATT by requiring stricter time limits and fallback procedures when the parties cannot agree to certain aspects such as the panel's composition or its terms of reference. Much more attention is given in the rules to third party participation. Initial experience demonstrates a great desire to use this opportunity to participate. But only "members" (i.e., nation-states or independent customs territories) can bring cases or participate formally. As in GATT, the panel receives oral and written arguments and "testimony," and formulates a report that is sent to the Dispute Settlement Body (DSB), where the parties may comment and urge changes.[33]

The major change in the DSU, however, is the elimination of "blocking" when the DSB considers the report. The report is deemed adopted unless

---

[33] See DSU, Articles 11–16, 33 ILM at 1233–1235. The DSB has the same members as the WTO General Council, except for its chairman.

there is a consensus against adoption (the "reverse consensus"), and, since the winning party could always object and block the consensus, the adoption is considered to be virtually automatic. The *quid pro quo* for this automaticity, however, is a provision that, for the first time, allows for an appeal. If an appeal is taken, then the report is not adopted. Instead, an appellate panel of three individuals, drawn from a permanent roster of seven individuals (with renewable four-year staggered terms),[34] considers the first-level report, receives arguments from the parties, and writes its own report. This report also is sent to the DSB where the same reverse consensus rule applies to adoption, again making it virtually certain to be adopted. It is this automaticity that worries some diplomats and critics of the WTO system, although in many other international tribunals automaticity, in the sense of no opportunity to block a report, also exists.

The DSU then has a series of detailed rules regarding an enforcement phase if a losing party is unwilling to carry out the recommendations of the panel as adopted by the DSB. These rules provide for "compensation" through trade measures, and for certain other pressures such as continuous monitoring to enhance the implementation of the dispute results.

In the US 1994 debate, some interests testified that the US should include in its implementing legislation certain measures regarding dumping law, even if those would appear to be vulnerable to dispute settlement procedure challenge at some future time.[35] Other witnesses argued against the WTO partly because the dispute settlement procedure was tougher, and no longer permitted a single nation to "block" acceptance of a panel report. There was criticism of the GATT panels ("decisions by three faceless bureaucrats in Geneva"), and, thus, of the likely form of the WTO panels. Criticism was targeted at the secrecy of the procedures, the lack of opportunity of private groups (nongovernment organizations, etc.) to offer views and evidence, the potential conflicts of interest of the panelists, and the possibility that the WTO secretariat lawyers would be biased and have too much influence on the panels, etc.[36] Indeed, although there have been important efforts to "open up" the WTO procedures (even those relating to decision-making discussed above), many constructive critics of the WTO feel there is much more that must be done.[37]

---

[34] See DSU, Article 17, 33 ILM at 1236–1237.

[35] See Results of the Uruguay Round Trade Negotiations: Hearings Before the Senate Finance Committee, 103rd Cong., 108 (1994) (testimony of Steven R. Appleton, representing the Semiconductor Industry Association).

[36] See The World Trade Organization and US Sovereignty: Hearings Before the Senate Committee on Foreign Relations, 103rd Cong. (1994) (June 14, 1994, testimony of John H. Jackson, Hessel E. Yntema Professor of Law, University of Michigan), available in 1994 WL 14188767.

[37] This author shares many, but not all, of the concerns expressed. See John H. Jackson, "World Trade Rules and Environmental Policies: Congruence or Conflict?" (1992) 49 *Washington and Lee Law Review* 1227.

A very important consideration affecting a nation's willingness to accept the WTO dispute settlement procedures is its view of the way the treaty and its institutions should play a role in that nation's international economic diplomacy. The US and many other nations have often expressed the view that the GATT and now the WTO treaty texts are vitally important to improving a rule-oriented international economic system that should enhance the predictability and stability of the circumstances of international commerce. This enhancement, in turn, should allow private entrepreneurs to plan better for longer term investment and other decisions. In short, a basic goal is to reduce the "risk premium" associated with commerce between nations with vastly differing governmental and cultural structures.[38] If a nation wishes to benefit from these policies, then it becomes difficult for it to oppose dispute settlement procedures when they impinge on it. There is a reciprocity element in these conditions, and this must be taken into account in reflecting on the weight to be given to sovereignty objections.

The US has explicitly made these considerations part of its diplomacy and has often expressed the view that the rules of the GATT and the WTO are vital for US commerce, particularly US exports.[39] The US was the most frequent initiator of dispute settlement procedures in the GATT and continues in the WTO with the same approach. It learned very early in the WTO history that to appear to "thumb its nose" at the dispute procedures posed very serious diplomatic risks to its status in the WTO and therefore to the potential usefulness of the WTO to the US.[40]

How does all this fit with the sovereignty objections? Again, it is abundantly clear that "sovereignty" is not a unitary concept, but is a series of particular considerations that I suggest are centered around the problem of allocation of power. Thus, when an objection is made to the US accepting the WTO because of the WTO dispute settlement procedures, the specific (decomposed) issues of that objection are substantially different from those regarding the problem of treaty norm application or the institutional structure of decision-making. In addition, the sovereignty objection really can be a series of specific objections about the nature or details of the dispute procedure. These in turn must be considered in the aggregate

---

[38] See, generally, e.g., Douglas C. North, *Institutions, Institutional Change and Economic Performance* (1990).

[39] See The World Trade Organization and US Sovereignty: Hearings Before the Senate Committee on Foreign Relations, 103rd Cong. (1994) (testimony by Rufus Yerxa, Deputy US Trade Representative), available in 1994 WL 14188843. See also, USTR Identification of Trade Expansion Priorities (Super 301) Pursuant to Executive Order 12901 (last modified, October 1, 1996) http://www.ustr.gov/reports/12901report.html.

[40] See John H. Jackson, "US Threat to New World Trade Order," *Financial Times*, May 23, 1995, 13; Ben Wildavsky, "The Big Deal" *National Journal*, June 24, 1995, at 1650; and Jagdish Bhagwati, "The US–Japan Car Dispute: A Monumental Mistake" (1996) *International Affairs* 261.

(unless there were options that allowed a nation to accept some details but not others), and that aggregate weighed against the policy advantages of belonging. "Sovereignty" thus is not a magical wand that one waves to ward off any entanglement in the international system. It is a policy-weighing process. And the policies most often address the question of allocation of power: should this nation accept the obligation to allow certain decisions affecting it (or its view of international economic relations) to be made by an international institution rather than retaining that power in the national government?

As heroic as they may appear, the dispute settlement procedures of the WTO have a number of features that are obviously designed to protect the sovereignty of the WTO members and to prevent too much power from being allocated to the dispute process. Many different illustrations could be described here, but only four subjects will be discussed to keep this text manageable. These four subjects are:

1. the obligation to comply with a panel ruling;
2. the legal precedent effect of a panel report;
3. the standard of review by which the WTO panels examine national government actions; and
4. the broad question of judicial activism or concerns about panels stretching interpretations to achieve certain policy results that they favor.

Of course, part of the background of these subjects is the detailed procedures or panel processes and the persons who are on the appellate body roster to be panels. The credibility of these procedures, and, thus, the likely willingness over time of members to accept panel results, is affected by the personnel and the content of the procedures. Of the seven roster members, for example, three are chosen from large trading powers (US, EU, and Japan), while the rest hail from smaller or less powerful members (Philippines, New Zealand, Egypt, and Uruguay). Since policy perceptions about sovereignty might sometimes differ between large and small nations, this majority could create some concerns (at least until practice suggests these are not troublesome) for larger members (who are the most frequent participants in the procedures).

1.   Legal effect and obligation of a panel or appeal report
One of the interpretive issues that has grown in importance since the WTO came into effect is whether the result of a dispute settlement process obligates the losing respondent to a complaint to change its laws or practices to conform to the panel recommendation. One might think the answer to this

should be obvious and affirmative, and certainly most other international tribunal procedures would embrace this result. However, the DSU has much language concerning enforcement and implementation and much of the focus of the language is on compensation. If a nation, particularly a large nation, has the option to perform or compensate, it may have the sense that in many cases brought by small countries, compensation could be relatively painless (small in amount). Thus, such a nation may feel its sovereignty is better protected by the availability of the compensation option.

In fact, US government officials testified to this effect in the Great 1994 Sovereignty Debate, and argued that no international body could require the US (not even in the loose sense of an international law norm) to do anything. In the view of this author, this interpretation is incorrect and not likely to be embraced by future panel reports. The language of the DSU includes a number of clauses that call for an obligation to perform according to panel findings. The DSU makes compensation only a fallback when performance does not occur, and keeps a matter under surveillance as long as performance has not occurred. Yet it was interesting that, as part of the sovereignty debate, US officials thought it would be useful to argue to the public and to the Congress as they did.[41]

2.   *Precedent or other effect of panel reports*

Some discussion about the precedent effect of GATT panels, and now WTO panels, has occurred. Under GATT it was not always clear what the legal effect of the GATT Council adopting a panel report was.[42] Clearly the general international law rule suggests that there is no strict precedential effect such as *stare decisis*. This author has argued that the real intended effect is only that of "practice," which over time and combined with other practice can have effects on interpretation. But concerns about this have been discussed in GATT councils (leading in some cases to reluctance to adopt a panel report which could be a bad precedent).[43]

The WTO and the DSU seem to attempt to foreclose the use of precedent for panel reports. The WTO text specifies a particular super-majority procedure for formal interpretations.[44] This seems to suggest that the

---

[41] See generally John H. Jackson, "The WTO Dispute Settlement Understanding: Misunderstandings on the Nature of Legal Obligation" (1997) 91 *American Journal of International Law* 60.

[42] See John H. Jackson, "The Legal Meaning of a GATT Dispute Settlement Report: Some Reflections" in Niels Blokker and Sam Muller (eds.), *Towards More Effective Supervision by International Organizations: Essays in Honour of Henry G. Schermers* (1994), 149.

[43] Discussions by the author with GATT Secretariat Personnel (1995).

[44] "The Ministerial Conference and the General Council shall have the exclusive authority to adopt interpretations of this Agreement and of the Multilateral Trade Agreements . . . The decision to adopt an interpretation shall be taken by a three-fourths majority of the members." WTO Agreement, Article IX(2), 33 ILM at 1148.

WTO system does not give power to the panels to create any formal interpretations, i.e. any formal precedents. Thus, the panel reports are binding only on the parties to the particular proceeding, much like the World Court rule.[45] Of course, the reports will have considerable persuasive effect, at least when well reasoned. Thus, in at least one WTO case won by multiple complainants against a respondent, the complainants reportedly argued most vigorously among themselves about which of several theories should be expressed in the report as the basis of the decision.

The WTO Charter provisions on interpretations can be combined with the thrust of some of the DSU language to reinforce the view that panel reports are not to act as formal interpretations. During the last months of the Uruguay Round negotiation (fall 1993), US negotiators were reportedly eager to prevent the panels from ruling on the WTO Charter itself, but in the end the DSU clearly provides the contrary view.[46] Here again one sees a sovereignty concern not itself significant enough to change a final decision to accept the treaty affecting a specific treaty detail.

3.   *Standard of review*

There are two standard-of-review problems in the WTO dispute settlement procedures: that of the Appellate Body review of first-level panel reports, and that of the standard of review of any WTO panel regarding judgments about member government actions that might be inconsistent with the treaty norms. It is the latter that will be taken up here.

The standard of review, related sometimes to, *inter alia*, the "margin of appreciation" concept,[47] is a critical element of allocating power between an international tribunal and a national government. This issue was very prominent in the "end game negotiations" of the Uruguay Round. Some negotiators supported a text that would embody a significant limitation on the degree to which WTO panels would second-guess national govern-

---

[45] For example and contrast, Article 94 of the UN Charter states: "Each Member of the United Nations undertakes to comply with the decision of the International Court of Justice in any case to which it is a party." Similarly, the Statute of the International Court of Justice, Article 59, implies such an obligation, stating: "The decision of the Court has no binding force except between the parties and in respect of that particular case." Statute of the ICJ, signed June 26, 1945, Article 59, 59 Stat. 1055; 3 Bevans 1179.

[46] "The rules and procedures of this Understanding shall also apply to consultations and the settlement of disputes between Members concerning their rights and obligations under the provisions of the Agreement Establishing the World Trade Organization." DSU, Article 1, 33 ILM at 1226. For reports on the negotiations in the Uruguay Round working group on dispute settlement, see *Inside US Trade*, October 1, 1993, at 7; November 5, 1993, at 1; November 19, 1993, at 19; November 26, 1993, at 1; and December 17, 1993, at 1.

[47] See R. St. J. Macdonald, "The Margin of Appreciation" in R. St. J. Macdonald *et al.* (eds.), *European System for the Protection of Human Rights* (1993), 83; Steven Croley and John H. Jackson, "WTO Dispute Procedures, Standard of Review, and Deference to National Governments" (1996) 90 *American Journal of International Law* 193.

ments on decisions regarding trade rules, such as antidumping rulings. The US negotiators tried to obtain treaty language that would follow the domestic US administrative law approach known as the *Chevron* doctrine.[48] Other nations objected, and in the end compromise language with considerable ambiguity was placed in the antidumping text but not applied to disputes on other matters (at least until a later study occurred). The DSU does not itself have an explicit text on this type of "standard of review" but there are some clauses that might support a cautious approach by the WTO panels.[49] In the first two appellate body reports, there is panel language that suggests such caution. One states, for example, that "WTO members have a large measure of autonomy to determine their own policies on the environment (including its relationship with trade), their environmental objectives and the environmental legislation they enact and implement."[50]

4.   Judicial activism or panel "overreaching"

Clearly there was some concern about the potential power of WTO panels. This was expressed in hearings during 1994, as well as in negotiations and discussions in various public and confidential forums. The other matters expressed above may sometimes influence panel caution in this regard, but some language in the DSU seems to be designed for the same end. In particular, the DSU says: "[r]ecommendations and rulings of the DSB cannot add to or diminish the rights and obligations provided in the covered agreements."[51] The proposal for a US national review panel to report on the correctness of WTO panel reports affecting the US could be another caution, as described below.

D.   The Uruguay Round, US law, and implications for sovereignty issues

Several significant issues of US constitutional and other law also, sometimes oddly, became embroiled in the sovereignty debate. Only four particular issues will be very briefly described here.

---

[48] Croley and Jackson, "WTO Dispute Procedures," 193 at 202.
[49] See, e.g., DSU, Article 3(2), 33 ILM at 1227.
[50] United States – Standards for Reformulated and Conventional Gasoline, Appellate Body Report and Panel Report, World Trade Organization, WT/DS2/9, May 20, 1996, at 30. See also Japan – Taxes on Alcoholic Beverages, Report of the Appellate Body, World Trade Organization, WT/DS8,10,11/AB/R, October 4, 1996, at 22. Both documents are available at World Trade Organization, Overview of the State-of-Play of WTO Disputes (last modified January 23, 1997) at http://www.wto.org/wto/dispute/bulletin.htm.
[51] DSU, Article 3(2), 33 ILM at 1227.

1.   The famous US section 301

A considerable amount of venom has been expressed by US trading partners towards US section 301.[52] This statute has a special role in the US constitutional division of power between the Congress and the President, delegating to the President the authority to retaliate with trade sanctions against certain "unreasonable or unfair" foreign government actions that damage US commerce. This statute has sometimes been used by the US to apply trade sanctions against other nations in a manner inconsistent with US treaty obligations, and major Uruguay Round participants were determined to rein in US unilateralism. This determination was part of the impetus for improved dispute settlement procedures and for the WTO Charter itself.

The US Congress made it very clear, however, that it would not tolerate changes in section 301, and the Executive negotiating position followed that mandate. Consequently, except for some minor procedural amendments, section 301 remains intact. Yet, in explaining its position (in ways too complex to recount here), the United States argued that section 301 could not be found inconsistent with US WTO obligations (in the absence of some specific action). Indeed, section 301 does call for use of the WTO dispute settlement procedures. This statute, however, was perhaps the most important political bellwether of the sovereignty considerations in the Congress during the 1994 debate.

2.   The treaty clause and the fast-track statutory approach

Another intriguing manifestation of sovereignty concerns was the interesting debate about the constitutionality of the fast-track procedure for approving the Uruguay Round and the WTO. Two levels of sovereignty concerns were raised in this context (demonstrating that the allocation of power concept goes deeper than just the federal level of a nation-state).[53] It

---

[52] See Trade Act of 1974, § 301, 19 USC § 2411 (1994). See, e.g., "Services of the European Commission" in *Report on US Barriers to Trade and Investment* (1994), 11–12.

[53] See S.2467, GATT Implementing Legislation: Hearings Before the US Senate Commerce, Science and Transportation Committee, 103rd Cong., 290–339 (1994) (statements and discussion of Laurence H. Tribe and Bruce Ackerman); Bruce Ackerman and David Golove, "Is NAFTA Constitutional?" (1995) 108 *Harvard Law Review* 4; Laurence Tribe, "Taking Text and Structure Seriously: Reflections on Free-Form Method in Constitutional Interpretation" (1995) 108 *Harvard Law Review* 6; "Statutory Procedure for Approval of the Uruguay Round Trade Negotiations and the WTO," treaty clause memorandum sent to various members of Congress and Executive branch officials, dated November 11, 1994. Signatories included Professors Bruce Ackerman, Yale University; Abram Chayes, Harvard University; Kenneth Dam, University of Chicago; Charles Fried, Harvard University; David Golove, Arizona University; Louis Henkin, Columbia University; Robert Hudec, University of Minnesota; John H. Jackson, University of Michigan; Harold Hongju Koh, Yale University; and Myres McDougal, Yale University (on file with author).

was argued that, despite various precedents to the contrary, there were sovereignty concerns when an international agreement required major national commitments and membership in an international organization that might involve yielding US sovereignty to global institutions. It was asserted, moreover, that the constitutional requirement that treaties be approved by a two-thirds vote of the Senate was the only appropriate procedure. In addition, regarding the second level of "sovereignty" arguments, it was argued that the purpose of the Senate treaty approval requirement was particularly to protect the sovereignty of US subfederal states. The Senate, it was argued, was a better protector of such states' rights since each state had equal representation there (two senators) and was traditionally, it was claimed, more assiduous in protecting states' rights.

This portion of the 1994 debate also involved various other constitutional arguments, and an interesting Senate Commerce Committee hearing in October with two debating law professors.[54] In the end, the fast-track procedure was followed, and the Senate voted seventy-six to twenty-four in favor of the statute with its delegation to the President. It can, thus, be argued that this was yet another precedent for following the statutory procedure (at least for trade treaties or other matters related to the Commerce Clause of the US Constitution), and was also an opinion by three-fourths of the US Senate favoring the constitutionality of the statutory approach.

3.   *Subfederal states in the United States*
The question of subfederal states of the United States received considerable attention in the 1994 Uruguay Round debate. This debate, along with the prior North American Free Trade Agreement (NAFTA) debate, were the first times since the origin of the GATT that such attention was given to state interests. A major concern of the states was the potential for a broad scope treaty like the Uruguay Round to invalidate many different state laws governing areas such as economic regulation, environmental affairs, product safety and health standards, etc. (insofar as these were left to the states by Congress or other federal bodies). An organization of state Attorneys-General posed "subfederal sovereignty objections" to the US Office of the Trade Representative, and this office worked with state officials to include language in the 1994 Uruguay Round Agreements Act[55] designed to protect state laws. State laws had already been subject to such

---

[54] See Detlev F. Vagts, "International Agreements, the Senate and the Constitution, Chapter 2: Constitutional Question" (1997) 36 *Columbia Journal of Transnational Law* 143.
[55] 108 Stat. 4809 (1994).

proceedings under the GATT in the Canadian challenge to state alcoholic beverage regulations. A GATT panel concluded that many of these state laws were inconsistent with GATT obligations such as the national treatment requirement that imports be treated no less favorably than domestic products.[56]

The result for the Uruguay Round Implementing Act was several lengthy sections that gave state government officials various procedural rights to participate and provide input into the US handling of WTO disputes affecting them. After this text was negotiated, state officials indicated satisfaction with the approach and removed their objections to US acceptance of the Uruguay Round treaty.[57]

4.   The proposed "WTO Dispute Settlement Review Commission"
One of the more explicit manifestations of sovereignty concerns, regarding power allocation in the 1994 debate was a compromise proposal between the US President and the Senate majority leader. A Democratic President needed votes in a Republican-dominated Senate to achieve passage of the Uruguay Round Agreements Act, and in late November 1994, a few days before the Congressional votes were scheduled, the majority leader proposed the idea of a statutory "Commission." This Commission would have been composed of five US federal judges who would review the adopted WTO panel reports adverse to the United States, judging them against a list of four particular criteria. The Commission would then advise the Congress whether it found any panel report to be contrary to any one of these criteria. If the Commission were to make determinations of the contrary nature for three reports, the Congress would consider a resolution to withdraw from the WTO (giving the requisite six-month notice required by the Uruguay Round agreements). This proposal (as of this writing in August 1997) has not become law, although a series of attempts were made to enact it in 1995 and 1996. Nevertheless, the proposal, its findings, and its criteria, all reveal an explicit concern for various aspects of the sovereignty objections discussed above.

---

[56] United States Measures Affect Alcoholic Malt Beverages, GATT Panel Report, adopted June 19, 1991, GATT Doc. No. DS23/R: GATT, *Basic Instruments and Selected Documents*, 39th Supplement, 206.

[57] See John H. Jackson *et al.*, *International Economic Relations: Cases, Materials and Texts* (3rd edn., 1995), 1168; Mattschaefer and Singer, "Multilateral Trade Agreements and US States: An Analysis of Potential GATT Uruguay Round Agreements," *Journal of World Trade*, December 1992, at 31; Statement of Administrative Action for the Uruguay Round Trade Agreements, Title I, Section 102, HR Doc. 103–316, at 15 (1994); Letter from Michael Carpenter (Attorney-General of Maine), Heidi Heitkamp (Attorney-General of North Dakota), Charles W. Burson (Attorney-General of Tennessee), to Michael Kantor (USTR), July 27, 1994 (on file with author).

The draft legislation[58] listed the following finding:

The continued support of the Congress for the WTO is dependent upon a WTO dispute settlement system that:
A) operates in a fair and impartial manner;
B) does not add to the obligations of or diminish the rights of the United States under the Uruguay Round agreements; and
C) does not exceed its authority, scope, or established standard of review.

The Bill therefore set forth four specific criteria for evaluating WTO dispute reports, asking whether the panel had:

1. exceeded its authority or terms of reference;
2. added to the obligations of, or diminished the rights of the United States;
3. acted arbitrarily or capriciously or engaged in misconduct, etc.; or
4. deviated from the applicable standard of review including that in Article 17.6 of the antidumping text.

Perhaps little needs to be added to the paragraphs quoted above; they clearly show the concerns about some aspects of the WTO dispute settlement system which relate to the broader power allocation concepts of sovereignty. Many observers felt that the final sanction of withdrawal would never be exercised by the Congress or signed into law by the President. And some observers felt that it was very unlikely that the Commission would ever find a WTO dispute report contrary to the criteria stated, although those criteria have significant ambiguities and could be interpreted in different ways depending on the judges who made up the Commission. Nevertheless, there was a perception, particularly among other members of the WTO, that the mere existence of this Commission could subtly influence the work of WTO panels, which might then be hesitant to take positions contrary to US interests, and thereby lose some of their impartiality. Some foreign diplomats suggested that it would be necessary for their governments to adopt a similar procedure to "redress this tilt."

IV.   Some concluding perspectives

Sovereignty, in practical terms, is still an important argument in many government policy debates. It has an emotional appeal and is often used in a blunt and undifferentiated way as a surrogate argument by opponents of

---

[58] A Bill to Establish a Commission to Review the Dispute Settlement Reports of the World Trade Organization and for Other Purposes, S.16, 104th Cong. (1995).

some government proposal. Yet when the context of some of the sovereignty arguments is analyzed in detail, it can be demonstrated that there are worthwhile policy issues raised at least in some circumstances, at least if we abandon some antiquated definitions of the concept of sovereignty. In this article, I examined sovereignty arguments and suggested that most often they raised policy issues about allocation of power, particularly as between international institutions or norms and national or even sub-federal levels of government.

When some of the policy debates are approached in this manner, it becomes clear that there are many facets and many details to the policy issue of appropriately allocating power. In the context of treaty acceptance, for example, questions are raised about the domestic law effect of international norms, about the nature of international decision-making processes that can generate secondary norms obligating the nation-state, about details of dispute settlement procedures affecting the credibility and efficiency of those procedures, and about questions of internal domestic allocation of power that are raised by international treaties, other norms, and institutions. When we examine some of these details in a "decomposed" or disaggregated way, we can more easily determine how to weigh some of the disadvantages of those details against the advantages of strengthened international norms and institutions. This process, in turn, may assist governments in evaluating the important policy considerations involved in participating in international institutions. This approach to sovereignty arguments may lead to better government decisions by forcing those who use sovereignty objections against policy proposals to make such objections more concrete and explicit so that they can be better compared to contrasting arguments.

Part VI

The Uruguay Round and beyond: perspectives and conclusions

Finally Part VI includes articles which review briefly the results of the 1986–1994 Uruguay Round of trade negotiations, and which point to new issues and to the future. Again selection necessarily was difficult. In a sense the three articles selected to be included here each point a slightly different but complementary way. The first of these (chapter 20) reviews the remarkable new institution created by the Uruguay Round, namely the WTO. The second then probes some fundamental issues of what has so far been the most important policy challenge to the GATT and the WTO, namely environmental policies. There are many new issues facing the WTO and some of these have been listed in the first article of this part. But when forced to limit a deeper discussion of a number of issues, this author felt it best to focus more deeply on one particular problem, that of the relation of environmental policies to the WTO system. Thus chapter 21 explores this problem. Finally, as promised in the introductory essay to Part I at the beginning of this book, a second portion of a recent article of this author which looks at the problems which the WTO will face in the future, is used to conclude this work.

20   The World Trade Organization: watershed innovation or cautious small step forward?*

1.   Introduction

On January 1, 1995, a new international organization came into being. Depending on one's perspective, the World Trade Organization (WTO) is either a modest enhancement of the General Agreement on Tariffs and Trade (GATT) which preceded it, or a watershed moment for the institutions of world economic relations embodied in the Bretton Woods system.

For twelve years, over 100 nations of the world have been participating in the largest and most complex negotiation concerning international economics in history (some would say the largest and most complex negotiation ever). Launched formally under GATT auspices in Punta del Este, Uruguay in September 1986 (after some years of preparation), the Uruguay Round negotiating results were formally signed at Marrakesh, Morocco on April 15, 1994, and ratified by a sufficient number of nations to bring those results into force on January 1, 1995. The results are embodied in a "document" of some 26,000 pages, most of which are detailed schedules of tariff, services trade, and other concessions. For the first time the GATT system includes major agreements on trade in services, and on trade-related intellectual property questions. Some fifty other portions of the agreement address subjects as diverse as antidumping, agricultural trade, subsidies, technical standards, textiles, and customs valuation. Included in this agreement are two important institutional measures: the Charter for a WTO, and a new set of dispute settlement procedures, both designed to assist in the effective implementation of the substantive rules established in the agreements.

2.   The GATT and its birth defects

. . .

---

* This chapter is based on John H. Jackson, "The World Trade Organization: Watershed Innovation or Cautious Small Step Forward?" (1995) *The World Economy* 11.

3.   The WTO

A.   *The genesis of the WTO*

The 1986 ministerial declaration of Punta del Este, containing the agenda and objectives for the Uruguay Round negotiation, did not include any explicit call for a new charter or organization, although it did establish negotiating groups including one for dispute settlement, and another for "Functioning of the GATT System." Despite this hesitancy, however, by 1990 there was considerable discussion of the need for an improved organizational structure for effective implementation of the Uruguay Round results. In December 1991, the Uruguay Round negotiators led by the GATT Director-General, Arthur Dunkel, prepared and released a draft text of treaty clauses which covered the entire Uruguay Round negotiation results up to that point, with indications of work yet to do. This was an important project with many implications. Included in this draft (for the first time) was a tentative draft of a new Charter for an organization – an MTO or Multilateral Trade Organization. This draft had a number of flaws, recognized by the US government and others, but through hard work the negotiators were able to revise the draft and iron out most of the flaws. In the December 1993 near final draft, the new organization was retitled the World Trade Organization (WTO). This Charter is included in the treaty embodying the results of the Uruguay Round, along with a major text of new procedures and rules for dispute settlement.

B.   *What is the WTO?*

With the new WTO Charter, the Uruguay Round results should provide a better institutional structure to fill the gap left in the Bretton Woods structure. Several general characteristics are noteworthy.

First, the Charter for the WTO can be described as a "mini-charter." It is devoted to the institutional and procedural structure that will facilitate and in some cases be necessary for the effective implementation of the substantive rules that have been negotiated in the Uruguay Round. The WTO is not an ITO (the 1948 draft ITO Charter which never came into force.) The WTO Charter text itself does not include substantive rules, but it incorporates the substantive agreements resulting from the Uruguay Round into "annexes." In many cases the criticism aimed at the WTO during the implementation debates was really criticism aimed at some of the substantive provisions of the Uruguay Round results, and should not be considered a criticism of the WTO institutional Charter.

Secondly, the WTO essentially will continue the GATT institutional ideas and many of its practices, in a form better understood by the public, media, government officials, and lawyers. To some extent, a number of the GATT "birth defects" are overcome in the WTO. The WTO Charter (XVI:I) expressly states the intention to be guided by GATT "decisions, procedures and customary practices" to the extent feasible. The practice of consensus is better defined and for the first time becomes a legal procedure in some important decisions, rather than just a practice.

Thirdly, the WTO structure offers some important advantages for assisting the effective implementation of the Uruguay Round. For example, a "new GATT 1994" is created to supersede the "old GATT." This procedure avoids the constraints of the amending clause of the old GATT which might make it quite difficult to bring the Uruguay Round into legal force. At the same time, the WTO ties together the various texts developed in the Uruguay Round and reinforces the "single package" idea of the negotiators, namely, that countries accepting the Uruguay Round must accept the entire package (with a few exceptions). No longer will the Tokyo Round approach of side codes, resulting in "GATT à la carte" be the norm.

The WTO Charter establishes (for the first time) the basic explicit legal authority for a Secretariat, a Director-General, and staff. It does this in a way similar to many other international organizations, and it also adds the obligation for nations to avoid interfering with the officials of the organization.

Another important aspect of the WTO structure is that it facilitates the extension of the institutional structure to the new subjects negotiated in the Uruguay Round, particularly services and intellectual property. Without some kind of legal mechanism such as the WTO, this would have been quite difficult to do since the GATT itself only applies to goods. The new GATT structure separates the institutional concepts from the substantive rules. The GATT 1994 will remain a substantive agreement (with many of the amendments and improvements developed throughout its history, including the Uruguay Round). The WTO has a broader context. Similarly the WTO will be able to apply a unified dispute settlement mechanism, and the Trade Policy Review Mechanism to all of the subjects of the Uruguay Round, for all nations who become members.

Fourthly, the WTO Charter offers considerably better opportunities for the future evolution and development of the institutional structure for international trade cooperation. Even though the WTO Charter is minimalist, the fact that there is provision for explicit legal status and the traditional organizational structure helps in this regard. With the WTO focusing on the institutional side, it also offers more flexibility for future inclusion of new negotiated rules or measures which can assist nations to face the constantly emerging problems of world economics.

C.   The legal structure of the WTO

The WTO Charter is confined to institutional measures, but the Charter explicitly outlines four important annexes which technically contain hundreds of pages of substantive rules. The annex structure is important and the different annexes have different purposes and different legal impacts (see Appendix A).

Annex 1

This contains the large texts, termed "Multilateral Trade Agreements," which comprise the bulk of the Uruguay Round results. All these are "mandatory," in the sense that these texts impose binding obligations on all members of the WTO. This reinforces the single package idea of the negotiators, departing from the Tokyo Round approach of "pick and choose" side texts, or "GATT à la carte." The Annex 1 texts include the following:

1. Annex 1A: GATT 1994, the revised and all-inclusive GATT agreement with related agreements or "codes," and the vast "schedules of concessions" that make up the large bulk of pages in the official treaty text. The schedules for each of the major trading countries, the US, Japan, and the European Union, each constitute a volume of printed tariff listings.
2. Annex 1B: GATS, the General Agreement on Trade in Services, with its schedules of specific commitments and Annexes.
3. Annex 1C: TRIPS, the Agreement on Trade-Related Intellectual Property measures.

Annex 2

This contains the dispute settlement rules, which are obligatory for all members, and which form (for the first time) an integrated and unified dispute settlement mechanism covering the WTO Charter, the agreements listed in Annex 1 and Annex 2, and is made available for agreements in Annex 4.

Annex 3

This annex contains the TPRM (Trade Policy Review Mechanism, in existence since 1988) by which the WTO will review the overall trade policies of each member on a periodic and regular basis, and report on those policies. The approach is not supposed to be "legalistic," and questions of consistency with WTO and annex obligations are not the focus; rather the focus is on transparency and the general impact of the trade policies, both on the country being examined and on its trading partners.

Annex 4

This annex contains four agreements which are "optional," and termed "Plurilateral Agreements." This is a slight departure from the single package ideal, but the agreements included tend to deal with subject matter which concerns a small number of countries, or is more "hortatory" in nature. Clearly this annex, to which addition may be made, provides some important flexibility for the WTO to evolve and redirect its attention and institutional support for new subjects that may emerge as important during the next few decades. The agreements currently included in Annex 4 cover trade in civil aircraft, government procurement, dairy products, and bovine meat.

Annex 1A is by far the largest and contains the GATT 1994, which is essentially the old GATT as modified by amendments, the Tokyo Round "codes" as renegotiated in the Uruguay Round, and some new Uruguay Round agreements. In addition to the GATT 1994, Annex 1A includes agriculture, sanitary and phytosanitary measures, textiles and clothing, technical barriers to trade, trade-related investment measures, Article VI (antidumping), customs valuation, pre-shipment inspection, rules of origin, import licensing, subsidies and countervailing measures, and safeguards, plus a series of "understandings" which further modify the GATT, and some ministerial "decisions and declarations." The tariff schedules (most of the 26,000 pages) are technically part of this annex. The relationship of many of these agreements listed above to GATT 1994 is somewhat murky.

Two of these agreements concern what are probably the most contentious of the "rules of conduct" clauses of the GATT, namely antidumping and subsidies/countervailing measures. One other concerns product standards (technical barriers) also addressed in the sanitary and phytosanitary agreement. As noted above, the legal relationship of these various GATT additions to the core GATT agreement itself is not always clear.

As impressive as the Uruguay Round results are, there are clearly a number of "leftover" issues which the WTO system will need to address during forthcoming years, in addition to overseeing a satisfactory implementation of the Uruguay Round results. The descriptions above hint at some of these, and other issues can be named. Together these include

1. enhancing and extending liberalization of trade in agricultural products;
2. future extensive negotiations on services;
3. further elaboration of the rules on subsidies;
4. further market access efforts;
5. further negotiations in the context of trade-related investment measures;
6. further negotiations concerning rules of origin;
7. greater integration of developing countries as well as monitoring the WTO/GATT rules to ensure fair treatment of those countries;
8. attention to the problems of antidumping rules and their compatibility with some of the Uruguay Round results; and
9. the problem of integrating the "economies in transition" (e.g., China, Russia, etc.) into the WTO system.

4.   Decision-making and the WTO: the "sovereignty" issues

The governing structure of the WTO follows part of the GATT 1947 model, but departs from it substantially. At the top there is a "Ministerial Conference" which meets not less than every two years. Next there are not one, but four "Councils." These include one "General Council," which seems to have overall supervising authority, can carry out many of the functions of the Ministerial Conference between Ministerial Conference sessions, and presumably meets at least as often as the GATT 1947 Council (monthly with exceptions). In addition, however, there is a council for each of the Annex 1 agreements, namely, a Council for Trade in Goods, a Council for Trade in Services, and a Council for Trade-Related Aspects of Intellectual Property Rights.

There is also a Dispute Settlement Body (DSB) to supervise and implement the dispute settlement rules in Annex 2. The WTO Charter provides that the "General Council shall convene as appropriate to discharge the responsibilities of the DSB." In the same manner there is a Trade Policy Review Body for the Trade Policy Review Mechanism.

There have been some allegations made that the WTO Charter is an important intrusion into "national sovereignty." Apart from the general problems of how to define "sovereignty" in a world that is increasingly interdependent, the WTO contains an elaborate matrix of decision-making procedures bounded by important constraints. Basically, there are five different techniques for making decisions or formulating new or amended rules of trade policy in the WTO: amendments to the agreements, decisions on various matters, "interpretations," waivers, and finally the negotiation and implementation of new agreements (see Appendix B).

A careful examination of the WTO Charter suggests that, apart from the addition of many new subjects to the substantive annexes, the WTO has no more real power than that which existed for the GATT under the previous agreements. This may seem surprising, but in fact the GATT treaty text contained language that was quite ambiguous, and could have been misused (but fortunately was not) to provide rather extensive powers. For example, in Article XXV of the GATT the Contracting Parties acting by majority vote were given the authority to take joint action "with a view to facilitating the operation and furthering the objectives of this agreement." This is very broad and ambiguous language.

Under the WTO Charter, although a majority of one-nation, one-vote is the fallback where consensus cannot be achieved, considerably more attention has been given to the question of decision-making in a number of different contexts, and certain restraints have been added, such as increasing the voting requirements for certain actions (to three-fourths of the members for many waivers and for formal interpretations), and a provision in the amending clauses that a country will not be bound by an amendment which it opposes if the amendment would "alter the rights and obligations of the members." Likewise, the waiver authority is more constrained and will be harder to abuse. Furthermore, formal "interpretations" "shall not be used in the manner that would undermine the amendment provisions." Thus there are more legal grounds than under GATT 1947 to challenge any potential overreaching on the part of the trade system's institutions. The protections for national sovereignty built into the WTO Charter rules on decision-making are substantially enhanced.

Regarding the practice of "consensus," as established for several decades in the GATT, several characteristics are worth noting. In the GATT, there is no explicit indication of a "consensus practice," and the word "consensus" is not used. The reason that the consensus practice developed was partly the uneasiness of governments about the loose wording of GATT decision-making powers, particularly that in GATT Article XXV. Partly because of this uneasiness, the practice developed of avoiding strict voting. Instead, the Contracting Parties have for several decades taken virtually all of their decisions by "consensus." Even when a formal vote was required (such as for a waiver), there would generally be a negotiation for a consensus draft text before such text was submitted to capitals for the formal vote.

In the practice of GATT, however, the word "consensus" was not defined. In the legal sense, if some sort of "consensus" could not be achieved, the fallback was the loose voting authority of the GATT. In the WTO Charter, however, consensus is defined (at least for some purposes) as the situation when a decision occurs and "no member, present at the meeting when the decision is taken, formally objects to the proposed decision." It should be noted that this is not the same as unanimity, since consensus is defeated only by a formal objection by a member present at

406   The Uruguay Round and beyond

the meeting. Thus, those absent do not prevent a consensus, nor does an abstention prevent a consensus. Furthermore, the practice in GATT and surely also in the WTO is that some countries who have difficulty with a particular decision, will nevertheless remain silent out of deference to countries with a substantially higher stake in the pragmatic economic consequences of the decision. Thus the consensus practice itself involves some deference to economic power. This has certainly been the practice in the GATT, and the WTO Charter provides that the WTO shall be guided by such "customary practices."

The WTO is considerably more explicit about the situation where consensus fails. In a few instances, a decision must be by consensus and there is no fallback to a majority vote (for example, adding plurilateral agreements to Annex 4, Article X(9), and amendments to the dispute settlement procedures in Annex 2). In many other situations, when consensus fails there is an explicit fallback vote, such as three-fourths of the membership. It is considered quite difficult to achieve such a heavy fallback vote as three-fourths of the membership (not three-fourths of those voting), since often 25 percent of the membership is not involved in a particular decision and may not show up at the meeting. Thus the protections of national sovereignty built into the WTO Charter rules on decision-making are substantially enhanced over that of the GATT.

The amending authority (Article X) is itself quite intricate and ingenious. It obviously has been carefully tailored to the needs of the participating nations related to each of the major multilateral agreements (GATT, GATS, and intellectual property). Amendments for some parts require unanimity. Other parts require two-thirds (after procedures in the Ministerial Conference and Councils seeking consensus for amendment proposals). In almost all cases, as mentioned above, when an amendment would "alter the rights and obligations," a member which refuses to accept the amendment is not bound by it. In such case, however, there is an ingenious procedure (partly following the model in GATT) whereby the Ministerial Conference can by three-fourths vote of the members require a member holding out to accept the amendment, or withdraw from the agreement, or remain a member with explicit consent of the Ministerial Conference (i.e., grant that member a waiver). It is therefore very hard to conceive of the amending provisions being used in any way to force a major trading country such as the United States, the European Union or Japan to accept altered rights or obligations. As stated above, the spirit and practice of GATT has always been to try to accommodate, through consensus negotiation procedures, the views of as many countries as possible, but certainly to give weight to views of countries who have power in the trading system. This is not likely to change.

There still exist some risks in the voting system, and practice under the WTO could be crucial in defining and constraining these risks. For example, bloc voting could develop and there have been hints that the European Union with its number of votes (equal to the number of its members who are also members of the WTO) and the votes of members of a series of association and affiliation agreements (all totaling more than a majority of GATT and now WTO members) could be tempted to use this voting strength to achieve some of its trade policy goals (such as a waiver or selection of officers).

5. Dispute settlement procedures

One of the many achievements of the GATT, despite its "birth defects," has been the development of a reasonably sophisticated dispute settlement process. The original GATT treaty contained very little on this, although it did specifically provide (in Articles XXII and XXIII) for consultation, and then submittal of issues to the GATT Contracting Parties. As time went on, however, the practice began to evolve more towards a "rule-oriented" system. For example, in the late 1950s the practice was introduced of a "panel" of individuals to make determinations and findings and recommend them to the Contracting Parties. Before that, disputes had been considered in much broader working parties comprised of representatives of governments.

During the next several decades, the Contracting Parties utilized the panel process more and more. Increasingly, the reports began to focus on more precise and concrete questions of "violations" of treaty obligations. At the end of the Tokyo Round in 1979, the GATT Contracting Parties adopted an understanding on dispute settlement which embraced some of these concepts, and embodied the practice concerning dispute settlement procedures which had developed during the previous decades.

In the 1980s, the dispute settlement panels were for the first time assisted by a new legal section of the GATT Secretariat. The panels began to write reports that were much more precise and better reasoned (and much longer!). Many countries, including the United States (which has been the largest single applicant for dispute settlement procedures in the GATT) found it useful to take issues to panels as part of their broader approach to trade diplomacy.

However, as might be expected given the history of GATT, there were a number of defects and problems in the dispute settlement process. Some of the problems were gradually overcome through practice in the GATT. But in the Uruguay Round December 1994 text, there is a major new section concerning dispute settlement procedures, the "Understanding on Rules and Procedures Governing the Settlement of Disputes."

The new text solves many, although not all, of the issues that have plagued the GATT dispute settlement system. It establishes a unified dispute settlement system for all parts of the GATT/WTO system, including the new subjects of services and intellectual property, thus precluding procedural controversies. It provides that all relevant parts of the Uruguay Round legal text can be considered in a particular dispute case, and it reaffirms the right of a complaining government to a panel process. Finally, it establishes a unique new appellate procedure. Thus, a panel report will effectively be deemed adopted by the new DSB, unless it is appealed by one of the parties to the dispute. If appealed, the dispute will go to an appellate panel. After the appellate body has ruled, its report will go to the DSB, but in this case it will be deemed adopted unless there is a consensus *against* adoption, and presumably that negative consensus can be defeated by any major objector. Thus the presumption is reversed, compared to the previous procedures, with the ultimate result that the appellate report will come into force as a matter of international law in virtually every case. The opportunity of a losing party to block adoption of a panel report will no longer be available.

6.   The WTO as a Bretton Woods partner

The combination of events and institutional developments of the last few years, with the NAFTA in North America, the EC evolution towards deepening and broadening integration, the extraordinarily elaborate Uruguay Round results, as well as developments in China and East Europe, probably amount to the most profound change in international economic relations, institutions, and structures since the origin of the Bretton Woods structure itself in the immediate post-war period. Inevitably of course, this raises the question of the role of the new WTO as part of the "new Bretton Woods system," as a partner to the International Monetary Fund (IMF) and the World Bank (IBRD).

It is therefore significant that for the first time we will have an explicit treaty-charter agreement establishing an international organization for trade, which can take its place beside the previously mentioned Bretton Woods organizations. This may seem a mere formalism, but it can have importance in orienting public and official perceptions and understandings. It could have a healthy influence in increasing the prestige of the trade organization and treaty system, and clearly that is one of the hoped-for results. No longer will government officials or the press have to run through the slalom of legal obstacles provided under the previous system, with its "provisional application," and its convoluted multiple dispute settlement procedures, as well as the difficult web of treaties that applied.

The new structure carries forward much complexity, but in terms of general understanding, the new WTO Charter should be considerably better. Furthermore, there are at least some indications in this structure of the need for the organization to pay attention to its "public image." In order for an organization which has such a potentially profound impact on economic affairs to succeed, it must give some attention to how it is understood by public constituencies in different cultures and economic systems.

An important defect of the previous system (a Bretton Woods system without an international trade organization) was perceived by many to be its lack of "coherence." This meant the lack of appropriate coordination and discussion between national government officials and international organizational officials who concentrated on monetary and lending questions, on the one hand, and those involved in the somewhat "messier" problems of trade in goods (involving many different interest groups and political/economic forces) on the other hand. One of the purposes of a new WTO is clearly to assist in providing this coherence, partly by establishing a higher profile, understandability, and prestige for the WTO, its officials, and national government officials accredited to it. If managed appropriately, there should be a considerably greater interchange among the three Bretton Woods institutions, possibly through certain joint committees, or at least through more attention to some issues such as how trade matters affect balance of payments or other monetary questions; and, *vice versa*, how monetary affairs, including exchange rate changes, can have great effects on trade policy.

Indeed, in recent years there has been a number of circumstances which have poignantly demonstrated the importance of the connection between monetary and trade policy. The bilateral trade tensions between the United States and Japan, and the ensuing dramatic exchange rate shifts, are one such example. The desires and advantages of some of the newly privatizing, or "marketizing" economies (Russia and other republics, China, etc.) also amply demonstrate this link, as economists and policy-makers stress the need for floating exchange rates in order for trade relations to be successful. Likewise problems of Latin American exchange rates, debt structure, and investment flows confirm the importance of this link.

Even in the GATT there was recognition of the monetary–trade link in several Articles. Countries who were GATT Contracting Parties but not members of the IMF had an obligation under GATT to enter into some sort of monetary framework agreement. Likewise, the GATT had provisions for trade measures linked to balance of payment difficulties.

A number of issues that are left over for future work will have important implications for the work of the World Bank and possibly the IMF. For example, antidumping and subsidy rules have often been contentious. Apparently there have occasionally been recommendations to developing countries to use these rules in a way that would seem less than optimal to trade specialists. It is hoped that the new institutional structure will create an environment of better coordination and mutual understanding between trade specialists and monetary specialists.

Likewise agriculture and food policy deserve much more attention, and so also do policies relating to commodities and commodity agreements. All of these can be substantially affected by monetary movements, particularly for some smaller countries.

Dispute resolution procedures are an important attribute of an international treaty "regime," and are looked upon as an essential component of effectively implementing treaty obligations so as to produce the degree of credibility for those obligations that makes them operate successfully in international economic relations. It is inevitable that some monetary issues will find their way into some disputes resolved through these procedures.

Other monetary and financial links to trade policy include:

1. the effects of exchange rate shifts on trade rules regarding financial services;
2. the methods of financial adjustment costs caused by liberalizing new trade rules;
3. questions on whether and when trade barriers and other distorting measures (such as subsidies) affect exchange rates or inhibit the ability of the monetary system to adjust;
4. the question of the responsibility of a balance of payments global *surplus* country to contribute to "re-balancing";
5. the question of the use of trade measures to offset balance-of-payments difficulties;
6. calculations of antidumping margins and subsidy impacts in the context of exchange rate shifts; and
7. the effects of debt on trade and monetary imbalances (and *vice versa*).

7.   Relation to domestic law of the US and other nations

. . .

8.   Reflections and perspectives: future prospects

A safe answer to the question asked in the title of this article, is "both." That is to say, the new WTO and the results of the Uruguay Round are both a modest step forward with regard to the institutional structure, and a watershed for the international economic system. The modest step can be seen in the WTO Charter as described above. The watershed, however, is the mere fact of creating a definitive institutional arrangement, combined with the extraordinary expanse of the Uruguay Round substantive negotiations. Clearly this marks a considerable departure from the hesitancy, tentativeness, and "provisional" nature of the GATT system. It puts in place a structure that will necessarily have to face an increasing number of problems during the next few decades.

Almost any reflective consideration of the rapidly increasing international economic interdependence leads to recommendations for increasing international cooperation in order to cope with the problems of interdependence. No longer can nations effectively implement their national economic regulations because of international constraints and implications. However, the more one turns to international cooperation institutions, the more it begins to be clear that attention must be paid to the "constitution" of these international institutions, just as extensive attention is given to national level "constitutions."

This raises issues about "governance," such as preventing abuse of power, effectively channeling important information to decision-makers, and giving constituencies the opportunity to be heard and to have influence on the decision-making processes. These concepts inevitably lead to questions about the appropriate distribution of power over economic affairs in the world, and the degree to which power should be located in an international institution, or a national/federal institution, or in subfederal or even very local governmental units. The word "subsidiarity" is sometimes used to describe these general concepts of distribution of power, and the opposing goals of keeping government decisions at levels closest to affected constituents, while empowering higher levels of government to take measures that affect broader segments of society.

The WTO as an institution continues to require attention in several respects. First, an important question is whether the new dispute settlement procedures will work effectively. There will indeed be temptations of some member nations, probably the largest, to ignore or undermine the results of dispute settlement procedures when those procedures do not entirely suit their interests. The dispute settlement procedure will lose credibility, and thus will fail in its primary purpose of establishing and maintaining a creditable "rule-oriented" system.

Secondly, the decision-making and voting procedures of the WTO, although much improved over the GATT, still leave much to be desired. It is not clear how the consensus practice will proceed, particularly given the large number of members. It may be necessary at some point to develop certain practices about voting to constrain misuse of the various voting rules.

Thirdly, with a likelihood of well over 120 nation members, the WTO must soon face up to its internal procedures for effective governance and administration. This suggests the need for some sort of steering group to guide and advise the Director-General, and other officers of the WTO, in developing priorities for agenda and secretariat work, as well as initiatives to meet new problems in the world. The question of such a steering group has been controversial in the past: every country that suspects it would not be a member of such a group tends to oppose its establishment. However, without such a group informal mechanisms arise that may be even more exclusive and biased to certain types of economic structures than would otherwise be desired by the membership. For example, the "quad" group consisting of the US, the EU, Japan, and Canada, has been very influential in the GATT system. Surely that influence will continue, but the question is will those four governments be joined by a broader group of representative governments while still maintaining a number small enough to be an effective guiding mechanism for the WTO?

Fourthly, an important institutional problem will be how to integrate into the WTO new or emerging subjects which arise in the future, such as the problem of environment and trade rules. The amending rules of the WTO may (as they did in GATT) turn out to be too rigid and difficult to fulfill. If that is the case, how will new subjects be integrated into the system? As mentioned above, it may be that new "plurilateral agreements" under Annex 4 will be a major device for this, but the more that occurs, the more we will go back to the old GATT difficulty of "à la carte" choices.

Fifthly, there is the broad and important issue of enhancing the public understanding of the WTO and its work. This leads to the subject of "transparency," commonly understood to mean adequate information and openness of the procedures, advocacy, meetings, etc., so that the media and scholarly endeavors can assist in informing the world public about the operation of the WTO.

Sixth, there has already been much comment about the "agenda" after the Uruguay Round, for the World Trading System. One question often raised is whether there should be another "round," or whether the procedures for pursuing future subjects should try to avoid rounds which tend to be complicated and cumbersome. The arguments in favor of rounds, however, may still prevail, namely that a larger round gives more opportunity for trade-offs between different subjects, and raises the issues to the highest level of national governments where definitive decisions can usually be made (whereas lower level officials and technicians would not be able to make such compromises).

Many participants will have great influence on the way the WTO responds to those issues, but the most significant influence will likely be that of the new Director-General of the WTO. His guidance and diplomacy will shape the early years of the WTO in ways that will have a profound impact on the longer term shape of its "constitution."

Without necessarily providing a complete inventory of substantive subjects issues to be faced in the future by the WTO (in addition to the so-called "left-over issues" mentioned in Part 3.C above), the following seem to be appropriately included on most lists.

1. A series of subjects, already newly facing the organization:
   - competition policy in relation to trade rules;
   - non-market economies, state trading, and economies in transition and their relation to the trading rules (e.g., China, Russia, etc.);
   - product (and service) standards and the use of science, raising questions of harmonization or other techniques of facilitating trade flows; and
   - cultural, social policy, and structural impediments to trade.
2. There are also a series of subjects called "link issues," which are subjects that are often separately considered, but which have important inter-linkages with trade. These include:
   - environmental rules and trade policy;
   - labor standards and rules and trade policy;
   - human rights and trade policy (including economic sanctions);
   - monetary policy and its relation to trade policy; and
   - arms control and nonproliferation issues and their relation to trade policy.
3. Apart from these subjects for a post-Uruguay Round agenda, there are certain basic GATT concepts that need to be reconsidered and possibly altered so that they will be more effective in the future economically interdependent world. These include:
   - the most-favored-nation clause (and problems of the free-rider);
   - regionalism and its relation to the multilateral system;
   - reciprocity and whether this concept can effectively handle the problems of rule-making;
   - national treatment and the need for minimum standards that go beyond nondiscrimination or "equal" treatment; and
   - antidumping rules (as previously mentioned) and the question of whether these rules are in reality "safeguards" or "escape clause" measures, rather than unfair trade measures.

In short, we have put in place an "evolutionary watershed" structure of institution and rules to round out the international economic system, but any close look quickly reveals that there is much more to do.

21   World trade rules and environmental policies: congruence or conflict?[*]

Introduction[1]

Proposition 1: Protection of the environment has become exceedingly important, and promises to be more important for the benefit of future generations. Protecting the environment involves rules of international cooperation, sanction, or both, so that some government actions to enhance environmental protection will not be undermined by the actions of other governments. Sometimes such rules involve trade restricting measures.

Proposition 2: Trade liberalization is important for enhancing world economic welfare and for providing a greater opportunity for billions of individuals to lead satisfying lives. Measures that restrict trade often will decrease the achievement of this goal.

These two propositions state the opposing policy objectives that currently pose important and difficult dilemmas for governments. This type of "policy discord" is not unique; there are many similar policy discords, at both the national and the international levels, that governments must confront.[2] Indeed, there is some evidence that environmental policy and trade policy are complementary, at least in the sense that increasing world welfare can lead to citizen demands and governmental actions to improve protection for the environment. The poorest nations in the world cannot

---

[*] This chapter is based on John H. Jackson, "World Trade Rules and Environmental Policies: Congruence or Conflict?" (1992) 49 *Washington and Lee Law Review* 4, 1227–1278.

[1] In connection with the subject of this paper, readers may want to examine the following other works by this same author: John H. Jackson, *Restructuring the GATT System* (1990); John H. Jackson, *World Trade and GATT* (1969); John H. Jackson, *The World Trading System: Law and Policy of International Economic Relations* (1989); John H. Jackson and William Davey, *Legal Problems of International Economic Relations: Cases, Materials and Text* (2nd edn., West Publishing, St. Paul, MN, 1986); and John H. Jackson et al., *Implementing the Tokyo Round: National Constitutions and International Economic Rules* (1984).

[2] An example of policy discord is the conflicting goals of providing adequate medical coverage while minimizing budget expenditures.

afford such protection, but as welfare increases protection becomes more affordable.[3]

An unfortunate development in public and interest group attention to trade and the environment is the appearance of hostility between proponents of the two different propositions stated above. The hostility is misplaced because both groups will need the assistance and cooperation of the other group in order to accomplish their respective policy objectives. Of course, some of this tension is typical of political systems. Political participants often seek to achieve opposing objectives and goals. Each side may endorse legitimate goals, but when the goals clash, accommodation is necessary.

To some extent, the conflicts between the trade liberalization proponents and the environmental protection proponents derive from a certain "difference in cultures" between the trade policy experts and the environmental policy experts. Oddly enough, even when operating within the framework of the same society, these different "policy cultures" have developed different attitudes and perceptions of the political and policy processes, and these different outlooks create misunderstandings and conflict between the groups.[4]

These problems are part of a broader trend of international economic relations that is posing a number of perplexing and troublesome situations for statesmen and policy leaders. Part of the difficulty inevitably results from the growth of international economic interdependence.[5] Such interdependence increases trade in both products and services across national borders and brings many benefits to participating countries. International interdependence also results in efficiencies and economies of scale that can raise world welfare (but not necessarily *everyone's* welfare, because some groups will be required to adjust in the face of increased competition).[6] This trend towards increased international economic interdependence requires a different sort of attitude towards government regulation. Within a nation, government regulations in such areas as consumer protection, competition policy, prudential measures (of banking and financial institutions), health and welfare (for example, alcohol and abortion control), and human rights (for example, prohibiting discrimination), are all designed by govern-

---

[3] Gene M. Grossman and Alan B. Krueger, *The Impacts of a North American Free Trade Agreement* (Discussion Papers in Economics No. 158, Woodrow Wilson School of Public and International Affairs, Princeton, NJ, 1991).

[4] The "culture of difference" is well described in Robert W. Jerome, "Traders and Environmentalists," *Journal of Commerce*, December 27, 1991, at 4A.

[5] See Jackson, *The World Trading System*, 2; John H. Jackson, "Transnational Enterprises and International Codes of Conduct: Introductory Remarks for Experts," Address Before International Bar Association Meeting in Berlin, August 27, 1980, in *Law Quadrangle Notes* 19 at 19–24.

[6] See, e.g., Peter B. Kenen, *The International Economy* (1985), 167–192.

ments to promote worthy policies that sometimes clash with market-oriented economic policies. When economic interdependence moves a number of these issues to the international scene, they become (at least in today's defective international system) much more difficult to manage. The circumstances and the broader scope of the international system create in many contexts (not just those concerning environmental policies) a series of problems and questions including:

1. general questions of the effectiveness of national "sovereignty" in the face of a need to cooperate with other countries to avoid some aspects of the "prisoners dilemma"[7] or "free-rider"[8] problems; unless there is cooperation, individual countries can profit from the efforts of other countries without contributing to those efforts, but in the longer run all may suffer;
2. perplexing questions of how new international rules should be made, questions that often involve voting procedures;
3. general questions of the appropriateness and degree to which national sovereignty will submit to international dispute settlement procedures to resolve differences on various policy matters;
4. problems of a single national sovereign using the extraterritorial reach of its regulation (sometimes termed unilateralism) to impose its will on the actions of other nations, or the citizens of other nations;
5. significant legitimate differences of view between nations as to economic structure, level of economic development, forms of government, appropriate role of government in economic activities, etc. Developing countries, for example, will have different views than on many "trade-off" matters, with developing countries generally arguing that environmental regulations unfairly restrain their economic development. They note that rich countries have benefited from decades or centuries of freedom

---

[7] "Prisoner's dilemma" refers to the hypothetical economic paradigm where two persons have partially opposing goals and might achieve a better result from cooperation than competition. The example often used is two prisoners being interrogated separately by a police official who is offering each one some advantage in return for confessing to a joint crime, or for giving information about the other's involvement in the crime. If the two cooperate and refuse to give any information, it is suggested that they may be in a better situation than if each tells on the other. In economic terms, countries, firms, or individuals could pursue competitive policies which, when pursued by everyone, cause aggregate damage to all (for example, competitive subsidization). The question then arises what would be the case if they cooperate so as to prevent the incentive to compete against each other with damaging policies.

[8] "Free-rider" refers to the situation where a group of countries agree to some discipline such as a restraint on using certain trade barriers. Under Most-Favored-Nation (MFN) they may be required to give the advantages of that discipline to other countries including countries that have not entered the specific agreement. Consequently, those countries that have not joined the agreement enjoy a benefit without submitting themselves to the discipline and are "free-riders."

from environmental protection rules, and that even today the rich countries are responsible for most of the world's pollution. Furthermore, poor countries argue that the imposition of environmental regulations threatens their economies with stagnation and populations with starvation.

All these circumstances and arguments occur in the context of a relatively chaotic and unstructured international system, which in many ways has not evolved adequately to keep up with the implications of growing international economic interdependence. This paper will probe the more specific issues of the relationship of international trade policy rules to environmental policies and rules,[9] primarily in the context of the General Agreement on Tariffs and Trade (GATT)[10] (which is the most important set of international trade policy rules). This will be done in the eight parts. Part I surveys the policies and certain rules of the GATT system and is followed by five parts that discuss areas of conflict between GATT policies and environmental policies. Part VII discusses institutional and dispute settlement issues and Part VIII draws conclusions about the relationship between trade policies and environmental policies.

The term "environmental policies" is defined very broadly for the purposes of this paper. It includes, for example, measures relating to health or health risks. The phrases "trade policies" and "trade liberalization" also are defined broadly to include not only trade in goods, but also trade in services.

I.   Objectives of trade rules and relation to environmental policy

The most significant and widespread rule system for international trade is the GATT system, which includes the GATT and over 200 ancillary treaties, as well as a number of other related arrangements and decisions. The GATT may soon be modified by the Uruguay Round,[11] so this paper will refer to the GATT/MTO system as broadly embracing the system as it is now and as it may emerge within a year or two. Of course, a number of

---

[9] The literature and documents discussing environmental policy are so voluminous and numerous that it is pointless to cite very much. Obviously the drafts for "Agenda 21" for the June 1992 conference in Rio de Janeiro are an important expression of environmental policies, as are the twenty-seven "Principles" set forth in a document for "Agenda item 9." The rather high generality of these expressions leave many questions open for further analytical works on detail.

[10] General Agreement on Tariffs and Trade, October 30, 1947, 61 Stat. A11, 55 UNTS 187.

[11] Draft Final Act Embodying the Results of the Uruguay Round of Multilateral Trade Negotiations, GATT Doc. MTN.TNC/W/FA, December 20, 1991 (hereinafter Dunkel Draft). An Agreement Establishing the Multilateral Trade Organization (MTO) is proposed in a Draft Charter in the Dunkel Draft, Annex IV. See Dunkel Draft, 91–101.

other treaties or arrangements, such as regional blocs like the proposed North American Free Trade Agreement (NAFTA),[12] are relevant to this discussion of "trade–environment policy discord," but most of the essential principles of the discord can be discussed in the context of GATT. Consequently, this paper will focus on the GATT/MTO rules and policies as worthy generic examples of problems that also occur in other contexts.

The basic policy underlying the GATT (and the broader "Bretton Woods system" established in 1944–1948) is well known.[13] The objective is to liberalize trade that crosses national boundaries, and to pursue the benefits described in economic theory as "comparative advantage." The notion of comparative advantage relates partly to the theories of economies of scale. When nations specialize, they become more efficient in producing a product (and possibly also a service). If they can trade their products or services for the different products or services that other countries specialize in producing, then all parties involved will be better off because countries will not waste resources producing products that other countries can produce more efficiently. The international rules are designed to restrain governmental interference with this type of trade.

There are exceptions to the general policy of liberalizing trade, one of which arises from the problem of "externalities," a concept that is closely associated with environmental protection. If a producer pollutes a stream during its manufacturing process, and there are no laws prohibiting such pollution, then it has imposed an "externality cost" on the world. The externality cost is the difference between the values of the unpolluted stream and the polluted stream. Because there is no law against polluting the stream, the cost is not recouped from the producer or passed on to the consumers of the product. This concept appears to be one of the most important core dilemmas or policy problems of the relationship between trade and environmental policies. Thus, much of the relationship is concerned with how environmental protection costs can be "internalized," to follow what is sometimes termed the "polluter pays principle."

The problem often boils down to the need to provide certain kinds of governmental rules or incentives that in certain ways either clash with the basic trade liberalization rules, or that alter them significantly. As soon as this occurs, however, there is a risk of undermining the GATT liberalization policies and rules. It is this "policy discord" that raises the difficult question of how to accommodate the competing values of trade liberalization on the one hand, and environmental protection on the other hand, without undermining the basic principles of both policy sets.

---

[12] North America Free Trade Agreement, September 6, 1992, US–Canada–Mexico, available in LEXIS, GENFED-EXTRA database; WL, NAFTA database.
[13] See Jackson, *World Trade and GATT*; and Jackson, *The World Trading System*.

The GATT trade liberalization policies that have been deemed fundamental for almost one-half of a century include the following.

1. Tariff reduction (GATT Article II): Originally the basic goal of the
GATT was to reduce tariffs. In this respect the GATT has been most
successful (particularly with respect to tariffs on industrial products
imported into industrial nations).[14] Indeed, in the last several years this
goal has had a profound influence on a number of countries that are not
industrialized.[15]

2. National treatment (GATT Article III): The national treatment rule
requires that nations, when applying their domestic taxes and regulations, treat imports no less favorably than they treat their domestically
produced goods (and services).

3. Most-favored-nation (MFN) (Article I): Nations are required to treat
other nation participants in the system (GATT members) equally with
respect to imports (or exports). Thus, under the GATT rules a nation
cannot discriminate (with some exceptions) between bicycle imports
from Japan and bicycle imports from Italy.

4. Nontariff barriers (NTBs): As the decades of GATT history passed, it
became increasingly clear that tariffs were no longer the major problem of trade barriers. Instead, so-called "nontariff barriers (NTBs)"
became much more important, and were addressed systematically for
the first time in the Tokyo Round of the 1970s which produced a series
of "codes" (special side treaties or agreements) that attempted to address some of the key NTB issues.[16] In the current Uruguay Round
negotiation, this process is being extended even further, and of course
new issues involving intellectual property and trade in services are
being added (with considerable complexity).[17] NTBs are very numerous, and new trade restriction and distortion techniques are constantly
arising.[18]

Arguably the current GATT system is not capable of handling the trade
liberalization problems of the forthcoming decades, and improvement will
be necessary. One major emerging problem is the effect of differences in
economic structures and cultures. Issues formerly thought to be well within
the exclusive terrain of national sovereignties, such as exchange rates and
taxing policies, now must be examined for their impact on trade liberalization or barriers.

[14] Jackson, *The World Trading System*, 115–131.
[15] See, e.g., Richard E. Feinberg, "Latin America: Back on the Screen," *International Economic Insights*, July–August 1992, 2 at 2–6.
[16] Jackson *et al.*, *Implementing the Tokyo Round*.   [17] Dunkel Draft.
[18] Jackson, *The World Trading System*, 130.

The GATT has established a new program to look systematically at governmental trade policies, called the Trade Policy Review Mechanism (TPRM).[19] In addition, the United States and Japan have bilaterally entered into a discussion process called Structural Impediments Initiative (SII)[20] that has probed very deeply into the two different societies and the systemic problems that affect trade flows between them (SII could very well be generalized gradually to include other groups of countries, and ultimately become part of the GATT TPRM). These procedures are part of a trend for the future, and, while environmental discussions could become a part of these procedures, further evolution will be needed.

Several recent important studies have tried to inventory some of the particular GATT system rules and clauses that have implications for environmental policy. Rather than repeat those inventories here, I refer to them in the footnotes,[21] and include some text in an Annex.[22] Needless to say, this area is very complex and important work needs to be done on understanding the particular relationship between a number of the GATT/MTO system rules on the one hand, and the environmental policies on the other hand.

A few "hypothetical" cases will demonstrate some of the possible policy clashes. In the cases below I use the initials "ENV" to indicate the environmentally "correct" country that imports (or exports), and the initials "EXP" to indicate the exporting country, and "IMP" to indicate an importing country.

1. ENV establishes a rule that requires a special deposit or tax on packaging which is not biodegradable, arguing that such packages are a danger for the environment. It so happens the ENV producers use a different package that is not so taxed. Only the packages from EXP are effected (in some cases it can be established that the tax imposed is in excess of that needed for the environmental protection).
2. ENV establishes a rule that requires any business firm which sells a product in the ENV market to establish a center that will recycle, or appropriately dispose of, the product when the ENV consumer is finish-

---

[19] See GATT Doc. Series C/RM/. . . and recent reports such as GATT Doc. C/RM/S/26A and B, June 12, 1992 (regarding Uruguay) and GATT Doc. C/RM/S/23A and B, November 7, 1991 (regarding the United States).

[20] Mitsuo Matsushita, "The Structural Impediments Initiative: An Example of Bilateral Trade Negotiations" (1991) 12 *Michigan Journal of International Law* 436.

[21] General Agreement on Tariffs and Trade, *International Trade* 90–91 (1992), 19–39; US Congress Office of Technology Assessment, *Trade and Environment: Conflicts and Opportunities* (1992); and Robert F. Housman and Durwood J. Zaelke, "Trade, Environment and Sustainable Development: A Primer" (1992) 15 *Hastings International and Comparative Law Review* 535.

[22] See Annex A, which includes the text of some of the relevant GATT provisions.

ed with the product's useful life. Such centers are relatively easy for domestic producers to establish, but much more difficult for importers (or exporters in EXP), and particularly difficult for EXP sellers of small quantities (which is often the case for new market entrants) to establish.

3. ENV establishes a subsidy for machinery purchased and used by domestic producers to assist in environmental protection (such as smoke stack cleaners). The subsidy could be in the form of special income tax depreciation deductions. When products from plants benefiting from the subsidy are exported, foreign countries such as IMP apply a countervailing duty to the exports to offset the benefits of the "subsidy."

4. ENV establishes a border tax (countervailing duty) on any electronics product that is imported from a country that does not have an environmental rule required by ENV. ENV argues that the lack of such a rule is in effect a "subsidy" when measured by economic principles of internalization and "polluter pays," and that the subsidy should be offset by a countervailing duty. EXP argues that, while its own method of pollution control is different, it is fully adequate and more efficient than ENVs and is also cheaper. Consequently, EXP argues either that its products should not incur the clean-up duty or that its environment can better withstand pollution activity.

5. ENV prohibits the importation of tropical hardwoods on the ground that imports of tropical hardwood products tend to induce deforestation in important tropical forest areas, and that such deforestation damages the world environment. ENV is a temperate zone nation with temperate forests, but does not apply any rule against temperate forest products, domestic or imported.

6. ENV has an important fishing fleet that captures salmon and herring. It also has an important fish processing industry. ENV establishes a rule against the exportation of the unprocessed salmon or herring caught within its territorial and protected zone area, arguing that landing those fish at its ports is necessary for an appropriate count of the fish supply. This count is needed for economic and environmental models designed to assist regulators in limiting the catch and promoting the growth of the fish supply. Local ENV fish-processing plants enjoy the benefit of avoiding competition for purchase of the fish by foreign processors in IMP.

7. ENV prohibits the sale of domestic or imported vegetables that have been genetically engineered to achieve certain characteristics, such as longer shelf life and better color. Its domestic industry does not use these genetically engineered plants, while certain foreign countries do. The foreign countries wish to export to ENV, arguing that the genetically engineered products are equal in every respect, and better in some

respects, to the safety and other characteristics of products that are not so engineered.

8. IMP establishes a rule against the importation of products from any producer in a foreign country that utilizes women in its factory. IMP argues that it is culturally offensive to its domestic producers to utilize women in their factories. Furthermore, because IMP prohibits the employment of women in factories, it feels obliged to prohibit the importation of goods that were produced from female labor.

A number of different trade policy problems are posed by the examples above and some of these will be discussed further under specific parts below. As a logical exercise one can use an unrealistic hypothetical to illustrate the conflict between trade policy and environmental policy. Imagine a country, ENV, establishing a rule that prohibits the importation of products from "any country that pollutes." Presumably that would cause virtually all trade to cease, totally undermining the GATT/MTO policies of liberalization. Although the example is extreme, one thing seems reasonably clear: the GATT/MTO system, and its policy and government specialists, need to change so as better to accommodate environmental policies. All too often during the past decade, it has appeared that the trade policy specialists have feared the incursion of the environmental policies on their terrain (partly because the environmental policies can be so easily used as an excuse for protectionism), and this fear has led to a certain attitude of "fending off," or other "lack of friendliness" towards environmental policies. Likewise, there has been a certain "unfriendliness" on the part of some of the environmental policy experts towards trade policies, reflected in large newspaper advertisements and "anti-GATT-zilla" posters![23]

The purpose of this paper is to probe the differences between the two policy sets, and to identify ways in which some of those differences can be narrowed. It is not possible to cover all of the problems that are involved in this clash, so I will focus on a selected number of key legal and institutional issues:

1. the problem of national treatment and its relation to product standards (Part II);
2. the problem of the general exceptions in GATT Article XX (Part III);
3. the related problem of the "process-product" characteristics that have been involved in the tuna/dolphin case, and concern with what is sometimes called the global commons (Part IV);
4. the intricate and elaborate problem of subsidies (Part V);

---

[23] See "SABOTAGE! of America's Health, Food Safety and Environmental Laws," *New York Times* (Midwest edition), April 20, 1992, at B5; see also Nancy Dunne, "Fears Over 'GATT-Zilla the Trade Monster'," *Financial Times*, January 30, 1992, at 3.

5. the subject of "competitiveness" (Part VI); and
6. a certain group of institutional problems related to the GATT/MTO system, including dispute settlement, transparency, and jurisprudence (Part VII).

II.   National treatment and product standards

One of the core principles of the GATT/MTO system of trade liberaliz-ation is the rule known as "national treatment," found in GATT Article III. The national treatment clause can be traced far back into treaties of centuries ago, and is applied to a number of different governmental activ-ities.[24] For purposes of a variety of governmental actions, it obligates a government to treat foreign products or persons the same as it treats its domestic products or persons. Before World War II, the national treatment clause was perhaps most commonly found in the Treaties of Friendship, Commerce, and Navigation (FCN Treaties), and in the context called for nondiscriminatory treatment by treaty parties with respect to citizens or firms of the other party to a treaty, operating within the territory of a treaty party. This principle has been applied extensively to issues of arrest and criminal process, and human rights.

In traditional international law practice there were two possible dimen-sions of national treatment. On the one hand, national treatment was deemed to be a rule of "nondiscrimination," requiring a government to treat aliens in a manner no less favorable than it treats its own citizens. However, under that approach, if its treatment of its own citizens was very bad (for example, arbitrary arrest or very poor jail conditions), similar treatment of foreigners would comply with the clause. Thus, there develop-ed a second aspect of national treatment under the phraseology and customary practice of certain treaty clauses that requires a certain mini-mum standard of treatment.

In general, the GATT national treatment clause (expressed in ten para-graphs of Article III, with certain exceptions built in) opted primarily for the nondiscrimination standard.[25] Thus it has been said that, while GATT requires a nation to tax and regulate imports from other GATT parties in a manner no less favorable than it treats its domestic product that is utterly foolish, it could also impose such a regulation on imported products. The government, for example, could prohibit the sale of both domestic and imported shampoo when the container showed a picture of a blond

[24] See Jackson, *World Trade and GATT*, 273–303; and Jackson and Davey, *Legal Problems of International Economic Relations*, 266, 483–537.
[25] See GATT Article III, 61 Stat. at A18, 55 UNTS at 204; see also the sources cited in note 23 above.

woman. Likewise, it could arguably prohibit the sale of domestic and imported products of the label contained any words in a language other than that of the importing country. Thus, the latter regulation often requires specialized labels on imports.

The GATT, however, does contain some language in paragraph 1 of Article III which states that regulations and taxes shall not be imposed in a way "so as to afford protection" against import competition. Thus, GATT contains some element of minimum standard that is related to principles of liberal trade. This type of minimum standard has resulted in an interpretation of Article III that prohibits government regulation even when it appears "on its face" to be nondiscriminatory, if in fact it is *de facto* discriminatory. An important case in United States jurisprudence of some decades ago struggled with this concept[26] and GATT panel cases and other discussions have made references to the problem of government regulation that affords effective protection, even though on its face it appears neutral.[27]

One example of *de facto* discriminatory regulation would be a regulation that imposed a higher tax on automobiles with greater horsepower and speed, when the importing country knew that its own automobile production tended to concentrate heavily in automobiles with lesser horsepower and speed. Likewise, a less favorable tax treatment for automobiles priced in excess of a certain amount of money, say $25,000, in circumstances where domestic production tended not to produce such higher priced autos while imports tended to concentrate on them, could be suspect. Clearly there are some difficult issues in these circumstances, particularly because governments may have a legitimate regulatory interest in classifying goods in certain ways, for example taxing luxury goods more heavily than daily staples. Thus, there are some delicate decisions that have to be made in interpreting GATT Article III.

Similar issues of interpretation arise in a number of "environmental" type cases. For example, an Ontario regulation[28] imposing a higher tax on the sale of beverages in aluminum containers than on other types of containers is arguably designed to help environmental matters. On the other hand, when it is discovered that very few Ontario-made beverages are sold in aluminum cans, while imports from the United States are very frequently sold in those containers, the regulation becomes suspect as a *de*

---

[26] Jackson and Davey, *Legal Problems of International Economic Relations*, 496; see Report of the GATT Panel, United States – Section 337 of the Tariff Act of 1930, GATT Doc. L/6439, para. 3.18, November 7, 1989, *Basic Instruments and Selected Documents*, 36th Supplement, 345 at 360.

[27] Jackson and Davey, *Legal Problems of International Economic Relations*, 483–537; and Report of the GATT Panel, United States – Alcoholic Beverages, GATT Doc. DS23/R, March 16, 1992.

[28] See, e.g., "Beer Blast," *Wall Street Journal*, August 4, 1992, at A14.

facto discrimination. The key issue then becomes one of determining who should decide whether the regulation is appropriate.

Even if a regulation is both *facially* nondiscriminatory and also *de facto* nondiscriminatory, some important issues about a "minimum standard" arise. The Beef Hormone Case, a current significant case between the United States and the European Community (EC) raised this issue.[29] In that case the EC had prohibited the sale of beef that had been grown with the assistance of artificial hormone infusions. The United States argued that it applied hormones by a method that was totally safe for human ingestion, and that the EC had no scientific basis for its regulation, which incidentally happened to hurt US exports of beef products to the EC. The EC replied that it had no obligation to provide a scientific justification for its regulation.

This dispute has festered. The United States pointed to a clause in the Tokyo Round Standards Code[30] that might have given some opportunity to require scientific justification for a product regulation. However, negotiators in the Uruguay Round have developed a draft phytosanitary text designed to provide some minimum standards for government regulation requiring "scientific principles" as justification.[31] This draft text has raised some serious concerns on the part of environmental policy experts in the United States and elsewhere. The experts worry that this text would inhibit national governments, or subfederal governmental units, from determining the appropriateness of a regulation that went beyond some minimum international standard. The language of the text itself does not seem to call for this, but the implication is that there will be an opportunity for exporting countries to challenge regulations of importing countries and to require importing countries to justify their regulations on the basis of "sound science." This raises substantial fears that GATT panels will tend to rule against regulations that go beyond a lowest common denominator of national environmental regulations in the GATT/MTN system.[32] This concern pushes the discourse into the question of institutions.

---

[29] See Janice Castro, "Why the Beef Over Hormones," *Time*, January 16, 1989, at 44.

[30] Agreement on Technical Barriers to Trade, GATT Doc. L/4812, November 12, 1979, *Basic Instruments and Selected Documents*, 26th Supplement, 8 at 8. Article 2, para. 2.1 states that: "Parties shall ensure that technical regulations and standards are not prepared, adopted or applied with a view to creating obstacles to international trade." *Ibid.*, 9. The Agreement also provides "technical expert groups" to assist dispute settlement panels. *Ibid.*, Annex 2, at 31.

[31] Dunkel Draft. See Text on Agriculture, Part C, which at para. 6 reads: "Contracting parties shall ensure that sanitary and phytosanitary measures are applied only to the extent necessary to protect human, animal or plant life or health, are based on scientific principles and are not maintained against available scientific evidence." *Ibid.*, § L, para. 6, at L.36.

[32] See Stewart Hudson, "Trade, Environment, and the Pursuit of Sustainable Development," Paper Prepared for World Bank Symposium on International Trade and Environment, Washington, DC, November 1991 (transcript available from author). Stewart Hudson is with the National Wildlife Federation, Washington, DC.

In summary, the GATT relatively easily accommodates national government environmental regulations that concern the characteristics of imported products. Thus, if a nation wishes to prohibit the sale of domestic and imported croissants which have a high cholesterol content, presumably this would be consistent with the GATT obligations of Article III. Under the Tokyo Round Standards Code and the Uruguay Round phytosanitary draft text approach there might be some opportunity to challenge the regulation. Nevertheless, it would seem that the national treatment standard would not be a major impediment or a major conceptual problem for environmental regulation, unless a requirement of scientific justification was interpreted to require such a high degree of justification as to inhibit unreasonably governments from imposing environmental standards. To ensure against that, it might be useful to have some interpretive notes for the Uruguay Round text.[33]

The minimum standard scientific justification approach can be very significant for the future of trade rules in the GATT/MTN system. For certain interests within a large country like the United States to argue that there should never be an international "second guess" (such as a tribunal process) of any national regulations in the environmental, or other area, could prevent important international cooperative measures to allow the trading system to evolve in a way to meet the new challenge. But there are some legitimate concerns on the part of the environmental policy advocates, and further work needs to be taken in the GATT/MTO context, some of which will extend over the next decade, to address those concerns. Briefly, the major concerns include:

1. the question of how difficult it will be to justify national or subfederal governmental unit regulations on environmental matters, in the context of international dispute settlement processes and a new treaty text that requires certain minimum standards of scientific justification for such regulations; and
2. the amount of latitude that will be granted to nation-states to impose environmental regulations that require higher standards than some international minimum.

III.   General exceptions in Article XX: health and conservation

The GATT contains an Article XX entitled "General Exceptions" which includes important provisions that override other obligations of the

[33] Some text in the October 7, 1992 NAFTA draft is of interest in connection with the burdens of scientific proof, for example Articles 904(3), 905(3), and 907, which are quoted in Annex C. The language specifies a right of governments to use a "higher level of protection" for the environmental international standards.

GATT, under certain circumstances defined in the Article. Again it is not practical or appropriate in this paper to deal with all of Article XX, but there are certain key measures that should be addressed. Quite often, concern for environmental matters focuses on paragraphs (b) and (g) of Article XX:[34]

(b) necessary to protect human, animal or plant life or health . . .
. . .
(g) relating to the conservation of exhaustible natural resources if such measures are made effective in conjunction with restrictions on domestic production or consumption . . .

The exceptions of Article XX are subject to some important qualifications in the opening paragraph of Article XX, however, which reads as follows:

Subject to the requirement that such measures are not applied in a manner which would constitute a means of arbitrary or unjustifiable discrimination between countries where the same conditions prevail, or a disguised restriction on international trade, nothing in this Agreement shall be construed to prevent the adoption or enforcement by any contracting party of measures.

To a large degree, these provisions provide a softened measure of "national treatment," and MFN obligations. They require governments that take measures which arguably qualify for the exceptions of Article XX to do so in such a way as to minimize the impacts mentioned in the opening paragraph. This has led some panel reports to interpret Article XX[35] to require nations to use the "least restrictive alternative" reasonably available to it as measures designed to support the goals of the exceptions of Article XX.

There are a number of important interpretive problems with respect to Article XX, and some of them are key to the environmental–trade liberalization clash. Two interpretive questions in particular stand out, namely the interpretation of the word "necessary," and the question of *whose health*, or *which exhaustible natural resources* can be the object of an acceptable national government regulation.

The word "necessary" clearly needs interpretive attention. It is partly interpreted by the "least restrictive alternative" jurisprudence mentioned above. Thus, if there are two or more alternatives that a government could

---

[34] GATT Article XX, 61 Stat. at 1460, 55 UNTS at 262; see Jackson and Davey, *Legal Problems of International Economic Relations* (Documents Supplement, 1989), 514; and US Congress Office of Technology Assessment, *Trade and Environment: Conflicts and Opportunities*, 32.

[35] Report of the GATT Panel, United States – Section 337 of the Tariff Act of 1930, GATT Doc. L/6439, para. 5.26, *Basic Instruments and Selected Documents*, 36th Supplement, 393; and General Agreement on Tariffs and Trade, Dispute Settlement Panel Report on Thai Restrictions on Importation of and Internal Taxes on Cigarettes, 30 ILM 1122 (1991).

use to protect human life or health, it is not "necessary" to choose the one that places more restrictions on trade, when an alternative that is equally efficient in protecting human life or health exists. This will obviously impose some restraint on the latitude that nations or subfederal governments have to impose regulations for environmental purposes.[36] On the other hand, it is considered important to prevent Article XX from becoming a large loophole that governments can use to justify almost any measures that are motivated by protectionist considerations. It is this slippery slope problem that worries many in connection with Article XX. The problem arises in a number of cases, including the packaging and fish examples that were discussed in the introduction.

The other interpretive problem is conceptually more difficult. When GATT Article XX provides an exception for measures necessary to protect human, animal, or plant life or health, should it be interpreted to mean only the life or health of humans within the importing country, or extend to the life or health of humans throughout the world? This interpretive problem is intimately related to the process-product characteristic difficulty. As far as this author can determine, Article XX has not been interpreted to allow a government to impose regulations to protect the life or health of humans, animals, or plants that exist outside of the government's own territorial borders. This problem was addressed, although somewhat ambiguously, in the tuna/dolphin case.[37] The problem is that of the typical slippery slope danger, combined with the concern that powerful and wealthy countries will impose their own views regarding environmental or other social or welfare standards on other parts of the world, even where such views may not be entirely appropriate. The term "eco-imperialism" has been coined for this problem.[38]

If a nation can prohibit the importation of goods from a poor third world country where the method of production is moderately dangerous to humans, why would a nation not also be able to prohibit the importation of goods produced in an environment that differs in many social or cultural attributes from its own society? Why should one country be able to use its trade laws to depart from the general liberal trade rules of the GATT/MTO system, to enforce its own view of how plant or animal life in the oceans (beyond territorial sea, or other jurisdictional limits), or to protect the ozone layer (as suggested in the tropical hardwoods hypothetical case)?

---

[36] General Agreement on Tariffs and Trade, Dispute Settlement Panel Report on United States Restrictions on Imports of Tuna, 30 ILM 1594 (1991).

[37] *Ibid.*

[38] Gijs M. DeVries, "How to Banish Eco-Imperialism," *Journal of Commerce*, April 30, 1992, at 8A.

Other countries may have a somewhat different view of the trade-off between economic and welfare values of production, and human life or health. Even in the industrial countries, there is tolerance of certain kinds of economic activity that almost inevitably will result in human deaths or injuries, an example being major construction projects for dams or bridges. These are tough issues, and ones that will require a lot of close and careful attention, presumably in the context not only of new rule making or treaty drafting, but also in the processes of interpretation through the dispute settlement mechanisms. Thus, once again, institutional questions become significant.

It has been argued by one author[39] that the drafting history of the GATT would lead to an interpretation of Article XX that would permit governments to take a variety of environmental measures and justify them under the general exceptions of GATT. While this view is interesting, and the research is apparently thorough, it is not entirely persuasive and overlooks important issues of treaty interpretation. Under typical international law, elaborated by the Vienna Convention on the Law of Treaties,[40] preparatory work history is an ancillary means of interpreting treaties. In the context of interpreting the GATT, we have more than forty years of practice since the origin of GATT, and we also have some very important policy questions raised by the "slippery slope arguments" mentioned above. Thus, unlike certain schools of thought concerning the United States Supreme Court's interpretation of the United States Constitution, it is this author's view that one cannot rely too heavily on the original drafting history.[41]

IV. The process-product problem: the tuna/dolphin case and the global commons question

An important conceptual "difficulty" of GATT is the so-called process-product characteristic problem, which relates closely to the Article XX exceptions and also to the national treatment obligations and other pro-

---

[39] Steve Charnovitz, "Exploring the Environmental Exceptions in GATT Article XX" (1991) 25 *Journal of World Trade* 37 at 37–55. A more recent article by Charnovitz, which has just come to the attention of this author and with which this author substantially agrees, is Steve Charnovitz, "Environmental and Labor Standards in Trade" (1992) 15 *World Economics* 335 at 335–356.

[40] Vienna Convention on the Law of Treaties, opened for signature May 23, 1969, entered into force January 27, 1980, UN Doc. A/CONF.39/27, Articles 31 and 32, 8 ILM 679 at 691–697.

[41] The criticism regarding some theories of interpretation refers to various doctrines of "original intent" in connection with theories of US Constitutional interpretation.

visions of GATT.[42] This issue is central to the so-called tuna/dolphin case[43] and needs to be explained.

Suppose that an importing country wishes to prohibit the sale of domestic or imported automobiles that emit more pollutants in their exhaust than permitted by a specified standard. Subject to the discussion in Part II, there seems to be little difficulty with this regulation. It relates to the characteristics of the product itself. If the product itself is polluting, then on a nondiscriminatory basis the government may prohibit its sale (or also prohibit its importation, as a measure to prohibit its sale).[44]

Suppose, on the other hand, that the government feels that an automobile plant in a foreign country is operated in such a way that it poses substantial hazards to human health, possibly through dangers of accidents from the machinery, pollutants or unduly high temperatures in the factory. On an apparently nondiscriminatory basis, the government may wish to impose a prohibition on the sale of domestic or imported automobiles that are produced in factories with certain characteristics. However, in this case it should be noted that the imported automobiles themselves are perfectly appropriate and do not have dangerous or polluting characteristics. Thus, the target of the importing country's regulation is the production "process." The key question under the GATT/MTO system is whether the importing country is justified either under national treatment rules of nondiscrimination, or the exceptions of Article XX (which do not require strict national treatment nondiscrimination as was discussed above). Trade policy experts are concerned that, if a nation is allowed to use the process characteristic as the basis for trade restrictive measures, then the result would be to open a Pandora's box of problems that could open large loopholes in the GATT. The following are some hypothetical illustrations of potential "process" problems further down the road.[45]

---

[42] Jackson and Davey, *Legal Problems of International Economic Relations*, 448, 514; Frederic L. Kirgis Jr., "Effective Pollution Control in Industrialized Countries: International Economic Disincentives, Policy Responses and the GATT" (1972) 70 *Michigan Law Review* 859; see also note 25 above.

[43] General Agreement on Tariffs and Trade, Dispute Settlement Panel Report on United States Restrictions on Imports of Tuna, 30 ILM 1594 (1991); see Jackson, *The World Trading System*, 197–199; GATT, *International Trade* 90–91, 27; and US Congress Office of Technology Assessment, *Trade and Environment: Conflicts and Opportunities*, 49; see also note 37 above.

[44] See notes 24–33 above and the accompanying text (discussing national treatment and product standards); see also Jackson and Davey, *Legal Problems of International Economic Relations*, 448 (citing the GATT Report on Belgian Family Allowances adopted by GATT Contracting Parties on November 7, 1952); and the GATT, Annex 1, 61 Stat. at A85–90; 55 UNTS at 292–305.

[45] See the sources cited in notes 20 and 38–40 above.

1. An importing country prohibits the sale of radios, whether domestic or imported, that are produced by workers who are paid less than a minimum amount of wages specified by the importing country. This minimum amount might be the importing country's own minimum wage, or it might be an amount considerably less but still substantial (in relation to poor countries).
2. An importing country that prohibits women from working in certain types of manufacturing plants also prohibits the importation of goods produced in similar plants that utilize women employees.
3. An importing country that specifies a weekly religious holiday, for example, Saturday or Sunday, prohibits the importation of goods produced in countries which do not observe such a holiday.
4. An importing country has strong political interests regarding the threat to marine mammals from certain fishing practices on the high seas, and thus prohibits the sale of products from both its domestic fishing industry and from foreign fishing if the products come from countries that permit the destructive fishing practices.

Obviously the tuna/dolphin case[46] relates to these issues. Although the GATT panel report is not entirely clear on this matter, it seems fair to say that there were two important objections to the US embargo on the importation of tuna. First, there is the question of "eco-imperialism," where one nation unilaterally imposes its fishing standards (albeit for environmental purposes) on other nations in the world without their consent or participation in the development of the standard. Secondly, there is the problem that the import embargo is inconsistent with the GATT rules unless there is some GATT exception that would permit the embargo. Of course, that exception relates to the "process-product" interpretation problem and therefore also to the problem in the national treatment rule (Article III) and the general exceptions of GATT (Article XX).

The approach in the GATT system so far has given great weight to this slippery slope concern, and thus tilted towards interpreting both the Article III (including some Article XI questions) and the Article XX exceptions to apply to the product standards and to life and health within the importing country, but not to extend these concepts and exceptions to "processes" outside the territorial limits of jurisdiction. The alternative which threatens to create the great loophole is a serious worry. The theories of comparative advantage which drive the policy of liberal trade, suggest that differences among nations are an important reason for trade. These can be differences of natural resources, as well as differences of cultural and population characteristics such as education, training, invest-

---

[46] See the sources cited in notes 20 and 38–40 above.

ment, and environment. To allow an exception to GATT to permit some governments unilaterally to impose standards on production processes as a condition of importation would substantially undermine these policy objectives of trade liberalization. On the other hand, trade sanctions, which include embargoes, are a very attractive and potentially useful means of providing enforcement of international cooperatively developed standards, including environmental standards.

Thus, there is an important trade-off that the GATT must face. It is not adequate, in this writer's view, for the GATT simply to say that trade should never be used as a sanction for environmental (or human rights, or antiprison labor) purposes. There are already a number of situations in which the GATT has at least tolerated, if not explicitly accepted, trade sanction type activity for what is perceived to be valid overriding international objectives.[47] What are the implications of this problem? To this writer, it seems clear that the GATT/MTO system must give specific and significant attention to this trade-off in order to provide for exceptions for environmental purposes. The exceptions should have well-established boundaries so as to prevent them from being used as excuses for a variety of protectionist devices or unilateral social welfare concerns. Possibly these exceptions should be limited to the situation where governments are protecting matters that occur within their territorial jurisdiction.

It may be feasible to develop an explicit exception in the GATT/MTO system, possibly by the waiver process which is reasonably efficient,[48] for a certain list of specified broad-based multilateral treaties. One of the concerns expressed about the tuna/dolphin case in GATT is the implications that it might have for the so-called "Montreal Protocol" concerning chlorofluorocarbons (CFCs) and the danger to the Earth's ozone layer. The Montreal Protocol[49] provides a potential future authorization of trade sanction measures against even nonsignatories for processes, not product characteristics, that violate the norms of the treaty. If the current rules of the GATT are interpreted to exclude exceptions for the process situation,

---

[47] Instances where the GATT has tolerated such uses include the imposition of trade sanctions on South Africa and Southern Rhodesia. Article XXI of GATT provides an exception for national security, and for measures in pursuance of a contracting party's "obligations under the United Nations Charter for the maintenance of international peace and security." GATT Article XXI, 61 Stat, at A63; 55 UNTS at 266. The GATT *Analytical Index* to Article XXI reports various practices that have been tolerated by the GATT system, including an Egyptian boycott against Israel, an EC action during the Falkland/Malvinas situation, and United States measures prohibiting trade involving Nicaragua.

[48] See Jackson, *World Trade and GATT*, 541–552; see also Annex B.

[49] Montreal Protocol on Substances That Deplete the Ozone Layer, September 16, 1987, entered into force January 1, 1989, 26 ILM 1550 (hereinafter the Montreal Protocol). See a description of this problem in US Congress Office of Technology Assessment, *Trade and Environment: Conflicts and Opportunities*, 43–46.

the Montreal Protocol Measures, except as among the signatories to the Montreal Protocol, would be contrary to GATT obligations.[50] It may take some time and study to develop the precise wording of an appropriate amendment or treaty exception for the GATT/MTO system for these environmental treaty cases, but in the short run for a limited period of years, it could be efficient to use a GATT waiver to clarify the issue as to specifically named treaties.[51]

In all likelihood, there are a sufficient number of signatories to the Montreal Protocol that are also GATT members so that a GATT waiver authorizing the trade measures contemplated in the Montreal Protocol could be adopted. Adoption of a waiver requires approval by two-thirds vote of the GATT contracting parties. But at the same time, it might be wise to go a few steps further and include in such a waiver several other specified treaties.[52] Obviously the waiver can also be amended in the future to add more specifically named treaties.

Even under such a waiver approach, there are still some important policy and treaty drafting questions that must be faced. For example, should the exception to the GATT be worded to apply only to the mandatory trade measures required by the specified environmental treaties? Or should it also be extended to those measures that are deemed discretionary but "authorized" by the environmental treaties? Or, would the GATT waiver even go one step further and authorize GATT members to take trade measures unilaterally to help enforce the substantive environmental norms contained in the environmental treaties, even when such environmental treaties do not have trade measures or sanctions indicated in their treaty texts?

V.   Subsidies

The problem of subsidies in international trade policy is perhaps the single most perplexing issue of the current world trading system, and one that is very complex. Some of the major controversies and negotiation impasses, such as the question of agriculture, relate to this problem. The

---

[50] Montreal Protocol. See US Congress Office of Technology Assessment, *Trade and Environment: Conflicts and Opportunities*, 44. The latter notes that the Montreal Protocol has seventy-nine members. GATT has more than 100 members, and a waiver requires two-thirds of those voting, which must include at least one-half of the total membership.

[51] Some language used in the NAFTA text suggests the possibility of a GATT waiver along the same lines as the NAFTA Article 104. See Annex C, Article 104.

[52] Apart from the Montreal Protocol, other treaties mentioned as candidates for a GATT waiver include the Basel Convention on the Control of Transboundary Movements of Hazardous Wastes and their Disposal, March 27, 1989, UN Doc. UNEP/IG. 80–83 (1989), reprinted in 28 ILM 657; and the Convention on International Trade in Endangered Species of Wild Fauna and Flora, March 3, 1973, 27 UST 1087; 993 UNTS 243.

GATT rules have become increasingly elaborate, and contain several different dimensions. Not only are there provisions in the GATT itself (Articles VI and XVI), but there is also the Tokyo Round "Code" on subsidies and countervailing duties which provides obligations to the signatories of that code.[53] It is not feasible in this paper to go into great detail about the subsidies question. Indeed, the subsidies question in relation to environmental policies may be one of the most intricate and difficult issues facing the world trading system during the next decade. Here I will only outline some of the major characteristics and problems of the potential clash between trade policies and environmental policies in relation to subsidies.

First, to look briefly at the subsidy trade rules,[54] the trade system has traditionally divided subsidies into two types: export subsidies (subsidies that apply only to exported products), and general subsidies (subsidies that apply to all products produced in the country, whether exported or not). The international system has imposed considerably more restraint on the use of export subsidies, thus deeming them to be particularly suspect.

Subsidies can have at least three different kinds of impact on international trade. Two of these relate to exports from a subsidizing country regardless of whether the subsidies are general or export subsidies. First, the subsidized exports can have an impact on an importing country, and the rules will often allow the importing country to impose a so-called "countervailing duty" to offset the effect of the subsidized imports. Secondly, subsidized exports may be introduced into a third country market to which a nonsubsidizing country is also exporting. In that case, the countervailing duty remedy is not available. The international system (GATT and the Subsidies Code) imposes specific international obligations on the use of certain kinds of subsidies, and it is this international obligation and its enforcement procedures (through dispute settlement) that is almost the only available remedy to the competing nonsubsidizing country in its complaint against the country that subsidizes. This international rule enforcement mechanism and dispute settlement process has been one of the most troublesome areas in the GATT, and there is considerable thought that the Tokyo Round Subsidies Code has largely failed in this respect. It should also be noted that the United States is the only major user of countervailing duties, although there is some evidence that other countries are now interested in increasing their use of them.

[53] Agreement on Interpretation and Application of Articles VI, XVI, and XXIII, GATT Doc. L/4812, November 12, 1979, *Basic Instruments and Selected Documents*, 26th Supplement, 56. The current number of signatories to this Convention is approximately twenty-five. See GATT Doc. L/6453 and addenda (through March 12, 1992).
[54] Jackson, *The World Trading System*, 249–273; Jackson, *World Trade and GATT*, 365–399; and Jackson and Davey, *Legal Problems of International Economic Relations*, 723–789.

The third influence of subsidies on trade is to inhibit imports into a subsidizing country. If an importing country subsidizes its domestic producers, these producers can often reduce their prices and thus inhibit imports that are not equally subsidized simply through increased price, quality, or other forms of competition. Indeed, the system is tilted against imports in that it permits a subsidizing importing country to subsidize its domestic product, and yet impose a countervailing duty on imports that are equally subsidized!

An underlying problem for all of these complex rules concerning subsidies is the definition of "subsidy" itself. The definition is often stated in very broad terms such that it would include governmental measures such as fire and police protection, roads, and schools. If the subsidy definition is so broad, the various trade response rules, particularly the countervailing duty, could totally undermine the liberal trading system. Thus, it has been necessary either to use a restricted definition of subsidy, or to define a "subset" of the broader set which subset is called "actionable" and thus subject to trade response measures.[55]

Having presented this all too brief outline of general trade subsidies rules in the GATT/MTO system, it is now important to turn to how they might apply in the environmental context. The following hypothetical cases can illustrate some of the problems that could occur:

1. Suppose an exporting country establishes a subsidy for certain of its manufacturing companies that allows them to receive grants or tax privileges for establishing environmental enhancement measures (such as machinery to clean up smoke or water emissions, or other capital goods for environmental or safety and health purposes). When those producers export their goods, the goods could be vulnerable to foreign nations imposing countervailing duties. Is this appropriate or should a special exception for environmental measures be carved out?
2. Suppose an exporting country lacks meaningful environmental rules, and exports goods into an importing country that has strict environmental rules for its manufacturers. The importing country's domestic industry will likely complain about what it perceives to be "unfair import competition." Can the importing country argue that the lack of environmental rules in the exporting country is the equivalent of a "subsidy" and impose a countervailing duty? Again this poses a slippery slope problem. Could such an importing country likewise impose countervailing duties against imports based on the argument that the imports were produced in a country that lacked competition policy

[55] Jackson, *The World Trading System*, 249–273; and Dunkel Draft (Draft Agreement on Subsidies and Countervailing Measures).

(antitrust laws)? Or lacked minimum standards of safety and health in the factories? This is a problem that closely relates to the process-product characteristic problem discussed in Part IV above.

3. Similarly, suppose a nation lacks environmental rules such that its domestic producers can produce goods cheaper than its competitors and thus compete to keep out goods that are imported from other countries that have substantial environmental rules. In that situation, the lack of environmental rules becomes an effective protectionist device.

Obviously these hypotheticals are not so "hypothetical." A good part of the discourse about the proposed NAFTA treaty expresses the concern that if Mexico lacks environmental rules it will have a competitive advantage *vis-à-vis* American or Canadian producers.[56] These problems illustrate the need for careful examination of the subsidy rules so as to design appropriate environmental exceptions or rules without destroying the advantages of the subsidy rules. These environmental exceptions or rules should probably include:

1. a modification to the definition of "actionable subsidy" to allow certain types of environment-enhancing government benefits and to exempt them from countervailing duties or other trade obligations;
2. a provision allowing trade restrictions, whether called "countervailing" or not, under the authority of other multilateral treaties designed to enforce certain international agreements; and
3. a recognition that, just because the environmental rules of an exporting nation are not as stringent as those of an importing nation, the latter should not apply "countervailing duties" based on a subsidy theory. On the other hand, international minimum standards might be formulated over time, possibly creating a benchmark required for goods to move freely in international trade.

VI.   Exports and competitiveness

Apart from the problems of the various technical rules of the GATT discussed above, there are also some important additional considerations for the relationship and possible effect of trade liberalization on environmental policies. One of those can be characterized as the question of "competitiveness." The situation is as follows: an exporting country has important environmental rules and standards, which its producers meet.

[56] "The Trade Accord," *New York Times*, August 13, 1992, at A2 and C3. See also the reports of discussions on the environment in the July 10, 1992 issue in relation to the NAFTA agreement in *Inside US Trade*.

These environmental efforts obviously have a cost, and the producers must bear those costs and build them into the price structure of the products that they export. These products compete in other countries with products from countries that do not have such environmental standards or efforts. This could be the case when the environmentalist country exports to a relatively nonenvironmentalist country, or when the two countries compete in some third market. Because the producers in the nonenvironmentalist country escape the cost of the environmental regulations, presumably they can produce at a lower cost and thus offer their product at a lower price. The concern of the producers in the environmentalist country is that this will be a form of competition for them that will be hard to meet and, thus, in their minds, is "unfair" because they are contributing to the world environment by their compliance with environmental standards.

This problem was touched on in the previous section when we discussed subsidies, but even apart from the rules of subsidies it can be an important problem, especially as it relates to political perceptions. Furthermore, because it is primarily a question of "export competitiveness," it does not get discussed in connection with many of the problems of national treatment, or the general exceptions to the GATT, which have been previously expressed. There are some GATT rules that cover exports, but they are not closely related to the problem posed here.

To some extent, this problem is similar to many other problems resulting from differences among societies. Some societies will have more stringent rules with respect to plant worker safety. Other societies will have stringent rules regarding family allowances or holidays. Still other societies will have minimum wages, and many other social measures can differ from society to society. As indicated earlier in this paper, attempts to use trade rules to make the world uniform in this regard could be futile and very damaging to the underlying policies of trade liberalization. Thus, the questions posed are whether environmental policies are substantially different than some of the other policies mentioned, and, if so, do they deserve a different kind of treatment in the world trading system.

First, it might be conceptually feasible to separate the environmental problems that affect only the environment of the country concerned (within its borders), from other problems that have an effect either across borders, or, even more broadly, on the world's environment (the global commons). It could be, and has been, argued that, because different countries vary in their degrees of environmental quality, and in the extent to which they tolerate environmental problems as a trade-off to gaining other benefits (such as eating better), that these issues can and should be left to the national sovereign states. Consequently, the international trading system ought not to try to redress or "harmonize" the different environmental approaches. Obviously there are many intricacies in this argument, and some of them have already been subjects of full papers elsewhere.[57]

Perhaps the more important question relates to the situation where the environmental degradation is of a type that impacts on the world as a whole, or at least on countries other than the acting or exporting nation. Here we have something of the "free-rider" problem, or the "prisoner's dilemma" issue, that points towards the need for international cooperation. Given the imperfections of the international system, and particularly its system for developing new rules (with its lowest common denominator constraints) environmental policy experts can legitimately argue that there must be some room for unilateral nation-state actions designed to support the world environment. This is perhaps the trickiest area for which to develop appropriate policy. It relates closely to the process-product characteristic question discussed above. Certainly the optimal approach would seem to be through broad-based multilateral treaties and rules, which then in turn raises the question of how to make such rules effective. This latter question quite often leads to a focus on trade sanctions as a means to make such rules effective, and as indicated earlier, an argument can be made that there should be an explicit exception in the GATT for certain kinds of trade actions to help enhance the effectiveness of international environmental rules, while preventing misuse of the exception.

Let us return for a moment to the first category of problems, those in which the environmental issues involve the environment only within the producing country, or the importing country which has competing producers that will benefit from lack of environmental rules In some of these cases, the importing country's political system would in fact desire some additional pressures on its decision-making processes to help induce the development of environmental rules. This is a common feature of the relationship of international action, particularly in the area of economic affairs, but also in the human rights area. In many cases, domestic leaders find it politically difficult to implement a preferred course of action unless there is some external pressure that helps them in their domestic advocacy, and also in some cases gives them an "excuse" for taking that action.

Some of this attitude certainly exists in the context of environmental rules,[58] and may in fact justify a broader approach in the GATT/MTO trading system. Thus, it could well be feasible and worthwhile, although time-consuming, to develop some rules in the trading system that impose

---

[57] See, e.g., Jagdish Bhagwati, "Why the Sins of One Economist Should Not Be Visited on All," *Financial Times*, February 18, 1992, at 21; "A Greener Bank," *Economist*, May 23, 1992, at 79 (discussing the World Bank's World Development Report, and mentioning a provocative memo by Lawrence Summers, the Bank's chief economist).

[58] These views on external pressure are expressed in private conversations with various foreign government officials, but are not generally stated in public, or in publications.

certain kinds of harmonizing minimum-level standards for environmental protection. In the alternative, rules that impose certain kinds of trade detriments, such as compensatory duties, on countries that do not adopt or enforce the harmonized or minimal environmental rules, might also be worthwhile.

VII.   The institutional problems: dispute settlement, transparency, and jurisprudence

The GATT is a rather strange and troubled institution. It was born with several birth defects because it was never meant to be an organization. Instead, it was intended that an International Trade Organization (ITO) Charter would come into effect that would provide the institutional framework, in which the GATT would be one part. Because of this troubled birth history, the GATT has always been deficient in the institutional clauses normally found in a treaty establishing an international organization.[59] These problems have become increasingly troublesome as world economic developments have gone beyond the rules provided by the GATT system. Some of these problems are being addressed in the current Uruguay Round GATT negotiation, and, if that is ultimately successful, it may help improve the institutional situation. Other GATT issues include problems of accepting new members, particularly those with different economic structures; the problem of assisting developing countries; the difficulty of facing up to some of the more newly appreciated issues that are affecting international trade flows, such as cultural and economic structural differences; questions of competition policy (antitrust); and, of course, environmental policies.

More broadly, the GATT generally suffers from institutional deficiencies in the two essential ingredients for an effective international organization, namely the making of new rules, and the provisions for making those rules effective through dispute settlement procedures. With respect to rule making, the GATT basically relies heavily on a consensus treaty-making process. With a membership that now exceeds 100 countries, this becomes extremely difficult. This difficulty is accentuated by the MFN obligations that give rise to a potential "free-rider" problem of nonsigning countries receiving the benefits of new agreements. This in turn tends to force negotiations towards a consensus for a new rule, into a "lowest common denominator" approach.

Likewise, the dispute settlement procedures of the GATT have been troubled. The actual GATT clauses setting them up are extremely sketchy. Nevertheless, through trial and error and general practice over four dec-

[59] See note 1 above, and particularly Jackson, *Restructuring the GATT System.*

ades, the GATT dispute settlement procedures have now developed into a remarkably full procedure that has been largely, but not totally, effective. Its effectiveness has been such, however, as to attract various interests who see in the GATT dispute settlement procedures an important attribute for subject matters that they would like to see placed under the GATT, such as the area of intellectual property.[60] Likewise, other trading arrangements, particularly some of the arrangements for trading blocs or free trade areas, have followed some of the general outlines of the GATT dispute settlement procedure, paying it the compliment of emulation.

The Uruguay Round negotiation currently sponsored by the GATT (the eighth since its origin) has been troubled. It was launched in September 1986, but is not yet complete. Nevertheless, in December 1991, the negotiating groups, through the coordination of the Secretariat and the Director-General, Arthur Dunkel, issued a tentative draft text of an entire package of agreements which could form the basis of the final negotiations towards a complete package to be approved. This is commonly called the "Dunkel Draft," and it contains two important institutional texts that relate to the problems discussed above. First, there is a charter for a Multilateral Trade Organization (MTO), which will provide some measure of improvement in the basic institutional structure of the GATT. It will not change such things as the structure of rule making, but it does provide, for the first time, a definitive legal treaty text to establish the organization, and put it on a sounder footing for future evolution. The existence of this text has been criticized by some interests in various participating countries, including some of the environmental interests. Some of this criticism is, I think, due to misunderstanding of the specific draft charter provisions and their relation to broader international law principles. Indeed, the draft charter is very minimal, and in many ways will result in no differences in the normal work of the organization, as compared to the existing organizational structure.[61]

Another important text in the Dunkel Draft is a draft agreement concerning revised dispute settlement procedures in the GATT. It should be noted that these dispute settlement procedures could exist independently of an MTO, if an MTO failed to come into being. However, an MTO does facilitate and help administer a broadened dispute settlement system that would now apply, not only to trade in goods, but also to intellectual property and trade in services. This procedure would provide a more effective "umbrella" for a single dispute settlement procedure and avoid some of the contentious problems of competing procedures that existed after the various Tokyo Round texts came into force.

---

[60] See "Symposium: Trade Related Aspects of Intellectual Property" (1989) 22 *Vanderbilt Journal of Transnational Law* 223; and Dunkel Draft, Annex III at 57.

[61] Dunkel Draft, 92.

Of course, there are those who would prefer not to have a more effective dispute settlement procedure, or, for that matter, a more effective organization. They see any such organization, or procedure at the international level, as a threat to their ability to achieve the results which they wish within a particular country. There is not much that can be said in response to that desire. In the view of this author, such a desire is somewhat irresponsible because the basic trends of world economic interaction, regardless of what happens in connection with new treaties, are such that some kinds of international cooperation and coordination are essential to avoid the rancorous and damaging disputes that are constantly arising between nations. International cooperation also provides the measure of predictability and stability that is essential for individual entrepreneurs and firms to act effectively. Often the action desired is investment, which depends on decisions that need a predictable rule system.

Several particular aspects of the legal effects of international actions should be clarified because there have been statements by various interest groups that suggest some misunderstanding about them. The first of these is the question of the domestic law application of international decisions of a GATT/MTO system. For the United States, it is very unlikely that any international GATT/MTO decision as to new rules (such as a new treaty) or a dispute settlement procedure result, would have direct application (self-executing effect) in United States law. Although some treaties can have self-executing effect in the United States, in recent years Congress has rather consistently negated such effect by provisions in its legislation approving the international trade treaties.[62] This result, incidentally, differs from country to country.

Many other countries are in the same position as the United States, such that the international treaty or international decisions will not automatically become part of their domestic law.[63] Instead, there must be an "act of transformation," which is some sort of domestic legal action that would implement the international rules or decisions. In the United States this could be an Act of Congress, or in cases where the power is delegated to the President, an action by the President or his delegatees. If the domestic law institutions fail to enact the appropriate transformation, the United States

---

[62] Trade Agreements Act of 1979, § 3(a) and (f), 19 USC § 2119(a) and (f) (1988); S. Rep. No. 249, 96th Cong., 1st Sess., 4, 36 (1979); Jackson et al., Implementing the Tokyo Round, 169–172; and Jackson, The World Trading System, 68, 75.

[63] See generally John H. Jackson, "Status of Treaties in Domestic Legal Systems: A Policy Analysis" (1992) 86 American Journal of International Law 310 at 310–340. The United Kingdom and Canada are generally considered "dualist" nations where treaties do not apply in domestic law, but must be implemented through parliamentary or other governmental acts of transformation. R. Higgins, "United Kingdom" in Francis G. Jacobs and Shelley Roberts (United Kingdom National Committee of Comparative Law) (eds.), The Effect of Treaties in Domestic Law (1987), 123.

or other country may be placed in contravention of international obligations. Such a situation, however, will not result in automatic domestic law change. To some extent this provides a certain escape hatch from inappropriate and overreaching international decisions. Needless to say this is a matter of considerable discussion and literature.[64]

A second potential misunderstanding of the legal situation relates to the effect of the GATT dispute settlement panel decisions. Under the current and proposed procedure, a "panel" will make its ruling in a report, and this report must be approved by the GATT Council. Under the new proposed procedures, this approval would be fairly automatic, subject to an appeal to a higher tribunal.[65] The GATT panel report is not binding until it is approved. After such approval, it is binding on the participant nations as a matter of international law, even though it does not directly become domestic law. In the case of the Canada–US Free Trade Agreement (FTA), and possibly some new FTA arrangements, there is one portion of the dispute settlement procedures available that does provide for direct, or nearly direct, application of the decisions of the tribunal. This is relatively rare and quite novel.[66]

Even with respect to international law obligations, the general international law rule is that the doctrine of precedent, or *stare decisis*, does not apply to rulings of international tribunals. Thus, the result of a panel report as between countries A and B, for example, is not technically a rule that obligates countries C and D, or even A and D. This leaves open the possibility that, through general international negotiating processes, or actions in a council of the GATT or MTO, the results of a panel report, even when approved, could be modified when applied to future cases. Nevertheless, it is true that panels do tend to follow prior panel decisions as a matter of persuasiveness and logical, consistent reasoning. In some cases, however, the panels have expressly departed from prior panel reports.[67]

What are the implications of all of this for environmental policy? First, as is fairly frequently noted in the text discussion in prior sections, many of the policy clashes that environmental policy has with trade policy point towards institutional questions. This is most importantly the case for the

---

[64] See note 60 above.

[65] Dunkel Draft, §§ S (Understanding on Rules and Procedures on Dispute Settlement) and T (Elements of an Integrated Dispute Settlement System).

[66] Free Trade Agreement, January 2, 1988, US–Canada, 27 ILM 293; HR Doc. No. 216, 100th Cong., 2nd Sess., 512 (1988).

[67] See Report of the GATT Panel, European Economic Community Restrictions on Imports of Dessert Apples, para. 12.1, GATT Doc. L/6491, June 22, 1989, *Basic Instruments and Selected Documents*, 36th Supplement, 93, 124. The Report states that: "The Panel . . . did not feel it was legally bound by all the details and legal reasoning of the 1980 Panel report." This is generally consistent with international law. See, e.g., Ian Brownlie, *Principles of Public International Law* (4th edn., 1990), 21.

dispute settlement processes of the GATT. It is in those processes that some of the interstitial decisions involving interpretation of current or future GATT/MTO treaties will be fought out. One example of that was the tuna/dolphin case, in which the panel itself noted that it would be inappropriate for the panel to make the requested interpretation of the GATT general exceptions of Article XX. It stated that such decisions should be made by the negotiators or the appropriate GATT bodies as a matter of treaty law alteration, rather than simply an interpretation of a panel.[68] In that sense, the tuna/dolphin case was praiseworthy, and in a broader sense should be praised even by the environmentalists who dislike the outcome. It suggests a certain amount of "judicial restraint." A contrary approach, with the panel seizing the issue and going forward with it, might in some future case be severely contrary to the interests of environmental policy.

Nevertheless, the environmentalists, apart from the question of precedent, have several legitimate complaints about the GATT dispute settlement procedures, among others. First, they note appropriately that the GATT lacks a certain amount of transparency. By that, we can understand that the GATT tends too often to try to operate in secrecy, attempting to avoid public and news media accounts of its actions. In recent years, this has become almost a charade, because many of the key documents, most importantly the early results of a GATT dispute settlement panel report, leak out almost immediately to the press. For purposes of gaining a broader constituency among the various policy interested communities in the world, gaining the trust of those constituencies, enhancing public understanding, as well as avoiding the "charade" of ineffective attempts to maintain secrecy, the GATT could go much further in providing for "transparency" of its process.

[68] General Agreement on Tariffs and Trade, Dispute Settlement Panel Report on United States Restrictions on Imports of Tuna, para. 6.3, 30 ILM 1594 at 1623 (1991) reads:

> The Panel further recalled its finding that the import restrictions examined in this dispute, imposed to respond to differences in environmental regulation of producers, could not be justified under the exceptions in Articles XX(b) or XX(g). These exceptions did not specify criteria limiting the range of life or health protection policies, or resource conservation policies, for the sake of which they could be invoked. It seemed evident to the Panel that, if the Contracting Parties were to permit import restrictions in response to differences in environmental policies under the General Agreement, they would need to impose limits on the range of policy differences justifying such responses and to develop criteria so as to prevent abuse. If the Contracting Parties were to decide to permit trade measures of this type in particular circumstances it would therefore be preferable for them to do so not by interpreting Article XX, but by amending or supplementing the provisions of the General Agreement or waiving obligations thereunder. Such an approach would enable the Contracting Parties to impose such limits and develop such criteria.

Secondly, there is criticism and concern that the GATT lacks the kind of expertise that would help it to make better decisions in dispute settlement processes. In particular, it is believed that the GATT lacks expertise in environmental issues. Again, there is considerable room for improvement in this regard, perhaps with procedures that would give panels certain technical assistance.

Finally, there is criticism of the GATT panel processes in that they (while operating in secret) fail to make provisions for the transmittal of arguments, information, and evidence from a variety of interested groups including nongovernment environmental policy groups. Once again, there should be ways that the GATT can improve on this problem.

Apart from the dispute settlement procedures, the overall institutional set-up of a GATT and a possible MTO could be likewise improved. In particular, transparency could be enhanced, perhaps by nongovernmental organizations (NGOs) as well as intergovernmental organizations (IGOs) gaining some share of participation in the GATT processes, possibly through an annual open meeting. Furthermore, as the GATT or MTO continue to evolve, procedures such as the already set-up TPRM might build in provisions for explicit attention to environmental concerns. It is clear that some of the GATT rules need to be changed. There are a variety of ways for them to be changed, some discussion on which is provided in Annex B.[69]

VIII.   Some conclusions

The discussions of this paper cover only the tip of the iceberg regarding the problematic relationship between world trade system policies and environmental policies. But in the light of those discussions, what can we say about the relationship of the two policy sets? Are they congruent or conflicting? The answer obviously is a bit of both.

In the broader long-term perspective there would seem to be a great deal of congruence. Some of that congruence derives from the economic and welfare enhancement of trade liberalization policies. Such welfare enhancement can in turn lead to enhancement of environmental policy objectives, as mentioned at the outset of this paper.

On the other hand, it is clear that the world trade policies and environmental policies do provide a certain amount of conflict. This conflict is not substantially different from a number of other areas where governmental policies have to accommodate the conflicting aims and goals of the policymakers and their constituents. Thus, to some degree it is a question of

[69] See Jackson, *World Trade and GATT*; and John H. Jackson, *Changing GATT Rules* (November 7, 1991) (appended as Annex B).

where the line will be drawn, or how the compromises will be made. In that sense, institutions obviously become very important because the decision-making process can tilt the decision results. If the world trade rules are pushed to their limit (for example, free trade with no exceptions for problems raised by environmental policies and actions affecting environments), clearly the trade rules will cause damage to environmental objectives. Likewise, if the environmental policies are pushed to their limit at the expense of the trading rules (so that governments will find it convenient and easy to set up a variety of restrictive trade measures, in some cases under the excuse of environmental policies), world trade will suffer.

Furthermore, there is no doubt that the "cultures" of the two policy communities (that of trade, and that of environment) differ in important ways. The trade policy experts have tended, over decades and perhaps centuries, to operate more under the practices of international diplomacy, which often means secrecy, negotiation, compromise, and to some extent behind the scenes catering to a variety of special economic interests. In addition, at the international level, because there is no overarching "sovereign leader," the processes are slow, faltering, and lend themselves to lowest common denominator results, or to diplomatic negotiations that agree to language without real agreement on substance.

On the other hand, the environmental policy groups, perhaps partly because they primarily operate on the national scene, have become used to using the processes of publicity and lobbying pressure on Congress or Parliaments, to which they have considerable access. There is, thus, a much broader sense of "participation" in the processes, which the international processes have not yet accommodated. Furthermore, the environmental policy groups, like many other groups working on the domestic level, have a sense of power achieved through successes in the legislative and public discussion processes. They feel somewhat frustrated with the international processes because those are sufficiently different to pose puzzling obstacles to the achievement of environmental goals.

This difference in culture is not inevitably permanent, and indeed the international processes need to accommodate more transparency and participation. This is true not only of the environmental case, but it is increasingly an important consideration for the broader way that international economic interdependence is managed. As more and more decisions that affect firms, citizens, and other groups, are made at the international level, it will be necessary for the international decision-making process to accommodate the goals of transparency, adequate expertise, and participation in the advocacy and rule making procedures.

To some extent, the rhetoric of some environmental policy advocates has been the rhetoric of antagonism to international organizations and procedures altogether. This, I suggest, is not constructive. The notion that the United States, for example, can or should impose unilaterally its environmental views and standards on other parts of the world, without any constraint from international rules or international dispute settlement procedures, is not likely to be a viable approach in the longer run. This means that in some cases when the United States submits (as it must, partly so as to get other countries reciprocally to submit) to international dispute settlement procedures, it will sometimes lose, and find itself obliged to alter its own domestic policy preferences. This has already been the case, and the United States has a mixed record of compliance with GATT rulings, although for a large powerful nation that record is not too bad.[70]

Apart from these longer run and institutional issues, there are matters that can be undertaken jointly by the trade and environmental policy communities, in the context of the GATT/MTO system. By way of reviewing some of the discussion in sections above, there seem to be two groups of actions that would be called for, the near-term, and the longer term.

Focusing first on the near-term actions, it seems feasible for the international trading system to accommodate some of the following actions or goals:

1. Greater transparency both in the rule making and in the dispute settlement procedures of the trading system is needed. This would call for more participation, greater opportunity for policy advocacy inputs, and for more openness in terms of publication of the relevant documents faster and in a way more accessible to interested parties.

---

[70] In a number of not too recent GATT panel cases that were brought by complaints against the United States, and in which the panel ruled that the US measures were inconsistent with GATT, the US subsequently revised its legislation or other measures in order to comply with the GATT panel report. See, e.g., Report of the GATT Panel, United States – Customs User Fee, GATT Doc. L/6264, February 2, 1988, *Basic Instruments and Selected Documents*, 35th Supplement, 245; United States Manufacturing Clause, GATT Doc. L/5609, May 5, 1984, *Basic Instruments and Selected Documents*, 31st Supplement, 74; Report of the GATT Panel, United States – Taxes on Petroleum and Certain Imported Substances, GATT Doc. L/6175, June 17, 1987, *Basic Instruments and Selected Documents*, 34th Supplement, 136; and Report of the GATT Panel, United States – Tax Legislation (DISC), GATT Doc. L/4422, November 12, 1976, *Basic Instruments and Selected Documents*, 23rd Supplement, 98. On the other hand, the United States has not complied with several other panel reports. In some cases, the United States has announced that it will accept the panel report and ultimately comply, but will wait until after the end of the Uruguay Round in case the Uruguay Round modifies the rule. See, e.g., Report of the GATT Panel, United States – Section 337 of the Tariff Act of 1930, GATT Doc. L/6439; Report of the Committee on Anti-Dumping Practices, GATT Doc. L/6609, *Basic Instruments and Selected Documents*, 36th Supplement, 435, 438 (addressing complaint of Sweden).

2. Greater access to participation in the processes is needed.
3. Some clarification is needed about the degree to which the international process will be allowed to intrude upon the scope of decision-making of national and subnational governments. For example, the "scope of review" of international GATT/MTO panels over national government regulatory decisions concerning the environment needs to be better defined. This is not an easy question, and it will not be solved quickly, but there probably needs to be some near-term accommodation through interpretive notes or otherwise in the Dunkel Draft texts, for example. Some of the NAFTA text's approach can be a useful example.
4. Finally, there will have to be some near-term rule accommodation by the GATT, by which I mean some adjustments or changes in those rules through one or another of the techniques for changing GATT rules (probably focusing on the waiver procedure) to establish a reasonably clear set of exceptions for certain multilateral environmental treaty provisions that call for trade action that would otherwise be inconsistent with the GATT/MTO rules.

Looking at the longer term, it is clear that there is a substantial agenda that must be addressed with regard to the intersection and potential clash of trade policies and environmental policies. The GATT/MTO system must develop mechanisms, including working parties and negotiations, to address these, and they will take time. The long-term agenda includes the following actions and goals.

1. The subsidies area will need substantial study and some kind of rule alteration to accommodate the respective interest.
2. Some type of more permanent exception will be needed either as an amendment or waiver embellishment of the Article XX exceptions of the GATT system, or possibly in the context of the national treatment rules. This can build upon the short-term rule alterations (for example, by waiver) mentioned above, with particular reference to the process-product characteristic question, so as to accommodate the broadly agreed international environmental policy provisions, such as those now contained in some treaties.
3. Undoubtedly the GATT/MTO dispute settlement procedure will continue to evolve, in the light of experience. Even if near-term provision is made for policy advocacy inputs from environmental policy experts, as time goes on and experience is obtained, there will need to be further adjustments in that procedure, possibly with some added limitations on the scope of the review of international panels over domestic national environmental provisions.

4. In particular, there needs to be some clarification about the rules and exceptions to accommodate national government unilateral imposition of environmentally justified rules that require or provide incentive for a higher standard of environmental protection than that for which the international community is able to develop a consensus.

It would be tragic if increased antagonism between the two policy groups occurred in such a way that the essential policy goals of both groups would be damaged unnecessarily. It is hoped that, with some of the clarifications of the policies outlined in this paper, combined with some of the institutional measures suggested, such antagonism can be largely avoided, or creatively channeled to promote a constructive accommodation of the discordant policy objectives.

22 Global economics and international economic law[*]

. . .

4.   Regulating cross-border economic activity

Earlier sections of this article noted the very broad range of subjects related to international economic law, and hinted at the problems facing governments who wish to regulate economic activity to achieve a wide variety of government objectives. Almost daily the news media suggest new or recurring problems of this type. The recent case of an airline merger involving Boeing and McDonnell-Douglas is an example of potential problems for nation-states attempting to regulate antitrust and competition policy.[1] Tainted foodstuff imports is another example.[2] The international "breakthrough" in early 1997 regarding a telecommunications international agreement is yet another example,[3] as is the banking crisis in Asia and various response attempts (often focusing on IMF activity).

In the financial services area, we also have to worry much more about problems of fiduciary relationships, prudential protection of consumers, and fraud, reminding us of the BCCI case. Other subjects include environment regulation, continuing work on agricultural trade, product standards, consumer protection in its broader ramifications, and securities regulation as we move into a twenty-four-hour market. If you begin to push the frontier of the subject, you have to think also of such things as labor regulations, labor standards, and even human rights.

---

[*] This chapter is based on John H. Jackson, "Global Economics and International Economic Law" (1998) 1 *Journal of International Economic Law* 1–23.
[1] See, e.g., Teresa Wyszomierski and Christopher Lingle, "Lessons of the Boeing Merger," *Journal of Commerce*, July 29, 1997 at 8.
[2] See, e.g., Stephanie Nall, "Meat Dispute Threatens to Spoil US–Europe Trade," *Journal of Commerce*, March 27, 1997 at 1; Stephanie Nall, "EU, US Sling Charges, Threats at One Another," *Journal of Commerce*, April 3, 1997 at 1.
[3] See, e.g., John Zarocostas, "US Urged to Back Telecom Accord," *Journal of Commerce*, February 14, 1997 at 1a.

Indeed, almost every conceivable area of economic activity which for one reason or another attracted governmental concern and often regulation, is now impacted by actual or potential international regulation of one kind or another. Thus we need to step back and ask what are the common elements of these many specific topics and often *ad hoc* government responses? The fundamental subject appears to be the question of the "regulation of economic behavior which crosses national borders." How should policy-makers (and scholars) approach this broad question? Are there some general principles of government regulatory activity which could be applied in most or all situations involving cross-border economic behavior? Can we develop some sort of general framework for policy analysis of this type? Here is a preliminary and tentative ("work in progress") attempt to do that.[4] These and many more questions can appropriately engage scholarly and policy-makers' attention for years to come.

Look first at a typical economic analysis of regulation.[5] Generally speaking market-oriented economists talk about avoiding governmental interference, except when there is something called "market failure."

As to market failure, the most familiar and the most commonly reiterated question in the economics literature are the problems of monopoly (competition policy); the problems of asymmetry of information (for instance, the consumer versus the expert sellers); and the problems of government distortions for a variety of reasons (and those get very, very troublesome because there are many different valid policy reasons why governments step in that do not have to do with the functioning of the market, and yet they cause distortions in the market). There is also the public goods problem, where the market cannot adequately give incentive for the creation of things that the public needs, because there is the opportunity for the whole public to use it, or capture it, i.e. to "free ride." This is a subject, of course, that is very close to intellectual property questions. And there are questions which are related to some of the others just mentioned, such as the question of distributive justice, or other alternative policies of governments.

One of the interesting features of this fairly traditional economic analysis is that it is almost always developed in the context of a single domestic economy. We must now ask: "What difference does it make that we are in the kind of international-linked world that we are in?" Look first at

---

[4] These thoughts are drawn partly from this author's following publications which may also interest the reader: John H. Jackson, *Hyman Soloway Lecture: The Uruguay Round, World Trade Organization, and the Problem of Regulating International Economic Behavior* (1995); John H. Jackson, "Reflections on Constitutional Changes to the Global Trading System" (1996) 70 *Chicago Kent Law Review* 511.

[5] See, e.g., Richard Lipsey, Paul Courant, Douglas Purvis, and Peter Steiner, *Microeconomics* (10th edn., 1993), especially Part 4.

monopoly, or competition policy. In some cases, you are really talking about a world economy; you are not talking about a national economy. That may change entirely your first judgment as to whether government intervention is necessary. For example, maybe there is a national monopoly, but, over time, borders have been thrown open to the product in such a way that the national monopoly really is no longer a market failure, because it has to struggle against the rest of the world. But, you can also see that the opposite conclusion is possible. It may be that things that do not look like they are a market failure domestically, when you look at or hypothesize a closed economy. However, when you move to the international system, because of various formal or informal linkages of various kinds, you may indeed find that there is market failure. And so, the international dimension of this creates the potential for different judgments on the question of whether we have the particular market failure or monopoly or competition policy questions.

Asymmetries of information is another case very ripe for difficulties enhanced by the international market. First of all, we have language differences worldwide, which makes it much harder for many persons to understand information. We have deep cultural differences where a "yes" means "no," a "no" means "maybe," and *vice versa*. We have a whole variety of factors: distance, different legal systems, the ability to enforce contracts in different ways, and so on. Thus, the asymmetries of information can give rise to many different conclusions, based on international activities.

Government distortions, of course, provide many possibilities. Are we beginning to face *international* government distortions? Are we beginning to face the regulations, for instance, of GATT, such as its textile system, as an illustration of how the international regulatory system begins to create distortions?

Public goods provide yet another set of market failure possibilities. There are many public goods in the worldwide *international* landscape. One is peace and security, peacekeeping in the United Nations for instance. Another is human rights. There are certain broader values than just economic market-oriented values. Thus again the international landscape would lead us to a conclusion that the market is not able to cope in the way that we think that it ought to.

Distributive justice suggests a variety of policies within the scope of a domestic market: progressive taxation, welfare, safety nets, a social market economy, etc. But, internationally, of course, we have this problem also: the developing countries argue for certain preferences. They argue for an international financial safety net, almost the equivalent of international bankruptcy.

So the next question is what should be the government response to market failure. In the economic literature, there are generally several kinds of responses that have been suggested – ways that governments can intervene. The government can tax. The government can subsidize. The government can regulate, create penalties for deviant behavior of various kinds. The government can try to alter various market incentives, such as by creating a system of permits, for instance, that are purchased or bid for, to allow certain environmental degradation under certain systems.

However, some of the governmental responses suggested in the event of national market failure cannot easily be used in a globalized situation. How is a government going to tax foreign people? Suppose a domestic government tries to regulate but a foreign government sees an opportunity to assist its own business participants by lax regulations, a so-called "race to the bottom" idea or "regulatory competition"? Thus many of the tools for government responses will not work in the same way in a globalized situation. And that forces us to consider the problems of regulatory competition, "race to the bottom," and downward harmonization, something that the environmentalists have warned about during the last few years. When one begins to analyze these situations, sometimes with the aid of game theory (particularly the so-called "prisoner's dilemma"),[6] one is pushed towards *international* cooperation as a necessary ingredient for handling these issues.

However, there are arguments for and against such internationalization. Governments may or may not be acting in the best interests of their society because of the distortions of governmental policy that are sometimes described by public choice theories. For example, a government leader wants to be reelected this autumn and therefore will not vote for a trade treaty. There is also a reverse side. An international institution can provide an additional buffer for national policy officials to make arguments in favor of the goals of an international institution. They can say that their nation is constrained by the international law and must obey these obligations.

However, there are risks in international cooperative activity or international "governance." Some of those risks are in the institutional details, such as the danger of decision rules like "consensus" that lead to the lowest common denominator approach that inhibits some countries from embracing higher standards concerning product safety or environmental considerations. There are situations where it is going to be very hard or impossible to achieve agreement because of the cultural differences and the economic diversities in the world. And we have to worry that some institu-

---

[6] Avinash K. Dixit and Barry J. Nalebuff, *Thinking Strategically* (1991).

tions can be abused, that when we yield "sovereignty" to some institutions, we could find that down the road (as has been alleged in some of the existing international organizations) there is corruption or misallocation of resources, or a distortion of the voting patterns.

Economists teach us that trade liberalization creates more goods or more welfare for everyone overall, but you cannot say that every particular person will be better off. There will be some winners and some losers. What do you do about the losers, particularly if they are disadvantaged? Who should bear adjustment costs? Beyond that, clearly there are goals that are not so oriented towards economics, such as keeping the peace, which is an important element of international relations theory and international economic theory.[7] So we have to construct the institutions that will follow or mediate among these and other goals such as human rights, crime abatement, drug traffic reduction, etc. These considerations thus pose various questions about whether the relevant international institutions are the appropriate place to resolve these issues.

Furthermore, even though globalization may affect a nation's decision as to "market failure" and the need for government intervention, that does not necessarily lead to the desirability of international intervention. It could be that the market failure consequences are confined to the domestic economy, even though they have been partly caused or influenced by globalization effects. Or, it could be that national government action could effectively "correct" the problem.

In a number of cases, the optimum approach could be some kind of international, or global, response, but the institution concerned may be weak, or so fraught with potential abuse that on a cost-benefit analysis you decide that you really cannot choose that institution for certain decisions. You may have to fall back on national governments for intervention, because of the dangers, or risks, of the international system. Sometimes the international system is so rigid because, for example, it is difficult to renegotiate a treaty that once a measure is in place it is virtually impossible to amend it. We have seen elements of that in the GATT, and maybe now in the WTO. When we look at international intervention, there are a series of different possibilities. There are also regional or unilateral possibilities, such as the nation-state acting through extraterritorial measures, or US section 301-type measures, of threatened sanctions or threatened retaliation.

Thus we must turn to the question of institution building, i.e. "constitution-making," at the international level. There are goals for the institutions that we might need and some of these goals are addressed, for example, in

---

[7] See Alan Sykes, "Comparative Advantage and the Normative Economics of International Trade Policy" (1998) 1 *Journal of International Economic Law* 25–48.

the WTO. It is not clear that the WTO is going to be able to succeed with respect to all these goals, however, but they deserve some thought.

One important goal is the concept of a rule-oriented system that provides the predictability and stability for the system for which many see a need for a variety of reasons, as we have already discussed.

However, there are other things to consider, such as whether an institutional structure recognizes and gives some deference to the real power configurations, so as to lead powerful governments to accept and implement the rules and decisions of the institution.

Other institutional goals include the participation of citizenry. We are clearly moving beyond elites in the conduct of international policy. The environmentalists again have begun to teach us about the necessity of having more open and more accessible procedures.[8]

In addition, there is the need for checks and balances. We have to be cautious about what we do institutionally and internationally in the regulatory area because we do not want the system to get out of hand. Often there is some confidence in national governments, and thus some worry about the delegation of "sovereignty." Perhaps there is a vestige of usefulness in the concept of "sovereignty" when it is used to express the concept of checks and balances against too much concentration of power in an international institution.

In Part 6 of this article, this analysis is built on and certain alternative institutional approaches to designing the "International Economic Constitution" explored.

5.   **Existing international economic institutions: the World Trade Organization and rule orientation**

The Bretton Woods conference of 1944 established the charters for the World Bank and the IMF. Participants at the 1944 conference recognized the need for a third institution for the subject of international trade, although they did not feel able at Bretton Woods to undertake a draft of that institution, partly because that conference was oriented towards monetary problems and was convened by and for the monetary authorities of the participating states rather than the trade authorities. Consequently one of the first tasks of the new United Nations and its Economic and Social Council (ECOSOC) in 1946 was to launch preparations for an International Trade Organization (ITO). But, as is well known, the ITO Charter (of Havana 1948) never came into force, because the United States Congress

---

[8] See, e.g., Daniel C. Esty, "Non-Governmental Organizations at the World Trade Organization: Cooperation, Competition, or Exclusion" (1998) 1 *Journal of International Economic Law* 123–148.

would not approve it.[9] Instead, the GATT, which for reasons partly relating to the constitutional structure of the US[10] had come into "provisional force," filled the gap left by the ITO failure, and became *de facto* the major trade treaty and institution for international trade relations and diplomacy. Despite this uneasy history and the "birth defects" of the GATT,[11] these institutions played a remarkably successful role for almost fifty years. Yet during the eighth major trade negotiating round of the GATT, it became apparent that a new institutional structure would be necessary, and thus the WTO was born, coming into effect on January 1, 1995.[12] In the short span of its new life, the WTO appears to be the prodigal child of the international trading system, already achieving a membership of more than 130 countries (with over 30 more negotiating for membership)[13] and over 105 dispute settlement procedures initiated under the new WTO rules for those procedures.

Significantly, it now seems clear that the WTO represents a further enhancement (compared to the GATT whose evolution was in this direction anyway)[14] in the direction of rule orientation. This is particularly demonstrated by the new WTO dispute settlement procedures.[15]

The full implications of the Uruguay Round (Uruguay Round) Agreement and its new institutions are undoubtedly not fully understood yet by any government which has accepted them. In the US during 1994 there was considerable discussion about the impact of the Uruguay Round treaty and the WTO on "US sovereignty."[16] While the term "sovereignty" has been much criticized as out of date and archaic, nevertheless, some of the issues in

---

[9] Susan A. Aaronson, *Trade and the American Dream: A Social History of Postwar Trade Policy* (1996).

[10] John H. Jackson, "The General Agreement on Tariffs and Trade in United States Domestic Law" (1967) 66 *Michigan Law Review* 249; see generally, John H. Jackson, *World Trade and the Law of GATT* (1969); and John H. Jackson, William Davey and Alan O. Sykes, *International Economic Relations* (3rd edn., 1995).

[11] John H. Jackson, "The Uruguay Round and the Launch of the WTO – Significance and Challenges" in Terence P. Stewart (ed.), *The World Trade Organization: The Multilateral Trade Framework for the 21st Century in the US Implementing Legislation* (American Bar Association, Section of International Law and Practice, 1996), chapter 1.

[12] Final Act Embodying the Results of the Uruguay Round of Multilateral Trade Negotiations, opened for signature April 15, 1994, Marrakesh, Morocco, 33 ILM 1140–1272 (1994). See also HR Doc. No. 316, 103rd Cong., 2nd Sess. (1994).

[13] See WTO website at http://www.unicc.org/wto. As of October 22, 1997, the WTO lists 132 members. Its "State of Play" document on disputes lists 105 disputes.

[14] John H. Jackson, *The WTO Constitution and Jurisprudence* (1998), see especially section 4.2 on "The GATT Dispute Settlement Procedure and its Evolution."

[15] These are principally set forth in the Dispute Settlement Understanding (DSU), which is Annex 2 to the WTO Charter in the Final Act of the Uruguay Round (note 12 above).

[16] John H. Jackson, "The Great 1994 Sovereignty Debate: United States Acceptance and Implementation of the Uruguay Round Results" in Jonathan Charney, Donald K. Anton, and Mary Ellen O'Connell (eds.), Essays in Honor of Louis Henkin (1998); also published in (1997) 36 *Columbia Journal of Transnational Law* 157–188.

this "great debate" are vital and contemporary. To a great extent these issues concern "allocation of power" as between a nation-state and an international regulatory system. To name a few examples, there are questions whether a product safety standard should be controlled by an international body, or a nation-state government, or even by subfederal government units. There are also questions about how to apply certain well-established international policies such as "most favored nation" treatment (nondiscrimination as between different nations) or "national treatment" (nondiscrimination as between domestic products or services and imported products or services). In addition there are questions about whether disputes about these and other issues should be resolved by an international body or not. In fact, a close analysis of sovereignty turns out to be very complex, and the subject can be "decomposed" into dozens of more specific issues.

Clearly acceptance of any treaty in some sense reduces the freedom of scope of national government actions. At the very least, certain types of actions inconsistent with the treaty norms would give rise to an international law obligation, and the amount of constraint might then vary with the institutional mechanisms for enforcement, but also with the national domestic government structure or political attitude towards international norms. Some skeptics might dismiss an international norm as ineffective and thus not constraining. But if a treaty norm were "self-executing" or "directly applicable" in a domestic legal system, it could have a greater constraining effect. Even without those effects, a treaty can have important domestic legal effects, such as influencing how domestic courts interpret domestic legislation. Beyond that, a treaty norm even without domestic legal effect can have weight in some domestic policy debates where some advocates will stress that positions contrary to their views would raise "serious international or treaty concerns." Thus the "sovereignty objection" can be seen to be directed more to the questions where a decision should be made, and what influences on that decision should be permitted.

Related both to the "sovereignty" question and to the promise of greater "rule orientation," the new dispute settlement procedures (and now practice and developing jurisprudence) seem demonstrably tilted towards rule orientation. Indeed speeches by international and national leaders indicate this and point to it with pride and satisfaction. Although the text of the DSU has clauses that arguably go both ways, if you read the DSU carefully and inventory the clauses that are relevant, you can easily come to the conclusion that the DSU opts for the rule-oriented procedure.[17]

---

[17] See, e.g., DSU Article 3(2), which in part reads: "The dispute settlement system of the WTO is a central element in providing security and predictability to the multilateral trading system." See also the speech of King Hassan II for the host government of the April 1994 Marrakesh ministerial meeting to conclude the Uruguay Round, where he said: "By

The issue of a nation-state's participation in an international dispute settlement procedure poses sovereignty questions of a different sort from those of institutional structure. If a nation has consented to a treaty and the norms it contains, why should it object to an external process which could rule on the consistency of that nation's actions with the treaty norms? It might be argued that such objections manifest a lack of intent to follow the norms, sort of accepting the treaty with fingers crossed behind the back. Indeed, there may be some elements of this thinking in this context. However, it could also be suggested that a nervousness about international dispute procedures reflects a government's desire to have some flexibility to resist future strict conformity to norms in certain special circumstances, particularly circumstances that could pose great danger to the essential national objectives. This is a sort of an "escape clause" idea, where a nation could accept norms with sincere intent to follow them except in the most severe and egregious cases of danger to the nation or to its political system. (Candidly though, it may also be noted that danger to the political fortunes of the ruling party in such a nation may take on great weight in these considerations.)

Apart from these "escape clause" notions, however, there is an institutional concern that the dispute procedures may not be objective, may be subject to procedural irregularities, may be overreaching, or may have other important defects that even other nations would recognize, but which are not redressed by the treaty or its institutional structure. This danger, either at the outset or developing at some later time, could legitimately constrain a nation's willingness to enter into stringent commitments to a dispute settlement procedure.

The major change in the DSU is the elimination of "blocking" when the Dispute Settlement Body (DSB) considers the report. Since the report is deemed adopted unless there is a "consensus" against adoption (the "reverse consensus") and since the "winning party" could always object, the adoption is considered to be virtually automatic. The *quid pro quo* for this automaticity, however, is the appeal which is now for the first time allowed. If an appeal is taken, then the report is not "adopted"; instead an appellate division of three individuals drawn from a permanent roster of seven individuals (with renewable four-year staggered terms)[18] considers the first-level report, receives arguments from the parties, and writes its own report. This report is also sent to the DSB where the same "reverse consensus" rule applies to adoption, again making it virtually certain to be

bringing into being the World Trade Organization today, we are enshrining the rule of law in international economic and trade relations, thus setting universal rules and disciplines over the temptations of unilateralism and the law of the jungle."

[18] DSU Article 17.

adopted. It is this "automaticity" that scares some diplomats and critics of the WTO system, although in many other international tribunals "automaticity" in the sense of no opportunity to block a report also exists.

How does all this fit the "sovereignty objections"? Again, it is abundantly clear that "sovereignty" is not a unitary concept, but rather a series of particular considerations centered around the problem of allocation of power. Thus when objection is made to the US accepting the WTO because of the WTO dispute settlement procedures, the specific ("decomposed") issues of that objection are substantially different from those regarding the problem of treaty norm application, or the institutional structure of decision-making. In addition, the sovereignty objection really could be a series of specific objections about the nature or details of the dispute procedure. These in turn must be considered in the aggregate (unless there were options which allowed a nation to accept some details but not others), and that aggregate weighed against the policy advantages of belonging. "Sovereignty" thus is not a magical wand that one waives to ward off any "entanglement" in the international system, but is rather a policy-weighing process.

6.   Future policy and future scholarship

Where may all this discussion lead? Obviously the previous sections suggest many implications for future directions of the international institutions. While the explicit focus has been on the new WTO, many of the matters discussed can and often should apply to other international economic regulatory and institutional entities and subject matter, whether monetary organizations or environmental treaties, or numerous other contexts. And these matters obviously have implications for policy and scholarly attention.

To attempt a complete inventory or a complete landscape of the potential directions and problems for the future would be folly, besides being inappropriate or unfeasible for this article. But a number of further matters can be mentioned for both policy consideration and scholarly attention. Among these would be attention to subjects logically building on the analysis developed in previous sections. One can, for example, mention some of the institutional questions and alternative possibilities needing exploration, partly summarizing matters discussed earlier in this article.

Assuming for the moment that a policy analysis of the various questions raised about appropriateness and difficulty of governmental market intervention suggests the necessity of taking international action or establishing some form of international cooperation, then it becomes necessary to explore a series of questions relating to the modalities of such international action or cooperation, including the possibility of designing institutions for that purpose.[19]

Clearly there are a number of different ways to approach the question of international effects on national markets. We can roughly inventory them under the subtopics of "unilateral," "bilateral," "regional," and "multilateral." Running through all of these levels ("vertical analysis") are several general questions, such as the following:

1. Should cooperative approaches be basically voluntary, or should they be binding (under international law)? If binding, should there be sanctions?
2. Should the emphasis on cooperation be procedural, or relate more substantively to the rules being applied?
3. With respect to substantive rules, should the approach be that of national treatment (nondiscrimination between domestic and imported goods), most favored nation (nondiscrimination among imported goods and exporting countries), or should there be some sort of minimum standards as the basis of a rule to apply?

In addition, one can explore several different "principles of managing interdependence" that would influence the techniques of cooperation:

1. Harmonization, a system that gradually induces nations towards uniform approaches to a variety of economic regulations and structures. An example would be standardization of certain product specifications. Another example would be uniformity of procedures for applying countervailing duties or escape clause measures.
2. Reciprocity, a system of continuous "trades" or "swaps" of measures to liberalize (or restrict) trade. The GATT negotiations are in this mold.
3. Interface, which recognizes that different economic systems will always exist in the world and tries to create the institutional means to ameliorate international tensions caused by those differences, perhaps through buffering or escape clause mechanisms.

Obviously a mixture of all these techniques is the most likely to be acceptable, but that still leaves open the question of what is the appropriate mixture. For example, how much should the "trade constitution" pressure nations to conform to some uniform "harmonized" approaches, or is it better simply to establish buffering mechanisms that allow nations to preserve diversity but try to avoid situations where one nation imposes burdens (economic or political) on other nations?

---

[19] See John H. Jackson, "Alternative Approaches for Implementing Competition Rules in International Economic Relations" (1994) *Aussenwirtschaft – Swiss Review of International Economic Relations* 225.

Closely connected to this previous point is an issue that may be loosely characterized as being similar to "federalism." This is the issue of the appropriate allocation of decision-making authority at different levels of government which are discussed in Part 4.

In order to regulate international economies today, there is a very high probability that the international community will turn towards the formation and designing of a treaty-based multilateral institution which could enable it appropriately and efficiently to respond to the problems of such regulation. Thus it is particularly important to begin thinking about some of the key questions that should be considered in designing international institutions. A series of "lawyer-type questions" then emerge, such as:

1. questions of rule-making at the international level, and whether procedures adequately consider some of the scientific and moral concerns involved in the subjects that are linked to trade;
2. questions of international dispute settlement procedures and to what extent they adequately consider opposing policy goals, or provide for appropriate advocacy from interested authorities and citizen groups;
3. questions of whether the international procedures incorporate adequate democratic processes including transparency, and right to be heard;
4. questions of the relation of international rules to domestic constitutional and other laws;
5. questions about the operation and procedures of national constitutional bodies and how these promote or inhibit international cooperation;
6. questions about the activity of interest groups, both those broadly oriented and those more oriented to specific interests or single issues, and how this activity relates to international institutions and procedures; and
7. questions concerning the problems of regulatory competition: governments seeking lower standards of regulation in order to attract economic activity to their societies (the "race to the bottom," or "race to the top," or in the US the "Delaware Corporation" problem).

These questions, which have perhaps become most apparent in the context of environment and competition policy, also relate to a long list of other potential policy areas that can cause clashes with international trade and other international economic policy goals. Such policy areas could certainly include:

- labor standards;
- commodity agreements and regulation;
- product standards (food, pharmaceutical, safety of goods etc.);

- insurance;
- banking and fiduciary institutions;
- investment protection;
- securities regulation and institutions;
- government procurement procedures and preferences;
- shipping and transport (including air transport);
- intellectual property protection and regulation; and
- taxation.

To close, the reader can probably see that the reflections in this article are consistent with ideas of a "pragmatist school" of international law scholarship.[20] The phrase "normative realist" has also been used, suggesting that scholars should feel some responsibility for moving the subject forward despite the difficulty and limitation of resources, and despite the sometimes pessimistic view point that mere "realism" can engender.

Let us hope that this will be the case, and take comfort in the observable fact that many fine scholars, young and older, are now embarked on some of these endeavors as well as other endeavors reflecting other appropriate priorities, as a burgeoning literature relevant to the subject of this article bears witness. There is reason to be optimistic that the combination of such scholarship and sensible policy-maker attention to it, will assist in repeating and continuing the relative success of the achievements of international economic institutions during the last fifty years.

[20] See, e.g., David Kennedy, "The International Style in Postwar Law and Policy: John Jackson and the Field of International Economic Law" (1995) 10 *American University Journal of International Policy* 671.

Select bibliography of the author's works

BOOKS

John H. Jackson, *World Trade and the Law of GATT* (1969) (Korean translation published in 1988)

John H. Jackson and Lee Bollinger, *Contract Law in Modern Society: Cases and Materials on Law of Contracts, Sales and Legal Methodology* (1973; 2nd edn., 1980)

John H. Jackson, Jean-Victor Louis, and Mitsuo Matsushita, *Implementing the Tokyo Round: National Constitutions and International Economic Rules* (1984)

John H. Jackson, Richard O. Cunningham, and Claude G. B. Fontheim, *International Trade Policy: The Lawyer's Perspective* (1985)

John H. Jackson, *International Competition in Services: A Constitutional Framework* (1988)

John H. Jackson and Edwin A. Vermulst, *Antidumping Law and Practice: A Comparative Study* (1989)

John H. Jackson, *Restructuring the GATT System* (1990) (Japanese translation published in 1990)

John H. Jackson, William J. Davey, and Alan O. Sykes Jr., *Legal Problems of International Economic Relations: Cases, Materials and Text on the National and International Regulation of Transnational Economic Relations* (1977; 2nd edn., 1986; 3rd edn., 1995)

John H. Jackson, *The World Trading System: Law and Policy of International Economic Relations* (1989; 2nd edn., 1997)

John H. Jackson and Alan O. Sykes Jr., *Implementing the Uruguay Round* (1997)

John H. Jackson, *The World Trade Organization: Constitution and Jurisprudence* (1998)

ARTICLES IN JOURNALS

John Jackson, "Eminent Domain – Procedure – Relation of Judge and Jury in Michigan Condemnation Proceedings" (1959) 58 *Michigan Law Review* 248

David W. Louisell and John H. Jackson, "Religion, Theology, and Public Higher Education" (1962) 50 *California Law Review* 751

John H. Jackson, "The Legal Framework of United Nations Financing: Peacekeeping and Penury" (1963) 51 *California Law Review* 751

John H. Jackson, "The Puzzle of GATT: Legal Aspects of a Surprising Institution" (1967) 1 *Journal of World Trade Law* 131

John H. Jackson, "The General Agreement on Tariffs and Trade in United States Domestic Law" (1967) 66 *Michigan Law Review* 249

John H. Jackson, "Notes and Comments: The New Economic Policy and United States International Obligations" (1972) 66 *American Journal of International Law* 110

John H. Jackson, "The Crumbling Institutions of the Liberal Trade System" (1978) 12 *Journal of World Trade Law* 93; also published at (1978) 22 *Law Quadrangle Notes* 14 (University of Michigan Law School)

John H. Jackson, "The Jurisprudence of International Trade: The DISC Case in GATT" (1978) 72 *American Journal of International Law* 747

John H. Jackson, "Governmental Disputes in International Trade Relations: A Proposal in the Context of GATT" (1979) 13 *Journal of World Trade Law* 1

John H. Jackson, "United States–EEC Trade Relations: Constitutional Problems of Economic Interdependence" (1979) 16 *Common Market Law Review* 453

John H. Jackson, "International Economic Problems and Their Management in the 21st Century" (1979) 9 *Georgia Journal of International and Comparative Law* 497

John H. Jackson, "The Birth of the GATT–MTN System: A Constitutional Appraisal" (1980) 12 *Law and Policy of International Business* 21

John H. Jackson, Jean-Victor Louis, and Mitsuo Matsushita, "Implementing the Tokyo Round: Legal Aspects of Changing Economic Rules" (1982) 81 *Michigan Law Review* 267 (preliminary version of the book published in 1984)

John H. Jackson, "Equality and Discrimination in International Economic Law (XI): The General Agreement on Tariffs and Trade" (1983) 37 *Yearbook of World Affairs* 224

John H. Jackson, "Perspectives on the Jurisprudence of International Trade: Costs and Benefits of Legal Procedures in the United States" (1984) 82 *Michigan Law Review* 1570 (preliminary version published at (1984) 74 *American Economic Review* 277; reprinted as "Pros and Cons of a Legalistic Trade System" (1985) 49 *Economic Impact* 53)

John H. Jackson, "Constructing a Constitution for Trade in Services" (1988) 11 *World Economy* 187

John H. Jackson, "Consistency of Export-Restraint Arrangements with the GATT" (1988) 11 *World Economy* 485

John H. Jackson, "National Treatment Obligations and Non-Tariff Barriers" (1989) 10 *Michigan Journal of International Law* 207

John H. Jackson, "State Trading and Nonmarket Economics" (1989) 23 *International Law* 89

John H. Jackson, "Perspectives on Countervailing Duties" (1990) 21 *Law and Policy of International Business* 739

John H. Jackson, "Status of Treaties in Domestic Legal Systems: A Policy Analysis" (1992) 86 *American Journal of International Law* 310

John H. Jackson, "Dolphins and Hormones: GATT and the Legal Environment for International Trade after the Uruguay Round" (1992) 14 *University of Arkansas at Little Rock Law Journal* 429

John H. Jackson, "GATT and the Future of International Trade Institutions" (1992) 18 *Brooklyn Journal of International Law* 11 (also published at (1992) 4

Michigan International Law Journal, Fall, 6)

John H. Jackson and William J. Davey, "Reform of the Administrative Procedures Used in US Antidumping and Countervailing Duty Cases" (1992) 6 *Administrative Law Journal of the American University* 399

John H. Jackson, "World Trade Rules and Environmental Policies: Congruence or Conflict?" (1992) 49 *Washington and Lee Law Review* 1227 (a shorter version was later published at (1993) 36 *Law Quadrangle Notes* 35 (University of Michigan Law School))

John H. Jackson, "Regional Trade Blocs and GATT" (1993) 16 *World Economy* 121

John H. Jackson, "Alternative Approaches for Implementing Competition Rules In International Economic Relations" (1994) 49 *Aussenwirtschaft – Swiss Review of International Economic Relations* 177

John H. Jackson, "The World Trade Organization: Watershed Innovation or Cautious Small Step Forward?" (1995) 18 *World Economy* 11

John H. Jackson, "International Economic Law: Reflections on the 'Boilerroom' of International Relations" (1995) 10 *American University Journal of International Law and Policy* 595

John H. Jackson and Steven P. Croley, "WTO Dispute Procedures, Standard of Review, and Deference to National Governments" (1996) 90 *American Journal of International Law* 193

John H. Jackson, "Reflections on International Economic Law" (1996) 17 *University of Pennsylvania Journal of International Economic Law* 17

John H. Jackson, "Reflections on Constitutional Changes to the Global Trading System" (1996) 72 *Chicago Kent Law Review* 511

John H. Jackson, "Los Procedimientos de Solucion de Diferencias en la OMC" (1996) 1 *Revista de Derecho Internacional Economico*, No. 2

John H. Jackson, "The World Trade Organization and the 'Sovereignty' Question" (1996) *Legal Issues of European Integration* 179 (law review of the Europa Instituut)

John H. Jackson, "Editorial Comment: The WTO Dispute Settlement Understanding – Misunderstandings on the Nature of Legal Obligation" (1997) 91 *American Journal of International Law* 60

John H. Jackson, "The Great 1994 Sovereignty Debate: United States Acceptance and Implementation of the Uruguay Round Results" (1997) 36 *Columbia Journal of Transnational Law* 157

John H. Jackson, "Global Economics and International Economic Law" (1998) 1 *Journal of International Economic Law* 1

John H. Jackson, "Dispute Settlement and the WTO: Emerging Problems" (1998) 1 *Journal of International Economic Law* 329

John H. Jackson and M. Bronckers, "Editorial Comment: Outside Counsel in WTO Dispute Processes" (1999) 2 *Journal of International Economic Law* 155

CHAPTERS IN BOOKS

John H. Jackson, "The General Agreement on Tariffs and Trade" in Walter S. Surrey and Don Wallace Jr. (eds.), *A Lawyer's Guide to International Business Transactions* (2nd edn., 1977), Part I, 41

John H. Jackson, "United States Policy Regarding Disruptive Imports from State Trading Countries or Government Owned Enterprises" in Don Wallace Jr. *et al.* (eds.), *Interface One* (1980), 1

John H. Jackson, "GATT Machinery and the Tokyo Round Agreements" in W. R. Cline (ed.), *Trade Policy in the 1980s* (1983), 159

John H. Jackson, "Multilateral and Bilateral Negotiating Approaches for the Conduct of US Trade Policies" in Robert M. Stern (ed.), *US Trade Policies in a Changing World Economy* (1987), 377

John H. Jackson, "Role of Supervisory Mechanisms in the Restructuring of the International Economic Order: Some Reflections" in P. van Dijk *et al.* (eds.), *Restructuring The International Economic Order: The Role of Law and Lawyers* (1987), 163

John H. Jackson, "United States" in Francis G. Jacobs and Shelley Roberts (eds.), *The Effect of Treaties in Domestic Law* (1987), 141

John H. Jackson, "Strengthening the International Legal Framework of the GATT–MTN System: Reform Proposals for the New GATT Round" in Ernst-Ulrich Petersmann and Meinhard Hilf (eds.), *The GATT Round of New Multilateral Trade Negotiations: Legal and Economic Problems* (1988; 2nd edn., 1991), 3

John H. Jackson, "Reflections on Restructuring the GATT" in Jeffrey J. Schott (ed.), *Completing the Uruguay Round: A Results-Oriented Approach to the GATT Trade Negotiations* (1990), 205

John H. Jackson, "Reflections on Restructuring the GATT" in Thomas Oppermann and Josef Molsberger (eds.), *A New GATT for the Nineties and Europe '92* (1991), 141

John H. Jackson, "The European Community and World Trade: The Commercial Policy Dimension" in William J. Adams (ed.), *Singular Europe: Economy and Polity of the European Community After 1992* (1992), 321

John H. Jackson, "US Constitutional Law Principles and Foreign Trade Law and Policy" in Meinhard Hilf and Ernst-Ulrich Petersmann (eds.), *National Constitutions and International Economic Law* (1993), 65

John H. Jackson, "National Constitutions, Transnational Economic Policy and International Law: Some Summary Reflections" in Meinhard Hilf and Ernst-Ulrich Petersmann (eds.), *National Constitutions and International Economic Law* (1993), 569

John H. Jackson, "World Trade Rules and Environmental Policies: Congruence or Conflict?" in Durwood Zaelke *et al.* (eds.), *Trade and the Environment: Law, Economics, and Policy* (1993), 219

John H. Jackson, "The Uruguay Round and the WTO: New Opportunities for the Bretton Woods System" in *Bretton Woods: Looking to the Future* (Bretton Woods Commission, 1994), C-219

John H. Jackson, "Managing the Trading System: The World Trade Organization and the Post-Uruguay Round GATT Agenda" in Peter B. Kenen (ed.), *Managing the World Economy: Fifty Years After Bretton Woods* (1994), 131

John H. Jackson, "Restructuring the GATT System" in Murray G. Smith and Debra P. Steger (eds.), *Trade Policy in the 1990s* (1994), 21

John H. Jackson, "The Legal Meaning of a GATT Dispute Settlement Report:

Some Reflections" in Niels Blokker and Sam Muller (eds.), *Towards More Effective Supervision by International Organizations: Essays in Honour of Henry G. Schermers* (1994), vol. I, 149

John H. Jackson, "Greening the GATT: Trade Rules and Environmental Policy" in James Cameron *et al.* (eds.), *Trade and the Environment: The Search for Balance* (1994), 39

John H. Jackson, "The World Trade Organization, Dispute Settlement, and Codes of Conduct" in Susan M. Collins and Barry P. Bosworth (eds.), *The New GATT: Implications for the United States* (1994), 63

John H. Jackson, "Dispute Settlement Procedures" in Organization for Economic Cooperation and Development (ed.), *The New World Trading System: Readings* (1995), 117

John H. Jackson, "From GATT to the World Trade Organization: Implications for the World Trading System" in Thomas Cottier (ed.), *GATT – Uruguay Round* (1995), 29

John H. Jackson, "Economic Law, International" in R. Bernhardt (ed.), *Encyclopedia of Public International Law* (1995), vol. 2, 20

John H. Jackson, "The WTO Dispute Settlement Procedures – A Preliminary Appraisal" in Jeffrey J. Schott (ed.), *The World Trading System: Challenges Ahead* (1996), 153

John H. Jackson, "Regulating International Economic Behavior – The WTO and the Challenge of Constructing Institutions to Manage Global Interdependence" in Ulrich Immenga *et al.* (eds.), *Festschrift für Ernst-Joachm Mestmacker* (1996), 611

John H. Jackson, "The Uruguay Round and the Launch of the WTO – Significance and Challenges" in Terence P. Stewart (ed.), *The World Trade Organization: The Multilateral Trade Framework for the 21st Century and US Implementing Legislation* (1996), 5

John H. Jackson, "International Legal Perspectives on Japan–North American Economic Frictions: Reflections on Problems of International Economic Relations" in Michael K. Young and Yuji Iwasawa (eds.), *Trilateral Perspectives on International Legal Issues: Relevance of Domestic Law and Policy* (1996), 263

John H. Jackson, "Regulating International Economic Behavior – Reflections on the Broader Setting of International Financial Markets and Institutions" in Joseph J. Norton and Mads Andenas (eds.), *Emerging Financial Markets and the Role of International Financial Organizations* (1996), 3

John H. Jackson, "Designing and Implementing Effective Dispute Settlement Procedures: WTO Dispute Settlement, Appraisal and Prospects" in Anne O. Krueger (ed.), *The WTO as an International Organization* (1998), 161

John H. Jackson, "The WTO Dispute Settlement Procedure: A Brief Overview" in *Proceedings of the ASIL/NVIR Fourth Hague Joint Conference – Contemporary International Law Issues: New Forms, New Applications* (1998), 384

John H. Jackson, "The WTO Dispute Settlement Understanding – Misunderstandings on the Nature of Legal Obligation" in James Cameron and Karen Campbell (eds.), *Dispute Resolution in the WTO* (1998), 69

John H. Jackson, "The Uruguay Round Results and National Sovereignty" in Jagdish Bhagwati and Mathias Hirsh (eds.), *The Uruguay Round and Beyond: Essays in Honor of Arthur Dunkel* (1998), 293

John H. Jackson, "Constituent Representation: Exploring the Context of the Key Policy Questions, Some Preliminary Observations" in Alan V. Deardorff and Robert M. Stern (eds.), *Constituent Interests and US Trade Policies* (1998), 311

John H. Jackson, "The Great 1994 Sovereignty Debate: United States Acceptance and Implementation of the Uruguay Round Results" in Jonathan I. Charney *et al.* (eds.), *Politics, Values and Functions: International Law in the 21st Century – Essays in Honor of Professor Louis Henkin* (1998), 149

SELECTED SHORTER ARTICLES, SPEECHES, AND MISCELLANEOUS WORKS

John H. Jackson, "Using the Computer for Simple Manipulations of Data and Information: A Suggested Program, Modern Uses of Logic in Law" (September 1964), 61

John H. Jackson, "Retrieval of International Legal Materials" (1964) 58 *American Journal of International Law* 980

John H. Jackson, "Book Review of Jurimetrics by Hans W. Baade" (1964) 52 *California Law Review* 441

John H. Jackson, "GATT as an Instrument for the Settlement of Trade Disputes" in *Proceedings of the American Society of International Law* (1967), 144

John H. Jackson, "Book Review of the Kennedy Round in American Trade Policy – The Twilight of the GATT by John W. Evans" (1972) 11 *Journal of Common Market Studies* 68

John H. Jackson, "The Trade Reform Act (Speech)" (1973) 6 *Case Western Reserve Journal of International Law* 107

John H. Jackson, "The Need for Negotiated Reforms (Speech)" (1975) 24 *American University Law Review* 1154 ("A symposium on Primary Resource Scarcity Effects on Trade and Investment")

John H. Jackson, "Comment, Colloquium on the Legal Aspects of a Projected New Economic Order" (1977) 24 *Netherlands International Law Review* 534

John H. Jackson and William J. Davey, 1978–1994 *Annual Memoranda for Teachers with Suggestions for Supplementary Materials to Accompany Legal Problems of International Economic Relations* (2nd edn., West Publishing Co., 1986)

John H. Jackson, "How is US Economic Policy Made?" (1978) 30 *Horizons USA* 54 (published by the International Communication Agency, Washington, DC)

John H. Jackson, "International Economic Policy and the US Constitution" (1978) 116 *Topic* 29 (published by the International Communication Agency, Washington, DC)

John H. Jackson, "The Constitutional Problems of the International Economic System and the Multilateral Trade Negotiation Results" in *Proceedings of the Annual Meeting of the American Society of International Law* (1979), 56 (also published in (1979) 24 *Law Quadrangle Notes*, Fall, 25 (University of Michigan Law School))

John H. Jackson, "Introduction: Perspectives on Anti-dumping Law and Policy" (1979) 1 *Michigan Yearbook of International Legal Studies* 1

John H. Jackson, "MTN and the Legal Institutions of International Trade, a report prepared at the request of the Subcommittee on International Trade, for the use of the Committee on Finance," United States Senate, 96th Congress, 1st Session (Committee Print, June 1979)

John H. Jackson, "Transnational Enterprises and International Codes of Conduct: Introductory Remarks for Experts" (1981) 25 *Law Quadrangle Notes*, Winter, 19 (University of Michigan Law School)

John H. Jackson, "International Legal Framework for Trade" in Nancy E. Eastam and Boris Krivy (eds.), *The Cambridge Lectures* 1981 (1982), 403

John H. Jackson, "Book Review of Taxing Unfair International Trade Practices by Greyson Bryan" (1982) 76 *American Journal of International Law* 435

John H. Jackson, "Book Review of International Trade Regulation: GATT, the United States and the European Communities by Edmund McGovern" (1983) 20 *Common Market Law Review* 622

John H. Jackson, "State Aid and Antidumping and Countervailing Duties (Panel Discussion)" in *Annual Proceedings of the Fordham Corporate Law Institute*: *Antitrust and Trade Policies of the European Economic Community* (1983), 29 and 136

John H. Jackson, "International Law" in *The Guide to American Law*: *Everyone's Legal Encyclopedia* (1983), 247

John H. Jackson, "Dispute Settlement Techniques Between Nations Concerning Economic Relations – With Special Emphasis on GATT" in T. E. Carbonneau (ed.), *Resolving Transnational Disputes Through International Arbitration* (Sixth Sokol Colloquium, 1984), 39

John H. Jackson, "Book Review of Protectionism and the European Community edited by E. L. M. Volker" (1984) 78 *American Journal of International Law* 993

John H. Jackson, "The Changing International Law Framework for Exports: The General Agreement on Tariffs and Trade" (1984) 14 *Georgia Journal of International and Comparative Law* 505

John H. Jackson, Testimony Before the Finance Committee of the United States Senate, November 21, 1985 (published as "Import Practices: Are They Really Unfair?" (1986) 30 *Law Quadrangle Notes*, Winter, 26 (University of Michigan Law School); also published as "Achieving a Balance in International Trade" (1986) 14 *International Business Lawyer*, April, 123)

John H. Jackson, "Comments on Institutional Arrangements for Managing the Canada/US Economic Relationship by John M. Curtis" in Deborah Fretz *et al.* (eds.), *Canada/United States Trade and Investment Issues* (Ontario Economic Council, Toronto, 1985), 158

John H. Jackson, "Book Review of Basic Documents on International Trade Law edited by Chia-Jui Cheng" (1987) 81 *American Journal of International Law* 570

John H. Jackson, "GATT and Recent International Trade Problems" (1987) 11 *Maryland Journal of International Law and Trade* 1 (remarks based on an address delivered at the University of Maryland School of Law School on October 1, 1986)

John H. Jackson, "Anticipating Trade Policy in 1987" (1987) 12 *Looking Ahead* 1

John H. Jackson, "In Memoriam – William Warner Bishop Jr. (1906–1987)" (1988) 22 *International Lawyer* 610

John H. Jackson, "Book Review of Law and Its Limitation in the GATT Multilateral Trade System by Olivier Long" (1988) 82 *American Journal of International Law* 653

John H. Jackson, "In Memoriam (a tribute to Professor William W. Bishop Jr.)" (1989) 10 *Michigan Journal of International Law* 24

John H. Jackson, "Symposium: Trade Related Aspects of Intellectual Property – Remarks of Professor John H. Jackson" (1989) 22 *Vanderbilt Journal of Transnational Law* 343

John H. Jackson, "Book Review of Foreign Affairs in English Courts by F. A. Mann" (1989) 83 *American Journal of International Law* 951

John H. Jackson, "Book Review of Developing Countries in the GATT Legal System by Robert E. Hudec" (1990) 84 *American Journal of International Law* 964

John H. Jackson, "EC '92 and Beyond: Comments from a US Perspective" (1991) 46 *Aussenwirtschaft: Swiss Review of International Economic Relations* 341

John H. Jackson, "GATT and the Future of International Trade Institutions" (1992) 4 *Michigan International Lawyer*, Fall, 6

John H. Jackson, "Friedman Award Address, Reflections on the Implications of NAFTA for the World Trading System" (1992) 30 *Columbia Journal of Transnational Law* 501

John H. Jackson, "Competition and Trade Policy, US Senate Committee on Judiciary, Chairman Senator Joseph R. Biden Jr. (Testimony for Hearing – June 18, 1992)" (published at (1992) 26 *Journal of World Trade* 111)

John H. Jackson, "Economic Governance in an Interdependent World: Lessons of Maastricht, GATT and NAFTA" in *Tenth International Trade Law Seminar Proceedings* (Department of Justice, Ottawa, October 15, 1992), 79

John H. Jackson, "Managing Economic Interdependence – An Overview" (1993) 24 *Law and Policy of International Business* 1025

Edith Brown Weiss and John H. Jackson, "Trade Environment and NAFTA: Introductory Remarks" (1993) 5 *Georgetown International Environmental Law Review* 515

John H. Jackson, "Testimony Prepared for the US Senate Finance Committee Hearing, March 23, 1994. Hearing on Uruguay Round Legislation" (US Government Printing Office, 1994)

John H. Jackson, "Testimony Prepared for the US Senate Committee on Foreign Relations, June 14, 1994. Hearing on the World Trade Organization and US Sovereignty" (US Government Printing Office, 1994)

John H. Jackson, Lecture for a Program "The Role of International Law in US Courts," Sponsored by the Federal Judicial Center for Federal Judges, Washington, DC, March 7–9, 1994

John H. Jackson, "Foreword" in Edwin A. Vermulst *et al.* (eds.), *Rules of Origin in International Trade: A Comparative Study* (1994)

John H. Jackson, "Commentary on Fair Trade, Reciprocity and Harmonization by Jagdish Bhagwati" in Alan V. Deardorff and Robert M. Stern (eds.), *Analytical and Negotiating Issues in the Global Trading System* (1994), 599

John H. Jackson, "US Threat to New World Trade Order," *Financial Times*, May 23, 1995, 17

John H. Jackson, "The New Constitution for the World Trading System – A WTO is Born," *IALS Bulletin*, No. 23 (Institute for Advanced Legal Studies, London, May 1996)

John H. Jackson, "Goodbye GATT, Hello WTO" (1996) 39 *Law Quadrangle Notes*, No. 3, 73 (University of Michigan Law School)

John H. Jackson, "Foreword, Perspectives on Regionalism in Trade Relations" (1997) 27 *Law and Policy of International Business* 873

John H. Jackson, "Appraising the Launch and Functioning of the WTO" (1997) 39 *German Yearbook of International Law* 20

John H. Jackson, "Keeping the President on the Fast Track" (1997) 40 *Law Quadrangle Notes*, No. 3, 74 (University of Michigan Law School)

John H. Jackson, *Preface, Les conséquences de la création de l'OMC pour les pays en développement* (Bérangère Taxil, 1998)

John H. Jackson, "International Economic Law and the Globalization Crisis," Lecture on the Occasion of the Professor's Inaugural to the Position of University Professor of Georgetown University, November 5, 1998

John H. Jackson, "Symposium on the First Three Years of the WTO Dispute Settlement System: Introduction and Overview" (1998) 32 *International Lawyer* 613

John H. Jackson et al., "Roundtable Summary and Looking to the Future: Summary of Presentations" (1998) 32 *International Lawyer* 943

Index of persons and authors

Index of subjects

abortion control, 415
access
  direct, 315
  market, 404
accession, 30, 32
  provisional, 31
act of state, 73
  act of transformation, 334, 337, 343, 344, 344, 346, 347, 349, 352, 353, 362, 364, 441
action(s)
  administrative, 141
  citizen, 54
  economic, 3
  escape clause, 270, 288
  executive, 26
  foreign government, 51
  government, 414
  import trade, 284
  international, 276, 438, 441
  national government, 136, 139, 357, 358
  noneconomic, 107
  protectionist, 80
  retaliatory, 63
activity, activities
  foreign policy, 285
  foreign governmental, 91
  government, 4, 78
  infrastructure, 96
  international economic, 51, 133, 278, 283
  international, 451
administrative
  actions, 141
  law, 139
  regime, 153
  regulation, 244
advancement
  economic, 169
advice and consent, 298, 304, 325, 352
advisory committees, 276
affairs

economic, 135, 279, 409, 411, 438
  environmental, 392
  foreign, 219, 265, 321
  foreign economic, 197, 200
  internal, 345
  international, 8, 52, 266, 278, 279
  international economic, 121, 265, 279
  military, 265, 279
  monetary, 409
agencies
  federal administrative, 145
agreement(s)
  bilateral, 59, 76
    executive, 228, 234, 236, 298, 299, 317, 320–322, 350
  explicit, 72
  floor-price, 80
  free trade area, 356
  free trade, 108, 122, 377
  GATT/WTO, 156
  goods, 38, 211, 295
  handshake, 267
  informal, 71
  intellectual property, 5
  interim, 64, 103, 104
    international, 35, 45, 53, 69, 72, 130, 135, 143, 155, 159, 211, 213, 222, 223, 225, 226, 232, 234, 235, 253, 265, 273, 275, 297–299, 302–304, 306, 314, 315, 317, 318, 323, 324, 326, 341, 349, 392, 449
  plurilateral, 179, 188, 190, 376, 383, 403, 406, 412
  preferential, 102, 103, 104, 109
  products, 36, 41, 97, 404
  sector, 89, 90
  settlement, 77
  sole executive, 320, 321
  subordinate, 300
    trade, 23, 62, 203, 207–209, 213, 218, 222, 224, 227, 229, 232, 233, 255, 377, 399, 449